D0206663

THE PERFORMANCE STUDIES READER

Second Edition

Reviews of the First Edition:

"Bial offers a wisely selected, coherent, and unified view of this major disciplinary field. A must for all students interested in knowing Performance Studies, and teachers wanting to make it accessible to a wider, more global audience." – Sudipto Chatterjee, University of California-Berkeley

"The great virtue of this anthology is that it is not attempting to delimit the boundaries of the field, but to open the avenues of future exploration." – Branislav Jakovljevic, Stanford University

The first edition of *The Performance Studies Reader* established itself as the leading anthology of key writings on the continually evolving field of performance studies. Bringing together contributions from a host of renowned artists and scholars, the Reader provided a lively and diverse collection of ideas suitable for undergraduates and beginning graduate students in performance studies, theater, cultural studies and related disciplines.

This updated and significantly enlarged Second Edition offers eight new chapters – for a total of 42 – on such important topics as devising theater, public memorial observances, and neurocognitive approaches to performance, as well as expanded introductory essays and internal cross-references. Widely used by students and scholars around the world as a stand-alone text, *The Performance Studies Reader, Second Edition* is also synchronized to the second edition of Richard Schechner's *Performance Studies: An Introduction*. Used together, the two volumes continue to provide a complete and integrated package for teaching and learning performance studies.

Henry Bial is Assistant Professor of Theatre and Film at the University of Kansas. He is the co-editor (with Carol Martin) of *Brecht Sourcebook* (2000), and the author of *Acting Jewish: Negotiating Ethnicity on the American Stage and Screen* (University of Michigan Press, 2005)

THE PERFORMANCE STUDIES READER

Second Edition

Edited by Henry Bial

Routledge
Taylor & Francis Group

LONDON AND NEW YORK

First edition published 2004 by Routledge

Second edition published 2007 by Routledge
2 Park Square, Milton Park, Abingdon, Oxon OX14 4RN

Simultaneously published in the USA and Canada
by Routledge
270 Madison Ave, New York, NY 10016

Reprinted 2008 (twice)

Routledge is an imprint of the Taylor & Francis Group, an informa business

Typeset in Perpetua by
RefineCatch Limited, Bungay, Suffolk
Printed and bound in Great Britain by
Cromwell Press, Trowbridge, Wiltshire

British Library Cataloguing in Publication Data
A catalogue record for this book is available from the British Library

Library of Congress Cataloging-in-Publication Data
The performance studies reader / edited by Henry Bial – 2nd ed.
p. cm.
Includes bibliographical references and index.
1. Theater – Anthropological aspects. 2. Performing arts. I. Bial, Henry, 1970–
PN2041.A57P49 2007   2006101417
791—dc22

ISBN10: 0–415–77274–5 (hbk)
ISBN10: 0–415–77275–3 (pbk)

ISBN13: 978–0–415–77274–7 (hbk)
ISBN13: 978–0–415–77275–4 (pbk)

To Christine Dotterweich Bial

CONTENTS

CONTENTS

CONTENTS

CONTENTS

CONTRIBUTORS

Barry Jean Ancelet is Professor of Francophone Studies and Folklore at the University of Louisiana at Lafayette. He has given papers and published articles and books on various aspects of Louisiana's Cajun and Creole cultures and languages, including *Cajun and Creole Music Makers* (University Press of Mississippi, 1984, 1999), *Cajun Country* (University Press of Mississippi, 1991), and *Cajun and Creole Folktales* (University Press of Mississippi, 1994). He has contributed to numerous documentary films and radio programs on Louisiana French culture, directs the annual Festival de Musique Acadienne component of Festivals Acadiens, and hosts "Rendez-vous des Cadiens," the weekly live radio show from the Liberty Theater in Eunice, Louisiana.

J.L. Austin (1911–1960) was a philosopher and linguist. He is credited with coining the term "performative" in a series of lectures at Harvard University in 1955, which were later published under the title *How To Do Things With Words* (Harvard University Press, 1962).

Eugenio Barba is the founder and director of Odin Teatret in Holstebro, Denmark, and of the International School of Theatre Anthropology. His most translated books are *Theatre: Solitude, Craft, Revolt* (Black Mountain Press, 1999), *The Paper Canoe* (Routledge, 1995), *Land of Ashes and Diamonds* (Black Mountain Press, 1999), and *The Secret Art of the Performer* (Routledge, 1991).

Gregory Bateson (1904–1980) was an anthropologist, cyberneticist, and communications theorist. His major works include *Steps to an Ecology of the Mind* (Ballantine, 1972) and *Mind and Nature* (Dutton, 1979).

Catherine Bell is the Bernard J. Hanley Professor of Religious Studies, and former department chair, at Santa Clara University, California. She is the author of *Ritual Theory, Ritual Practice* (Oxford University Press, 1992) and *Ritual: Perspectives and Dimensions* (Oxford University Press, 1997), and the forthcoming *Teaching Ritual* (AAR Teaching Religion Series, Oxford, 2007). The author of many articles on aspects of Chinese popular religion, she is currently working on a book project entitled *Believing*.

John Bell is a scholar, performer, and teacher whose work focuses on puppet, mask, and performing object theater as well as political theater and street performance. He began his theater work with Bread and Puppet Theater, and currently works as part of the Great Small Works theater collective. He is the author of *Strings, Hands, Shadows: A Modern Puppet History* (Detroit Institute of the Arts, 2000), the forthcoming *American Puppet Modernism*, and editor of *Puppets, Masks, and Performing Objects* (MIT Press, 2001).

Homi K. Bhabha is Anne F. Rothenberg Professor of Humanities at Harvard University, director of the Humanties Center at Harvard, and the Distinguished Visiting Professor in the Humanities at University College, London. The author of *The Location of Culture* (Routledge 1994) and editor of the essay collection *Nation and Narration* (Routledge 1990), Bhabha is currently at work on *A Measure of Dwelling*, a theory of vernacular cosmopolitanism forthcoming from Harvard University Press and *The Right to Narrate*, forthcoming from Columbia University Press.

Henry Bial (editor) is Assistant Professor of Theatre and Film at the University of Kansas. He is the author of *Acting Jewish: Negotiating Ethnicity on the American Stage and Screen* (University of Michigan Press, 2005), and co-editor (with Carol Martin) of *Brecht Sourcebook* (Routledge, 2000).

Rhonda Blair, Professor of Theatre at Southern Methodist University, has published in *Performance and Cognition* (Routledge, 2006), *Upstaging Big Daddy* (University of Michigan Press, 1993), *Method Acting Reconsidered* (Palgrave, 2000), *Tennessee Williams: A Casebook* (Routledge, 2001), and *Metamorphos*, among others. She is co-editor, with Bruce McConachie and Raynette Halvorsen Smith, of *Perspectives on Teaching Theatre* (Peter Lang, 2001). Some of Blair's more recent performance work has included a political cabaret trilogy – *American Jesus* (solo), *American Burka*, and *Dreaming America: In the Bunker with George* – created in collaboration with Echo Theatre.

Bertolt Brecht (1898–1956) was a German playwright, director, and performance theorist. His major works include *The Threepennny Opera* (1928), *Mother Courage and Her Children* (1941), and *The Caucasian Chalk Circle* (1948). Many of Brecht's theoretical writings were translated into English by John Willett in the collection *Brecht On Theatre* (Methuen, 1964).

Judith Butler is Maxine Elliot Professor in the Departments of Rhetoric and Comparative Literature at the University of California, Berkeley. She received her Ph.D. in Philosophy from Yale University in 1984. She is the author of *Antigone's Claim: Kinship Between Life and Death* (Columbia University Press, 2000), *Hegemony, Contingency, Universality*, with Ernesto Laclau and Slavoj Žižek (Verso Press, 2000), *Subjects of Desire: Hegelian Reflections in Twentieth-Century France* (Columbia University Press, 1987), *Gender Trouble: Feminism and the Subversion of Identity* (Routledge, 1990), *Bodies That Matter: On the Discursive Limits of "Sex"* (Routledge, 1993), *The Psychic Life of Power: Theories of Subjection* (Stanford University Press, 1997), *Excitable Speech* (Routledge, 1997), as well as numerous articles and contributions on philosophy and feminist and queer theory. Her recent book, *Giving an Account of Oneself* (Fordham University Press, 2005) is a critique of ethical violence and an effort to formulate a theory of responsibility for an opaque subject.

Marvin Carlson, Sidney E. Cohn Professor of Theatre and Comparative Literature at the Graduate Center of the City University of New York, has received the ATHE Career Achievement Award, the George Jean Nathan Award for Dramatic Criticism, the Joseph A. Calloway Prize, and the ASTR Distinguished Scholarship Award. In 2005, he received an honorary doctorate from the University of Athens. He has published widely in theatre history and theory, performance studies and dramatic literature.

Dwight Conquergood (1949–2004) was Professor of Performance Studies at Northwestern University. An ethnographer who conducted extensive field research in refugee camps overseas and in immigrant neighborhoods in Chicago, Conquergood co-produced two award-winning documentaries based on his Chicago urban field research: *Between Two Worlds: The Hmong Shaman in America* (1985) and *The Heart Broken in Half* (1990). He consulted with the International Rescue Committee and other human rights organizations working on the death penalty, as well as with public defenders working on capital cases, and taught at the Bryan R. Shechmeister Death Penalty College, School of Law, Santa Clara University.

Marco De Marinis teaches Theatre History and Performance Semiology at the University of Bologna. He is a member of Eugenio Barba's International School of Theatre Anthropology, and the author of *The Semiotics of Performance* (Indiana University Press, 1993).

Jacques Derrida (1930–2004) was an Algerian-born French philosopher, considered the pioneer of "deconstruction" in the humanities. His many influential works include *Of Grammatology* (Editions de Minuit, 1967; Eng. Johns Hopkins University Press, 1976), *Writing and Difference* (Editions de Seuil, 1967; Eng. University of Chicago Press, 1978), *Margins of Philosophy* (Editions de Minuit, 1972; Eng. University of Chicago Press, 1982).

Alyda Faber is Assistant Professor of Theology at Atlantic School of Theology in Halifax, Canada. Her research and teaching interests include religion and film, feminist theory and theology, and violence as a category for theological reflection. She is working on a book project on religion and film, on the question of how certain strains of religious and ethical subjectivity contribute to spectator theory.

Johannes Fabian is professor of cultural anthropology at the University of Amsterdam. Previously, he taught at Northwestern and Wesleyan Universities and at the National University of Zaire in Lubumbashi. He did research on religious movements, language, work, and popular culture in the Shaba mining region of Zaire (1966–7, 1972–4, 1985, 1986). In his theoretical and critical work, he addressed questions of epistemology and of the history of anthropology, especially in his *Time and the Other: How Anthropology Makes its Object* (Columbia University Press, 1983, 2002). His books include *Power and Performance* (University of Wisconsin Press, 1990), *Time and the Work of Anthropology* (Routledge, 1991), and *Anthropology with an Attidude* (Stanford University Press, 2001).

Neal Gabler is the author of *An Empire of Their Own: How the Jews Invented Hollywood* (Crown, 1988), *Winchell: Gossip, Power, and the Culture of Celebrity* (Knopf, 1994), *Life The Movie: How*

Entertainment Conquered Reality (Knopf, 1998), and *Walt Disney: The Triumph of the American Imagination* (Knopf, 2006).

Clifford Geertz is Professor Emeritus in the School of Social Science at the Institute for Advanced Study. He has conducted extensive ethnographical research in Southeast Asia and North Africa. He has also contributed to social and cultural theory and been influential in turning anthropology toward a concern with the frames of meaning within which various peoples live out their lives. He has worked on religion, most particularly Islam, on bazaar trade, on economic development, on traditional political structures, and on village and family life. He is at present working on the general question of ethnic diversity and its implications in the modern world.

Erving Goffman (1922–82) was among the first scholars to make comprehensive studies of performance in everyday life. His books include *The Presentation of Self in Everyday Life* (Doubleday, 1959), *Interaction Ritual* (Aldine, 1967), and *Frame Analysis* (Harper & Row, 1974).

Guillermo Gómez-Peña is a performance artist, writer, and a Contributing Editor to *TDR: The Journal of Performance Studies*. His most recent book is *Ethno-Techno: Writings on Performance, Activism, and Pedagogy* (Routledge, 2005).

Jerzy Grotowski (1933–1999) was a Polish theatre director, performer trainer, and theorist, and founding director of the Polish Laboratory Theatre. His book *Towards A Poor Theatre* (Odin Teatrets Forlag, 1968) has been widely influential on theatre training around the world.

Frances Harding is Lecturer in African Drama in the Department of African Languages and Cultures at the School of Oriental and African Studies (SOAS), University of London. She has worked in theatre in several African countries, particularly in Nigeria, and writes on different aspects of theatre and performance in Africa, and has edited the volume *The Performance Arts in Africa* (Routledge, 2002).

Johan Huizinga (1872–1945) was a Dutch historian and an early theorist of play. His work includes *Homo Ludens* (Pantheon, 1940).

Shannon Jackson is Professor of Rhetoric and Professor and Chair of Theater, Dance, and Performance Studies at the University of California, Berkeley. She has published and performed in numerous journals, theatres, collections, and galleries. Her book on performance and American social reform, *Lines of Activity* (University of Michigan Press, 2000), received Honorable Mention for the John Hope Franklin Prize from the American Studies Association. Her second book, *Professing Performance* (Cambridge University Press, 2004), received Best Book prizes from the Association for Theatre in Higher Education and the National Communication Association. She is currently at work on a new manuscript titled *Social Works: The Infrastructural Politics of Performance*.

Allan Kaprow (1927–2006) helped to develop the "Environment" and "Happening" in the late 1950s and 1960s, as well as their theory. His Happenings – some 200 of them – evolved over the years, until they were nearly indistinguishable from ordinary life. He published extensively and was, at the time of his death, Professor Emeritus in the Visual Arts Department of the University of California, San Diego.

Barbara Kirshenblatt-Gimblett is University Professor and Professor of Performance Studies at the Tisch School of the Arts, New York University, where she chaired her department for over a decade. She is the recipient of numerous grants and awards, among them the Guggenheim fellowship. She is the author of *Destination Culture: Tourism, Museums, and Heritage* (University of California Press, 1998).

Jill Lane is Assistant Professor in the Department of Spanish and Portuguese at New York University, and Associate Director of the Hemispheric Institute of Performance and Politics. She is the author of *Blackface Cuba, 1840–1895* (University of Pennsylvania Press, 2005) and co-editor, with Peggy Phelan, of *The Ends of Performance* (New York University Press, 1998). She has previously taught at Ohio State University and at Yale University.

Michael Atwood Mason is an anthropologist and exhibit developer at the Smithsonian's National Museum of Natural History, where he was a co-curator of the permanent *African Voices* exhibition. He is the author of *Living Santería: Rituals and Experiences in Afro-Cuban Religion* (Smithsonian Institution Press, 2002).

Jon McKenzie is Associate Professor of English and Coordinator of Modern Studies at the University of Wisconsin–Milwaukee. He is the author of *Perform or Else: From Discipline to Performance* (Routledge, 2001) and numerous essays, including "Performance and Globalization," "Global Feeling: (Almost) All You Need is Love," and "Democracy's Performance." He is currently working on a second book, titled *Performance Inc: Global Performativity and Mediated Resistance*, and co-editing the collection *Contesting Performance: Global Genealogies of Research*.

Vsevolod Meyerhold (1874–1940) was a Russian actor and director who developed a system of acting known as "biomechanics" which emphasized the kinetic potential of the human body through highly-stylized movement. His writings on performance have been translated into English by Edward Braun as *Meyerhold on Theatre* (Methuen, 1969).

Isidore Okpewho is State University of New York Distinguished Professor of the Humanities at Binghamton University. He is the author of numerous scholarly works on African literature and performance, including *Once Upon a Kingdom* (Indiana, 1998), *African Oral Literature* (Indiana, 1992), and *Oral Performance in Africa* (Editor, Spectrum Books, 1990), as well as the award-winning novels *Tides* (Longman, 1993) and *The Last Duty* (Longman, 1976). His latest novel, *Call Me By My Rightful Name* (Africa World Press, 2004), about African-American ancestral memory, is built around a focal African praise poem. He is currently writing a critical-cultural study of *The Ozidi Saga*, an Ijo epic from southern Nigerian, against the backdrop of the present environmental crisis in the Nigerian delta.

Andrew Parker is Professor of English at Amherst College. He recently edited and co-translated Jacques Ranciere's *The Philosopher and His Poor* (Duke University Press, 2004).

Peggy Phelan is the Ann O'Day Maples Chair in the Arts and Professor of Drama, Stanford University. She is the author of the Survey essays for *Art and Feminism*, edited by Helena Reckitt (Phaidon, 2001) and *Pipilotti Rist* (Phaidon, 2001). She is also the author of *Mourning Sex: Performing Public Memories* (Routledge, 1997) and *Unmarked: The Politics of Performance* (Routledge, 1997). She co-edited *The Ends of Performance* (New York University Press, 1997) with Jill Lane, and with the late Lynda Hart, she co-edited *Acting Out: Feminist Performances* (University of Michigan Press, 1993). Currently she is writing a book entitled *Twentieth Century Performance*, to be published by Routledge.

Jack Santino is Professor of Folklore and Popular Culture at Bowling Green State University. He has been President of the American Folklore Society and Editor of the *Journal of American Folklore*. His documentary film, *Miles of Smiles, Years of Struggle: The Untold Story of the Black Pullman Porter* (1983), co-produced with Paul Wagner, received four Emmy awards. He has published extensively in the field of ritual, festival, and celebration, including most recently *Signs of War and Peace: Social Conflict and the Public Use of Symbols in Northern Ireland* (Palgrave Macmillan, 2000) and an edited volume, *Spontaneous Shrines and the Public Memorialization of Death* (Palgrave Macmillan, 2006).

Richard Schechner is University Professor and Professor of Performance Studies at New York University. He founded The Performance Group and is currently the founding artistic director of East Coast Artists. He is the editor of *TDR: The Drama Review* and the author of many books, including *Between Theatre and Anthropology* (University of Pennsylvania Press, 1985), *Performance Theory* (revised edition Routledge, 2003), and *Performance Studies: An Introduction* (revised edition Routledge, 2006).

Eve Kosofsky Sedgwick is the author of several books, including *Epistemology of the Closet* (University of California Press, 1990) and *Touching Feeling: Affect, Pedagogy, Performativity* (Duke University Press, 2003). She teaches in the Ph.D. Program in English at CUNY Graduate Center.

Lee Strasberg (1901–1982) was co-founder of the Group Theatre, and one of the United States' best-known acting teachers. He was the author of *Strasberg at the Actor's Studio* (Viking, 1968) and A *Dream of Passion: The Evolution of the Method* (Little, Brown, 1987).

Brian Sutton-Smith is Professor of Education, Emeritus, at the University of Pennsylvania. A pioneer in the scholarly study of play, he is the author of *The Ambiguity of Play* (Harvard, 1998), *Toys as Culture* (Gardner, 1986), and numerous other books and essays.

Diana Taylor is Professor of Performance Studies and Spanish at New York University. She is the author of *Theatre of Crisis: Drama and Politics in Latin America* (University Press of Kentucky, 1991), *Disappearing Acts: Spectacles of Gender and Nationalism in Argentina's "Dirty War"* (Duke University Press, 1997), and most recently *The Archive and the Repertoire: Performing Cultural Memory in the Americas* (Duke University Press, 2003), which won the Outstanding Book Award from the Association of Theatre in Higher Education, and the Katherine Singer Kovacs Prize from the Modern Language Association. She directs the Hemispheric Institute of Performance and Politics, funded by the Ford Foundation and the Rockefeller Foundation.

Edith (Edie) Turner is Lecturer in Anthropology at the University of Virginia, and editor of the journal *Anthropology and Humanism*. Her books include *Experiencing Ritual* (University of Pennsylvania Press, 1992), *The Hands Feel It* (Northern Illinois University Press, 1996), *Among the Healers* (Praeger, 2005), and *Heart of Lightness* (Berghahn, 2006).

Victor Turner (1917–1983) was a Scottish-born anthropologist. His major works include *The Ritual Process* (Aldine, 1969), *Dramas, Fields, and Metaphors* (Cornell University Press, 1974), and *From Ritual to Theatre* (PAJ, 1982).

W.B. Worthen is J. L. Styan Collegiate Professor of Drama in the Department of English Language and Literature at the University of Michigan. He is the author of many articles on drama and performance theory, and of several books, including *The Idea of the Actor* (Princeton, 1984), *Modern Drama and the Rhetoric of Theater* (California, 1992), *Shakespeare and the Authority of Performance* (Cambridge, 1996), *Shakespeare and the Force of Modern Performance* (Cambridge, 2003), and *Print and the Poetics of Modern Drama* (Cambridge, 2006). He is the editor of *The Wadsworth Anthology of Drama* (formerly *The Harcourt Anthology of Drama*), and is past editor of *Theatre Journal* and past co-editor of *Modern Drama*. He is currently writing a book tentatively titled *Reading Drama: Between Poetry and Performance*.

Mary Zimmerman is Professor of Performance Studies at Northwestern University. She is a member of the Lookingglass Theatre Company and is an Artistic Associate of the Goodman Theatre. She is the winner of a Tony Award for Best Direction of her own adaptation of the *Metamorphoses*, and recipient of a MacArthur Fellowship.

ACKNOWLEDGEMENTS

Acknowledgements from the First Edition

There are many people whom I must thank for their support and assistance in this project. First among these is Richard Schechner. It was Richard who first articulated the need for a collection to complement his *Performance Studies: An Introduction*, and he has been the biggest supporter of this project from its inception. He has been an invaluable source of advice and guidance, from the initial selection of articles to the final form of the manuscript. Without Richard's unflagging support, this project would not have come to fruition. Talia Rodgers of Routledge has been similarly instrumental in shepherding this book from idea to proposal to the final product which you now hold in your hand. I also thank Carol Martin, who taught me how to do this when we co-edited the *Brecht Sourcebook*. If there is anything lacking in the present volume, it should be blamed on my inadequate learning, not on Carol's excellent teaching.

I thank the many gifted teachers and students in the Department of Performance Studies at New York University, where I earned my Ph.D. What I know of Performance Studies has been shaped primarily by their words and deeds. Though I could list them by the dozens, I particularly wish to thank my classmates Cindy Brizzell, Stephanie Marlin-Curiel, and Dan Bacalzo. My colleagues in the Department of Theatre and Dance at the University of New Mexico have also provided invaluable support – this is doubly true of those in the Theatre area: Eugene Douglas, David Jones, Jim Linnell, Susan Pearson-Davis, and Digby Wolfe. Special thanks are due my department Chairs, Denise Shultz and Judith Bennahum, for providing the time and resources I needed to complete this project. UNM graduate students Michael Halloran and Kristen Smith, as well as my longtime friend Mark Giordano, were of great help in transcribing much of the previously-published material to disc.

Finally, I thank my parents, Ernest and Martha Bial, my wife Christine, to whom this book is dedicated, and my daughters Anna and Emily, for their infinite love and patience.

Additional acknowledgements for the Second Edition

In addition to those thanked above, the following people have contributed specifically to the development and preparation of this second edition. First again is Richard Schechner. His tireless and remarkable efforts in revising and updating *Performance Studies: An Introduction* (2006) helped to occasion this volume, and his support and advice continue to be essential. At Routledge, Minh Ha Duong has championed the project with a combination of patience and good humor that has been invaluable. Also at Routledge, Talia Rodgers, Moira Taylor, and Katherine Davey have worked to ensure the continued synchronicity between this *Reader* and Schechner's *Performance Studies*. Special thanks are due to the many wonderful teachers around the world who have used *The Performance Studies Reader* in their classrooms and offered me their feedback and suggestions as I prepared this second edition. These include (but are not limited to): Pamela Cheek, Iris Smith Fischer, David Jortner, Jennifer Parker-Starbuck, Keith Peacock, James Thompson, and Celestine Woo. This edition has also benefited from the lively questions, opinions, and enthusiasms of my students at the University of New Mexico and (since 2005) the University of Kansas.

The Department of Theatre and Film and the College of Liberal Arts and Sciences at the University of Kansas provided necessary support in the form of faculty research funds and essential infrastructure. Out of many wonderful colleagues at Kansas, I especially acknowledge the advice and consultation of Jonathan Boyarin, John Gronbeck-Tedesco, Mechele Leon, and John Staniunas. Julie Noonan provided significant assistance in preparing the manuscripts of the new chapters, and in catching errors from the first edition.

On a personal note, I continue to be blessed with a supportive, patient, and loving family. To my parents Martha and Ernest Bial, my daughters Emily and Anna, and my wife Christine, still the best thing to happen to me in performance studies: thank you.

Permissions

The authors and publishers represented in this collection have been exceedingly generous with their time and assistance in securing reprint rights to their work. I gratefully acknowledge permission to publish articles and extracts as follows:

Richard Schechner, "Performance studies: the broad spectrum approach," *TDR* 32: 3 (T119, Fall 1988), pp, 4–6. © 1988 by New York University and the Massachusetts Institute of Technology. Reprinted by permission of MIT Press and the author.

W.B. Worthen, "Disciplines of the text/sites of performance," *TDR* 39: 1 (T145, Spring 1995), pp. 13–28. © 1995 by New York University and the Massachusetts Institute of Technology. Reprinted by permission of MIT Press and the author.

Jon McKenzie, "The liminal norm" from *Perform or Else*, pp. 49–53. © 2001 by Jon McKenzie. Reproduced by permission of Taylor & Francis Books UK and the author.

Shannon Jackson, "Professing performances: disciplinary genealogies," *TDR* 45: 1 (T169, Spring 2001), pp. 84–95. © 2001 by New York University and the Massachusetts Institute of Technology. Reprinted by permission of MIT Press and the author.

Barbara Kirshenblatt-Gimblett, "Performance studies." © 2002 by Barbara Kirshenblatt-Gimblett. Reprinted by permission of the author.

John Bell, "Performance studies in an age of terror," *TDR* 47: 2 (T178, Summer 2003), pp. 6–8. © 2003 by New York University and the Massachusetts Institute of Technology. Reprinted by permission of MIT Press and the author.

Erving Goffman, "Performances: belief in the part one is playing" from *The Presentation of Self in Everyday Life*, pp. 17–24. © 1959 by Erving Goffman. Used by permission of Doubleday, a division of Random House, Inc.

Clifford Geertz, "Blurred genres: the refiguration of social thought" from *Local Knowledge*, pp. 26–30. © 1983 by Clifford Geertz. Reprinted by permission of the author.

Marvin Carlson, "What is performance?" from *Performance: A Critical Introduction*, pp. 1–7. © 1996 by Marvin Carlson. Reproduced by permission of Taylor & Francis Books UK and the author.

Neal Gabler, "Life the movie" from *Life The Movie: How Entertainment Conquered Reality*, pp. 4–7. © 1998 by Neal Gabler. Used by permission of Alfred A. Knopf, a division of Random House, Inc.

Peggy Phelan, "Marina Abramović: witnessing shadows," *Theatre Journal* 56: 4 (2004), pp. 569–577. © 2004 by The Johns Hopkins University Press. Reprinted with permission of The Johns Hopkins University Press and the author.

Victor Turner, "Liminality and communitas" from *The Ritual Process*, pp. 94–106. © 1969 by Victor Turner. Reprinted by permission of Transaction Publishers.

Catherine Bell, " 'Performance' and other analogies" from *Ritual Theory, Ritual Practice*, pp. 37–46. © 1992 by Catherine Bell. Used by permission of Oxford University Press, Inc. and the author.

Michael Atwood Mason, " 'The blood that runs through the veins': the creation of identity and a client's experience of Cuban-American *santería dilogún* divination," *TDR* 37: 2 (T138, Summer 1993), pp. 119–130. © 1993 by New York University and the Massachusetts Institute of Technology. Reprinted by permission of MIT Press and the author.

Alyda Faber, "Saint Orlan: ritual as violent spectacle and cultural criticism," *TDR* 46: 1 (T173, Spring 2002), pp. 145–156. © 2002 by New York University and the Massachusetts Institute of Technology. Reprinted by permission of MIT Press and the author.

Jack Santino, "Performative commemoratives, the personal, and the public: spontaneous shrines, emergent ritual," originally published in slightly different form as "Performative commemoratives, the personal, and the public: spontaneous shrines, emergent ritual, and the field of folklore (AFS presidential plenary address, 2003)," *Journal of American Folklore* 117 (Fall 2004), pp. 363–372. © 2004 by the Board of Trustees of the University of Illinois. Used with permission of the University of Illinois Press and the Author.

Johan Huizinga, "The nature and significance of play as a cultural phenomenon" from *Homo Ludens*, pp. 1–5. © 1950 by Roy Publishers. Reprinted by permission of Beacon Press, Boston.

Gregory Bateson, "A theory of play and fantasy" from *Steps to an Ecology of the Mind*, pp. 177–93. © 1972 by Chandler Publishing Co. Reprinted by permission of The University of Chicago Press.

Brian Sutton-Smith, "The ambiguity of play" from *The Ambiguity of Play*, pp. 52–60. Copyright © 1997 by the President and Fellows of Harvard College. Reprinted by permission of Harvard University Press.

Allan Kaprow, "Just doing," *TDR* 41: 3 (T155, Fall 1997), pp. 101–106. © 1997 by New York University and the Massachusetts Institute of Technology. Reprinted by permission of MIT Press.

Barry Jean Ancelet, "Falling apart to stay together: deep play in the Grand Marais Mardi Gras," *Journal of American Folklore* 114 (Spring 2001), pp. 144–153. © 2001 by the American Folklore Society. Reprinted by permission of the American Folklore Society and the author.

John L. Austin, "How to do things with words: lecture II" from *How to do Things with Words*, edited by J.O. Urmson and Marina Sbisa, pp. 12–24, Cambridge, Mass.: Harvard University Press, Copyright © 1962, 1975 by the President and Fellows of Harvard College. Reprinted by permission of Harvard University Press.

Jacques Derrida, "Signature event context" from *Margins of Philosophy*, translated by Alan Bass, pp. 325–327. © 1982 by the University of Chicago. Reprinted by permission of the University of Chicago Press.

Judith Butler, "Performative acts and gender constitution: an essay in phenomenology and feminist theory," *Theatre Journal* 40: 4 (1988), pp. 519–531. © 1988 by The Johns Hopkins University Press. Reprinted with the permission of The Johns Hopkins University Press and the author.

Andrew Parker and Eve Kosofsky Sedgwick, "Introduction" to *Performativity and Performance*, pp. 1–18. © 1995 by Andrew Parker and Eve Kosofsky Sedgwick. Reproduced by permission of Routledge/Taylor & Francis Group, LLC and the authors.

Johannes Fabian, "Theatre and anthropology, theatricality and culture," *Research in African Literatures* 30: 4 (1999), pp. 24–31. Reprinted by permission of Indiana University Press and the author.

Bertolt Brecht, "A dialogue about acting" from *Brecht on Theatre*, edited and translated by John Willett, pp. 26–29. Translation copyright © 1964, renewed 1992 by John Willett. Reprinted by permission of Hill & Wang, a division of Farrar, Straus and Giroux, LLC. [US rights] A&C Black [UK rights] and Suhrkamp Verlag [world rights].

Jerzy Grotowski, "The actor's technique" from *Towards a Poor Theatre*, pp. 173–183. © 1968 by Jerzy Grotowski and Odin Teatrets Forlag. Reprinted by permission of Odin Teatret.

ACKNOWLEDGEMENTS

Lee Strasberg, "A dream of passion" from *A Dream of Passion*, pp. 149–51. Copyright © 1987 by Davada Enterprises. Reprinted by permission of Little, Brown and Company, Inc.

Frances Harding, "Presenting and re-presenting the self: from not-acting to acting in African performance," *TDR* 43: 2 (T162, Summer 1999), pp. 118–135. © 1999 by New York University and the Massachusetts Institute of Technology. Reprinted by permission of the MIT Press.

Rhonda Blair, "Reconsidering Stanislavsky: feeling, feminism, and the actor," *Theatre Topics* 12: 2 (2002), pp. 177–190. © 2002 by The Johns Hopkins University Press. Reprinted with permission of The Johns Hopkins University Press and the author.

Vsevolod Meyerhold, "First attempts at a stylized theatre" from *Meyerhold in Theatre*, translated and edited by Eduard Braun, pp. 49–58. © 1969 by Eduard Braun. Reprinted by permission of A&C Black.

Isidore Okpewho, "The oral artist: training and preparation" from *African Oral Literature*, pp, 21–25. © 1992 by Isidore Okpewho. Reprinted by permission of Indiana University Press and the author.

Marco De Marinis, "The performance text" from *The Semiotics of Performance*, translated by Áine O'Healy, pp. 47–59. © 1993 by Indiana University Press. Reprinted by permission of Indiana University Press and the author.

Eugenio Barba, "The deep order called turbulence: the three faces of dramaturgy," *TDR* 44: 4 (T168, Winter 2000), pp. 56–66. © 2000 by New York University and the Massachusetts Institute of Technology. Reprinted by permission of MIT Press and the author.

Mary Zimmerman, "The Archaeology of Performance," *Theatre Topics* 15: 1 (2005), pp. 25–35. © 2005 by The Johns Hopkins University Press. Reprinted with permission of The Johns Hopkins University Press and the author.

Victor Turner with Edie Turner, "Performing ethnography" from *The Anthropology of Performance* by Victor Turner, pp. 139–155. © 1986 by PAJ Publications. Reprinted by permission of Edie Turner.

Homi K. Bhabha, "Of mimicry and man" from *The Location of Culture*, pp. 85–92. © 1994 by Homi K. Bhabha. Reproduced by permission of Taylor & Francis Books UK and the author.

Guillermo Gómez-Peña, "Culturas-in-extremis: performing against the cultural backdrop of the mainstream bizarre" © 2003 by Guillermo Gómez-Peña. Reprinted by permission of the author. An earlier version of this essay appeared under the title "The new global culture" in *TDR* 45: 1 (T169, Spring 2001), pp. 7–30. © 2001 by Guillermo Gómez-Peña.

Jill Lane, "Reverend Billy: preaching protest and post-industrial flânerie," *TDR* 46: 1 (T173, Spring 2002), pp. 60–3, 73–84 (excerpted with the permission of the author). © 2002 by New York University and the Massachusetts Institute of Technology. Reprinted by permission of MIT Press and the author.

Dwight Conquergood, "Performance studies: interventions and radical research," *TDR* 46: 2 (T174, Summer 2002), pp. 145–156. © 2002 by New York University and the Massachusetts Institute of Technology. Reprinted by permission of MIT Press.

Diana Taylor, "Translating Performance," *Profession 2002* (2002), pp. 44–50. © 2002 by the Modern Language Association of America. Reprinted by permission of the Modern Language Association of America and the author. This essay also appears in similar form on pp. 1–15 of Taylor's *The Archive and the Repertoire: Performing Cultural Memory in the Americas* (Duke University Press, 2003).

INTRODUCTION

Henry Bial

There are people who already know, or think they know, what performance studies is. This book is not for them. This book is for the people who like *not knowing*, who find the uncertainty of unmapped terrain exhilarating. This is also true of the field itself. What makes performance studies unique is that it shares the characteristics of its object: performance. Just as performance is contingent, contested, hard to pin down, so too is its study. For the most part, those of us who consider ourselves "performance studies people" like it that way. As Diana Taylor writes in this volume, "I find its [performance's] very undefinability and complexity reassuring" (see page 385). The positive promise of performance studies – its potential to illuminate, instruct, and inspire – is enhanced, not diminished, by this ever-present uncertainty.

Therefore, I will not attempt in this introduction to define the field of performance studies. As Barbara Kirshenblatt-Gimblett writes, "Performance Studies starts with a set of concerns and objects and ranges widely for what it needs by way of theory and method" (see page 43). Hence, the only definition that is universally applicable to the field is a tautology: performance studies is what performance studies people do. The purpose of this book is to collect in one volume numerous examples of what performance studies people do, allowing readers to find their own place at this movable feast of ideas.

Of course, one of the things performance studies people do is attempt to define our field of study; but as you will see from the essays in the first section of this book, all such definitions are themselves *performative*. That is, they are not descriptions of an already-existing body of knowledge, but attempts to create a knowledge-formation by defining, explaining, and discussing it. As Shannon Jackson notes in this volume, disciplinary labels such as theater, speech, and performance studies should be viewed "less as stably referential terms than as discursive sites on which a number of agendas, alliances, and anxieties collect" (see page 40). Assembling an anthology with the title *The Performance Studies Reader* carries with it many of the same concerns. There will be many readers who will question why certain texts have been included, why others have been left out. This is true of all anthologies, but it is especially true in this case. This book is intended as an inclusive, rather than exclusive, introduction to performance studies. The absence of certain texts or authors from these pages should not be construed as a banishment of those ideas from the performance studies realm.

The term *Performance Studies Reader* refers not only to this book, but to you, the reader, and to me, the editor. I have been reading performance studies, as a student and as a teacher, for about a dozen years: not very long by some people's standards, too long by others'. As a graduate student in New York University's Department of Performance Studies in the mid-1990s, I frequently thought: 1) this field is really exciting, and 2) this field is really confusing. It is exciting to read and write within an intellectual community that includes theatrical practitioners and critics, anthropologists, folklorists, sociologists, and cultural theorists. It is exhilarating to watch new worlds of inquiry open in the spaces between these more established disciplines. It is a special kind of rush to set out in pursuit of an object-of-study that is as elusive, temporal, and contingent as performance. To be a performance studies reader is to work without a net, to walk on hot coals, to search in a dark alley at midnight for a black cat that isn't there. We are the lovers on Keats' Grecian urn, eternally in pursuit.

But the flipside of finding oneself at the center of such an intellectual vortex is the tendency – especially for the newcomer – toward disorientation. How does one idea relate to another? Where do academic disciplines overlap? Is performance studies properly a discipline at all, or is it a kind of way station, an academic version of Grand Central Terminal, where ideas and idea-makers brush up against each other on the way from one place to another? "Your attention please, this is the final boarding call for Cultural Studies, making all local stops including Women's Studies, African Studies, Asian Studies, Queer Theory, and Cultural Studies. If you're not going to Cultural Studies, you're on the wrong train!" And even if readers know, or think they know, how to connect the dots from where they've come from to where they are to where they would like to go, it is not always easy to stick to the path, given the converging and diverging rush of words, images, and performances that swirl about in every direction.

And I subsequently thought: someday, when I am a professor, I shall write a book which organizes the myriad disciplines and dissents of performance studies into a neat, coherent narrative, while still respecting the complexity of this interdisciplinary and intercultural project. This book would serve as a map of the complex and ever-changing landscape of the field. It would survey the terrain from above, assisting students and other visitors in orienting themselves, and reminding more experienced readers how they got there. This was, perhaps, an over-ambitious goal for a student, but performance studies is an enterprise which encourages (not to say induces) such ambition. In a landscape where boundaries are blurred and borders routinely violated, where your view changes with each step, who is immune to the temptation to simply set out in search of the Emerald City?

Richard Schechner got there first. Of course, he had a head start. As one of the pioneers of the field, the person who coined the very term "Performance Studies," Schechner was the ideal person to write *Performance Studies: An Introduction* (Routledge, 2002), now in its second edition (2006). In that book – which this volume is meant to accompany – Schechner charts the evolution and development of the field, from its intellectual roots in theater, anthropology, and other disciplines through fundamental concepts such as ritual, play, and performativity, to comprehensive discussions of the act of performing, of performance processes, and of global and intercultural performances. Though, as Schechner notes, "The one overriding and underlying assumption of performance studies is that the field is wide open" (1),

Performance Studies: An Introduction gives students a stable frame of reference against which their own avenues of inquiry can be measured.

Because *The Performance Studies Reader* is designed as a companion to Schechner's *Performance Studies*, you will find the essays in this volume organized into eight parts, one part keyed to each chapter of Schechner's text. In that way, teachers of performance studies can use the two books in concert (or employ each independently, if they so desire). The material in each part expands or comments upon the ideas contained in the corresponding chapter: "What is performance studies?," "What is performance?," "Ritual," "Play," "Performativity," "Performing," "Performance processes," and "Global and intercultural performance."

But it is very important to note that the articles in *The Performance Studies Reader* do not repeat or rehash the material in Schechner's text, nor are they dependent on it. Rather, taken as a group, these writings provide an even more expansive kind of introduction to Performance Studies as an academic discipline. If *Performance Studies: An Introduction* is the coherent guide to the field that I longed for as a student, *The Performance Studies Reader* is a more experiential and immediate map of the area, drawn from street-level. It navigates the discipline by introducing readers to key thinkers in the field. These thinkers in turn identify the major landmarks of "PS Land." Used either by itself or in conjunction with Schechner's book, the *Reader* encourages teachers and students to discover their own pathways from one to another. Some of these landmarks look different close up than they do on the larger map; some stand at the very limits of the field; a few stand outside the boundaries which performance studies scholars usually draw, beckoning readers to stretch further.

In other words, this *Reader* is both a supplement to Schechner's *Performance Studies* and a means to providing a qualitatively different reading and learning experience. Ideally the two volumes will work together handsomely, providing the basis for "a compact course in performance studies" (Schechner 2006: ix).

Within these pages, you will find acknowledged "classics" – works whose canonical status in performance studies is rarely challenged – such as Erving Goffman's "Performances: belief in the part one is playing" from *The Presentation of Self in Everyday Life* and J.L. Austin's "Lecture II" from *How to Do Things With Words*. You will also find works so current that the ink is barely dry, such as Mary Zimmerman's "The archaeology of performance" and Diana Taylor's "Translating performance." You will find work by the "stars" of the field, and you will find work by scholars whose names may be new to you. You will find short excerpts from book-length works, and a handful of journal articles reprinted in their entirety. If you've previously used the first edition of this *Reader*, you will find all the same articles here, along with eight new pieces (one for each Part) selected especially for the current edition. These new chapters have been selected with an eye toward keeping the *Reader* current with the emerging field: seven of the eight have been published since 2001. For those using the *Reader* in conjunction with *Performance Studies: An Introduction*, all eight are listed as "suggested readings" in the second edition of Schechner's text.

Because performance studies draws healthily on its eclectic roots and branches, the authors of the works collected here often assume a familiarity on behalf of the reader with ideas and works that may be outside your experience. To help you along, each part begins with a brief introduction which contextualizes the articles in that part and explains their relationship to one other. At the end of each chapter, you will find cross-references to other articles in the *Reader*; like everything else in performance studies, the thematic divisions between parts of this book are provisional and contested; there are numerous ways to connect the articles and ideas in this collection, and readers are encouraged to seek out those paths that speak to them the loudest. You may also note that within each thematic part, the articles are arranged chronologically, so that you can more easily follow the historical evolution of certain concepts.

Finally, I sincerely invite you to experience the wonders of being a performance studies reader. This book is offered as a resource for anyone who wishes to chart a path through the field of performance studies, and for anyone who wishes to get lost in it.

Part I

WHAT IS PERFORMANCE STUDIES?

Richard Schechner writes, "Theoretically, performance studies is wide open; practically, it has developed in a certain way" (Schechner 2006: 1). This "certain way" has, in the academy, been shaped in large part by institutional imperatives. In the 1980s and 1990s, university theater departments began to rethink their mission. Teachers of theater and dance, and of speech communication saw their traditional European and American curriculum growing gradually disconnected with the increasingly multi-cultural and media-driven world of the professional performing arts. At the same time, the shift of colleges and universities toward a corporate model (the university delivers a "product" to student-consumers) placed increased pressure on all disciplines to assert their relevance in the global marketplace.

The essays in this section trace the development of performance studies as an academic discipline in response to these challenges. As the editor of *TDR: The Journal of Performance Studies* and a professor at New York University's Department of Performance Studies (the first of its kind), Schechner became the leading advocate for this paradigm shift. Schechner's 1988 essay "Performance studies: the broad spectrum approach" calls for a "wholesale reconstruction of curricula" to include the study of performance in ritual and social contexts. For those who would still study aesthetic performance, Schechner and others suggested a de-emphasizing of literary, text-based criticism in favor of performance-based analysis. W.B. Worthen explores the debate around text and performance in "Disciplines of the text/sites of performance" (1995). Drawing on the work of literary theorists such as Roland Barthes, Worthen shows how the disciplinary evolution of performance studies raises important questions about authorship and originality.

Jon McKenzie's "The liminal-norm," excerpted from his 2001 book *Perform Or Else*, notes another distinguishing characteristic of performance studies as an academic enterprise: it is self-consciously positioned as "liminal" – between two states of being (e.g. between theater and ritual), and belonging to neither. Because this liminal position is often understood as a space for transgression or resistance (ideas and acts that go against the mainstream), many performance studies scholars have come to consider social activism a defining characteristic of the field. McKenzie, whose goal is to develop a "general theory of performance," here explores some of the implications of this "challenge of efficacy." Like McKenzie, Shannon Jackson turns a critical eye on the university and how resistance to traditional disciplinary structures helped shape contemporary performance studies. Her 2001 essay "Professing performances: disciplining genealogies" traces the genealogy of the field back to the establishment of performing arts departments in American universities in the early twentieth century.

In "Performance studies," Barbara Kirshenblatt-Gimblett surveys the development of the field since its establishment in the early 1980s. This essay – a detailed account of where performance studies has been, and where it may be headed – is based on a 1999 report given to the Rockefeller Foundation by Kirshenblatt-Gimblett, the first Chair of NYU's Department of Performance Studies (1981–1993), and was revised and updated in 2002. To close Part I, John Bell's "Performance studies in an age of terror" (2003) revisits Schechner's call for curricular change, arguing for the utility of performance studies as a framework for the analysis of twenty-first century global culture. Through the provocative suggestion that both terrorism and the responses to it can be understood as performance, Bell's essay anticipates questions of definition that are further explored in Part II.

Students and other newcomers to performance studies may find this intellectual history daunting or abstract. The concern with disciplinary boundaries and interdisciplinary formations may seem too far removed from what we ordinarily call performance. Scholars writing about how scholarship is practiced may seem excessively reflexive. Yet it is important to remember that how we structure our thoughts is often a determining factor in what we are able to think, and what we are able to think *about*. Moreover, as the essays in this section demonstrate, this self-awareness of the issues and methods that shape our work has defined performance studies as a field for its entire existence. This is not simply a function of performance studies' genesis in a reflexive, postmodern era. Such self-awareness is an essential characteristic of performance itself.

1

PERFORMANCE STUDIES
The broad spectrum approach

Richard Schechner

It's April 1988. I've been traveling a lot these past few months – India, China, Ann Arbor, Texas, Chicago. And I've seen lots of performances ranging from *jingju* (Beijing Opera) to performance art, from classic dramas to rehearsals of new works by students. I've listened to what people from several cultures and several regions of the United States have to say about the future of the live performing arts: how they are taught, practiced, evaluated; what their recent history has been; and what their near future might be. I've observed classes and performances; spoken to, and debated with, artists, students, and teachers.

The impression I get is that colleagues in India and China are searching through their alternatives concerning training, scholaring, and producing both classic and new works. Although the situation in each of these vast multicultural countries is distinct, and there are many problems, there appears to be agreement on two fronts. First, that a working relationship has to exist between those who are training theater workers and professionals in the field. Second, that performance – as distinct from any of its subgenres like theatre, dance, music, and performance art – is a broad spectrum of activities including at the very least the performing arts, rituals, healing, sports, popular entertainments, and performance in everyday life.

The training of professional performing artists does not coincide with the way either theater and dance majors or performance studies students are educated. In too many American colleges and universities the training of professionals and the educating of majors has been conflated, to the detriment of both professional training and the education of young people who are "interested in" dance and theater but will never earn their living as performing arts professionals.

In my travels I met too many students who were sullen or angry. Entering as wide-eyed freshmen preparing for professional careers or as graduate students expecting to become university-level teachers, they are ripening into extremely disillusioned people. Jobs either as theater workers or as teachers are precious few (see Comments in [*TDR* journal] T113 and T114). The regional theater, television, and film industries are not going to grow much. As far as teaching is concerned, even with the expected wave of retirements coming during the next fifteen years there is little chance that performing arts departments will expand significantly from their current base. I met many faculty who were entrenched, marking time, and scared of the future.

As for the broad spectrum approach – treating performative behavior, not just the performing arts, as a subject for serious scholarly study – this idea is just beginning to make some headway among the academic establishment. In too many American theater and dance departments there is an almost bitter resistance to the broad spectrum approach. Academic inertia crushes thinking that goes beyond the Western traditions of drama or dance and beyond the idea of the performing arts as activities that take place on theater stages.

What needs to be discussed is a wholesale reconstruction of curricula both within performing arts departments and in the university at large. Performing arts departments need to expand their areas of study so that the training of would-be professionals is only a part of what they do. The number of new actors, choreographers, dancers, directors, designers, costumers, and techies should be reduced until the supply more nearly fits the demand. Training and production programs should be reorganized along the lines I outlined in my Comment in [TDR] T116. Instead of training unemployable performance workers, theater and dance departments should develop courses that show how performance is a key paradigm in many cultures, modern and ancient, non-Western and Euro-American.

Performing arts curricula need to be broadened to include courses in performance studies. What needs to be added is how performance is used in politics, medicine, religion, popular entertainments, and ordinary face-to-face interactions. The complex and various relationships among the players in the performance quadrilog – authors, performers, directors, and spectators – ought to be investigated using the methodological tools increasingly available from performance theorists, social scientists, and semioticians. Courses in performance studies need to be made available not only within performing arts departments but to the university community at large. Performative thinking must be seen as a means of cultural analysis. Performance studies courses should be taught outside performing arts departments as part of core curricula.

How hard will it be to get universities to use performance studies as part of their core curricula? At Stanford, the faculty has voted to include studies of non-Western and minority cultures and feminism as part of the required core "civilization" course. How will this be achieved? I recommend a performance studies approach. It is no accident that when nations wish to improve their relations they most often begin by exchanging performing artists. This is because performances both express particular cultural traits and are enjoyable. They are "from somewhere" definite, but they give pleasure everywhere. Exciting, robustly intellectual world-civilization courses can be built around studying dance, theater, rituals, popular entertainments, and sports – buttressed by necessary readings in history and literature, and accompanied by spirited discussions.

Are the teachers of such courses at present available? Can today's theater and dance departments be handed the assignment of developing core curriculum performance studies courses? For the most part, no. The shift I am talking about will emerge gradually. NYU's Department of Performance Studies is a good beginning. The movement toward developing performance studies departments and courses by Northwestern, Brown, and Wisconsin Universities, and at Franklin and Marshall College and several other institutions is encouraging. Young teachers coming from these programs need to be placed as performance studies specialists not only in theater and dance departments but in history, English, women's studies, communications, anthropology, sociology, area studies, popular culture, and ethnomusicology departments. Dialog has to open between performance studies specialists and those who are responsible for planning undergraduate core curricula.

I realize that what I've been saying may sound self-serving. Here I am, a member of NYU's Performance Studies Department; and here I am, editor of *TDR: A Journal of Performance Studies*. But the urgent activities of NYU's department and of *TDR* can also be read as evidence that my colleagues and I are willing to put up so that we don't have to shut up. We are working toward what I have roughly outlined above.

I believe that if the study of performance does not expand and deepen, going far beyond both the training of performance workers and the Western tradition of drama and dance, the whole academic performing arts enterprise constructed over the past half-century or so will collapse. The happy alternative is to expand our vision of what performance is, to study it not only as art but as a means of understanding historical, social, and cultural processes.

READER CROSS-REFERENCES

Worthen, McKenzie, Jackson, Kirshenblatt-Gimblett, J. Bell – implications of the broad spectrum approach on college and university curricula.

Geertz, C. Bell – views of the expanded notion of performance from the disciplinary standpoint of anthropology

Fabian, Turner and Turner, Conquergood – on performance as a means of understanding historical, social, and cultural processes

Taylor – translating "performance studies" into other languages

2

DISCIPLINES OF THE TEXT

Sites of performance[1]

W.B. Worthen

> What is in fact curious about all these gestures, these angular and abruptly abandoned attitudes, these syncopated modulations formed at the back of the throat, these musical phrases that break off short, these flights of elytra, these rustlings of branches, these sounds of hollow drums, these robot squeakings, these dances of animated manikins, is this: that through the labyrinth of their gestures, attitudes, and sudden cries, through the gyrations and turns which leave no portion of the stage space unutilized, the sense of a new physical language, based upon signs and no longer upon words, is liberated. These actors, with their geometric robes seem to be animated hieroglyphs.
>
> Antonin Artaud (1958: 54)

Observing the Balinese dancers, Antonin Artaud undertakes a complex act of intercultural reading. On the one hand, what impresses Artaud is the immediacy of the performers, the sense in which their performance is not an act of re-presentation, but instead a kind of "pure theater, where everything, conception and realization alike, has value, has existence only in proportion to its degree of objectification *on the stage*" (1958: 53). At the same time, though, Artaud also sees their performance hollowing out the dancers, objectifying them: they become "animated manikins" making "robot squeakings"; they undergo a thorough and "systematic depersonalization" (58). Although their gestures "make useless any translation into logical discursive language," Artaud's account of the dancers nonetheless attempts such a translation: their movements demonstrate the value "of a certain number of perfectly learned and above all masterfully applied conventions," they have the "evocative power of a system," a system that verges, surprisingly enough, on "mathematics" (55). Artaud, the theorist of "no more masterpieces," working to evacuate the logos-like authority of scripted texts, nonetheless *reads* the Balinese dancers' bodies, produces these bodies and their performance as a *text*.[2]

Artaud's reading is arresting for other reasons, too, not least for its imperial dimension: we might suspect that the Balinese bodies become texts so readily because, for Artaud, the Balinese are already just things. I open with Artaud's wild ethnology in order to tease out some contemporary assumptions about the relationship between texts and performances, assumptions that structure some of the fault lines that run through the various disciplinary and institutional formations that claim the study of drama/theatre/performance today: cultural studies, English, literature, performance studies, theatre history, theatre studies. Like many negotiations, boundary wars are as much a contest of authority and power as of "truth" or "method" – recall the 1993 American Theatre for Higher Education (ATHE) squabble about admitting Performance Studies as a FORUM member, or the summons in recent ads for *TDR: The Drama Review,* "The Journal of Performance Studies" to "Join the move to performance studies!" Here, I want to explore the relationship between texts, textuality, and performance as an issue deeply inflected by notions of authority – not so much professional authority, but the stabilizing, hegemonic functioning of the Author itself. I am interested in the ways that notions of authority are covertly inscribed in recent discussions of performance, often at just those moments when the supposedly liberating "textuality" of performance is most urgently opposed to that Trojan horse of the absent author, the text. Reconsidering how, or whether, texts are actually *opposed* to performances is one way to rethink the disciplinary instruments that map the contours of drama/theatre/performance studies today.

As Clifford Geertz has remarked, "The great virtue of the extension of the notion of text beyond things written on paper or carved into stone is that it trains attention on precisely this phenomenon: on how the inscription of action is brought about, what its vehicles are and how they work, and on what the fixation of meaning from the flow of events – history from what happened, thought from thinking, culture from behavior – implies for socio-logical interpretation" (1983: 31).[3] Geertz envisions a continuum between texts and the textuality of behavior, one that enables us to read performances as texts, analyze how performances signify, and to interrogate the subsequent rewriting of those performances, the "fixation" of their meanings in texts. In theatre studies, however, a surprisingly romantic sentimentality tends to creep into this issue, opposing "performance" (transgressive, multi-form, revisionary) to the (dominant, repressive, conventional, and canonical) domain of the "text." It's odd that texts should be regarded in this way (where would intertextuality come from without texts?), and this incoherence perhaps suggests that *texts* are not what is really at issue, but how they are construed as vessels of authority, of canonical values, of hegemonic consensus.

Part of this confusion stems from three interlaced ways we think of a "text": (1) as a canonical vehicle of authorial intention; (2) as an intertext, the field of textuality; (3) as a material object, the text in hand. In "From Work to Text," his now classic celebration of textuality, Roland Barthes provides a convenient discrimination between the first two senses, one that informs contemporary discussions of the textuality of performance. Barthes describes an "epistemological slide" (1988: 155) in the conception of written texts, from "the traditional notion of the *work*" to the more relativized sense of the *text* (156), and then characterizes several features and consequences of this slippage. The *work,* that "fragment of substance, occupying a part of the space of books (in a library for example)" (156–7), is the vehicle for authorized cultural reproduction, a "signified" approached through inter-pretation; the *work* discloses a "secret, ultimate, something to be sought out" (158). The *text,* on the other hand, is the field of production rather than interpretation; its "field is that of the signifier," governed by a metonymic rather than a hermeneutic logic, best approached through "the activity of associations, contiguities, carryings-over," through "*playing*" (158).[4] As an object of authorized interpretation, the *work* is, finally, "normally the object of a consumption" (161); the *text* is not an object but a field, "that *social* space which leaves no language safe, outside, nor any subject of the enunciation in position as judge, master, analyst, confessor, decoder" (164). If the *work* is authorized, interpreted, consumed, the *text* is encountered as a field of "play, activity, production, practice" (162). It's not surprising that Barthes's opposition between the *work* (authoritarian, closed, fixed, single, consumed) and the *text* (liberating, open, variable, traced by intertexts, performed) proves so useful to contemporary discourse about performance, in part because Barthes's sense of the *text* is self-consciously performative. Barthes's *text* is the field of the signifier, of textuality, of play, of production – and, of course, of *jouissance*, "a pleasure without separation" (164). Where interpretation is earnest, concerned with fidelity and obedience, performance is insouciant, rewriting and disseminating the words of the text in various ways. Contemporary "studies" – cultural, literary, theatre, and performance – have gained analytical and theoretical leverage from this textualization of performance, the sense that performed events operate discursively, and that meanings arise from the slippage and interplay between signifying formalities. Yet despite the widespread application of "textuality" to reading the body and performance, these two conceptions of the text (text-as-*work*, text-as-*textuality*) often become blurred, compacted in one another, and compacted with that third sense of text, the material words on the page. This confusion most often takes place precisely when an opposition between text and performance is invoked to mark different disciplinary accounts of drama and performance, and the different institutional fields in which the study and practice of drama, theatre, and performance take place.

Stage vs. page, literature vs. theatre, text vs. performance: these simple oppositions have less to do with the relationship between writing and enactment than with power, with the ways that we authorize performance, ground its significance. Not surprisingly, both strategies of authorization – literary and performative – share similar assumptions, what we might call a rhetoric of origin/essence. This rhetoric appears to ground the relationship between text and performance, a relationship that is always conceived, as John Rouse suggests, as "a question both of the possible and the allowable" (1992: 146). From the "literary" perspective, the meaning, and so the authority, of performance is a function of how fully it expresses the meanings, gestures, themes located ineffably in the structures of the work, which is taken both as the ground and origin of performance and as the embodiment of authorial intention, the work. Though performance may discover meanings or nuances not immediately available through "reading" or "criticism," these meanings are nonetheless seen as latent potentialities located in the words on the page, the traces of the authorial work. The performative perspective generally avails itself of the same emphasis on origins: stage production is, in a sense, the final cause for the writing of plays, which gain their fullest, their essential meaning only in the circumstances for which they were originally intended: theatrical performance. Stanley Wells epitomizes this position in his "General Introduction" to the 1984 Oxford *William Shakespeare: The Complete Works*: "Nevertheless, it is in performance that the plays lived and had their being. Performance is the end to which they were created, and in this edition we have devoted our efforts to recovering and presenting texts of Shakespeare's plays as they were acted in the London playhouses which stood at the centre of his professional life" (1984: xxxvii).[5] (It might be noted that this argument traces authorial intention in the generalized practices of the stage.) Much as the text-centered view essentializes and universalizes reading or interpretive practice (the meanings of the play are then *in* the text, regardless of the ways we have been conditioned to read them), so this view essentializes and universalizes notions of stage performance (the meanings of the play emerge *on* the stage, regardless of how we have been conditioned to produce or read them). The text here is merely the signifier of the essentially performative nature of the play, an enabling accident of the performance.

I have phrased this dichotomy crudely, in part to suggest how notions of legitimacy and authority persist in thinking about dramatic performance. Think of acting students, for example, dismissing some baroque interpretation of *Hamlet* or *Godot* as unactable, not assimilable to the contemporary (i.e., "natural") discourse of stage production, and so illegitimate to the study of drama. Or of theatre reviewers (or literary scholars) dismissing some "experimental" production of *Agamemnon* as "experimental," trendy, somehow not "faithful" to the meaning, intention of the originating text. Or of stage directors talking about letting the stage release the intentions of the author; of the more theatrically oriented stage directions of the new *Oxford Shakespeare*; of the American Repertory Theatre (ART) *Endgame* debacle.[6] The desire to ground the meaning of theatrical production by attributing its authority either to the work or to the institutions of the stage afflicts both the popular and the academic conception of theatrical meaning.

Part of the problem in the way that text and performance are conceived has to do with reductive assumptions of the formal consistency of published texts, of texts as material objects that house the *work* of the author. For although it is now conventional to see performance as traced by a variety of gestural, figural, and ideological textualities, the notion that there *is* a text to produce onstage is surprisingly resistant to change. And yet recent controversies in textual studies – bibliography as it was once called – over the relationship between texts as material objects and notions of the authorial *work* have sharply undermined the supposed authority (intentional or otherwise) of *the* text. Much of this work in English studies surrounds the production of Shakespearean dramatic texts, the ways in which the history of editorial practice – from Heminge and Condell's publication of the folio *Works* of Shakespeare in 1623, through the "scientific" bibliography of W.W. Greg (1954) and Fredson Bowers (1964) – has been designed to produce books that claim to embody the "original" or at best a close approximation to the author's intended inscription, a fleshing out of the spiritualized *work*. But as Leah Marcus asks,

> What if, rather than flowing effortlessly and magically from Shakespeare's mind onto the unalterable fixity of paper, the plays were from the beginning provisional, amenable to alterations by the playwright or others, coming to exist over time in a number of versions, all related, but none of them an original in the pristine sense

promised by Heminge and Condell? Nothing we know about the conditions of production in the Renaissance playhouse allows us to hope for single authoritative versions of the plays.

(1988: 44)[7]

Marcus suggests that the notion of a printed text as the embodiment of the organic unity of an author's "work" is foreign to the circumstances of Renaissance publishing, and perhaps to all textual production, in Shakespeare's era.[8]

But the "textual condition" – in Jerome McGann's apt phrase – haunts all texts, not only those produced in the early modern period. For as McGann suggests, "a 'text' is not a 'material thing' but a material event or set of events, a point in time (or a moment in space) where certain communicative interchanges are being practiced" (1991: 21). In this sense, no single printed text corresponds to the authorial *work,* which can only be conceived as "the global set of all texts and poems which have emerged in the literary production and reproduction process" (32) – texts which are, of course, necessarily contradictory of one another, usually in their linguistic as well as in their material elements. The *work* is always absent, an ideal construction assigned to an equally absent "author." Much as the "author's name manifests the appearance of a certain discursive set and indicates the status of this discourse within a society and a culture" (Foucault 1979: 147), so the *work* is a site of regulation, containment, a way to fix and stabilize meanings by predetermining the range of appropriate interpretation, of licensed reading. Yet the *work* is never present in the text; the text is its signifier and its supplement, signifying the *work*'s absence at the same time that it locates a material space for it, here, in and not in this particular materialization, this book. What Barthes means by *text* is in some sense more like what we usually mean by performance: a production of a specific state of the text in which a variety of intertextual possibilities are realized. In this sense, performance has the same relation to the material *text* (the printed text, the text on the page) that the text has to the authorial *work*: the performance signifies an absence, the precise fashioning of the text's absence, at the same time that it appears to summon it into being, to produce it as performance (remembering that reading is as much a performance, a production of the text, as a stage performance is).[9] The material text, the text as object, deconstructs the *work* even before we encounter it, play it, produce it as reading, criticism, enactment.

Though eccentric in the history of publishing, in many ways dramatic texts are normative of the "textual condition." The contemporary controversy surrounding Shakespearean editing may seem like a special case, but it's really not: the publication of a play is usually guaranteed to produce a text that violates any sense of a stable relation between published "text," organic "work," and authorial "intention." As Philip Gaskell has remarked in his study of Tom Stoppard's *Travesties,* contemporary plays often exist in several quite different, equally "authoritative" printed versions: a preproduction text, a text published in conjunction with the premiere, subsequent editions published after later productions, texts incorporating revisions which may or may not have been made directly by the author, collected editions, acting editions (1978).[10] The acting editions common in the theatre usually include much nonauthorial material (property plots, for example), but even trade editions include text of dubious provenance; stage directions (which often derive from the practice of the initial production) are notably suspect – though many directors (but not scholars or critics) regard them as dispensable anyway.[11] The publisher generally prescribes the overall format of the play on the page; plays are much less conventionalized in their layout than novels, but are not usually susceptible to the kinds of idiosyncratic layout that frequently accompany modern poetry (Ntozake Shange and Heiner Müller are two exceptions that prove this rule). A publisher's production team will generally determine the punctuation and positioning of speech prefixes, the amount of space between speeches, the typography, location, and positioning of stage directions, and so on.[12] And, of course, plays now appear in a variety of electronic formats, which enable "readers" both to read a text and to view video performances more or less simultaneously on a computer screen. These accidentals may seem truly incidental to the integrity of the *work*, but they are only incidental if we regard the printed text as the poorly materialized body of the work's spirit. If, on the other hand, we are interested in how texts are produced in the world, these accidents are the record of that production – they encode the publisher's sense of the audience and purpose of the volume, as well as the means by which it will be read, be *performed*. To read *Endgame* in the familiar Grove Press edition, in the double-column format of a drama anthology, or on a computer screen – where, of course, the reader may be able to interact with, change the text while reading it – is to recognize how deeply the material form of the text affects the kinds of attention we bring to bear on it, the ways we read it. The material text determines the sense of the *work* that we may finally achieve.[13]

To see the book itself as a production complicates traditional notions of the authority of meaning, since any *work* turns out not to be the origin of the text, but its effect, an effect of a panoply of performances, of textualizations. Indeed, it might be argued that to engage the text textually, to think of the text as a production of the work, is to attribute to the text (and to its performance as reading) the functions of performance: that performance works rhetorically, to accomplish "the *appearance of substance*," the "compelling illusion" of a motivating identity which is, of course, always absent (Butler 1990: 271). By locating the *work* in the text, rather than seeing it as an effect, an ascription derived from the text, the "text vs. performance" argument makes an odd eventuality possible: the unacknowledged importation of the kinds of authority associated with the *work* into the performance itself. Performance becomes the place where the Author is realized, that "principle of closure, of semiotic inhibition, employed in the conflict of interpretations to privilege certain readings and control 'unruly meanings' " (Berger 1987: 153).

Although this spectral movement of cultural authority from the *work* to the performance is visible in a variety of places, the example I would like to develop here is taken from a discussion of intercultural performance – just the kind of discussion which we might expect to dispel notions of the authority of the *work* in performance. In a fine article on a kathakali production of *King Lear,* Phillip Zarrilli describes how Australian playwright David McRuvie and French actor-director Annette Leday collaborated with the Kerala State Arts Academy, using "a group of highly regarded senior kathakali artists" (1992: 18) to stage a production of Shakespeare's play. This is an important and suggestive piece of work, and Zarrilli both documents and interrogates a range of intercultural issues arising from the production –

working arrangements between producers and performers, the play's reception in both European and Malayali press, and the reactions of two institutionalized custodians of canonicity (the Shakespeare industry/press, on the one hand, and the kathakali performers and audiences on the other). Both Zarrilli and the producers have a delicate and nuanced sense of how this intercultural performance exchange might work, and of how it actually did work. Yet at the same time, in both the producers' conception and to a lesser extent in Zarrilli's account, the interculturalism of the *Kathakali King Lear* depends on relatively essentialized notions of text and performance: "Leday and McRuvie wanted the production to speak equally to both its original audiences. For Malayalis the production was intended to provide a kathakali experience of one of Shakespeare's great plays and roles. Assuming that many in the European audience would know Shakespeare's play, the production was intended as an accessible way of experiencing kathakali" (19). And yet it is precisely this notion of origin that is undone – as it must be – by the process of production. Neither *King Lear* nor kathakali were produced here/both *King Lear* and kathakali were produced here. Zarrilli notes that McRuvie's "reelaboration of the *King Lear* text to conform with kathakali's theatrical criteria . . . radically transformed the original. The typed English adaptation ran barely twenty pages for the two-hour-plus performance. The action focused exclusively on Lear and his three daughters. The Gloucester subplot was completely cut, as were Kent, Cornwall, and Albany" (19–20).[14] Similarly, kathakali discourse had to be altered as well: the narrative, sung dialog, and gestural passages that structure kathakali performance had to be simplified, and the roles of *King Lear* needed to be adapted to the conventional types of kathakali characterization, exerting a certain pressure on each.

Characterizing the British response to the performance, Zarrilli notes that one review described it as having "little to do with Shakespeare"; it had equally little to do with kathakali in a traditional sense (27). What is surprising, then, is that given the extraordinary reelaboration of *both* textual modes, the producers and Zarrilli claim to be trying to reproduce some essential "experience," via the intercultural discourse of *Kathakali King Lear*. The fissuring of the text is not really at issue: the work for this production was in many senses not unlike the cutting and reelaborating necessary for any production, even those that work to encode themselves as "faithful" to the text. In some essentials, this *King Lear* is no less and no more "Shakespeare's" *King Lear* than Peter Brook's famous *Endgame*-inspired production, or the plays produced by Edward Bond or Howard Barker under different titles (*Lear*, *Seven Lears*). As Terry Eagleton has argued, "text and production are distinct formations – different material modes of production, between which no homologous or 'reproductive' relationship can hold. They are not two aspects of the same discourse – the text, as it were, thought or silent speech and the production thought-in-action, articulate language; they constitute distinct kinds of discourse, between which no simple 'translation' is possible" (1978: 66). We have to forego, then, the notion that any production speaks the text in some unmediated, or faithfully mediated way. All productions betray the text, all texts betray the idealist *work*. Although McRuvie and Leday scorn "some hypothetically universal realm of communication" (Zarrilli 1992: 36), their test of intercultural performance is finally predicated on some hypothetically stable and universal "content" to be communicated. "King Lear" remains, even with the cast cut, the plot changed, the language changed, and so on; kathakali can be experienced in some essential manner, even when the formal and cultural traditions of the performance have been altered.

What makes this project – for all its ambition, for all the excitement and promise it holds – finally disappointing is that the "experiment," far from testing the condition of performance (intercultural or otherwise), merely confirms it; or, to be more precise, it confirms the conditions of authority and authorization animating much Western performance. McRuvie and Leday rewrite, "transgress" the written text, but texts are always a field of transgression; at the same time, they see their activity as authorized by its fidelity to the *work* – Shakespeare's work, kathakali tradition. Much as texts always point to an absent origin, so the *Kathakali King Lear* points to an absence as well: kathakali, *King Lear*. To say that the *Kathakali King Lear* rewrites but preserves Shakespeare's play is to understand performance in fundamentally conservative terms, underwritten less by the "text" than by the phantom Author who haunts and exceeds it. How the "author" or "intention" or "meaning" is said to fill that absence is, I would argue, where the politics of performance, and the hegemony of literature, exert themselves.[15] How does thinking about texts, authority, and performance in this way relate to the bondage of our disciplinary evocations of drama and performance? Eagleton's remarks on text and performance as incommensurable modes of production imply that, rather than locating the authority of performance in the text *or* its enactment, we need instead to interrogate the practices – critical, histrionic, directorial – that claim this homology, that forge a specific kind of produced meaning onstage. This clearly dialectical interrogation may sound easier to accomplish than it is; I'd like, finally, to illustrate this difficulty by considering some of the disciplinary claims of "performance studies." Performance studies has, of course, provocatively challenged many assumptions about what performance is, where performance is, and how performances signify. By expanding the investigation of performance into the social and cultural sphere, and by interrogating a range of performance modes, forms, and occasions, performance studies participates in the kind of disciplinary remapping characteristic of intellectual life in the *fin de siècle*. Like other questions of representation – gender studies, queer theory, postcolonial studies, semiotics, to name just a few – performance studies takes place in a variety of institutional locations not currently labeled "performance studies" departments. This seems to me not a disabling situation, though it is certainly a disempowering one within the institutional structure of the university, and the way to combat it – to inaugurate the "move to performance studies" – is, of course, to suggest that performance studies constitutes a "new paradigm."

In its particular blending of ethnology with literary and cultural theory, as well as in the productive eclecticism it sponsors, performance studies has certainly brought new questions into view, new ways of thinking, writing, and teaching into practice. But to define this "new paradigm" in opposition to theatre studies – or, indeed, to the other "paradigms" from which performance studies often draws its theoretical armature and methodological practice – is, finally, to reinscribe performance studies with at least some of the analytical hierarchies its practitioners would contest. In his now notorious paper first delivered at the 1992 ATHE convention in Atlanta, Richard Schechner suggests that "theatre as we have known and practiced it – the staging of written dramas – will be the string quartet of the twenty-first century: a beloved but extremely limited genre, a subdivision of performance," and so calls for a conceptual remapping of our current disciplinary and institutional horizons: "The new paradigm is 'performance,' not theatre. Theatre departments should become 'performance departments'" (1992: 8, 9). Schechner is certainly right to view performance as "about more than the enactment of Eurocentric drama," and I am in sympathy – though, obviously, not in complete agreement – with his sense that "performed acts, whether actual or virtual, *more than the written word*, connect and negotiate the many cultural, personal, group, regional, and world systems comprising today's realities" (9, my emphasis). I don't want to go into Schechner's sense of this "new paradigm" here, however, in part because this brief, occasional essay gives a poor accounting of it – largely multiplying "objects" of study (that is, merely expanding the turf) under the banner of "intercultural" performance, rather than articulating the conceptual paradigm that would offer new modes of analysis and explanation, a new sense of what *counts* and of how it counts in the identification, analysis, and explanation of performance. This is not an unusual problem in the interdisciplinary world, and it afflicts most areas of the humanities at the moment – expanding the canon of literature, history, art, and so on has challenged the notion of a single embracing paradigm in ways that have yet to be resolved.[16]

Where Schechner's new paradigm seems most fairly to evoke a Kuhnian conceptual revolution is in the area of pedagogy, how performance – especially intercultural performance, the hallmark of performance studies in Schechner's formulation – will be taught. The basic premise of this innovation is a familiar split, an opposition between *reading* and *doing*: "It is not only a question of studying different cultures from a scholarly perspective, but of seeing and doing rituals, dramas, celebrations, and festivals from Africa, Asia, Europe, Native America, and Latin America"; "Students need to practice various kinds of social customs, dress, religious observances, and aesthetics" (9). The learning of the body is critical to any education, but Schechner's dichotomy between reading and doing is suspiciously evocative of the dichotomy between texts and performances, and suggests how difficult it is to articulate a new paradigm through a merely binary rhetoric.[17]

What are the consequences of conceiving reading as the domain of textual domination, of the explicit transmission of the repressive and canonical authority of dominant culture, and of performance as the means of evading such authority? In "Dramatic Ritual/Ritual Drama: Performative and Reflexive Athropology," Victor Turner describes his collaboration with Schechner in a performance/anthropology workshop that offers one version of this pedagogy. In this workshop, participants (Turner, his wife Edith Turner, and students both of performance and of anthropology) enacted various rituals of the Ndembu people, who had been the subject of much of Turner's anthropological fieldwork and analysis. Turner was, naturally, sensitive to the limitations of this experiment: "Surely, at so many removes, must not the whole performance have seemed highly artificial, inauthentic? Oddly enough, according to the students, it did not" (1982: 96). The fact that *authenticity* is at issue here is revealing, and troubling. Although there is an intertextual element to this workshop, "performance" is finally a mode of fidelity – to the offstage authority of the *work* being reproduced here, the authentic Ndembu ritual. At the moment that this performance becomes truly intercultural and intertextual – when, we might say, the rituals of NYU and the Ndembu finally deconstruct one another, subvert notions of authorized performance altogether – it loses its value for Turner, precisely because that "authentic" other disappears from view, is replaced by a performance whose only authority is in the performance itself. Attempting to perform a girls' puberty ritual – which takes place in a culture in which inheritance was matrilineal but "politics was mainly in the hands of males" (1982: 97–8) – the performers tried to get inside the "affective dimension" of the ritual through a kind of intercultural performance "framing":

> They began a rehearsal with a ballet, in which women created a kind of frame with their bodies, positioning themselves to form a circle, in which the subsequent male political action could take place. Their idea was to show that action went on within a matrilineal sociocultural space. Somehow this device didn't work – there was a covert contemporary political tinge in it which denatured the Ndembu sociocultural process. This feminist mode of staging ethnography assumed and enacted modern ideological notions in a situation in which those ideas are simply irrelevant.
>
> (1982: 97)

Irrelevant to whom? This performance is "irrelevant" only if we believe that performance can achieve authenticity, that it can become (unlike the *text*) the faithful vehicle of the immanent, authorized *work*. Much as the *Kathakali King Lear* is haunted by notions of Shakespearean authority imported at precisely the moment that "text" is opposed to "performance," so here Ndembu rituals assume the status of a *work*, which governs the performance as its "signified": the performance is relegated to the status of interpretation, a means of echoing meanings which already exist elsewhere rather than being a site for the production of meaning, a site where the ways in which meaning is produced can be interrogated, inspected, performed. Turner's students, in a manner of speaking, might as well have been staging scenes from *Hamlet* in an English class.

Although Turner wants to oppose reading and doing here, escaping the deadly authority of the text for the exploratory activity of live – and enlivening – performance, his performing bodies are, in effect, *readers* of the most conventional kind, searching in their performance to reproduce not merely the "text" of Ndembu ritual – which, like all other texts, deconstructs the thing it represents – but the absent, authoritative, authoritarian *work*. Their bodies, in a sense, become like the bodies of Artaud's Balinese, not a site of intertextual production, nor of intercultural dissonance; performance is the site for the reproduction of authority, the authority of the innate meaning of Ndembu ritual. I don't mean to suggest that the use of performance in teaching, or intercultural performance, or performance studies itself must necessarily fail to fulfill the promise of a "new paradigm": indeed, the promise of this shifting can be felt precisely in the variety of work that can be characterized as "performance studies."[18] But I do mean to suggest how difficult it is to discover such a paradigm without understanding the notions of "paradigm" and "discipline" we use to frame and authorize our activities in a sufficiently dialectical manner. New paradigms are often ghosted by their history in ways that are difficult to recognize, acknowledge, and transform; to understand "performance studies" through a simple opposition between text and performance is to remain captive to the spectral disciplines of the past. Both texts and performances are materially unstable registers of signification, producing "meaning" inter-textually in ways that deconstruct notions of intention, fidelity, authority, present meaning. At the same time, texts and performances retain the gesture of such semiosis, and dis-cussions of both text and performance remain haunted by the desire for authorization. If I have fairly captured even part of the complexity of this situation, it should be clear that no simple opposition between text and performance – or, I would argue, between the "paradigms" we constitute to frame them – will be sufficient to capture the rich, contra-dictory, incommensurable ways that they engage one another. Given this difficulty, I think we should be eager not to foreclose understanding, to preempt new critical practice, by reaching too quickly and irritably for the certainty that notions of "paradigm" and "discipline" appear to offer. At this moment of undisciplined, interdisciplinary flux, euphoria, uncertainty, mystery, and doubt, perhaps what's called for is a little negative capability.

NOTES

1 I would like to thank Oscar G. Brockett for inviting me to give an earlier version of this paper at the 1993 American Society for Theater Research annual convention, and Shannon Jackson, of the Performance Studies Department at Northwestern University, for taking the time to read and comment on an earlier draft. Finally, my thanks – come what may – to Richard Schechner for putting this "forum" together.

2 On the notion that the theater of cruelty is a noninterpretive theater, see Derrida (1978: 245).

3 Dominick LaCapra, among others, has criticized the "excessively homogenizing" aspect of Geertz's "anthropological model" when it is applied to "societies which in the modern period have been sources of both emulation and imperialistic imposition on the rest of the world"; he also suggests that Geertz's "insistence on the autonomy of symbolic forms may avoid reductionism at the price of regressing to precritical idealism" (1988: 378). Despite the conventional opposition between the repressive text and transgressive performance, the concept of textuality and of the discourse of behavior have critically enabled the contemporary discussion of performance, theatrical and otherwise. A genealogy of the textualization of performance might trace the impact of Saussurean linguistics in the "human sciences," first felt in France in the 1950s, and then in Anglo-American scholarship and theory in the 1960s; the elaboration of semiotic and semiological analysis in literature, the arts, and culture generally, especially Jacques Derrida's sense of the interminable play of signifiers, of there being no "outside" or "beyond" the text; Jacques Lacan's formulation of the unconscious as a language; the ramifications of Louis Hjelmslev's articulation of the "subject" of discourse; related notions of the subject traced and textualized by ideological production associated with Louis Althusser, Göran Therborn, and others; and – most urgently in feminist theory, in gay and lesbian work, and in studies of the production of "race," ethnicity, and colonial subjects in performance – the ways the body itself is taken as a site of representation, traced by textualities that both encode and "naturalize" the body while at the same time framing the possibility of performative subversion.

4 Moreover, while the *work* is bound to the irreducible, single voice of the author, the *text* "is plural as . . . it accomplishes the very plural of meaning, an *irreducible* (and not merely an acceptable) plural. The Text is not a co-existence of meanings but a passage, an overcrossing; thus it answers not to an interpretation, even a liberal one, but to an explosion, a dissemination" (Barthes

1988: 159). To read the *work*, then, is to be "caught up in a process of filiation. [. . . T]he author is reputed the father and the owner of his work: literary science therefore teaches *respect* for the manuscript and the author's declared intentions, while society asserts the legality of the relation of author to work (the '*droit d'auteur*' or 'copyright,' in fact of recent date since it was only really legalized at the time of the French Revolution)" (160–1). The *text,* on the other hand, "reads without the inscription of the Father. [. . . T]he metaphor of the Text is that of the *network*" (161).

5 Michael Vanden Heuvel presents a more subtle version of this distinction: "dramas are written within an aesthetic and semiotic framework that includes theatricality or spectacle" (1993: 160–1).

6 Gerald Rabkin describes this controversy in detail. "Director JoAnne Akalaitis and the ART producers essentially adhered to the letter of the printed text despite a few cuts and alterations," but set the play in "a desolate length of subway tunnel replete with derelict cars and the detritus of modern technological civilization" rather than in Beckett's "bare interior." Barney Rossett (his American agent at the time) informed Beckett of the production and threatened legal action. When the play opened in December 1984, the program included disclaimers by Beckett and Rossett, as well as a statement by the ART Artistic Director, Robert Brustein: this was the compromise that prevented legal action (1987: 146–8).

7 Marcus continues,

> Shakespeare wrote his own name in many different ways; his spelling of other words appears also to have been unregularized in the extreme. His dramatic language was "prelexical," to use Margreta de Grazia's apt phrase, in that it failed to conform to codified notions of language which had not yet been invented. He appears to have punctuated quite sparsely, opening the playtexts up to a variety of 'senses' rather than establishing a single governing interpretation. We have no reason to suppose that the larger structures of the plays were less malleable and open to the proliferation of meaning.
>
> (1988: 44–5)

8 In their fine recent article on "The materiality of the Shakespearean text," Margreta de Grazia and Peter Stallybrass argue that the materiality of Renaissance texts – the "old typefaces and spellings, irregular line and scene divisions, title pages and other paratextual matter" – insists "upon being looked *at*, not seen *through*. Their refusal to yield to modern norms bears witness to the specific history of the texts they make up, a history so specific that it cannot comply with modern notions of correctness and intelligibility" (1993: 256–7). In an era in which a play might appear under several different titles, and in which even Shakespeare's signature can be conceived as "a collaborative field, not the private property of a single individual" (278), it is difficult to maintain the Enlightenment regard for print as the transparent vehicle of the immanent authorial *work*.

9 In a powerful reading of August Wilson's *Ma Rainey's Black Bottom*, Sandra L. Richards argues that performance traditions – the traditions of blues performance, in this case – while literally absent from the written text often provide the means for "filling" moments otherwise apparently "blank" on the page. I am grateful to Sandra Richards for sharing the text of her 1993 English Institute essay with me.

10 Gerald Rabkin develops this issue, and a reading of Barthes's "From work to text," in relation to the specific texts of theatrical production, and issues of copyright and censorship. He notes, for example, that performers and directors accept "the text's privilege" in a variety of ways, not least at those moments – ignoring stage directions, for instance – where they seem to oppose the authority of the text.

> That privileging, however, is not necessarily accepted by theatre discourse's truncation of 'manuscript into the unique signifier, the *script*. Unlike critics, most actors and directors rarely talk about the text; they talk of the script which they hold in their hands as they rehearse. The script is inscribed, it may indeed be published, but it carries a provisional authority. The script is something to be used and discarded as its textuality is corporealized in performance.
>
> (1985: 150)

It should be remarked, though, that if the script is taken as a vehicle of authority, discarding it does not do away with that privilege; it has merely been rewritten into the corporeal discourse of the stage.

11 It is also important to note that editions change text depending on the venue; Trevor Griffith's play *Comedians* is a case in point. Early in the play, Gethin Price recites this limerick to the other comedians-in-training of the play: "There was a young lady called Pratt/ Who would hang from the light by her hat/ With a frightening cough/ She would jerk herself off/ By sinking her teeth in her twat" (Faber edition, 1976a: 17–18; Grove Press edition, 1976b: 18–19). The Samuel French edition, which advertises the American production of the play at the Music Box Theatre, alters the limerick, presumably for American audiences: "There was a young lady called Hunt/ Who had a remarkable stunt/ With a frightening cough/ She would jerk herself off/ By sinking her teeth in her cunt" (Samuel French edition, 1976c: 19). The fact that *this* limerick was altered, rather than many other culturally specific points in the dialog, points precisely to the ways that the text embodies notions of audience and reception, not merely authorial expression or intention: the producers of the play, and the publishers of its American acting edition, have clearly felt that "translating" this misogynist limerick is essential to the play's "meaning" in ways that other British English/American English inconsistencies are not.

12 In part this problem is a function of the rise of playwrights to the social status of "authors," and the desire – of the playwright, his or her estate, publishers, the culture industry – to preserve and promote an authoritative edition: the various editions of Oscar Wilde's *The Importance of Being Earnest* are a good example here, as are the fortunes of playwrights whose careers were made by publishing their plays – Shaw, Ibsen, Beckett, for example.

13 As McGann rightly has remarked,

> To read, for example, a translation of Homer's *Iliad* in the Signet paperback, in the edition published by the University of Chicago Press, in the Norton Critical Edition, or in the limited edition put out by the Folio Society (with illustrations), is to read Homer's *Iliad* in four very different ways. Each of these texts is visually and materially coded for different audiences and different purposes.
>
> (1991: 115)

14 Zarrilli also implies that the nine scenes of the play included some material not in Shakespeare's version – "the wedding and departure of Cordelia and France," for instance (1992: 20).

15 One dimension of Zarrilli's piece I haven't addressed here is its political dimension, the politics of such adaptation and reproduction. What does it mean to produce a text like *King Lear* in this manner, what are the vectors of power that undergird or inform this activity, and do those vectors alter depending on the site of performance? What possibilities for resistance – political, cultural, performative – are encoded in the relationship between the canonicity of texts and the canonicity of performance modes, and in the contestatory strategies of authorization this production presumes?

16 Schechner is clear that the subject of intercultural performance "is the difficulties brought up by multiculturalism, the misunderstandings, broken languages, and failed transactions occurring when and where cultures collide, overlap, or pull away from each other" (1992: 7). Performance

studies attempts to resolve this situation largely through accumulation: "performance studies" will include the study of "different cultures from a scholarly perspective"; how "performances are used in politics, medicine, sports, religion, and everyday life"; the "four great realms of performance: . . . entertainment, education, ritual, and healing"; the relationship between "authors, performers, directors, and spectators"; the whole range of performance activity – training, preparations, warm-ups, performing, cool down, and aftermath"; and the entire range of "popular entertainment – . . . rock concerts, discos, electioneering, wrestling, congames and stings, college and professional sports, vogueing, street theater, parades, demonstrations, and a panoply of religious rituals ranging from staid old church services to hot gospel sings, to the rituals of Asian and African religions, to the practices of New Age Shamanism" (9–10). Several disciplines have long had some interest in what Schechner describes as "popular entertainment," though without a paradigmatic commitment to performative signification. For a recent attempt to forge a rapprochement between theater studies and performance studies, see Dolan (1993).

17 This dichotomy, it might be noted, is enshrined in the "*TDR* Writers' Guidelines" (1993) as well, where potential contributors are informed that "We are not interested in drama as such, the analysis of playtexts with no reference to their actual life in performance," as though the text and one's reading of it were only a kind of virtual reality, not a performance, not the actual life of the text or of the reader.

18 As in other fields – literary criticism and theory, or cultural studies, for instance – which have drawn methods, interpretive priorities and practices, and even objects of inquiry from other "disciplines," it becomes particularly difficult to insist on a single "paradigm" of disciplinary inquiry. Consider, for example, the various ways in which "ethnography" and "performance" are constructed by Dwight Conquergood (1992), Margaret Thompson Drewal (1992), and Richard Schechner (1992); or the interrelationship between cultural history, theater history, literary criticism, ethnography, and performance in Joseph Roach's understanding of performance genealogy (1992); or of Peggy Phelan's articulation of performance, cultural critique, and psychoanalysis (1993).

REFERENCES

Artaud, Antonin (1958) "On the Balinese theater." In *The Theater and Its Double*, translated by Mary Caroline Richards, 53–67. New York: Grove Press.

Barthes, Roland (1988) "From work to text." In *Image/Music/Text*, translated by Stephen Heath, 155–64. New York: Farrar, Straus, and Giroux.

Berger, Harry, Jr. (1987) "Bodies and texts." *Representations* 17 (Winter): 144–66.

Bowers, Fredson (1964) *Bibliography and Textual Criticism*. Oxford: Clarendon Press.

Butler, Judith (1990) "Performative acts and gender constitution: an essay in phenomenology and feminist theory." In *Performing Feminisms: Feminist Critical Theory and Practice*, edited by Sue-Ellen Case, 270–82. Baltimore: Johns Hopkins University Press.

Clifford, James (1988) *The Predicament of Culture: Twentieth-Century Ethnography, Literature, and Art*. Cambridge: Harvard University Press.

Conquergood, Dwight (1992) "Performance theory, Hmong shamans, and cultural politics." In *Critical Theory and Performance*, edited by Janelle G. Reinelt and Joseph R. Roach, 41–64. Ann Arbor: University of Michigan Press.

Derrida, Jacques (1978) "The theatre of cruelty and the closure of representation." In *Writing and Difference*, translated by Alan Bass, 232–50. Chicago: University of Chicago Press.

Dolan, Jill (1993) "Geographies of learning: theatre studies, performance, and the 'performative'." *Theatre Journal* 45, 4: 417–41.

Drewal, Margaret Thompson (1992) *Yoruba Ritual: Performers, Play, Agency*. Bloomington: Indiana University Press.

Eagleton, Terry (1978) *Criticism and Ideology*. London: Verso.

Foucault, Michel (1979) "What is an author?" In *Textual Strategies*, edited by Josué V. Harari, 141–60. Ithaca: Cornell University Press.

Gaskell, Philip (1978) *From Writer to Reader: Studies in Editorial Method*. Oxford: Oxford University Press.

Geertz, Clifford (1983) "Blurred genres: the refiguration of social thought." In *Local Knowledge: Further Essays in Interpretive Anthropology*. New York: Basic Books.

de Grazia, Margreta, and Peter Stallybrass (1993) "The materiality of the Shakespearean text." *Shakespeare Quarterly* 44, 3 (Fall): 255–83.

Greg, W.W. (1954) *The Editorial Problem in Shakespeare: A Survey of the Foundations of the Text*. Oxford: Clarendon Press.

Griffiths, Trevor (1976a) *Comedians*. London: Faber and Faber.

—— (1976b) *Comedians*. New York: Grove Press.

—— (1976c) *Comedians: A Play in Three Acts*. New York: Samuel French.

LaCapra, Dominick (1988) "Culture and ideology: from Geertz to Marx." *Poetics Today* 9, 2: 377–94.

Marcus, Leah (1988) *Puzzling Shakespeare: Local Reading and Its Discontents*. Berkeley: University of California Press.

McGann, Jerome J. (1991) *The Textual Condition*. Princeton: Princeton University Press.

Phelan, Peggy (1993) *Unmarked: The Politics of Performance*. London and New York: Routledge.

Rabkin, Gerald (1985) "Is there a text on this stage? Theatre/authorship/interpretation." *Performing Arts Journal* 9, 2.3 (PAJ26/27): 2–3, 142–59.

Richards, Sandra L. (1993) "Writing the absent potential: drama, performance, and the canon of African American literature." Unpublished manuscript.

Roach, Joseph (1992) "Mardi Gras Indians and others: genealogies of American performance." *Theatre Journal* 44, 4: 461–83.

Rouse, John (1992) "Textuality and authority in theater and drama: some contemporary possibilities." In *Critical Theory and Performance*, edited by Janelle G. Reinelt and Joseph R. Roach, 146–57. Ann Arbor: University of Michigan Press.

Schechner, Richard (1992) "A new paradigm for theater in the academy." *TDR* 36, 4 (T136): 7–10.

TDR (1993) "*TDR* Writers' Guidelines." *TDR* 36, 3 (T135): n.p.

Turner, Victor (1982) "Dramatic ritual/ritual drama: performative and reflexive anthropology." In *From Ritual to Theatre: The Human Seriousness of Play*, 89–101. New York: PAJ Publications.

Vanden Heuvel, Michael (1993) "Textual harassment: teaching drama to interrogate reading." *Theatre Topics* 3, 2: 159–66.

Wells, Stanley (1984) "General introduction." *William Shakespeare: The Complete Works*, edited by Stanley Wells and Gary Taylor, xiii–xxxvii. New York and Oxford: Oxford University Press.

Zarrilli, Phillip B. (1992) "For whom is the king a king? Issues of intercultural production, perception, and reception in a *Kathakali King Lear*." In *Critical Theory and Performance*, edited by Janelle G. Reinelt and Joseph R. Roach, 16–40. Ann Arbor: University of Michigan Press.

READER CROSS-REFERENCES

Schechner – on the need for a new, interdisciplinary way of teaching and studying performance

Geertz – also cautions against the limits of an interdisciplinary approach

De Marinis – on the semiotic definition of "text" as it relates to performance

Turner and Turner – describe a ritual re-enactment similar to the one cited by Worthen

Conquergood – notes the bias of Western academics toward text-based inquiry, and the political implications of that bias

Zimmerman – on the status of the text and "the work" in her process of devising theatre

3

THE LIMINAL-NORM

Jon McKenzie

Let us again assemble two paradigms of efficacy, two models of cultural performance legible from our readings. In the first, efficacy grounds itself in embodied transgressions, in practices honed by theater, ritual, and other trainings of the body. Performance here is between theater and ritual: its limen is the theatricalization of ritual and the ritualization of theater. Face-to-face encounters, site-specific events, the co-presencing of individual and social bodies – these instantiate the transformative power of performance in the first decades of performance studies, prior even to its appellation. The second model of efficacy, that of resistance, takes off from the discourses of critical theory and the experiments of performance art: its cutting edge is the theory of practice and the practice of theory. Mediated encounters, parodic appropriations, bodies constructed by and through discourse: increasingly (though not exclusively) these have come to make up the efficacy of performance in the last two decades. Passing between the two models, the challenge of efficacy turns itself outside in: from transgressing a totalitarian power from an outside site to resisting a hegemonic power from within that very power arrangement.

Theater and ritual have in no way been left behind in this passage from transgressive to resistant efficacy. They remain two of the most important objects of study, and while their role as models has diminished, it has not been eliminated. Today, the field of cultural performance and the paradigm of performance studies cannot be *thought* without citing theater and ritual. They remain, as it were, specific and historical touchstones for any general theory of cultural performance. Theater continues to offer an important formal reference for conceptualizing cultural performance; in addition, theater departments and organizations such as the Association for Theatre in Higher Education and the American Society for Theatre Research provide important bases for its teaching and research. Similarly, the discipline of anthropology continues to provide performance scholars with important methodological approaches, especially those related to ethnographic fieldwork.

Furthermore, between theory and performance art, liminality remains one of the most frequently cited attributes of performative efficacy. Carlson, for instance, closes his 1996 survey with a section entitled "Conclusion: what is performance?", which ends with the following definition, one that touches upon both liminality and theatricality:

[Performance] is a specific event with its liminoid nature foregrounded, almost invariably clearly separated from the rest of life, presented by performers and attended by audiences both of whom regard the experience as made up of material to be interpreted, to be reflected upon, to be engaged in – emotionally, mentally, and perhaps even physically. This particular sense of occasion and focus as well as the overarching social envelope combine with the physicality of theatrical performance to make it one of the most powerful and efficacious procedures that human society has developed for the endlessly fascinating process of cultural and personal self-reflexion and experimentation.[1]

Scholars also continue to stress the liminality or "in betweenness" of the paradigm itself. In a 1998 essay, "What is performance studies anyway?", Schechner writes: "Performance studies is 'inter' – in between. It is intergeneric, interdisciplinary, intercultural – and therefore inherently unstable. Performance studies resists or rejects definition. As a discipline, PS cannot be mapped effectively because it transgresses boundaries, it goes where it is not expected to be. It is inherently 'in between' and therefore cannot be pinned down or located exactly."[2] Liminality, then, remains key to articulating the efficacy of both cultural performance and performance studies, whether that efficacy be conceived as transgressive or resistant.

Cutting-edge practices, fringe groups and marginalized peoples, border crossings, transgressions of boundaries and limits – these can and have been theorized in terms of liminality. What is performance? What is performance studies? "Liminality" is perhaps the most concise and accurate response to both of these questions. Paradoxically, the persistent use of this concept within the field *has made liminality into something of a norm*. That is, we have come to define the efficacy of performance and of our own research, if not exclusively, then very inclusively, in terms of liminality – that is, a mode of activity whose spatial, temporal, and symbolic "in betweenness" allows for social norms to be suspended, challenged, played with, and perhaps even transformed. The concept has not simply been applied to performances; it has also helped us to *construct* objects of inquiry by guiding the selection of activities to be studied, their formal analysis, and their political evaluation. And as we have seen, the liminal rite of passage also functions as a striking emblem of the paradigm itself, both of its initiation and of its subsequent development.

To underscore the normative dimension of liminality, I have come to call it the *liminal-norm*. More generally, the liminal-norm operates in any situation where the valorization of liminal transgression or resistance itself becomes normative – at which point theorization of such a norm may become subversive. I made up the term "liminal-norm" not long after reading another citation of rites of passage, this one by Michel Foucault. In an interview entitled "Rituals of exclusion," Foucault discusses how capitalist norms are inscribed pedagogically:

There is the first function of the university: to put students out of circulation. Its second function, however, is one of integration. Once a student has spent six or seven years of his life within this artificial society, he becomes "absorbable": society can consume him. Insidiously, he will have received the values of this society. He will have been given socially desirable models of behavior, so that this ritual of exclusion will finally take on the value of inclusion and recuperation or reabsorbtion. *In this sense, the university is no doubt little different from those systems in so-called primitive societies in which the young men are kept outside the village during their adolescence, undergoing rituals of initiation which separate them and sever all contact between them and real, active society. At the end of the specified time, they can be entirely recuperated or reabsorbed.*[3]

In other words, the very same rituals which performance scholars have long cited in theorizing the efficacy of performance, Foucault cites to explain the university's normative function within contemporary society.[4]

Turner himself recognized the conservative function that liminal rites of passage ultimately play in agrarian, pre-industrial societies, where they almost always reinforce existing social structures. Turning to cultural performances found in industrial societies, he came to distinguish the liminal from the liminoid, the latter referring to cultural activities found in "advanced" societies marked by the sharp separation of labor and leisure.[5] However, there is little doubt that Turner's interest and passion lay in the anti-structural elements he theorized in both liminal and liminoid activities, and it was these elements which he stressed in his critical dialogue with Schechner and other performance scholars (elements Foucault does not mention in the text cited above, although elsewhere he does emphasize the importance of "limit-experiences" to his own theoretical work).[6]

The liminal-norm is important here for several interrelated reasons. *First,* it demonstrates how forces of normativity can become mutational, and vice versa. In his ethnographic research, Turner recognized that the liminal practices of Ndembu society could lead to either schism or reinforcement of existing social structures, with reinforcement being the most common outcome. However, as liminality was generalized across the emerging field of cultural performance – that is, as it was re-cited, decontextualized, and recontextualized – the relatively rare instances of schism and radical transformation quickly came to the fore as performance scholars sought to theorize the efficacy of cultural performance during the social unrest found in North America and Western Europe during the 1960s and early 1970s. Liminality almost exclusively became a space and time of transgression and subversion; thus, a concept and practice primarily associated with normative forces had become the embodiment of mutational forces. However, the very success of this generalization process inevitably produced the normalizing effects already noted: the concept of liminality has helped to guide the selection and construction of objects as well as their analysis and evaluation, and in addition it has shaped Performance Studies' image of itself, the self-representation of the paradigm in relation to both the academy and society at large. Again, re-citation, decontextualization, and recontextualization, only here liminal efficacy has become a liminal-norm.

Second, the liminal-norm also suggests that any given conceptual model, even one constructed and deployed to theorize transgression or resistance, is necessarily limited in terms of both its formal and its functional resistance, is necessarily limited in terms of both its formal and its functional aspects. This does not imply that one must – or even can – avoid modelization or generalization altogether. As indicated earlier, the formation of theoretical concepts presupposes movements of generalization, as does the emergence of a research paradigm such as performance studies. The challenge, then, is not to abandon conceptual modelization, but rather to inscribe this movement within one's specific situation, to fold generalization back on itself in order to avoid reducing performance to any one model, be it theater or ritual or performance art or such theoretical models as formalism, psycho-analysis, feminism, deconstruction, queer theory, or postcolonial theory. These models have all been extremely productive to the study of cultural performance, yet all have their own perspectives, their own limits. The task is thus also to multiply the models at one's disposal while at the same time opening up these models to their "own" alterity. To cite yet another model: Félix Guattari describes schizoanalysis as a process of "metamodelisation," one that, "rather than moving in the direction of reductionist modelisations which simplify the complex, will work toward its complexification, its processual enrichment, toward the consistency of its virtual lines of bifurcation and differentiation, in short towards its ontological heterogeneity."[7] I have attempted here to analyze the workings of not one but several models crucial to the emergence and development of performance studies. In doing so, I have focused special attention on liminal rites of passage because they are a particularly rich and productive model of the paradigm's movement of generalization. This modelization process I have nicknamed the "passage to paradigm." In other words, liminal rites provide us with *a* (and not *the*) metamodel of the paradigm, one that I have tried to crack open by citing its normative and mutational dimensions, as well as other models and movements.

Third, as a metamodel, the liminal-norm can help us resituate the borders and limits of performance studies itself. This resituation or displacement of borders is crucial to the challenge guiding our entire project, the rehearsal of a general theory of performance. This project entails challenging performance studies, that is, challenging ourselves. By focusing on liminal activities, on transgressive and resistant practices, or, more generally, upon socially efficacious performances, we have overlooked the importance of *other* per-formances, performances whose formalization and study also took off in the United States and which have since gone global. These other performances are not metaphorical displacements of theatrical or cultural activities, though they are certainly and mistakenly can be reduced to them. Nor would we describe these other performances as primarily transgressive or resistant; far from it. As we shall see, their function is for the most part highly normative, so normative in fact that one might justifiably align them with the Establishment, the System, the Machine – in short, with the very institutions and forces against which cultural performance has directed much of its efficacious efforts over the past half-century. But recognizing one's own involvement with these normative performances is, paradoxically, essential to making such efforts more diverse, more concrete, more efficacious. It is also essential to our general theory.

The development of such a theory is highly problematic. Carlson writes that if we "consider performance as an essentially contested concept, this will help us to understand the futility of seeking some overarching semantic field to cover such seemingly disparate usages as the performance of an actor, of a schoolchild, of an automobile."[8] I agree. But at stake in such usages is not simply different meanings of the term "performance," but also entirely different sets of discourses and practices, different infrastructures and histories, different paradigms of performance. More profoundly, what's at stake in our general theory is not an overarching semantic field of performance, but rather an underworldly stratum of performative power and knowledge, a pragmatic formation upon which all this contesting of performance unfolds. The question "What is performance?" perhaps remains inescapable, especially when surveying a paradigm or defining a field, but to map different terrains of this stratum – which is less a metaphysical foundation than an onto-historical sedimentation of forces – a more urgent question becomes "*which* performance?"

Philosophically speaking, to pose the question "What is?" presupposes a unified form while promising a single, correct answer, while the question "Which one?" assumes a multiplicity of forces that must be *actively* interpreted and evaluated.[9] This will be my assumption. Rehearsing a general theory of performance, we must not only use different concepts, nor only contest and critique them; we must also *create* concepts, *initiate* models, *launch* movements of generalization. Performance studies scholars have obviously created multiple and diverse concepts and continue to do so. However, this multiplicity and diversity are themselves largely determined by our paradigmatic perspective, which I have called here the challenge of efficacy. Direct, or rather internal, analysis of this perspective can only proceed so far, for we cannot easily get a perspective on our perspective, on the critical and affective investments in a field we have constructed and to some extent been constructed through. To open an angle on what amounts to our paradigmatic presuppositions and prejudices, we must turn elsewhere, for "prejudices are found by contrast, not by analysis."[10] Our rehearsal of a general theory must thus seek out other sites, other premises, other performances.

NOTES

1 Marvin Carlson. *Performance: A Critical Introduction*. London: Routledge, 1996, 198–9.
2 Richard Schechner. "What is performance studies anyway?" *The Ends of Performance*. Ed. Peggy Phelan and Jill Lane. New York: New York University Press, 1998, 360.
3 Michel Foucault. *Foucault Live (Interviews, 1966–84)*. Trans. John Johnston. Ed. Sylvève Lotringer. New York: Semiotext(e), 1989, 66, my emphasis.
4 Significantly, Foucault also pejoratively characterizes the university environment as a "fictitious, artificial and quasi-theatrical" one in which "the student is given a gamelike way of life." See "Rituals of exclusion." In *Foucault Live (Interviews 1966–84)*. Trans. John Johnston. Ed. Sylvève Lotringer. New York: Semiotext(e), 1989, 65.
5 See Turner's essay "From liminal to liminoid, in play, flow, and ritual: an essay in comparative symbology,." In *From Ritual to Theater: The Human Seriousness of Play*. New York: PAJ Publications, 1982. Within performance studies, "liminoid" has never been as widely accepted a term as "liminal."
6 See the interview "The experience-book." In *Remarks on Marx: Conversations with Duccio Trombadori*. Trans. R. James Goldstein and James Cascalto. New York: Semiotext(e), 1991.
7 Félix Guattari, *Chaosmosis: An Ethico-Aesthetic Paradigm*. Trans. Paul Bains and Julian Pefanis. Bloomington: Indiana University Press, 1995, 61.
8 Carlson. *Performance*, 5.

9 For a discussion of the differences between the Platonic (formal) question "What is?" and the Nietzschean ("forceful") question "Which one?" or "What is it *for me?*," see Gilles Deleuze, *Nietzsche and Philosophy*. Trans. Hugh Tomlinson. New York: Columbia University Press, 1983, 75–8.

10 Paul Feyerabend. *Against Method: Outline of an Anarchistic Theory of Knowledge*. London;: Verso, 1978, 31.

READER CROSS-REFERENCES

Jackson – on the opposition of performing arts to traditional academic disciplines
Carlson – McKenzie directly refers to his definition of performance
Turner – definition of liminality
Phelan – liminality in performance art

4

PROFESSING PERFORMANCES
Disciplinary genealogies

Shannon Jackson

In 1905, Professor George Lyman Kittredge, Chairman of the English department at Harvard University, dropped a note to his colleague Professor George Pierce Baker. The latter had been concerned that one of Kittredge's new hires might have designs on the teaching of "the drama" and thus designs on Baker's own curricular territory. Kittredge sought to mollify Baker's anxiety. "You may feel quite secure," he wrote, "as to any cutting into your special field" (in Baker, 19 March 1905). The sentence reproduced the content and form of an all-too-familiar interaction between empowered chairman and paranoid colleague. And, as is often true of such interactions, it also revealed a hint of intellectual condescension within its gesture of institutional assurance, one that left flexible whether the word "special" had the connotation of the extraordinary, the narrow, or the peripheral.

Lately, I have been looking at documents surrounding individuals like George Pierce Baker and other white academic American men – Hiram Corson at Cornell, Brander Matthews at Columbia, Thomas Dickinson at Wisconsin, Frederick Koch at North Carolina, Thomas Wood Stevens at Carnegie Tech – who figure prominently in the early institutionalization of "performance" in the United States. This is to trace something that most often called itself drama at that point, later dance, sometimes rhetoric, oratory, or speech. Spending so much time with such documents would have been inconceivable to me a few years ago and is still sometimes only barely sustainable. What does sustain me is an interest in understanding their implications for the institutionalization of performance studies now. My effort is a little different from others that have speculated on the future of our field. Rather than venturing into what the 1999 conference of Performance Studies International (PSi) called "the hinterlands," this article is a return to areas already mapped – fortressed castles such as theatre departments, speech departments, and literature departments – seeing in them less stability and more cartographical complexity than it might always be expedient for performance studies scholars to acknowledge. Investigating issues of performance's institutionalization is lamentably not always the same as investigating developments in performance scholarship. Indeed, this study came out of my naïve frustration in recognizing how little the institutional operations with which performance studies contends seem to "know" what performance studies scholarship says it "knows." Confronting mechanisms such as department divisions, school divisions, job placement, graduation requirements, building infrastructures, curricular breakdowns, and departmental divisions of labor has thus provoked my heretofore inconceivable research. Part of a larger project that will explore a number of institutional relationships among performance and other fields such as anthropology, folklore, classics, cultural studies, and more, these reflections will focus on only one historical network of relations between speech, theatre, and literature. I hope that my reasons for picking up this corner of the rug will become clear as I continue. Rather than defending or rejecting terms such as "drama" or "theatre" or "speech" or "literature," I am most interested in thinking about how such concepts become discursive touchstones for certain kinds of principles that fare better or worse at different historical moments in the academy. Often this is about re-casting stories that we already know about past disciplinary history into a differently aimed kind of argument.

What I have decided and will schematically argue is that such institutional questions and their very complicated histories turn out to unsettle the somewhat oppositional epistemology driving, for instance, the provocative title of the 1999 Performance Studies International conference: "'Here be Dragons': Mapping the Undiscovered Realms of Performance Studies." I am neither the first nor the last person to deconstruct our "dragon" metaphor and the quest for the "undiscovered realms" that permeated that gathering. But consider in this light Baker's paranoia and his concern about remaining "special." It derived of course from a particular kind of marginality, one that wants recognition but not in a form that jeopardizes its self-constructed identity as an outsider. In our current discourse, there is a danger now of turning such an internally conflicted predicament into a jealously held position. There is a strange paradox in the attempt to position oneself as an inhabitant of unclaimed territory, for the gesture itself not only maps that territory but also stakes the claim. It simultaneously suggests that no one was there before, disavowing its relationship to the practices of earlier, colonial cartographers. Nevertheless, the divisions, buildings, maps, and curricular structures generated in the early professing of performance remain in altered forms today. Even though Baker and his like developed their special field into a highly mapped terrain from which many of us would say that we are departing, we still unevenly enjoy and endure its operations, discourses, and professional privileges. As such, a con-sideration of institutional history can, in Brechtian fashion, be an illuminating exercise in defamiliarization. It further demonstrates how saturated oppositional discourse is with what it claims not to be and how necessary the notion of the dragon-filled zone is to the idea of a dragon-free zone. At the same time, and even more pointedly for a field enamored of its renegade status, such institutional history illustrates how over-written (or over-mapped) the position of the dragon is by the castle it might claim to be storming.

In my opening anecdote of 1905, Chairman Kittredge and Professor Baker inhabited an English department that was in the midst of an intellectual transformation in the field of literary studies. As such, they were also negotiating the interpersonal conflicts and inter-office paranoias that drive and derive from such intellectual changes. The late nineteenth to early twentieth century was a period of debate, change, retrenchment, and more debate as US colleges and universities grappled with their relationship to a changing American society. They argued over access to higher education for women, for newer immigrants, for

African-Americans, and for the children of both the industrial bourgeoisie and the working classes. As numerous historians of higher education have demonstrated, this period would also usher in the era of "professionalism," an economic and discursive formation that differently but pervasively inflected both professors' sense of their students' educational goals and their own sense of their positions as "career academics." The always conflicted position of the academic thereby came to inhabit another type of conflicted situation with which we are now quite familiar, though not necessarily reconciled. As the role of the US university was increasingly positioned as preparation for entrance into the managerial classes, academics worked to maintain a separate social position outside the so-called professions while simultaneously legitimating themselves curricularly and institutionally within professionalizing terms. Humanities professors in particular tried to create and maintain a legitimating sphere of cultural capital, a realm that distinguished itself both from the manual training of vocational schools as well as the nonmanual technical training of preprofessional schools. At the same time, and noteworthy in various discussions about what the "i" in PSi might mean, US bastions of higher education worked to figure out what it meant to be a specifically "American" university, alternately disavowing and reproducing the structures and intellectual movements developed in foreign lands (where of course "foreign" meant the ever so exotic countries of England, France, and Germany).

The story of the professionalization of literature within this situation is quite interesting and has already been told a few times, though I find the retelling of this story with an eye to a performance genealogy even more intriguing. Literature was in danger of not faring very well within professionalist modes of legitimation. As John Guillory (1993) and Gerald Graff (1987) have argued, it thus manifestly had to make itself "rigorous," to become a science based in evidence, an object of knowledge with clear rules to replace nebulous belletrism. German philology entered and/or was imported precisely to lend the study of literature this necessary positivism, a specialist training in historical research, etymology, and the accumulation of facts that pushed to develop a science of the literary and thus to assure all involved that literature professors really had an object of study. To give this some contemporary institutional significance, Graff and Guillory both situate current training in "theory" on a historical plane with philology (with New Criticism in between). Thus, despite the fact that philology and most critical theory are very different in the content of their intellectual assumptions, they occupy a similar structural position from the perspective of professional history; they both serve a similar function in the mechanics of professionalization and scholarly "training" within the arts and humanities. Such manifest rigor also warded off feminizing discourses of delegitimation that derived from the university's changing demographics of class, ethnicity, and gender. Philology kept literature from appearing to be a sentimental field that appealed only to coeds. At the same time, however, philology was criticized. It was accused of being too scientific, of being over-specialized, and of compromising the experience of literature. Occasionally, its American critics appealed to nationalist allegiances by accusing its followers of slavishly imitating the Europeans, more specifically the Germans. As such, philology anticipated many subsequent "theory" movements accused of being specialist, jargon-ridden, and ruinous to the humanities – or of being French. This kind of history certainly defamiliarizes 1999 *New York Times* debates on the role of "specialized language."[1] Indeed, such institutional and disciplinary genealogies expose a constant cycle of rotation and disavowal where one era's "specialization" becomes the next era's "common sense"; groundbreaking theoretical movements look like dunder-headed empiricism to subsequent generations.

By 1905, George Lyman Kittredge had emerged as one of the foremost practitioners of literary philology in the United States. As such, the moment when Chairman Kittredge dropped his administrative note was also a moment when the promoter of a then "trendy" intellectual movement – philology – was in the midst of exercising a position of institutional power. As Susan Harris Smith (1997) has suggested, however, the position of "drama" (and its teachers) within this literary transformation was an ambivalent one. Dramatic literature, especially drama performed, risked associations with the feminine, the primitive, and the commercial in a way that threatened the profession of literature's redefined story about itself. Something similar held true for Baker's original field of rhetoric, whose emphasis on oral communication would, in English departments, increasingly transmogrify into the teaching of written communication. From there came the phenomenon of the composition class, a teaching responsibility increasingly placed on the lower rungs of the literature profession's academic ladder. Indeed, in some institutions, the denigration or excision of "drama" and "speech" was fundamental to the intellectual redefinition and professional rise of the literary. The categories of drama, speech, and theatre thus functioned ambivalently, on the one hand heightening vulnerabilities over the cultural capital of literary studies while, on the other hand, threatening to derail the new scientific rigor of literature's gendered professionalization. Whether theatre and rhetoric could transcend these associations and/or be recuperated along rigorous philological lines was still debatable in the early twentieth century. Hence the condescending assurance and hedged institutional protectiveness of a trendy philologist like Kittredge vis-à-vis a rhetoric-cum-drama professor like Baker.[2]

Baker's background was similar to many of his contemporary pro-performance colleagues at other universities. Though twenty years later Baker would become the founder of the oft-renowned Yale School of Drama, at the turn of the century he was a teacher of rhetoric in an English department. He was a professor whose interests in oral pedagogy had trans-mogrified from a respectable focus on argumentation to a curious fixation on the oral performance of the drama, proceeding apace down a slippery slope that went from the oral performance of Shakespeare to the oral performance of "drama other than Shakespeare," to the promotion of campus play production, to the fostered creation of so-called "original" plays by the students themselves. He was something of a dragon at Harvard's gate. As most of us teaching in the United States know at least indirectly, Baker was one of a cohort of individuals – often couched as heroic in the departmental chronicles of theatre – who broke from English to form separate departments. What is less incorporated, however, is under what principles that disciplinary break happened and, more to the point, how that history situates and so defamiliarizes the disciplinary reunions performance studies is attempting to effect now.

While the stories of particular persons and institutions vary enormously, Baker's location paralleled that of a number of his pro-performance colleagues and serves as an index of a larger epistemological and institutional fallout around the professing of performance.

Arguing for drama and performance against and yet within the already conflicted field of the English department produced multiple ambivalences. I will consolidate a few issues under three conundra in order to give a sense of their contemporary relevance: (1) the institutional tension around the "interdisciplinarity" of performance, (2) the hypercontextuality of the performed event as an object of knowledge, and (3) the legitimation of oral and theatrical "practice" as a valued educational activity. Without being able to recount fully the professional histories of "generalism" and "specialization" in the space of the present article, it is perhaps generally understood that the principles behind departmentalization, curriculum reform, funding, and resource allocation do not always keep step with the heterogenous models, methods, and bibliographic citations that appear in interdisciplinary scholarship. This is something we all know and can knee-jerkedly critique the Institution for inhibiting. But the disconnect between institutional structure and interdisciplinary rhetoric is particularly stark and, I think, a little bit chastening in light of Baker's concern about his "special field." Of course, it came out of a fear of Chairman Kittredge's brand of interdisciplinary engagement, one that rationalized disciplinary takeover in the name of interdisciplinary expansion. Though they didn't use the word "interdisciplinary" at the time, this colonialist model – the "every field shall become (like) mine" model of interdisciplinarity – is perhaps somewhat familiar to theatre scholars such as Jill Dolan (1992) who critique other fields for "the midnight raiding" of theatre studies. However, the direction of such a critique shifts with an awareness of academic theatre's various stages of institutionalization. Baker was still somewhat traumatized by his experience at Harvard when he founded the Yale School of Drama, one whose model other universities would replicate. There, he would fend off fears of colonialist interdisciplinarity with his own paradoxical brand of isolationist interdisciplinarity, constantly celebrating the theatre for being a form that integrated literature, art history, and the study of human behavior while simultaneously creating a structure that short-circuited interaction with the university departments that specialized in the study of literature, art history, and human behavior. Thus, the rhetoric of disciplinary multiplicity coexisted surprisingly easily with a practice of institutional singularity, a fact that should stall any easy assumptions about what "interdisciplinarity" means to theatre and performance studies now.

Disjunctures among disciplines and institutions appear in other places. Writing in 1903 as the first professor of dramatic literature in the United States, Brander Matthews of Columbia University published treatises such as *A Study of the Drama* (1910) that exemplify performance's epistemological predicament and that laid the foundations for the antitraditional break that would eventually become the tradition of theatre studies methodology. In assuring their colleagues that theatre had a right to separate institutional status, scholars reproduced turn-of-the-century conventions of historical singularity and progressive continuity, mapping new principles of similarity and difference on which the "itself" of theatre could rest securely. It was in such a professionalizing university climate, by extension, that the evolutionary paradigm of "from ritual to theatre" became invoked and later routinized. As performance studies scholars seek to undo the ideological, national, and global consequences of such a construct, it is probably equally important to remember its institutional expediency; knowledge was made more teachable, useful, and justifiable to a professionalizing university when it took shape in the clear categories and progressive arcs of a delineated "survey."

Furthermore, occupying the liminal position of the legitimated margin, while Matthews and like-minded souls occasionally pitted themselves against philological trendiness, they most often borrowed and adapted its methods. Theatre scholars took philology's emphasis on historical research and on the conventions of literary transmission to rationalize the investigation of such "extra-literary" realms as street layouts, building configurations, set designs, managerial structures, actors, and audiences. Indeed, to a philological method acutely preoccupied with the accumulation of "facts," the circumstances of the performed event offered an endless supply of discoverable data, even if they were not always the kind of facts that most literary philologists were interested in or skilled at discovering. Theatre's excessive contextuality thus called literary philology's bluff to such a degree that the former could not remain under the umbrella of the latter.

This kind of disciplinary past foregrounds a number of discontinuous genealogies that are of concern to present institutional discussions. First of all, it reminds us of how saturated the "origin" of positivist theatre history (remember those buildings, those ticket prices, those actor biographies) is with the discipline of literary studies – and with a once-trendy enterprise within literary studies at that. It resituates, for instance, a recent theatre history conference in which a panel asked the question "Is jargon really necessary?" The question forgets theatre history's historical alliance with a turn-of-the-century methodology that was accused in its own time of being over-specialized and employing an anti-humanist and jargon-ridden vocabulary. Admittedly, when trends in literary studies turned toward New Criticism and its decontextualizing practices of close reading in the 1940s, the con-textualized study of theatre made it more securely "the opposite" of the literary. At the same time, the ever-changing discipline of literature suggests that those who routinely denounce the literary study of theatre and performance might want to be clearer about which "literary" they mean.

From another direction, this genealogy also stalls the easy alignments and differentiations that are sometimes drawn in current self-labeled progressive contexts of cultural study. This is to ask what it means for performance studies scholars to meet cultural theorists, many of whom were originally trained as literary theorists and whose institutional pre-decessors once found it necessary to excise performance from a self-legitimating equation. What does it mean for all of these disconnected or disavowedly connected scholars to form contemporary connections? Whether gathered under the banner of structuralism or poststructuralism, materialism or new historicism, reader-response or speech act theory, such cultural studies arenas generally argue against the notion of a pure aesthetic form, knowable outside of a context of production. The methodological direction of this kind of cultural critique means something particular for a performance genealogy. What one realizes is that, as individuals trained in different disciplines, we also enter with different historic institutional privileges. As such, we might have different notions of what the hinter-land is. One person's discovery turns out to be another's disciplinary home. One would-be dragon may look, from another's angle of vision, like the occupant of a historically well-appointed castle. All may be embedded in histories with different assumptions about who they are fighting. There is not, for instance, an unproblematic equivalence between cultural theory's critique of New Criticism's conservatism and performance studies' critique of theatre history's conservatism. Besides enduring a retroactive ahistoricism in the conservative appellation, theatre history cannot be adequately critiqued for ignoring the "new" methodological dicta of cultural studies. Indeed, theatre has long been a form where text was less easily sliced from something like context and where the apparatus of production was all-too frustratingly difficult to disavow. Matthews was theorizing the importance of audience response long before Wolfgang Iser (1980, 1989; to say nothing of John Fiske 1987, 1989) elaborated on reception theory. This does not mean that there is not a great deal to critique in theatre studies but rather that the direction of the critique – one that homogenizes and assumes equal solidity in all that is already mapped – can sometimes be misplaced. This disciplinary complexity is thus another moment when it is not quite clear who is playing rebellious dragon to whose fortressed castle. As certain contemporary strains of performance studies seek alliances with certain strains of literary studies – in theoretical models, in progressive politics, in journals, in curricula, conferences, bibliographies, hirings, and graduate placements – it will be important to investigate such blind spots and to be careful not to perpetuate the disabling institutional structures from which they derive.

Other genealogical investigations produce different kinds of defamiliarizing moments. Consider briefly two different kinds of arguments for the legitimation of oral performance or performance "practice" in the academy. On the one hand, one can look at someone like Hiram Corson at Cornell for whom the oral performance of literature was synonomous with a nearly spiritualized encounter (Graff and Warner 1989: 90). Mapping his interest in this pedagogical mode to prevailing binaries of the day, Corson ended up arguing for oral performance by opposing it to philology, riding an antispecialist and antitheoretical sentiment (at a time of course when historical research was "theoretical"), casting performance as the realm of the unmediated and the unrigorous. The success of Corson's argument produced new institutional structures whose limits – as we debate the legacy of oral interpretation in performance studies – we now face in current debates over the institutional future of performance studies. Meanwhile, a second strain of academic performance studies came as part of the break of drama/theatre from English departments. As pro-performance theatre professors argued for new buildings and the apparati of theatre-making, it is quite clear in retrospect how much the pro-performance discourse threatened the shaky class politics of redefining universities. When Baker and Thomas Wood Stevens – who started a theater department within the engineering-oriented environment of Carnegie Tech – argued for performance "practice," they employed a language of workshops, labs, and industrial "plants," of workmanlike ingenuity, of craft, trade, and daily labor that came dangerously close to a discourse of manual training (Stevens 1913–25). As such, they tread close to the realm of the vocational school from which many a university was eager to distance itself and even farther from the humanist discourse of cultural capital that would have ensured that theatre was, after all, a "humanity." Breaking free from literature meant that speech and theatre gained the success of institutional autonomy, but it also short-circuited their connection to the literature and humanities departments' claims of "cultural capital" in rationalizing their role in the academy.

This transformation was one of many reasons why the discourse of nonacademic professionalization – the claim of a somewhat shaky bridge to economic capital rather than to cultural capital – became part of how speech and theatre departments began to talk about themselves. Theatre came to include courses on audition techniques. Speech communication departments began to teach organizational communication and tips for on-camera broadcasting. Such departments became places where the teaching faculty were engaged in different spheres of professionalization, many of them outside of the academy. In such departments, issues of interdisciplinarity are often erroneously elided with issues of inter-professionality – and they, I would submit, turn out not to be the same thing. A union between an artist and a scholar turns out not to be entirely equivalent to a union between a literature scholar and a philosopher, for the interdisciplinary encounter of the latter is compounded by further differences in professionalization, standards of career success, and models of productivity that underpin the former. However, it would be disingenuous for arts and humanities academics to distance themselves self-righteously from such "preprofessional" developments without recognizing how imbricated such arguments for their alternative are in a notion of cultural capital – even cultural capital that calls itself progressive in content. Such cultural pedagogy occurs in that nebulous space that is not manual training and not nonmanual technical training; as such, its critique of preprofessional "vocationalism" also needs to reckon with its own unique class and institutional location – as well as its own imbrication in a discourse of professionalism.

Once again, who is the dragon here?

Finally, I think that we can find help in sorting through these conundra by testing them next to related arguments on the role of technical and practical training in humanist fields. In *The Employment of English* (1998), Michael Berubé has joined and advanced a larger conversation on the status of composition within the English department, asking us to consider the class politics of literary professionalization and to reconceive courses in writing technique so that they become central to the cultural work of a progressive literary education. Similarly, in a 1997 issue of MLA's publication *Profession*, Russell Berman echoes others by asking colleagues to question the denigrated position of language teaching in foreign literature departments – "the line of class division, corresponding precisely to the distribution of rewards by the university, that runs through all our departments" – and to argue against a conception of second-language proficiency as a "merely technical skill" (63–4). Faculty and graduate students in theatre and performance studies can make use of these arguments, it seems to me, appropriating them to think through with more complexity the much-beleaguered theory/practice division that undergirds our field and to consider the class politics that this division reifies. Furthermore, the kinship among composition, language teaching, and theatre training suggests that we might want to be more vigilant about our uses of the word "practice" – another unstably referential term – and to track instead the discontinuous histories of labor, professionalism, technical training, vocation, and cultural and economic capital in which such a materialist term is embedded. Finally, since many humanists can be found revising the very structure of humanities education and research, it may be that theatre's historic ill fit as a humanistic field could now provide an intriguing site for conducting this revision. In a 1999 issue of *The Chronicle of Higher*

Education, once English professor now Vice Provost Cathy Davidson asks the provocative question "What if scholars in the humanities worked together, in a lab?" It occurs to me that theatre faculty have been approaching something like this lab-based model for quite some time. While the fact that we did so contributed to our status as not-quite-humanists, such current creative rethinking about the nature and function of the humanities might realign our connection to the term.

Institutional history suggests that there are several maps operating simultaneously and, moreover, that there might be a more unacknowledged interdependence between castles and hinterlands than a homogenized oppositional discourse allows. Disciplinary genealogy is neither a celebratory search for origins nor a self-satisfied rejection of the stodgy. It is, after Foucault, a means of approaching the past to unsettle the heretofore stable. Writing such a genealogy often means revisiting categories that performance studies itself resists or de-centers – words such as "drama," "theatre," "speech," or "literature." If we think of such labels – and others such as "theory," "practice," "interdisciplinary" – less as stably referential terms than as discursive sites on which a number of agendas, alliances, and anxieties collect, then I think that the institutionalization of performance studies and the institutionalization of something like "theatre" or "speech" or "literature" turn out to have more to do with each other than current conversations let on. Such terms function inconsistently at different times and at different places; they are invoked out of convenience at moments when knowledges need reorganization or when vague institutional developments require some discursive support. As such, they also sustain a network of disavowed connection and disavowed difference, an array of blind spots, synecdochic fallacies, and reinvented wheels. In such a complicated space, one scholar's experiment turns out to be another's tradition; one scholar's core comes back as another's periphery. One field finds it too expedient to cast a dominant form as marginal in order to prop up its own centrality; another finds it too expedient to cast a marginal form as dominant in order to better stage its own rebellion. Rather than wholly succumbing to the language of the new, it seems to me at least as interesting theoretically and secure institutionally for performance studies to expose the historical entanglements of the already-was and thus still-still-kind-of-is. It seems important to show how disciplinary breaks were saturated with the terms of the field that they were fleeing and to suggest that contemporary innovations sometimes derive from arenas that once devalued that which they now celebrate. Institutional history also suggests that assumptions of the "special" status of performance studies, enticing as they are, could do with a genealogical jolt.

NOTES

1 After the journal *Philosophy and Literature* awarded its Bad Writing Award to Judith Butler and Homi Bhabha in December 1998, articles and editorials debated the function of theory and specialist language. See, for instance, the *New York Times* articles in the "Arts and Ideas" section of 27 February 1999 and on the editorial page of 3 March 1999 and 20 March 1999.

2 Theater's gendered association received institutional reinforcement from the fact that it was Radcliffe women's college rather than Harvard that initially supported George Pierce Baker's courses in playwriting. Baker's efforts to disentangle himself from this association was partially successful (he eventually taught playwriting at Harvard) but only after producing a self-defensive, masculinist argument for theatre's legitimacy.

SELECTED BIBLIOGRAPHY

Baker, George Pierce (1894–1925a) Numerous essays. Personal and Professional Archives. Theater Collection, Harvard University.

—— (1894–1925b) George Pierce Baker Papers. Sterling Library, Yale University.

Barish, Jonas (1979) *The Antitheatrical Prejudice*. Berkeley: University of California Press.

Berlin, James (1987) *Rhetoric and Reality: Writing Instruction in American Colleges, 1900–35*. Carbondale: Southern Illinois University Press.

Berman, Russell (1997) "Reform and continuity: graduate education toward a foreign cultural literacy." *Profession*: 61–74.

Berubé, Michael (1998) *The Employment of English: Theory, Jobs, and the Future of Literary Studies*. New York: New York University Press.

Brenkman, John (1987) *Culture and Domination*. Ithaca, NY: Cornell University Press.

Bourdieu, Pierre (1988) *Homo Academicus*. Translated by Peter Collier. London: Basil Blackwell.

Butler, Judith (1999) "A 'Bad Writer' Bites Back." *New York Times*, March 20.

Carlson, Marvin (1996) *Performance: A Critical Introduction*. New York: Routledge.

Davidson, Cathy (1999) "What if scholars in the humanities worked together, in a lab?" *Chronicle of Higher Education*, 28 May: B4.

Dolan, Jill (1992) "Geographies of learning: theater studies, performance, and the 'performative.' " *Theater Journal* 45, 1: 417–41.

Eagleton, Terry (1996) [1983] *Literary Theory: An Introduction*. Oxford: Basil Blackwell.

Fiske, John (1987) *Television Culture*. New York: Routledge.

—— (1989) *Understanding Popular Culture*. Boston: Unwin Hyman.

Flynn, Joyce (1989) "A complex causality of neglect." *American Quarterly* 41, 1 (March): 123–7.

Foucault, Michel (1972) *The Archaeology of Knowledge*. New York: Pantheon Books.

Graff, Gerald (1987) *Professing Literature: An Institutional History*. Chicago: University of Chicago Press.

Graff, Gerald, and Reginald Gibbons, eds. (1985) *Criticism in the University*. Evanston, Ill.: Northwestern University Press.

Graff, Gerald, and Michael Warner, eds. (1989) *The Origins of Literary Studies in America: A Documentary Anthology*. New York: Routledge.

Guillory, John (1993) *Cultural Capital: The Problem of Literary Canon Formation*. Chicago: University of Chicago Press.

Iser, Wolfgang (1980) *The Act of Reading: A Theory of Aesthetic Response*. Baltimore, Md: Johns Hopkins University Press.

—— (1989) *Prospecting: From Reader Response to Literary Anthropology*. Baltimore, Md: Johns Hopkins University Press.

Kinne, Wisner Payne (1954) *George Pierce Baker and the American Theatre*. Cambridge, Mass.: Harvard University Press.

Koch, Frederick (1897–1944) Selected essays. Personal and Professional Papers. The Southern Historical Collection. Wilson Library, University of North Carolina–Chapel Hill.

Lee, Josephine (1999) "Disclipining theater and drama in the English department: some reflections on 'performance' and institutional history." *Text and Performance Quarterly* 19, 2 (April): 145–58.

Matthews, Brander (1910) *A Study of the Drama*. New York: Houghton Mifflin Company.

—— (1917) *These Many Years: Recollections of a New Yorker*. New York: C. Scribner.

Nelson, Cary (1997) *Manifesto of a Tenured Radical*. New York: New York University Press.

Ohmann, Richard (1976) *English in America*. New York: Oxford University Press.

Roach, Joseph (1999) "Reconstructing theater/history." *Theatre Topics* 9, 1 (March): 3–10.

Smith, Dinitia (1999) "When ideas get lost in bad writing," *New York Times*, 27 February.

Smith, Susan Harris (1989) "Generic hegemony: American drama and the canon." *American Quarterly* 41, 1 (March): 112–21.

—— (1997) *American Drama: The Bastard Art*. Cambridge: Cambridge University Press.

Stevens, Thomas Wood (1913–25) Numerous essays. Personal and Professional Papers. University Library, University of Arizona.

—— (1914) "A school of the theater arts." *The Drama*: 635–9.

Stray, Christopher (1998) *Classics Transformed: Schools, Universities, and Society in England, 1830–1960*. Oxford: Clarendon Press.

Veysey, Laurence R. (1965) *The Emergence of the American University*. Chicago: University of Chicago Press.

Wilkerson, Margaret (1991) "Demographics and the academy." In *The Performance of Power: Theatrical Discourse and Politics*, edited by Sue-Ellen Case and Janelle Reinelt, 238–41. Iowa City: Iowa University Press.

Williams, Raymond (1952) *Drama from Ibsen to Eliot*. London: Chatto & Windus.

—— (1968a) *Drama from Ibsen to Brecht*. London: Chatto & Windus.

—— (1968b) [1954] *Drama in Performance*. London: C.A. Watts.

Williams, Simon (1999) "The challenge to professional training and development." In *The Performance of Power: Theatrical Discourse and Politics*, edited by Sue-Ellen Case and Janelle Reinelt, 242–8. Iowa City: Iowa University Press.

READER CROSS-REFERENCES

Schechner, J. Bell – on performing arts curricula

McKenzie – how performance studies as a discipline is self-consciously oppositional to traditional disciplinary structures

Kirshenblatt-Gimblett – an institutional history of performance studies

Parker and Sedgwick – the geneaology of performativity, a fundamental concept in performance studies

Conquergood – on how performance studies can challenge traditional academic hierarchies

Taylor – explores the genealogy of the term "performance"

5

PERFORMANCE STUDIES

Barbara Kirshenblatt-Gimblett

The field of Performance Studies takes performance as an organizing concept for the study of a wide range of behavior. A postdiscipline of inclusions, Performance Studies sets no limit on what can be studied in terms of medium and culture. Nor does it limit the range of approaches that can be taken. A provisional coalescence on the move, Performance Studies is more than the sum of its inclusions. While it might be argued that "as an artform, performance lacks a distinctive medium" (Carroll 1986: 78), embodied practice and event is a recurring point of reference within Performance Studies.

Performance Studies starts from the premise that its objects of study are not to be divided up and parceled out, medium by medium, to various other disciplines – music, dance, dramatic literature, art history. The prevailing division of the arts by medium is arbitrary, as is the creation of fields and departments devoted to each. Most of the world's artistic expression has always synthesized or otherwise integrated movement, sound, speech, narrative, and objects. Moreover, the historical avant-garde and contemporary art have long questioned these boundaries and gone about blurring them. Such confounding of categories has not only widened the range of what can count as an artmaking practice, but also given rise to performance art that is expressly not theatre and art performance that dematerializes the art object and approaches the condition of performance (Carroll 1986; see also Sayre 1989; Schimmel *et al.* 1998). Performance Studies takes its lead from such developments. This field is not only intercultural in scope and spirit, but also challenges aesthetic hierarchies and analyzes how they are formed. Performance Studies encompasses not only the most valorized, but also the least valued, cultural forms within these hierarchies.

Like other new knowledge formations (Cultural Studies, Visual Culture, Postcolonial Studies, Gender Studies), Performance Studies starts with a set of concerns and objects and ranges widely for what it needs by way of theory and method. Performance Studies has made common cause with, and is contributing to, the many fields from which it draws. By theorizing embodiment, event, and agency in relation to live (and mediated) perform- ance, Performance Studies can potentially offer something of a counterweight to the emphasis in Cultural Studies on literature and media, text as an extended metaphor for culture, and enrich the discussion of discourse, representation, the body (to be distinguished from embodiment), and identity. One can even discern what might be called a performative turn in contemporary cultural, aesthetic, and political theory.[1] Ray Birdwhistell argued that "Performance is an inherent constituent of all communication" (Birdwhistell 1970, in Sullivan 1986: 7), while Dell Hymes suggested that " 'It is through the study of performance' that one could look forward to an integration of the social sciences and humanities" (Hymes 1975, in Sullivan 1986: 3). The possibilities are signaled by Peggy Phelan, who writes that "To date . . . there has been little attempt to bring together the specific epistemological and political possibilities of performance as it is enacted in what are still known, for better or worse, as 'theater events' and the epistemological and political openings enabled by the 'performative' invoked by contemporary theory" (Phelan 1993: 15). She is referring here to the work of J.L. Austin and, based on his concept of performative utterances, the efforts of Judith Butler and others to theorize gender and sexuality.

During the last two decades Performance Studies programs have been established in the United States, Australia, England, Wales, France, and Brazil, among others.[2] Increasingly, individual Performance Studies courses are being included in existing theatre history and speech and communication curricula, as well as in folklore, anthropology, ethnomusicology, art history, literature, history, cultural studies, and area studies programs including American, Asian, and Africana, among others. There are several indications that the field has come of age, including a series of highly successful international conferences during the 1990s, the formation of professional associations,[3] several specialized journals,[4] and an increasing number of programmatic essays, textbooks, readers, and book series.[5]

While they converge at many points, these programs and organizations offer at least three different paradigms for the field, thanks both to their particular disciplinary genealogies and to their visions for the future.[6]

Broad spectrum approach (New York University)

In 1980, New York University's Graduate Department of Drama changed its name to Department of Performance Studies. The change of name followed almost twenty years of preparation, much of it recorded in the pages of *TDR: The Drama Review* and the writings of Richard Schechner. Schechner has long advocated a broad spectrum approach:

> We believe that if the study of performance does not expand and deepen – going far beyond both the training of performance workers and the Western tradition, far beyond the analysis of dramatic literature – the academic, performing-arts enterprise constructed over the past half century or so will collapse. A happier alternative is to widen our vision of performance, studying it not only as art but as a means of understanding historical, social, and cultural processes.
>
> (see pages 7–9 in this volume for full text)

NYU's program developed in the context of contemporary experimental performance, with links to the historical avant-garde. Its faculty (Richard Schechner, Michael Kirby, Brooks McNamara) were themselves active in the Off Off Broadway movement. To align their artistic practice with their pedagogy, they abandoned a traditional currriculum in

European and American drama and theatre and set out to create an innovative Performance Studies program almost from scratch. Euro-American theatre would thenceforth find its place within an intercultural, intergeneric, and interdisciplinary intellectual project as one of many objects of study. Taking their lead from the historical avant-garde and contemporary experimental performance, NYU's faculty was determined that Western theatre and the dramatic text would not be at the center of the new Performance Studies curriculum, though it continues to play an important role. As Schechner stated: "Performance is a very inclusive notion of action; theatre is only one node on a continuum that reaches from ritualization in animal behavior (including humans) through performances in everyday life – greetings, displays of emotion, family scenes, and so on – to rites, ceremonies and performances: large-scale theatrical events" (Schechner 1977: 1). Writing ten years later, Peggy Phelan articulated the notion that animated the establishment of Performance Studies at New York University as follows: "Was 'theatre' an adequate term for the wide range of 'theatrical acts' that intercultural observation was everywhere revealing? Perhaps 'performance' better captured and conveyed the activity that was provoking these questions. Since only a tiny portion of the world's cultures equated theatre with written scripts, performance studies would begin with an intercultural understanding of its fundamental term, rather than enlisting intercultural case studies as additives, rhetorically or ideologically based postures of inclusion and relevance" (Phelan and Lane 1998: 3).

Aesthetic communication approach
(Northwestern University)

The name changes at Northwestern University chart the movement over the course of more than a century from a nineteenth-century Department of Elocution to a Department of Oral Interpretation, which, in 1984, became the Department of Performance Studies. Much of Northwestern speech, communication, rhetoric, and oral interpretation curriculum remains intact even as new courses in Performance Studies proper have been added. Northwestern's program "produces research and creative work in the performance of literature; the adaptation and staging of texts, particularly narrative works; cultural studies and ethnography; performance theory and criticism; performance arts and dance theatre; and the practice of everyday life."[7] It does so in a spirit that has been characterized as inclusionary, noncanonical, "democratic and counterelitist" – Performance Studies "celebrate[s] the performative nature of human communication" (Pelias and VanOosting 1987: 221).

If NYU initially enlarged the concept of theatre to include many other kinds of performance, Northwestern expanded the notion of literature in terms of text, broadly conceived, to include not only literature but also "cultural texts." The two programs differ in several other important ways. First, NYU took a revolutionary approach to the transformation of a drama department into a Performance Studies one, whereas at Northwestern University and elsewhere the shift from oral interpretation to performance studies tends to be understood as evolutionary:

What may be said with certainty is that paradigm shift [from oral interpretation to performance studies], if such it is, is *not* a revolutionary denial of oral interpretation as the antecedent schema. Rather, the new nomenclature affirms the study and performance of literary texts as central to, but not limiting, its theory and methodology. Hence, the paradigmatic relationship between oral interpretation and performance studies might display the performance of literature as the central circle in a concentric figure widening out to include social dramas, rituals, storytelling, jokes, organizational metaphors, everyday conversations, indeed any communication act meeting the criteria of aesthetic discourse.

(Pelias and VanOosting 1987: 229)

Second, NYU has made performance the umbrella under which all kinds of performance can be and are studied, and, at least in theory and despite its history as a drama department, none has precedence. In contrast, within speech and communication field, the metaphor of concentric circles places the performance of literature at the center. Stated another way, performance studies becomes a "subunit within speech communication" (Strine *et al.* 1990).

Ethnoscenology (University of Paris VIII)

The third and most recent model of Performance Studies is that of Ethnoscenology, whose mission is "to avoid any form of ethnocentrism in the study of the performing arts and practices in their cultural, historical, social context" by refusing to privilege the "Western theatre model." The object of study is "the organized human performing practices (OHPP)" of all cultures. Ethnoscenology's transdisciplinary perspective brings together "scientific disciplines devoted to the exploration and analysis of human behavior" (ethology, psychology, neurobiology, cognitive sciences, anthropology, ethnomusicology); humanities; performers and their practical knowledge; and "the proper implicit and explicit local paradigm." Inspired by Marcel Mauss's notion of techniques of the body and Eugenio Barba's Theatre Anthropology, Ethnoscenology rejects mind/body dualism and integrates the cognitive and the somatic. In contrast with Northwestern's paradigm, Ethnoscenology does not take text as its point of departure, but rather the "knowing body" and the corporal dimension of performance.[8] Consistent with NYU's Performance Studies paradigm, contemporary experimental performance continues to animate the Ethnoscenology enterprise.

New directions/sources of creativity

New directions and sources of creativity within Performance Studies arise from the living, breathing symbiosis between aesthetic practices and the study of them. There is an active interchange between theory and practice, scholar and artist, art form and knowledge formation. New objects of study, particularly the unruly objects of contemporary art, destabilize not only what counts as art but also how they and all that came before them might be studied. Performance Studies is not simply a more encompassing version of theatre studies.

What is at stake is not inclusiveness per se, for inclusions are often structured in ways that reproduce the conditions of their exclusion. Rather, Performance Studies picks up the gauntlet thrown down by resistant artistic and cultural practices. This requires the fashioning, however provisional, of a (post)disciplinary subject adequate to the task. It is in that spirit that Performance Studies questions the relationship between disciplinary formations, disciplinary subjects, and their objects of study.

Performance is a more welcoming and productive concept for a truly intercultural field of study than concepts that are more tightly bound up with culturally specific divisions of the arts by medium and genre, as is the case with theatre, for example. This is not to underestimate the historical conditioning of the term performance. As is true of any keyword, "the problem of its meanings" are "inextricably bound up with the problems it [is] being used to discuss" (Williams 1983: 15). Performance has a long history and wide range of meanings in everyday English usage, from high performance in technology and performance measures in management and finance to the legally defined performance requirements of contracts. Only recently has the word performance entered other languages, almost exclusively to designate performance art. It is essentially untranslatable. *Dictionary of the Theatre: Terms, Concepts, and Analysis* (Pavis 1998), which was translated from French, provides no entry for the term performance, though it does include entries for performance analysis, performance art, and performance text.[9]

An expanded view of performance requires more than simply adding to the inventory of what has historically been considered theatre (or oral interpretation). It requires a reconceptualization of performance in light of each and every inclusion. In other words, performance is a responsive concept, rather than a procrustean bed. It is not simply a big tent under which all may gather, but an organizing concept under revision in light of the many activities to which it is addressed. Those activities may be taken for granted, part of the quotidian world. They may derive from traditions with great historical depth and theories about themselves, to mention only the *Natyashastra* for India and Zeami for Japan. Or, they may arise from contemporary experimentation, whether Happenings, performance art, postmodern dance, or installation art. This set of possibilities is as vital for artists as it is for scholars.

As Schechner is quick to note, "long before scholars took an interest, artists had an expanded view of performance. From futurism through dadaism, in the arts and rituals of many non-Western cultures, in the practice and ideas of Vsevelod Meyerhold, Antonin Artaud, John Cage, Suzuki Tadashi, Anna Halprin, and Allan Kaprow (to name just a very few)" (Schechner 1990: 16). Oskar Schlemmer, who developed the Bauhaus theatre during the 1920s, laid out just such an expanded view in his "Scheme for Stage, Culture, and Popular Entertainment, According to Place, Person, Genre, Speech, Music, Dance" (in Gropius 1996: 19). This scheme integrated the sermon, Wagner, mass gymnastics, ancient tragedy, and circus within a utopian vision of what theatre of the future might become. As Schlemmer's scheme suggests, when the historical avant-garde and postwar experimentalists mounted their opposition, they turned to all that was outside prevailing categories of art. Artaud declared, "No more masterpieces," Marinetti proclaimed, "The distinction of the senses is arbitrary," and decades later, Kaprow would propose, "nonart is more art than Art art."

Such radical artistic practices produce notions of performance of special interest to Performance Studies. A lively interchange between scholars and artists (and a blurring of the distinction) has informed the theatre anthropology (Eugenio Barba), intercultural performance (Peter Brook), poor theatre (Jerzy Grotowski), environmental theatre (Richard Schechner), theatre of the oppressed (Augusto Boal), reverse anthropology (Guillermo Gómez-Peña), and the Los Angeles Festival (Peter Sellars). (See Schechner 1993; Pavis 1996; Jeyifo 1996; Bharucha 1997.) As such artists look to everyday life, industry, popular culture, and ritual, to the outmoded and the repudiated, and to other cultures, so too do the scholars who study them. Noel Carroll encapsulates how Performance Studies emerged from such developments:

> The repudiation of mainstream theater led performance artists to seek out, resurrect, and adopt forms of theatrical performance overshadowed or forgotten as parts of our theatrical heritage because of the dominance of the well-made play. This maneuver itself was heralded by Artaud's interest in Balinese ritual. As a result, since the sixties, experimentation in performance art has embraced revivals of circus, nightclub acts, ritual, storytelling, masques, mime, puppetry, stand-up comedy, television game shows, and talk shows. Indeed, a new academic category, Performance Studies, has been developed, replacing Drama, in order to accomodate the proliferation of the new paratheatrical avant-garde while also documenting the history of the forgotten theatrical forms from which avant-garde performance art is drawing its inspiration.
>
> (Carroll 1986: 77)

Not only are some artists theorists in their own right, but also the symbiosis between artists and theorists has been consequential for artmaking (see Clifford 1988).

Science and technology

Performance as an organizing idea has been responsive not only to new modes of live action, but also new technologies. Citing mediated performance art, Philip Auslander (1992) takes issue with the assumption of human agents, live bodies, and presence as organizing concepts for Performance Studies. According to Jon McKenzie (1994: 86), virtual reality and the technologies that produce it make "the distinction between human and technological performance . . . increasingly problematic." Both can be understood in terms of "experience design" (88). If boundaries are to be blurred, why not also the line between live and mediated performance? Artists cross that line and Performance Studies has followed suit. One result can be seen in Stephen Kaplin's "puppet tree," which plots the distance between performer and object all the way from Balinese shadow plays to computer generated figures and virtual objects (Kaplin 1999).

Technology is integral to the history of performance. First, the theatre itself can be understood as a machine, to cite only the extraordinary stage machinery of the Baroque theatre. Its inner workings are related to ship technologies, as can be seen at Drottningholm, near Stockholm, where shipbuilders applied their knowledge of ropes and wooden winches, pulleys, and capstans to create the inner workings of one of the best-preserved Baroque theatres in the world. Scene design is related to the history of what Jonathan Crary calls "techniques of the observer." Second, the body itself has been imagined as an intelligent performing machine, from historical automata, whose mechanisms are related to those of clocks, to the microchip, which "has replaced clockworks as the intelligence driving performing objects" (Tillis 1999; see also Sussman 1999).

Performance is integral to the history of technology. The notion of *gestural knowledge* is critical to an understanding of bodies of practice in the laboratory. Otto Sibum, Research Director at the Max Planck Institut für Wissenschaftsgeschichte, defines gestural knowledge and its value for a history of science as follows:

> Despite the fact that one often knows the outcome of the historical experiments through publications of note book entries, undertaking to perform the experiment remains a highly valuable, investigative study, acting on a trial basis. It will become obvious that getting the experiment to work demands a great deal of embodied capabilities, many of which are no longer known at all well. Therefore success in repeating the trial depends above all on the improvisational work and knowledge of the researcher. Material objects (as well as accompanying texts) serve as a kind of choreography for this performance because they provide partial direction of our thinking and acting . . . gestural knowledge in doing the experiment represents a resource in its own right, which complements the usually static representations of past practices like historical texts and material objects. *Doing* the experiment, and recognizing the troubles encountered in getting it to work, creating an awareness of the behaviour of the historical experimenter and the practices, possibly unarticulated, which are indispensable for the performance of the experiment. This acquired gestural knowledge can serve as a heuristic device in developing interpretations of the existing textual representations of the historical experiment.
>
> (Sibum 1995: 28)

Sibum explores how *instruments of precision* molded *gestures of accuracy*, taking as a case in point the brewing industry in England and Benjamin Joule's experiments to find an exact way of measuring heat. In other words, the issue is not whether or not to uphold a particular definition of performance over and against media and technology, but rather to work with the relationships between them. Critical to the history of Performance Studies is, for example, the cybernetic thinking of Gregory Bateson, who was drawing from the field of communications engineering long before the digital revolution of our time. (See Bateson 1972 for essays spanning four decades.)

Objects, ideas, knowledge industries

At a time when media – and, in particular, digital technologies – have altered our relationship to the material world, including our very own bodies, Performance Studies has much to offer to an understanding of materiality, embodiment, sensory experience, liveness, presence, and personhood as they bear on being-in-the-world and as they are mediated by technologies old and new.[10] As the volume of information increases and with it the artificial intelligence necessary to manage it, Performance Studies seeks to understand the kinds of knowledge that are located in the body. Fruitful contributions to this topic include Marcel Mauss's *techniques of the body*; Otto Sibbum's *gestural knowledge*; Pierre Bourdieu's *habitus*; and Paul Connerton's *body memory*. This is not to essentialize the body as technology's other, but rather to redefine and resituate the issues, including the technologizing of the body, the question of its boundaries, its history, and much that might once have been taken for granted about corporeality, somaticism, and the senses.[11]

If the body is one site of performance analysis, objects are another. As suggested above, object performance provides a particularly rich arena for the relationship between people and things. This, among other themes, is taken up by Performance Studies scholars working on museums. The museum and the theatre are historically related, in connection not only with the architectural form of the memory palace but also with Protestant opposition to theatre. Museums, in this context, are one response to what Jonas Barish has called the anti-theatrical prejudice. They might be considered a form of Protestant theatre. A grand instance of object performance, the museum stands in an inverse relationship to the theatre. In theatre, spectators are stationary and the spectacle moves. In the museum, spectators move and the spectacle is still (until recently). Exhibition is how museums stage knowledge. They do this by the way they arrange objects, broadly conceived, in space and by how they install the visitor. The experience, however visual it may be, is corporeal. The key sense – so key that it is invariably overlooked – is propriocepsis or how the body knows its own boundaries and orientation in space. The museum is an archeological site for excavating the history of the body, understood in these terms. If anything, technologies of virtual reality, for example, have heightened awareness and required more sophisticated theories of embodiment. (See Moser and MacLeod 1996.)

The museum, particularly the natural history, science, and techology museum, is an archive of outmoded knowledge formations that have sedimented themselves in collections, catalogues, storage arrangements, particular modes of display, and the historically formed dispositions of its viewers. Many fields were once housed in museums. They were based upon collections formed in the course of research and provided the foundation for analysis. As those fields migrate to the laboratory and the university, a tension arises in museums between the historical value of old collections and the challenges of presenting new knowledge that is not collection based. In the process, museums have changed their relationship not only to their collections but also to exhibition as a medium. If anything, museums and their exhibitions have become more theatrical – even operatic – than ever. In the way they do what they are about – I have in mind museums of redress such as Holocaust museums – they are more performative than ever. They have also become prime sites for applying new technologies of information and display, to the point that museums are established without collections and exhibitions may not feature objects. (See Kirshenblatt-Gimblett 1998.) This does not spell the end of objects. Rather, the question of the role and meaning of things requires attention to objecthood and materiality in an era so concerned with information and virtuality.

Cultural equity

Because of the inclusionary spirit of Performance Studies (and the theoretical concern with what "inclusion" presumes), the field is particularly attuned to issues of place, personhood, cultural citizenship, and equity. Artists and scholars concerned with *intercultural performance* deal with these issues by bringing diverse performance cultures into conversation and collaboration with one another. At the same time, Performance Studies scholars are developing theories of heritage as a mode of cultural production that have implications for cultural policy dealing with preservation and equity in a variety of contexts. (See Kirshenblatt-Gimblett 1995 [Appendix B] and 1998.) It could be said, for example, that heritage is a way of producing the local for export, tourism being a global market for this commodity. Or, put another way, processes of globalization produce the local, while altering the very nature and value of the local. Issues of equity and social justice inform the work of activists, both artists and scholars, concerned with a wide range of issues, from labor, immigration, and homelessness to homophobia, racism, AIDS, violence, and censorship. (See Boal 1998; Cohen-Cruz 1998; Muñoz 1999; Thiong'o 1998; Kondo 1997; Piper 1996; and Taylor 1996.)

Performance Studies is a promising context for exploring issues of culture and creativity in relation to the challenges of 20th century science and technology, changing knowledge industries, shifting configurations of the global and local, and issues of equity and social justice.

NOTES

1 Performance now appears as a keyword in several lexicons. See, for example, Pavis 1998 and Lentricchia and McLaughlin 1995. See also, *The Johns Hopkins Guide to Literary Theory and Criticism* http://www.press.jhu.edu/books/hopkins guide to literary theory/b-index.html, where a search for the keyword *performance* brought up such entries as Semiotics, Drama Theory, Speech Acts, Linguistics and Language, Discourse Analysis, Anthropological Theory and Criticism, and Psychoanalytic Theory and Criticism (The Post-Lacanians). The term also appears in business, legal, medical, technology, and computer lexicons. See http://www.onelook.com/cgi-bin/cgiwrap/bware/dofindt.cgi?word=performance&type=type a. On the notion of performance in legal thought, see Hibbitts 1992.

2 Among the institutions that have established performance studies programs are Indiana University (Bloomington), University of Sidney, University of Warwick, Centre for Performance Research at the University of Wales. At the University of Paris VIII and Salvador de Bahia, Jean-Marie Pradier has created his own version of Performance Studies under the banner of Ethnoscenology. See Pradier 2001. See also the new Hemispheric Institute of Performance and Politics, a innovative consortium of artists, scholars, and institutions in the Americas, organized by Diana Taylor. Founding members are in Brazil, Peru, and the United States. http://lrw.net/~hemisphere/index2.html

3 During the 1980s, a Performance Studies focus group was established within ATHE (Association for Theatre in Higher Education) and a Performance Studies Division was formed within the Speech Communication Association. Last year, PSi Performance Studies International was formally constituted at the fifth annual Performance Studies Conference.

4 *TDR: The Drama Review, A Journal of Performance Studies*, which is edited by Richard Schechner at New York University and published by MIT Press, was established in 1956 as *Tulane Drama Review*. *Performing Arts Journal*, edited by Bonnie Maranca and Gautam Dasgupta and published by Johns Hopkins University Press, was established in 1976. *Women and Performance: A Journal of Feminist Theory*, established in 1983, is edited and published at New York University. *Performance Research*, which is edited by Richard Gough at the University of Wales and published by Routledge, was established in 1995. *LIMEN: an electronic journal dedicated to the performance paradigm* was published by the Centre of Theatre Practice/Kaos Theatre and Murdoch University during the mid-1990s.

5 Among the presses supporting a Performance Studies book series are Routledge and University of California Press. See the attached Bibliography for programmatic essays, readers, and textbooks.

6 Such paradigms pose a challenge to existing fields of study, particularly theater and oral interpretation. See Schechner 1990; Dolan 1993; Worthen 1995; Lee 1999.

7 Northwestern University, *The Graduate School Bulletin 1997/1999*, Performance Studies. http://www.nwu.edu/graduate/bulletin/programs/speech/spch-pfst.html.

8 This discussion is based on Pradier's 2001 article "Ethnoscenology: the flesh is spirit."

9 Rather than provide an entry for *performance*, this *Dictionary* refers the reader to the term *spectacle*, which is offered as the French translation of *performance*. However, a chart comparing *spectacle* (French) and *performance* (English) explains that "the generic notion of 'spectacle' and 'spectacularity' is missing in the English *performance*," without suggesting what is missing from *spectacle* (French) (Pavis 1998: 256). Similar incommensurabilites are found in other languages as well.

10 The increasingly technologized body, on the one hand, and the question of personhood in digital media, on the other, are lively areas of concern within Performance Studies. See for example, the special issue of *Women and Performance* devoted to "Sexuality and cyberspace: performing the digital body," http://www.echonyc.com/~women/Issue17/index.html.

11 See, for example, the special issue of *Performance Research* (1999) devoted to food and performance.

BIBLIOGRAPHY

Artaud, Antonin (1988) "An end to masterpieces." In *Antonin Artaud: Selected Writings*, ed. Susan Sontag, 252–9. Berkeley: University of California Press.

Auslander, Philip (1992) *Presence and Resistence: Postmodernism and Cultural Politics in Contemporary American Performance*. Ann Arbor: University of Michigan Press.

Austin, J. L. (1980) *How to Do Things With Words*. New York: Oxford University Press.

Barba, Eugenio, and Nicola Saravese (1991) *A Dictionary of Theatre Anthropology: The Secret Art of the Performer*. London: Routledge.

Barish, Jonas (1981) *The Anti-Theatrical Prejudice*. Berkeley: University of California Press.

Bateson, Gregory (1972) *Steps to an Ecology of Mind*. New York: Ballantine.

Bauman, Richard, and Charles Briggs (1990) "Poetics and performance as critical perspectives on language and social life." *Annual Review of Anthropology* 19: 59–88.

Beeman, William O. (1993) "The anthropology of theater and spectacle." *Annual Review of Anthropology* 22: 369–93.

Bharucha, Rustom (1997) "Negotiating the river: intercultural interactions and interventions." *TDR: The Drama Review* 41, 3 (T155): 31–8.

Boal, Augusto (1998) *Legislative Theatre: Using Performance to Make Politics*. London: Routledge.

Butler, Judith P. (1993) *Bodies that Matter: On the Discursive Limits of "Sex."* New York: Routledge.

Carlson, Marvin (1996) *Performance: A Critical Introduction*. New York: Routledge.

Carroll, Noel (1986) "Performance." *Formations* 3, 1: 63–81.

Clifford, James (1988) *The Predicament of Culture*. Cambridge: Harvard University Press.

Cohen-Cruz, Jan, ed. (1998) *Radical Street Performance: An International Anthology*. New York: Routledge.

Connerton, Paul (1989) *How Societies Remember*. Cambridge: Cambridge University Press.

Conquergood, Dwight (1989) "Poetics, play, process, and power: the performative turn in anthropology." *Text and Performance Quarterly* 1: 82–95.

—— (1991) "Rethinking ethnography: towards a critical cultural politics." *Communications Monographs* 58, June: 179–94.

Crary, Jonathan (1992) *Techniques of the Observer*. Cambridge: Massachusetts Institute of Technology Press.

Dolan, Jill (1993) "Geographies of learning: theatre studies, performance, and the 'performative.' " *Theatre Journal* 45, December: 417–41.

Drewal, Margaret Thompson (1991) "The state of research on performance in Africa." *African Studies Review* 34, 3: 1–64.

Gómez-Peña, Guillermo (1993) *Warrior For Gringostroika*. St. Paul: Graywolf Press.

Gropius, Walter, and Arthur S. Wensinger, eds. (1996) *The Theater of the Bauhaus*. Baltimore: Johns Hopkins University Press.

Grotowski, Jerzy (1968) *Towards a Poor Theatre*. Holstebro: Odin Teatrets Forlag.

Hibbitts, Bernard J. (1992) " 'Coming to our senses': communication and legal expression in performance cultures." *Emory Law Journal* 41, 4: 874–960.

Hymes, Dell (1975) "Breakthrough into performance." In *Folklore: Performance and Communication*, eds. Dan Ben-Amos and Kenneth Goldstein, 11–74. Hague: Mouton.

Jeyifo, Biodun (1996) "The reinvention of theatrical tradition: critical discourses on interculturalism in the African theatre." *The Intercultural Performance Reader*, ed. Patrice Pavis, 149–61. New York: Routledge

Kaplin, Stephen (1999) "The puppet tree: a model for the field of puppet theatre." *TDR: The Drama Review* 43, 3: 28–35.

Kirshenblatt-Gimblett, Barbara (1995) "The aesthetics of everyday life." *Conversations before the End of Time*, ed. Suzi Gablik, 410–33. New York: Thames and Hudson.

—— (1998) *Destination Culture: Tourism, Museums, and Heritage*. Berkeley: University of California Press.

Kondo, Dorinne (1997) *About Face: Performing "Race" in Fashion and Theater*. New York: Routledge.

Lee, Josephine (1999) "Disciplining theater and drama in the English Department: some reflections on 'performance' and institutional history." *Text and Performance Quarterly* 19, 2: 145–58.

Lentricchia, Frank, and Thomas McLaughlin, eds. (1995) *Critical Terms for Literary Study*. 2nd edn. Chicago: University of Chicago Press.

Mauss, Marcel (1979) "Body techniques." *Sociology and Psychology: Essays by Marcel Mauss*, 95–123. London: Routledge & Kegan Paul.

McKenzie, Jon (1994) "Virtual reality: performance, immersion, and the thaw." *TDR: The Drama Review* 38, 4 (T144): 83–106.

Moser, Mary Anne, and Douglas MacLeod, eds. (1996) *Immersed in Technology: Art and Virtual Environments*. Cambridge: Massachusetts Institute of Technology Press.

Muñoz, José Esteban (1999) *Disidentifications: Queers of Color and the Performance of Politics*. Minneapolis: University of Minnesota Press.

Pavis, Patrice, ed. (1996) *The Intercultural Performance Reader*. New York: Routledge.

—— (1998) *Dictionary of the Theatre: Terms, Concepts, and Analysis*, trans. Christine Shantz. Toronto: University of Toronto.

Pelias, Ronald J., and James VanOosting (1987) "A paradigm for performance studies." *Quarterly Journal of Speech* 73: 219–31.

Phelan, Peggy (1993) *Unmarked: The Politics of Performance*. New York: Routledge.

Phelan, Peggy, and Jill Lane, eds. (1998) *The Ends of Performance*. New York: New York University Press.

Piper, Adrian (1996) *Adrian Piper: Out of Order, Out of Sight*. Cambridge: Massachusetts Institute of Technology Press.

Pradier, Jean-Marie (2001) "Ethnoscenology: the flesh is spirit." *New Approaches to Theatre Studies and Performance Analysis: The Colston Symposium*, ed. Günter Berghaus, 61–81. Tübingen: Niemayer Verlag.

Roach, Joseph R. (1996) *Cities of the Dead: Circum-Atlantic Performance*. New York: Columbia University Press.

Sayre, Henry (1995) "Performance." *Critical Terms for Literary Study*, eds. Frank Lentricchia and Thomas McLaughlin, 91–104. Chicago: University of Chicago Press.

Sayre, Henry M. (1989) *The Object of Performance: The American Avant-Garde Since 1970*, 101–44. Chicago: University of Chicago Press.

Schechner, Richard (1977) *Essays on Performance Theory 1970–1976*. New York: Drama Book Specialists.

—— (1985) *Between Theater and Anthropology*. Philadelphia: University of Pennsylvania Press.

—— (1990) "Performance studies: the broad spectrum approach." *Phi Betta Kappa Phi Journal*, summer: 15–16.

—— (1993) *The Future of Ritual: Writings on Culture and Performance*. New York: Routledge.

Schimmel, Paul *et al.* (1998) *Out of Actions: Between Performance and the Object, 1949–1979*. Los Angeles and New York: Museum of Contemporary Art and Thames and Hudson.

Sibum, Heinz Otto (1995) "Working experiments: a history of gestural knowledge." *Cambridge Review* 116, 2325: 25–37.

Stern, Carol Simpson, and Bruce Henderson (1993) *Performance: Texts and Contexts*. New York: Longman.

Strine, Mary Susan, Beverly Whitaker Long, and Mary Frances Hopkins (1990) "Research in interpretation and performance studies: trends, issues, priorities." *Speech Communication: Essays to Commemorate the 75th Anniversary of the Speech Communication Association*, eds. Gerald M. Phillips and Julia T. Wood, 181–204. Carbondale: Southern Illinois University Press.

Sullivan, L. (1986) "Sound and senses: toward a hermeneutics of performance." *History of Religions* 26, 1: 1–33.

Sussman, Mark (1999) "Performing the intelligent machine: deception and enchantment in the life of the automaton chess player." *TDR: The Drama Review* 43, 3 (T163): 81–96.

Taylor, Diana (1996) *Disappearing Acts: Spectacles of Gender and Nationalism in Argentina's Dirty War*. Durham: Duke University Press.

Taylor, Diana, and Juan Villegas, eds. (1994) *Negotiating Performance: Gender, Sexuality, and Theatricalism in Latin/o America*. Durham: Duke University Press.

Thiong'o, Ngugi wa (1998) *Penpoints, Gunpoints, and Dreams: The Performance of Literature and Power in Post-colonial Africa*. New York: Oxford University Press.

Tillis, Steve (1999) "The art of puppetry in the age of media production." *TDR: The Drama Review* 43, 3 (T163): 182–95.

Williams, Raymond (1983) *Keywords: A Vocabulary of Culture and Society*. Rev. edn. New York: Oxford University Press.

Worthen, W. B. (1995) "Disciplines of the text/sites of performance." *TDR: The Drama Review* 35, 1: 13–28.

Zarrilli, Phillip (1986) "Toward a definition of performance studies: part I." *Theatre Journal* 38, 3: 372–6.

—— (1986) "Toward a definition of performance studies: part II. *Theatre Journal* 38, 4: 493–6.

READER CROSS-REFERENCES

Schechner – the broad spectrum approach to performance studies

Goffman, Gabler – the study of everyday life as performance

Bateson, Blair – applications of cognitive science to the study of performance

Austin, Butler, Parker and Sedgwick – the epistemological connection between philosophical and theatrical understandings of performativity

Fabian, Turner and Turner, Conquergood – issues of intercultural performance

Gómez-Peña, Lane – artistic responses to globalization

J. Bell, Santino, Taylor – the potential of performance studies to reconceptualize contemporary issues and events

6

PERFORMANCE STUDIES IN AN AGE OF TERROR

John Bell

I remember in 1992 at a conference of the Association for Theatre in Higher Education (ATHE), Richard Schechner arguing in a keynote speech that the whole concept of theater as a separate, self-contained discipline was no longer relevant. Schechner predicted that theater or drama departments themselves would eventually face extinction, to be superseded (of course) by more broadly focused concepts (and departments?) of performance studies. The advantage of this, it seemed to me at the time, would be that we would no longer have to pursue the charade that live, text-based realistic performance (reverently known as "The Drama") was as central a modern cultural form as it had appeared to have been from the nineteenth century until, say, 1928, when Broadway theater production reached its numerical highpoint; or certainly until 1940, by which time Thornton Wilder had written to Gertrude Stein that Hollywood had finally surpassed Broadway (Stein 1996: 254).

However, a decade has gone by and I think Schechner underestimated the conservative nature of academic thought processes and academic change, because the academic study of The Drama is still central, and performance studies is still considered by many to be a fringe discipline seeking to dilute time-honored boundaries among performance forms and their concomitant standards of artistic greatness. The curious monster of performance studies, of course, *wants* to cross boundaries and consider the Western dramatic tradition not simply in solipsistic terms, but in the context of world culture, popular performance, mass-media spectacle, and the performative rituals of contemporary life.

What does this have to do with our post-9/11 world?

Five days after the destruction of the World Trade Center, the celebrated modernist composer Karlheinz Stockhausen landed in a heap of trouble by allowing his analysis of art-making to be applied to the recent events in Manhattan. In a Hamburg press conference about a new 28-hour-long performance cycle entitled *Licht*, Stockhausen explained how the piece incorporated such traditional characters from the Western cultural pantheon as Saint Michael, Eve ("the mother of life"), and Lucifer ("the prince of light") (Zander 2002). Stockhausen's inspired artistic sense saw these figures not simply as outdated metaphors of "cultural history," as a reporter put it, but as persistent, contemporary forces. Stockhausen offered as an example that Lucifer "is very present [. . .] in New York at the moment," and then went on to make a colossal public relations blunder by referring to the destruction of the World Trade Center as Lucifer's handiwork: "*das größte Kunstwerk, das es je gegeben hat*" – "the greatest work of art there has ever been" (in Hilferty 2002). Of course, all hell broke loose as a result of Stockhausen's analogy, and the 73-year-old composer was termed, among other things, a lunatic. Stockhausen claimed he had been quoted out of context, and that his reference to Lucifer as "the cosmic spirit of rebellion, of anarchy," who "uses his high degree of intelligence to destroy creation" had been misunderstood (Stockhausen in Deutsch 2001).

My point here is not to defend Stockhausen, but to point out a big problem concerning the concept of "art," because it is specifically the word "art" that made the composer's comments so obscene, so clueless. (They would have been just as obscene if he had termed the events of 9/11 "theater" or "drama.") This is because by 2001 modernist and post-modernist notions of what art is, what artists do, and what functions art serves in Western culture were overwhelmingly dominated by the image of the artist as an isolated romantic genius who creates objects, sounds, or events that by definition can only connect to our lives as high-end cultural products.

Would it have been considered any less obscene for Stockhausen to call the destruction of the World Trade Center "performance"? Not "performance *art*," because that postmodern formal tradition is also often lovingly restricted to isolated and impenetrable cultural products, but "performance" in, say, Schechner's terms, as "twice-behaved behavior." I'm not sure if by doing so Stockhausen would have avoided media outrage, but I want to argue that the term "performance" is invaluable for understanding not only what the 9/11 terrorists did, but also for understanding much of what has happened before and after 9/11, and what will happen in the years to come as the United States develops its worldwide "war on terrorism."

Using the tools of performance studies to analyze how calculated violence is employed in media-saturated society is not an insult to the memories of those who died, but an essential means of understanding the undeniably symbolic level at which global conflict is now being played out. It is clear that such vivid terms as "Axis of Evil," "Homeland Security," and "Weapons of Mass Destruction" have been put into play with full cognizance of their semiotic value, and we will only understand the actual implications of these concepts and the actions connected to them – performatives all – if we are able to comprehend them on an equally sophisticated level of analysis.

The concept of performance, and our studies of performance, can help us understand and respond to these new exigencies. From the temporary public shrines that sprouted up all over Manhattan immediately after 9/11 (so wonderfully documented and chronicled by Barbara Kirshenblatt-Gimblett (2003)); to the public protests, marches, and rallies all over the world that have followed 9/11 in almost weekly regularity; to the conscious manipulation of the threat of terror by the United States government both at home and abroad in highly professional propaganda campaigns; and finally to the onset of a global war without end on the part of our "world's largest army," the idea of performance offers concepts, means of analysis, and methods of action which can help us figure out where we are and what we ought to do – certainly better than concepts of "art" or "drama" and "theater," which seem to be, consciously or unconsciously, now scrupulously estranged from the things of import that happen around us.

In other words, at the onset of the twenty-first century, the idea of performance and the young tradition of performance studies are critical to any understanding of our present situation. We can use and develop the tools of performance studies to explain to ourselves and to others what is going on around us. The analytic frameworks of "theater," "drama," and "art" analysis clearly don't allow us this opportunity, as Stockhausen's experience shows. But performance studies does.

REFERENCES

Deutsch, R.W. (2001) "Stockhausen replies to critics of his comments on U.S. tragedy." *Red Ludwig.com*, 25 September: http://www.redludwig.com/news/archive/092501.html (6 March 2002).

Hilferty, Robert (2002) "The greatest work of art in the entire cosmos." *Andante*, 23 December: http://www.andante.com/article/article.cfm?id=14377 (8 January 2003).

Kirshenblatt-Gimblett, Barbara (2003) "Kodak Memories." *TDR* 47: 1 (T177): 11–48.

Stein, Gertrude (1996) *The Letters of Gertrude Stein and Thornton Wilder*. Edited by Edward M. Burns and Ulla E. Dydo, New Haven: Yale University Press.

Zander, Margarete (2002) "Journalist for NDR clears Stockhausen of making statements." Stockhausen-Verlag, 6 March: http://www.stockhausen.org/zander.html (8 January 2003).

READER CROSS-REFERENCES

Schechner — the shift from "drama" to performance studies
Goffman, Gabler — everyday events as performance
Santino — public shrines as a response to September 11, 2001
Kaprow — the blurred boundary between life and art

Part II

WHAT IS PERFORMANCE?

The term "performance" most commonly refers to a tangible, bounded event that involves the presentation of rehearsed artistic actions. We may, for example, attend *a* performance of a play, a dance, or a symphony. We can extend this idea of *a* performance to other events that involve a performer (someone doing something) and a spectator (someone observing something): a clergy member's performance of a religious service, an athlete's performance on the court, a politician's performance in a debate. Performance may also be understood more generally as any activity that involves the presentation of rehearsed or pre-established sequences of words or actions. Schechner calls this "restored behavior" or "twice-behaved behavior."

But performance is also a concept, a way of understanding all types of phenomenon. Shakespeare's idea that "all the world's a stage" is not new; it was probably not new to Shakespeare. But the idea of the world as performance has become increasingly relevant throughout the last century, displacing an earlier idea of the world as a book. While the language we use to describe this worldview often borrows from the stage (actors, roles) it is important to remember that understanding the world as performance can mean both more and less than understanding the world as "theater."

In his 1959 book *The Presentation of Self in Everyday Life*, anthropologist Erving Goffman explored how much of our everyday social interactions consist of pre-established patterns or routines. In the section excerpted here, "Belief in the part one is playing," Goffman draws on theatrical language (*show, audience, setting*) to describe the various expressive tools which individuals employ to indicate social status, noting that these everyday life performances may be "cynical" (intended to deceive) or "sincere" (intended to reflect "reality"). Goffman was one of the first (among many) social scientists to turn to the theater for a framework with which to interpret non-theatrical behavior. Conversely, many of Goffman's contemporaries in the humanities were turning to social theories to help analyze theatrical and literary events. Writing in 1983, Clifford Geertz ("Blurred genres: the refiguration of social thought") casts a critical eye on these interdisciplinary borrowings and what they may suggest for the subsequent study of performance.

One of the most thorough recent attempts to define performance in the field of performance studies is Marvin Carlson's 1996 book *Performance: A Critical Introduction*. In his introduction, "What is performance?," excerpted here, Carlson dissects several different uses of the term, while recognizing its "essential contestedness" (see p. 70). Carlson's consideration of performance art as a genre reminds us that the term "performance" does not always connote fiction or artifice. Used in contrast to "theater" or "drama," "performance" makes a claim to authenticity.

Neal Gabler, in an excerpt from *Life the movie* (1988), brings us back to the question of performance in everyday life. Like Goffman, Gabler suggests that social roles are performed, but Gabler takes it a step further, declaring "after decades of public-relations contrivances and media hype, [. . .] life has *become* art, so that the two are now indistinguishable" (see p. 76). This proposition is put to the test in a more oppositional way by performance artists such as Marina Abramović who enact everyday behaviors for audiences in art galleries and elsewhere. Peggy Phelan's 2004 essay considers Abramović's work with an eye toward issues of consciousness, liveness, and the artist's body. How and why are these issues essential to performance?

As the chapters in this section demonstrate, the limits of what is performance and what can be considered *as* performance are not fixed. The boundaries between performance and not performance are constantly being tested, challenged, and remapped by artists and theorists alike. This dynamic and flexible characterization of our object of study is one of the hallmarks of performance studies.

7

PERFORMANCES
Belief in the part one is playing

Erving Goffman

When an individual plays a part he implicitly requests his observers to take seriously the impression that is fostered before them. They are asked to believe that the character they see actually possesses the attributes he appears to possess, that the task he performs will have the consequences that are implicitly claimed for it, and that, in general, matters are what they appear to be. In line with this, there is the popular view that the individual offers his performance and puts on his show "for the benefit of other people." It will be convenient to begin a consideration of performances by turning the question around and looking at the individual's own belief in the impression of reality that he attempts to engender in those among whom he finds himself.

At one extreme, one finds that the performer can be fully taken in by his own act; he can be sincerely convinced that the impression of reality which he stages is the real reality. When his audience is also convinced in this way about the show he puts on – and this seems to be the typical case – then, for the moment at least, only the sociologist or the socially disgruntled will have any doubts about the "realness" of what is presented.

At the other extreme, we find that the performer may not be taken in at all by his own routine. This possibility is understandable, since no one is in quite as good an observational position to see through the act as the person who puts it on. Coupled with this, the performer may be moved to guide the conviction of his audience only as a means to other ends, having no ultimate concern in the conception that they have of him or of the situation. When the individual has no belief in his own act and no ultimate concern with the beliefs of his audience, we may call him cynical, reserving the term "sincere" for individuals who believe in the impression fostered by their own performance. It should be understood that the cynic, with all his professional disinvolvement, may obtain unprofessional pleasures from his masquerade, experiencing a kind of gleeful spiritual aggression from the fact that he can toy at will with something his audience must take seriously.[1]

It is not assumed, of course, that all cynical performers are interested in deluding their audiences for purposes of what is called "self-interest" or private gain. A cynical individual may delude his audience for what he considers to be their own good, or for the good of the community, etc. For illustrations of this we need not appeal to sadly enlightened showmen such as Marcus Aurelius or Hsun Tzû. We know that in service occupations practitioners who may otherwise be sincere are sometimes forced to delude their customers because their customers show such a heartfelt demand for it. Doctors who are led into giving placebos, filling station attendants who resignedly check and recheck tire pressures for anxious women motorists, shoe clerks who sell a shoe that fits but tell the customers it is the size she wants to hear – these are cynical performers whose audiences will not allow them to be sincere. Similarly, it seems that sympathetic patients in mental wards will sometimes feign bizarre symptoms so that student nurses will not be subjected to a disappointingly sane performance.[2] So also, when inferiors extend their most lavish reception for visiting superiors, the selfish desire to win favor may not be the chief motive; the inferior may be tactfully attempting to put the superior at ease by simulating the kind of world the superior is thought to take for granted.

I have suggested two extremes: an individual may be taken in by his own act or be cynical about it. These extremes are something a little more than just the ends of a continuum. Each provides the individual with a position which has its own particular securities and defenses, so there will be a tendency for those who have traveled close to one of these poles to complete the voyage. Starting with lack of inward belief in one's role, the individual may follow the natural movement described by Park:

> It is probably no mere historical accident that the word person in its first meaning, is a mask. It is rather a recognition of the fact that everyone is always and every-where, more or less consciously, playing a role . . . it is in these roles that we know each other; it is in these roles that we know ourselves.[3]

> In a sense, and in so far as this mask represents the conception we have formed of ourselves – the role we are striving to live up to – this mask is our truer self, the self we would like to be. In the end, our conception of our role becomes second nature and an integral part of our personality. We come into the world as individuals, achieve character, and become persons.[4]

This may be illustrated from the community life of Shetland.[5] For the last four or five years the island's tourist hotel has been owned and operated by a married couple of crofter origins. From the beginning, the owners were forced to set aside their own conceptions as to how life ought to be led, displaying in the hotel a full round of middle-class services and amenities. Lately, however, it appears that the managers have become less cynical about the performance that they stage; they themselves are becoming middle class and more and more enamored of the selves their clients impute to them.

Another illustration may be found in the raw recruit who initially follows army etiquette in order to avoid physical punishment and eventually comes to follow the rules so that his organization will not be shamed and his officers and fellow soldiers will respect him.

As suggested, the cycle of disbelief-to-belief can be followed in the other direction, starting with conviction or insecure aspiration and ending in cynicism. Professions which the public holds in religious awe often allow their recruits to follow the cycle in this direction, and often recruits follow it in this direction not because of a slow realization that they are deluding their audience – for by ordinary social standards the claims they make may be quite valid – but because they can use this cynicism as a means of insulating their inner selves from contact with the audience. And we may even expect to find typical careers of faith, with the individual starting out with one kind of involvement in the performance he is required to give, then moving back and forth several times between sincerity and cynicism before completing all the phases and turning-points of self-belief for a person of his station. Thus, students of medical schools suggest that idealistically oriented beginners in medical school typically lay aside their holy aspirations for a period of time. During the first two years the students find that their interest in medicine must be dropped so that they may give all their time to the task of learning how to get through examinations. During the next two years they are too busy learning about diseases to show much concern for the persons who are diseased. It is only after their medical schooling has ended that their original ideals about medical service may be reasserted.[6]

While we can expect to find natural movement back and forth between cynicism and sincerity, still we must not rule out the kind of transitional point that can be sustained on the strength of a little self-illusion. We find that the individual may attempt to induce the audience to judge him and the situation in a particular way, and he may seek this judgment as an ultimate end in itself, and yet he may not completely believe that he deserves the valuation of self which he asks for or that the impression of reality which he fosters is valid. Another mixture of cynicism and belief is suggested in Kroeber's discussion of shamanism:

> Next, there is the old question of deception. Probably most shamans or medicine men, the world over, help along with sleight-of-hand in curing and especially in exhibitions of power. This sleight-of-hand is sometimes deliberate; in many cases awareness is perhaps not deeper than the foreconscious. The attitude, whether there has been repression or not, seems to be as toward a pious fraud. Field ethnographers seem quite generally convinced that even shamans who know that they add fraud nevertheless also believe in their powers, and especially in those of other shamans: they consult them when they themselves or their children are ill.[7]

Front

I have been using the term "performance" to refer to all the activity of an individual which occurs during a period marked by his continuous presence before a particular set of observers and which has some influence on the observers. It will be convenient to label as "front" that part of the individual's performance which regularly functions in a general and fixed fashion to define the situation for those who observe the performance. Front, then, is the expressive equipment of a standard kind intentionally or unwittingly employed by the individual during his performance. For preliminary purposes, it will be convenient to distinguish and label what seem to be the standard parts of front.

First, there is the "setting," involving furniture, décor, physical layout, and other background items which supply the scenery and stage props for the spate of human action played out before, within, or upon it. A setting tends to stay put, geographically speaking, so that those who would use a particular setting as part of their performance cannot begin their act until they have brought themselves to the appropriate place and must terminate their performance when they leave it. It is only in exceptional circumstances that the setting follows along with the performers; we see this in the funeral cortege, the civic parade, and the dream-like processions that kings and queens are made of. In the main, these exceptions seem to offer some kind of extra protection for performers who are, or who have momentarily become, highly sacred. These worthies are to be distinguished, of course, from quite profane performers of the peddler class who move their place of work between performances, often being forced to do so. In the matter of having one fixed place for one's setting, a ruler may be too sacred, a peddler too profane.

In thinking about the scenic aspects of front, we tend to think of the living room in a particular house and the small number of performers who can thoroughly identify themselves with it. We have given insufficient attention to assemblages of sign-equipment which large numbers of performers can call their own for short periods of time. It is characteristic of Western European countries, and no doubt a source of stability for them, that a large number of luxurious settings are available for hire to anyone of the right kind who can afford them. One illustration of this may be cited from a study of the higher civil servant in Britain:

> The question how far the men who rise to the top in the Civil Service take on the "tone" or "color" of a class other than to which they belong by birth is delicate and difficult. The only definite information bearing on the question is the figures relating to the membership of the great London clubs. More than three-quarters of our high administrative officials belong to one or more clubs of high status and considerable luxury, where the entrance fee might be twenty guineas or more, and the annual subscription from twelve to twenty guineas. These institutions are of the upper class (not even of the upper middle) in their premises, their equipment, the style of living practiced there, their whole atmosphere. Though many of the members would not be described as wealthy, only a wealthy man would unaided provide for himself and his family space, food and drink, service, and other amenities of life to the same standard as he will find at the Union, the Travellers', or the Reform.[8]

Another example can be found in the recent development of the medical profession where we find that it is increasingly important for a doctor to have access to the elaborate scientific stage provided by large hospitals, so that fewer and fewer doctors are able to feel that their setting is a place that they can lock up at night.[9]

If we take the term "setting" to refer to the scenic parts of expressive equipment, one may take the term "personal front" to refer to the other items of expressive equipment, the items that we most intimately identify with the performer himself and that we naturally expect will follow the performer wherever he goes. As part of personal front we may include: insignia of high office or rank; clothing; sex, age, and racial characteristic; size and looks; posture; speech patterns; facial expressions; bodily gestures; and the like. Some of these vehicles for conveying signs, such as racial characteristics, are relatively fixed and over a span of time do not vary for the individual from one situation to another. On the other hand, some of these sign vehicles are relatively mobile or transitory, such as facial expression, and can vary during a performance from one moment to the next.

NOTES

1 Perhaps the real crime of the confidence man is not that he takes money from victims but that he robs all of us of the belief that middle-class manners and appearance can be sustained only by middle-class people. A disabused professional can be cynically hostile to the service relation his clients expect him to extend to them; the confidence man is in a position to hold the whole "legit" world in this contempt.

2 See Taxel, op. cit. [Harold Taxel, "Authority structure in a mental hospital ward" (unpublished master's thesis, Department of Sociology, University of Chicago, 1953)], 4. Harry Stack Sullivan has suggested that the tact of institutionalized performers can operate in the other direction, resulting in a kind of *noblesse-oblige* sanity. See his "Socio-psychiatric research," *American Journal of Psychiatry*, x, 987–8:

> A study of "social recoveries" in one of our large mental hospitals some years ago taught me that patients were often released from care because they had learned not to manifest symptoms to the environing persons; in other words, had integrated enough of the personal environment to realize the prejudice opposed to their delusions. It seemed almost as if they grew wise enough to be tolerant of the imbecility surrounding them, having finally discovered that it was stupidity and not malice. They could then secure satisfaction from contact with others, while discharging a part of their cravings by psychotic means.

3 Robert Ezra Park, *Race and Culture* (Glencoe, Ill.: Free Press, 1950), 249.
4 Ibid., 250.
5 Shetland Isle study [research conducted by Goffman in a Shetland Island farming community. Reported in part in Goffman, "Communication conduct in on island community" (unpublished PhD dissertation, Department of Sociology, University of Chicago, 1953)].
6 H.S. Becker and Blanche Greer, "The fate of idealism in medical school," *American Sociological Review*, 23, 50–6.
7 A.L. Kroeber, *The Nature of Culture* (Chicago: University of Chicago Press, 1952), 311.
8 H.E. Dale, *The Higher Civil Service of Great Britain* (Oxford: Oxford University Press, 1941), 50.
9 David Solomon, "Career contingencies of Chicago physicians" (unpublished PhD dissertation, Department of Sociology, University of Chicago, 1952), 74.

READER CROSS-REFERENCES

Kirshenblatt-Gimblett, Gabler – subsequent takes on the performance of everyday life
Kaprow – the blurring of art and life from the artist's point of view
Faber, Harding – the presentation of self in ritual contexts
Butler – gender as part of the presentation of self
Phelan – the self framed as art
Santino – the commemorative uses of setting

8

BLURRED GENRES

The refiguration of social thought

Clifford Geertz

The drama analogy for social life has of course been around in a casual sort of way – all the world's a stage and we but poor players who strut and so on – for a very long time. And terms from the stage, most notably "role," have been staples of sociological discourse since at least the 1930s. What is relatively new – new, not unprecedented – are two things. First, the full weight of the analogy is coming to be applied extensively and systematically, rather than being deployed piecemeal fashion – a few allusions here, a few tropes there. And second, it is coming to be applied less in the depreciatory "mere show," masks and mummery mode that has tended to characterize its general use, and more in a constructional, genuinely dramaturgical one – making, not faking, as the anthropologist Victor Turner has put it.

The two developments are linked, of course. A constructionalist view of what theater is – that is, poiesis – implies that a dramatistic perspective in the social sciences needs to involve more than pointing out that we all have our entrances and exits, we all play parts, miss cues, and love pretense. It may or may not be a Barnum and Bailey world and we may or may not be walking shadows, but to take the drama analogy seriously is to probe behind such familiar ironies to the expressive devices that make collective life seem anything at all. The trouble with analogies – it is also their glory – is that they connect what they compare in both directions. Having trifled with theater's idiom, some social scientists find themselves drawn into the rather tangled coils of its aesthetic.

Such a more thoroughgoing exploitation of the drama analogy in social theory – as an analogy, not an incidental metaphor – has grown out of sources in the humanities not altogether commensurable. On the one hand, there has been the so-called ritual theory of drama associated with such diverse figures as Jane Harrison, Francis Fergusson, T.S. Eliot, and Antonin Artaud. On the other, there is the symbolic action – "dramatism," as he calls it – of the American literary theorist and philosopher Kenneth Burke, whose influence is, in the United States anyway, at once enormous and – because almost no one actually uses his baroque vocabulary, with its reductions, ratios, and so on – elusive. The trouble is, these approaches pull in rather opposite directions: the ritual theory toward the affinities of theater and religion – drama as communion, the temple as stage; the symbolic action theory toward those of theater and rhetoric – drama as persuasion, the platform as stage. And this leaves the basis of the analogy – just what in the theatron is like what in the agora – hard to focus. That liturgy and ideology are histrionic is obvious enough, as it is that etiquette and advertising are. But just what that means is a good deal less so.

Probably the foremost proponent of the ritual theory approach in the social sciences right now is Victor Turner. A British formed, American re-formed anthropologist, Turner, in a remarkable series of works trained on the ceremonial life of a Central African tribe, has developed a conception of "social drama" as a regenerative process that, rather like Goffman's of "social gaming" as strategic interaction, has drawn to it such a large number of able researchers as to produce a distinct and powerful interpretive school.

For Turner, social dramas occur "on all levels of social organization from state to family." They arise out of conflict situations – a village falls into factions, a husband beats a wife, a region rises against the state – and proceed to their denouements through publicly performed conventionalized behavior. As the conflict swells to crisis and the excited fluidity of heightened emotion, where people feel at once more enclosed in a common mood and loosened from their social moorings, ritualized forms of authority – litigation, feud, sacrifice, prayer – are invoked to contain it and render it orderly. If they succeed, the breach is healed and the status quo, or something resembling it, is restored; if they do not, it is accepted as incapable of remedy and things fall apart into various sorts of unhappy endings: migrations, divorces, or murders in the cathedral. With differing degrees of strictness and detail, Turner and his followers have applied this schema to tribal passage rites, curing ceremonies, and judicial processes; to Mexican insurrections, Icelandic sagas, and Thomas Becket's difficulties with Henry II; to picaresque narrative, millenarian movements, Caribbean carnivals, and Indian peyote hunts; and to the political upheaval of the 1960s. A form for all seasons.

This hospitableness in the face of cases is at once the major strength of the ritual theory version of the drama analogy and its most prominent weakness. It can expose some of the profoundest features of social process, but at the expense of making vividly disparate matters look drably homogeneous.

Rooted as it is in the repetitive performance dimensions of social action – the re-enactment and thus the reexperiencing of known form – the ritual theory not only brings out the temporal and collective dimensions of such action and its inherently public nature with particular sharpness; it brings out also its power to transmute not just opinions but, as the British critic Charles Morgan has said with respect to drama proper, the people who hold them. "The great impact [of the theater]," Morgan writes, "is neither a persuasion of the intellect nor a beguiling of the senses . . . It is the enveloping movement of the whole drama on the soul of man. We surrender and are changed." Or at least we are when the magic works. What Morgan, in another fine phrase, calls "the suspense of form . . . the incompleteness of a known completion" is the source of the power of this "enveloping movement," a power, as the ritual theorists have shown, that is hardly less forceful (and hardly less likely to be seen as otherworldly) when the movement appears in a female initiation rite, a peasant revolution, a national epic, or a star chamber.

Yet these formally similar processes have different content. They say, as we might put it, rather different things, and thus have rather different implications for social life. And though ritual theorists are hardly incognizant of that fact, they are, precisely because they are so concerned with the general movement of things, ill equipped to deal with it. The great dramatic rhythms, the commanding forms of theater, are perceived in social processes of all sorts, shapes, and significances (though ritual theorists in fact do much better with the cyclical, restorative periodicities of comedy than the linear, consuming progressions of tragedy, whose ends tend to be seen as misfires rather than fulfillments). Yet the individuating details, the sort of thing that makes *A Winter's Tale* different from *Measure for Measure*, *Macbeth* from *Hamlet*, are left to encyclopedic empiricism: massive documentation of a single proposition – *plus ça change, plus c'est le même changement*. If dramas are, to adapt a phrase of Susanne Langer's, poems in the mode of action, something is being missed: what exactly, socially, the poems say.

This unpacking of performed meaning is what the symbolic action approaches are designed to accomplish. Here there is no single name to cite, just a growing catalogue of particular studies, some dependent on Kenneth Burke, some on Ernst Cassirer, Northrop Frye, Michel Foucault, or Emile Durkheim, concerned to say what some bit of acted saying – a coronation, a sermon, a riot, an execution – says. If ritual theorists, their eye on experience, tend to be hedgehogs, symbolic action theorists, their eye on expression, tend to be foxes.

Given the dialectical nature of things, we all need our opponents, and both sorts of approach are essential. What we are most in want of right now is some way of synthesizing them. In my own analysis of the traditional Indic polity in Bali as a "theater state" – cited here not because it is exemplary, but because it is mine – I have tried to address this problem. In this analysis I am concerned, on the one hand (the Burkean one), to show how everything from kin group organization, trade, customary law, and water control to mythology, architecture, iconography, and cremation combines to a dramatized statement of a distinct form of political theory, a particular conception of what status, power, authority, and government are and should be: namely, a replication of the world of the gods that is at the same time a template for that of men. The state enacts an image of order that – a model for its beholders, in and of itself – orders society. On the other hand (the Turner one), as the populace at large does not merely view the state's expressions as so many gaping spectators but is caught up bodily in them, and especially in the great, mass ceremonies – political operas of Burgundian dimensions – that form their heart, the sort of "we surrender and are changed" power of drama to shape experience is the strong force that holds the polity together. Reiterated form, staged and acted by its own audience, makes (to a degree, for no theater ever wholly works) theory fact.

But my point is that some of those fit to judge work of this kind ought to be humanists who reputedly know something about what theater and mimesis and rhetoric are, and not just with respect to my work but to that of the whole steadily broadening stream of social analyses in which the drama analogy is, in one form or another, governing. At a time when social scientists are chattering about actors, scenes, plots, performances, and personae, and humanists are mumbling about motives, authority, persuasion, exchange, and hierarchy, the line between the two, however comforting to the puritan on the one side and the cavalier on the other, seems uncertain indeed.

READER CROSS-REFERENCES

Schechner, Conquergood – the need for an interdisciplinary approach to performance
Turner – main proponent of ritual theory
C. Bell, Fabian – follow Geertz in examining the utility of performance as an anthropological concept
Ancelet – cites Geertz' work on deep play
J. Bell, Phelan, Kaprow – "art" as blurred genre in social thought

9

WHAT IS PERFORMANCE?

Marvin Carlson

The term "performance" has become extremely popular in recent years in a wide range of activities in the arts, in literature, and in the social sciences. As its popularity and usage have grown, so has a complex body of writing about performance, attempting to analyze and understand just what sort of human activity it is. For the person with an interest in studying performance, this body of analysis and commentary may at first seem more of an obstacle than an aid. So much has been written by experts from such a wide range of disciplines, and such a complex web of specialized critical vocabulary has been developed in the course of this analysis, that a newcomer seeking a way into the discussion may feel confused and overwhelmed.

In their very useful 1990 survey article "Research in interpretation and performance studies: trends, issues, priorities," Mary Strine, Beverly Long, and Mary Hopkins begin with the extremely useful observation that performance is "an essentially contested concept." This phrase is taken from W. B. Gallie's *Philosophy and the Historical Understanding* (1964), in which Gallie suggested that certain concepts, such as art and democracy, had disagreement about their essence built into the concepts themselves. In Gallie's terms: "Recognition of a given concept as essentially contested implies recognition of rival uses of it (such as oneself repudiates) as not only logically possible and humanly 'likely,' but as of permanent potential critical value to one's own use or interpretation of the concept in question."[1] Strine, Long, and Hopkins argue that performance has become just such a concept, developed in an atmosphere of "sophisticated disagreement" by participants who "do not expect to defeat or silence opposing positions, but rather through continuing dialogue to attain a sharper articulation of all positions and therefore a fuller understanding of the conceptual richness of performance."[2] In his study of the "post-structured stage," Erik MacDonald suggests that "performance art has opened hitherto unnoticed spaces" within theatre's representational networks. It "problematizes its own categorization," and thus inevitably inserts theoretical speculation into the theatrical dynamic.[3]

The present study, recognizing this essential contestedness of performance, will seek to provide an introduction to the continuing dialogue through which it has recently been articulated, providing a variety of mappings of the concept, some overlapping, others quite divergent. Recent manifestations of performance, in both theory and practice, are so many and so varied that a complete survey of them is hardly possible, but this [study] attempts to offer enough of an overview and historical background to single out the major approaches and sample significant manifestations in this complex field, to address the issues raised by the contested concepts of performance and what sorts of theatrical and theoretical strategies have been developed to deal with these issues.

My own background is in theatre studies, and my emphasis will be on how ideas and theories about performance have broadened and enriched those areas of human activity that lie closest to what has traditionally been thought of as theatrical, even though I will not be devoting a great deal of attention to traditional theatre as such, but rather to that variety of activities currently being presented for audiences under the general title of "performance" or "performance art." Nevertheless, in these opening remarks it might be useful to step back at least briefly from this emphasis and consider the more general use of the term "performance" in our culture, in order to gain some ideas of the general semantic overtones it may bear as it circulates through an enormous variety of specialized usages. I should perhaps also note that although I will include examples of performance art from other nations, my emphasis will remain on the United States, partly, of course, because that is the center of my own experience with this activity, but, more relevantly, because, despite its international diffusion, performance art is both historically and theoretically a primarily American phenomenon, and a proper understanding of it must, I believe, be centered on how it has developed both practically and conceptually in the United States.

"Performing" and "performance" are terms so often encountered in such varied contexts that little if any common semantic ground seems to exist among them. Both the *New York Times* and the *Village Voice* now include a special category of "performance" – separate from theatre, dance, or films – including events that are also often called "performance art" or even "performance theatre." For many, this latter term seems tautological, since in simpler days all theatre was considered to be involved with performance, theatre being in fact one of the so-called "performing arts." This usage is still much with us, as indeed is the practice of calling any specific theatre event (or for that matter specific dance or musical event) a "performance." If we mentally step back a moment from this common practice and ask what makes performing arts performative, I imagine the answer would somehow suggest that these arts require the physical presences of trained or skilled human beings whose demonstration of their skills is the performance.

I recently came across a striking illustration of how important the idea of public display of technical skill is to this traditional concept of "performance." At a number of locations in the United States and abroad, people in period costume act out improvised or scripted events at historical sites for tourists, visiting schoolchildren, or other interested spectators – a kind of activity often called "living history." One site of such activity is Fort Ross in Northern California, where a husband and wife, dressed in costumes of the 1830s, greet visitors in the roles of the last Russian commander of the fort and his wife. The wife, Diane Spencer Pritchard, in her role as "Elena Rotcheva," decided at one time to play period music on the piano to give visitors an impression of contemporary cultural life. But later she abandoned this, feeling, in her words, that it "removed the role from living-history and placed it in the category of performance."[4] Despite taking on a fictive personality, dressing in period clothes, and "living" in the 1830s, Ms. Pritchard did not consider herself "performing" until she displayed the particular artistic skills needed to give a music recital. Normally human agency is necessary for a "performance" of this sort (even in the theatre we do not speak of how well the scenery or the costumes performed), but the public demonstration of particular skills can be offered by nonhuman "performers," so that, for example, we commonly speak of "performing" dogs, elephants, horses or bears.[5]

Despite the currency of this usage, most of her audience probably considers Ms. Pritchard to be performing as soon as she greets them in the costume and character of a long-dead Russian pioneer. Pretending to be someone other than oneself is a common example of a particular kind of human behavior that Richard Schechner labels "restored behavior," a title under which he groups actions consciously separated from the person doing them – theatre and other role playing, trances, shamanism, rituals.[6] Schechner's useful concept of "restored behavior" points to a quality of performance not involved with the display of skills, but rather with a certain distance between "self" and behavior, analogous to that between an actor and the role the actor plays on stage. Even if an action on stage is identical to one in real life, on stage it is considered "performed" and off stage merely "done." Hamlet, in his well-known response to the Queen concerning his reactions to his father's death, distinguishes between those inner feelings that resist performance and the actions that a man might play" with a consciousness of their signifying potential.

Hamlet's response also indicates how a consciousness of "performance" can move from the stage, from ritual, or from other special and clearly defined cultural situations into everyday life. Everyone at some time or another is conscious of "playing a role" socially, and recent sociological theorists [. . .] have paid a good deal of attention to this sort of social performance.

The recognition that our lives are structured according to repeated and socially sanctioned modes of behavior raises the possibility that all human activity could potentially be considered as "performance," or at least all activity carried out with a consciousness of itself. The difference between doing and performing, according to this way of thinking, would seem to be not in the frame of theatre versus real life but in an attitude – we may do actions unthinkingly, but when we think about them, this introduces a consciousness that gives them the quality of performance. This phenomenon has been perhaps most searchingly analyzed in the various writings of Herbert Blau, to which we also will return later.

So we have two rather different concepts of performance, one involving the display of skills, the other also involving display, but less of particular skills than of a recognized and culturally coded pattern of behavior. A third cluster of usages takes us in rather a different direction. When we speak of someone's sexual performance or linguistic performance or when we ask how well a child is performing in school, the emphasis is not so much on display of skill (although that may be involved) or on the carrying out of a particular pattern of behavior, but rather on the general success of the activity in light of some standard of achievement that may not itself be precisely articulated. Perhaps even more significantly, the task of judging the success of the performance (or even judging whether it is a performance) is in these cases not the responsibility of the performer but of the observer. Ultimately, Hamlet himself is the best judge of whether he is "performing" his melancholy actions or truly "living" them, but linguistic, scholastic, even sexual performance is really framed and judged by its observers. This is why performance in this sense (as opposed to performance in the normal theatrical sense) can be and is applied frequently to non-human activity – TV ads speak interminably of the performance of various brands of automobiles, and scientists of the performance of chemicals or metals under certain conditions. I observed an amusing conflation of the theatrical and mechanical uses of this term in an advertisement by the MTA (Metropolitan Transportation Authority) on the New York subway in October 1994, when the subway was celebrating ninety years of service. This was billed as "New York City's longest running performance."

If we consider performance as an essentially contested concept, this will help us to understand the futility of seeking some overarching semantic field to cover such seemingly disparate usages as the performance of an actor, of a schoolchild, of an automobile. Never-theless, I would like to credit one highly suggestive attempt at such an articulation. This occurs in the entry on performance by the ethnolinguist Richard Bauman in the *International Encyclopedia of Communications*.[7] According to Bauman, all performance involves a conscious-ness of doubleness, through which the actual execution of an action is placed in mental comparison with a potential, an ideal, or a remembered original model of that action. Normally this comparison is made by an observer of the action – the theatre public, the school's teacher, the scientist – but the double consciousness, not the external observation, is what is most central. An athlete, for example, may be aware of his own performance, placing it against a mental standard. Performance is always performance *for* someone, some audience that recognizes and validates it as performance even when, as is occasionally the case, that audience is the self.

When we consider the various kinds of activity that are referred to on the modern cultural scene as "performance" or performance art," these are much better understood in relation to this over-arching semantic field than to the more traditional orientation suggested by the piano-playing Ms. Pritchard, who felt that so long as she was not displaying a virtuosic skill she could not be "performing." Some modern "performance" is centrally concerned with such skills (as in the acts of some of the clowns and jugglers included among the so-called "new vaudevillians"), but much more central to this phenomenon is the sense of an action carried out *for* someone, an action involved in the peculiar doubling that comes with consciousness and with the elusive "other" that performance is not but which it constantly struggles in vain to embody.

Although traditional theatre has regarded this "other" as a character in a dramatic action, embodied (through performance) by an actor, modern performance art has, in general, not been centrally concerned with this dynamic. Its practitioners, almost by definition, do not base their work upon characters previously created by other artists, but upon their own bodies, their own autobiographies, their own specific experiences in a culture or in the world, made performative by their consciousness of them and the process of displaying them for audiences. Since the emphasis is upon the performance, and on how the body or self is articulated through performance, the individual body remains at the center of such presentations. Typical performance art is solo art, and the typical performance artist uses little of the elaborate scenic surroundings of the traditional stage, but at most a few props, a bit of furniture, and whatever costume (sometimes even nudity) is most suitable to the performance situation.

It is not surprising that such performance has become a highly visible – one might almost say emblematic – art form in the contemporary world, a world that is highly self-conscious, reflexive, obsessed with simulations and theatricalizations in every aspect of its social awareness. With performance as a kind of critical wedge, the metaphor of theatricality has moved out of the arts into almost every aspect of modern attempts to understand our condition and activities, into almost every branch of the human sciences – sociology, anthropology, ethnography, psychology, linguistics. And as performativity and theatricality have been developed in these fields, both as metaphors and as analytic tools, theorists and practitioners of performance art have in turn become aware of these developments and found in them new sources of stimulation, inspiration, and insight for their own creative work and the theoretical understanding of it.

Performance art, a complex and constantly shifting field in its own right, becomes much more so when one tries to take into account, as any thoughtful consideration of it must, the dense web of interconnections that exists between it and ideas of performance developed in other fields and between it and the many intellectual, cultural, and social concerns that are raised by almost any contemporary performance project. Among them are what it means to be postmodern, the quest for a contemporary subjectivity and identity, the relation of art to structures of power, the varying challenges of gender, race, and ethnicity, to name only some of the most visible of these.

NOTES

1 W.B. Gallie, *Philosophy and the Historical Understanding*, New York: Schocken Books, 1964, 187–8.

2 Mary S. Strine, Beverly Whitaker Long, and Mary Frances Hopkins, "Research in interpretation and performance studies: trends, issues, priorities," in Gerald Phillips and Julia Wood (eds.), *Speech Communications: Essays to Commemorate the Seventy-Fifth Anniversary of the Speech Communication Association*, Carbondale: Southern Illinois University Press, 1990, 183.

3 Erik MacDonald, *Theater at the Margins: Text and the Post-Structured Stage*, Ann Arbor: University of Michigan Press, 1993, 175.

4 Diane Spencer Pritchard, "Fort Ross: from Russia with love," in Jan Anderson (ed.), *A Living History Reader*, vol. 1, Nashville, Tenn.: American Association for State and Local History, 1991, 53.

5 Like most uses of "performance," this one has been challenged, particularly by the noted semiotician of the circus Paul Bouissac. Bouissac argues that what seems to be performance is actually an invariable natural response to a stimulus provided by a trainer who "frames" it as performance. In Bouissac's words, the animal does not "perform," but "negotiates social situations by relying on the repertory of ritualized behavior that characterizes its species" ("Behavior in context: in what sense is a circus animal performing?," in Thomas Sebeok and Robert Rosenthal (eds.), *The Clever Hans Phenomenon: Communication with Horses, Whales, Apes, and People*, New York: New York Academy of Sciences, 1981, 24). This hardly settles the matter. As we shall see, many theorists of *human* performance could generally accept Bouissac's alternate statement, and moreover anyone who has trained horses or dogs knows that, even accounting for an anthropomorphic bias, these animals are not simply negotiating social situations, but are knowingly repeating certain actions for physical or

emotional rewards, a process that, to me at least, seems to have important features in common with human performance.

6 Richard Schechner, *Between Theater and Anthropology*, Philadelphia: University of Pennsylvania Press, 1985, 35–116.
7 Richard Bauman in Erik Barnouw (ed.), *International Encyclopedia of Communications*, New York: Oxford University Press, 1989.

READER CROSS-REFERENCES

Schechner – performance as an organizing principle for academic inquiry
Goffman – the presentation of self in everyday life
Faber, Kaprow, Gómez-Peña, Lane – performance art
Parker and Sedgwick – the contestedness of the term "performativity"
Taylor – the untranslatability of the term "performance"
Phelan – the role of the live in defining performance

10

LIFE THE MOVIE

Neal Gabler

To compare life to a movie is not to say, as the cliché has it, that life imitates art, though surely there is truth to that. Nor is it to say that life has devised its own artistic methods and thus reversed the process – art imitates life – though that also is true, as one can see from the number of novels, movies, and television programs that have been inspired by real-life events. Rather it is to say that after decades of public-relations contrivances and media hype, and after decades more of steady pounding by an array of social forces that have alerted each of us personally to the power of performance, life has *become* art, so that the two are now indistinguishable from each other. Or, to rework an aphorism of the poet Stéphane Mallarmé, the world doesn't exist to end in a book; when life is a medium, books and every other imaginative form exist to end in a world.

One need look no further than the daily news to realize how true this is now. It does not minimize the media excesses of the penny press, the yellow press and the original tabloids, to recognize that [in recent years] the news has become a continuous stream of what one might call "lifies" – movies written in the medium of life, projected on the screen of life, and exhibited in the multiplexes of the traditional media, which are increasingly dependent upon the life medium. The murder trial of former football star O.J. Simpson, the life and death of Diana, Princess of Wales, the ongoing soap-operatic sagas of Elizabeth Taylor or television talk show hostess Oprah Winfrey, the shooting of Long Island housewife Mary Jo Buttafuoco by her husband's seventeen-year-old paramour, the bombing of the federal office building in Oklahoma City by right-wing dissidents, the repeated allegations of extramarital dalliances by President Bill Clinton, to name only a handful of literally thousands of episodes life generates – these are the new blockbusters that preoccupy the traditional media and dominate the national conversation for weeks, sometimes months or even years at a time, while ordinary entertainments quickly evanesce.

But however much we may be preoccupied with them, it is not just these "lifies" that make life a movie. As Boorstin observed, the deliberate application of the techniques of theater to politics, religion, education, literature, commerce, warfare, crime, *everything*, has converted them into branches of show business, where the overriding objective is getting and satisfying an audience. Acting like a cultural Ebola virus, entertainment has even invaded organisms no one would ever have imagined could provide amusement.

Dr. Timothy Leary, onetime proponent of hallucinogens, turned his death into entertainment by using his computer Web page to chronicle his deterioration from prostate cancer, a show which ended with a video of him drinking a toxic cocktail in what he called a "visible, interactive, suicide." A group of teenage thugs in Washington, DC, videotaped their depredations, even posing for the camera after beating a victim while an "audience" of bystanders cheered. And one enterprising entrepreneur converted a former Nazi command post on the eastern front in Poland into a theme resort, while another planned an amusement park outside Berlin with the motif of East Germany under communism. What traditional entertainment always promised was to transport us from our daily problems, to enable us to escape from the travails of life. Analyzing the mechanism through which this was achieved, literary scholar Michael Wood in his book *America in the Movies* [1989] described our films as a "rearrangement of our problems into shapes which tame them, which disperse them to the margins of our attention," where we can forget about them. This is what we really mean when we call entertainment "escapist": We escape from life by escaping into the neat narrative formulas in which most entertainments are packaged. Still, with movies there was always the assumption that the escape was temporary. At the end of the film one had to leave the theater and reenter the maelstrom of real life.

When life itself is an entertainment medium, however, this process is obviously altered. Lewis Carroll, commenting on a vogue among nineteenth-century cartographers for ever larger and more detailed maps, once cautioned that the maps might get so large they would interfere with agriculture, and waggishly suggested that the earth be used as a map of itself instead. Carroll's is an apt analogy for the new relationship between entertainment and life. By conflating the two and converting everything from the kidnapping of the Lindbergh baby to the marital misadventures of Elizabeth Taylor into entertainments that transport us from our problems, we need never leave the theater's comfort. We can remain constantly distracted. Or, put another way, we have finally learned how to escape from life into life.

While there are certainly those who will disapprove, one is almost compelled to admit that turning life into escapist entertainment is a perversely ingenious adaptation to the turbulence and tumult of modern existence. Why worry about the seemingly intractable problems of society when you can simply declare "It's morning in America," as President Reagan did in his 1984 reelection campaign, and have yourself a long-running Frank Capra movie right down to the aw-shucks hero? Why fret over the lack of national purpose during the doldrums of the post-Cold War era when you can convert a shooting war into a real-life war movie that reaffirms your destiny, as America did in 1991 with the Gulf War? Movies have always been a form of wish fulfillment. Why not life?

READER CROSS-REFERENCES

Goffman – earlier formulation of performing in everyday life
Carlson – on self-conscious display of virtuosity
Phelan, Faber, Santino – the overlapping spheres of life, art, and media
Gómez-Peña, Lane – the globalizing force of entertainment culture

11

MARINA ABRAMOVIĆ: WITNESSING SHADOWS

Peggy Phelan

Born in 1946 in Belgrade, Yugoslavia, Marina Abramović might be too old to qualify as an "It girl" – but certainly she is enjoying a new level of concentrated attention, if not quite celebrity. Her performance in New York's Sean Kelly Gallery in November 2002, *The House with the Ocean View*, won the New York Dance and Performance Award (the Bessie) and Best Show in a Commercial Gallery from the International Association of Art Critics. The same performance was featured on HBO's *Sex and the City* during its sixth season in 2003, and the *New York Times* ran four pieces about Abramović's performance, including a short interview in the Sunday *Magazine* (the world's largest circulating magazine).[1]

Abramović has been positioning herself for this kind of fame for some time now. She won the Golden Lion Award for Best Artist at the 1997 Venice Biennale for *Balkan Baroque*, her meditative and mournful performance installation about the disaster in the Balkans. Before that, her collaborative walk with Ulay across the Great Wall of China (1986) commanded a lot of attention as well. But those pieces were celebrated for the endurance and strength they required. In 1998, Abramović began to change her image, and to some degree, her work as well. The cover of her extraordinary catalog, *Marina Abramović: Artist Body*, features a photograph of her romping on a beach holding a beach ball aloft.[2] This same image adorns the espresso cups designed by Illy and sometimes now available on eBay™. Posing more in the mode of a movie star than an ordeal artist, Abramović's recent photographs might have helped stoke her fame, but they are not responsible for it. Abramović's fame and its ties to the market – while not entirely unwelcome, I'm sure – sit uneasily with some of the premises of her art. Or to put it slightly differently, the gap between the art Abramović makes and the form of its most recent celebration raises interesting questions about both art and capital in the new century.

Abramović came of age as an artist in the 1970s, still performance art's most serious and daring decade. But unlike Chris Burden, Vito Acconci, Carolee Schneemann, Adrian Piper, or Dennis Oppenheim, all of whom were working in the capitalist United States in the early 1970s, Abramović was exploring performance art in Belgrade under Tito's regime. A significant aspect of the US-based performance art of the early 1970s defined itself in opposition to the commodity based art market. Attempting to create art that had no object, no remaining trace to be sold, collected, or otherwise "arrested," performance artists of the 70s were working against the accumulative logic of capital. Adrian Piper articulated the problems with commodity-based art in 1970:

> All around me I see galleries and museums faltering or closing as the capitalist structure on which they are based crumbles. This makes me realize that art as a commodity isn't such a good idea after all. That the value of an artwork has somehow become subject to monetary rather that aesthetic interest. That inconceivable amounts of money are lavished on objects, while artists expend their energy in plumbing and secretarial work in order to support themselves and their art. That by depending on a gallery to package and sell his [sic] product, the artist becomes a parasite who produces work tailored to sell rather than innovate. That the artist as parasite necessarily dies when the host dies. That all this wouldn't seem so inevitable if artists had the same social and financial status as all other civil servants who provide a service to their community.[3]

Some 30 years on, Piper's survey of the crumbling art market seems almost quaint. The connection between the parasite and host, however, has only gained in power as art and capital have become ever more intimate. Antonia Fraser's video *Untitled* (2003) makes this parasitic relationship depressingly clear. Shown at the Friedrich Petzel Gallery in New York from June 10 to July 9, 2004, *Untitled* is a video documenting a collector and Fraser having sex. According to the gallery's website, Fraser suggested the idea and asked the gallery to find the collector:

> *Untitled*, 2003 was initiated in 2002 when Andrea Fraser approached Friedrich Petzel Gallery to arrange a commission with a private collector on her behalf. The requirements for the commission were to include a sexual encounter between Fraser and a collector, which would be recorded on videotape, with the first exemplar of the edition going to the participating collector. The resulting videotape is a silent, unedited, 60-minute document shot in a hotel room with a stationary camera and existing lighting.[4]

The three all seem to have gotten what they wanted: the gallery got some videos (copies of the exemplar/y sexual encounter?); Fraser got a big payday (the collector paid US$20,000) and a lot of press; and the collector got to be both patron and collector (and he appears to have enjoyed the sex). The price for copies of the video, Fraser reports, rose during the exhibition in New York.[5]

While Fraser and the Petzel Gallery seem to have hoped that the work would be seen as part of Fraser's ongoing interest in "institutional critique," her examination of the political economy of the art world – the literal enactment of the relationship between art and prostitution – robs the performance of art. The utter loss of metaphor at the center of the video action, a kind of check-the-box rehearsal of common heterosexual positions, collapses the crucial division, the central frame necessary to sustain the conversation between art and life. More depressing still, when I contacted the gallery to inquire if the collector wore a condom and if Fraser had an orgasm – both issues central to the "institutional critique" of heterosexuality and its representations – the gallery told me they would not answer my questions because they were "not relevant to the work."[6] Great art accumulates relevance and meaning as it moves beyond the control of its creators; weak art decides in advance what the piece is about. Constraining critical discussion about what is and is not relevant to contemporary art not only makes things dull and boring, it reveals a lack of faith in the quality of the art work.

While the literalism attendant upon acting out simple analogical propositions such as "art is like prostitution" has haunted performance art from the start, the limitations of this literalism have been long ignored by performance theorists. Indeed, it could be argued that performance theory has celebrated the incipient literalism of the form. Piper again: "The immediacy of the artist's presence as art-work/catalysis confronts the viewer with a broader, more powerful, and more ambiguous situation than discrete forms or objects."[7] While I agree entirely with Piper, the ever-growing cultural uneasiness with "ambiguous situations" in the United States – an anxiety especially evident in Bush's White House – has meant that what began in the seventies as an energetic examination of the often arbitrary line between art/life has turned into an erasure of that line entirely. Without a robust sense of "life" as something other than art, the terms collapse into one another and we are left with an all-performance-all-the-time reality, a reality that risks making art nothing more than a mode of documentation.

Perhaps, then, it should not surprise us that video documentation of Fraser's perform-ance would sit so congenially within the commodity fetishism that still inspires the art market (and all other markets). Fraser's video, however, seems already dated and passé, especially in relation to work that views the art market as a subsidiary, rather than central, motivation for making art. In the case of Marina Abramović's *The House with the Ocean View*, commercial marketing seems decidedly beside the point, for reasons we shall see shortly. While I do not believe it is possible to think of performance art as somehow "beyond" or "outside" the art market, I do continue to believe that one of the most politically radical aspects of live art is its resistance to commodity form.

In her early solo pieces, Abramović, like Piper, considered performance art a laboratory for experiments in consciousness. But whereas Piper was interested in how consciousness might be changed by politically progressive and sophisticated performance, Abramović was interested in pushing her own consciousness to its limit. She began to realize that exploring consciousness required a willingness to be unconscious. In *Rhythm 2* and *Rhythm 5*, both made in 1974, she lost consciousness during her performance, once intentionally and once accidentally. In *Rhythm 5*, Abramović constructed a five-pointed star made from wood shavings soaked in gasoline. She lit the star and then walked around it, cutting her hair and nails and throwing them into each end of the star. She then lay down inside the star; not realizing that the flames would consume all of the oxygen in the inner area of the star, she lost consciousness. In *Rhythm 2*, she took drugs designed for treating catatonia and schizo-phrenia, passing out from the latter. In retrospect, perhaps these works might seem more sensational than illuminating, but performing these extreme acts gave Abramović an insight into the line between strength and vulnerability, and the oxymoronic nature of "solo" performance. In *Rhythm 5*, for example, a doctor in the audience realized that her clothes were on fire and that she was not moving, and he pulled her out of the burning star. Rather than being chastened by the need for rescue, however, Abramović dedicated herself to designing performances in which her own individual consciousness was not necessary for the completion of the event itself. She said, "After this performance, I ask[ed] myself how to use my body in and out of consciousness without interrupting the performance."[8] Deciding that her art was quite literally more important than her mind, she created performances in which her conscious presence was both a provocative anchoring point and strangely irrelevant, if not quite completely expendable.

Working in another tradition, Andy Warhol came to a similar conclusion. When he often said, "anyone can make my art," he meant both that his actual presence was not needed for the execution of his mechanical art and that anyone who stepped in would, of course, be making Warhols (and not, say, Phelans). In this statement, Warhol straddles both the democratic ideal of "we are all artists" and retains the proprietary economy of power in the marketplace – even in the Warholian democracy, "my" is paramount.

Admittedly, it is a bit jarring to think of Warhol and Abramović as allies since, on the surface at least, their work seems so absolutely different. But while they took different routes to arrive at the notion that they were not necessary to completing their work, and while they had different reasons for believing in the impersonality of art, their mutual conviction that the artist's consciousness is not necessary for art is worth pondering. Warhol's grand environmental tour de force *Shadows* (1978) shares a surprising trait with Abramović's *The House with the Ocean View*. Auratic and abstract, literal and expansive, both art works operate in an economy predicated on the belief that emptying out and erasing the self and the objects used to sustain that self (from food to plastic form) paradoxically creates extraordinary abundance. But the price of this abundance might well be a kind of vast emptiness, a glimpse of the threshold between form and formlessness, between knowing and unknowing, between life and death.

Warhol famously claimed that "good business is the best art," a conviction he arrived at shortly after he was shot by Valerie Solanas.[9] Having started his professional career as a commercial artist, Warhol became a fine artist, then aspired to be a business artist. His Factory and film production work were signs of his desire to think of art as a mode of commerce. But while this aspiration has often been viewed as crass and cynical, most of the art he actually made is subtle, complicated, and astonishingly sophisticated. *Shadows* is among his most brilliant works. Commissioned by the Lone Star Foundation (now the Dia Center for the Arts), Warhol's *Shadows* was first exhibited in January 1979. Twenty years later, Dia again exhibited the installation (1998–99). In both installations, 60 of the 102 panels of the work were hung edge to edge and close to the floor. The paintings are each 76 × 52 inches and range in color from Day-Glo™ green to mud-like brown. In the 1998 99 exhibition, they covered the entire circumference of the lower part of Dia's large room. Attending the first exhibition, Julian Schnabel observed, "There is almost nothing on them. Yet they seem to be pictures of something."[10] While accounts of what that something is vary, one can safely say the abstract paintings, like shadows themselves, capture what

Wallace Stevens aptly described as "the nothing that is not there, and the nothing that is."[11] Standing in a room surrounded by their colors, one feels enveloped in negative reflection. The preservation and stylization of a lost light source, remade into a vast chamber of new light, color, and texture, has an alchemical feel. The screens seem to confirm and extend to vision the poststructuralist phrase, "the presence of absence." Trevor Fairbrother has linked *Shadows* to Warhol's *Skulls*, and suggests that both are meditations on death.[12] I find them less somber and dark than *Skulls*, primarily because they refuse to take definitive shape or to yield some knowable underlying object of which they are a reflection. They function as copies for which no original can be deduced. The serialization of the image of negative reflection bespeaks a resistance to the consolations of form, even while the repetition elegantly composes a mesmerizing environment of texture, scale, and color.[13] In 1981, three years after completing the series, Warhol composed a self-portrait called *The Shadow*, suggesting that his own identity was the distillation of the history of his own negative reflections. The dizzying force of Warhol's environment (he referred to the serialized *Shadows* as "disco décor") comes from the realization that one spends all one's time looking at them and sees both the effort to see and the paintings' repeated refusal to yield anything but that effort. When I saw *Shadows* at Dia in 1999, I was aware both of my effort to "get" the paintings, and the energetic pursuit made by other viewers with me in the space to grasp the source of the paintings' power. This shared sense of effort (a sense that encompassed failure but was somehow exhilarating rather than defeating) was part of what made these works essentially environmental and theatrical. This effort cannot be sold and displayed, but it is central to Warhol's best art.

Abramović's *House* might best be seen as a late flowering of environmental theater, a bloom based on a radical paring away of the noise and general hubbub usually associated with such work. Abramović lived in the Sean Kelly Gallery for 12 days, fasting and refraining from talking, reading, or writing. As Thomas McEvilley notes, Abramović's decision to live in the gallery repeats and extends similar decisions made by performance artists in the seventies, including Chris Burden, Linda Montano, Gerard Richter, Gilbert and George, and others.[14] But in these works, the artists performed "for" the audience, rather than "with" the audience.

In Abramović's installation, the public was invited to the gallery to participate in what she called "an energy dialogue." This consisted primarily of an exchange of gaze between the artist and her spectators (usually one at a time). This exchange, in turn, was observed by the other viewers.[15] Abramović spent her time moving across three stages, each suspended about six feet from the floor, and buttressed with center ladders with butcher knives for rungs. The stage to the viewer's left had a toilet and shower, the center stage had a wooden table and chair with a large crystal embedded in its back, and the right stage had a wooden platform for a bed. Each day the artist wore a different color linen jacket and trousers. A metronome was also usually clicking throughout the performance. Whether one calls it environmental theater or social sculpture, *House* extends something of the repetition and serialization at work in Warhol's *Shadows* into the realm of live art. While Warhol was operating within the economy of the object and setting up repeating copies of the same image, Abramović was theatricalizing the repetitive everyday acts of sleeping, showering, eliminating waste, and sitting at a table. But these acts, each perhaps an homage to the quotidian, did not render the performance a literal treatment of these common acts. On the contrary, the symbolic and metaphorical associations were dense, ranging from Kafka's *Hunger Artist* to the prayerful acts of a Sufi mystic. The accumulation of associations and meanings people brought to bear on the art quite literally added to its energetic force.[16]

At the core of Abramović's *House* is the belief that live performance might illuminate the mutual and repeated attempt to grasp, if not fully apprehend, consciousness as simultaneously intensely personal and immensely vast and impersonal. While many spiritual traditions – especially Zen Buddhism – postulate similar relationships to consciousness, Abramović's art is fundamentally theatrical in the sense that it depends on an audience. Moreover, the public nature of Abramović's meditation rendered the performance an experiment in intersubjectivity. Intersubjective experience has been theorized, idealized, disdained, and celebrated for a long time, but rarely has it been offered as the centerpiece of a five-day-long performance.

Emmanuel Levinas argues that it is in the face-to-face encounter that ethics is distilled.[17] Abramović's performance is couched in markedly different language, but the ideas are startlingly similar. *The House with the Ocean View* combines themes and methods Abramović has developed and nurtured over 30 years of performance practice. While it would be false to call *House* the culmination of Abramović's study – she plans to continue working on this performance and to do it again – nonetheless, the performance consolidated certain concepts in live art that I think are worth untangling.

These concepts include the still complex relationship between the commodity and live art. In the 12 years since I wrote "The ontology of performance: representation without reproduction," the technology capable of broadcasting live art has grown enormously.[18] Now we have streaming video, webcasts, digital video, and other media able to record and circulate live events. These technologies can give us something that closely resembles the live event, but they remain something other than live performance. In terms of performance's ontological question, streaming video functions in the way a still photograph works: it conveys the work but it is not the live event itself.

Performance remains a compelling art because it contains the possibility of both the actor and the spectator becoming transformed during the event's unfolding. People can often have significant and meaningful experiences of spectatorship watching film or streaming video. But these experiences are less interesting to me because the spectator's response cannot alter the pre-recorded or the remote performance, and in this fundamental sense, these representations are indifferent to the response of the other. Interactivity holds more promise, but thus far most of the technology delimits in advance the kinds of interaction possible between audience members and performers. (Some of this reminds me of the illusionary notion of "letting the audience decide" the endings of certain plays. Essentially, theatrical casts rehearsed multiple endings and then picked which of the prescribed actions they would offer in response to the audience's "choice.")

In live performance, the potential for the event to be transformed in unscripted ways by those participating (both the artists and the viewers) makes it more exciting to me. This is precisely where the liveness of performance art matters. Of course, a great number of performances do not approach this potential at all, and many spectators and performers have no interest in this aspect of the live event. But the possibility of mutual transformation of both the observer and the performer within the enactment of the live event is extraordinarily important, because this is the point where the aesthetic joins the ethical.[19] The ethical is fundamentally related to live art because both are arenas for the unpredictable force of the social event.

This aspect of live performance makes consideration of the commodity object secondary at best. While the logic of capital certainly produces ethical considerations, the particular force of live performance concerns the ethical and the aesthetic *tout court*. *The House with the Ocean View* illuminates the pivotal oscillation between the ethical and the aesthetic. Emptying herself out, becoming physically smaller in front of our eyes, Abramović managed to invoke the economy of literal (female) sacrifice and (pseudo)-martyrdom, but also to sidestep them. (Although it would be hard to deny that there was a spiritual, if not exactly religious, cast to the whole event, in part because the three raised stages resembled altars.) At the end of her 12-day performance, Abramović came down from the stage and addressed her viewers. She explained that she thought of her piece as a response to the events of 9/11. She said, "I want to dedicate this work to New York and to the people of New York. In a city that has no time I wanted to create an island of time." By remaining silent for 12 days and inviting viewers to join her in that silence, she gave some observers the opportunity to dwell within their own memories of the events of that calamitous day for the first time.

Jacques Lacan claimed that love is a giving of what one does not have.[20] In giving time to those who had none in the fevered frenzy of that morning, Abramović also gave them, and gave us, love. Addressing both those who came to see her in the gallery and those who had ceased to see, *The House with the Ocean View* was perched between the specific concentration of the here and now of 12 days in New York, and the more complicated and abstract pull of the history of war and geography. This abstraction was not so much a lesson in the facts of different wars and terrorist acts; it was more a meditation about the vastness of intent, cause, and meaning.

In making the world her stage, RoseLee Goldberg suggests that Abramović also created "without a doubt one of the most important live art works in decades."[21] Part of what makes the work so powerful is its inability to be communicated or exhausted by the commentary it generates.[22] One can describe the setting and the physical movements of the performance, but the art that made this *House* took place in the spaces between the spaces we saw, in the eyes and minds of the artist and the viewers who sat silently and were transformed. A celebration and dramatization of liminality, *House* resists the commodity and logic of discrete forms that fuel the art market. In saying this, I am not saying that no objects will be sold, or that the performance is "beyond" the market. But I am saying that there are other kinds of capital at work in this piece.

The performance can be celebrated and made famous. But can it be understood? I attended the performance on two different days, gave a talk about it at the Tate Modern, and have written about it here and elsewhere.[23] But I do not think I have begun to approach what really occurred in the performance, primarily because I was a witness to something I did not see and cannot describe. I was in the realm of Warhol's *Shadows*, seeing the trace of a history of negative reflections that refused to find form.

The condition of witnessing what one did not (and perhaps cannot) see is the condition of whatever age we are now entering. Whether we call this period "the post-postmodern age" or "the age of terrorism," it is characterized both by an intimate reawakening to the fragility of life and a more general sense of connection to one another that exceeds simple geo-physical, ideological, or cultural proximity. If Levinas is right, and the face-to-face encounter is the most crucial arena in which the ethical bond we share becomes manifest, then live theater and performance might speak to philosophy with renewed vigor. So far the language of this conversation has been largely nonverbal. Becoming fluent will require practice, patience, humility, and the recognition that the social body, like our own all-too-human body, is both stronger than we guessed and unbearably tender. The connec-tion between the social body and the mortal body is defiantly metaphorical. The meta-phorical link, however, is fused by the literal physical body – whether the body of a suicide bomber or of an earnest artist – as its actions and inactions make vivid the drama we face every moment of this, our dismaying young century.

NOTES

1 Steven Henry Madoff, "A viewable fast, enforced by knives," *New York Times*, November 10, 2002; Roberta Smith, "When seeing is not only believing, but also creating," *New York Times*, November 22, 2002; Steven Henry Madoff, "Reflecting on an ordeal that was also art," *New York Times* November 28, 2002; and Catherine Saint Louis, "What were they thinking: the way we live now," *New York Times Magazine*, December 15, 2002.
2 Marina Abramović, *Artist Body: Performances 1969–1998* (Milan: Charta, 1998).
3 Adrian Piper, "Talking to myself: the ongoing autobiography of an art object," in *Out of Order, Out of Sight: Selected Writings in Meta-Art, 1968–1992, Volume 1* (Cambridge: MIT Press, 1996), 40.
4 See http://www.petzel.com.
5 Jerry Saltz, "Super theory woman": http://www.Artnet.com (July 2004).
6 E-mail reply from Maureen Sarro, Director, Friedrich Petzel Gallery, July 20, 2004.
7 Piper, "Talking to Myself", 42–43.
8 Abramović, *Artist Body*, 69.
9 Andy Warhol, *The Philosophy of Andy Warhol: From A to B and Back Again* (New York: Harcourt Brace & Company, 1975), 92.
10 Julian Schnabel, "Preface," *Andy Warhol: Shadow Paintings* (New York: Gagosian Gallery, 1989), 4.
11 Wallace Stevens, "The snow man," in *Harmonium* (New York: Alfred A. Knopf, 1923), 24.
12 Trevor Fairbrother, "Skulls," in *The Work of Andy Warhol* (Seattle: Bay Press, 1989), 95–114.
13 For further discussion see Lynne Cooke, "Andy Warhol's Shadows": http://www.diachelsea.org/exhibs/warhol/shadows/.
14 Thomas McEvilley, "Performing the present tense," in *Marina Abramović: The House with the Ocean View* (Milan: Charta, 2003), 167–69.
15 For a fuller discussion, see *Marina Abramović: The House with the Ocean View*, which includes essays by Thomas McEvilley, Cindy Carr, RoseLee Goldberg, Chrissie Iles, and Peggy Phelan.
16 This accumulation of reference and range of meaning might be seen in direct contrast to Fraser's *Untitled*, in which both the artist and the gallery seek to patrol the frameworks through which the art might be seen.

17 Emmanuel Levinas, *Ethics and Infinity: Conversations with Philippe Nemo*, trans. Richard Cohen (Pittsburgh: Duquense University Press, 1985).

18 Peggy Phelan, "The ontology of performance: representation without reproduction," in *Unmarked: The Politics of Performance* (New York: Routledge, 1993), 146–66.

19 For a fuller discussion of the ethical and the aesthetic see "Performance, live culture and things of the heart: Peggy Phelan in conversation with Marquard Smith," *The Journal of Visual Culture*, 2(3) (2003): 291–302.

20 Jacques Lacan, "The signification of the phallus," in *'crits: A Selection*, trans. Alan Schneider (New York: W. W. Norton & Company, 1977), 281–92.

21 RoseLee Goldberg, "The theater of the body," in *Marina Abramović: The House with the Ocean View* (Milan: Charta, 2003), 157.

22 In addition to the commentaries already cited in the *New York Times* and the 2003 Charta catalog devoted to the piece, other significant essays include: James Westcott, "Marina Abramović: *The House with the Ocean View,*" *The Drama Review* 47(3) (T179): 129–36; and Laurie Anderson, "Marina Abramović," *Bomb Magazine* 84, http://www.bombsite.com/abramovic/abramovic.html. This essay includes a wide-ranging interview – more of a conversation – between the artists.

23 Peggy Phelan, "On seeing the invisible," in *Marina Abramović: The House with the Ocean View* (Milan: Charta, 2003), 171–79. The essay will also appear in *Live*, ed. Adrian Heathfield (London: The Tate Modern, 2004).

READER CROSS-REFERENCES

Carlson – performance art

Gómez-Peña – performance art's relationship to mediatization

Faber – the ordeal art of Orlan

Gabler – life as art

Kaprow, Lane – performances that resist commercialization

Part III

RITUAL

Rituals are performances that provide structure and continuity to our lives. They are a means of ordering the world to fit our perception. We perform rituals to mark the passage of time (harvest festivals, birthday parties), to transform our social status (weddings, graduations), or to ensure good fortune (blessings, certain prayers). In this way, rituals provide us with a sense of control over an uncertain existence. Rituals are based on repetition, and though most rituals change somewhat over time, we look to them as fixed points from which we measure the rest of our experience. Generally speaking, rituals exemplify and reinforce the values and beliefs of the group that performs them. Conversely, communities are defined by the rituals they share.

Though virtually all performances contain some ritualized behavior, ritual itself is a particular kind of performance. It emphasizes efficacy over entertainment, adherence to tradition over technical virtuosity. Ritual has "real" consequences. Religious or sacred rituals express or enact belief, connecting the participants to a spiritual power. Secular rituals, while not specifically religious, nevertheless invoke the authority of some concept larger than the individual: the state, the community, tradition. Even a private individual ritual such as one's daily grooming routine takes on enhanced significance as a means of defining oneself in relation to society at large.

In disciplinary terms, ritual is where theater and anthropology overlap. It is the art of performance mobilized in the service of a social or religious imperative. In "Liminality and communitas" (1969), anthropologist Victor Turner emphasizes the liminal, or in-between, status of the ritual subject, suggesting that this aspect of ritual can lead to a feeling of *communitas*, a social bond between the participants. This is illustrated with an example from the rite of passage performed by the Ndembu tribe of Zambia. For Turner, rituals are part of "social dramas" that allow a culture to maintain a balance between what he calls "structure and anti-structure." Catherine Bell, in " 'Performance' and other analogies" (1992), considers the impact of Turner and others' performance analysis on ethnography. While agreeing that performance can be a powerful lens through which to view ritual, Bell cautions that its utility is limited, because the performance analogy contains intrinsic assumptions about participant-observation, meaning, and efficacy that may affect our ability to understand a culture.

Michael Atwood Mason's " 'The blood that runs through the veins' " (1993) and Alyda Faber's "Saint Orlan" (2002) provide detailed descriptions of contemporary ritual practice. Mason examines a traditional Afro-Cuban ritual, *Santería Dilogún* divination, exploring how it can provide comfort and reassurance to those in crisis. Faber, by contrast, considers an oppositional ritual, the violent manipulation of religious imagery by French performance artist Orlan. Finally, in this section, Jack Santino's "Performative commemoratives: the personal, and the public" (2004) considers an emerging class of rituals which are designed for public display, and which invite participation from a general audience. Such performances, which often memorialize victims of violence, challenge traditional notions of *communitas* and suggest new understandings of the relationship between ritual and performativity.

Taken collectively, these essays show us that the colloquial use of "ritual" to mean *pro forma* or "without impact" is far from the truth. Ritual, both as a cultural practice and as a lens through which to understand performances of various kinds, continues to shape our lives, and to affect communities large and small throughout the world.

12

LIMINALITY AND COMMUNITAS

Victor Turner

Form and attributes of rites of passage

In this chapter I take up a theme I have discussed briefly elsewhere (Turner, 1967: 93–111), note some of its variations, and consider some of its further implications for the study of culture and society. This theme is in the first place represented by the nature and characteristics of what Arnold van Gennep (1909) has called the "liminal phase" of *rites de passage*. Van Gennep himself defined *rites de passage* as "rites which accompany every change of place, state, social position and age." To point up the contrast between "state" and "transition," I employ "state" to include all his other terms. It is a more inclusive concept than "status" or "office", and refers to any type of stable or recurrent condition that is culturally recognized. Van Gennep has shown that all rites of passage or "transition" are marked by three phases: separation, margin (or *limen*, signifying "threshold" in Latin), and aggregation. The first phase (of separation) comprises symbolic behavior signifying the detachment of the individual or group either from an earlier fixed point in the social structure, from a set of cultural conditions (a "state"), or from both. During the intervening "liminal" period, the characteristics of the ritual subject (the "passenger") are ambiguous; he passes through a cultural realm that has few or none of the attributes of the past or coming state. In the third phase (reaggregation or reincorporation), the passage is consummated. The ritual subject, individual or corporate, is in a relatively stable state once more and, by virtue of this, has rights and obligations vis-à-vis others of a clearly defined and "structural" type; he is expected to behave in accordance with certain customary norms and ethical standards binding on imcumbents of social position in a system of such positions.

Liminality

The attributes of liminality or of liminal *personae* ("threshold people") are necessarily ambiguous, since this condition and these persons elude or slip through the network of classifications that normally locate states and positions in cultural space. Liminal entities are neither here nor there; they are betwixt and between the positions assigned and arrayed by law, custom, convention, and ceremonial. As such, their ambiguous and indeterminate attributes are expressed by a rich variety of symbols in the many societies that ritualize social and cultural transitions. Thus, liminality is frequently likened to death, to being in the womb, to invisibility, to darkness, to bisexuality, to the wilderness, and to an eclipse of the sun or moon.

Liminal entities, such as neophytes in initiation or puberty rites, may be represented as possessing nothing. They may be disguised as monsters, wear only a strip of clothing, or even go naked, to demonstrate that as liminal beings they have no status, property, insignia, secular clothing indicating rank or role, position in a kinship system – in short, nothing that may distinguish them from their fellow neophytes or initiands. Their behavior is normally passive or humble; they must obey their instructors implicitly, and accept arbitrary punishment without complaint. It is as though they are being reduced or ground down to a uniform condition to be fashioned anew and endowed with additional powers to enable them to cope with their new station in life. Among themselves, neophytes tend to develop an intense comradeship and egalitarianism. Secular distinctions of rank and status disappear or are homogenized. The condition of the patient and her husband in *Isoma* had some of these attributes – passivity, humility, near-nakedness – in a symbolic milieu that represented both a grave and a womb. In initiations with a long period of seclusion, such as the circumcision rites of many tribal societies or induction into secret societies, there is often a rich proliferation of liminal symbols.

Communitas

What is interesting about liminal phenomena for our present purposes is the blend they offer of lowliness and sacredness, of homogeneity and comradeship. We are presented, in such rites, with a "moment in and out of time," and in and out of secular social structure, which reveals, however fleetingly, some recognition (in symbol if not always in language) of a generalized social bond that has ceased to be and has simultaneously yet to be fragmented into a multiplicity of structural ties. These are the ties organized in terms either of caste, class, or rank hierarchies or of segmentary oppositions in the stateless societies beloved of political anthropologists. It is as though there are here two major "models" for human interrelatedness, juxtaposed and alternating. The first is of society as a structured, differentiated, and often hierarchical system of politico-legal-economic positions with many types of evaluation, separating men in terms of "more" or "less." The second, which emerges recognizably in the liminal period, is of society as an unstructured or rudimentarily structured and relatively undifferentiated *comitatus*, community, or even communion of equal individuals who submit together to the general authority of the ritual elders.

I prefer the Latin term "communitas" to "community", to distinguish this modality of social relationship from an "area of common living." The distinction between structure and communitas is not simply the familiar one between "secular" and "sacred," or that, for example, between politics and religion. Certain fixed offices in tribal societies have *many* sacred attributes; indeed, every social position has *some* sacred characteristics. But this "sacred" component is acquired by the incumbents of positions during the *rites de passage*, through which they changed positions. Something of the sacredness of that transient humility and modelessness goes over, and tempers the pride of the incumbent of a higher position or office. This is not simply, as Fortes (1962: 86) has cogently argued, a matter of giving a general stamp of legitimacy to a society's structural positions. It is rather a matter of giving recognition to an essential and generic human bond, without which there could be *no* society. Liminality implies that the high could not be high unless the low existed, and he who is high must experience what it is like to be low. No doubt something of this thinking, a few years ago, lay behind Prince Philip's decision to send his son, the heir apparent to the British throne, to a bush school in Australia for a time, where he could learn how "to rough it."

Dialectic of the developmental cycle

From all this I infer that, for individuals and groups, social life is a type of dialectical process that involves successive experience of high and low, communitas and structure, homogeneity and differentiation, equality and inequality. The passage from lower to higher status is through a limbo of statuslessness. In such a process, the opposites, as it were, constitute one another and are mutually indispensable. Furthermore, since any concrete tribal society is made up of multiple personae, groups, and categories, each of which has its own developmental cycle, at a given moment many incumbencies of fixed positions coexist with many passages between positions. In other words, each individual's life experience contains alternating exposure to structure and communitas, and to states and transitions.

The liminality of an installation rite

One brief example from the Ndembu of Zambia of a *rite de passage* that concerns the highest status in that tribe, that of the senior chief Kanongesha, will be useful here. It will also expand our knowledge of the way the Ndembu utilize and explain their ritual symbols. The position of senior or paramount chief among the Ndembu, as in many other African societies, is a paradoxical one, for he represents both the apex of the structured politico-legal hierarchy and the total community as an unstructured unit. He is, symbolically, also the tribal territory itself and all its resources. Its fertility and freedom from drought, famine, disease, and insect plagues are bound up with his office, and with both his physical and moral condition. Among the Ndembu, the ritual powers of the senior chief were limited by and combined with those held by a senior headman of the autochthonous Mbwela people, who made submission only after long struggle to their Lunda conquerors led by the first Kanongesha. An important right was vested in the headman, named Kafwana, of the Humbu, a branch of the Mbwela. This was the right to confer and periodically to medicate the supreme symbol of chiefly status among tribes of Lunda origin, the *lukanu* bracelet, made from human genitalia and sinews and soaked in the sacrificial blood of male and female slaves at each installation. Kafwana's ritual title was *Chivwikankanu*, "the one who dresses with or puts on the *lukanu*." He also had the title *Mama yaKanongesha*, "mother of Kanongesha," because he gave symbolic birth to each new incumbent of that office. Kafwana was also said to teach each new Kanongesha the medicines of witchcraft, which made him feared by his rivals and subordinates – perhaps one indication of weak political centralization.

The *lukanu*, originally conferred by the head of all the Lunda, the Mwantiyanvwa, who ruled in the Katanga many miles to the north, was ritually treated by Kafwana and hidden by him during interregna. The mystical power of the *lukanu*, and hence of the Kanongesha-ship, came jointly from Mwantiyanvwa, the political fountainhead, and Kafwana, the ritual course: its employment for the benefit of the land and the people was in the hands of a succession of individual incumbents of the chieftainship. Its origin in Mwantiyanvwa symbolized the historical unity of the Ndembu people, and their political differentiation into subchiefdoms under Kanongesha; its periodic medication by Kafwana symbolized the land – of which Kafwana was the original "owner" – and the total community living on it. The daily invocations made to it by Kanongesha, at dawn and sunset, were for the fertility and continued health and strength of the land, of its animal and vegetable resources, and of the people – in short, for the commonweal and public good. But the *lukanu* had a negative aspect; it could be used by Kanongesha to curse. If he touched the earth with it and uttered a certain formula, it was believed that the person or group cursed would become barren, their land infertile and their game invisible. In the *lukanu*, finally, Lunda and Mbwela were united in the joint concept of Ndembu land and folk.

In the relationship between Lunda and Mbwela, and between Kanongesha and Kafwana, we find a distinction familiar in Africa between the politically or militarily strong and the subdued autochthonous people, who are nevertheless ritually potent. Iowan Lewis (1963) has described such structural inferiors as having "the power or powers of the weak" (111). One well-known example from the literature is to be found in Meyer Fortes' account of the Tallensi of northern Ghana, where the incoming Namoos brought chieftainship and a highly developed ancestral cult to the autochthonous Tale, who, for their part, are thought to have important ritual powers in connection with the earth and its caverns. In the great Golib Festival, held annually, the union of chiefly and priestly powers is symbolized by the mystical marriage between the chief of Tongo, leader of the Namoos, and the great earth-priest, the Golibdaana, of the Tale, portrayed respectively as "husband" and "wife." Among Ndembu, Kafwana is also considered, as we have seen, symbolically feminine in relation to Kanongesha. I could multiply examples of this type of dichotomy many times from African sources alone, and its range is world-wide. The point I would like to stress here is that there is a certain homology between the "weakness" and "passivity" of liminality in diachronic transitions between states and statuses, and the "structural" or synchronic inferiority of certain personae, groups, and social categories in political, legal, and economic systems. The "liminal" and the "inferior" conditions are often associated with ritual powers and with the total community seen as undifferentiated.

To return to the installation rites of the Kanongesha of the Ndembu: The liminal component of such rites begins with the construction of a small shelter of leaves about a mile away from the capital village. This hut is known as *kafu* or *kafwi*, a term Ndembu derive from *ku-fwa*, "to die," for it is here that the chief-elect dies from his commoner state. Imagery of death abounds in Ndembu liminality. For example, the secret and sacred site where novices are circumcised is known as *ifwilu* or *chifwilu*, a term also derived from *ku-fwa.* The chief-elect, clad in nothing but a ragged waist-cloth, and a ritual wife, who is either his senior wife (*mwadyi*) or a special slave woman, known as *lukanu* (after the royal bracelet) for the occasion, similarly clad, are called by Kafwana to enter the *kafu* shelter just after sundown. The chief himself, incidentally, is also known as *mwadyi* or *lukanu* in these rites. The couple are led there as though they were infirm. There they sit crouched in a posture of shame (*nsonyi*) or modesty, while they are washed with medicines mixed with water brought from Katukang'onyi, the river site where the ancestral chiefs of the southern Lunda diaspora dwelt for a while on their journey from Mwantiyanvwa's capital before separating to carve out realms for themselves. The wood for this fire must not be cut by an ax but found lying on the ground. This means that it is the product of the earth itself and not an artifact. Once more we see the conjunction of ancestral Lundahood and chthonic powers.

Next begins the rite of *Kumukindyila*, which means literally "to speak evil or insulting words against him"; we might call this rite "The reviling of the chief-elect." It begins when Kafwana makes a cut on the underside of the chief's left arm – on which the *lukanu* bracelet will be drawn on the morrow – presses medicine into the incision, and presses a mat on the upper side of the arm. The chief and his wife are then forced rather roughly to sit on the mat. The wife must not be pregnant, for the rites that follow are held to destroy fertility. Moreover, the chiefly couple must have refrained from sexual congress for several days before the rites.

Kafwana now breaks into a homily, as follows:

> Be silent! You are a mean and selfish fool, one who is bad-tempered! You do not love your fellows, you are only angry with them! Meanness and theft are all you have! Yet here we have called you and we say that you must succeed to the chieftainship. Put away meanness, put aside anger, give up adulterous intercourse, give them up immediately! We have granted you chieftainship. You must eat with your fellow men, you must live well with them. Do not prepare witchcraft medicines that you may devour your fellows in their huts – that is forbidden! We have desired you and you only for our chief. Let your wife prepare food for the people who come here to the capital village. Do not be selfish, do not keep the chieftainship to yourself! You must laugh with the people, you must abstain from witchcraft, if perchance you have given it already! You must not be killing people! You must not be ungenerous to people!
>
> But you, Chief Kanongesha, Chifwanakenu ["son who resembles his father"] of Mwantiyanvwa, you have danced for your chieftainship because your predecessor is dead [i.e. because you killed him]. But today you are born as a new chief. You must know the people, O Chifwanakenu. If you were mean, and used to eat your cassava mush alone, or your meat alone, today you are in the chieftainship. You must give up your selfish ways, you must welcome everyone, you are the chief! You must stop being adulterous and quarrelsome. You must not bring partial judgments to bear on any law case involving your people, especially where your own children are involved. you must say: "If someone has slept with my wife, or wronged me, today I must not judge his case unjustly. I must not keep resentment in my heart."

After this harangue, any person who considers that he has been wronged by the chief-elect in the past is entitled to revile him and most fully express his resentment, going into as much detail as he desires. The chief-elect, during all this, has to sit silently with downcast head, "the pattern of all patience" and humility. Kafwana meanwhile splashes the chief with medicine, at intervals striking his buttocks against him (*kumubayisha*) insultingly. Many informants have told me that "a chief is just like a slave (*ndung'u*) on the night before he succeeds." He is prevented from sleeping, partly as an ordeal, partly because it is said that if he dozes off he will have bad dreams about the shades of dead chiefs, "who will say that he is wrong to succeed them, for has he not killed them?" Kafwana, his assistant, and other important men, such as village headmen, man-handle the chief and his wife – who is similarly reviled – and order them to fetch firewood and perform other menial tasks. The chief may not resent any of this or hold it against the perpetrators in times to come.

Attributes of liminal entities

The phase of reaggregation in this case comprises the public installation of the Kanongesha with all pomp and ceremony. While this would be of the utmost interest in study of Ndembu chieftainship, and to an important trend in study of Ndembu chieftainship, and to an important trend in current British social anthropology, it does not concern us here. Our present focus is upon liminality and the ritual powers of the weak. These are shown under two aspects. First, Kafwana and the other Ndembu commoners are revealed as privileged to exert authority over the supreme authority figure of the tribe. In liminality, the underling comes uppermost. Second, the supreme political authority is portrayed "as a slave," recalling that aspect of the coronation of a pope in Western Christendom when he is called upon to be the "*servus servorum Dei.*" Part of the rite has, of course, what Monica Wilson (1957: 46–54) has called a "prophylactic function." The chief has to exert self-control in the rites that he may be able to have self-mastery thereafter in face of the temptations of power. But the role of the humbled chief is only an extreme example of a recurrent theme of liminal siutations. This theme is the stripping off of preliminal and postliminal attributes.

Let us look at the main ingredient of the *Kumukindyila* rites. The chief and his wife are dressed identically in a ragged waist-cloth and share the same name – *mwadyi*. This term is also applied to boys undergoing initiation and to a man's first wife in chronological order of marriage. It is an index of the anonymous state of "initiand." These attributes of sexlessness and anonymity are highly characteristic of liminality. In many kinds of initiation where the neophytes are of both sexes, males and females are dressed alike and referred to by the same term. This is true, for example, of many baptismal ceremonies in Christian or syncretic sects in Africa: for example, those of the *Bwiti* cult in the Gabon (James Fernandez; personal communication). It is also true of initiation into the Ndembu funerary association of *Chiwila*. Symbolically, all attributes that distinguish categories and groups in the structured social order are here in abeyance; the neophytes are merely entities in transition, as yet without place or position.

Other characteristics are submissiveness and silence. Not only the chief in the rites under discussion, but also neophytes in many *rites de passage* have to submit to an authority that is nothing less than that of the total community. This community is the repository of the whole gamut of the culture's values, norms, attitudes, sentiments, and relationships. Its representatives in the specific rites – and these may vary from ritual to ritual – represent the generic authority of tradition. In tribal societies, too, speech is not merely communication but also power and wisdom. The wisdom (*mana*) that is imparted in sacred liminality is not just an aggregation of words and sentences; it has ontological value, it refashions the very being of the neophyte. That is why, in the Chisungu rites of the Bemba, so well described by Audrey Richards (1956), the secluded girl is said to be "grown into a woman" by the female elders – and she is so grown by the verbal and nonverbal instruction she receives in precept and symbol, especially by the revelation to her of tribal *sacra* in the form of pottery images.

The neophyte in liminality must be a *tabula rasa*, a blank slate, on which is inscribed the knowledge and wisdom of the group, in those respects that pertain to the new status. The ordeals and humiliations, often of a grossly physiological character, to which neophytes are submitted represent partly a destruction of the previous status and partly a tempering of their essence in order to prepare them to cope with their new responsibilities and restrain them in advance from abusing their new privileges. They have to be shown that in themselves they are clay or dust, mere matter, whose form is impressed upon them by society.

Another liminal theme exemplified in the Ndembu installation rites is sexual continence. This is a pervasive theme of Ndembu ritual. Indeed, the resumption of sexual relations is usually a ceremonial mark of the return to society as a structure of statuses. While this is a feature of certain types of religious behavior in almost all societies, in preindustrial society, with its strong stress on kinship as the basis of many types of group affiliation, sexual continence has additional religious force. For kinship, or relations shaped by the idiom of kinship, is one of the main factors in structural differentiation. The undifferentiated character of liminality is reflected by the discontinuance of sexual relations and the absence of marked sexual polarity.

It is instructive to analyze the homiletic of Kafwana, in seeking to grasp the meaning of liminality. The reader will remember that he chided the chief-elect for his selfishness, meanness, theft, anger, witchcraft, and greed. All these vices represent the desire to possess for oneself what ought to be shared for the common good. An incumbent of high status is peculiarly tempted to use the authority vested in him by society to satisfy these private and privative wishes. But he should regard his privileges as gifts of the whole community, which in the final issue has an overright over all his actions. Structure and the high offices provided by structure are thus seen as instrumentalities of the common weal, not as a means of personal aggrandizement. The chief must not "keep his chieftainship to himself." He "must laugh with the people," and laughter (*ku-seha*) is for the Ndembu a "white" quality, and enters into the definition of "whiteness" or "white things." Whiteness represents the seamless web of connection that ideally ought to include both the living and the dead. It is right relation between people, merely as human beings, and its fruits are health, strength, and all good things. "White" laughter, for example, which is visibly manifested in the flashing of teeth, represents fellowship and good company. It is the reverse of pride (*winyi*), and the secret envies, lusts, and grudges that result behaviorally in witchcraft (*wuloji*), theft (*wukombi*), adultery (*kushimbana*), meanness (*chifwa*), and homicide (*wubanji*). Even when a man has become a chief, he must still be a member of the whole community of persons (*antu*), and show this by "laughing with them," respecting their rights, "welcoming every-one," and sharing food with them. The chastening function of liminality is not confined to this type of initiation but forms a component of many other types in many cultures. A well-known example is the medieval knight's vigil, during the night before he receives the accolade, when he has to pledge himself to serve the weak and the distressed and to meditate on his own unworthiness. His subsequent power is thought partially to spring from this profound immersion in humility.

The pedagogics of liminality, therefore, represent a condemnation of two kinds of separation from the generic bond of communitas. The first kind is to act only in terms of the rights conferred on one by the incumbency of office in the social structure. The second is to follow one's psychobiological urges at the expense of one's fellows. A mystical character is assigned to the sentiment of humankindness in most types of liminality, and in most cultures this stage of transition is brought closely in touch with beliefs in the protective and punitive powers of divine or preterhuman beings or powers. For example, when the Ndembu chief-elect emerges from seclusion, one of his subchiefs – who plays a priestly role at the installation rites – makes a ritual fence around the new chief's dwelling, and prays as follows to the shades of former chiefs, before the people who have assembled to witness the installation:

> Listen, all you people. Kanongesha has come to be born into the chieftainship today. This white clay [*mpemba*], with which the chief, the ancestral shrines, and the officiant will be anointed, is for you, all the Kanongeshas of old gathered together here. [Here the ancient chiefs are mentioned by name.] And, therefore, all you who have died, look upon your friend who has succeeded [to the chiefly stool], that he may be strong. He must continue to pray well to you. He must look after the children, he must care for all the people, both men, and women, that they may be strong and that he himself should be hale. Here is your white clay. I have enthroned you, O chief. You, O People, must give forth sounds of praise. The chieftainship has appeared.

The powers that shape the neophytes in liminality for the incumbency of new status are felt, in rites all over the world, to be more than human powers, though they are invoked and channeled by the representatives of the community.

REFERENCES

Fortes, Meyer (1962) "Ritual and office," in Max Gluckman (ed.), *Essays on the Ritual of Social Relations*. Manchester: Manchester University Press.

Lewis, Iowan M. (1963) "Dualism in Somali notions of power," *Journal of the Royal Anthropological Institute*, vol. 93, part I.

Richards, Audrey I. (1956) *Chisungu*, London: Faber and Faber.

Turner, Victor (1967) *The Forest of Symbols*, Ithaca: Cornell University Press.

Van Gennep, Arnold (1909) *The Rites of Passage* (trans. Monika B. Vizedom and Gabrielle L. Caffee), London: Routledge and Kegan Paul.

Wilson, Monica (1957) *Rituals of Kinship among the Nyakyusa*, London: Oxford University Press.

READER CROSS-REFERENCES

Schechner – close collaborator

McKenzie – on liminality as a defining concept for performance studies

Geertz, C. Bell, Fabian, Conquergood – implications of Turner's ritual theory for anthropological and ethnographic practice

Mason, Faber, Santino, Ancelet – descriptions of specific rituals

Turner and Turner – with wife and collaborator Edie Turner, on the value of reenacting ritual for instructional purposes

13

"PERFORMANCE" AND OTHER ANALOGIES

Catherine Bell

In recent years the notion of "cultural performance" has become increasingly popular as a category and general approach. This popularity appears to have been nourished by a variety of sources. Foremost among these are Kenneth Burke's notion of "dramatism," V. Turner's work on social dramas, the multiplication of categories such as "civil ceremonial" and "secular rites," work on the sociology of role playing along with Erving Goffman's interaction rituals, and, last but not least, perhaps, J.L. Austin's and John Searle's analyses of "speech acts."[1]

In its own way, performance theory signals a strong dissatisfaction with the traditional categories brought to the study of ritual. At the same time, however, its focus on ritual, theater, or sports as 'genres' or 'universals' of performance appears to involve the construction of very traditional types of relationships and categories.[2] Some performance theorists have explicitly aspired "to transcend such conventional dichotomies as oral and written, public and private, doing and thinking, primitive and modern, sacred and secular."[3] Clearly these dichotomies have contributed to the perception that theoretical analysis is failing to convey something important about how ritual activities are generated and experienced. Grimes has rued how "foreign" ritual has become for us, while V. Turner echoed D.H. Lawrence's quip that "analysis presupposes a corpse."[4] Turner, in particular, repeatedly argued that a "living quality frequently fails to emerge from our pedagogics."[5] More specifically, Sherry Ortner suggests that frustration with structural linguistics was responsible for this turning to how language communicates via performance.[6] Robert Wuthnow supports this idea by explicitly contrasting dramaturgical and structural approaches to analyzing culture. The former, he argues, which focuses on ritual in the broadest sense, is able to incorporate the social dimension lost to structural analysis."[7] For Wuthnow, the dramaturgical approach recasts the problem of meaning by affording a shift from analysis of the subjective or semantic meaning of symbols to analysis of the conditions under which symbolic acts are meaningful."[8]

Despite their insights into the problems of ritual theory, neither Wuthnow nor the others cited effectively break free of a theoretical framework in which activity is seen as dramatizing or enacting prior conceptual entities in order to reaffirm or reexperience them.

Grimes, for example, argues "the primacy of the human body" in ritual studies, but he equates this primacy with the body's "capacity to *enact* social roles and body forth cultural meanings."[9] Although the notion of performance appears to many to offer some solution to the way in which theory fails to grasp action, as a whole the contributions of performance theory and terminology to the formulation of an approach that does not dichotomize doing and thinking remain somewhat obscure. Indeed, the performance approach appears to suggest a further exaggeration of the structured relations between thinking theorist and acting object which I have already examined.

Performance theorists frequently base themselves on two interrelated points originally articulated by Singer. First, as noted previously, people "think of their culture as encapsulated within discrete performances, which they can exhibit to outsiders as well as to themselves." Second, such performances constitute for the outside observer "the most concrete observable units of the cultural structure" – since each performance "has a definitely limited time span, a beginning and an end, an organized program of activity, a set of performers, an audience, and a place and occasion of performance."[10] Although such statements do not constitute an agenda for systematic analysis, they are more than a simple application of the "drama analogy," with its whole system of terms, relationships, and assumptions.[11] Singer did not merely suggest an approach to ritual that guarantees direct access to native units of experience and clear observation of sociocultural processes; he also defined culture itself in terms of those very activities that appear to provide such clear access and observation. That is, cultural performances are the ways in which the cultural content of a tradition "is organized and transmitted on particular occasions through specific media."[12] Thus, these performances are the specific and particular manifestations ('instances') of culture aside from which culture is just an abstract category."[13] However, if culture is the giving of performances, then culture is that which is given to an "audience" or the outside theorist who has joined it. Researchers and theorists are repositioned in performance theory: no longer peering in through the window, they are now comfortably seated as members of the audience for whom the performance is being presented. As such, the theorist-observer has become an important participant, one who is integral both to the actors' ability to act culturally (i.e. to perform) and to their ability to understand their own culture (since such understanding is the result of expressing their general cultural orientations in discrete ritual activities).

In some cases, performance theory appears to promote an even more intense mode of participation. In discussing ritual and social drama, for example, Turner calls for the "performance of ethnography" by both anthropologists and professional actors.[14] John MacAloon refers to the "performance" given by academic participants at a symposium that resulted in the book he subtitled "Rehearsals Toward a Theory of Cultural Performance."[15] Grimes finds that the activities of scattered experiments in improvisational theater are "crucial both to the practice and study of religion, particularly ritual studies."[16]

This enhanced participation of the scholar-observer takes an interesting form in Grimes's development of the project of "ritual criticism." Ritual criticism is loosely modeled on the relationship of literary criticism to literature and on cultural-critical developments in anthropology (as described by Marcus and Fischer). Moreover, Grimes's critical evaluation of ritual can be conducted in a variety of ways: through indigenous forms of emic criticism, etic forms by scholars or foreign critics, and even criticism of one religious tradition by another. In another formulation, he contrasts the criticism practiced by rites and ritualists themselves with the critical activities of "ritologists."[17] The position of the critical observer, Grimes suggests, should be neither scientifically neutral nor theologically normative; the purpose of critical observation is to aid in the recognition of ritual exploitation on the one hand or appropriate revision and borrowing of ritual practices on the other.[18] It appears that two concerns are central to Grimes's project: first, an appreciation of the inadequacy of earlier models of participant-observer relations and, second, a real sense of shared purpose between participants and critics. What Jennings saw as a shared "epistemological" project, Grimes would appear to embrace as a shared project of both cultural critique and reflexive self-observation.

Performance terminology has been used in a wide variety of ways. By far the most cautious performance position was laid out by the British anthropologist Gilbert Lewis. According to Lewis, our tendency to be preoccupied with the intellectual aspects of responses to ritual (i.e. deciphering the meaning of its coded messages) leads us to over-look more immediate sensory responses. He suggests "likening" ritual to the performance of a play or a piece of music, but he cautions against using such insights into ritual to define it.[19]

If Lewis has been the most cautious of those who invoke performance, then V. Turner was certainly one of the most enthusiastic. Yet Turner's late work on ritual and performance remains fundamentally within the framework of his early theory of ritual as the transformational dialectic of structure and antistructure (or organization and communitas) to serve as a vehicle for unfolding social dramas.[20] Social dramas are embodied in ritual, where they have paradigmatic functions that make clear the deepest values of the culture. In Turner's view, such paradigmatic functions also serve to provide the outsider with a "limited area of transparency in the otherwise opaque surface of regular, uneventful social life."[21] This is the same "window of ritual" evoked by Geertz.

Performance theory probably has one of its most sophisticated presentations in the work of Stanley Tambiah. Tambiah explicitly reacts against the opposition of thought and action and suggests that the devaluation of action embedded in the distinction can be redressed by a focus on performance.[22] Like Ortner and Wuthnow, he argues that the social dimension becomes more accessible through performance theory. Tambiah is particularly concerned, in fact, that the significance of the semantic structure of words and acts not lead us to ignore the significance of social relations both within the ritual itself and within the larger context of the rite.[23] He breaks with the Durkheimian approach developed by Gluckman and V. Turner in arguing that ritual does not evoke feelings or express the mental orientation of individuals in any sort of direct and spontaneous way. Rather, he emphasizes the formalism of ritual as having a distancing effect that serves to articulate and communicate attitudes of institutionalized communication.[24] Tambiah's appreciation for the social dimension also leads him to amend Austin and Searle by explicating the necessary social conditions under which "saying is doing" and ritual is "a mode of social action."[25] Saying is just saying and formalized acts are idiosyncratic, he argues, unless they conform to established social conventions and subject themselves to judgments of legitimacy.[26]

Tambiah distinguishes three ways in which ritual is performative: (1) it involves doing things, even if the doing is saying in the Austinian sense; (2) it is staged and uses multiple media to afford participants an intense experience; and (3) it involves indexical values in the sense laid out by Pierce. The indexical features of ritual are seen in its graded scale of ostentatiousness, the choice of site, the degree of redundancy or elaboration, and so on, all of which present and validate the social hierarchy indirectly depicted by them. As a system of communication, ritual involves both indexical features that refer to the social hierarchy and symbolic features that refer to the cosmos. Indeed, Tambiah goes on to elaborate a series of opposing features mobilized in ritual, including semantic/referential components versus pragmatic components, form versus content, the cultural and the universal, and indexical symbolism versus indexical iconicity.[27] Thus, despite his focus on performance and his concerns about the thought–action dichotomy, he also is drawn into the familiar dilemma of setting out to transcend one bifurcation only to generate others that find their integration in ritual as a mechanism for fusing theoretical distinctions.[28]

Performance theory rests of course on the slippery implications of an extended metaphor, specifically the analogy between ritual activities and the acts of performing and dramatizing. While it offers a new descriptive vantage point on aspects of ritual activities, as a paradigm or model it is gravely disadvantaged in several ways. First, the increased naturalization of the outside observer that is obtained in the very definition of act as performance takes the relationship between subject and object constructed by the theorist and inscribes it into the nature of the object itself. In other words, ritual comes to be seen as performance in the sense of symbolic acts specifically meant to have an impact on an audience and entreat their interpretive appropriation. Second, the notion of performance as a theoretical tool for approaching certain activities comes to be used as descriptive of the fundamental nature of those activities; in other words, a model of ritual activity provides the criteria for what is or is not ritual. Third, although performance may become a criterion for what is or is not ritual, insofar as performance is broadly used for a vast spectrum of activities, there is no basis to differentiate among ways of performing. An initial focus on the performative aspects of ritual easily leads to the difficulty of being unable to distinguish how ritual is not the same as dramatic theater or spectator sports.[29]

Rappaport attempts to avoid some of these problems when he maintains that ritual is not drama, although performance, like formality, is a sine qua non of ritual.[30] In this way he holds on to the primacy of doing and acting that a performance focus promises, but he does not succumb to the slippage of explaining by analogy. In a somewhat similar vein, Emily Ahern also challenges the description of ritual as a dramatization that is meant to affect the participants as opposed to the external world.[31] In so doing, she points to an interesting problem inherent in the performance metaphor: Since performance theory denies any validity to indigenous claims that certain actions *affect* the gods, the harvest, or anything beyond the dispositions of the actors and audience, how much epistemological sharing can there actually be between Chinese participants and Western interpreters concerning the type of project at stake in a Chinese "soul-settling" ceremony?

Performance theorists, of course, argue that what ritual does is communicate (and hence it does not secure the intercession of deities, pacify the dead, or encourage rain, etc.) and it is through this function that ritual indirectly affects social realities and perceptions of those realities. However, when performance theory attempts to explain such communication it must fall back on ritual activity as depicting, modeling, enacting, or dramatizing what are seen as prior conceptual ideas and values. The meaningfulness of ritual that such interpretations attempt to explicate has nothing to do with the efficacy that the ritual acts are thought to have by those who perform them. The idiom of communication through symbolic acts maybe a corrective to the notion of magic, but it does little to convey what these acts mean to those involved in them.

In his famous discussion of "blurred genres," Geertz looks at three popular analogies adopted by the social sciences to interpret social behavior."[32] He begins with the "game" analogy, then goes on to explore the "drama" analogy, and finally turns to the "text" analogy. The drama analogy, he suggests, affords an appreciation of certain features of action, specifically its temporality, collectivity, public nature, and power to transmute not just opinions but people themselves. However, it lumps all types of social action together as having the same form without any ability to appreciate the differences in content. The game and text analogies likewise illuminate certain features and confuse others. All of these analogies, he argues, are examples of a cases-and-interpretations approach to social theory, rather than the older laws-and-instances approach. Thus, they are concerned with interpretation and meaning – specifically, what "all the usual objects of social-scientific interest" mean to those who are immediately involved in them."[33] Yet it is not at all clear that this actually is the type of meaning derived from the theoretical deployment of these analogies. While Geertz finds that "religious symbols . . . reek of meaning," Tambiah has his doubts.[34] Tambiah rejects such "intentionality" theories as inadequate to the interpretation of formalized and conventionalized action and finds the various conceptions of meaning in anthropology a "deadly source of confusion."[35] With the exception of Tambiah, however, the popularity of performance metaphors and theories represents something of a consensus about "meaning" as a specifically hermeneutical conception.

In the same vein, Marcus and Fischer suggest that the popularity of ritual as a theoretical focus is based on how readily a public performance can be *read like a text*.[36] The text analogy is used explicitly in Alton Becker's study of Indonesian *wayang* performances as "text-building." It is more implicit in James Fernandez's study (with its echoes of Boas and Burke) of ritual as the strategic deployment of a metaphor.[37] In both cases, however, the interpretative hermeneutic brought to bear on ritual approaches the rite as if it were a text. In his essay "Deep Play," Geertz also explicitly approaches ritualized activities as a text to be decoded."[38] Yet he concludes his later comparison of blurred genres with a recognition of the particular dangers and implausibility of the text analogy. Its application to action is, Geertz argues, an example of "a thorough-going conceptual wrench."[39] Hinting at the problems involved in the readiness to decode ritual, Geertz nearly echoes some of Tambiah's reservations after all.

Paul Ricoeur has argued both systematically and pointedly that meaningful action" is indeed like a text, delineating criteria for textuality that meaningful action also fulfills.[40] For the most part, however, the textual analogy is usually applied with much less clarity. Moreover, the analogy tends to be based not on the assertion of a similarity between texts and rites but on the similarity of the interpretive position of the theorist in each case. In fact, if we think in terms of the mode of interpretation rather than the similarities of such objects as rite, drama, and text, the text analogy can be seen to underlie the drama analogy and be quite basic to performance theory.

Certainly there is a general tendency in the social sciences to "textualize" the objects of its concern. Such textualization, according to Jameson, is "a methodological hypothesis whereby the objects of study of the human sciences . . . are considered to constitute so many texts which we *decipher* and *interpret,* as distinguished from the older view of those objects as realities or existants or substances which we in one way or another attempt to know."[41] We textualize, he implies, not because rites are intrinsically like texts, but because we approach both looking for meaning as something that can be deciphered, decoded, or interpreted. Developing Geertz's contrast between "law-and-instances" and "cases-and-interpretation" styles of analysis, one might suppose that the shift in cultural studies away from the model of science and the dogma of scientific objectivity has been essentially based on an interpretive–textual model.[42]

Yet the interpretive project, whether conducted in literary criticism or anthropology, carries some important assumptions. Foremost among them are the assumptions that the text (rite or another example of meaningful social action) is autonomous and unified, on the one hand, and that its latent meaning is fully accessible to a close reading of its manifest form on the other."[43] Both assumptions present problems when it comes to the avowed benefits of a performance approach to ritual. For example, the emphasis on the *activity* of ritual which performance theory attempts to develop may actually be something of an illusion. The interpretive endeavor requires, and assumes, that activity encodes something. As the foregoing thought–action argument illustrated, the assumed existence of such a "something," the latent meaning of the act, once again devalues the action itself, making it a second-stage representation of prior values.

It has been suggested that the reasons for the shift to a performance approach, with its underlying interpretive–textual paradigm, are the perceived failures of earlier models and the greater explanative power, particularly in terms of social dimensions, of the new paradigm. The performance paradigm deserves a thorough assessment of its "merits as a concept," as Leach would say, and the results might vindicate this explanation of its popularity. Yet it is also possible to see some basis for its popularity in the distinctive imagery of performance theory (that of a sensitive and appreciative participant interpreter, not a coldly detached, analytic scientist) and in the greater obscurity of the slippage involved (how much more readily "performance" slips from being a tool for analysis to being a feature of the object and thereby validates an approach and a whole discourse). While it is this type of slippage that affords the expedient logic on which many theories of ritual are based, this imagery is an equally powerful incentive for ritual studies.

NOTES

1 Kenneth Burke, *The Philosophy of Literary Form*, 3rd edn (Berkeley: University of California Press, 1973), originally published in 1941; Victor Turner, *Dramas, Fields and Metaphors* (Ithaca, NY: Cornell University Press, 1974); Sally F. Moore and Barbara G. Myerhoff, eds., *Secular Ritual* (Amsterdam: Van Gorcum, 1977); Erving Goffman, *Interaction Ritual* (Garden City, NY: Doubleday, 1967); J.L. Austin, *How to Do Things With Words* (Cambridge: Harvard University Press, 1962); and John R. Searle, *Speech Acts* (Cambridge: Cambridge University Press, 1969). For a good discussion of the various roots of performance theory, see Lawrence E. Sullivan, "Sounds and senses: toward a hermeneutics of performance," *History of Religions* 26, 1 (1986): 2–14.

2 On the various "genres" of performance, see Richard Schechner and Willa Appel, eds., *By Means of Performance: Intercultural Studies of Theater and Ritual* (Cambridge: Cambridge University Press, 1989), 3.

3 John J. MacAloon, *Rite, Drama, Festival, Spectacle: Rehearsals Toward a Theory of Cultural Performance* (Philadelphia: Institute for the Study of Human Issues, 1984), 1.

4 Grimes, *Beginnings in Ritual Studies*, introduction, no pagination; Victor Turner, *From Ritual to Theater: The Human Seriousness of Play* (New York: Performing Arts Journal Publications, 1982), 89.

5 V. Turner, *From Ritual to Theater*, 89.

6 Ortner, "Theory in anthropology since the sixties," *Comparative Studies in Society and History* 26 (1984): 144.

7 Robert Wuthnow, *Meaning and Moral Order* (Berkeley: University of California Press, 1987), 11–15. He also considers two other approaches which he characterizes as subjective and institutional.

8 Wuthnow, 344.

9 Ronald L. Grimes, "Ritual studies," in *The Encyclopedia of Religion*, vol. 12, ed. Mircea Eliade (New York: Macmillan, 1987), 423. Emphasis added.

10 Singer, *Traditional India*, Philadelphia: American Folklore Society, 1959, xiii.

11 On the drama analogy, see Geertz's "Blurred genres: the refiguration of social thought," in *Local Knowledge: Further Essays in Interpretive Anthropology* (New York: Basic Books, 1983), 19–35. [Also see pages 64–7 in this volume – Ed.]

12 Singer, *Traditional India*, xii.

13 In her book *Sherpas Through Their Rituals* (Cambridge: Cambridge University Press, 1978), Sherry Ortner echoes Singer's definitions of culture and provides another very intelligent definition of ritual that is still governed by the three homologized structural patterns.

14 Turner, *From Ritual to Theater*, 89–101.

15 MacAloon, 3.

16 Grimes, *Beginnings in Ritual Studies*. See Grimes's discussion of the role of the theorist as a critic of ritual in "Ritual criticism and reflexivity in fieldwork," *Journal of Ritual Studies* 2, 2 (1988): 217–39.

17 Grimes, "Ritual criticism," 221 and 235. Also see his recent book *Rutal Criticism: Case Studies in Its Practice, Essays on Its Theory* (Columbia: University of South Carolina Press, 1990).

18 Grimes, "Ritual criticism," 218.

19 Lewis, 8, 22, 33–4, 38.

20 MacAloon, 3.

21 Victor Turner, *From Ritual to Theater*, 82; and his *Schism and Continuity in African Society* (Manchester: Manchester University Press, 1957), 93, quoted in MacAloon, 3.

22 Stanley J. Tambiah, "A performative approach to ritual," *Proceedings of the British Academy* 65 (1979): 113–69, particularly 120.

23 Tambiah, "A performative approach to ritual," 115; also see Stanley J. Tambiah, "The magical power of words," *Man*, n.s. 3, 2 (1968): 180, 189.

24 Tambiah, "A performative approach to ritual," 124.

25 Tambiah, "A performative approach to ritual," 119 and 122.

26 Tambiah, "A performative approach to ritual," p. 127.

27 Tambiah, "A performative approach to ritual," pp. 153–4, 158, and 166.

28 Tambiah, "A performative approach to ritual," 139, on the fusion of form and content.

29 Geertz, Local Knowledge, 19–35.

30 Roy A. Rappaport, Ecology, Meaning and Religion (Richmond, Cal.: North Atlantic Books, 1979), 176–7.

31 Emily M. Ahern, "The problem of efficacy: strong and weak illocutionary acts," Man, n.s. 14, 1 (1979): 1–17.

32 Geertz, Local Knowledge, 19–35.

33 Geertz, Local Knowledge, 22.

34 Clifford Geertz, Negara: The Theatre State in Nineteenth Century Bali (Princeton: Princeton University Press, 1980), 105.

35 Tambiah, "A performative approach to ritual," 123–4, 132.

36 George E. Marcus and Michael M. J. Fischer, Anthropology as Cultural Critique (Chicago: University of Chicago Press, 1986), 61.

37 James W. Fernandez, "Persuasions and performances: of the beast in every body . . . and the metaphors of everyman," Daedalus 101, 1 (1972): 39–60 (also published in Clifford Geertz, ed., Myth, Symbol and Culture (New York: Norton, 1971), 39–60). Also James W. Fernandez, "The performance of ritual metaphors," in The Social Use of Metaphor: Essays on the Anthropology of Rhetoric, ed. J. David Sapir and J. Christopher Crocker (Philadelphia: Unversity if Pennsylvania Press, 1977), 100–31.

38 Geertz, The Interpretation of Cultures, 412–53.

39 Geertz, Local Knowledge, 30.

40 Paul Ricoeur, "The model of the text: meaningful action considered as a text," Social Research 38 (Autumn 1971): 529–62.

41 Frederic Jameson, "The ideology of the text," Salmagundi 31–2 (Fall 1975/Winter 1976): 205.

42 Two recent studies of orality, textuality, and performance highlight some other tensions that come to light in performance theory: while William A. Graham's Beyond the Written Word: Oral Aspects of Scripture in the History of Religions (Cambridge: Cambridge University Press, 1987) is concerned to demonstrate the oral and performative dimensions of scriptural texts, Stuart H. Blackburn's Singing of Birth and Death: Texts in Performance (Philadelphia: University of Pennsylvania Press, 1988) is concerned to argue the importance of texts for oral performance. If their analyses are correct, the first is a justified corrective to an exaggerated stress on textuality and the second to a similar exaggeration of orality. For a demonstration of a comparable set of emphases in recent interpretations of the Javanese slametan, see Mark. R. Woodward's corrective to Geertz's aproach in "The slametan: textual knowledge and ritual performance in Central Javanese Islam," History of Religions 28, 1 (1988): 54–89. Although performance theory does not appear to offer any resolutions of these oral–text tensions, it may well prove to be a very useful arena in which the larger issues of orality and textuality loom more clearly and may be engaged more directly. This can be seen, for example, in a spate of ethnographies, represented by Joel C. Kuipers's Power in Performance: The Creation of Textual Authority in Weyewa Ritual Speech (Philadelphia: University of Pennsylvania Press, 1990), or M. E. Combs-Schilling's Sacred Performances: Islam, Sexuality and Sacrifice (New York: Columbia University Press, 1989).

43 See Jonathan Culler, The Pursuit of Signs: Semiotics, Literature and Deconstruction (Ithaca, NY: Cornell University Press, 1981), especially chapter 1. Culler goes on to question "interpretation" as the goal of a critic's work. Also see Dowling's discussion of Freud's influence on the notion of latent meaning in Jameson's The Political Unconscious (Ithaca, NY: Cornell University Press, 1981), 36.

READER CROSS-REFERENCES

Schechner – the shift to performance theory

Worthen, Jackson, Fabian, Conquergood – issues of "text" as applied to non-theatrical performances

Turner – whom Bell cites as the foremost proponent of performance as an anthropological concept

Goffman – role-playing in non-theatrical contexts

Geertz – shares concerns about the validity of performance analogy

Ancelet – application of Geertz' concept of deep play

Santino – the application of ritual theory to public displays of mourning

Austin – source of Tambiah's performative approach to ritual

14

"THE BLOOD THAT RUNS THROUGH THE VEINS"

The creation of identity and a client's experience of Cuban-American *Santería Dilogún* divination

Michael Atwood Mason

A woman in Washington, DC, cannot sleep at night. She is restless, nervous; her eyes dart about searching the darkness for a clue to her discomfort. She is about to leave town, move back to her mother's house after many years away. She realizes that she needs help. Early the next morning, she calls a friend; through him, she makes an appointment to consult an *oriaté*, a diviner and priest in the Afro-Cuban religious tradition of *la Regla de Ocha*.[1]

When she and her friend arrive at the diviner's house, she rings the bell for the upstairs apartment and is let in by a small Cuban woman who explains that her husband, the oriaté, is still in the shower. Together, they climb the stairs. The visitors are asked to sit with the newborn baby; the television broadcasts professional wrestling. At the left corner of the far wall, the woman sees the shrine to the *oricha*, the deities of la Regla de Ocha. Two bookcases stand side by side, one for the woman who answered the door and one for the oriaté; on the shelves are soup tureens in various colors. These tureens contain the sacred stones, or *otanes*, physical manifestations of the oricha. Symbols for each oricha surround the tureens: There is Obatalá's white cowtail switch, traditional African symbol of authority, perfect for the senior oricha. The bookcase in the corner has a large blue and white tureen on top, with blue carnations next to the tureen; it is for Yemayá, mother of the oricha and ruler of the sea. There is Oyá's black cowtail switch – perfect for the only oricha not afraid of the dead – and with it her copper crown and nine tools. There is the *batea Changó*, a wooden covered bowl that rests on top of an overturned wooden mortar; *Changó* is the majestic king. The tureens all have food around them. Yellow pastries are for Ochún, the flowing goddess of rivers and love. The watermelon at the base of the bookcases is for Yemayá. In the right corner stands a small, low table covered with white cloth and containers of water; this is the *bóveda*, the shrine of the dead, and next to it rest several dolls to represent important spirits.

After a while, the oriaté appears from the back of the apartment and the woman and her friend follow him into the kitchen. Seated at a table, the diviner has in front of him a small, flat reed basket; on the basket lie twenty-one cowrie shells, with their rounded side removed so they can fall up or down. There are also some hard candies and a small red and black clay figure. This is Eleguá Oníkokó, the god of speech and the knower of destiny. As he prepares the tiny table, the diviner asks the woman if she is married to the man who has come with her.

"No," she responds.
"Hermanos? (Siblings?)" counters the diviner.
"No."
"Oh, just friends," he says laughing.

The oriaté begins to chant prayers in Lucumí, a dialect of Yoruba that is used as a liturgical language in Ocha. As he prays, he dips his fingers into a small glass of water and dribbles it on Eleguá and on the shells, another manifestation of the oricha. After this, he rubs the shells together in his hands and then in small circles on the basket. He holds the shells to the woman's forehead and shoulders. After finishing with this procedure, the oriaté raps on the basket three times as three is the sacred number associated with Eleguá. He drops the shells and counts those that land with their serrated "mouths" up. Five. Oché is the name of this odu, or figure. He begins to describe the situations that the figure reveals; he uses a proverb, and describes Ochún, who rules this odu. He gathers the cowries again and again drops them. Eleven cowries land with their "mouths" up; Ojuani is the figure through which San Lázaro speaks. It portends much danger. Again the diviner described the specific situation, but now he is focusing on the entire double-figure, Oché Ojuani. He uses proverbs, gives advice, and asks more questions about the woman's social situation. She responds to all his inquires, elaborating on the details of her life.

The oriaté again raps on the table three times. "*Iré, Eleguá?* Does the figure carry good luck, Eleguá?" Oché. He throws again to clarify. Oché again. He explains that Oché Meji, as this figure is called, is the only figure to carry luck here; the woman is very lucky and the diviner seems amazed. He interprets this figure in the same manner as before. Proverbs, advice, questions, stories. The process repeats as the diviner discovers what kind of good luck the woman has. He asks about her family; she responds that she is about to return to her mother's house, which is torn by anguish. The mother has recently broken up with a long-time lover; the sister has recently tried to commit suicide; the woman is troubled by her feelings and cannot seem to find a solution to her problems. The oriaté finds out which oricha will help the woman and what sacrifice should be offered. Each time he throws the shells, he has new advice and new questions for the woman. With each throw, she relaxes a little more.[2]

The woman, María, is troubled; even if she is just trying to learn more about herself, at some level she is in crisis. The divination ritual helps clarify her position in the social and supernatural worlds. After her situation is clarified, she is able to act, to make a sacrifice that plants her squarely in the larger cosmological context. The ritual of *dilogún* divination just described synthesizes a multitude of experiences within the client and provides a method for action.

My goal here is to understand one aspect of the experience of the client. In using a phenomenological approach that allows the field experience as data to speak to me (see Jackson 1989: 4), the even under study becomes enmeshed in my own vision of the other people involved in the field experience; we experience the divination together (see Devereaux 1967: 20); the meanings emerge from that shared experience.

This shared experience, however, cannot be fully communicated. Although many factors make this the case, perhaps radical empiricism addresses the most significant. Experience, as lived by real people, never fits perfectly into categories of thought or anthropological and folkloric models; experience overflows the concepts used to describe and understand it (see Sartre 1969: 49). Similarly, the experience of another person is always inaccessible. We cannot completely know the experience of another person; we can only understand the expressions of their experience, the symbols used to represent life. These idioms exist in different genres and I have tried to gather as many representations of divination experiences as possible. I have been "read" by the *dilogún*, interviewed many other people who have been read and many diviners, and watched the process repeatedly; the involvement leads to a double goal: to present divination in a way that fits with these various commentaries by friends and informants and to present it in a way that resonates with my own understanding of the tradition and experience.

After finishing the chanted prayers, the oriaté raps on the basket three times to summon Eleguá. He drops the shells and counts the ones that land "mouth" up. Five. Oché. "Thanks be to Ochún. Oché speaks of the blood that runs in the veins (*la sangre que corre por las venas*) and you must guard everything inside, do you understand me?"

The interior world of the client, almost invisible to the diviner's eyes, troubles her and presents danger. From the beginning of the *consulta* (consultation), the client's inner world needs attention. Her own emotional, social, and historical positions become the focus of the consulta, which reveals the present crisis, its supernatural solution, and the destiny of the client (see Brandon 1983: 222). Destiny, as construed in the Regla de Ocha, occupies an important space and encompasses all past actions, present troubles and the future (Cabrera 1980: 197). The cowrie shells and the diviner confront the client with her own experience.

Divination apparently reduces anxiety and provides a basis for action; this is a truism. But the method by which divination clarifies situations and offers solutions remains unclear. In this case, the figure, the single fall of the shells (Velasquez 1990b), implies a specific proverb which the diviner and then María can employ as an essential and inexhaustible interpretive frame for the problem at hand. Despite some variation in the Regla de Ocha, Oché regularly evokes "The blood that runs through the veins."[3] Advice follows the proverb and accompanies the rhetorical question "Do you understand me?"

The diviner again gathers the shells. Eleven. Oché-Juani. He asks about troubles with the police; María says no, no problems with the police. The diviner continues to explain that she must guard against troubles with the police. She resists this idea and seems unrelated to what is happening, amused and almost uninvolved. He says that it could be someone in the family.

"Are there problems with your family?"

María must confront the blood that runs through all the veins of her life. The questions asked of the client in this specific consulta reveal the common concerns and crises that compel people to visit the diviner. The interior – her body, her emotions, thoughts, her spiritual concerns – surface almost immediately and become a central context and concern of the session. Is she worried? Always thinking about today's business? And tomorrow's? Is she healthy? Has she visited a doctor? When a person's health fails, she often visits a diviner.

The next questions relate María to the larger society; frequently, it seems, members of the Cuban-American community interact with the police and the court system. Putting aside the causes of this interesting and disturbing phenomenon, it is important to note this concern with the more institutionalized parts of American culture. Is there trouble with the police? Are you in trouble with the law? The Oché-Juani figure suggests being caught at something, being trapped. When María replies with surprise and hesitates to agree, the diviner suggests that perhaps it is someone in the family; this connection of the individual to her social surrounding implies a sense of self different from that of Euro-Americans. The boundaries of the self are not limited to the individual, but encompass family and the political environment. The trouble that brings the client to the oricha may be a problem in her own life or a problem in the life of a family member; a problem in the family creates a problem for the individual.

After María hesitates once again, the oriaté once more asks, "Have you had problems with your family?" Attention now bears on the family itself. María quickly says that she does not have problems but her sister has been troubled (*yo no tengo problemas, pero hay problemas con mi hermana*). The details of the trouble are revealed: María's sister has been fighting with her mother. A problem emerges that is significant and disturbing to the client.

"The blood that runs through the veins" is mapped on to different levels of the client's life. Oché-Juani suggests that there is a problem somewhere, and in fact few people visit a diviner unless a problem exists. The blood can be the literal blood of the client; the relationships within a family can also be construed as its life, its blood; and the members of a society are as its lifeblood. The life of the body, the family, and the whole society merge in the proverb. The visual part of the metaphor – the blood coursing through the veins – unites the different realms of potential crisis.

> Pictorializing in this way we can inspect the organizing images that are at play in ritual performance and see how microcosm and macrocosm, inner things and outer things, centers and peripheries, upper things and lower things, time-present and time-past are related. For out of such parts are wholes constructed.
>
> (Fernandez 1986: 165)

The image applies to each area of social life – the body, the family, and the polity – and further exploration, through cowrie shell divination, offers a solution to the problem. The metaphor, which emerges from the extraordinarily diverse choices possible in cowrie divination, is activated by the fall of the sign Oché and becomes meaningful and useful in comprehending the immediate circumstances. Thus a dialectic begins in which the shells, as the mouths of the oricha and through the oriaté, suggest the contours of the problematic situation, and María responds positively and negatively until a consensus emerges. For María to be at peace, to be in balanced relationships, and to live productively, her blood must run smoothly.[4]

The problems at hand, the lack of money, the appearance and sense of failure as she returns home, and the anxiety of that return — all of these elements create stress. María changes her normal behavior and seeks out a different community in which to find answers, to develop solutions; a breach of normalcy occurs (Turner 1988: 74). She leaves the Anglo-dominated world in which she usually lives and works and finds an alternative community that, at least to some extent, resembles the Puerto Rican society of her mother's family. The crisis continues as she struggles for clarity and a path of action. María performs a social drama with a cast of one, although not completely alone because her friend accompanies her. She frames this event as meaningful and important; several facts evidence the importance of the ritual to her. At a time when she struggles financially, María pays the diviner a ritual fee (*derecho*) of $25; this money represents an important investment as it could have been used to buy something more physically essential. At the end of the day, after returning from the bookstore where she holds a part-time job to augment the income of her full-time job as an editor for a nonprofit organization, María discussed the consulta at length with me and recorded much of it in her journal; she also requested that I make a copy of the field tape for her so she could review the reading later. The monetary sacrifice and the desire to consider the reading repeatedly and in detail indicate its import as part of a larger drama in María's life, and that it is an "extraordinary experience" for her (see Abrahams 1986: 60). She explains, "I enjoyed what he said about me, you know, I like participating in things like that . . . I, I just took it as an opportunity to learn more about myself" (Hernandez 1991).

> "Are there problems in your family?" asks the oriaté.
> "I don't have problems, but there are problems with my sister."
> "Problems she has had with, with your mother?"
> "Yes. They fight a lot."
> "Are you married?" he asks.
> "No," she responds quickly.
> "Do you have a boyfriend?"
> "No," again quickly.
> "Have you had one?"
> "I used to have one."

Through many questions, the diviner asks María to tell him things about herself. She responds quickly and, in general, candidly. When asked about problems with the law, she laughs. When asked about troubles in the family, she answers the question and adds useful and pertinent information. The questions and answers significantly add to the ritual (cf. Fitzgerald 1975: 227); this diviner blends the information that he sees in the sign of the shells with what the client reveals (Velasquez 1990b).

These questions offer, in the course of the consulta, an opportunity for self-revelation. Frequently a person volunteers not just a bit of helpful information, as María does, but whole narratives about the troubling situation; if the diviner hits on a relevant concern, the client can expose as much or as little of the circumstances as she chooses; she can externalize as much or as little of her interior self as she chooses. When asked if she has visited a doctor, María responds that she has not, and then asks if the problems with "*lo interior*" (the interior) are "physical or mental or emotional or spiritual" (Velasquez 1990a); she asks the oriaté to clarify the idea of the interior as she attempts to understand better its importance and meaning.

While many people reveal the details of their personal lives in response to the diviner's questions, no one is required to say anything. Commonly, a person gives no clarification of his reasons for coming to the diviner; the client whispers a questions to the shells and, thus, the diviner cannot manipulate the client (cf. Bascom 1969: 68–9 and 1980: 5). Still, even in the extreme case where the client refuses to aid the diviner, questions are answered.

In my fieldwork, as I said, I have had several consultas with the cowries. I have tried different strategies to see what effect, if any, they had on the readings.[5] I have had readings in which I spoke little after each question; in others I provided only the information requested, only answered the questions; in still others, I used the questions as opportunities to speak candidly and at length about my concerns and feelings. Each degree of participation produced readings with a distinct character. When revealing only what was asked directly, the readings were brief and laborious; essentially the diviner defined my experience solely by what the shells suggested. Here, I had to refrain from speaking; it seemed as though the oriaté was arbitrarily defining my situation as I struggled silently to evaluate whether his definition fit my experience. When I offered detailed accounts of important issues in my life, the readings left me feeling renewed, refreshed, and with a sense of having revealed myself;[6] these readings seemed to flow naturally. Despite the differing tones, however, it is important to remember that in each case the structure of the ritual remained the same and it was my experience that changed; not only did the ritual structure my experience,[7] it provided options for different kinds of experience.

These different kinds of involvement and experience within the ritual structure suggest that the person being "searched" (*registrado*) can experience what I will call "reflective flow." In the literature on experience, authors commonly posit a dichotomous and dialectical relationship between reflexivity and reflection about experiences on the one hand and uninterpreted, uninterrupted experience on the other (see Csikszentmihaly and Robinson 1990; Turner 1986: 42 and 1988: 86). In many situations, especially in ritual, there exists a kind of experience that is equally reflective and fluid. In the consulta, the client is objectified and her life is defined and narrated by the oriaté, creating an intense sense of self-consciousness (Abrahams 1986: 56), but actions and responses to questions still transpire in a natural and comfortable way. Here reflexivity and flow are simultaneous as María answers questions about herself; she "restores behavior" as she narrates a different and more detailed version of her life (Schechner 1985: 35). Although her presentation of self occurs in the discontinuous format of question and answers, she performs her life in a comfortable, fluid manner. Of central importance here is the role of ritual. Erving Goffman presents a valuable vision of ritual:

> In brief, a play keys life, a ceremonial keys an event . . . Once it is seen that ceremonials have a consequence that scripted dramas and even contests do not, it is necessary to admit that the engrossment and awe generated by these occasions vary greatly among participants.
>
> (Goffman 1974: 58)

Although in a given ritual or ceremony not all the participants have the same experiences, I am arguing for the possibility that some people will experience reflective flow, where they are hyperconscious of their actions and still not self-consciously inhibited.[8]

But as María answers the oriaté's questions and performs herself, she also reveals the fundamental diversity of her own experiences. In the example that opens this section, she comments about many things in a short time; the exchange transpires in about four seconds. Despite its brevity, the exchange uncovers many aspects of her life. First she positions herself socially: she is not married nor does she have a boyfriend. The fact that she has had a boyfriend indexes her sexual tendencies; she is either bisexual or heterosexual. This exchange also contrasts two specific times in María's life. She responds, "I used to have one [a boyfriend]"; this period of her life, of her past, contrasts with the present when she lacks that kind of companionship and intimacy. More generally, this issue of the past and present is especially important to Cuban-Americans living in exile, who make up the vast majority of practitioners of Ocha; the present in the United States often contrasts drastically with the past in Cuba.

Other questions index different aspects of her life. The questions about her family again touch on social relationships, and she states that she has a sister, that her mother is alive and the two of them do not always get along. Her position in the family appears as central to the reading. At another moment, when the oriaté gives her advice, she assents to the fact that she is constantly worried about the future, that she is troubled inside. The diviner "said some things that I think are true about my personality" (Hernandez 1991).

She reveals herself as a "multiple presence" of "infinite layers" (Trinh 1989: 94): Past and present, social life internalized and external. These differences, all part of María's life, do not annul identity but aid in its creation; her experience of herself includes all these times and relationships, not to mention the feelings that she has about them, and it is precisely these remembered historical moments and specific relationships that make her most naturally and completely herself. Like Gayatri Spivak, "I do not intend a simplistic definition of identity (1990: 38)"; instead I offer questions about the "experiencing subject" (see Bruner 1986: 9).

An experiencing subject can be seen as a function of social relationships; individuals are equated with their social roles. María is a *woman*, a *writer*, a *lover*, a *daughter*, and a *Puerto Rican-American* whose father is from the northwestern United States and whose mother is from Puerto Rico. Each of these social positions has traditional behavior attached to it; she is none of these things in isolation. Yet, paradoxically, María is all these things at once. Similarly she fits into many rhetorical positions; she is *I* when speaking and *you* when addressed (cf. Lacan 1978: 298); she occupies no singular position in social life or discourse. Still, her identity and subjectivity can be seen "as an emergent property of historicized experience" (Alcoff 1988: 431). Thus, María as an experiencing subject exists in a specific historical context that acts as a frame and helps create meaning. She experiences herself and the events of her life through all of these different lenses.

> The self cannot, therefore be treated as a thing among things; it is a function of our involvement with others in a world of diverse and ever-altering interests and situations.
>
> (Jackson 1989: 3)

Social roles and groups frame what people experience and thus give their experiences specific kinds of meaning, but this meaning is never final, exclusive or determinate. Yet neither María nor her experience can be reduced to these facts of social life, she is more than the sum total of her social positions. I have tried to describe both general experiences of divination and those specific to her.

The oriaté discovers which oricha will help the woman and the sacrifice that should be offered. Ochún, the ruler of the sign Oché, will help María. "Acuaró, Ochún? (A sacrifice of partridges, Ochún?) Six followed by seven shells. Obarra-Dí. Yes, a sacrifice of partridges will clear the road."

The shells speak and tell María that Ochún, who rules "sweet" water, honey, love, passion, and lo interior, will come to her aid; to gain this assistance, María must make an *ebó* (sacrifice) to Yalorde (a praise-name for Ochún). The sacrifice will re-establish the balance between the supernatural world and the human world; this lack of balance between the worlds causes the troubles. The act of sacrifice, then, becomes an essential moral act. To sacrifice is to create balance and evoke healing; after sacrificing to Ochún, María is more likely to receive Her help and call on Her in the future. Thus the establishment and maintenance of relationships with the oricha represent an important part of destiny, as construed by members of the Regla de Ocha.[9]

As a point of contact between these two domains, the sacrifice acts to unite the two. Divination and the subsequent sacrifices often objectify the immediate and subjective situation, recast it in a large, mythological context, and provide a route for action (see Jackson 1989: 66), but my interest here is the method of the recasting. As I have already made clear, the various parts of the client's life come to the fore during a *consulta de dilogún*. Rather than attempting to simplify any singular problem, the reading records a series of conflicts and tensions within the client. Although predominantly verbal, the ritual orchestrates different kinds of experience to intensify the crisis (see Kapferer 1986: 194). Here, the divination figures evoke or "contain", as the diviners say, certain proverbs. These proverbs lead to questions that personalize the situation and involve the client in the reading; also contained in the figures are stories of mythical characters and their troubles. Advice, culled from the generalities of the proverb and the stories, instructs the client how to live, what to do and what not to do, how to interact with the family, and how to win the help of the oricha. Each turn represents a subtle variation in the theme at hand. The blood that runs in the veins can be any kind of internal problem, but each question intensifies the issues, even if it only provides an example of what the client is not experiencing. Although the problems that plague the client are not solved, that is, there is no guarantee that María's sister and mother will stop fighting and that María will stop worrying, the reading intensifies the situation.

Indigenously, the problems' cause lies in some imbalance between the supernatural and human worlds. After this intensification of the realities of life, the diviner offers a method to transcend the situation. "Ochún wants partridges," he tells her. Each oricha has particular foods: Ochún is partial to fish, partridges, eggs, shrimp, oranges, and pastries. The conflicts are further intensified by the deity wanting something. Not only is María worried about her family and finances, she now has to concern herself with the demands of the goddess. These demands are numbered along with her other concerns but carry a different weight. This problem can be solved: a sacrifice to Ochún.

The diviner carefully evokes the problems of the client but does not solve them. In reality he cannot solve her problems, nor can he make her stop worrying. The issues remain in their original tension but are more explicit and are now juxtaposed with the new problem – the sacrifice. This intensification and clarification forces the client to identify more and more with the reality of the situation (see Lévi-Strauss 1979: 321, 323). The sacrifice, as a method to solve one problem, becomes a catharsis for all the tensions discussed during the consulta.[10]

With each throw the woman relaxes a little. Because she lacks the time and money to return to the oriaté and sacrifice the partridges, she goes to a river, the home of Ochún, and offers five yellow candles, five oranges, and five chocolate chip cookies.[11]

NOTES

1 This article is based on fieldwork done for the District of Columbia Commission on the Arts and Humanities.

2 A transcription and translation of this divination session can be found in Mason (1992).

3 Although some diviners disagree about the proverbs that accompany specific figures, Oché seems to be associated universally with the same proverb. For examples where the same figure carries different proverbs, see Ecún (1988: 131) versus Gonzalez-Wippler (1989: 130).

4 It is interesting to note here that divination can be seen as a quintessential negotiation between structure and agency. The shells speak through the diviner; the figure that appears refers to traditional materials and interpretations, and the client either accepts or rejects this understanding of the situation. This reading of the ritual, of course, examines only the structural interaction of the diviner and the client while ignoring the larger traditional frame of the ritual itself.

5 Jackson's work on radical empiricism suggests using the ethnographer's experience as primary data (1989: 4). I have offered this information as an addition to the other data presented here.

6 It is not surprising that I feel as if I have been seen by another person after retelling the stories of my life; Sandra Dolby-Stahl has argued forcefully that the personal experience narrative functions frequently to create intimacy (see Dolby-Stahl 1977 and 1989: 37–43).

7 See Munn (1969) on the ritual structuring of personal experience.

8 I have used the occasion of this paper about the experience of the client of *dilogún* divination to express the possibility of reflective flow. The idea emerged over a long period of time as I reflected

upon my experiences of important rituals in my own life The issue as it appears here and applies to an anthropology of experience was greatly clarified through repeated conversations with Rory P.B. Turner, whose help and friendship I gratefully acknowledge.

9 See Bascom (1980: 35) for the Yoruba view of destiny and its relationship to divination. See also Murphy (1981), which posits this relationship as fundamental to the ritual system of *santería*.

10 This interpretation of sacrifice only works for the consulta; other sacrifices are made in an Regla de Ocha that are not structurally related to catharsis. The best example is the large annual sacrifices on the anniversary of initiation (see Brown 1989: 419–32).

11 It is important to notice that María did conform to the diviner's instructions. Instead of returning to him, she alters the sacrifice and offers Ochún foods that she likes. This alteration of tradition can be seen as a resistance to the oriaté's position of power: Although María accepts the information that she received from him, she chooses to perform a private sacrifice that does not include him. María explains, "I did offer Ochún some oranges and some chocolate chip cookies and some candles. . . . I just told her [Ochún] that I had somehow made a promise to her that I hadn't kept and that I was trying to keep my promise which is what he [José] said . . . I did it to show my respect. I took it to be a serious moment" (Hernandez 1991).

REFERENCES

Abrahams, Roger (1986) "Ordinary and extraordinary experience," in *The Anthropology of Experience*, edited by V. Turner and E. Bruner, 45–72, Urbana: University of Illinois Press.

Alcoff, Linda (1988) "Cultural feminism versus post-structuralism: the identity crisis in feminist theory," *Signs* 13: 405–36.

Bascom, William (1969) *The Yoruba of Southwestern Nigeria*, New York: Holt, Rinehart and Winston.

—— (1980) *Sixteen Cowries*, Bloomington: Indiana University Press.

Brandon, George (1983) *The Dead Sell Memories*, Ann Arbor: University Microfilms International.

Brown, David (1989) "Garden in the machine: Afro-Cuban sacred art and performance in urban New Jersey and New York," unpublished doctoral dissertation, Yale University.

Bruner, Edward (1986) "Experience and its expression," in *The Anthropology of Experience*, edited by V. Turner and E. Bruner, 3–30, Urbana: University of Illinois Press.

Cabrera, Lydia (1980) *Yemayá y Ochún*, Miami: Colección de Chicherikú.

Cortez, Enrique (n.d.) *Manual del Italero de la Religion Yoruba*, n.p.

Csikszentmihaly, Mihaly and Rick E. Robinson (1990) *The Art of Seeing: An Interpretation of the Aesthetic Encounter*, Malibu: J.P. Getty Museum, Getty Center for Education on the Arts.

Devereaux, George (1967) *From Anxiety to Method in the Behavioral Sciences*, The Hague: Mouton.

Dolby-Stahl, Sandra (1977) "The personal narrative as folklore," *Journal of the Folklore Institute* 14: 9–30.

—— (1989) *Literary Folkloristics and the Personal Narrative*, Bloomington: Indiana University Press.

Ecún, Obá (1988) *Addimú: Ofrenda a los Orichas*, Miami: Editorial SIBI.

Fernandez, James (1986) "The argument of images and the experience of returning to the whole," in *The Anthropology of Experience*, edited by V. Turner and E. Bruner, 159–87, Urbana: University of Illinois Press.

Fitzgerald, Dale (1975) "The language of ritual events among the Ga of Southern Ghana," in *Sociolinguistic Dimensions of Language Uses*, edited by B. Blount and M. Sanches, 205–34, New York: Academic Press.

Goffman, Erving (1974) *Frame Analysis: An Essay on the Organization of Experience*, New York: Harper and Row.

Gonzalez-Wippler, Migene (1989) *Introduction to Seashell Divination*, New York: Original Publications.

Hernandez, María (1991) Interview with author, 15 May, telephone interview in Bloomington, Ind., and Albuquerque, NM.

Jackson, Michael (1989) *Paths toward a Clearing: Radical Empiricism and Ethnographic Inquiry*, Bloomington: Indiana University Press.

Kapferer, Bruce (1986) Performance and the structuring of meaning and experience," in *The Anthropology of Experience*, edited by V. Turner and E. Bruner, 159–87, Urbana: University of Illinois Press.

Lacan, Jacques (1978) *Ecrits: A Selection*, translated by A. Sheridan, New York: Norton.

Lévi-Strauss, Claude (1979) The effectiveness of symbols," in *The Reader in Comparative Religion*, edited by W. Lessa and E. Vogt, 318–27, New York: Harper and Row.

Mason, Michael Atwood (1992) " 'The blood that runs in the veins': experience and performance in Cuban-American *santería* divination," unpublished MA thesis, Indiana University.

Munn, Nancy (1969) "Symbolism in ritual context: aspects of symbolic action," in *Handbook of Social and Cultural Anthropology*, edited by J.J. Honigman, 579–612, Chicago: Rand-McNally.

Murphy, Joseph (1981) *The Ritual System of Cuban Santería*, Ann Arbor: University Microfilm International.

Sartre, Jean-Paul (1969) "Itinerary of a thought," *New Left Review* 58: 43–66.

Schechner, Richard (1985) *Between Theater and Anthropology*, Philadelphia: University of Pennsylvania Press.

Spivak, Gayatri (1990) *The Post-Colonial Critic: Interviews, Strategies, Dialogues*, New York: Routledge.

Trinh, T. Minh-Ha (1989) *Woman, Native Other*, Bloomington: Indiana University Press.

Turner, Victor (1986) "Dewey, Dilthey, and drama: an essay in the anthropology of experience," in *The Anthropology of Experience*, edited by V. Turner and E. Bruner, 159–87, Urbana: University of Illinois Press.

—— (1988) *The Anthropology of Performance*, New York: PAJ Publications.

Velasquez, José (1990a) Divination session with María Hernandez, taped by author, 26 May, Washington, DC.

—— (1990b) Interview with author, 18 October, Washington, DC.

READER CROSS-REFERENCES

Geertz, Turner, C. Bell – ritual and performance

Faber, Santino, Ancelet – describe different types of ritual

Grotowski, Barba – mystic elements in theatrical performance

Gómez-Peña – intercultural encounters

15

SAINT ORLAN

Ritual as violent spectacle and cultural criticism

Alyda Faber

Saint Orlan, as the French performance artist named herself in 1971, has created a series of widely publicized surgical performances called *The Reincarnation of Saint Orlan*. Her practice of self-directed violence creates a spectacle that violates the viewer and establishes her body as "a site of public debate" (Orlan 1998: 319). By violence I mean acts that threaten the body as a sensorium of pain and injury, both physical and psychic. My interpretion of Orlan's project as violence does not entail moralizing against violence, that is, considering violence within an ethical framework of clear distinctions of good and evil. Orlan's work challenges such categorical distinctions. The artist's use of cosmetic surgery as a medium for artistic expression amplifies the social pressures on women to conform to narrowly defined patriarchal standards of beauty. In fact, her work exposes the violence of these beauty standards insofar as her "reincarnation" project embodies these practices to excess.

Since 1990, Orlan has had nine cosmetic surgeries; each has been videotaped and directed as a performance (see Augsburg 1998; Davis 1997; Rose 1993). Each surgery has a theme, which Orlan develops by reading from philosophical, literary, or psychoanalytic texts as she is operated on, and all participants in the surgery-performances are dressed in costumes created by famous fashion designers Paco Rabamme, Franck Sorbier, Miyaké, and Lan Vu. Orlan often holds iconic props, such as a devil's pitchfork, and some surgeries are accompanied by dancers. Her first four surgeries involved liposuction: reduction and reshaping of her ankles, knees, hips, buttocks, waist, and neck. Orlan considers the seventh surgery, titled *Omniprésence* (1993), the most significant. This surgery was broadcast live to 15 art galleries in several different countries, and viewers could ask Orlan questions during the operation. A postperformance gallery installation of *Omniprésence* featured 41 images contrasting a computer-generated image of Orlan (a composite of selected features from classical paintings of Diana, Mona Lisa, Psyche, Venus, and Europa) with daily photos of Orlan as she recovered from surgery, her face bandaged, swollen, discolored, and scarred. Also in the aftermath of each performance Orlan makes relics of her body tissue, enclosing inside the reliquaries pieces of scalp with hair attached, clumps of fat, and bloody bits of gauze, which she sells for as much as 10,000 francs (US $1,400).

Surgeries seven, eight, and nine mark a radicalization of Orlan's surgical projects: the formation of a "mutant body" (Orlan 1999). To this end, Orlan had an implant inserted at each temple, creating two bumps on her head (*Omniprésence*, 1993), and the largest breast implants possible for her anatomy. Orlan anticipated a tenth and final surgery to take place in Japan, to construct an immense nose that would begin in the middle of her forehead, in the style of a pre-Columbian Mayan mask. The *Reincarnation* project was intended to terminate with Orlan's request to an advertising agency to give her a new name, and her subsequent application for a legal name change. In 1997 she revised her original plans for concluding the project and began a collaborative work with Pierre Zovilé of Montreal, entitled *Self-Hybridations* (see Ayers 1999; Zovilé 1998). Together they create digital images that combine Orlan's features with features that reflect beauty standards from other cultures and eras, including skull deformations, scarification, and squints. In an interview with Robert Ayers, in which she discusses her *Self-Hybridation* project, Orlan says that she plans to augment her virtual reconstruction work with two further surgeries: "one which is quite involved and the other which is lighter, more poetic, but I'd like these to be the apotheosis of all my operations." Orlan does not disclose the nature of the first surgery except to say that it is an unprecedented procedure intended to intensify her faculties. The second surgery will simply be "opening up and closing the body" while Orlan observes with serenity and dispassion (Ayers 1999: 182).

Orlan calls her work "blasphemous." She deliberately creates and embodies visual parodies of Christian martyrdom by assuming cruciform positions on the operating table. These images reinforce Orlan's excessive appropriation and embodiment of the rituals of feminine beauty that pressure women to seek an unattainable physical perfection. Her intention is to expose the invisible practice of cosmetic surgery, "desacralizing the surgical act and making a private act transparent, public" (Orlan 1998: 322). It seems to me, however, that she also resacralizes surgery by deepening the ritual aspects of cosmetic surgery, and by creating visceral and grotesque images that evoke sensations of awe and horror to elicit the sacred dimensions of the experience.

In this way, Orlan's work resembles that of the French philosopher Georges Bataille (1897–1962). In his writings, Bataille documents his attempts to stay inside the experience of violence through a sustained practice of internalized sacrifice. Following Christian hagiographies, yet creating his own heterodox mysticism of violence in opposition to them. Bataille seeks a dissolution of self-presence through practices of sexual orgies, drunkenness, and meditation upon photographs of a contemporary torture victim. In these practices, he finds himself "undone like flowing sand," pouring out his energies in a wanton expenditure that defies habitual human economies of measured exchanges. This temporary dissolution of self into nature, existing "in the world like water in water" (Bataille 1989 [1973]: 19) embodies a loss of subject–object distinctions sustained by cognition. Bataille evokes a certain catastrophic grace inside human flesh: "Everything broken, and a feeling of inexorability – which I love. . . . Unprotected, consenting, ecstatic: *as if blood poured from my eyes*" (1988 [1961]: 77). For Bataille, the flesh in its aversive pain and its domestic abyss of possible death is a violating, horrifying, joyous encounter with the sacred. In his writings, he creates himself as a sacred figure of this vivifying and terrifying proximity to death in life.

Through her cosmetic surgeries, Orlan embodies a similar risk-filled venture that threatens habitual human economies of bodily integrity, thus opening painful sensations of the ungovernable flesh, of the "body-machine" (1998: 322) for the spectator. This is to say that the violent spectacle of her surgeries creates an experience of the kind of vertiginous attraction–repulsion that Bataille calls a sacred apotheosis of the wanton sordid flesh.

While Orlan seems more interested in the self's negotiations with and disappearance into technology – rather than into nature – like Bataille, Orlan enacts the transformation of self into a sacred figure and art. Her art dissolves distinctions between subject and object, author and work, in and through her transformations of her own body as a work of art, within the framework of a self-appointed saintliness. Catherine Bell's understanding of ritualization in *Ritual Theory, Ritual Practice* (1992) and Edith Wyschogrod's conception of a transgressive saintliness in *Saints and Postmodernism* (1990) are particularly illuminating with respect to this aspect of Orlan's project. Both works suggest ways to interpret Orlan's self-designated saintliness through their attention to the creation of religious meanings and the significance of the body for religious ritual and imaginative acts.

For Bell, the body and its actions are the foundation of ritual practice: "It is the unrecognized primacy of the body in a ritualized environment that distinguishes ritualization from other social strategies" (1992: 180). The centrality of the body to ritual means that "ritualization is a particularly mute form of activity. It is designed to do what it does without bringing what it is doing across the threshold of discourse or systematic thinking" (93). Ritualization orders the ambiguities and indeterminacies of experience into distinctions between good and evil, light and dark, spirit and flesh, above and below, inside and outside. This dualistic framework evokes what Bell calls a "redemptive hegemony," an understanding of ultimate power and order in the world. The ritual agent learns this redemptive order through embodied practices. For example, in a Catholic mass, *kneeling* embodies submission to a power above oneself (rather than *representing* submission). The ritual agent participates in this practice while interpreting its symbolism. The framework for understanding the world created through ritualization is then used by individuals to interpret experiences beyond the ritual space.

The embodied, prediscursive aspects of ritualization described by Bell have relevance to the postmodern saint as described by Edith Wyschogrod. Wyschogrod responds to the contemporary impasse of contested ethical theories by proposing as an alternative the "flesh-and-blood" saint. Such a person responds to the needs of the Other, attempting to alleviate the mental or physical suffering of the needy without consideration of the pain it causes her or himself. Saintliness evokes an imperative to imitate, through the saint's embodiment of excessive love and generosity toward the Other. This desire on the part of the saint incorporates the "pain and wounding of desire, its restlessness, its instability and obsessiveness" (Wyschogrod 1990: 146). Wyschogrod argues that the saint's communication of love, generosity, and compassion "depends upon the human body as an unsurpassable condition of meaning" (59), which is similar to Bell's understanding of how ritualization conveys ambiguous and indeterminate meaning. The meaning the saint conveys must be interpreted as art, and is only truly perceived when an imitator extends the saint's movements into her own life. Yet postmodern saints, in Wyschogrod's view, may also embody the excesses of contemporary society and its practices of unrestrained desire, which Wyschogrod refers to as "saints of depravity." I argue that Orlan invests her body with the kind of plastic significance that contemporary patriarchal capitalist societies encourage, a parodic saintliness that reveals the debility and pain of such a body, and not a saintliness meant as a model to imitate.

Orlan communicates her art using the medium of her body, and, as both Bell and Wyschogrod suggest, the primacy of the body as a means of communication creates meaning that cannot be limited to or by propositional discourse. Orlan's art develops a transgressive form of prediscursive communication by creating a spectacle of violence. As Kathy Davis notes, "While Orlan begins her performances by apologizing to her audience for causing them pain, this is precisely her intention" (1997: 172). Orlan states that art is not meant to be decoration for apartments: we have plants, aquariums, furniture, and curtains that serve this purpose. Art must disturb both artist and viewer, forcing us to question its deviance and its social project (Orlan 1999). Her art is not in the least decorative. Watching video or film footage of her surgical performances is an acutely painful experience. At the Festival International du Film sur l'Art held in Montreal from 13 to 17 March 2001, I attended a premiere screening of Stephan Oriach's documentary *ORLAN, Carnal Art* (2001), billed as "surgical performances for the not-so-queasy [pour estomacs solides]." Without the breaks provided by commentary on her work by art critics, I was certain I could not have sustained the intense pressure I felt in my gut as I looked at images of her surgery. People in the audience around me were gasping, closing their eyes, recoiling at images of her punctured and opened body: a surgeon inserts an epidural needle into her spine, saws the skin on her leg following the lines he has drawn on her flesh, empties the contents of a needle into her cheek, slices into her lips, probes a tube into a fleshly hole under her chin, moves an oblong implement around under her cheeks, cuts the skin around her ear and moves the skin around like a flap.

Orlan refers to her art as a "parodic style, the grotesque, and the ironic" (1998: 321). In my view, Orlan uses a medium of violence against her own body to create uncontestable images of the opened body that force the attention of the spectators and to establish the authority of her own political protest. Following both Bell's and Wyschogrod's arguments about ritual and saintly acts as radically corporeal. Orlan's impotence *and* her self-assertion during her surgeries embody in an extreme way how cultural messages are imprinted on our flesh – with possibly violent repercussions.

Cosmetic surgery is an ambiguous, ritualized violence that, in Orlan's practice of it, creates ritual that evokes horror, pain, chaos, and disorder in the spectator – the counterpoint of the "redemptive hegemony" that Bell describes. Orlan's surgeries blend capitulation to social "advertising" of the female body with resistance to those impositions. During her performance-surgeries, Orlan is both active director and passive object under the surgeon's knife. She recites from texts as long as she is able, evoking an impression of "an autopsied corpse that continues to speak, as if detached from its body" (Orlan 1998: 321). Her reference to her own perverse appearance as a life-like corpse is not gratuitous: for Orlan, art is a matter of life and death, and she is conscious of the risks of disfigurement and paralysis that she faces with each surgery.

Orlan's performances challenge the patriarchal imperative to control the body, since she consents to becoming the object of surgery even while remaining a conscious participant or subject of the process. In this way, she exposes the unacknowledged suffering that comes with any attempt to achieve the images of women as portrayed in advertising by fashion models. Orlan's opened body exposes her audience to the body's passivity and receptivity to pain and wounding, and also, in this case, its complicity in the wounding. As cultural critique, Orlan's performances expose the pain caused by heedless capitulation to the male desire for a sculpted body. As Susan Bordo argues, this desire to reshape the body is "an industry and an ideology fuelled by fantasies of rearranging, transforming, and correcting, an ideology of limitless improvement and change, defying the historicity, the mortality, and indeed, the very materiality of the body" (1993: 245). Orlan's performances command attention because she puts her own body at risk in order to create awareness of the extent to which we all discipline our own bodies, in more or less painful ways, to conform to current social norms. In Wyschogrod's terms, Orlan's saintly self-sacrifice to the surgical practices used to reshape her plastic body paradoxically becomes her strongest form of communication.

Orlan is often asked about the pain she suffers, which she explains away as peripheral to her project: "Carnal Art does not desire pain, does not seek pain as a source of purification, and does not perceive pain as Redemption" (1998: 319). She presents her body as a monument to an excessive social desire for physical transformation, to evoke pain in the spectator and to force questions about the body in contemporary capitalist society. Grotesque images of her surgery-performances are intended to reverberate through the spectator's body as something "burnt and bitten into . . . consciousness" (Eliot 1968: 571). Orlan seems to want her spectators to come to an awareness of social impressions upon the body in the same prediscursive way that culture forms our bodily habits and disciplines. Violence forces upon spectators a visceral understanding:.

> Few images force us to close our eyes: death, suffering, the opening of the body. . . . Here the eyes become black holes in which the image is absorbed willingly or by force. There images plunge in and strike directly where it hurts without passing through the habitual filters, as if the eyes no longer had any connection with the brain.
>
> (Orlan 1998: 315)

The authority of her protest against the imposition of unattainable feminine beauty standards depends upon reiterated images of violence to her own body as it is probed, cut, suctioned, stuck, and sliced with surgical implements. As with ritualization, the power of these images resides in their prediscursive reverberations in and through the body of the spectator. And, as Bell points out, the ambiguity of such communication means that it is open to a wide range of interpretation.

The ambiguity and indeterminacy of Orlan's embodied communication means that she can be interpreted as either rejecting or conforming to prevailing cultural standards of feminine beauty. While she is clearly opposed to the commercialization of art and the commodification of feminine beauty standards, she nonetheless sells reliquaries of her body tissues, in effect selling her flesh. She acts as a parodic exemplum of the pressures that women feel to conform to beauty standards by working exclusively at the transformation of her body. The early surgeries fit within the cosmetic intentions of this kind of surgery, and it is only from the seventh surgery on that she begins to create a mutant body in parodic fulfillment of feminine beauty standards. She explains that the first surgeries were performed by male surgeons who wanted to keep her "cute." Orlan embodies the fantasy of a self-orchestrated and limitless transformation of the body, yet she contrasts fluid, computer generated images of herself with those images created by her own "body-machine" (1998: 322), which are entirely unpredictable and uncontrollable. Orlan's fantasies of self-transformation seem to dematerialize the body, yet at the same time her patient documentation of her cosmetic surgeries and the process of recovery from these operations expose "plastic surgery as a lengthy, laborious, imprecise, and imperfect material process rather than a quick and easy result" (Augsburg 1998: 291), thereby recovering the fleshly weight of the body.

Orlan chooses to be a parodic exemplar of an unrestrained desire to transform the body. Because of her ambiguous embodied communication, she runs the risk of reinstating the very ideologies she protests in her attempt to open – through violent spectacle – public debate about power and disempowerment in and through the feminine body. Orlan's work also intimates an important possibility within her performance of a saintliness of depravity. She creates a religious framework, albeit blasphemous, that disrupts common patterns of religious meaning limited to a redemptive order, and intimates a sacred meaning for embodied experiences of negativity, disorder, pain, violence, and bodily disintegration.

REFERENCES

Augsburg, Tanya (1998) "Orlan's performative transformations of subjectivity," in *The Ends of Performance*, edited by Peggy Phelan and Jill Lane, 285–314, New York: New York University Press.

Ayers, Robert (1999) "Serene and happy and distant: an interview with Orlan," *Body in Society* 5, 2: 171–84.

Bataille, Georges (1988 [1961]) *Guilty*, translated by Bruce Boone, Venice, Cal.: Lapis Press.

—— (1989 [1973]) *Theory of Religion*, translated by Robert Hurley, New York: Zone Books.

Bell, Catherine (1992) *Ritual Theory, Ritual Practice*, New York: Oxford University Press.

Bordo, Susan (1993) *Unbearable Weight: Feminism, Western Culture, and the Body*, Berkeley: University of California Press.

Davis, Kathy (1997) " 'My body is my art: cosmetic surgery as feminist utopia?", in *Embodied Practices: Feminist Perspectives on the Body*, edited by Kathy Davis, 168–81, London: Sage Publications.

Eliot, George (1968) *Middlemarch*, edited by Gordon S. Haight, Boston: Houghton Mifflin Company.

Orlan (1998) "Intervention," in *The Ends of Performance*, edited by Peggy Phelan and Jill Lane, 315–27, New York: New York University Press.

—— (1999) "Conference excerpts," from ". . . This is my body . . . this is my software . . .," 4 November, <http://www.civc.fr/creation_artistique/online/orlan/conference.html> (10 October 2001).

ORLAN, Carnal Art (2001) Produced and directed by Stephan Oriach, 75 minutes, Myriapodus Films, 35 mm.

Rose, Barbara (1993) "Is it art? Orlan and the transgressive act," *Art in America* 81, 2 (February): 82–7.

Wyschogrod, Edith (1990) *Saints and Postmodernism: Revisioning Moral Philosophy*, Chicago: University of Chicago Press.

Zovilé, Pierre (1998) "Refiguration-self hybridation: a collaborative work in the cyberspace," 14 October, <http://www.isea.qc.ca/webcast/montreal/zovile.html> (10 October 2001).

READER CROSS-REFERENCES

Carlson – on performance art

Goffman, Gabler, Kaprow – the self presented as art

Turner, C. Bell – connecting ritual and performance

Mason – a different kind of ritual

Butler – the performance of the female body

Grotowski, Strasberg, Harding, Barba – the commitment of the performer's whole self to the performance

Phelan – another example of ordeal art

Ancelet – ritual use of violence

16

PERFORMATIVE COMMEMORATIVES, THE PERSONAL, AND THE PUBLIC

Spontaneous Shrines, Emergent Ritual

Jack Santino

I recently attended a ceremony at Bowling Green State University called "Operation Transformation," held in memory of victims of domestic violence. The event was sponsored by the BGSU Women's Center and was held inside a Christian chapel on campus. In front of the prominent cross were 22 votive candles in purple glasses – purple being the designated color of mourning; 22 victims were being remembered.

This was the opening event of a month-long public display of 22 two-dimensional silhouettes, each shrouded in black cloth. October 1, 2003 was the unveiling. As each effigy was unveiled, an individual woman read the stories of the deceased in the first person and the present tense: "My name is _____ . I am __ years old and have __ children. On _____ I was shot to death in front of my children by my estranged husband. My name is _____ ; remember my name." Audience members included family members of the victims and BGSU students. Overcome with emotion, some of the women reading the brief biographies had trouble maintaining their composure. The victims and the audience members were young and old, black, white, and Latino. All were from the surrounding area.

This ritualistic event, the unveiling, simultaneously memorialized deceased individuals and drew attention and tried to mobilize action toward a social problem, that is, domestic violence. Both aspects – the personal identity of the victims and the social malignancy that led to their deaths – were emphatically manifest in the presentation. The readers called attention to the life stories and personal relationships of the victims, and the entire event was presented in the context of domestic violence as a gendered crime. Moreover, the ceremony borrowed heavily from traditional Christian ritual.

This kind of public memorialization of death toward a social end seems to be a growing phenomenon. The AIDS quilt is an example, as are the demonstrations of the Madres de la Plaza – calling attention to the disappeared in Argentina and Chile, the Bloody Sunday commemorations in Northern Ireland, gang memorial walls, roadside crosses, and all the other "spontaneous shrines" (as I term them) that we see. Central to all of these phenomena is the conjunction of the performative memorializing of personal deaths in the framework of the social conditions that caused those deaths with the commemorative or celebratory. (To commemorate is, in a sense, to celebrate something or someone. I use the terms equivalently, but not interchangeably.) In a sense, death has always been publicly memorialized. Think of the funeral procession of hearse and cars down the street; the rituals held in houses of worship and in cemeteries. In these and other cases, though, participation in the ritual activities is restricted to a particular group – family and friends, for instance. I refer to the tendency to commemorate a deceased individual in front of an undifferentiated public that can then become participatory if it so chooses. First, then, I explore the concept of the public, beginning with rituals generally found in public, and not just rituals concerned with death and mourning.

Rituals in public

Historian Samuel Kinser cites the slaughtering of "steers and other animals before the Pope and other Roman notables after a parade through the city," as reported in a document circa AD 1140, as the earliest report of festive customs held prior to Lent, that is, Mardi Gras or carnival (Kinser 1990: 3). This is clearly an expressive public event in that it is a festive or ritual act carried out in a public place. Public places can be either indoors or outdoors – a church or a plaza, for instance. In many ritual events, audiences are present but are restricted to, for example, only women or men, or friends and relatives. In a sense, all rituals are public, in that an audience of some kind is necessary to witness and validate the changes wrought by the ritual – or, at least, proclaimed by it. Here we think of ritual as dramatic social enactments that are thought by the participants to have some transformational or confirmatory agency and that they derive this power from an overarching para-human authority, such as a deity, the state, or an institution such as a university – rather than ritual in the sense of custom or, even more broadly, routine. The movement in scholarship (e.g., performance studies) toward ritual as public display – that is, applying theories derived from the study of ritual to contemporary public display events – parallels the social development of performative actions intended to produce change that will be seen by a broad and undifferentiated public. Most official rituals do not have general audiences – you have to be invited to attend or be a member of the group involved. In events such as the Operation Transformation project, however, we see public ritualistic events that invite participation from a broad audience.

The concept of public display clearly is a broad one. Roger Abrahams suggests it with reference to events such as "the parade, the pageant, or the ball game . . . expositions and meets, games and carnivals and auctions" (1981: 303–4), using the term to refer to "planned-for public occasions" in which "accumulated feelings may be channeled into contest, drama, or some other form of display" and that also includes "actions and objects [that] are invested with meaning and values [that] are put on display" (303). Don Handelman suggests that we deal with the problem of imprecise terminologies such as "ritual," "festival," "spectacle," "rite," and so forth, by developing taxonomies and analytical methodologies based on the events' designs – that is, according to what the

126

particular event is intended to accomplish socially (1990). Ronald L. Grimes presents the term "public ritual" as an inclusive category "capable of including most examples of civil and secular ritual" (1982). In a study of a series of "living celebrations" that I curated for the Smithsonian Institution in the early 1980s, I called the staged presentations of traditional cultures, designed in part by the participants who were themselves members of the community whose traditions were being represented, "rites of public presentation" (Santino 1988), a concept related both to the ideas of public display and also to Barbara Myerhoff's concept of "definitional ceremonies" (1978: 185–6). I made the point that, although the nature of celebratory and ritualistic events was necessarily transformed when staged in a museum setting for an audience that would not otherwise participate in them or be familiar with them in their own lives, the events in question became ritualistic in a different way – not simply because they were theatrical, but because, although they were presented to the public as a kind of entertainment (however edifying), in practice, they turned out to be something else, a hybrid form where audiences actually participated in rites that were foreign to them. The role of the audience members was transformed from passive observer, as at the theater, to active participant, as at a ritual. Cristina Sánchez Carretero has examined this phenomenon of public (and private) events being transformed by institutional presentation for the edification of a broad audience of people outside the tradition (2003). One important aspect of public display is the domain in which groups choose certain events from their own culture through which to publicly present themselves as a group to outsiders: at a museum, university, festival, and so on.

Problematizing the "public"

I have referred above to at least three senses of the term "public": (1) done before an audience; (2) performed in institutionalized contexts such as universities or museums for people unfamiliar with the tradition; and (3) set out before a spectatorship whose make-up is fluid and unpredictable. Nevertheless, the concept of "public" needs to be further problematized. For instance, on June 2, 1995, I visited a rag well, that is, a holy well with healing properties, in Dungiven, County Derry, Northern Ireland. This one is surrounded – indeed, almost obscured – by trees and bushes on which were tied rags, strings, ropes, and other pieces of cloth left by previous visitors as votive offerings. The well is located close to the ruins of the medieval priory of St. Mary, overlooking a spectacular view of the valley below, but is easily missed as one walks onto the grounds. Once seen, however, it is unforgettable. The outer branches are unadorned. Only inside the copse, the thicket, or the "scrubbery" as they say in Ulster, surrounding the well itself, are the thick, twisted, gnarled, and dense branches covered by rags of all sorts and colors of materials. It is both a wall made of rags and branches and an environment, a space into which one must enter to get to the small rock basin with its holy water. Most of the rags are faded and in various stages of disintegration. Perhaps people leave these in the belief that, as the rags disintegrate, the illness to which they correspond will also fade. To see it, however, people have to know where it is. My friend and I each left a token of our presence – I tore my handkerchief in two, and we tied them to branches. Broadly speaking, as tokens of our having visited, the rags are at least in part, memorials.

It is clear that the motivations leading to such public acts of memorialization are many and complex, having to do with sickness, belief, personal devotion, attempts to influence that which is beyond human control, and also a need to demonstrate to an audience one does not know that one participated, that one contributed to this monument, and that one was there, albeit anonymously. Ironically, this rag well is strikingly visual, yet one cannot see it under usual circumstances. Memorialization or commemoration is one aspect of the display of cloth here. Performativity – the intent to effect a cure, to make something happen – is another. Both aspects may be present simultaneously in the actions of any one individual who leaves such a token at this place. J.L. Austin assigned the term "performative utterances" to those statements that accomplish a social change, statements such as "I do," "I now pronounce you husband and wife," or "I christen this ship" (1962). These statements, often found in rites of passage, cause the effect they pronounce. Here I extend the term from utterances to events that attempt to cause social change.

Public decorating for and ritual marking of special times and places is, of course, a well-known phenomenon internationally. Beyond the obvious examples of domestic and institutional decoration for important religious and calendrical occasions should be added the tendencies to ritualize present absences, such as the use of yellow ribbons to denote concern for hostages or green willows to denote awareness of absent lovers. Likewise, the deceased have been ritualized in most societies for which we have evidence. When death is sudden, untimely, or unexpected, as in automobile accidents, for instance, some cultures have found it appropriate to mark the place where the death occurred (for a general discussion of commemorations, see Gillis (1994)). Roadside crosses are found extensively throughout the American Southwest and Latin America for instance, as well as in many European countries. In the last decades of the twentieth century, this custom has been adapted internationally. No longer a regional tradition, the marking of the place of a shocking death with a spontaneous shrine consisting of flowers and personal memorabilia has become part of the global expressive repertoire, seen most dramatically at the site of the Oklahoma City bombing, in London and Paris after the death of Princess Diana, and in New York after September 11, 2001. In all these examples, the ribbons, flowers, and personal items reference a person or a group in a remarkable or significant condition of absence: hostage, distant lover, soldier sent to war, dead celebrity, or martyred leader. Just as important, they express an attitude toward that condition and the larger contexts in which they exist: support for the soldiers' cause, faithfulness toward a lover, or condemnation of violence. The attitudes expressed are also intended to be shared by those who view the artifacts – to convince or to have an effect on the aggregate spectatorship. Thus, these displays can be said to be performative and are frequently done in conjunction with public events, such as silent witness gatherings. It is their performative aspects that necessitate they be displayed in public. With most deaths, private mourning and flowers at the grave are sufficient. When the site of an untimely death, or its metaphorical analogue, is so adorned, the element of performativity is being exercised through these spontaneous shrines. We can see a duality in the yellow ribbon displays and the rag wells, but in spontaneous shrines the duality is expressly that they both commemorate deceased individuals and simultaneously suggest an attitude toward a related public issue.

The examples of such "performative commemoratives" are legion in the contemporary world, as I have indicated already. From the Mourning Wall in Oklahoma City, created in response to the bombing of a federal building, to memorial walls commemorating the deaths of gang members or the school shootings in Littleton, Colorado, in 1999, spontaneous shrines and the public marking of the places where death occurred have become a primary response. They are no longer emergent. They have clearly become a contemporary mourning ritual or tradition under certain circumstances – that of untimely death. Concomitantly, newspapers and other media frequently (ritualistically?) feature these shrines as part of their coverage of these events. Here, the media helps spread the tradition, much as David Waldstreicher, following Benedict Anderson (1983), argues that Independence Day customs were nationalized and standardized by print journalism (1997). Moreover, televised "watches" of the life-cycle events and funerals of public figures such as Princess Diana or John F. Kennedy, Jr., have become part of the rituals themselves (Dayan and Katz 1992). How these traditions have coalesced and spread at this point in history is an important question (see Santino 1992b, 1999), but we should also remember that the actual instances of ritual commemoration are specific to particular times, places, cultures, societies, and people. Here we can see personal, popular actions – the laying of flowers and wreaths – melded with international media coverage in an interesting conjunction of the intensely personal with the global.

On the other hand, actions such as leaving a piece of rag at a holy well, although it may imply the presence of a deity or a supernatural being as a witness, may simply be thought of as a direct (magical) act in which the rag corresponds to the affliction. The presence of the rag implies a potential audience of future visitors to the well. This points to the fact that ritual in the stricter sense of the term is instrumental: it is believed to be able to effect change. Healing rituals may or may not be successful, but they are thought to be potentially efficacious, regardless of the outcome. Rites of passage are generally accepted among scholars as a social mechanism of status change, although we probably all have had the experience of undergoing some life cycle event – a birthday, maybe, or a confirmation – that we felt meant nothing to us. I would suggest that what we analytically call rituals are emically efficacious. Thus, they appear to outsiders as largely, even primarily, metaphorical, symbolic, and expressive, regardless of how functional they are thought to be among participants. For devout Roman Catholics, for instance, the bread and wine of the mass is truly, literally, transformed into the body and blood of Christ. For Pentecostals, the Holy Spirit is genuinely present during their services. The problem arises precisely in the kinds of literature to which we have been referring, in which other cultural performances are generally categorized along with ritual, or as ritual itself. Analytically they share symbolic ceremonialism, cultural patterning, and framing, but for the participants a ritual is a conscious means to a desired end and less a doing for its own sake (Schieffelin 1998). Further, as was mentioned in the case of the rag well, there are multiple intentions involved.

The rag well described above is a prime example of a custom that involves public display, although the well itself is hidden and hard to find. One must either know where it is or deliberately seek it out. Thus, the clientele for this healing well are self-selected. On the other hand, a parade in a city or town will be witnessed by many people who do not set out to watch it. Similarly, a display of festive decoration on the facade of a building, a yellow ribbon, or a spontaneous shrine will be seen by an indiscriminate audience of passers-by. The term "public" here has to do with spectatorship, witness, participation, and social transformation, as well as a Habermasian sense of shared civic interest (Habermas 1992). Performative commemoratives – spontaneous shrines – invite participation, unlike the funeral procession one happens to run across. They also invite interpretation. Once set out before an undifferentiated public, the polysemy inherent in these assemblages allows for a broad range of readings and associations by passers-by, regardless of the initial intentions of the originators.

I have long been interested in issues of public display and public display events. I developed the term "folk assemblage," or simply "assemblage," to help theorize my early considerations of holiday decorations, particularly for Halloween, as well as the display of yellow ribbons (Santino 1986, 1992b). I attempted to put a lot of the ideas together in my more recent study of Northern Ireland, titled *Signs of War and Peace: Social Conflict and the Public Uses of Symbols in Northern Ireland* (2001). A great deal of public-display activities, such as parades, and materials, such as murals, are found in Northern Ireland, and I found it to be an ideal place to study its various usages.

It was in Northern Ireland in 1992, while studying Halloween there, that I first became personally and professionally involved in spontaneous shrines. My colleague at the Ulster Folk and Transport Museum, Michael McCaughan, had seen a large display of flowers and notes at the site of a recent paramilitary killing. After discussing it, we went to the site together. McCaughan, a photographer, took some pictures. Later, he was asked to develop an exhibition of his photographs.

When McCaughan asked me to contribute an essay to the exhibition catalogue, I purposely set out to develop an appropriate term and vocabulary for the phenomenon. I decided on "spontaneous shrines" for several reasons (Santino 1992a). At that time, to my knowledge, the press had not yet begun to use the condescending and inaccurate term "makeshift memorials." I use the word "spontaneous" to indicate the unofficial nature of these shrines. For example, a 14-year-old girl may decide to place a note and a rose at the site of her father's unexpected murder by a paramilitary gunman in Belfast. No one told her to. These are not instigated by church or state. They are truly "popular," that is, of the people, or in that sense, "folk." And I use the word "shrine" because these are more than memorials. They are places of communion between the dead and the living (thus, the notes left there). They are sites of pilgrimage, as Sylvia Grider has noted (2001). They commemorate and memorialize, but they do far more than that. They invite participation even from strangers. They are "open to the public."

This moves us to another point – the political nature of spontaneous shrines. I suggest that the shrines personalize public and political issues and, in personalizing them, are political themselves, even in the absence of overt political sloganeering, as in Northern Ireland. Spontaneous shrines are silent witnesses. Further, they reflect and comment on public and social issues. The Malice Green site in Detroit, where an African-American man was killed while in police custody, is a comment on police brutality. Roadside crosses reflect road conditions and drunk-driving issues. September 11 shrines reflect on terrorism or political violence. In Northern Ireland, they reflect and implicitly comment on paramilitary violence by forcing recognition of the havoc it wreaks on ordinary people. The question of intentionality versus spectator interpretation is germane here, because observers' readings and associations will vary from those of the creators. Moreover, the relative degree of performativity versus commemoration varies from assemblage to assemblage, as well as among different types of public memorializations. The intent of a roadside cross may be primarily commemorative, though it might be viewed as a warning by passing motorists; the performances of the Bloody Sunday protesters in Northern Ireland or the Mothers of the Plaza in South America are intentionally political, but involve the commemoration of the lives of specific, victimized individuals. All of these examples involve both performativity and commemoration to a greater or lesser degree. One can view these dimensions as two ends of a continuum, along which any particular instance of public memorialization of death and spontaneous shrine might be placed, according to its emphasis.

It is said that, in war, a combatant is trained to depersonalize the enemy, to demonize the enemy in order to be able to kill with little or no remorse. Spontaneous shrines act in the opposite way, performing the opposite task. They insist on the personal nature of the individuals involved in these issues and the ramifications of the actions of those addressed by the shrines. You don't think drunk driving is a problem? My daughter was killed – here, at this spot – because of it. Teenage drinking? Responsible for the deaths of a carload of kids – right here. The county doesn't want to spend money on road improvement? Look at all the crosses along this stretch of road. You are carrying out a holy war? You killed my father. Paramilitaries are killing people in the name of freedom? The IRA killed my wife. That's not a Taig or a Prod – that's my husband, my father, my brother. You are conducting wars against terrorism? You killed my mother, my sister, my daughter.

Now: defend your actions, your politics, in light of that. We, who build shrines and construct public altars or parade with photographs of the deceased, will not allow you to write off victims as mere regrettable statistics. We insist; the shrines insist – by their disruption of the mundane environment, their calling attention to themselves – that we acknowledge the real people, the real lives lost, and the devastation to the commonwealth that these politics hold. By translating social issues and political actions into personal terms, the shrines are themselves political statements. Much of their communicative power is derived from their personalization of the public (i.e., performativity) just as a great deal is drawn from the language of mortuary ritual, of death and dying (i.e., of commemoration). They are, I believe, the voice of the people.

The shrines insert and insist upon the presence of the absent people. They display death in the heart of social life. These are not graves awaiting occasional visitors and sanctioned decoration. Instead of a family visiting a grave, the "grave" comes to the "family" – that is, the public, all of us. We are all family, mutually connected, interdependent. Spontaneous shrines both construct the relationship between the deceased and those who leave notes and memorabilia, and present that relationship to visitors. This is manifested in the notes and in the nature of the gifts that are brought, left, and publicly displayed: a high-school jacket, dog tag, or old report card indicate fellow student, comrade soldier, or bereaved parent. The gifts have personal meaning, and this is indicative – that is, they index the nature of the relationship, real or (as with Princess Diana and other celebrities) imagined. Imagined, but no less felt.

Spontaneous shrines place deceased individuals back into the fabric of society, into the middle of areas of commerce and travel, and into everyday life as it is being lived. Traditional societies have always done this, as in the Latino Day of the Dead rituals and celebrations, at traditional Irish wakes, at New Orleans jazz funerals, or at rural and regional homecomings and Decoration Day traditions. It seems as if people are reacting to the mass industrialization of death and the alienation of contemporary society with new folk traditions, rituals, and celebrations.

There is much more to be investigated, of course, beyond the scope of this presentation. Family members and friends usually create these spontaneous shrines. Roadside shrines appear to be largely Christian in that they frequently feature a cross as the dominant symbol (though not always). Is shrine too narrow a word? Does it exclude non-Christians? Do members of other faiths, or no religion at all, create these as well? They certainly did in New York after September 11. Would "spontaneous sacralization" be more accurate? It is more unwieldy, and "performative commemoratives" is a larger conceptual categorization.

What about race and gender? How and when do they factor in? Spontaneous shrines seem to be created by women and men of various races and backgrounds. Still, these are questions that need to be examined. Here, I have focused on the dynamics of spontaneous shrines that combine memorialization of deceased individuals with their topicality regarding social issues, and that use funerary tradition to address larger, causative, social problems.

NOTE

This essay, originally subtitled "Spontaneous shrines, emergent ritual, and the field of folklore," was given as the Presidential Plenary Address to the 2003 meeting of the American Folklore Society.

REFERENCES

Abrahams, Roger D. (1981) "Shouting match at the border: the folklore of display events," in *"And Other Neighborly Names": Social Process and Cultural Image in Texas Folklore*, ed. Richard Bauman and Roger D. Abrahams, pp. 303–21. Austin: University of Texas Press.

Anderson, Benedict R. (1983) *Imagined Communities: Reflections on the Origin and Spread of Nationalism*. London: Verso Editions/NLB.

Austin, J.L. (1962) *How to Do Things with Words*. Cambridge, Mass.: Harvard University Press.

Ben-Amos, Dan (1972) "Toward a definition of folklore in context," in *Toward New Perspectives in Folklore*, ed. Amirico Paredes and Richard Bauman, pp. 3–15. Austin: University of Texas Press.

Dayan, Daniel, and Elihu Katz (1992) "Defining media events: high holidays of mass communication," in *Media Events: The Live Broadcasting of History*, pp. 1–24. Cambridge, Mass.: Harvard University Press.

Gillis, John R. (ed.) (1994) *Commemorations: The Politics of National Identity*. Princeton, N.J.: Princeton University Press.

Grider, Sylvia (2001) "Spontaneous shrines: preliminary observations regarding the spontaneous shrines following the terrorist attacks of September 11, 2001," *New Directions in Folklore*, 4(2): http://www.temple.edu/isllc/newfolk/shrines.html (accessed October 10, 2003).

Grimes, Ronald D. (1982) "The lifeblood of public ritual: fiestas and public exploration projects," in *Celebration: Studies in Festivity and Ritual*, ed. Victor Turner, pp. 272–83. Washington, D.C.: Smithsonian Institution Press.

Habermas, Jurgen (1992) "Citizenship and national identity: some reflections on the future of europe," *Praxis International*, 12(1): 1–19.

Handelman, Don (1990) *Models and Mirrors: Towards an Anthropology of Public Events*. Cambridge: Cambridge University Press.

Kinser, Samuel (1990) *Carnival American Style: Mardi Gras at New Orleans and Mobile*. Chicago: University of Chicago Press.

Myerhoff, Barbara (1978) *Number Our Days*. New York: Simon and Schuster.

Sánchez Carretero, Cristina (2003) "The Day of the Dead: dying days in Toledo, Ohio?" in *Holidays, Ritual, Festival, Celebration, and Public Display*, ed. Cristina Sánchez Carretero and Jack Santino, pp. 173–90. Alcalá, Spain: University of Alcalá Press.

Santino, Jack (1986) "The folk assemblage of autumn: tradition and creativity in Halloween folk art," in *Folk Art and Art Worlds*, ed. John Michael Vlach and Simon Bronner, pp. 151–69. Ann Arbor, Mich.: UMI Research Press.

—— (1988) "The tendency to ritualize: the living celebrations series as a model for cultural presentation and validation," in *The Conservation of Culture: Folklorists and the Public Sector*, ed. Burt Feintuch, pp. 118–31. Lexington: University Press of Kentucky.

—— (1992a) "'Not an unimportant failure:' rituals of death and politics in Northern Ireland," in *Displayed in Mortal Light*, ed. Michael McCaughan, Antrim, Northern Ireland: Antrim Arts Council.

—— (1992b) "Yellow ribbons and seasonal flags: the folk assemblage of war," *Journal of American Folklore*, 105(415): 19–33.

—— (1999) "Public protest and popular style: resistance from the right in Northern Ireland and South Boston," *American Anthropologist*, 101(3): 515–28.

—— (2001) *Signs of War and Peace: Social Conflict and the Public Use of Symbols in Northern Ireland*. New York: Palgrave.

Schieffelin, Edward L. (1998) "Problematizing performance," in *Ritual, Performance, Media*, ed. Felicia Hughes-Freeland, pp. 194–207. London: Routledge.

Waldstreicher, David (1997) *In the Midst of Perpetual Fetes: The Making of American Nationalism, 1776–1820*. Chapel Hill, N. C.: University of North Carolina Press.

READER CROSS-REFERENCES

Schechner, C. Bell – use of ritual as a term in performance studies

J. Bell – spontaneous shrines as a response to September 11, 2001

Mason, Ancelet – describe traditional rituals

Turner – rites of passage

Austin, Derrida, Butler, Parker and Sedgwick – on performative acts

Conquergood – the importance of the popular

Part IV

PLAY

To play means to do something that is neither "serious" nor "real." Yet play is nonetheless important, for it demands risks and promises rewards that may have consequences for our everyday lives. We play to escape, to step out of everyday existence, if only for a moment, and to observe a different set of rules. We play to explore, to learn about ourselves and the world around us. Play may be formal and organized, as in a professional football game, or informal and unpredictable, as with children in a park. Play can be competitive or cooperative, goal-oriented or open-ended. Play may involve an erosion or inversion of social status (as in the Trinidad Carnival). It may involve lying and deceit (as in a confidence game). Often the thrill of risk is itself the reward for playing, as in gambling, sky-diving, and other activities which pit the player's skill and determination against the vagaries of chance.

In performance studies, play is understood as the force of uncertainty which counterbalances the structure provided by ritual. Where ritual depends on repetition, play stresses innovation and creativity. Where ritual is predictable, play is contingent. But all performances, even rituals, contain some element of play, some space for variation. And most forms of play involve pre-established patterns of behavior. Hence, as Schechner writes, "performance may be defined as ritualized behavior conditioned/permeated by play" (2006: 89).

One of the first modern scholars to analyze play was Dutch historian Johan Huizinga. In "The nature and significance of play as a cultural phenomenon" (1950 [1938]), Huizinga presents the argument that play is an intrinsic element of human culture. "[L]aw and order, commerce and profit, craft and art, poetry, wisdom and science," he writes, "[a]ll are rooted in the primeval soil of play" (p. 140). In "A theory of play and fantasy" (1972), Gregory Bateson examines the role of play in communication, and of communication in play. Play involves "real" words and actions that are paradoxically "not-real" because they are "framed" within the context of play. Bateson seeks to understand how people do and do not recognize such "frames" and paradoxes as a means toward a greater understanding of the human psyche. The essay concludes with the recognition that such paradoxes are necessary for further development – we need to play in order to adapt, survive, and evolve. Play theorist Brian Sutton-Smith, in "The ambiguity of play" (1997), offers a counterpoint to Bateson by casting a critical eye on how the rhetoric of play infuses scientific and cultural discourse.

Exploring concepts such as "the play of the gods" and "the universe at play," Sutton-Smith asks whether the seemingly infinite expansion of the term "play" to all aspects of existence is appropriate or desirable, and what its implications may be for the study of play.

Play can lead to art, and vice versa, as illustrated in "Just doing" (1997) by artist Allan Kaprow. In this essay, itself a playful and selective assemblage of his earlier writings, Kaprow describes the creative process as series of games and diversions. "Play, of course," he writes, "is at the heart of experimentation" (p. 161). Play can also be at the heart of rituals that preserve and defend a community's culture. Barry Jean Ancelet's "Falling apart to stay together" (2001) describes how "deep play" (play that involves significant risk to the player) functions in the preservation of one of the United States' oldest ritual performance traditions, Louisiana's Cajun Country Mardi Gras.

17

THE NATURE AND SIGNIFICANCE OF PLAY AS A CULTURAL PHENOMENON

Johan Huizinga

Play is older than culture, for culture, however inadequately defined, always presupposes human society, and animals have not waited for man to teach them their playing. We can safely assert, even, that human civilization has added no essential feature to the general idea of play. Animals play just like men. We have only to watch young dogs to see that all the essentials of human play are present in their merry gambols. They invite one another to play by a certain ceremoniousness of attitude and gesture. They keep to the rule that you shall not bite, or not bite hard, your brother's ear. They pretend to get terribly angry. And – what is most important – in all these doings they plainly experience tremendous fun and enjoyment. Such rompings of young dogs are only one of the simpler forms of animal play. There are other, much more highly developed forms: regular contests and beautiful performances before an admiring public.

Here we have at once a very important point: even in its simplest forms on the animal level, play is more than a mere physiological phenomenon or a psychological reflex. It goes beyond the confines of purely physical or purely biological activity. It is a *significant* function – that is to say, there is some sense to it. In play there is something "at play" which transcends the immediate needs of life and imparts meaning to the action. All play means something. If we call the active principle that makes up the essence of play "instinct", we explain nothing; if we call it "mind" or "will" we say too much. However we may regard it, the very fact that play has a meaning implies a non-materialistic quality in the nature of the thing itself.

Psychology and physiology deal with the observation, description, and explanation of the play of animals, children, and grown-ups. They try to determine the nature and significance of play and to assign it its place in the scheme of life. The high importance of this place and the necessity, or at least the utility, of play as a function are generally taken for granted and form the starting-point of all such scientific researches. The numerous attempts to define the biological function of play show a striking variation. By some the origin and fundamentals of play have been described as a discharge of superabundant vital energy, by others as the satisfaction of some "imitative instinct", or again as simply a "need" for relaxation. According to one theory play constitutes a training of the young creature for the serious work that life will demand later on. According to another it serves as an exercise in restraint needful to the individual. Some find the principle of play in an innate urge to exercise a certain faculty, or in the desire to dominate or compete. Yet others regard it as an "abreaction" – an outlet for harmful impulses, as the necessary restorer of energy wasted by one-sided activity, as "wish-fulfillment", as a fiction designed to keep up the feeling of personal value, etc.[1]

All these hypotheses have one thing in common: they all start from the assumption that play must serve something which is *not* play, that it must have some kind of biological purpose. They all enquire into the why and the wherefore of play. The various answers they give tend rather to overlap than to exclude one another. It would be perfectly possible to accept nearly all the explanations without getting into any real confusion of thought – and without coming much nearer to a real understanding of the play-concept. They are all only partial solutions of the problem. If any of them were really decisive it ought either to exclude all the others or comprehend them in a higher unity. Most of them only deal incidentally with the question of what play is *in itself* and what it means for the player. They attack play direct with the quantitative methods of experimental science without first paying attention to its profoundly aesthetic quality. As a rule they leave the primary quality of play as such virtually untouched. To each and every one of the above "explanations" it might well be objected: "So far so good, but what actually is the *fun* of playing? Why does the baby crow with pleasure? Why does the gambler lose himself in his passion? Why is a huge crowd roused to frenzy by a football match?" This intensity of, and absorption in, play finds no explanation in biological analysis. Yet in this intensity, this absorption, this power of maddening, lies the very essence, the primordial quality of play. Nature, so our reasoning mind tells us, could just as easily have given her children all those useful functions of discharging superabundant energy, of relaxing after exertion, of training for the demands of life, of compensating for unfulfilled longings, etc., in the form of purely mechanical exercises and reactions. But no, she gave us play, with its tension, its mirth, and its fun.

Now this last-named element, the *fun* of playing, resists all analysis, all logical interpretation. As a concept, it cannot be reduced to any other mental category. No other modern language known to me has the exact equivalent of the English "fun." The Dutch "aardigkeit" perhaps comes nearest to it (derived from "aard" which means the same as "Art" and "Wesen"[2] in German, and thus evidence, perhaps, that the matter cannot be reduced further). We may note in passing that "fun" in its current usage is of rather recent origin. French, oddly enough, has no corresponding term at all; German half makes up for it by "Spass" and "Witz" together. Nevertheless it is precisely this fun-element that characterizes the essence of play. Here we have to do with an absolutely primary category of life, familiar to everybody at a glance right down to the animal level. We may call play a "totality" in the modern sense of the word, and it is as a totality that we must try to understand and evaluate it.

Since the reality of play extends beyond the sphere of human life it cannot have its foundations in any rational nexus, because this would limit it to mankind. The incidence of play is not associated with any particular stage of civilization or view of the universe. Any thinking person can see at a glance that play is a thing on its own, even if his language possesses no general concept to express it. Play cannot be denied. You can deny, if you like, nearly all abstractions: justice, beauty, truth, goodness, mind, God. You can deny seriousness, but not play.

But in acknowledging play you acknowledge mind, for whatever else play is, it is not matter. Even in the animal world it bursts the bounds of the physically existent. From the point of view of a world wholly determined by the operation of blind forces, play would be altogether superfluous. Play only becomes possible, thinkable, and understandable when an influx of *mind* breaks down the absolute determinism of the cosmos. The very existence of play continually confirms the supra-logical nature of the human situation. Animals play, so they must be more than merely mechanical things. We play and know that we play, so we must be more than merely rational beings, for play is irrational.

In tackling the problem of play as a function of culture proper and not as it appears in the life of the animal or the child, we begin where biology and psychology leave off. In culture we find play as a given magnitude existing before culture itself existed, accompanying it and pervading it from the earliest beginnings right up to the phase of civilization we are now living in. We find play present everywhere as a well-defined quality of action which is different from "ordinary" life. We can disregard the question of how far science has succeeded in reducing this quality to quantitative factors. In our opinion it has not. At all events it is precisely this quality, itself so characteristic of the form of life we call "play," which matters. Play as a special form of activity, as a "significant form," as a social function — that is our subject. We shall not look for the natural impulses and habits conditioning play in general, but shall consider play in its manifold concrete forms as itself a social construction. We shall try to take play as the player himself takes it: in its primary significance. If we find that play is based on the manipulation of certain images, on a certain "imagination" of reality (i.e. its conversion into images), then our main concern will be to grasp the value and significance of these images and their "imagination." We shall observe their action in play itself and thus try to understand play as a cultural factor in life.

The great archetypal activities of human society are all permeated with play from the start. Take language, for instance — that first and supreme instrument which man shapes in order to communicate, to teach, to command. Language allows him to distinguish, to establish, to state things; in short, to name them and by naming them to raise them into the domain of the spirit. In the making of speech and language the spirit is continually "sparking" between matter and mind, as it were, playing with this wondrous nominative faculty. Behind every abstract expression there lies the boldest of metaphors, and every metaphor is a play upon words. Thus in giving expression to life man creates a second, poetic world alongside the world of nature.

Or take myth. This, too, is a transformation or an "imagination" of the outer world, only here the process is more elaborate and ornate than is the case with individual words. In myth, primitive man seeks to account for the world of phenomena by grounding it in the Divine. In all the wild imaginings of mythology a fanciful spirit is playing on the borderline between jest and earnest. Or finally, let us take ritual. Primitive society performs its sacred rites, its sacrifices, consecrations, and mysteries, all of which serve to guarantee the well-being of the world, in a spirit of pure play truly understood.

Now in myth and ritual the great instinctive forces of civilized life have their origin: law and order, commerce and profit, craft and art, poetry, wisdom and science. All are rooted in the primeval soil of play.

The object of the present essay is to demonstrate that it is more than a rhetorical comparison to view culture *sub specie ludi*. The thought is not at all new. There was a time when it was generally accepted, though in a limited sense quite different from the one intended here: in the seventeenth century, the age of world theatre. Drama, in a glittering succession of figures ranging from Shakespeare and Calderón to Racine, then dominated the literature of the West. It was the fashion to liken the world to a stage on which every man plays his part. Does this mean that the play-element in civilization was openly acknowledged? Not at all. On closer examination this fashionable comparison of life to a stage proves to be little more than an echo of the Neo-platonism that was then in vogue, with a markedly moralistic accent. It was a variation on the ancient theme of the vanity of all things. The fact that play and culture are actually interwoven with one another was neither observed nor expressed, whereas for us the whole point is to show that genuine, pure play is one of the main bases of civilization.

NOTES

1 For these theories, see H. Zondervan, *Het Spel bij Dieren, Kindern, en Volwassen Menschen* (Amsterdam, 1928), and F. J. J. Buytendijk, *Het Spel van Mensch en Diet als openbaring van levensdriften* (Amsterdam, 1932).
2 Nature, kind, being, essence, etc. Trans.

READER CROSS-REFERENCES

Schechner, Kirshenblatt-Gimblett – the inclusion of play in performance studies
Bateson – the importance of play in communication and thought
Sutton-Smith – play as a concept in philosophy, science, and other disciplines
Taylor – the translatability of technical terms

18

A THEORY OF PLAY AND FANTASY

Gregory Bateson

This research was planned and started with an hypothesis to guide our investigations, the task of the investigators being to collect relevant observational data and, in the process, to amplify and modify the hypothesis.

The hypothesis will here be described as it has grown in our thinking.

Earlier fundamental work of Whitehead, Russell,[1] Wittgenstein,[2] Carnap,[3] Whorf,[4] etc., as well as my own attempt[5] to use this earlier thinking as an epistemological base for psychiatric theory, led to a series of generalizations:

(1) That human verbal communication can operate and always does operate at many contrasting levels of abstraction. These range in two directions from the seemingly simple denotative level ("The cat is on the mat"). One range or set of these more abstract levels includes those explicit or implicit messages where the subject of discourse is the language. We will call these metalinguistic (for example, "the verbal sound 'cat' stands for any member of such and such class of objects," or "The word 'cat' has no fur and cannot scratch"). The other set of levels of abstraction we will call metacommunicative (e.g. "My telling you where to find the cat was friendly," or "This is play"). In these, the subject of discourse is the relationship between the speakers.

It will be noted that the vast majority of both metalinguistic and metacommunicative messages remain implicit; and also that, especially in the psychiatric interview, there occurs a further class of implicit messages about how metacommunicative messages of friendship and hostility are to be interpreted.

(2) If we speculate about the evolution of communication, it is evident that a very important stage in this evolution occurs when the organism gradually ceases to respond quite "automatically" to the mood-signs of another and becomes able to recognize the sign as a signal: that is, to recognize that the other individual's and its own signals are only signals which can be trusted, distrusted, falsified, denied, amplified, corrected, and so forth.

Clearly this realization that signals are signals is by no means complete even among the human species. We all too often respond automatically to newspaper headlines as though these stimuli were direct object-indications of events in our environment instead of signals concocted and transmitted by creatures as complexly motivated as ourselves. The nonhuman mammal is automatically excited by the sexual odor of another; and rightly so, inasmuch as the secretion of that sign is an "involuntary" mood-sign; i.e. an outwardly

141

perceptible event which is a part of the physiological process which we have called a mood. In the human species a more complex state of affairs begins to be the rule. Deodorants mask the involuntary olfactory signs, and in their place the cosmetic industry provides the individual with perfumes which are not involuntary signs but voluntary signals, recognizable as such. Many a man has been thrown off balance by a whiff of perfume, and if we are to believe the advertisers it seems that these signals, voluntarily worn, have sometimes an automatic and autosuggestive effect even upon the voluntary wearer.

Be that as it may, this brief digression will serve to illustrate a stage of evolution – the drama precipitated when organisms, having eaten of the fruit of the Tree of Knowledge, discover that their signals are signals. Not only the characteristically human invention of language can then follow, but also all the complexities of empathy identification, projection, and so on. And with these comes the possibility of communicating at the multiplicity of levels of abstraction mentioned above.

(3) The first definite step in the formulation of the hypothesis guiding this research occurred in January, 1952, when I was in the Fleishhacker Zoo in San Francisco to look for behavioral criteria which would indicate whether any given organism is or is not able to recognize that the signs emitted by itself and other members of the species are signals. In theory, I had thought out what such criteria might look like – that the occurrence of metacommunicative signs (or signals) in the stream of interaction between the animals would indicate that the animals have at least some awareness (conscious or unconscious) that the signs about which they metacommunicate are signals.

I knew, of course, that there was no likelihood of finding denotative messages among nonhuman mammals, but I was still not aware that the animal data would require an almost total revision of my thinking. What I encountered at the zoo was a phenomenon well known to everybody: I saw two young monkeys *playing*, i.e. engaged in an interactive sequence of which the unit action or signals were similar to but not the same as those of combat. It was evident, even to the human observer, that the sequence as a whole was not combat, and evident to the human observer that to the participant monkeys this was "not combat."

Now, this phenomenon, play, could only occur if the participant organisms were capable of some degree of metacommunication, i.e. of exchanging signals which would carry the message "this is play."

(4) The next step was the examination of the message "This is play," and the realization that this message contains those elements which necessarily generate a paradox of the Russellian or Epimenides type – a negative statement containing an implicit negative metastatement. Expanded, the statement "This is play" looks something like this: "These actions in which we now engage do not denote what those actions *for which they stand* would denote."

We now ask about the italicized words, "*for which they stand*." We say the word "cat" stands for any member of a certain class. That is, the phrase "stands for" is a near synonym of "denotes." If we now substitute "which they denote" for the words "for which they stand" in the expanded definition of play, the result is: "These actions, in which we now engage, do not denote what would be denoted by those actions which these actions denote." The playful nip denotes the bite, but it does not denote what would be denoted by the bite.

According to the Theory of Logical Types such a message is of course inadmissable, because the word "denote" is being used in two degrees of abstraction, and these two uses are treated as synonymous. But all that we learn from such a criticism is that it would be bad natural history to expect the mental processes and communicative habits of mammals to conform to the logician's ideal. Indeed, if human thought and communication always conformed to the ideal, Russell would not – in fact could not – have formulated the ideal.

(5) A related problem in the evolution of communciation concerns the origin of what Korzybski[6] has called the map–territory relationship: the fact that a message, of whatever kind, does not consist of those objects which it denotes ("The word 'cat' cannot scratch us"). Rather, language bears to the objects which it denotes a relationship comparable to that which a map bears to a territory. Denotative communication as it occurs at the human level is only possible *after* the evolution of a complex set of metalinguistic (but not verbalized)[7] rules which govern how words and sentences shall be related to objects and events. It is therefore appropriate to look for the evolution of such metalinguistic and/or metacommunicative rules at a prehuman and preverbal level.

It appears from what is said above that play is a phenomenon in which the actions of "play" are related to, or denote, other actions of "not play." We therefore meet in play with an instance of signals standing for other events, and it appears, therefore, that the evolution of play may have been an important step in the evolution of communication.

(6) *Threat* is another phenomenon which resembles play in that actions denote, but are different from, other actions. The clenched fist of threat is different from the punch, but it refers to a possible future (but at present nonexistent) punch. And threat also is commonly recognizable among nonhuman mammals. Indeed it has lately been argued that a great part of what appears to be combat among members of a single species is rather to be regarded as threat (Tinbergen,[8] Lorenz[9]).

(7) Histrionic behavior and deceit are other examples of the primitive occurrence of map–territory differentiation. And there is evidence that dramatization occurs among birds: a jackdaw may imitate her own mood-signs (Lorenz[10]), and deceit has been observed among howler monkeys (Carpenter[11]).

(8) We might expect threat, play, and histrionics to be three independent phenomena all contributing to the evolution of the discrimination between map and territory. But it seems that this would be wrong, at least so far as mammalian communication is concerned. Very brief analysis of childhood behavior shows that such combination as histrionic play, bluff, playful threat, teasing play in response to threat, histrionic threat, and so on form together a single total complex of phenomena. And such adult phenomena as gambling and playing with risk have their roots in the combination of threat and play. It is evident also that not only threat but the reciprocal of threat – the behavior of the threatened individual – is a part of this complex. It is probable that not only histrionics but also spectatorship should be included within this field. It is also appropriate to mention self-pity.

(9) A further extension of this thinking leads us to include ritual within this general field in which the discrimination is drawn, but not completely, between denotative action and that which is to be denoted. Anthropological studies of peace-making ceremonies, to cite only one example, support this conclusion.

In the Andaman Islands, peace is concluded after each side has been given ceremonial freedom to strike the other. This example, however, also illustrates the labile nature of the frame "This is play," or "This is ritual." The discrimination between map and territory is always liable to break down, and the ritual blows of peace-making are always liable to be mistaken for the "real" blows of combat. In this event, the peace-making ceremony becomes a battle (Radcliffe-Brown[12]).

(10) But this leads us to recognition of a more complex form of play; the game which is constructed not upon the premise "This is play" but rather around the question "Is this play?" And this type of interaction also has its ritual forms, e.g. in the hazing of initiation.

(11) Paradox is doubly present in the signals which are exchanged within the context of play, fantasy, threat, etc. Not only does the playful nip not denote what would be denoted by the bite for which it stands, but, in addition, the bite itself is fictional. Not only do the playing animals not quite mean what they are saying but, also, they are usually communicating about something which does not exist. At the human level, this leads to a vast variety of complications and inversions in the fields of play, fantasy, and art. Conjurers and painters of the *trompe l'oeil* school concentrate upon acquiring a virtuosity whose only reward is reached after the viewer detects that he has been deceived and is forced to smile or marvel at the skill of the deceiver. Hollywood film-makers spend millions of dollars to increase the realism of a shadow. Other artists, perhaps more realistically, insist that art be nonrepresentational; and poker players achieve a strange addictive realism by equating the chips for which they play with dollars. They still insist, however, that the loser accept his loss as part of the game.

Finally, in the dim region where art, magic, and religion meet and overlap, human beings have evolved the "metaphor that is meant," the flag which men will die to save, and the sacrament that is felt to be more than "an outward and visible sign, given unto us." Here we can recognize an attempt to deny the difference between map and territory, and to get back to the absolute innocence of communication by means of pure mood-signs.

(12) We face then two peculiarities of play: (a) that the messages or signals exchanged in play are in a certain sense untrue or not meant; and (b) that that which is denoted by these signals is nonexistent. These two peculiarities sometimes combine strangely to a reverse a conclusion reached above. It was stated (4) that the playful nip denotes the bite, but does not denote that which would be denoted by the bite. But there are other instances where an opposite phenomenon occurs. A man experiences the full intensity of subjective terror when a spear is flung at him out of the 3D screen or when he falls headlong from some peak created in his own mind in the intensity of nightmare. At the moment of terror there was no questioning of "reality," but still there was no spear in the movie house and no cliff in the bedroom. The images did not denote that which they seemed to denote, but these same images did really evoke that terror which would have been evoked by a real spear or a real precipice. By a similar trick of self-contradiction, the film-makers of Hollywood are free to offer to a puritanical public a vast range of pseudosexual fantasy which otherwise would not be tolerated In *David and Bathsheba*, Bathsheba can be a Troilistic link between David and Uriah. And in *Hans Christian Andersen*, the hero starts out accompanied by a boy. He tries to get a woman, but when he is defeated in this attempt, he

returns to the boy. In all of this, there is, of course, no homosexuality, but the choice of these symbolisms is associated in these fantasies with certain characteristic ideas, e.g. about the hopelessness of the heterosexual masculine position when faced with certain sorts of women or with certain sorts of male authority. In sum, the pseudohomosexuality of the fantasy does not stand for any real homosexuality, but does stand for and express attitudes which might accompany a real homosexuality or feed its etiological roots. The symbols do not denote homosexuality, but do denote ideas for which homosexuality is an appropriate symbol. Evidently it is necessary to re-examine the precise semantic validity of the interpretations which the psychiatrist offers to a patient, and, as preliminary to this analysis, it will be necessary to examine the nature of the frame in which these interpretations are offered.

(13) What has previously been said about play can be used as an introductory example for the discussion of frames and contexts. In sum, it is our hypothesis that the message "This is play" establishes a paradoxical frame comparable to Epimenides' paradox. This frame may be diagramed thus:

> All statements within this
> frame are untrue.
>
> I love you.
>
> I hate you.

The first statement within this frame is a self-contradictory proposition about itself. If this first statement is true, then it must be false. If it be false, then it must be true. But this first statement carries with it all the other statements in the frame. So, if the first statement be true, then all the others must be false; and vice versa, if the first statement be untrue then all the others must be true.

(14) The logically minded will notice a *non-sequitur*. It could be urged that even if the first statement is false, there remains a logical possibility that some of the other statements in the frame are untrue. It is, however, a characteristic of unconscious or "primary-process" thinking that the thinker is unable to discriminate between "some" and "all," and unable to discriminate between "not all" and "none." It seems that the achievement of these discriminations is performed by higher or more conscious mental processes which serve in the nonpsychotic individual to correct the black-and-white thinking of the lower levels. We assume, and this seems to be an orthodox assumption, that primary process is continually operating, and that the psychological validity of the paradoxical play frame depends upon this part of the mind.

(15) But, conversely, while it is necessary to invoke the primary process as an explanatory principle in order to delete the notion of "some" from between "all" and "none," this does not mean that play is simply a primary-process phenomenon. The discrimination between "play" and "nonplay," like the discrimination between fantasy and nonfantasy, is certainly a function of secondary process, or "ego." Within the dream the dreamer is usually unaware that he is dreaming, and within "play" he must often be reminded that "This is play."

Similarly, within dream or fantasy the dreamer does not operate with the concept "untrue." He operates with all sorts of statements but with a curious inability to achieve metastatements. He cannot, unless close to waking, dream a statement referring to (i.e. framing) his dream.

It therefore follows that the play frame as here used as an explanatory principle implies a special combination of primary and secondary processes. This, however, is related to what was said earlier, when it was argued that play marks a step forward in the evolution of communication – the crucial step in the discovery of map–territory relations. In primary process, map and territory are equated; in secondary process, they can be discriminated. In play, they are both equated and discriminated.

(16) Another logical anomaly in this system must be mentioned: that the relationship between two propositions which is commonly described by the word "premise" has become intransitive. In general, all asymmetrical relationships are transitive. The relationship "greater than" is typical in this respect; it is conventional to argue that if A is greater than B, and B is greater than C, then A is greater than C. But in psychological processes the transitivity of asymmetrical relations is not observed. The proposition P may be a premise for Q; Q may be a premise for R; and R may be a premise for P. Specifically, in the system which we are considering, the circle is still more contracted. The message "All statements within this frame are untrue" is itself to be taken as a premise in evaluating its own truth or untruth. (Cf. the intransitivity of psychological preference discussed by McCulloch.[13] The paradigm for all paradoxes of this general type is Russell's[14] "class of classes which are not members of themselves." Here Russell demonstrates that paradox is generated by treating the relationship "is a member of" as an intransitive.) With this caveat, that the "premise" relation in psychology is likely to be intransitive, we shall use the word "premise" to denote a dependency of one idea or message upon another comparable to the dependency of one proposition upon another which is referred to in logic by saying that the proposition P is a premise for Q.

(17) All this, however, leaves unclear what is meant by "frame" and the related notion of "context." To clarify these, it is necessary to insist first that these are psychological concepts. We use two sorts of analogy to discuss these notions: the physical analogy of the picture frame and the more abstract, but still not psychological, analogy of the mathematical set. In set theory the mathematicians have developed axioms and theorems to discuss the rigor the logical implications of membership in overlapping categories or "sets." The relationships between sets are commonly illustrated by diagrams in which the items or members of a larger universe are represented by dots, and the smaller sets are delimited by imaginary lines enclosing the members of each set. Such diagrams then illustrate a topological approach to the logic of classification. The first step in defining a psychological frame might

be to say that it is (or delimits) a class or set of messages (or meaningful actions). The play of two individuals on a certain occasion would then be defined as the set of all messages exchanged by them within a limited period of time and modified by the paradoxical premise system which we have described. In a set-theoretical diagram these messages might be represented by dots, and the "set" enclosed by a line which would separate these from other dots representing nonplay messages. The mathematical analogy breaks down, however, because the psychological frame is not satisfactorily represented by an imaginary line. We assume that the psychological frame has some degree of real existence. In many instances, the frame is consciously recognized and even represented in vocabulary ("play," "movie," "interview," "job," "language," etc.). In other cases, there may be no explicit verbal reference to the frame, and the subject may have no consciousness of it. The analyst, however, finds that his own thinking is simplified if he uses the notion of an unconscious frame as an explanatory principle; usually he goes further than this and infers its existence in the subject's unconscious.

But while the whole analogy of the mathematical set is perhaps over-abstract, the analogy of the picture frame is excessively concrete. The psychological concept which we are trying to define is neither physical nor logical. Rather, the actual physical frame is, we believe, added by human beings to physical pictures because these human beings operate more easily in a universe in which some of their psychological characteristics are externalized. It is these characteristics which we are trying to discuss, using the externalization of an illustrative device.

(18) The common functions and uses of psychological frames may now be listed and illustrated by reference to the analogies whose limitations have been indicated in the previous paragraph:

(a) Psychological frames are exclusive, i.e. by including certain messages (or meaningful actions) within a frame, certain other messages are excluded.

(b) Psychological frames are inclusive, i.e. by excluding certain messages certain others are included. From the point of view of set theory these two functions are synonymous, but from the point of view of psychology it is necessary to list them separately. The frame around a picture, if we consider this frame as a message intended to order or organize the perception of the view, says, "Attend to what is within and do not attend to what is outside." Figure and ground, as these terms are used by gestalt psychologists, are not symmetrically related as are the set and nonset of set theory. Perception of the ground must be positively inhibited and perception of the figure (in this case the picture) must be positively enhanced.

(c) Psychological frames are related to what we have called "premises." The picture frame tells the viewer that he is not to use the same sort of thinking in interpreting the picture that he might use in interpreting the wallpaper outside the frame. Or, in terms of the analogy from set theory, the messages enclosed within the imaginary line are defined as members of a class by virtue of their sharing common premises or mutual relevance. The frame itself thus becomes a part of the premise system. Either, as in the case of the play frame, the frame is involved in the evaluation of the messages which it contains, or the frame merely assists the mind in understanding the contained messages by reminding the thinker that these messages are mutually relevant and the messages outside the frame may be ignored.

(d) In the sense of the previous paragraph, a frame is metacommunicative. Any message which either explicitly or implicitly defines a frame *ipso facto* gives the receiver instructions or aids in his attempt to understand the messages included within the frame.

(e) The converse of (d) is also true. Every metacommunicative or metalinguistic message defines, either explicitly or implicitly, the set of messages about which it communicates, i.e. every metacommunicative message is or defines a psychological frame. This, for example, is very evident in regard to such small metacommunicative signals as punctuation marks in a printed message, but applies equally to such complex metacommunicative messages as the psychiatrist's definition of his own curative role, in terms of which his contributions to the whole mass of messages in psychotherapy are to be understood.

(f) The relation between psychological frame and perceptual gestalt needs to be considered, and here the analogy of the picture frame is useful. In a painting by Rouault or Blake, the human figures and other objects represented are outlined. "Wise men see outlines and therefore they draw them." But outside these lines, which delimit the perceptual gestalt or "figure," there is a background or "ground" which in turn is limited by the picture frame. Similarly, in set-theoretical diagrams, the larger universe within which the smaller sets are drawn is itself enclosed in a frame. This double framing is, we believe, not merely a matter of "frames within frames" but an indication that mental processes resemble logic in *needing* an outer frame to delimit the ground against which the figures are to be perceived. This need is often unsatisfied, as when we see a piece of sculpture in a junk shop window, but this is uncomfortable. We suggest that the need for this outer limit to the ground is related to preference for avoiding the paradoxes of abstraction. When a logical class or set of items is defined — for example, the class of matchboxes — it is necessary to delimit the set of items which are to be excluded, in this case, all those things which are not matchboxes. But the items to be included in the background set must be of the same degree of abstraction, i.e. of the same "logical type" as those within the set itself. Specifically, if paradox is to be avoided, the "class of matchboxes" and the "class of nonmatchboxes" (even though both these items are clearly not matchboxes) must not be regarded as members of the class of nonmatchboxes. No class can be a member of itself. The picture frame, then, because it delimits a background, is here regarded as an external representation of a very special and important type of psychological frame — namely a frame whose function is to delimit a logical type. This, in fact, is what was indicated above when it was said that the picture frame is an instruction to the viewer that he should not extend the premises which obtain between the figures within the picture to the wallpaper behind it.

But it is precisely this sort of frame that precipitates paradox. The rule for avoiding paradoxes insists that the items outside any enclosing line be of the same logical type as those within, but the picture frame, as analyzed above, is a line dividing items of one logical type from those of another. In passing, it is interesting to note that Russell's rule cannot be stated without breaking the rule. Russell insists that all items of inappropriate logical type be exluded (i.e. by an imaginary line) from the background of any class, i.e. he insists upon the drawing of an imaginary line of precisely the sort which he prohibits.

(19) This whole matter of frames and paradoxes may be illustrated in terms of animal behavior, where three types of message may be recognized or deduced: (a) Messages of the sort which we here call mood-signs; (b) messages which simulate mood-signs (in play, threat, histrionics, etc.); and (c) messages which enable the receiver to discriminate between mood-signs and those other signs which resemble them. The message "This is play" is of this third type. It tells the receiver that certain nips and other meaningful actions are not messages of the first type.

The message "This is play" thus sets a frame of the sort which is likely to precipitate paradox: it is an attempt to discriminate between, or to draw a line between, categories of different logical types.

(20) This discussion of play and psychological frames establishes a type of triadic constellation (or system of relationships) between messages. One instance of this constellation is analyzed in paragraph 19, but it is evident that constellations of this sort occur not only at the nonhuman level but also in the much more complex communication of human beings. A fantasy or myth may simulate a denotative narrative, and, to discriminate between these types of discourse, people use messages of the frame-setting type, and so on.

(21) In conclusion, we arrive at the complex task of applying this theoretical approach to the particular phenomena of psychotherapy. Here the lines of our thinking may most briefly be summarized by presenting and partially answering these questions:

(a) Is there any indication that certain forms of psychopathology are specifically characterized by abnormalities in the patient's handling of frames and paradoxes?

(b) Is there any indication that the techniques of psychotherapy necessarily depend upon the manipulation of frames and paradoxes?

(c) Is it possible to describe the process of a given psychotherapy in terms of the interaction between the patient's abnormal use of frames and the therapist's manipulation of them?

(22) In reply to the first question, it seems that the "word salad" of schizophrenia can be described in terms of the patient's failure to recognize the metaphoric nature of his fantasies. In what should be triadic constellations of messages, the frame-setting message (e.g. the phrase "as if") is omitted, and the metaphor or fantasy is narrated and acted upon in a manner which would be appropriate if the fantasy were a message of the more direct kind. The absence of metacommunicative framing which was noted in the case of dreams (15) is characteristic of the waking communications of the schizophrenic. With the loss of the ability to achieve the more primary or primitive message. The metaphor is treated directly as a message of the more primary type. [. . .]

(23) The dependence of psychotherapy upon the manipulation of frames follows from the fact that therapy is an attempt to change the patient's metacommunicative habits. Before therapy, the patient thinks and operates in terms of a certain set of rules for the making and

understanding of messages. After successful therapy, he operates in terms of a different set of such rules. (Rules of this sort are in general unverbalized, and unconscious both before and after.) It follows that, in the process of therapy, there must have been communication at a level *meta* to these rules. There must have been communication about a *change* in rules.

But such a communication about change could not conceivably occur in messages of the type permitted by the patient's metacommunicative rules as they existed either before or after therapy.

It was suggested above that the paradoxes of play are characteristic of an evolutionary step. Here we suggest that similar paradoxes are a necessary ingredient in that process of change which we call psychotherapy.

The resemblance between the process of therapy and the phenomenon of play is, in fact, profound. Both occur within a delimited psychological frame, a spatial and temporal bounding of a set of interactive messages. In both play and therapy, the messages have a special and peculiar relationship to a more concrete or basic reality. Just as the pseudo-combat of play is not real combat, so also the pseudolove and pseudohate of therapy are not real love and hate. The "transfer" is discriminated from real love and hate by signals invoking the psychological frame; and indeed it is this frame which permits the transfer to reach its full intensity and to be discussed between patient and therapist.

The formal characteristics of the therapeutic process may be illustrated by building up a model in stages. Imagine, first, two players who engage in a game of canasta according to a standard set of rules. So long as these rules govern and are unquestioned by both players, the game is unchanging, i.e. no therapeutic change will occur. (Indeed many attempts at psychotherapy fail for this reason.) We may imagine, however, that at a certain moment the two canasta players cease to play canasta and start a discussion of the rules. Their discourse is now of a different logical type from that of their play. At the end of this discussion, we can imagine that they return to playing but with modified rules.

This sequence of events is, however, still an imperfect model of therapeutic interaction, though it illustrates our contention that therapy necessarily involves a combination of discrepant logical types of discourse. Our imaginary players avoided paradox by separating their discussion of the rules from their play, and it is precisely this separation that is impossible in psychotherapy. As we see it, the process of psychotherapy is a framed interaction between two persons, in which the rules are implicit but subject to change. Such change can only be proposed by experimental action, but every such experimental action, in which a proposal to change the rules is implicit, is itself a part of the ongoing game. It is this combination of logical types within the single meaningful act that gives to therapy the character not of a rigid game like canasta but, instead, of an evolving system of interaction. The play of kittens or otters has this character.

(24) In regard to the specific relationship between the way in which the patient handles frames and the way in which the therapist manipulates them, very little can at present be said. It is, however, suggestive to observe that the psychological frame of therapy is an analogue of the frame-setting message which the schizophrenic is unable to achieve. To talk in "word salad" within the psychological frame of therapy is, in a sense, not pathological. Indeed the neurotic is specifically encouraged to do precisely this, narrating his dreams and

free associations so that patient and therapist may achieve an understanding of this material. By the process of interpretation, the neurotic is driven to insert an "as if" clause into the productions of his primary process thinking, which productions he had previously deprecated or repressed. He must learn that fantasy contains truth.

For the schizophrenic the problem is somewhat different. His error is in treating the metaphors of primary process with the full intensity of literal truth. Through the discovery of what these metaphors stand for he must discover that they are only metaphors.

(25) From the point of view of the project, however, psychotherapy constitutes only one of the many fields which we are attempting to investigate. Our central thesis may be summed up as a statement of the necessity of paradoxes of abstraction. It is not merely bad natural history to suggest that people might or should obey the Theory of Logical Types in their communications; their failure to do this is not due to mere carelessness or ignorance. Rather, we believe that the paradoxes of abstraction must make their appearance in all communication more complex than that of mood-signals, and that without these paradoxes the evolution of communication would be at an end. Life would then be an endless interchange of stylized messages, a game with rigid rules, unrelieved by change or humor.

NOTES

1 A.N. Whitehead and B. Russell, *Principia Mathematica*, 3 vols., 2nd edn., Cambridge: Cambridge University Press, 1910–13.
2 L. Wittgenstein, *Tractatus Logico-Philosophicus*, London: Harcourt Brace, 1922.
3 R. Carnap, *The Logical Syntax of Language*, New York: Harcourt Brace, 1937.
4 B.L. Whorf, "Science and linguistics," *Technology Review*, 1940, 44: 229–48.
5 J. Ruesch and G. Bateson, *Communication: The Social Matrix of Psychiatry*, New York: Norton, 1951.
6 A. Korzybski, *Science and Sanity*, New York: Science Press, 1941.
7 The verbalization of these metalinguistic rules is a much later achievement which can only occur after the evolution of a nonverbalized meta-metalinguistics.
8 N. Tinbergen, *Social Behavior in Animals with Special Reference to Vertebrates*, London: Methuen, 1953.
9 K.Z. Lorenz, *King Solomon's Ring*, New York: Crowell, 1952.
10 Ibid.
11 C.R. Carpenter, "A field study of the behavior and social relations of howling monkeys," *Comparative Psychological Monographs*, 1934, 10: 1–168.
12 A.R. Radcliffe-Brown, *The Andaman Islanders*, Cambridge: Cambridge University Press, 1922.
13 W.S. McCulloch, "A heterarchy of values, etc.," *Bulletin of Mathematical Biophysics*, 1945, 7: 89–93.
14 Whitehead and Russell, op. cit.

READER CROSS-REFERENCES

Huizinga – the significance of play in human culture
Sutton-Smith – play as a concept in philosophy, science, and other disciplines
Austin, Derrida – repetition and metacommunication in speech
Harding, De Marinis, Turner and Turner – how performance may be framed
Blair – uses cognitive approach to analyze the process of acting
Ancelet – threat in a context of play

19

THE AMBIGUITY OF PLAY
Rhetorics of fate

Brian Sutton-Smith

Vicissitudes of fortune, which spares neither man nor the proudest of his works, which buries empires and cities in a common grave.

Edward Gibbon

Children are a lottery in the modern concept of progress.

after Frech

The ancient rhetorics of play, fate, power, identity, and frivolity are so called because they are of more ancient origin than the modern rhetorics, progress, the imaginary, and the self. The latter three can be traced to major historical concepts of the past two hundred years, those being the Enlightenment, romanticism, and individualism, while the ancient rhetorics have antecedents throughout history. But there are additional differences as well. The ancient rhetorics tend to be about groups rather than individuals. And in general, those who believe in one or more of the modern rhetorics of play tend to discount the ancient rhetorics as play forms. In part this is because the older rhetorics are less socialized, more crude, and less in synchrony with modern rational life, though this is somewhat more true of fate and frivolity than of power and identity. Nevertheless the violence of the power rhetorics and the carnivalesque quality of the rhetorics of identity are also often seen as beyond the pale of civilized credibility, as are the excesses of gambling and the travesties of folly. Additionally, these older forms of play are typically more obligatory than they are optional. They therefore offend the modern sensibility that play must be associated with voluntariness. The ancient rhetorics have more extrinsic motivation about them and imply that play can be coercive. The modern rhetorics state, contrarily, that play is an exercise of freedom. But to admit that play can be coercive is to deprive "freedom" of its legitimacy as a universal definition, so many moderns would prefer the alternative of denying that gambling and football and carnival are really play at all; they can be called addiction, violence, and orgy instead. There is also a deep reluctance to associate children with any of these ancient rhetorics. The point of view taken in this work, however, is that all of the rhetorics, whether modern or ancient, are based on or are simulacra of play forms, and all should be taken into account in any truly empirical examination of the character and functioning of play.

The first rhetoric of the ancient group, the rhetoric of fate, is the most pervasive of all play rhetorics but the least publicly ideologized in modern times. It is at the heart of the most ancient of religions (animism and mysticism) and is at the deepest level of even modern minds, because life and death are, after all, fateful, not rational and not escapable. This chapter deals with various forms of fate as play, such as the attributions that the gods are at play, that the universe is at play, that our brains are at play, and finally that we are creatures of the play of fortune and luck, as exemplified by games of chance. There is a sense in which the irrevocability of fate leaves no answers except the most desperate and universal of human answers, which is that one might perhaps escape by luck or its personified equivalent, God's favor. Luck is very much fate's last hope. It is the play of the last chance. It is the play of everyman. Though pitiful, it is the only recourse in the mortal situation, unless of course we really do rise by works rather than by grace. From a secular point of view, then, to be mortal is ultimately to be without hope, but in the game model of this predicament, there is a slight lottery like hope. The odds, though long, might occasionally be with us in the more confined worldly domain of chance. In this sense it is useful to think of games of chance not only as models of the irrevocability of fate but also as fate fantasied (though in Florida, as they say, the probability of winning the state lottery is the same as the chance of being hit by lightning three times – but then, as they also say, there is a lot of lightning in Florida).

Perhaps it can be said that the ones who lose at games of chance are at least playfully in control of the circumstances of their own losing. This is the definition of play – the illusion of mastery over life's circumstances – once offered by the great scholar of child play Erik Erikson. In his words, the purpose of play is "to hallucinate ego mastery" (1956: 185). If such "illusory mastery" is indeed the spirit or motivation behind adults' play in games of chance, as it is an account of children's play, then it is surely a definition of play that escapes the limitations of the progress rhetoric. Play as an irrational act of gaining pleasure through one's own illusions is hardly consistent with the rationality of the rhetoric of progress. Of course if children and gamblers were put in a separate category of existence, then progressivists would not regard this reference to "illusion" as the ultimate definition of play. The discontinuity between adult and child play would be a discontinuity between rational adults and the collective group of irrational gamblers and nonrational children. Given the laws and prohibitions against gamblers and children throughout Western history, this negative collective category of children and gambling adults has actually existed, even though the groups are seldom theoretically linked in the present mordant way.

But calling the masteries of play in childhood or adulthood forms of hallucination or illusion is itself an epistemological discourse that implies something defective about them. This discourse implies that those who master their lives in more realistic ways are more mature or more adequate persons, and this may or may not be empirically true. Given that there is nothing more characteristic of human achievement than the creation of illusory cultural and theorctical worlds, as in music, dance, literature, and science, then children's and gamblers' full participation in such play worlds can be seen not as a defect, or as compensation for inadequacy, but rather as participation in a major central preoccupation of humankind. The modern computer-age habit of calling these "virtual worlds" rather than illusory worlds highlights this move toward a more positive, if narrower, epistemological attitude about their function. As we now see the creation of human meanings as central to human culture, we can give more primary appreciation to these manifestations in our artists, our children, and our gamblers (Hymes 1974). We might borrow from Steiner the view that the issue is no longer whether there is superior reality versus inferior play, but whether the play is itself merely ordinary or a case of "brilliant virtuality" (1995). The rhetoric of fate is a real threat to the rhetoric of progress, because the concept of virtuality promises to put adults and children in the same Indic world.

The play of the gods

I move now to an array of examples in which play exemplifies not our own autonomy but our being controlled by some fate. The concept that play originates in the activities of the gods is well illustrated by O'Flaherty, who says, in her book *Dreams, Illusions and Other Realities* (1984), "This is a book about myths, dreams and illusion. It is about the ways in which they are alike, the ways in which they are different, and what each teaches us about reality. Transformations of one sort or another are the heart of myths" (3). She goes on to show how, in Hindu mythology, the world is at play in the hands of the gods, and dreaming and playfulness are forms of reality treated as seriously as the so-called commonsense world. Play, like dreams, is not a secondary state of reality, as it is with us, but has primacy as a form of knowing. O'Flaherty says: "In India the realm of mental images is not on the defensive. Common sense has a powerful lobby there, as it has with us, but it does not always have everything its own way. Reality has to share the burden of proof with unreality in India, and it is by no means a foregone conclusion that reality will win" (304).

Handelman (1992) brings these ideas to bear on the issue of play when he says:

> In Indian cosmology, play is a top down idea. Passages to play and their premises are embedded at a high level of abstraction and generality. The qualities of play resonate and resound throughout the whole. But more than this, qualities of play are integral to the very operation of the cosmos. To be in play is to reproduce time and again the very premises that inform the existence of this kind of cosmos . . . Now in cosmologies where premises of play are not embedded at a high level and are not integral to the organization of the cosmos, as in Western society, the phenomenon of play seems to erupt from the bottom. By bottom up play I mean that play often is phrased in opposition to, or as a negation of, the order of things. This is the perception of play as unserious, illusory and ephemeral, but it is also the perception of play as subversive and resisting the order of things.
>
> (12)

Schechner (1988), beginning with the same Hindu materials as O'Flaherty and extrapolating probably from his own iconoclastic career in theater direction, suggests that if we look more closely at Western play, particularly what he calls "dark play" and what I have called elsewhere "cruel play" (Sutton-Smith 1982) and the "masks of play" (Sutton-Smith and Kelly-Byrne 1984), there are some strong similarities with the Indian tradition. He agrees that for moderns play has low status, whereas in Hindu metaphysics it is indeed the divine process of creation; and whereas for moderns play is framed as not real, for Hindus it is one of multiple realities, all transformable into each other. However, when he shifts this discourse from a concern with metaphysical and cultural forms to the more ontological or psychological plane, then it is possible to see modern parallels between our own play behavior, particularly in what he calls our dark play, and that of the Hindus. Thus while Handelman might wish to deny it, Schechner contends that playing is for us, as for the Hindus,

> a creative destabilizing action that frequently does not declare its existence, even less its intentions. Playing is a mood, an attitude, a force. It erupts or one falls into it. It may persist for a long time as specific games, rites, and artistic performances do – or it comes and goes suddenly – a wisecrack, an ironic glimpse of things, a bend or crack in behavior. It's wrong to think of playing as the interruption of ordinary life. Consider instead playing as the underlying, always there, continuum of experience. Ordinary life is netted out of playing but play continually squeezes through even the smallest holes of the work net . . . work and other activities constantly feed on the underlying ground of playing, using the play mood for refreshment, energy, unusual ways of turning things around, insights, breaks, opening and especially looseness.
>
> (1988: 16–18)

Here we have Schechner borrowing from his readings in Hindu metaphysics an interpretation of play as a highly transforming and powerful, often irrational experience, which he apparently presumes to be universal. In this he goes beyond the typical Western tradition of play interpretation, although there are some scholars who are attempting to do similar things within Western theology. They believe that the Christian God can be seen as a creative player (Berger 1969; Miller 1969; Moltmann 1972; Nemoianu and Royal 1992). But on closer analysis they seem to be talking about a fairly rational creator, whereas Schechner, like Nietzsche, has a fairly irrational and secular player in mind. In sum, while in part accepting Handelman's dichotomy of up and down, Schechner injects into the bottom-up Western psychological play attitude a more comprehensive and heteronymous theory of play's role than Handelman's cultural bottom-up implies.

On Schechner's behalf it might be added that dreams, daydreams, and illusions could be included as a part of his bottom-up view in Western thought, particularly as this seems to be the case neurologically, as will be shown later. There is enough known about these oneiric phenomena to see that they have a kind of pervasiveness and automaticity of their own. They do seem to resist attempts to make the good things in life always a part of conscious control and choice. They constantly present us with other images of ourselves that seem to persist despite our desire to the contrary, so that even if we are usually reluctant to give dreams the ontological status of play, they do constantly permeate our thinking – and it is not certain that when this happens it is not itself a kind of play of mind. What makes interpretation more difficult is that what permeates minds day by day, "the underlying, always there, continuum of experience," is usually referred to as daydreaming, reverie, or rumination. Is play to be the name for all of these, as Schechner implies? Or is play to be only the more active next step that is taken willfully with these daydreams, to turn them into controlled fantasies or imaginings? There is truly a sense in which a mind plays its own recordings and has its own streams of consciousness, very little of which is actively under control. But human passivity in these respects contrasts with the active nature usually attributed to waking play and usually thought to be essential to most modern definitions of play. One can see how the passivity or receptivity of the Hindu in face of the metaphysical universe at play could mingle quite easily with the Hindu ontological sense of the individual mind at daydreaming play. Play could then be thought to be mainly a phenomenon to be experienced top down rather than actively manipulated bottom up. Typical Western definitions, by contrast, make the player a more entrepreneurial kind of being. And this allows Westerners to divide off the "daydream stuff" as a less credible part of the mind. But Schechner's alternative suggests that if the Western concept of play, no matter how controlling, does rest on a bedrock of dreams, that would be a much more comprehensive bottom-up idea than most modern play theorists have in mind. A further advantage of Schechner's broad view might be that it could help account for the way in which players quickly become highly absorbed in their own play. The message "this is play" lets go a flood of internally instigated emotion and involvement. The continuity between such impelling automata and the more behavioral matters of play might well account for the ever present and sudden surge of ready engagement in virtual play experience.

Without confusing Schechner's ontological usage with the Hindu metaphysical usage, it can be proposed that the breadth of play he suggests for these secular nonmythic times provides a *broad play* rhetoric. In what follows, the modern broad play rhetoric will be presented as one that encompasses all the mind materials of dreams, daydreams, tropes, and active play forms. Contrarily the *narrow play* rhetoric will speak for the more limited rhetorics of progress, power, identity, and the self . . . . Briefly, these can be called the broad and narrow versions of play. In the broad version, everything is play that is clearly not of an immediate adaptive usefulness. In the narrow version, nothing is play unless contemporaneously so named. Most things, in this narrow version, are not play. Dreams are dreams, daydreams are daydreams, imagination is imagination (though it can become imaginative play), spectators are just spectators of someone else playing, and metaphors are simply figures of speech, unless we actually play with them. Children do many things that are not play, such as exploring, practicing, exercising, learning, imitating, problem solving, and all the art activities that are art, not play.

The universe at play

The broader definition, in which either the gods or our own brains influence us playfully beyond our control, has about it an externality not likely to be popular in modern everyday parlance. Of similar externality are those views of the universe that see it too as being at play. In the hard sciences the concept of play is constantly being applied as a metaphor or a metaphysic to handle the inconstancy, indeterminism, unpredictability, or chaos of basic physical processes throughout the universe. There is a daunting similarity between some of these views of the universe and some of the ways neurologists are beginning to talk about the brain. They are, universe and brain, both more or less beyond control, and all one can do is try to understand the rules by which they operate. Perhaps one of the fascinations of games of chance is that they mirror both physical nature and human nature more adequately than we want to believe.

I am grateful for Spariosu's assemblage of the play theories of the play-oriented Nobel Prize-winning physical scientists, and I quote here briefly from his extended accounts (1989). Jacques Monod contends that "life on earth is entirely a matter of chance . . . essentially unpredictable" (217). Eigen and Winkler state that "everything that happens in our world resembles a vast game in which nothing is determined in advance but the rules, and only the rules are open to objective understanding . . . chance and necessity underlie all events. The history of play goes back to the beginnings of time . . . chance and rules are the elements of play. Once begun by the elementary particles, atoms, molecules, play is carried on by our brain cells. Man did not invent play. But it is 'play and only play that makes man complete' " (224). Erwin Schrodinger goes considerably further when he sees science itself as belonging to the play sphere, not just driven by the logic of adaptation: "Play, art and science are the spheres of human activity where the action and aim are not rule determined by the aims imposed by the necessities of life" (275). For Schrodinger, science is a rhetorical product of its age no less than all the other ideological rhetorics of the particular time and place. Werner Heisenberg takes a similar position on the comparability of art (and play) and science as complementary modes of knowledge. The most playful of modern science philosophers, however, is Paul Feyerabend, who likens science to the play of infants with language: "It is a bricolage of experimentation . . . initial Playful activity is an essential prerequisite of the final act of understanding . . . new scientific practice needs time to develop its conceptual tools and its empirical data by playing with them, that is, by constantly repeating and combining them until they become common usage or reality" (295).

In his analysis Spariosu is able to show that even with this openness of science to the metaphor of play, the majority of the scientific philosophers are still dominated by a rational and progressive view of how science and art or play will proceed together. Like Kant and Schiller, they do not really allow for imagining as a subversive activity or allow themselves to be seriously attracted to an irrational view of the universe. Even Feyerabend, who comes closest to Nietzsche's view of the playful universe as a constant struggle between antagonistic powers, is still more moderate than Nietzsche. In his own pluralistic and idealistic notion of a post-scientific world, Feyerabend suggests there can be balance, with different subcultural powers observing a certain amount of fair play in relation to each other.

REFERENCES

Berger, P.L. (1969) *A Rumor of Angels: Modern Society and the Rediscovery of the Supernatural*, Garden City, NY: Doubleday, Anchor Books.

—— (1992) "Passages to play: paradox and process," *Play and Culture* 5, 1: 1–19.

Handelman, D. (1990) *Models and Mirrors: Toward an Anthropolgy of Public Events*, Cambridge: Cambridge University Press.

Hymes, F. (ed.) (1974) *Reinventing Anthropology*, New York: Vintage.

Miller, D.L. (1969) *Gods and Games*, New York: World.

Moltmann, J. (1972) *Theology of Play*, New York: Harper and Row.

Nemoianu, V. and R. Royal (1992) *Play, Literature and Religion*, Albany: State University of New York Press.

O'Flaherty, W.D. (1984) *Dreams, Illusions, and Other Realities*, Chicago: University of Chicago Press.

Schechner, R. (1988) "Playing," *Play and Culture* 1, 1: 3–27.

Spariosu, M. (1989) *Dionysus Reborn*, Ithaca: Cornell University Press.

Steiner, W. (1995) *The Scandal of Pleasure*, Chicago: University of Chicago Press.

Sutton-Smith, B. (1982) "Play theory and the cruel play of the nineteenth century," in *The World of Play*, ed. P.E. Manning, West Point, NY: Leisure Press.

Sutton-Smith, B. and D. Kelly-Byrne (1984) *The Masks of Play*, West Point, NY: Leisure Press.

READER CROSS-REFERENCES

Schechner—play as an element of the broad spectrum approach to performance studies

Jackson, McKenzie – disciplinary rhetorics

Geertz – has addressed play from an anthropological standpoint

Huzinga – the significance of play in human culture

Bateson – play in communication and thought processes

Derrida – uncertainty in philosophical and linguistic discourse

Zimmerman – the unexpected in the creative process

20

JUST DOING

Allan Kaprow

For years I've been trying to pick up my shadow on a sunny day, to put it in my pocket for a rainy day. I remember to do this now and then. It's been difficult. And to tell the truth, I've never succeeded. The shadow changes as I bend over, and I can't quite compress it to fit into my jeans.

(*All Mine*, 1987–)

*

On the same subject, I and a friend, the musician Jean-Charles Francois, did small events for each other in the 1980s to provide some diversion from our administrative duties at the University of California, San Diego. We did them together, usually just the two of us, sometimes with a few others. This one involved our going out to the hills east of the university campus. The idea was that one of us would follow the other without saying a word, only making sure to step constantly on the shadow of the other, no matter where he went.

In practice, since the leader would go over boulders, around cactus, and up and down ravines, the length and relative position of the shadow changed. Sometimes it was in front of him, if he was walking away from the sun. In that case, it was a bit tricky; the follower had to jump in front of the leader and walk backwards to keep the shadow in view, making quick changes as the leader swung around to different directions. According to plan, the leader had no obligation to the follower.

At certain moments, for example, when walking up a ravine, the shadow would be shortened by the angle of the ground. Then we would find ourselves nearly on top of one another, our shoes touching. When the follower lost contact with the shadow (as it frequently happened), he would loudly bang together two stones he carried in his hands – again, as per plan.

This single sound marked the moment when we exchanged positions: the follower became the leader. But of course, since contact was lost so often, and the distances kept changing, it all got pretty unclear as to who was what. Nevertheless, it was very formally executed.

(*Tail Wagging Dog*, 1985)

*

Ludwig Thurmer, Barbara Glas, Coryl Crane, and I were together in Berlin. Ludwig and Barbara had a new baby. We went for a walk to look for some new grass, since it was spring. Soon we found a perfect field of young shoots. Coryl and Barbara, carrying her baby, walked slowly into it, leaving clear footprints. Ludwig and I followed, placing our shoes exactly in the same depressions. But before each step, we reached behind us to lift up the flattened blades of grass, so that no marks were left. Afterwards, looking at the field, it was very odd; it seemed that we'd never been there.

(*Walking Light on the World*, 1982)

*

A few years ago, a group joined me for a workshop in experimental art. A large room was set aside for us. After the usual introductions (whose conventional form – "My name is . . ." – we soon saw as an "event"), we decided to play with the light switch. The idea was that anyone in the room could get up from where they were sitting and turn off the lights. How long it would take was unplanned. Then, anyone could turn it on. Then off. Then on, and so forth. Long periods of time followed. Although there were no guidelines about silence, no one spoke. You could hear people breathing. We peeked at one another, trying to anticipate who would make the next move. Sometimes we stared at someone, challenging them, to see who would wait the longest.

People got up and played with the switch, flicking the light, or archly changing it back and forth, as if to convey some message. Equally, there were 15 minutes or more of doing nothing. The only advice given in advance was that anyone could leave the room when they had to. The experiment would end when no one remained. After about two and a half hours I had to give a talk elsewhere. There were nine in the room when I left. I went to the airport after the lecture and never heard when the room became empty.

(*On/Off*, 1994)

*

The playground for experimental art is ordinary life. But playing in this ordinary world does not mean including even more features of the commonplace than we are already used to finding in exhibitions, concerts, poems, dances, films, and performances. Such appropriations are the traditional strategies that turn life into art. No matter how much life we confront in them, their standard contexts never allow us to forget art's higher station. In contrast, the experimental artist who plays with the commonplace does so in the very midst of crossing the street or tying a shoelace. There is no excerpting and reenacting them on a stage, no documenting them for a show. Art is thus easily forgotten. And that is the condition for experimentation: the art is the forgetting of art.

For John Cage, an experimental action in music was one whose outcome couldn't be known in advance (my paraphrase). Musical and nonmusical sound ("noise") were equally welcome, along with their unpredictable arrangements. But, for the most part, Cage's experimental music was still music, and took place in the concert situation. Art was automatically affirmed despite Cage's commitment to the stuff of life. But that was the 1950s and it was a big step into the vernacular.

Today, we may say that experimental art is that act or thought whose identity as art must always remain in doubt. Not only does this hold for anyone who plays with the "artist"; it holds especially for the "artist"! The experiment is not to possess a secret artistry in deep disguise; it is not knowing what to call it at any time! As soon – and it is usually very soon – as such acts and thoughts are associated with art and its discourses, it is time to move on to other possibilities of experimentation.

*

A woman agreed that she needed guidance. Her friends proposed to give it by moving her in the right directions. So she just stood and waited to be moved. Her friends had a discussion and decided on some right directions for her; that is, out the door, down the stairs, along a river . . . They moved her by pulling, shoving, dragging, and carrying her in the right directions. They set aside some days for this, as their decisions were quite serious. And, naturally, there were some disagreements. But the woman was patient and just waited until they agreed on what to do.

(*Help Is Always Welcome*, 1990)

*

In answer to my suggestion to Brian Dick – that he might like to do the stupidest thing he could think of, and then the smartest – he hung a roomful of big pickles from a ceiling, wrapping them with electric wire attached to the house current. When he turned on the switch, the pickles glowed and sent out blue sparks before burning out and smelling bad. Then, for his "smartest" thing, he repeated the whole procedure the next day.

(1990)

*

Play, of course, is at the heart of experimentation. Elsewhere, I've pointed out the crucial difference in the English language between playing and gaming (1993: 110–26). Gaming involves winning or losing a desired goal. Playing is open-ended and, potentially, everybody "wins." Playing has no stated purpose other than more playing. It is usually not serious in content or attitude, whereas gaming, which can also involve playing if it is subordinated to winning, is at heart competitive.

*

Experimentation also involves attention to the normally unnoticed. I scratch my ear when it itches. I notice the itch, notice my scratching, and notice when the itching stops, if it does. I attend to my raised arm and my fingers pulling at my ear (it's the left one), while discussing politics. But mostly, I scratch itches without noticing. I learned as a child not to scratch an itch in public, and now that I intentionally notice that I do so anyway, the whole action looms large. It's a little strange, and my conversation about politics loses interest as itching and scratching shine brighter. In other words, attention alters what is attended. Playing with everyday life often is just paying attention to what is conventionally hidden.

*

For example, we all know about those creeps who telephone someone and breathe a lot but don't say anything. Five friends and I decided to play with heavy breathing on the telephone.

161

We exchanged numbers and were free to call any of them at any time for the next three days. All we were to do was breathe heavily for as long as we wished, or until we were cut off. Sometimes a phone would just ring and ring. It was never clear if the person was out or was refusing to pick up the receiver. Sometimes we would reach an answering machine, and we had to decide if we wanted to breathe for the recording. It was the same uncertainty when we were at home: Was the phone ringing because it was an expected business call, or was it going to be heavy breathing? Would the phone ring in the middle of the night? How long could we keep from giggling?

Once, I reached the mother-in-law of one of the group. She listened to me breathing for a moment and screamed in Italian that I was a pervert and worse, before slamming down the receiver. The funny thing about this caper was that you couldn't tell from the breathing who was telephoning.

(*Touching Someone*, 1991)

*

If the analytically inclined still want to know why to play at everyday life, an answer might go like this: Experimental art is the only kind of art that Anglo-America can call its own. This American culture has long rejected the fine arts as irrelevant and devoid of honest labor. "Idle hands make devil's work." Experimental art, as described here, is the one kind of art that can affirm and deny art at the same time. It is the one kind of art that can claim as value no value! It is in agreement with American philistinism and its throwaway materialism – while it is free to enact a sort of "native" creativity in the play of ordinary life (c.f. John Dewey). The one caveat is that it must not be called art.

*

I woke up one day and had an idea. I would dig a bucket of dirt from the garden, and I'd put the bucket of dirt and a shovel in my truck. On some future day, I'd trade my dirt for someone else's dirt. A month went by and I didn't think about it. Usually, every week, I go on Wednesdays to sit at the Zen Center in San Diego. So, one Wednesday, I remembered the bucket of dirt. I asked Ben Thorsen, who lived there at the time, "Can I have a bucket of dirt? Don't worry, I'll give you a bucket of good garden dirt in return." I told him about the rich compost in the garden. He looked at me and started to laugh. "Sure, there's plenty of dirt." He pointed in all directions.

I went to get the bucket of dirt and shovel. When I came back Ben said, "I've got a better idea. Let's crawl under the Zen Center and get the dirt from just below the seat of our teacher [Charlotte Joko Beck]. That'll be heavy-duty Buddhist dirt!" I agreed it was a very good idea. We got a flashlight and squeezed our way under the floor of the house, dragging the bucket and shovel behind us. It was cramped, with maybe 15 inches of clearance, filthy dirty, cobwebs everywhere. But we couldn't determine the exact spot we were looking for. So Ben said he would go back out and would tap on the floor above; I could move over to where his taps were coming from, and tap back to him. That's what we did. At the right place under the floor, I scooped out a hole in the dreadful dirt that was only construction remnants. Replacing it with my garden dirt would be an improvement,

162

I thought uncharitably. In any case, the heavy-duty Buddhist vibes were the main consideration. So I wiggled out with the stuff and brushed off my clothes.

Ben was thoroughly amused by then and said, "What are you doing this for?" I said, "Oh, it's what I like to do. No big deal." He said, "Well, I guess it's no sillier than sitting on a cushion for hours doing nothing" (as we seem to do at the Center). We talked for some time about the meaning of life.

Some weeks passed, and I stopped at the local farm stand where I bought my fruit and vegetables. I asked the woman there, "Can I have a bucket of your dirt? I'll give you one in return." She stared at me. "You want a bucket of dirt? From here? Why?" She pointed to the barren clay of the roadside. She thought she hadn't heard me right. I said "It's heavy-duty Buddhist dirt," and I told her the story.

She was clearly impressed with the Buddhist part. "I thought you were an artist." I said to her yes and that this was what I did. "I thought you were a college professor." "Sure. I teach this sort of thing, trading dirt." "They pay you for it?" she asked me. Then she thought a moment. "But it's not serious; it's what my grandson does." She gestured toward the child playing on the floor with cornhusks. "What's serious?" I said to her.

So we had a long talk about the meaning of life while I dug a hole at the side of the road. As I was about to pour the Buddhist dirt into it, she tossed some dry seeds into the bucket. I said "What did you do that for?" "Why not? It can't hurt," she said.

(The dirt trading and the stories went on for three years. It had no real beginning or end. The stories began to add up to a very long story, and with each retelling they changed. When I stopped being interested in the process [it coincided with my wife and I having to move after our rental property was sold], I put the last bucket of dirt back into the garden.)

(*Trading Dirt*, 1982–5)

REFERENCE

Kaprow, Allan (1993) "The education of the un-artist," part 2, in *Essays on the Blurring of Art and Life*, Berkeley: University of California Press.

READER CROSS-REFERENCES

Goffman, Gabler – the blurring between art and life
Huizinga, Bateson, Sutton-Smith – academic discourses of play
Phelan, Faber, Grotowski, Brecht, Strasberg, Zimmerman – playing with the quotidian in the service of art

21

FALLING APART TO STAY TOGETHER
Deep play in the Grand Marais Mardi Gras

Barry Jean Ancelet

As a social game, Mardi Gras ultimately reaffirm the status quo, perhaps nudging it along conservatively toward change, instead of undermining it or threatening it with genuine chaos as Bakhtin has suggested (Ancelet 1993; Davis 1975: 97–123; Le Roy Ladurie 1979: 316; Lindahl 1996). The Cajun Country Mardi Gras in southern Louisiana has been shown to be a powerful definer of its *petit monde* by visiting and extracting a commitment from those who belong to the social hub of the region or neighborhood (Ancelet 1992; Lindahl 1996). In this article, I examine the dramatic play that underlies one particular Mardi Gras ritual, the one that takes place in Grand Marais, Louisiana. In addition to fulfilling the usual functions of the Louisiana country Mardi Gras, in visiting the neighborhood and extracting a show of social commitment in the form of a donation of gumbo ingredients or money, this community's version of the celebration includes an intense dramatic ritual that chronically and impulsively spills over into something like what Clifford Geertz has called "deep play" (1973). The result of this practice seems to be a reaffirmation of the tradition; it engages all players to reach an intensified level of commitment to the game itself by requiring them to cooperate in pulling it back from the brink of apparent disaster. In his study of Balinese cockfighting, Geertz pointed out that there were real issues and tensions driving the play associated with this social ritual. What on the surface appears to be a purely ludic affair can have serious undercurrents that reflect community realities and concerns. Yet outside observers with no attachment to the community have frequently mistaken the surface play at face value, describing various versions of the Mardi Gras as a colorful, chaotic frenzy (Ancelet 1989).

I have been interested in South Louisiana's Cajun Country Mardi Gras since 1977. I addressed the blurring of the participant and observer roles available to me during my first experience on the Mamou run that same year, in an American Folklore Society conference paper entitled "The Mamou Mardi Gras from behind the mask: problems of the ethnic folklorist working in his own community." Since then I have participated in various Mardi Gras runs on horseback, in a wagon, in a truck, and on foot. I have observed, photographed,

164

and reported on 24 different versions of the country Mardi Gras, some all white, some all black, some mixed; some all men, some all women, some mixed; some all adults, some all children, some mixed; some on horseback, some in wagons, some on four-wheelers, some on foot, most in some combination. With that possible variation in mind, generally, masked (or painted) and costumed revelers gather on a designated day before Ash Wednesday, the first day of the Lenten season, usually on Tuesday (Mardi Gras) but in some cases on Saturday (Samedi Gras) or Sunday (Dimanche Gras). They travel together through the countryside, usually circling the town, sometimes approaching the town from a designated gathering point out in the country, collecting the ingredients for a communal gumbo to be eaten at the end of the day. Specific elements, such as masking and costuming strategies, singing styles, and begging practices, change from place to place as towns and country settlements give shape to their own versions of the celebration.

In the two-day Grand Marais run, participants run on Saturday and Sunday. They disguise themselves with painted faces instead of masks. Participants and organizers explain that masks are prohibited in Jeff Davis Parish, but this may in fact have more to do with history and tradition than statutes.[1] They also identify themselves by wearing some sort of hat or cap, usually with a feather attached to it. Runners visit houses in the working-class neighborhoods of Jennings and visit farmsteads in the rural countryside north of town and west of Bayou Nezpiqué, an area known as Grand Marais. They also stop traffic on the road between houses. They approach houses and cars in positions of supplication, on their knees or crawling, with hats in hand to beg for any contribution, including money for their gumbo fund to help pay for the communal meal they will make available to all on Tuesday night. Black-faced *nègres* with braided burlap whips vigorously enforce the "law" of the undisguised *capitaine* (captain) during the mock trials and subsequent ritual floggings of designated participants – improvised for especially generous households or individual contributors. If the capitaine judges that enough money has been donated to the gumbo fund, he orders his group of *soldats* (soldiers), also called *sauvages* (Indians), to sit in a circle and sing the traditional questing and drinking song, which describes a bottle and glass of liquor that are slowly emptying in the depths of winter and must be refilled:

Mardi Gras, d'ayoù viens-tu?	Mardi Gras, where do you come from?
Tout alentour du fond d'hiver.	All around the depths of winter.
Mardi Gras, d'ayoù viens-tu?	Mardi Gras, where do you come from?
Tout alentour du fond d'hiver.	All around the depths of winter.
Je viens de l'Angleterre, o mon cher, o mon cher.	I come from England, oh my dear, oh my dear.
Je viens de l'Angleterre.	I come from England.
Tout alentour du fond d'hiver.	All around the depths of winter.
O Mardi Gras, quoi portes-tu?	Oh Mardi Gras, what do you bring?
Tout alentour du fond d'hiver.	All around the depths of winter.
O Mardi Gras, quoi portes-tu?	Oh Mardi Gras, what do you bring?
Tout alentour du fond d'hiver.	All around the depths of winter.
J'apporte la bouteille, o mon cher, o mon cher.	I bring the bottle, oh my dear, oh my dear.
Tout alentour du fond d'hiver.	All around the depths of winter.

O la bouteille est bue.	Oh the bottle is drunk.
Tout alentour du fond d'hiver.	All around the depths of winter.
O la bouteille est bue.	Oh the bottle is drunk.
Tout alentour du fond d'hiver.	All around the depths of winter.
Il reste que le plein verre, o mon cher,	Only the full glass remains, oh my dear,
o mon cher.	oh my dear.
Il reste que le plein verre.	Only the full glass remains.
Tout alentour du fond d'hiver.	All around the depths of winter.
O le plein verre est bu.	Oh the full glass is drunk.
Tout alentour du fond d'hiver.	All around the depths of winter.
O le plein verre est bu.	Oh the full glass is drunk.
Tout alentour du fond d'hiver.	All around the depths of winter.
Il reste que la rinçure, o mon cher,	Only the dregs remain, oh my dear,
o mon cher.	oh my dear.
Il reste que la rinçure.	Only the dregs remain.
Tout alentour du fond d'hiver.	All around the depths of winter.
O la rinçure est bue.	Oh the dregs are drunk.
Tout alentour du fond d'hiver.	All around the depths of winter.
O la rinçure est bue.	Oh the dregs are drunk.
Tout alentour du fond d'hiver.	All around the depths of winter.
O *ring* et *rang* et ma bouteille, et ma bouteille,	Oh ring and rang and my bottle, and my bottle,
O *ring* et *rang* et ma bouteille qui s'en va.	Oh ring and rang and my bottle is dwindling.
Les Acadiens sont pas si fous	The Acadians are not so foolish
De se laisset sans boire un coup.	As to leave each other without having a drink.
Toute chanson qui passe à fin	Every song that reaches an end
Méirite un petit coup à boire.	Is worth having a little drink.

Afterward, the capitaine and his assistant improvise charges against a few of the participants, accusing them of such trumped-up transgressions as not singing the song properly or approaching the house or donor inappropriately. The capitaine designates the "accused" by collecting their hats. There is a brief mock trial, based on circular logic that flees from the truth. The capitaine always wins, and the condemned are then ordered to lie face down in alternating directions. Invariably they add to the play, creating confusion by deliberately lining up wrong, that is, crossed or in the same direction. The nègres then whip the accused vigorously as they yell to each other to "get right." The guilty will sometimes turn several times at the same time to find themselves still wrong, as the nègres continue their whipping. Other soldats may crawl over the accused to ostensibly protect their "brothers" from the blows, which can be surprisingly earnest. This, however, can be a mixed blessing at best, as the accused are often lying face down on gravel or cement driveways. Eventually, the capitaine gets them right and gives them a preordained number of ritual taps, usually less severe than the lashings they have already received. The nègres are basically the capitaine's lieutenants. They carry out his orders without question. They can also be beaten by the capitaine or his assistant if they transgress one of the rules designed to define their performance. As lead beggars, they are to approach each house on their knees with hats in hand. And they are not to question the capitaine's choice of soldats to be whipped.

Beyond the already intense nature on the surface of this ritualistic play, there is an even deeper level of play (cf. Geertz 1973) in the Grand Marais Mardi Gras. This deep play is initiated by a crisis that apparently jeopardizes the celebration itself. These crises are then incorporated into the Mardi Gras, providing participants an opportunity to shift into another level of improvisation, a level that far surpasses the level of improvisation routinely performed for the homeowners as part of the "normal" Mardi Gras visit.

The first time I saw this deeper level of play emerge was in 1993 at the Tuesday evening gumbo supper and dance, during which participants have no painted faces and wear no costumes other than hats decorated with symbolic flowering branches, and whippers have what they call "dress whips," part of what Le Roy Ladurie describes as the third, "redressive" stage of carnival, representing the end of festivities and the beginning of reintegration into normal life (1979: 306). During that year's closing ceremony, at which were gathered all participants as well as members of the community who contributed to the Mardi Gras, someone proposed that Capitaine Wallace should be whipped for having lost the flag that served as his standard at one point during Sunday's run. At the mock trial that necessarily ensued, Capitaine Wallace and his lieutenants valiantly explained that Wallace had indeed been separated from his flag but that this was because it had been stolen by one of the soldats, that this was not his fault, and that the thief more properly should be whipped. The soldats countered with the undeniable point that the guilty one had been whipped plenty for his transgression during Sunday's run but that it remained true that the capitaine had lost the flag, betraying one of his primary responsibilities to clearly identify himself as the responsible party and negotiator to all the households that the Mardi Gras visited.

Up to this point, the improvised trials of the evening had resembled those performed for homeowners and donors throughout the countryside. In this instance, however, the accusation called the capitaine himself into question, and the trial headed into new and potentially dangerous territory. The outcome of the trial was determined as soon as the accusation was first brought up, an eventuality that the initial accusers may not have taken into consideration. After many convoluted arguments, Capitaine Wallace, in typical Mardi Gras fashion acting as both judge and accused, eventually announced that his condemnation was indeed justified. According to the rules of the game that they found themselves making up as they went along, the capitaine could choose to designate a lieutenant to receive his whipping in his place. Dallas, a formidable man and the run's most vigorous whipper, was understandably concerned that the soldats might try to take advantage of the situation by exacting a measure of revenge if he were chosen. Apparently unwilling to take the chance, Dallas left the circle of soldats, declaring that he would not participate in the whipping of the capitaine. At this point, the play shifted into a deeper mode. Dallas had broken the ritual circle and defied the game itself. After considerable protesting and confusion, the game went on without Dallas. Capitaine Wallace declared that he would accept his own flogging. Though well into his 70s, Capitaine Wallace remained both physically and mentally sturdy, an excellent horseman, a powerful man, and a born leader with a commanding presence that was never challenged. Yet, on this occasion, for the purposes of the game, he slipped into another of his personae, an apparently frail and fragile old man who regularly complained, especially in the weeks preceding each Mardi Gras, that his age and failing health made his continued participation in this rigorous ritual questionable. There was a clear sense of awe as the venerable capitaine handed over the banner to his assistant capitaine and went down onto the floor with much ado and dramatic difficulty. From his prone position, he put on quite a show in response to the symbolic taps given to him by the remaining lieutenants, quivering in mock pain though the whips were hitting much more floor than him.

Capitaine Wallace's improvisation was not without precedent. He explained later, in 1996, that there is an existing procedure for whipping the capitaine and the nègres:

Capitaine Wallace: Yeah, I'll have to do it. The others can't do it.

Barry Ancelet: That's to keep things in order?

CW: Yeah, if you didn't do that, you let the others do it, you know, it'd be too much of it. It don't work. So it's always been the way it was done. If the nègres have got to be whipped, it has to be the capitaine or the co-capitaine, his assistant.

BA: Somebody above him?

CW: Yeah, you see, one of the leaders.

BA: Now, can the capitaine ever get whipped?

CW: The capitaine can at the dance over there, but it has to be the next guy in command. That's the only one. Because if you go down, people like Dallas, they're going to get you. You can believe, you're going to get it.

But for the purposes of the game, everyone inside and outside the circle seemed to feel that this was a particularly vulnerable time as this potentially volatile game, which can exist only under the absolute control of its strong leader, was apparently leaderless for the moment. Afterward, all were reassured when Capitaine Wallace abandoned the temporary role he had donned for the occasion and rose from the floor to resume his position of absolute power at the head of the circle.

With order apparently restored, Dallas sought to return to the circle. But his leaving had broken a ritual trust. All players now shifted gears to participate in a remarkable improvised mock trial to deal with the matter of his desertion. They used the game itself to deal with a problem that was quite real and that threatened to deprive the Mardi Gras of one of its most valued members. Negotiating from the edge of the circle, Dallas was eventually allowed to reenter with the understanding that he would stand trial for his transgression. He was, of course, convicted in due course and condemned to be flogged. He thus found himself in position to receive the potentially harsh treatment he was earnestly trying to avoid in the first place. Understanding that the game was flirting with disaster if there were genuine revenge or a genuine mutiny, Capitaine Wallace declared that he would take care of the sentence himself and administered a modest whipping to the relief of everyone involved.

Members of the community watching this spectacle were mightily entertained. Even nonparticipants knew of Dallas's notoriously fierce whippings and found that turning the tables on him was hilarious. The ostensible purpose of such play is precisely to generate laughter in the community. No members of the community indicated any awareness of the close call that the ritual had endured. Members of the group did not articulate an overt understanding of the potential danger of the situation at the time. In fact, there was an audible sigh of relief from participants upon the discovery of a viable solution. Nor did anyone respond to questions about the situation later. But events in subsequent years seem to indicate that this level of play may actually be cultivated, consciously or subconsciously, by the group or parts of the group, not only to satisfy a desire for greater thrills but to reaffirm the group by creating a need for it to negotiate between cohesion and disintegration or dissolution.

Another year, Dallas, the enforcer, was temporarily entrusted with the moneybag used to hold donations during the day. According to the rules, the bag is the responsibility of the capitaine, whose role it is to represent the players to the community they are visiting. As master of the game, he is the only person who can be expected to control such serious matters as negotiating visits and guarding the group's booty. Otherwise occupied for a moment during this particular day, Capitaine Wallace delegated to his toughest lieutenant the responsibility for returning the moneybag to the vehicle accompanying the ride for safekeeping. On his way, some of the soldats succeeded in distracting Dallas and spirited away the bag. This lapse genuinely jeopardized the accountability of the capitaine, and thus the Mardi Gras, vis-à-vis those working to collect the funds and those contributing to the communal gumbo. The soldats who pilfered the bag came immediately to show it off to Capitaine Wallace, who promptly summoned Dallas before him. Dallas was accused of losing track of the bag and was immediately found guilty by the same kangaroo court logic as that which convicted Capitaine Wallace in the previous episode. The soldats were punished for stealing the bag – but so was Dallas for losing it. This time, however, the sentence was to be carried out on the road, in public and in process.

It became immediately clear that whipping a whipper *in media res* was a highly unusual turn of events. Once the game got this far, no one knew exactly how to proceed, for it had not happened before. Confused over the procedure for such an unanticipated event, the players then engaged in considerable negotiation concerning how this was to be done and by whom. It was determined after considerable discussion that only the capitaine and the co-capitaine could participate in the administration of the sentence. Dallas also invoked the right not to be whipped alone. Someone pointed out that Troy, another lieutenant, had been observed without a hat during the same visit, and he was pressed into service as Dallas's partner in crime and punishment. It was also determined that Dallas and Troy must be disarmed to receive their sentence, and their whips were removed with considerable gravity and circumstance along with their hats, as per the tradition. Even then, the two bareheaded and unarmed condemned lieutenants lay down in the circle only to come back up or roll over at least 20 times to negotiate another fine point, hands in the air as if attempting to hold off the inevitable. The tension was palpable. These were not just any participants but, in fact, leaders being court-martialed – and not back at headquarters, as in the previous example, but in the field. A refusal by Dallas or Troy to accept the terms of the sentence would have amounted to a mutiny and would have led to a breakdown in the game. Soldats who might use the opportunity to obtain revenge for their own harsh treatment during the day tried to negotiate a role for themselves in the process. Several of them added to the confusion of the moment, taking advantage of the traditional practice of "protecting" those to be whipped by crawling over them, taking special care to crush the lieutenants into the ground as they went. After several tenuous minutes, Capitaine Wallace finally succeeded in guiding the group through these uncharted waters. Both men stoically accepted the sentence and their flogging with grace. The crisis was resolved, and all continued the day with the structure of the game intact and the roles of the players reaffirmed after this hair-raising performance. People at the house thought that the whole scene was hilarious. A few of the more experienced soldats and whippers, including John and Wilson, confided through nervous smiles that they were relieved to get out of that fix with all members still in the game. They knew how close they had come to a meltdown of the core, but their faith in the ability of the game to ultimately prevail was confirmed.

The following year, Troy accidentally bumped his father-in-law Wilson, knocking him from his horse while roughhousing during a rare charge up to a house. Some murmured that this was the first time in 20 years that someone had fallen from a horse during the Mardi Gras. Slightly injured and genuinely embarrassed, Wilson tearfully announced his resignation from the group at the lunch stop near his own home. There was a moment of awkward silence. Faced with the imminent loss of a valued member of the team, the men did the only thing they could figure out to do. They applauded Wilson, thanking him for his years of service. Troy protested that he, and not Wilson, should resign because he was the cause of the trouble. Then a most remarkable thing happened. One of the soldats sitting in the circle took off his hat and threw it into the center – then another and another, until all the men were bareheaded. Then some of the older men who do not usually participate in the floggings, including the driver of the wagon and the old man who looks after the horses during the stops, took off their hats and threw them into the circle as well. And then the entire group – over 30 men – lay face down on the ground for a mass whipping, spontaneously offering themselves in atonement. The frenzy went on for a long time.

Threatened with the loss of two of their most respected members, the soldats reacted with a heartfelt attempt to collectively atone for the transgression in a remarkable show of solidarity. What had started as quite real had been forced into game-threatening play by the sheer momentum of the group, which then turned this problem into an opportunity to reaffirm itself. Wilson and Troy were so touched that they remounted after the lunch break and finished the day. Next year, both were back in the saddle. Once again, the game was questioned and preserved by the players. This time, a real problem had started the process. That real problem was eventually co-opted and transformed into game-threatening play. Once that happened, though, it was then defused, and the game was reaffirmed once again.

Crises such as these have occurred at some point during each of the years that I have observed this version of the Mardi Gras. In some cases, the crisis seems to have been first improvised as part of the game and then turned into a structural problem when it tripped over the game's usual boundaries. In other cases, the crisis seems to have started as a real problem that was eventually defused when the group co-opted it to turn it into a game. In each case, the crisis appeared to threaten the very structure of the game, thus placing the game itself in apparent jeopardy. The challenge in each case, then, was to restore the game by reaffirming or redefining its rules and the roles of the players. This deep play occurs during the improvised mock trials that are part of a typical house visit or during the more stylized mock trials that are part of the Tuesday evening dance and gumbo supper at the American Legion Hall in Jennings, but the primary audience is clearly the players themselves.

The need for this chronic reaffirmation may come from the real identity crisis expressed frequently by Capitaine Wallace in interviews with members of the press, folklorists, and anyone who will listen. The Grand Marais Mardi Gras never totally disbanded during the World War II years, as happened with other runs such as the well-known Mamou and Church Point models. Those big horseback runs were eventually revived by community leaders, such as attorney Paul Tate in Mamou and Dr. R.L. Savoy in Church Point, who redefined the Mardi Gras runs to enable them to exist in contemporary terms. Whipping, for example, once a common feature of most Mardi Gras celebrations, was eliminated. The Grand Marais run, on the other hand, continued throughout the war years and did not need to be revived or redefined. Here, the celebration has weathered considerable social criticism, especially in the town of Jennings, part of the territory of the Grand Marais run, from segments of society that are genuinely embarrassed by what appear to be politically incorrect aspects of the tradition, including its blackface components and its apparent violence through flogging and aggressive behaviors among the participants (David Marcantel, personal communication, 1990). Capitaine Wallace often insists on the importance of preserving the specific nature of the run and tries to avoid diluting it or having it drift stylistically toward other runs. Wallace is especially concerned with the future of the run when he will no longer be able to provide the leadership it takes to pull off this improvisational wonder. It is clear that no written (or oral) description could be produced to guide the next generation in the practice of this tradition. One learns to improvise by improvising. The deep play that emerges each year may represent Capitaine Wallace's demand for an expression of renewed commitment to the game itself from its players.

In 1998, Capitaine Wallace finally gave his troupe the ultimate test, retiring from his position as master of the game. This act, together with a series of other challenges, including the unavailability of other key members of the band, caused the run to be cancelled that year. In 1999, however, spurred on by the runners as well as their extended families and neighbors, who all found that they missed what the run did for the community, the run was successfully revived under Capitaine Francis, a considerably younger member of the group with years of experience as a whipper. Former Capitaine Wallace looked anything but former, though, as he stood next to Capitaine Francis, advising him at every turn, helping to lead the song, and especially helping to improvise the play that is at the heart of this ritual. The image of passing the torch would be ineffective in describing this transition. Instead, it was more like a father running along with his child who was just learning to ride a bicycle, guarding against disaster, just in case. Eventually, Wallace withdrew from his strident supervising role under pressure from several members of the group and from several of their wives, who provide much of the support structure for the run, and especially his own sister, Laura. The community felt it necessary to see whether or not Capitaine Francis could lead the group on his own. He did. There was considerable improvisation during the day, though perhaps not as intense as before.

The deepest play I observed under Capitaine Francis's early leadership was the whipping of Troy, a longtime member of the circle, who was unable to run because he was in training to become a police officer but who was in attendance at every house along the way as an observer. It was clearly painful for all concerned to have Troy outside the circle. At one point during what is traditionally one of the most important visits of the day, at the Landry family compound, it was "discovered" that Troy had paid his dues for the year, as though he were running. Capitaine Francis had him hauled into the circle, demanded his hat, and cleverly accused him of running Mardi Gras incognito. As an observer, Troy was unpainted and not in costume, but the edge between performance and observation, already thin in his case, had been blurred by one of the soldats who had bumped Troy's face with his own, thus marking him with a little paint and adding to the available confusion. He was tried and, of course, convicted. He was whipped in an emotional and touching frenzy that included his being covered by everyone in the circle. He and many participants were visibly moved to tears, as the play reinforced Troy's inclusion in the participant circle. With this incident, young Capitaine Francis demonstrated his ability to improvise beyond the circle, that is, beyond the game, though in a relatively safe way. If the nature of the game survives this change of leadership, eventually this capitaine will be tested with the same sort of deep play that Wallace so deftly survived for years. And if the nature of the game survives, the tests he will face will be different every year, requiring him to lead the group in improvising a creative and ingenious solution to preserve the Mardi Gras.

This, then, is a game within a game, and the goal of this inner game is to save the game itself, to confirm through innovation the rules and roles necessary for this ritual of apparent social disorder to continue to function. Geertz's analysis of the social function of deep play among Balinese cockfighters (1973) is based on similar issues, though the stakes are obviously different. There is not necessarily a veritable social restructuring involved in this Mardi Gras play, as appears to be the case in Geertz's example, nor does the chaotic inversion of this Mardi Gras risk spilling over into real life, as happened in Romans in 1579 and 1580 (Le Roy Ladurie 1979). In those two cases of what Geertz has called "deep play," real-life social relationships were negotiated under the surface of a cultural game. Serious social status is at stake in the deep play of the cockfighters described by Geertz. Le Roy Ladurie's study of the Romans Mardi Gras shows how that town's feuding factions used the deep play of their Mardi Gras as a cover for a real power struggle that eventually ended in civil upheaval. This betrayal of the game's integrity and intent ultimately led to the demise of the Mardi Gras in that community. Though there are certainly social issues at play in the Grand Marais Mardi Gras, as in most, the "deep play" described here is play for the sake of the preservation and dynamic regeneration of the game itself. It is internally directed improvisational theater primarily by and for the actors – the participants themselves – rather than for the spectators. Though the spectators get to watch, and some can even be brought into the circle, it seems that only those who are privy to the relationships and issues in play are aware of the nature of this deeper play or of the stakes involved. Actual crises threaten to escalate the pretend chaos inherent in the Mardi Gras into what appears to be genuine chaos. Yet, upon closer examination, the crises actually seem to be a deeper level of pretense that seeks instead to reaffirm the game itself. This is border maintenance not along the outside edges of the Mardi Gras to prevent an explosion but, rather, at its very heart to prevent an implosion.

NOTE

1 According to LS [Louisiana Statute] 14: 313, masking in public is prohibited statewide, but events such as Halloween and Mardi Gras are specifically exempted from this prohibition. The chief deputy of the Jeff Davis Parish Sheriff's Office and the chief of police of the City of Jennings both confirmed that there is currently no parish statute or city ordinance further limiting masking on the local level. The current version of the state law apparently dates from the 1960s. An earlier version of the state law from the 1920s was broader and deliberately left enforcement up to local officials. According to Louisiana historian Carl Brasseaux, officials in the Jennings area at that time elected to use the statute to inhibit Ku Klux Klan activities. This may have contributed to a change in cultural practice from masking to face painting at one point, although there is no longer a legal reason to avoid masks. Ironically, planned Klan activities are also now exempted from this prohibition in the current version of the law.

REFERENCES

Ancelet, Barry Jean (1977) "The Mamou Mardi Gras from behind the mask: problems of the ethnic folklorist working within his own community," paper presented at the American Folklore Society Annual Meeting.

—— (1989) "Mardi Gras and the media: who's fooling whom?" *Southern Folklore*, 46(3): 211–219.

—— (1992) "Singing outlaws and beggars with whips: variety in the South Louisiana Mardi Gras," paper presented at the American Folklore Society Annual Meeting.

—— (1993) "Playing the other: ritual reversal in the South Louisiana Country Mardi Gras," paper presented at the American Folklore Society Annual Meeting.

Davis, Nathalie Zémon (1975) *Society and Culture in Early Modern France*. Stanford: Stanford University Press.

Geertz, Clifford (1973) *The Interpretation of Cultures: Selected Essays*. New York: Basic Books.

Le Roy Ladurie, Emmanuel (1979) *Le Carnaval de Romans*, trans. Mary Feeney. New York: George Braziller (original: Paris: Gallimard, 1979).

Lindahl, Carl (1996) "Bakhtin's carnival laughter and the Cajun Country Mardi Gras," *Folklore*, 107: 57–70.

READER CROSS-REFERENCES

Geertz – coined the term "deep play"

Bateson, Sutton-Smith – offer frameworks and terms for describing the play event

Turner – the role of ritual in creating and sustaining community

Barba – harnessing turbulence and chaos in the service of dramaturgy

Part V

PERFORMATIVITY

Performativity is a term layered with multiple meanings. On one level, it is a variation on theatricality: something which is "performative" is similar – in form, in intent, in effect – to a theatrical performance. This use of the term is invoked by those who wish to describe a performance without the connotations of artifice or superficiality that accompany the word "theatrical." On another level, the term "performative" refers to a specific philosophical concept concerning the nature and potential of language. Linguistic philosopher J.L. Austin, in a series of lectures delivered at Harvard University in 1955, defined the "performative" as an utterance that does not make a statement – i.e., that does not express truly or falsely an already-existing condition – but in fact performs an action. This is a situation in which, to use Austin's words, "to *say* something is to *do* something" (see p. 177). Austin's lectures were published in 1962 as *How to Do Things With Words*, one chapter of which is excerpted in this section. Significantly, however, Austin excludes theatrical speech from his discussion, because it does not seriously reflect the intent of the speaker.

The nature of language was also a paramount concern for Jacques Derrida, whose 1971 lecture "Signature event context" (English translation published 1982) is excerpted here. Derrida directly addresses Austin's attempt to exclude speech uttered by an actor on stage from the general theory of the performative (see p. 181), suggesting that what Austin objects to in such "parasitic" speech is its "citational" quality: it refers to something outside itself, to an event or procedure that is beyond the experience of the speaker. Yet, says Derrida, because it depends on "conventional procedure," Austin's performative is always citational. Moreover, as Derrida's larger theory of language presupposes a gap or slippage (*différance*) between intent and reception in all speech, dramatic dialogue is less a case of "special circumstances" (p. 181) than "the determined modification of a general citationality – or rather, a general iterability" (p. 184). Derrida agrees that stage speech *is* different from ordinary speech, but that this difference is merely one of degree. Derrida's formulation of all speech as "iteration" – re-statement of that which has been said before – offers a rationale for understanding *all* language as performance, and in so doing offers the possibility of unifying the two meanings of performativity: speech/behavior as performance meets speech/behavior as action.

Perhaps the most remarkable synthesis of these two meanings of performativity is expressed in Judith Butler's 1988 essay "Performative acts and gender constitution." Butler explains that gender is not a condition which one *has*, but is in fact "an identity tenuously constituted in time" – that is, a social role which one *performs*. In arguing that gender is constituted through performative acts, Butler ascribes to gender the contingent and temporal qualities of performance as understood in theater and anthropology. At the same time, in theorizing the possibility of using such acts as a strategy for the cultural transformation of gender norms, she draws upon the philosophical understanding of performativity: the acts which constitute gender are not expressive of a reality; they constitute that reality through their performance.

In their "Introduction to *Performativity and Performance*" (1993), Andrew Parker and Eve Kosofsky Sedgwick seek to further unify the theatrical and philosophical discourses around performativity. Austin, they point out, discounts theatrical performance as incapable of sustaining performative speech. Yet, in order for Austin's performative to be effective, it must have certain performance-like qualities: namely, there must be an audience (listener), and the speech act must conform to a pre-established pattern. Re-reading Austin in light of Derrida as well as later psychoanalytic and post-structuralist theories, Parker and Sedgwick find that the link between linguistic performativity and theatrical performance "emerges [. . .] as an active question" (p. 204).

Another implication of these ideas is explored in Johannes Fabian's "Theater and anthropology, theatricality and culture" (1999). Fabian, an anthropologist, traces his own and his discipline's relationship to concepts of language, theatricality, and identity, arguing in favor of performance ("practical theatricality") as a means of promoting intercultural understanding.

22

HOW TO DO THINGS WITH WORDS
Lecture II

J.L. Austin

We were to consider, you will remember, some cases and senses (only some, Heaven help us!) in which to *say* something is to *do* something; or in which *by* saying or *in* saying something we are doing something. This topic is one development – there are many others – in the recent movement towards questioning an age-old assumption in philosophy – the assumption that to say something, at least in all cases worth considering, i.e. all cases considered, is always and simply to *state* something. This assumption is no doubt unconscious, is no doubt precipitate, but it is wholly natural in philosophy apparently. We must learn to run before we can walk. If we never made mistakes how should we correct them?

I began by drawing your attention, by way of example, to a few simple utterances of the kind known as performatories or performatives. These have on the face of them the look – or at least the grammatical make-up of "statements"; but nevertheless they are seen, when more closely inspected, to be, quite plainly, *not* utterances which could be "true" or "false." Yet to be "true" or "false" is traditionally the characteristic mark of a statement. One of our examples was, for instance, the utterance "I do" (take this woman to be my lawful wedded wife), as uttered in the course of a marriage ceremony. Here we should say that in saying these words we are *doing* something – namely, marrying, rather than *reporting* something, namely *that* we are marrying. And the act of marrying, like, say, the act of betting, is at least *preferably* (though still not *accurately*) to be described as *saying certain words*, rather than as performing a different, inward and spiritual, action of which these words are merely the outward and audible sign. That this is so can perhaps hardly be *proved*, but it is, I should claim, a fact.

It is worthy of note that, as I am told, in the American law of evidence a report of what someone else said is admitted as evidence if what he said is an utterance of our performative kind: because this is regarded as a report not so much of something he said, as which it would be hear-say and not admissible as evidence, but rather as something he did, an action of his. This coincides very well with our initial feelings about performatives.

So far, then, we have merely felt the firm ground of prejudice slide away beneath our feet. But now how, as philosophers, are we to proceed? One thing we might go on to do, of course, is to take it all back: another would be to bog, by logical stages, down. But all this must take time. Let us first at least concentrate attention on the little matter already mentioned in passing – this matter of "the appropriate circumstances." To bet is not, as I pointed out in passing, merely to utter the words "I bet, etc.": someone might do that all right, and yet we might still not agree that he had in fact, or at least entirely, succeeded in betting. To satisfy ourselves of this, we have only, for example, to announce our bet after the race is over. Besides the uttering of the words of the so-called performative, a good many other things have as a general rule to be right and to go right if we are to be said to have happily brought off our action. What these are we may hope to discover by looking at and classifying types of case in which something *goes wrong* and the act – marrying, betting, bequeathing, christening, or what not – is therefore at least to some extent a failure: the utterance is then, we may say, not indeed false but in general *unhappy*. And for this reason we call the doctrine of *the things that can be and go wrong* on the occasion of such utterances the doctrine of the *Infelicities*.

Suppose we try first to state schematically – and I do not wish to claim any sort of finality for this scheme – some at least of the things which are necessary for the smooth or "happy" functioning of a performative (or at least of a highly developed explicit performative, such as we have hitherto been alone concerned with), and then give examples of infelicities and their effects. I fear, but at the same time of course hope, that these necessary conditions to be satisfied will strike you as obvious.

(A.1) There must exist an accepted conventional procedure having a certain conventional effect, that procedure to include the uttering of certain words by certain persons in certain circumstances, and further,

(A.2) the particular persons and circumstances in a given case must be appropriate for the invocation of the particular procedure invoked.

(B.1) The procedure must be executed by all participants both correctly and

(B.2) completely.

(Γ.i) Where, as often, the procedure is designed for use by persons having certain thoughts or feelings, or for the inauguration of certain consequential conduct on the part of any participant, then a person participating in and so invoking the procedure must in fact have those thoughts or feelings, and the participants must intend so to conduct themselves,[1] and further

(Γ.2) must actually so conduct themselves subsequently.

Now if we sin against any one (or more) of these six rules, our performative utterance will be (in one way or another) unhappy. But, of course, there are considerable differences between these "ways" of being unhappy – ways which are intended to be brought out by the letter-numerals selected for each heading.

The first big distinction is between all the four rules A and B taken together, as opposed to the two rules Γ (hence the use of Roman as opposed to Greek letters). If we offend against any of the former rules (A's or B's) – that is, if we, say, utter the formula incorrectly, or if, say, we are not in a position to do the act because we are, say, married already, or it is the purser and not the captain who is conducting the ceremony, then the act in question, e.g. marrying, is not successfully performed at all, does not come off, is not achieved. Whereas in the two Γ cases the act *is* achieved, although to achieve it in such circumstances, as when we are, say, insincere, is an abuse of the procedure. Thus, when I say "I promise" and have no intention of keeping it, I have promised but. . . . We need names for referring to this general distinction, so we shall call in general those infelicities A.1–B.2 which are such that the act for the performing of which, and in the performing of which, the verbal formula in question is designed, is not achieved, by the name MISFIRES; and on the other hand we may christen those infelicities where the act is achieved ABUSES (do not stress the normal connotations of these names!). When the utterance is a misfire, the procedure which we purport to invoke is disallowed or is botched; and our act (marrying etc.) is void or without effect etc. We speak of our act as a purported act, or perhaps an attempt – or we use such an expression as "went through a form of marriage" by contrast with "married." On the other hand, in the Γ cases, we speak of our infelicitous act as "professed" or "hollow" rather than "purported" or "empty," and as not implemented, or not consummated, rather than as void or without effect. But let me hasten to add that these distinctions are not hard and fast, and more especially that such words as "purported" and "professed" will not bear very much stressing. Two final words about being void or without effect. This does not mean, of course, to say that we won't have done anything: lots of things will have been done – we shall most interestingly have committed the act of bigamy – but we shall *not* have done the purported act, viz. marrying. Because, despite the name, you do not when bigamous marry twice. (In short, the algebra of marriage is BOOLEAN.) Further, "without effect" does not here mean "without consequences, results, effects."

Next, we must try to make clear the general distinction between the A cases and the B cases among the misfires. In both of the cases labeled A there is *misinvocation* of a procedure – either because there is, speaking vaguely, no such procedure, or because the procedure in question cannot be made to apply in the way attempted. Hence infelicities of this kind A may be called *Misinvocations*. Among them, we may reasonably christen the second sort – where the procedure does exist all right but can't be applied as purported – *Misapplications*. But I have not succeeded in finding a good name for the other, former, class. By contrast with the A cases, the notion of the B cases is rather that the procedure is all right, and it does apply all right, but we muff the execution of the ritual, with more or less dire consequences: so B cases as opposed to A cases will be called *Misexecutions* as opposed to Misinvocations: the purported act is *vitiated* by a flaw or hitch in the conduct of the ceremony. The Class B.1 is that of Flaws, the Class B. 2 that of Hitches.

We get, then, the scheme shown overleaf.[2]

I expect some doubts will be entertained about A.1 and Γ.2; but we will postpone them for detailed consideration shortly.

But before going on to details, let me make some general remarks about these infelicities. We may ask:

(1) To what variety of "act" does the notion of infelicity apply?
(2) How complete is this classification of infelicity?
(3) Are these classes of infelicity mutually exclusive?

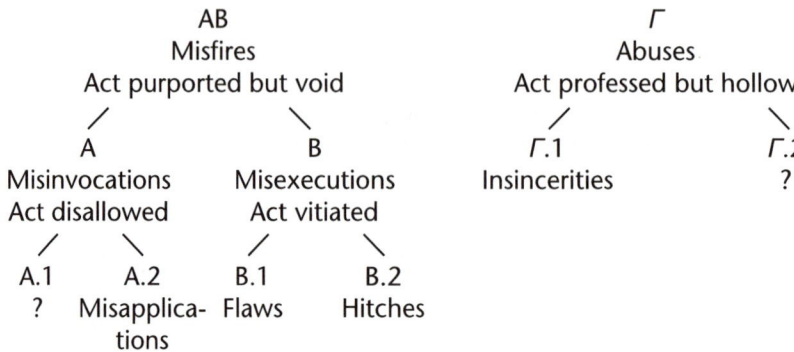

Infelicities

	AB		Γ	
	Misfires		Abuses	
	Act purported but void		Act professed but hollow	
A		B	Γ.1	Γ.2
Misinvocations		Misexecutions	Insincerities	?
Act disallowed		Act vitiated		
A.1	A.2	B.1	B.2	
?	Misapplica-tions	Flaws	Hitches	

Let us take these questions in (that) order.

(1) How widespread is infelicity?

Well, it seems clear in the first place that, although it has excited us (or failed to excite us) in connection with certain acts which are or are in part acts of *uttering words*, infelicity is an ill to which *all* acts are heir which have the general character of ritual or ceremonial, all *conventional* acts: not indeed that *every* ritual is liable to every form of infelicity (but then nor is every performative utterance). This is clear if only from the mere fact that many conventional acts, such as betting or conveyance of property, can be performed in non-verbal ways. The same sorts of rule must be observed in all such conventional procedures – we have only to omit the special reference to verbal utterance in our A. This much is obvious.

But, furthermore, it is worth pointing out – reminding you – how many of the "acts" which concern the jurist are or include the utterance of performatives, or at any rate are or include the performance of some conventional procedures. And of course you will appreciate that in this way and that writers on jurisprudence have constantly shown themselves aware of the varieties of infelicity and even at times of the peculiarities of the performative utterance. Only the still widespread obsession that the utterances of the law, and utterances used in, say, "acts in the law", *must* somehow be statements true or false has prevented many lawyers from getting this whole matter much straighter than we are likely to and I would not even claim to know whether some of them have not already done so. Of more direct concern to us, however, is to realize that, by the same token, a great many of the acts which fall within the province of Ethics are *not*, as philosophers are too prone to assume, simply in the last resort *physical movements*: very many of them have the general character, in whole or part, of conventional or ritual acts, and are therefore, among other things, exposed to infelicity.

Lastly we may ask – and here I must let some of my cats on the table – does the notion of infelicity apply to utterances *which are statements*? So far we have produced the infelicity as characteristic of the *performative* utterance, which was "defined" (if we can call it so much) mainly by contrast with the supposedly familiar "statement." Yet I will content myself here with pointing out that one of the things that has been happening lately in philosophy is that close attention has been given even to "statements" which, though not false exactly nor yet "contradictory," are yet outrageous. For instance, statements which refer to something which does not exist as, for example, "The present King of France is bald." There might be a temptation to assimilate this to purporting to bequeath something which you do not own. Is there not a presupposition of existence in each? Is not a statement which refers to something which does not exist not so much false as void? And the more we consider a statement not as a sentence (or proposition) but as an act of speech (out of which the others are logical constructions), the more we are studying the whole thing as an act. Or, again, there are obvious similarities between a lie and a false promise. We shall have to return to this matter later.[3]

(2) Our second question was: How complete is this classification?

(i) Well, the first thing to remember is that, since in uttering our performatives we are undoubtedly in a sound enough sense "performing actions," then, as actions, these will be subject to certain whole dimensions of unsatisfactoriness to which all actions are subject but which are distinct – or distinguishable – from what we have chosen to discuss as infelicities. I mean that actions in general (not all) are liable, for example, to be done under duress, or by accident, or owing to this or that variety of mistake, say, or otherwise unintentionally. In many such cases we are certainly unwilling to say of some such act simply that it was done or that he did it. I am not going into the general doctrine here: in many such cases we may even say the act was "void" (or voidable for duress or undue influence) and so forth. Now I suppose some very general high-level doctrine might embrace both what we have called infelicities *and* these other "unhappy" features of the doing of actions – in our case actions containing a performative utterance – in a single doctrine; but we are not including this kind of unhappiness – we must just remember, though, that features of this sort can and do constantly obtrude into any particular case we are discussing. Features of this sort would normally come under the heading of "extenuating circumstances" or of "factors reducing or abrogating the agent's responsibility," and so on.

(ii) Second, as *utterances* our performatives are *also* heir to certain other kinds of ill which infect *all* utterances. And these, likewise, though again they might be brought into a more general account, we are deliberately at present excluding. I mean, for example, the following: a performative utterance will, for example, be *in a peculiar way* hollow or void if said by an actor on the stage, or if introduced in a poem, or spoken in soliloquy. This applies in a similar manner to any and every utterance – a sea-change in special circumstances. Language in such circumstances is in special ways – intelligibly – used not seriously, but in ways *parasitic* upon its normal use – ways which fall under the doctrine of the *etiolations* of language. All this we are *excluding* from consideration. Our performative utterances, felicitous or not, are to be understood as issued in ordinary circumstances.

(iii) It is partly in order to keep this sort of consideration at least for the present out of it that I have not here introduced a sort of "infelicity" – it might really be called such – arising out of "misunderstanding." It is obviously necessary that to have promised I must normally

(A)   have been *heard* by someone, perhaps the promisee;
(B)   have been understood by him as promising.

If one or another of these conditions is not satisfied, doubts arise as to whether I have really promised, and it might be held that my act was only attempted or was void. Special precautions are taken in law to avoid this and other infelicities, e.g. in the serving of writs or summonses. This particular very important consideration we shall have to return to later in another connection.

(3) Are these cases of infelicity mutually exclusive? The answer to this is obvious.

(a) No, in the sense that we can go wrong in two ways at once (we can insincerely promise a donkey to give it a carrot).

(b) No, more importantly, in the sense that the ways of going wrong "shade into one another" and "overlap", and the decision between them is "arbitrary" in various ways.

Suppose, for example, I see a vessel on the stocks, walk up and smash the bottle hung at the stem, proclaim "I name this ship the *Mr. Stalin*" and for good measure kick away the chocks; but the trouble is, I was not the person chosen to name it (whether or not – an additional complication – *Mr. Stalin* was the destined name; perhaps in a way it is even more of a shame if it was). We can all agree

(1) that the ship was not thereby named;[4]
(2) that it is an infernal shame.

One could say that I "went through a form of" naming the vessel but that my "action" was "void" or "without effect," because I was not a proper person, had not the "capacity," to perform it: but one might also and alternatively say that, where there is not even a pretense of capacity or a colorable claim to it, then there is no accepted conventional procedure; it is a mockery, like a marriage with a monkey. Or again one could say that part of the procedure is getting oneself appointed. When the saint baptized the penguins, was this void because the procedure of baptizing is inappropriate to be applied to penguins, or because there is no accepted procedure of baptizing anything except humans? I do not think that these uncertainties matter in theory, though it is pleasant to investigate them and in practice convenient to be ready, as jurists are, with a terminology to cope with them.

NOTES

1 It will be explained later why the having of these thoughts, feelings, and intentions is not included as just one among the other "circumstances" already dealt with in (A).

2 [Austin from time to time used other names for the different infelicities. For interest some are here given: A.x, Non-plays; A.2, Misplays; B, Miscarriages; B.r, Misexecutions; B.2, Non-executions; Γ, Disrespects; Γ.1, Dissimulations; Γ.2, Non-fulfillments, Disloyalties, Infractions, Indisciplines, Breaches. J. O. U.]

3 See p. 47 ff. J. O. U.

4 Naming babies is even more difficult; we might have the wrong name and the wrong cleric – that is, someone entitled to name babies but not intended to name this one.

READER CROSS-REFERENCES

Jackson, Kirshenblatt-Gimblett, Taylor – use of the term "performative" in performance studies

Butler, Santino – expansion of the performative act beyond speech

Derrida, Parker and Sedgwick – explore the implications of this lecture, especially Austin's attempt to exclude "parasitic" speech from consideration in his theory of the performative

Carlson, Fabian – alternate uses of "performative"

23

EXCERPT FROM "SIGNATURE EVENT CONTEXT"[*]

Jacques Derrida

Therefore, I ask the following question: is this general possibility necessarily that of a failure or a trap into which language might *fall*, or in which language might lose itself, as if in an abyss situated outside or in front of it? What about *parasitism*? In other words, does the generality of the risk admitted by Austin *surround* language like a kind of *ditch*, a place of external perdition into which locution might never venture, that it might avoid by remaining at home, in itself, sheltered by its essence or *telos*? Or indeed is this risk, on the contrary, its internal and positive condition of possibility? this outside its inside? the very force and law of its emergence? In this last case, what would an "ordinary" language defined by the very law of language signify? Is it that in excluding the general theory of this structural parasitism, Austin, who nevertheless pretends to describe the facts and events of ordinary language, makes us accept as ordinary a teleological and ethical determination (the univocality of the statement – which he recognizes elsewhere remains a philosophical "ideal," pp. 72–73 – the self-presence of a total context, the transparency of intentions, the presence of meaning for the absolutely singular oneness of a speech act, etc.)?

For, finally, is not what Austin excludes as anomalous, exceptional, "non-serious,"[1] that is, *citation* (on the stage, in a poem, or in a soliloquy), the determined modification of a general citationality – or rather, a general iterability – without which there would not even be a "successful" performative? Such that – a paradoxical, but inevitable consequence – a successful performative is necessarily an "impure" performative, to use the word that Austin will employ later on when he recognizes that there is no "pure" performative.[2]

Now I will take things from the side of positive possibility, and no longer only from the side of failure: would a performative statement be possible if a citational doubling did not eventually split, dissociate from itself the pure singularity of the event? I am asking the question in this form in order to forestall an objection. In effect, it might be said to me: you cannot allege that you account for the so-called graphematic structure of locution solely on the basis of the occurrence of failures of the performative, however real these failures might be, and however effective or general their possibility. You cannot deny that there are also performatives that succeed, and they must be accounted for: sessions are opened, as Paul Ricoeur did yesterday, one says "I ask a question," one bets, one challenges, boats are launched, and one even marries occasionally. Such events, it appears, have occurred. And were a single one of them to have taken place a single time, it would still have to be accounted for.

I will say "perhaps." Here, we must first agree upon what the "occurring" or the event-hood of an event consists in, when the event supposes in its allegedly present and singular intervention a statement which in itself can be only of a repetitive or citational structure, or rather, since these last words lead to confusion, of an iterable structure. Therefore, I come back to the point which seems fundamental to me, and which now concerns the status of the event in general, of the event of speech or by speech, of the strange logic it supposes, and which often remains unperceived.

Could a performative statement succeed if its formulation did not repeat a "coded" or iterable statement, in other words if the expressions I use to open a meeting, launch a ship or a marriage were not identifiable as *conforming* to an iterable model, and therefore if they were not identifiable in a way as "citation"? Not that citationality here is of the same type as in a play, a philosophical reference, or the recitation of a poem. This is why there is a relative specificity, as Austin says, a "relative purity" of performatives. But this relative purity is not constructed *against* citationality or iterability, but against other kinds of iteration within a general iterability which is the effraction into the allegedly rigorous purity of every event of discourse or every speech act. Thus, one must less oppose citation or iteration to the noniteration of an event, than construct a differential typology of forms of iteration, supposing that this is a tenable project that can give rise to an exhaustive program, a question I am holding off on here. In this typology, the category of intention will not disappear; it will have its place, but from this place it will no longer be able to govern the entire scene and the entire system of utterances. Above all, one then would be concerned with different types of marks or chains of iterable marks, and not with an opposition between citational statements on the one hand, and singular and original statement-events on the other. The first consequence of this would be the following: given this structure of iteration, the intention which animates utterance will never be completely present in itself and its content. The iteration which structures it a priori introduces an essential dehiscence and demarcation. One will no longer be able to exclude, as Austin wishes, the "non-serious," the *oratio obliqua*, from "ordinary" language. And if it is alleged that ordinary language, or the ordinary circumstance of language, excludes citationality or general iterability, does this not signify that the "ordinariness" in question, the thing and the notion, harbors a lure, the teleological lure of consciousness whose motivations, indestructible necessity, and systematic effects remain to be analyzed? Especially since this essential absence of intention for the actuality of the statement, this structural unconsciousness if you will, prohibits every saturation of a context. For a context to be exhaustively determinable, in the sense demanded by Austin, it at least would be necessary for the conscious intention to be totally present and actually transparent for itself and others, since it is a determining focal point of the context. The concept of or quest for the "context" therefore seems to suffer here from the same theoretical and motivated uncertainty as the concept of the "ordinary," from the same metaphysical origins: an ethical and teleological discourse of consciousness. This time, a reading of the connotations of Austin's text would confirm the reading of its descriptions; I have just indicated the principle of this reading.

Différance, the irreducible absence of intention or assistance from the performative statement, from the most "event-like" statement possible, is what authorizes me, taking into account the predicates mentioned just now, to posit the general graphematic structure of every "communication." Above all, I will not conclude from this that there is no relative specificity of the effects of consciousness, of the effects of speech (in opposition to writing in the traditional sense), that there is no effect of the performative, no effect of ordinary language, no effect of presence and of speech acts. It is simply that these effects do not exclude what is generally opposed to them term by term, but on the contrary presuppose it in dyssemetrical fashion, as the general space of their possibility.

NOTES

* Editor's note: this chapter is excerpted from "Signature event context," a communication to the Congrès international des Sociétés de philosophie de langue française, Montreal, August 1971. Page numbers cited in the text refer to J.L. Austin, *How to Do Things with Words* (New York: Harvard University Press, 1962).

1 The very suspect value of the "non-serious" is a frequent reference (see, e.g., pp. 104, 121). It has an essential link with what Austin says elsewhere about the *oratio obliqua* (pp. 70–71) and about *mime*.

2 From this point of view one might examine the fact recognized by Austin that "the same sentence is used on different occasions of utterance in both ways, performative and constative. The thing seems hopeless from the start, if we are to leave utterances as they stand and seek for a criterion" (p. 67). It is the graphematic root of citationality (iterability) that provokes this confusion, and makes it "not possible," as Austin says, "to lay down even a list of all possible criteria" (ibid.).

READER CROSS-REFERENCES

Austin – defines the performative speech act
Butler – expands upon Derrida's ideas of citation and iterability
Parker and Sedgwick – further explore the idea of "parasitism"
Taylor – cites Derrida's analysis of iterability

24

PERFORMATIVE ACTS AND GENDER CONSTITUTION

An essay in phenomenology and feminist theory

Judith Butler

Philosophers rarely think about acting in the theatrical sense, but they do have a discourse of "acts" that maintains associative semantic meanings with theories of performance and acting. For example, John Searle's "speech acts," those verbal assurances and promises which seem not only to refer to a speaking relationship, but to constitute a moral bond between speakers, illustrate one of the illocutionary gestures that constitutes the stage of the analytic philosophy of language. Further, "action theory," a domain of moral philosophy, seeks to understand what it is "to do" prior to any claim of what one *ought* to do. Finally, the phenomenological theory of "acts," espoused by Edmund Husserl, Maurice Merleau-Ponty, and George Herbert Mead, among others, seeks to explain the mundane way in which social agents *constitute* social reality through language, gesture, and all manner of symbolic social sign. Though phenomenology sometimes appears to assume the existence of a choosing and constituting agent prior to language (who poses as the sole source of its constituting acts), there is also a more radical use of the doctrine of constitution that takes the social agent as an *object* rather than the subject of constitutive acts.

When Simone de Beauvoir claims, "one is not born, but, rather, *becomes* a woman," she is appropriating and reinterpreting this doctrine of constituting acts from the phenomenological tradition.[1] In this sense, gender is in no way a stable identity or locus of agency from which various acts proceed; rather, it is an identity tenuously constituted in time – an identity instituted through a *stylized repetition of acts*. Further, gender is instituted through the stylization of the body and, hence, must be understood as the mundane way in which bodily gestures, movements, and enactments of various kinds constitute the illusion of an abiding gendered self. This formulation moves the conception of gender off the ground of a substantial model of identity to one that requires a conception of a constituted *social temporality*. Significantly, if gender is instituted through acts which are internally discontinuous, then the *appearance of substance* is precisely that, a constructed identity, a performative accomplishment which the mundane social audience, including the actors themselves, come to believe and to perform in the mode of belief. If the ground of gender identity is the

187

stylized repetition of acts through time, and not a seemingly seamless identity, then the possibilities of gender transformation are to be found in the arbitrary relation between such acts, in the possibility of a different sort of repeating, in the breaking or subversive repetition of that style.

Through the conception of gender acts sketched above, I will try to show some ways in which reified and naturalized conceptions of gender might be understood as constituted and, hence, capable of being constituted differently. In opposition to theatrical or phenomenological models which take the gendered self to be prior to its acts, I will understand constituting acts not only as constituting the identity of the actor, but as constituting that identity as a compelling illusion, an object of *belief*. In the course of making my argument, I will draw from theatrical, anthropological and philosophical discourses, but mainly phenomenology, to show that what is called gender identity is a performative accomplishment compelled by social sanction and taboo. In its very character as performative resides the possibility of contesting its reified status.

I Sex/gender: feminist and phenomenological views

Feminist theory has often been critical of naturalistic explanations of sex and sexuality that assume that the meaning of women's social existence can be derived from some fact of their physiology. In distinguishing sex from gender, feminist theorists have disputed causal explanations that assume that sex dictates or necessitates certain social meanings for women's experience. Phenomenological theories of human embodiment have also been concerned to distinguish between the various physiological and biological causalities that structure bodily existence and the *meanings* that embodied existence assumes in the context of lived experience. In Merleau-Ponty's reflections in *The Phenomenology of Perception* on "the body in its sexual being," he takes issue with such accounts of bodily experience and claims that the body is "an historical idea" rather than "a natural species."[2] Significantly, it is this claim that Simone de Beauvoir cites in *The Second Sex* when she sets the stage for her claim that "woman" and, by extension, any gender is an historical situation rather than a natural fact.[3]

In both contexts, the existence and facticity of the material or natural dimensions of the body are not denied, but reconceived as distinct from the process by which the body comes to bear cultural meanings. For both de Beauvoir and Merleau-Ponty, the body is understood to be an active process of embodying certain cultural and historical possibilities, a complicated process of appropriation which any phenomenological theory of embodiment needs to describe. In order to describe the gendered body, a phenomenological theory of constitution requires an expansion of the conventional view of acts to mean both that which constitutes meaning and that through which meaning is performed or enacted. In other words, the acts by which gender is constituted bear similarities to performative acts within theatrical contexts. My task, then, is to examine in what ways gender is constructed through specific corporeal acts, and what possibilities exist for the cultural transformation of gender through such acts.

Merleau-Ponty maintains that the body is not only an historical idea but a set of possibilities to be continually realized. In claiming that the body is an historical idea, Merleau-Ponty means that it gains its meaning through a concrete and historically mediated expression in the world. That the body is a set of possibilities signifies (a) that its appearance in the world, for perception, is not predetermined by some manner of interior essence, and (b) that its concrete expression in the world must be understood as the taking up and rendering specific of a set of historical possibilities. Hence, there is an agency which is understood as the process of rendering such possibilities determinate. These possibilities are necessarily constrained by available historical conventions. The body is not a self-identical or merely factic materiality; it is a materiality that bears meaning, if nothing else, and the manner of this bearing is fundamentally dramatic. By dramatic I mean only that the body is not merely matter but a continual and incessant *materializing* of possibilities. One is not simply a body, but, in some very key sense, one does one's body and, indeed, one does one's body differently from one's contemporaries and from one's embodied predecessors and successors as well.

It is, however, clearly unfortunate grammar to claim that there is a "we" or an "I" that does its body, as if a disembodied agency preceded and directed an embodied exterior. More appropriate, I suggest, would be a vocabulary that resists the substance metaphysics of subject–verb formations and relies instead on an ontology of present participles. The "I" that is its body is, of necessity, a mode of embodying, and the "what" that it embodies is possibilities. But here again the grammar of the formulation misleads, for the possibilities that are embodied are not fundamentally exterior or antecedent to the process of embodying itself. As an intentionally organized materiality, the body is always an embodying *of* possibilities both conditioned and circumscribed by historical convention. In other words, the body *is* a historical situation, as de Beauvoir has claimed, and is a manner of doing, dramatizing, and *reproducing* a historical situation.

To do, to dramatize, to reproduce, these seem to be some of the elementary structures of embodiment. This doing of gender is not merely a way in which embodied agents are exterior, surfaced, open to the perception of others. Embodiment clearly manifests a set of strategies or what Sartre would perhaps have called a style of being, or Foucault "a stylistics of existence." This style is never fully self-styled, for living styles have a history, and that history conditions and limits possibilities. Consider gender, for instance, as *a corporeal style*, an "act," as it were, which is both intentional and performative, where "performative" itself carries the double-meaning of "dramatic" and "non-referential."

When de Beauvoir claims that "woman" is a historical idea and not a natural fact, she clearly underscores the distinction between sex, as biological facticity, and gender, as the cultural interpretation or signification of that facticity. To be female is, according to that distinction, a facticity which has no meaning, but to be a woman is to have *become* a woman, to compel the body to conform to an historical idea of "woman," to induce the body to become a cultural sign, to materialize oneself in obedience to an historically delimited possibility, and to do this as a sustained and repeated corporeal project. The notion of a "project," however, suggests the originating force of a radical will, and because gender is a project which has cultural survival as its end, the term *"strategy"* better suggests the situation of duress under which gender is a performance with clearly punitive consequences. Discrete genders are part of what "humanizes" individuals within contemporary culture; indeed, those who fail to do their gender right are regularly punished. Because there is neither an "essence" that gender expresses or externalizes nor an objective ideal to which gender aspires; because gender is not a fact, the various acts of gender create the idea of gender, and without those acts there would be no gender at all. Gender is, thus, a construction that regularly conceals its genesis. The tacit collective agreement to perform, produce, and sustain discrete and polar genders as cultural fictions is obscured by the credibility of its own production. The authors of gender become entranced by their own fictions whereby the construction compels one's belief in its necessity and naturalness. The historical possibilities materialized through various corporeal styles are nothing other than those punitively regulated cultural fictions that are alternately embodied and disguised under duress.

How useful is a phenomenological point of departure for a feminist description of gender? On the surface it appears that phenomenology shares with feminist analysis a commitment to grounding theory in lived experience, and in revealing the way in which the world is produced through the constituting acts of subjective experience. Clearly, not all feminist theory would privilege the point of view of the subject (Kristeva once objected to feminist theory as "too existentialist"),[4] and yet the feminist claim that the personal is political suggests, in part, that subjective experience is not only structured by existing political arrangements, but effects and structures those arrangements in turn. Feminist theory has sought to understand the way in which systemic or pervasive political and cultural structures are enacted and reproduced through individual acts and practices, and how the analysis of ostensibly personal situations is clarified through situating the issues in a broader and shared cultural context. Indeed, the feminist impulse, and I am sure there is more than one, has often emerged in the recognition that my pain or my silence or my anger or my perception is finally not mine alone, and that it delimits me in a shared cultural situation which in turn enables and empowers me in certain unanticipated ways. The personal is thus implicity political inasmuch as it is conditioned by shared social structures, but the personal has also been immunized against political challenge to the extent that public/private distinctions endure. For feminist theory, then, the personal becomes an expansive category, one which accomodates, if only implicitly, political structures usually viewed as public. Indeed, the very meaning of the political expands as well. At its best, feminist theory involves a dialectical expansion of both of these categories. My situation does not cease to be mine just because it is the situation of someone else, and my acts, individual as they are, nevertheless reproduce the situation of my gender, and do that in various ways. In other words, there is, latent in the personal is political formulation of feminist theory, a supposition that the life-world of gender relations is constituted, at least partially, through the concrete and historically mediated *acts* of individuals. Considering that "the" body is invariably transformed into his body or her body, the body is only known through its gendered appearance. It would seem imperative to consider the way in which this gendering of the body occurs. My suggestion is that the body becomes its gender through a series of acts which are renewed, revised, and consolidated through time. From a feminist point of view, one might try to reconceive the gendered body as the legacy of sedimented acts rather than a predetermined or foreclosed structure, essence, or fact, whether natural, cultural, or linguistic.

The feminist appropriation of the phenomenological theory of constitution might employ the notion of an *act* in a richly ambiguous sense. If the personal is a category which expands to include the wider political and social structures, then the *acts* of the gendered subject would be similarly expansive. Clearly, there are political acts which are deliberate and instrumental actions of political organizing, resistance collective intervention with the broad aim of instating a more just set of social and political relations. There are thus acts which are done in the name of women, and then there are acts in and of themselves, apart from any instrumental consequence, that challenge the category of woman itself. Indeed, one ought to consider the futility of a political program which seeks radically to transform the social situation of women without first determining whether the category of woman is socially constructed in such a way that to be a woman is, by definition, to be in an oppressed situation. In an understandable desire to forge bonds of solidarity, feminist discourse has often relied upon the category of woman as a universal presupposition of cultural experience which, in its universal status, provides a false ontological promise of eventual political solidarity. In a culture in which the false universal of "man" has for the most part been presupposed as coextensive with humanness itself, feminist theory has sought with success to bring female specificity into visibility and to rewrite the history of culture in terms which acknowledge the presence, the influence, and the oppression of women. Yet, in this effort to combat the invisibility of women as a category feminists run the risk of rendering visible a category which may or may not be representative of the concrete lives of women. As feminists, we have been less eager, I think, to consider the status of the category itself and, indeed, to discern the conditions of oppression which issue from an unexamined reproduction of gender identities which sustain discrete and binary categories of man and woman.

When de Beauvoir claims that woman is an "historical situation," she emphasizes that the body suffers a certain cultural construction, not only through conventions that sanction and proscribe how one acts one's body, the "act" or performance that one's body is, but also in the tacit conventions that structure the way the body is culturally perceived. Indeed, if gender is the cultural significance that the sexed body assumes, and if that significance is codetermined through various acts and their cultural perception, then it would appear that from within the terms of culture it is not possible to know sex as distinct from gender. The reproduction of the category of gender is enacted on a large political scale, as when women first enter a profession or gain certain rights, or are reconceived in legal or political discourse in significantly new ways. But the more mundane reproduction of gendered identity takes place through the various ways in which bodies are acted in relationship to the deeply entrenched or sedimented expectations of gendered existence. Consider that there is a sedimentation of gender norms that produces the peculiar phenomenon of a natural sex, or a real woman, or any number of prevalent and compelling social fictions, and that this is a sedimentation that over time has produced a set of corporeal styles which, in reified form, appear as the natural configuration of bodies into sexes which exist in a binary relation to one another.

II Binary genders and the heterosexual contract

To guarantee the reproduction of a given culture, various requirements, well-established in the anthropological literature of kinship, have instated sexual reproduction within the confines of a heterosexually based system of marriage which requires the reproduction of human beings in certain gendered modes which, in effect, guarantee the eventual reproduction of that kinship system. As Foucault and others have pointed out, the association of a natural sex with a discrete gender and with an ostensibly natural "attraction" to the opposing sex/gender is an unnatural conjunction of cultural constructs in the service of reproductive interests.[5] Feminist cultural anthropology and kinship studies have shown how cultures are governed by conventions that not only regulate and guarantee the production, exchange, and consumption of material goods, but also reproduce the bonds of kinship itself, which require taboos and a punitive regulation of reproduction to effect that end. Lévi-Strauss has shown how the incest taboo works to guarantee the channeling of sexuality into various modes of heterosexual marriage,[6] Gayle Rubin has argued convincingly that the incest taboo produces certain kinds of discrete gendered identities and sexualities.[7] My point is simply that one way in which this system of compulsory heterosexuality is reproduced and concealed is through the cultivation of bodies into discrete sexes with "natural" appearances and "natural" heterosexual dispositions. Although the ethnocentric conceit suggests a progression beyond the mandatory structures of kinship relations as described by Lévi-Strauss, I would suggest, along with Rubin, that contemporary gender identities are so many marks or "traces" of residual kinship. The contention that sex, gender, and heterosexuality are historical products which have become conjoined and reified as natural over time has received a good deal of critical attention not only from Michel Foucault, but from Monique Wittig, gay historians, and various cultural anthropologists and social psychologists in recent years.[8] These theories, however, still lack the critical resources for thinking radically about the historical sedimentation of sexuality and sex-related constructs if they do not delimit and describe the mundane manner in which these constructs are produced, reproduced, and maintained within the field of bodies.

Can phenomenology assist a feminist reconstruction of the sedimented character of sex, gender, and sexuality at the level of the body? In the first place, the phenomenological focus on the various acts by which cultural identity is constituted and assumed provides a felicitous starting point for the feminist effort to understand the mundane manner in which bodies get crafted into genders. The formulation of the body as a mode of dramatizing or enacting possibilities offers a way to understand how a cultural convention is embodied and enacted. But it seems difficult, if not impossible, to imagine a way to conceptualize the scale and systemic character of women's oppression from a theoretical position which takes constituting acts to be its point of departure. Although individual acts do work to maintain and reproduce systems of oppression, and, indeed, any theory of personal political responsibility presupposes such a view, it doesn't follow that oppression is a sole consequence of such acts. One might argue that without human beings whose various acts, largely construed, produce and maintain oppressive conditions, those conditions would fall away, but note that the relation between acts and conditions is neither unilateral nor unmediated.

There are social contexts and conventions within which certain acts not only become possible but become conceivable as acts at all. The transformation of social relations becomes a matter, then, of transforming hegemonic social conditions rather than the individual acts that are spawned by those conditions. Indeed, one runs the risk of addressing the merely indirect, if not epiphenomenal, reflection of those conditions if one remains restricted to a politics of acts.

But the theatrical sense of an "act" forces a revision of the individualist assumptions underlying the more restricted view of constituting acts within phenomenological discourse. As a given temporal duration within the entire performance, "acts" are a shared experience and "collective action." Just as within feminist theory the very category of the personal is expanded to include political structures, so is there a theatrically based, and, indeed, less individually oriented view of acts that goes some of the way in defusing the criticism of act theory as "too existentialist." The act that gender is, the act that embodied agents *are* inasmuch as they dramatically and actively embody and, indeed, *wear* certain cultural significations, is clearly not one's act alone. Surely, there are nuanced and individual ways of *doing* one's gender, but *that* one does it, and that one does it *in accord with* certain sanctions and proscriptions, is clearly not a fully individual matter. Here again, I don't mean to minimize the effect of certain gender norms which originate within the family and are enforced through certain familial modes of punishment and reward and which, as a consequence, might be construed as highly individual, for even there family relations recapitulate, individualize, and specify pre-existing cultural relations; they are rarely, if ever, radically original. The act that one does, the act that one performs, is, in a sense, an act that has been going on before one arrived on the scene. Hence, gender is an act which has been rehearsed, much as a script survives the particular actors who make use of it, but which requires individual actors in order to be actualized and reproduced as reality once again. The complex components that go into an act must be distinguished in order to understand the kind of acting in concert and acting in accord which acting one's gender invariably is.

In what senses, then, is gender an act? As the anthropologist Victor Turner suggests in his studies of ritual social drama, social action requires a performance which is *repeated*. This repetition is at once a reenactment and reexperiencing of a set of meanings already socially established; it is the mundane and ritualized form of their legitimation.[9] When this conception of social performance is applied to gender, it is clear that although there are individual bodies that enact these significations by becoming stylized into gendered modes, this "action" is immediately public as well. There are temporal and collective dimensions to these actions, and their public nature is not inconsequential; indeed, the performance is effected with the strategic aim of maintaining gender within its binary frame. Understood in pedagogical terms, the performance renders social laws explicit.

As a public action and performative act, gender is not a radical choice or project that reflects a merely individual choice, but neither is it imposed or inscribed upon the individual, as some post-structuralist displacements of the subject would contend. The body is not passively scripted with cultural codes, as if it were a lifeless recipient of wholly pre-given cultural relations. But neither do embodied selves pre-exist the cultural conventions which essentially signify bodies. Actors are always already on the stage, within the terms of the performance. Just as a script may be enacted in various ways, and just as the play requires both text and interpretation, so the gendered body acts its part in a culturally restricted corporeal space and enacts interpretations within the confines of already existing directives.

Although the links between a theatrical and a social role are complex and the distinctions not easily drawn (Bruce Wilshire points out the limits of the comparison in *Role-Playing and Identity: The Limits of Theatre as Metaphor*[10]), it seems clear that, although theatrical performances can meet with political censorship and scathing criticism, gender performances in non-theatrical contexts are governed by more clearly punitive and regulatory social conventions. Indeed, the sight of a transvestite on stage can compel pleasure and applause, while the sight of the same transvestite on the seat next to us on the bus can compel fear, rage, even violence. The conventions which mediate proximity and identification in these two instances are clearly quite different. I want to make two different kinds of claims regarding this tentative distinction. In the theatre, one can say, "this is just an act," and de-realize the act, make acting into something quite distinct from what is real. Because of this distinction, one can maintain one's sense of reality in the face of this temporary challenge to our existing ontological assumptions about gender arrangements; the various conventions which announce that "this is only a play" allows strict lines to be drawn between the performance and life. On the street or in the bus, the act becomes dangerous, if it does, precisely because there are no theatrical conventions to delimit the purely imaginary character of the act. Indeed, on the street or in the bus, there is no presumption that the act is distinct from a reality; the disquieting effect of the act is that there are no conventions that facilitate making this separation. Clearly, there is theatre which attempts to contest or, indeed, break down those conventions that demarcate the imaginary from the real (Richard Schechner brings this out quite clearly in *Between Theatre and Anthropology*[11]). Yet in those cases one confronts the same phenomenon, namely that the act is not contrasted with the real, but *constitutes* a reality that is in some sense new, a modality of gender that cannot readily be assimilated into the pre-existing categories that regulate gender reality. From the point of view of those established categories, one may want to claim, but oh, this is *really* a girl or a woman, or this is *really* a boy or a man, and further that the *appearance* contradicts the *reality* of the gender, that the discrete and familiar reality must be there, nascent, temporarily unrealized, perhaps realized at other times or other places. The transvestite, however, can do more than simply express the distinction between sex and gender, but challenges, at least implicitly, the distinction between appearance and reality that structures a good deal of popular thinking about gender identity. If the "reality" of gender is constituted by the performance itself, then there is no recourse to an essential and unrealized "sex" or "gender" which gender performances ostensibly express. Indeed, the transvestite's gender is as fully real as that of anyone whose performance complies with social expectations.

Gender reality is performative, which means, quite simply, that it is real only to the extent that it is performed. It seems fair to say that certain kinds of acts are usually interpreted as expressive of a gender core or identity, and that these acts either conform to an expected gender identity or contest that expectation in some way. That expectation, in turn, is based upon the perception of sex, where sex is understood to be the discrete and factic datum of primary sexual characteristics. This implicit and popular theory of acts and gestures as *expressive* of gender suggests that gender itself is something prior to the various acts, postures, and gestures by which it is dramatized and known; indeed, gender appears to the popular imagination as a substantial core which might well be understood as the spiritual or psychological correlate of biological sex.[12] If gender attributes, however, are not expressive but performative, then these attributes effectively constitute the identity they are said to express or reveal. The distinction between expression and performativeness is quite crucial, for if gender attributes and acts, the various ways in which a body shows or produces its cultural signification, are performative, then there is no pre-existing identity by which an act or attribute might be measured; there would be no true or false, real or distorted acts of gender, and the postulation of a true gender identity would be revealed as a regulatory fiction. That gender reality is created through sustained social performances means that the very notions of an essential sex, a true or abiding masculinity or femininity, are also constituted as part of the strategy by which the performative aspect of gender is concealed.

As a consequence, gender cannot be understood as a *role* which either expresses or disguises an interior "self," whether that "self" is conceived as sexed or not. As performance which is performative, gender is an "act," broadly construed, which constructs the social fiction of its own psychological interiority. As opposed to a view such as Erving Goffman's which posits a self which assumes and exchanges various "roles" within the complex social expectations of the "game" of modern life,[13] I am suggesting that this self is not only irretrievably "outside," constituted in social discourse, but that the ascription of interiority is itself a publically regulated and sanctioned form of essence fabrication. Genders, then, can be neither true nor false, neither real nor apparent. And yet, one is compelled to live in a world in which genders constitute univocal signifiers, in which gender is stabilized, polarized, rendered discrete and intractable. In effect, gender is made to comply with a model of truth and falsity which not only contradicts its own performative fluidity, but serves a social policy of gender regulation and control. Performing one's gender wrong initiates a set of punishments both obvious and indirect, and performing it well provides the reassurance that there is an essentialism of gender identity after all. That this reassurance is so easily displaced by anxiety, that culture so readily punishes or marginalizes those who fail to perform the illusion of gender essentialism should be sign enough that on some level there is social knowledge that the truth or falsity of gender is only socially compelled and in no sense ontologically necessitated.[14]

III Feminist theory: beyond an expressive model of gender

This view of gender does not pose as a comprehensive theory about what gender is or the manner of its construction, and neither does it prescribe an explicit feminist political program. Indeed, I can imagine this view of gender being used for a number of discrepant political strategies. Some of my friends may fault me for this and insist that any theory of gender constitution has political presuppositions and implications, and that it is impossible to separate a theory of gender from a political philosophy of feminism. In fact, I would agree, and argue that it is primarily political interests which create the social phenomena of gender itself, and that without a radical critique of gender constitution feminist theory fails to take stock of the way in which oppression structures the ontological categories through which gender is conceived. Gayatri Spivak has argued that feminists need to rely on an operational essentialism, a false ontology of women as a universal in order to advance a feminist political program.[15] She knows that the category of "women" is not fully expressive, that the multiplicity and discontinuity of the referent mock and rebel against the univocity of the sign, but suggests it could be used for strategic purposes. Kristeva suggests something similar, I think, when she prescribes that feminists use the category of women as a political tool without attributing ontological integrity to the term, and adds that, strictly speaking, women cannot be said to exist.[16] Feminists might well worry about the political implications of claiming that women do not exist, especially in light of the persuasive arguments advanced by Mary Anne Warren in her book *Gendericide*.[17] She argues that social policies regarding population control and reproductive technology are designed to limit and, at times, eradicate the existence of women altogether. In light of such a claim, what good does it do to quarrel about the metaphysical status of the term, and perhaps, for clearly political reasons, feminists ought to silence the quarrel altogether.

But it is one thing to use the term and know its ontological insufficiency and quite another to articulate a normative vision for feminist theory which celebrates or emancipates an essence, a nature, or a shared cultural reality which cannot be found. The option I am defending is not to redescribe the world from the point of view of women. I don't know what that point of view is, but whatever it is, it is not singular, and not mine to espouse. It would only be half right to claim that I am interested in how the phenomenon of men's or women's point of view gets constituted, for while I do think that those points of views are, indeed, socially constituted, and that a reflexive genealogy of those points of view is important to do, it is not primarily the gender episteme that I am interested in exposing, deconstructing, or reconstructing. Indeed, it is the presupposition of the category of woman itself that requires a critical genealogy of the complex institutional and discursive means by which it is constituted. Although some feminist literary critics suggest that the presupposition of sexual difference is necessary for all discourse, that position reifies sexual difference as the founding moment of culture and precludes an analysis not only of how sexual difference is constituted to begin with but how it is continuously constituted, both by the masculine tradition that preempts the universal point of view, and by those feminist positions that construct the univocal category of "women" in the name of expressing or, indeed, liberating a subjected class. As Foucault claimed about those humanist efforts to liberate the criminalized subject, the subject that is freed is even more deeply shackled than originally thought.[18]

Clearly, though, I envision the critical genealogy of gender to rely on a phenomenological set of presuppositions, most important among them the expanded conception of an "act" which is both socially shared and historically constituted, and which is performative in the sense I previously described. But a critical genealogy needs to be supplemented by a politics of performative gender acts, one which both redescribes existing gender identities and offers a prescriptive view about the kind of gender reality there ought to be.

196

The redescription needs to expose the reifications that tacitly serve as substantial gender cores or identities, and to elucidate both the act and the strategy of disavowal which at once constitute and conceal gender as we live it. The prescription is invariably more difficult, if only because we need to think a world in which acts, gestures, the visual body, the clothed body, the various physical attributes usually associated with gender, *express nothing*. In a sense, the prescription is utopian, but consists in an imperative to acknowledge the existing complexity of gender which our vocabulary invariably disguises and to bring that complexity into a dramatic cultural interplay without punitive consequences.

Certainly, it remains politically important to represent women, but to do that in a way that does not distort and reify the very collectivity the theory is supposed to emancipate. Feminist theory which presupposes sexual difference as the necessary and invariant theoretical point of departure clearly improves upon those humanist discourses which conflate the universal with the masculine and appropriate all of culture as masculine property. Clearly, it is necessary to re-read the texts of Western philosophy from the various points of view that have been excluded, not only to reveal the particular perspective and set of interests informing those ostensibly transparent descriptions of the real, but to offer alternative descriptions and prescriptions; indeed, to establish philosophy as a cultural practice, and to criticize its tenets from marginalized cultural locations. I have no quarrel with this procedure, and have clearly benefited from those analyses. My only concern is that sexual difference should not become a reification which unwittingly preserves a binary restriction on gender identity and an implicitly heterosexual framework for the description of gender, gender identity, and sexuality. There is, in my view, nothing about femaleness that is waiting to be expressed; there is, on the other hand, a good deal about the diverse experiences of women that is being expressed and still needs to be expressed, but caution is needed with respect to that theoretical language, for it does not simply report a pre-linguistic experience, but constructs that experience as well as the limits of its analysis. Regardless of the pervasive character of patriarchy and the prevalence of sexual difference as an operative cultural distinction, there is nothing about a binary gender system that is given. As a corporeal field of cultural play, gender is a basically innovative affair, although it is quite clear that there are strict punishments for contesting the script by performing out of turn or through unwarranted improvisations. Gender is not passively scripted on the body, and neither is it determined by nature, language, the symbolic, or the overwhelming history of patriarchy. Gender is what is put on, invariably, under constraint, daily and incessantly, with anxiety and pleasure, but if this continuous act is mistaken for a natural or linguistic given, power is relinquished to expand the cultural field bodily through subversive performances of various kinds.

NOTES

1 For a further discussion of de Beauvoir's feminist contribution to phenomenological theory, see my "Variations on sex and gender: Beauvoir's *The Second Sex*," *Yale French Studies* 172 (1986).

2 Maurice Merleau-Ponty, "The body in its sexual being," in *The Phenomenology of Perception*, trans. Colin Smith (Boston: Routledge and Kegan Paul, 1962).

3 Simone de Beauvoir, *The Second Sex*, trans. H.M. Parshley (New York: Vintage, 1974), 38.

4 Julia Kristeva, *Histoire d'Amour* (Paris: Editions Denoel, 1983), 242.

5 See Michel Foucault, *The History of Sexuality: An Introduction*, trans. Robert Hurley (New York: Random House, 1980), 154: "the notion of 'sex' made it possible to group together, in an artificial unity, anatomical elements, biological functions, conducts, sensations, and pleasures, and it enabled one to make use of this fictitious unity as a causal principle."

6 See Claude Lévi-Strauss, *The Elementary Structures of Kinship* (Boston: Beacon Press, 1965).

7 Gayle Rubin, "The traffic in women: notes on the 'political economy' of sex," in *Toward an Anthropology of Women*, ed. Rayna R. Reiter (New York: Monthly Review Press, 1975), 178–85.

8 See my "Variations on sex and gender: Beauvoir, Witting, and Foucault," in *Feminism as Critique*, ed. Seyla Benhabib and Drucila Cornell (London: Basil Blackwell, 1987 [distributed by the University of Minnesota Press]).

9 See Victor Turner, *Dramas, Fields, and Metaphors* (Ithaca: Cornell University Press, 1974). Clifford Geertz suggests in "Blurred genres: the refiguration of thought," in *Local Knowledge, Further Essays in Interpretive Anthropology* (New York: Basic Books, 1983), that the theatrical metaphor is used by recent social theory in two, often opposing, ways. Ritual theorists like Victor Turner focus on a notion of social drama of various kinds as a means for settling internal conflicts within a culture and regenerating social cohesion. On the other hand, symbolic action approaches, influenced by figures as diverse as Emile Durkheim, Kenneth Burke, and Michel Foucault, focus on the way in which political authority and questions of legitimation are thematized and settled within the terms of performed meaning. Geertz himself suggests that the tension might be viewed dialectically; his study of political organization in Bali as a "theater-state" is a case in point. In terms of an explicitly feminist account of gender as performative, it seems clear to me that an account of gender as ritualized public performance must be combined with an analysis of the political sanctions and taboos under which that performance may and may not occur within the public sphere free of punitive consequence.

10 Bruce Wilshire, *Role-Playing and Identity: The Limits of Theatre as Metaphor* (Boston: Routledge and Kegan Paul, 1981).

11 Richard Schechner, *Between Theatre and Anthropology* (Philadelphia: University of Pennsylvania Press, 1985). See, especially, "News, sex, and performance," 295–324.

12 In *Mother Camp* (Englewood Cliffs: Prentice-Hall, 1974), Anthropologist Esther Newton gives an urban ethnography of drag queens in which she suggests that all gender might be understood on the model of drag. In *Gender: An Ethnomethodological Approach* (Chicago: University of Chicago Press, 1978), Suzanne J. Kessler and Wendy McKenna argue that gender is an "accomplishment" which requires the skills of constructing the body into a socially legitimate artifice.

13 See Erving Goffman, *The Presentation of Self in Everyday Life* (Garden City: Doubleday, 1959).

14 See Michel Foucault's edition of *Herculine Barbin: The Journals of a Nineteenth Century French Hermaphrodite*, trans. Richard McDougall (New York: Pantheon Books, 1984) for an interesting display of the horror evoked by intersexed bodies. Foucault's introduction makes clear that the medical delimitation of univocal sex is yet another wayward application of the discourse on truth-as-identity. See also the work of Robert Edgerton in *American Anthropologist* on the cross-cultural variations of response to hermaphroditic bodies.

15 Remarks at the Center for Humanities, Wesleyan University, Spring, 1985.

16 Julia Kristeva, "Woman can never be defined," trans. Marilyn A. August, in *New French Feminisms*, ed. Elaine Marks and Isabelle de Courtivron (New York: Schocken, 1981).

17 Mary Anne Warren, *Gendericide: The Implications of Sex Selection* (New Jersey: Rowman and Allanheld, 1985).

18 Ibid.; Michel Foucault, *Discipline and Punish: The Birth of the Prison*, trans. Alan Sheridan (New York: Vintage Books, 1978).

READER CROSS-REFERENCES

Kirshenblatt-Gimblett – notes Butler's contribution to performance studies

Goffman, Gabler – the social and theatrical construction of the self

Phelan, Faber – oppositional and gendered performance art

Austin – defines the performative speech act

Parker and Sedgwick – theatrical and philosophical ideas of performativity

Harding – display of the gendered body in Africa

Derrida – concept of citation provides a mechanism for performance of gender

Blair – warns against discarding all biological understandings of behavior

25

INTRODUCTION TO *PERFORMATIVITY AND PERFORMANCE*

Andrew Parker and Eve Kosofsky Sedgwick

When is saying something doing something? And how is saying something doing something? If they aren't coeval with language itself, these questions certainly go as far back, even in European thought, as – take your pick – Genesis, Plato, Aristotle. Proximally, posed explicitly by the 1962 publication of the British philosopher J.L. Austin's *How to Do Things With Words,* they have resonated through the theoretical writings of the past three decades in a carnivalesque echolalia of what might be described as extraordinarily productive cross-purposes. One of the most fecund, as well as the most under-articulated, of such crossings has been the oblique intersection between performativity and the loose cluster of theatrical practices, relations, and traditions known as performance. The English Institute conference at which these essays were presented was an attempt, at a moment full of possibilities, to take stock of the uses, implications, reimagined histories, and new affordances of the performativities that are emerging from this conjunction.

That these issues reverberated through what has been, historically, a conference on English literature is only one of the many signs of theoretical convergence that has, of late, pushed performativity on to center stage. A term whose specifically Austinian valences have been renewed in the work of Jacques Derrida and Judith Butler, performativity has enabled a powerful appreciation of the ways that identities are constructed iteratively through complex citational processes.[1] If one consequence of this appreciation has been a heightened willingness to credit a performative dimension in all ritual, ceremonial, scripted behaviors, another would be the acknowledgment that philosophical essays themselves surely count as one such performative instance.[2] The irony is that, while philosophy has begun to shed some of its anti-theatrical prejudices, theater studies have been attempting, meanwhile, to take themselves out of (the) theater. Reimagining itself over the course of the past decade as the wider field of performance studies, the discipline has moved well beyond the classical ontology of the black box model to embrace a myriad of performance practices, ranging from stage to festival and everything in between: film, photography, television, computer simulation, music, "performance art," political demonstrations, health care, cooking, fashion, shamanistic ritual . . .[3]

Given these divergent developments, it makes abundant sense that performativity's recent history has been marked by cross-purposes. For while philosophy and theater now share "performative" as a common lexical item, the term has hardly come to mean "the same thing" for each.[4] Indeed, the stretch between theatrical and deconstructive meanings of "performative" seems to span the polarities of, at either extreme, the *extroversion* of the actor, the *introversion* of the signifier. Michael Fried's opposition between theatricality and absorption seems custom-made for this paradox about "performativity": in its deconstructive sense, performativity signals absorption; in the vicinity of the stage, however, the performative is the theatrical.[5] But in another range of usages, a text like Lyotard's *The Postmodern Condition* uses "performativity" to mean an extreme of something like *efficiency* – postmodern representation as a form of capitalist efficiency – while, again, the deconstructive "performativity" of Paul de Man or J. Hillis Miller seems to be characterized by the *dis*linkage precisely of cause and effect between the signifier and the world.[6] At the same time, it's worth keeping in mind that, even in deconstruction, more can be said of performative speech-acts than that they are ontologically dislinked or introversively nonreferential. Following on de Man's demonstration of "a radical estrangement between the meaning and the performance of any text" (298), one might want to dwell not so much on the nonreference of the performative, but rather on (what de Man calls) its necessarily "aberrant" relation to its own reference – the torsion, the mutual perversion, as one might say, of reference and performativity.

Significantly, perversion had already made a cameo appearance in *How to Do Things With Words* in a passage where the philosophical and theatrical meanings of performative actually do establish contact with each other.[7] After provisionally distinguishing in his first lecture conservatives from performatives – statements that merely describe some state of affairs from utterances that accomplish, in their very enunciation, an action that generates effects – Austin proceeded to isolate a special property of the latter: that if something goes wrong in the performance of a performative, "the utterance is then, we may say, not indeed false but in general *unhappy*" (14). Such "infelicity," Austin extrapolated, "is an ill to which *all* acts are heir which have the general character of ritual or ceremonial, all *conventional* acts" (18–19). But if illness was understood here as intrinsic to and thus constitutive of the structure of performatives – a performative utterance is one, as it were, that always may get sick – elsewhere Austin imposed a kind of quarantine in his decision to focus exclusively, in his "more general account" of speech-acts, on those that are "issued in ordinary circumstances":

> [A] performative utterance will, for example, be *in a peculiar way* hollow or void if said by an actor on the stage, or if introduced in a poem, or spoken in soliloquy. This applies in a similar manner to any and every utterance – a sea-change in special circumstances. Language in such circumstances is in special ways – intelligibly – used not seriously, but in ways *parasitic* upon its normal use – ways which fall under the doctrine of the *etiolations* of language. All this we are *excluding* from consideration.
>
> (22)

This passage, of course, forms the heart of Derrida's reading of Austin in "Signature event context": where Austin sought to purge from his analysis of "ordinary circumstances" a range of predicates he associated narrowly with theater, Derrida argued that these very predicates condition from the start the possibility of any and all performatives. "For, finally," asked Derrida, "is not what Austin excludes as anomalous, exceptional, 'nonserious,' that is, *citation* (on the stage, in a poem, or in a soliloquy), the determined modification of a general citationality – or rather, a general iterability – without which there would not even be a 'successful' performative?" (*Margins*, 325). Where Austin, then, seemed intent on separating the actor's citational practices from ordinary speech-act performances, Derrida regarded both as structured by a generalized iterability, a pervasive theatricality common to stage and world alike.

Much, of course, has long since been made of Austin's parasite, which has gone on to enjoy a distinguished career in literary theory and criticism. And Derrida's notion of a generalized iterability has played a significant role in the emergence of the newly expanded performance studies. Yet what, to our knowledge, has been underappreciated (even, apparently, by Derrida) is the nature of the perversion which, for Austin, needs to be expelled as it threatens to blur the difference between theater and world. After all these years, in other words, we finally looked up "etiolation" and its cognates in our handy Merriam-Webster, and were surprised to discover the following range of definitions:

> **etiolate** (vt): 1) to bleach and alter or weaken the natural development of (a green plant) by excluding sunlight; 2) to make pale and sickly <remembering how drink hardens the skin and how drugs etiolate it – Jean Stafford>; 3) to rob of natural vigor, to prevent or inhibit the full physical, emotional, or mental growth of (as by sheltering or pampering) <the shade of Poets' walk, a green tunnel that has etiolated so many . . . poets – Cyril Connolly>
>
> **etiolated** (adj): 1) grown in absence of sunlight, blanched; lacking in vigor or natural exuberance, lacking in strength of feeling or appetites, effete <etiolated poetry>
>
> **etiolation** (n): 1) the act, process or result of growing a plant in darkness; 2) the loss or lessening of natural vigor, overrefinement of thought or emotional sensibilities: decadence
>
> **etiology** (n): a science or doctrine of causation or of the demonstration of causes; 2) all the factors that contribute to the occurrence of a disease or abnormal condition

What's so surprising, in a thinker otherwise strongly resistant to moralism, is to discover the pervasiveness with which the excluded theatrical is hereby linked with the perverted, the artificial, the unnatural, the abnormal, the decadent, the effete, the diseased. We seem, with Austinian "etiolation," to be transported not just to the horticultural laboratory, but back to a very different scene: the Gay 1890s of Oscar Wilde. Striking that, even for the dandyish Austin, theatricality would be inseparable from a normatively homophobic thematics of the "peculiar," "anomalous, exceptional, 'nonserious.'"

If the performative has thus been from its inception already infected with queerness, the situation has hardly changed substantially today. The question of when and how saying something is doing something echoed, to take one frighteningly apt example, throughout C-SPAN's coverage of the debates surrounding the Pentagon's 1993 "don't ask, don't tell, don't pursue" policy on lesbians and gay men in the US military. The premise of the new policy is:

> Sexual *orientation* will not be a bar to service unless manifested by homosexual *conduct*. The military will discharge members who engage in homosexual conduct, defined as a homosexual act, a *statement* that the member is homosexual or bisexual, or a marriage or attempted marriage to someone of the same gender.[8]

"Act," "conduct," and "statement" pursue their coercively incoherent dance on the ground of identity, of "orientation." Since the unveiling of the policy, all branches of government have been constrained to philosophize endlessly about what kind of *statement* can constitute "homosexual *conduct*," as opposed to orientation, and hence trigger an investigation aimed at punishment or separation. Performativity – as any reader of Austin will recognize – lives in the examples. Here is an example of a US Congressman imitating J.L. Austin:

> Representative Ike Skelton, a Missouri Democrat who heads the House [Armed Services Military Forces and Personnel] subcommittee, asked [the Joint Chiefs of Staff] for reactions to four situations: a private says he is gay; a private says he thinks he is gay; an entire unit announces at 6:30 A.M. muster that they are all gay; a private frequents a gay [bar] every Friday night, reads gay magazines and marches in gay parades. He asked what would happen in each situation under the new policy.[9]

Such highly detailed interrogations of the relation of *speech* to *act* are occurring in the space of a relatively recent interrogation of the relation of *act* to *identity*. "Sexual orientation will not be a bar to service unless manifested by homosexual conduct" – contrast these fine discriminations with the flat formulation that alone defined the issue until 1993: "Homosexuality is incompatible with military service." In response to many different interests, the monolith of "homosexuality" has diffracted into several different elements that evoke competing claims for legitimation or censure. Unlikely as the influence may seem, the new policy is clearly founded in a debased popularization of Foucauldian and post-Foucauldian work in the history of sexuality. Probably through the work of legal scholars involved in gay/lesbian advocacy, the queer theorists' central distinction between same-sex sexual *acts* and historically contingent gay/lesbian *identities* has suddenly become a staple of public discourse from Presidential announcements to the call-in shows (assuming it's possible at this point to distinguish between the two). Yet the popularization of this analytic tool has occurred through an assimilation of it to such highly phobic formulations as the Christian one, "Hate the sin but love the sinner." (Was it for this that the careful scholarship of the past decade has traced out the living and dialectical linkages and gaps between same-sex acts and queer and queer-loving identities? – all of which need to be nurtured and affirmed if any are to flourish.)

A variety of critiques of agency, as well, have begun to put interpretive pressure on the relations between the individual and the group as those are embodied, negotiated, or even ruptured by potent acts of speech or silence. Viewed through the lenses of a postmodern deconstruction of agency, Austin can be seen to have tacitly performed two radical condensations: of the complex producing and underwriting relations on the "hither" side of the utterance, and of the no-less-constitutive negotiations that comprise its uptake. Bringing these sites under the scrutiny of the performative hypothesis, Austin makes it possible to see how much more unpacking is necessary than he himself has performed. To begin with, Austin tends to treat the speaker as if s/he were all but coextensive – at least, continuous – with the power by which the individual speech-act is initiated and authorized and may be enforced. (In the most extreme example, he seems to suggest that war is what happens when individual citizens declare war! [40, 156].) "Actions can only be performed by persons," he writes, "and obviously in our cases [of explicit performatives] the utterer must be the performer" (60). Foucauldian, Marxist, deconstructive, psychoanalytic, and other recent theoretical projects have battered at the self-evidence of that "obviously" – though in post-Foucauldian theory, in particular, it seems clear that the leverage for such a critique is available precisely in the space opened up by the Austinian interest in provisionally distinguishing what is being said from the fact of the saying of it.[10]

If Austin's work finds new ways to make a deconstruction of *the performer* both necessary and possible, it is even more suggestive about the "thither" side of the speech-act, the complex process (or, with a more postmodernist inflection, the complex space) of uptake. Austin's rather bland invocation of "the proper context" (in which a person's saying something is to count as doing something) has opened, under pressure of recent theory, on to a populous and contested scene in which the role of silent or implied witnesses, for example, or the quality and structuration of the bonds that unite auditors or link them to speakers, bear as much explanatory weight as do the particular speech-acts of supposed individual speech agents. Differing crucially (as, say, theater differs from film?) from a more familiar, psychoanalytically founded interrogation of *the gaze*, this interrogation of the space of reception involves more contradictions and discontinuities than any available account of interpellation can so far do justice to; but interpellation may be among the most useful terms for beginning such an analysis. (In the Congressional hearings on "don't ask, don't tell," a lively question was this: if a drill sergeant motivates a bunch of recruits by yelling "Faggots!" at them, is it permissible for a recruit to raise his hand and respond, "Yes, sir"?) It is in this theoretical surround that the link between performativity and performance in the theatrical sense has become, at last, something more than a pun or an unexamined axiom: it emerges, as in many of the essays collected here, as an active question.

The most classic Austinian examples (those unceasing invocations of the first person singular present indicative active) open up newly to such approaches. "I dare you," for instance, gets classified cursorily, along with "defy," "protest," "challenge," in Austin's baggy category of the behabitives, which "include the notion of reaction to other people's behavior and fortunes and of attitudes and expressions of attitudes to someone else's past conduct or imminent conduct" (160–1). But to do justice to the performative force of "I dare you," as opposed to its arguably *constative* function of expressing "attitudes," requires a disimpaction of the scene, as well as the act, of utterance. To begin with, while "I dare you" ostensibly involves only a singular first and a singular second person, it effectually depends as well on the tacit requisition of a third person plural, a "they" of witness – whether or not literally present. In daring you to perform some foolhardy act (or else expose yourself as, shall we say, a wuss), "I" (hypothetically singular) necessarily invoke a consensus of the eyes of others. It is these eyes through which you risk being seen as a wuss; by the same token, it is *as* people who share with me a contempt for wussiness that these others are interpellated, with or without their consent, by the act I have performed in daring you.

Now, these people, supposing them real and present, may or may not in fact have any interest in sanctioning against wussiness. They might, indeed, themselves be wussy and proud of it. They may wish actively to oppose a social order based on contempt for wussitude. They may simply, for one reason or another, not identify with my contempt for wusses. Alternatively they may be skeptical of my own standing in the ongoing war on wussiness – they may be unwilling to leave the work of its arbitration to me; may wonder if I harbor wussish tendencies myself, perhaps revealed in my unresting need to test the w-quotient of others. For that matter, you yourself, the person dared, may share with them any of these skeptical attitudes on the subject; and may additionally doubt, or be uninterested in, *their* authority to classify you as wuss or better.

Thus, "I dare you" invokes the presumption, but *only* the presumption, of a consensus between speaker and witnesses, and to some extent between all of them and the addressee. The presumption is embodied in the lack of a formulaic negative response to being dared, or to being interpellated as witness to a dare. The fascinating and powerful class of negative performatives – disavowal, renunciation, repudiation, "count me out" – is marked, in almost every instance, by the asymmetrical property of being much less prone to becoming conventional than the positive performatives. Negative performatives tend to have a high threshold. (Thus Dante speaks of refusal – even refusal through cowardice – as something "great.")[11] It requires little presence of mind to find the comfortable formula "I dare you," but a good deal more for the dragooned witness to disinterpellate with, "Don't do it on my account."

Nonetheless such feats are possible, are made possible by the utterance itself; and to that extent it is necessary to understand any instance of "I dare you" as constituting a crisis quite as much as it constitutes a discrete act. For in daring you, in undertaking through any given iteration to reinscribe a set of presumptive valuations more deeply, and thereby to establish more firmly my own authority to wield them, I place under stress the consensual nature both of those valuations and of my own authority. To have my dare greeted with a witnesses' chorus of "Don't do it on our account" would radically alter the social, the political, the interlocutory (I-you-they) space of our encounter. So, in a different way, would your calmly accomplishing the dare and coming back to me, before the same witnesses, with the expectation of my accomplishing it in turn.

NOTES

1 Jacques Derrida, "Signature event context," in *Margins of Philosophy*, trans. Alan Bass (Chicago, 1982); Judith Butler, *Gender Trouble: Feminism and the Subversion of Identity* (New York, 1990), and *Bodies that Matter: On the Discursive Limits of "Sex"* (New York, 1993).

2 An exemplary instance of this acknowledgment would be Shoshan Felman, *The Literary Speech Act*, trans. Catherine Porter (Ithaca, 1983), which undertakes both a speech-act reading of *Don Juan* and a theatrical reading of Austin.

3 Among the many texts that reflect this transformation, see Sue-Ellen Case, ed., *Performing Feminisms* (Baltimore, 1990); Richard Schechner, *Between Theater and Anthropology* (Philadelphia, 1985); Michael Taussig, *Mimesis and Alterity* (New York, 1993); and Victor Turner, *The Anthropology of Performance* (Baltimore, 1985). . . . On the ontological distinctions that circumscribe traditional notions of theatrical space, see Philippe Lacoue-Labarthe, "Theatrum analyticum," *Glyph* 2 (1977), 122–43, and Geoffrey Bennington, *Lyotard: Writing the Event* (New York, 1988): "A theatre involves three limits or divisions or closures. First, the outside walls of the building itself. The 'real world' is outside, the theatre inside . . . Within the theatre comes a second limit or division, separating the stage from the audience, marking off the place observed and the place from which it is observed. . . . A third essential limit separates the stage from the wings or back-stage" (10–11).

4 For an extension of this discussion, see Eve Kosofsky Sedgwick, "Queer performativity: Henry James's *The Art of the Novel*," *GLQ* 1 (1993), 2, from which the remainder of this paragraph is taken.

5 Michael Fried, *Absorption and Theatricality: Painting and Beholder in the Age of Diderot* (Berkeley, 1980).

6 Jean-François Lyotard, *The Postmodern Condition: A Report on Knowledge*, trans. Geoff Bennington and Brian Massumi (Minneapolis, 1984); J. Hillis Miller, *Tropes, Parables, Performatives: Essays on Twentieth-Century Literature* (Durham, 1991); Paul de Man, *Allegories of Reading: Figural Language in Rousseau, Nietzsche, Rilke, and Proust* (New Haven, 1979).

7 J.L. Austin, *How to Do Things With Words* (Cambridge, Mass., 1975).

8 "Text of Pentagon's new policy guidelines on homosexuals in the military," *New York Times* (20 July 1993), A16 (national edition), emphasis added.

9 Eric Schmitt, "New gay policy emerges as a cousin of status quo," *New York Times* (22 July 1993), A14 (national edition).

10 Foucault writes, for instance, about sexuality:

> The central issue . . . is not to determine whether one says yes or no to sex, whether one formulates prohibitions or permissions, whether one asserts its importance or denies its effects . . . but to account for the fact that it is spoken about . . . What is at issue, briefly, is the overall "discursive fact."
>
> (*The History of Sexuality, Vol. 1: An Introduction*, trans. Robert Hurley [New York, 1978]).

The Foucauldian move is not, of course, identical to Austin's distinction between the (true or false) constatation of an utterance, and its performative force – a de-emphasis of yes versus no – is not the same as a de-emphasis of true versus false. The two moves are congruently structured, however; they invoke and reward very similar interpretive skills. We might say that both Austin and Foucault train readers to identify and perform the kind of figure/ground reversals analyzed by the Gestalt psychology of the first half of the twentieth century. Austin, for instance, abandoning the attempt to distinguish between some utterances that are intrinsically performative and others that are intrinsically constative, finally offers a substitute account, applicable to any utterance, that is couched in terms (such as the curious intransitive verb "to abstract") of perception and attention: "With the constative utterance, we abstract from the illocutionary . . . aspects of the speech act, and we concentrate on the locutionary . . . With the performative utterance, we attend as much as possible to the illocutionary force of the utterance, and abstract from the dimension of correspondence with facts" (145–6).

11 "*Il gran rifiuto*," in the *Inferno*, III, 60. See also Cavafy's poem "Che fece . . . il gran rifiuto," in Edmund Keeley and Philip Sherrard, trans., George Savidis, ed., *C.P. Cavafy: Collected Poems*, revised edn. (Princeton, 1992), 12.

READER CROSS-REFERENCES

Austin – the originator of the concept of performative speech acts

Butler – a more expansive and radical notion of the performative

De Marinis – semiotic interpretation vis-à-vis performance

Schechner, McKenzie, Jackson, Taylor – performance studies terminology

Derrida – ideas of citation and iterability make possible more radical understandings of performativity

J. Bell – application of performance studies to contemporary political issues

26

THEATER AND ANTHROPOLOGY, THEATRICALITY AND CULTURE[1]

Johannes Fabian

I A confession

I am not a theater-goer. There are years between the plays I occasionally take in because friends take me along. In 1997, during a stay in New York, I did have what was for me a busy season: in Brooklyn, I saw a Peter Brook play based on Sacks' *The Man Who Mistook . . . .* Then I went to a triple header, including a Woody Allen piece, in the Village, and finally there was a Shakespeare play, with free admission, by a group of young actors in the basement of Dean and de Luca's coffee shop. I left after the first act. The actors were unable or unwilling to adjust to the intimacy of the room and made a shouting match of the occasion. It was embarrassing. In fact, embarrassment may be the main reason for my apparent lack of interest. I am embarrassed by most institutionalized theater in my own society as I am embarrassed by church services I must attend for a confirmation, a wedding, or a funeral. In German, I would translate embarrassing as *peinlich*, a cognate of painful, something that hurts.

A few years ago, I was thrilled to see my seven-year-old daughter share my feelings. Together with her mother they had decided to attend at least one of three lectures I was invited to present in the Jefferson Rotunda at the University of Virginia. She appeared to enjoy the crowd in this strange, solemn environment until I approached the lectern. When I began to speak she tried to hide under her mother's skirts.

I am not going to analyze this response, but I should make my confession more complete and perhaps more intriguing. I have never known this feeling of embarrassment when, as an ethnographer of contemporary African culture in Zaire/Congo, I attended scores of impro-vised plays performed by a troupe of popular actors; or when I spent countless hours with members of religious movements engaged in teaching, prayer, and ecstatic experiences. The question of why this is so I shall leave unanswered. I remain unconvinced by the obvious explanation: as an anthropologist, I can maintain a kind of distance I do not have from my own culture. Such a response would run against everything I have tried to accomplish in my field.

II A trajectory

It is safe to assume that something that becomes a consuming interest in one's later professional life had its origin in early dreams and experiences. As to dreams, I don't recall ever wanting to be an actor, or even pretending to be one in the games we played as children. I do have vivid memories of a circus show we once put on in an arena built from the rubble that, three years after the bombs had fallen, still covered much of the street where we lived. I had no act, though; I was the impresario and announcer, or, rather, one of several who claimed that role.

As to early experiences, my memories of acting and pretending go deeper. They are tied to learning to speak a foreign language. My parents were bilingual but I grew up at first speaking German only. We lived in a region that eventually became a part of Poland, a process that had not yet become a fact when I was eight years old. Within what must have been weeks I spoke Polish. Perhaps I was prepared, having heard from early childhood the sound of another Slavic language, a Moravian dialect spoken by the adults in my family; and there must have been some gradual acquisition of linguistic competence. But my memory tells me nothing about acquiring anything and a lot about joining something; hanging out, playing along in an ongoing piece, pretending that there was nothing strange about mustachioed men kissing ladies' hands and young mothers openly nursing their children. I felt proud and excited about being talked to in Polish and being able to respond. (My accomplishment lasted for about a year; then we moved to the West and Polish became the only one of many languages I had to learn during my life of which I retained nothing but fragments – most of them, incidentally, performative bits and pieces such as swear words, proverbs, lines of songs. . . .)

Thus, some of my earliest experiences with theatricality in the sense of pretending, putting on an act, playing a role, I made in extraordinary situations where cultures came in contact, if that describes the political upheavals of the time, and where mastering contact was a matter of survival. Intercultural relations, I must have learned then, however unknowingly, happen in a tension between pride (or "honesty," "identity") and vanity ("make-believe," "showing off"). A lateral thought: What does it mean when Christian traditions in our Western culture declare pride and vanity sinful? Is righteousness worth the price of missed opportunities to learn?

In the trajectory I am trying to trace I took the next step as a student of sociology and social anthropology when I encountered the concepts of actor and role, both central to structuralist-functionalist theory. True, the sociological concept "actor" was derived from action, not from acting; still, a role was a role, to be learned, assumed, and played by actors. I never liked these concepts and terms. At best, they are dead metaphors; at worst, they make a routine of the theatricality of social life. . . . I have been equally distrustful of drama as a root metaphor for society or history. In sociological theory, I felt then, and understand better now, these concepts are most of the time used in a flat, positive, undialectical manner. They deny what they appear to affirm: that social and cultural relations are better understood when tensions, even contradictions, between action and acting, life and theater, are acknowledged.

By the time Victor Turner became known for doing just that (acknowledging tensions), I had decided to avoid theatrical metaphors. Eventually, it was trying to understand matters such as timing and shared time in communicative events that made me discover that much of cultural knowledge is performative rather than informative and that this has consequences for the way we think of ethnography. In the end, I rejoined Turner when I realized that the ethnographer, as he put it, really is an ethnodramaturg. In our fieldwork we are occasions for, sometimes producers of, cultural performances that may range from reciting a set of kinship terms to putting on a full-blown ritual spectacle. It was by fortunate accident rather than design that a troupe of actors helped me to gain and formulate these insights in the performative nature of much of culture.[2]

III Culture, theatricality, and anthropology

The significance of theater in multicultural situations would seem to depend on the theatricality of the culture. I would like to address this issue as an anthropologist (rather than as someone claiming special expertise in multicultural theater). I will do this with a recent *trouvaille* from readings on the history of exploration and early ethnography of Central Africa. My source is *Sur le Haut-Congo*, by Camille Coquilhat, published in 1888. The author was an officer of the Congo Free State. He took part in campaigns of "pacification" along the Congo River preparatory to occupation. As an observer and student of the populations that were to be colonized, he was more than equal to travelers and writers whom we now count as early anthropologists; as a writer he had moments that make one think of Joseph Conrad. At one point Coquilhat recounts the visit of two explorers and missionary pioneers, George Grenfell and Thomas Comber, to the station he commanded. They claimed to have seen among the "natives"

> la preuve d'un certain art dramatique. Ils racontent comme suit une "présentation" qu'ils déclarent fort agréable et qui dura plusieurs heures.

> [proof of a certain dramatic art. They, the missionaries, then tell of a "presentation" that, they declare, was quite pleasant and lasted for several hours.]

(156)

This is how, according to Coquilhat, the missionaries described the event:.

> Le spectacle commença par des danses agiles auxquelles succéda un acte évoquant dans le style grec; le "choeur" était gracieusement représenté par des petites filles de huit à douze ans. Un brancard d'étrange aspect était porté sur les épaules de quatre hommes. Il supportait, caché sous une couverture en flanelle rouge, un corps ou un objet invisible. Assise à l'une de ses extrémités, une gentille fillette regardait grave et triste. Ce brancard, qui était fait de bambous, fut déposé à terre et entouré par le choeur. Un air plaintif fut chanté, par une femme qui se plaça sur le côté de la civière. Nous ne pûmes comprendre grand'chose à ses paroles, mais

nous saisîmes ce fréquent refrain: Kawa-Ka, "Il n'est pas mort." Au bout d'un certain temps, les charmes de l'incantation furent considérés comme ayant opéré et le drap rouge se prit à onduler. On le releva et l'on mit à jour une jeune fille toute tremblante, comme si elle se trouvait dans un état aigu d'épilepsie. Deux personnes s'approchèrent et, la prenant par le bras, ils remirent sur ses pieds. [The missionaries state:] Cette représentation avait été donnée pour être agréable aux blancs.

To which Coquilhat adds:.

Je suis un peu tenté de croire que, dans cette occurrence, les indigènes ont simplement imité une de leurs nombreuses cérémonies de superstition.

[The spectacle began with some agile dances followed by an act evocative of the Greek style; the "chorus" was graciously represented by small girls between eight and twelve years. Four men carried a strange looking stretcher on their shoulders. On it was, hidden under a red flannel blanket, a body or some invisible object. A gentle little girl sat at one end of the bier, looking serious and sad. This stretcher, which was made of bamboo, was put down on the ground and the chorus placed itself around it. A woman took her position alongside the litter and sang a plaintive tune. We did not understand much of what she said but caught an often repeated refrain: "Kawa-Ka, He is not dead." After a certain time, the incantation was considered to have had its effect, and the red cover began to undulate. It was removed and revealed a young girl shaking all over, as if she were in the midst of an epileptic seizure. Two persons approached, took the girl by her arms and put her on her feet. The missionaries add: This representation had been made to please the whites.]

To which Coquilhat adds:.

[I'm a bit tempted to believe that, in this case, the natives simply imitated one of their numerous superstitious cermonies.]

(156)

Event classified and put aside. What happened? The missionary explorers reported on what they experienced as a theatrical performance. They suspected the intention behind it: what they saw was a self-presentation by this culture, put on to "please" them – to make them feel welcome, to entertain and perhaps enlighten them. When they compared what they saw to Greek tragedy, they built an intercultural bridge. Coquilhat, our protoanthropologist, manages, in one sentence, to shore up cultural distance by labeling the event superstitious *and* to deny the Africans creativity when he qualifies the performance as merely imitative of some ritual.

   Briefly, I suggest that the text tells us two important things about theatricality and encounters between cultures:[3]

- If allowed, people will let us get to know them by performing (parts of) their culture. Such knowledge – let us call it performative – demands participation (at least as an audience) and therefore some degree of mutual recognition.
- In a frame of mind I called "informative," that is, one that admits as knowledge only what is based on data first gathered and then controlled by the collector, performances need to be dismissed because they are threatening to any enterprise, project, or institution that depends for its existence on maintaining distance and control. Most nation-states, many religions and academic disciplines are of that kind.

It follows, then, that admitting theater as a source of intercultural knowledge involves recognition, not only of performative next to informative knowledge, but also of anarchic vs. hierarchic conceptions of knowledge. Only then can we begin to gain knowledge of other cultures through participative play and playful mimesis. Given the state of the world, it is safe to expect that such performative commingling would be regarded as subversive by most of the institutions on which our societies are built.

IV Theater and intercultural relations

Can theatricality (performativeness in communication, skills of representation, invention of forms of presentation, actual performances) be a means to achieve the aim of better intercultural relations? Again, it is hard to imagine how the answer to this could be negative. Still, there is a danger that must be avoided, which is to instrumentalize theatricality. That it can be instrumentalized we know from the uses to which it has been put, for instance, by fascist and other totalitarian regimes.

Perhaps the real question – and this was what the preceding scene should have prepared us for – is to find out whether theatricality can be a source as well as a mode of knowledge. Dancers, musicians, and actors may have the answer and be able to perform it. We anthropologists are expected, or doomed, to produce a discourse about it – which I am not going to do here, except to suggest that events like the one reported and commented on by Coquilhat may lead us to progress from a fairly well-understood issue – the role of theatricality and performance in gaining knowledge of other cultures – to pondering the possibility and reality of truly intercultural knowledge. This is a problem that will force us to question the very concept of culture as defining identity. Taking theatricality seriously may lead us to doubt the equation of social existence with cultural identity. We should ponder a thesis that can be put as follows:

> If "to be or not to be" is the question, then "to be *and* not to be" – to me the most succinct conception of performance – might be the answer.[4]

V An afterthought on anthropology and theater

That anthropologists have been fascinated by drama as a form of social action, as reflecting the nature of rituals, as illuminating the structure of societal processes is well known. But what about tragedy and comedy? The history of our discipline suggests that tragedy (drama that ends badly) preceded drama (which never really ends) as the key trope of encounter between Us and Them: early reports of encounters with so-called "savages," even many later inquiries of "natives," convey a sense of doom. Cultures and societies we Westerners study are destined to disappear, a belief supported by many texts. My current favorite quotation comes from Leo Frobenius, who concluded his dirge for *Das sterbende Africa: Die Seele eines Erdteils* (*Dying Africa: The Soul of a Continent*) with this appeal to students of Africa's past:

> Grabt!
> Aber achtet darauf, dass die Scherben nicht euch begraben.
> Erlebt!
> Unter jenen, die durch uns sterben.
> Sterben müssen.
> Erlebt es vor ihrem Tode.
> Damit ihr die Wiederaufstehung verstehen lernt!

> [Keep digging! But see to it that the shards don't bury you.
> Experience life.
> Among those who die through us.
> Must die.
> Experience it before they die.
> So that you learn to understand resurrection.]

> (503)

Though it would take more than one striking text to prove this, I think that anthropological discourse in general, and many accounts specifically, lean to a tragic mode of emplotment. Where is comedy in anthropology? Not in the funny stories anthropologists sometimes tell, nor in a growing number of ethnographies of humor, clowning, and such; as a trope helping us to understand the nature of our discipline, comedy must probably be sought as a comedy of intercultural errors, of mistaken identities, that confuse and complicate relations. . . . Any decent fieldworker knows how funny culture can be when it bungles because it has lost its certainties, its territory; pidgins and similar transcultural languages often are hilarious. But comedy in relations between cultures is something we are just beginning to explore. It is not a subject that is likely to flourish under conditions of political correctness. Laughter is my final cue here:

> Sie lachen über meinen Enthusiasmus für die Wilden beinahe so wie Voltaire über Rousseau, dass ihm das Gehen auf Vieren so wohl gefiele; glauben Sie nicht, dass ich deswegen unsre sittlichen und gesitteten Vorzüge, worin es auch sei, verachte. Das menschliche Geschlect ist zu einem Fortgange von Scenen, von Bildung, von Sitten bestimmt; wehe dem Menschen, dem die Scene misfällt, in der er auftreten, handeln und sich verleben soll. Wehe aber auch dem Philosophen über

Menschheit und Sitten, dem seine Scene die einzige ist, und der die erste immer auch als die schlechteste verkennet! Wenn alle mit zum Ganzen des fortgehenden Schauspiels gehören, so zeigt sich in jeder eine neue, sehr merkwürdige Seite der Menschheit . . .

[You laugh about my enthusiasm for the savage, almost like Voltaire ridiculed Rousseau saying that he must like walking on all fours; don't believe that I therefore despise our moral and well-behaved advantages, wherever they may be found. Humanity is destined to a progression of scenes, of education, of custom; pity on the person who dislikes the scene in which he must appear, act, and live out his life! Pity also on the philosopher of humanity and customs who has no scene but his own and who mistakes the first one always for the worst. If all of them belong to the whole of the ongoing spectacle, then, in every one of them there reveals itself a new and quite remarkable side of mankind.]

(Herder n.d., 2: 15)

This is not, as some might argue, a plea for cultural relativism. Here Herder asks for a kind of understanding that is based on tolerating oneself as well as others and he envisages the need for tolerance with the help of a theatrical notion: Being part of humanity means acting in a scene that is part of a larger play.

Going beyond what Herder states, but trying to be faithful to the spirit of his thought, let me conclude with another thesis: The greatest challenge for intercultural tolerance is not to accept, on some philosophical or political principle, those deep values and beliefs that are presumed to keep a culture together. That is easy, at least for the liberal-minded. Moral and political multiculturalism are the privilege of the powerful and the protected. Courage, imagination, and practice are needed to meet otherness in its everyday theatrical forms of self-presentation with all its tricks and props, postures and poses, masks and costumes, white-face and black-face. I am not about to argue for an either–or position, but I think that Enlightenment ideals of refinement, rational simplicity, and clarity, and the temptation to equate truth and value with purity and honesty need to be countered by a Romantic appreciation of *Verkleidung*, disguise and dressing up for many roles. If, as a result of such universalized yet practical theatricality, theater "runs the risk of losing its characteristics and essence,"[5] so be it. I already confessed I am not much of a theater-goer.

NOTES

1 First presented as a contribution to a symposium on "Theatre in a multicultural society," organized by the International School of Theatre Anthropology, 3–5 May 1996, Copenhagen. I wish to thank Eugenio Barba and Kirsten Hastrup for inviting me to this memorable event.
2 Documented and analyzed in my *Power and Performance*.
3 Explored in greater detail in my *Out of Our Minds*.
4 I later learned that this thesis has been attributed by some to the painter Francis Bacon.
5 This was a fear expressed in a programmatic statement prepared by the organizers of the Copenhagen symposium.

REFERENCES

Coquilhat, Camille (1888) *Sur le Haut-Congo*, Paris: J. Lebègue.

Fabian, Johannes (1990) *Power and Performance: Ethnographic Explorations through Proverbial Wisdom and Theater in Shaba, Zaire*, Madison: University of Wisconsin Press.

—— (2000) *Out of Our Minds: Reason and Madness in the Exploration of Central Africa*, Berkeley: University of California Press.

Frobenius, Leo (1928) *Das sterbende Africa: Die Seele eines Erdteils [Dying Africa: The Soul of a Continent]*, Frankfurt: Societätsdruckerei.

Herder, J. G. (n.d.) *Auszug aus einem Briefwechsel über Ossian und Lieder alter Völker, Vol. 2: Herders Werke*, Leipzig: Verlag des Bibliographischen Instituts.

READER CROSS-REFERENCES

Austin, Butler, Derrida, Parker and Sedgwick – on the meanings of performativity

Schechner, Geertz, Turner and Turner, Conquergood, Taylor – performance as a means to facilitate intercultural understanding

Harding, Okpewho – on performance and performer training in Africa

Bhabha – intercultural relations in colonized societies

Gómez-Peña – comedy in relations between cultures

Part VI

PERFORMING

For every kind of performance there is a different kind (and often many kinds) of performing. Performing happens in everyday life, in the home, in the workplace, in sports and games, in the arts, and in sacred and secular ritual. Any time you take on a role, tell a story, or simply enact a bit of restored behavior, you are performing. This does not mean that you are "faking" or being untrue to your "real self." As the essays in Part II ("What is Performance?") and Part V ("Performativity") show, performing often involves the utmost sincerity. Sincere or "believed-in" performing is the basis of virtually all social interaction. Performance studies encompasses all these branches of performing. However, the essays in this section specifically address the theory and practice of performing in theatrical contexts: that is, the theory and practice of acting. If we recognize that virtually all human behavior involves performing, then we can think of the theatre as a kind of laboratory where actors and directors stage experiments to help us better understand ourselves. Some of these experiments are described in the following pages.

In the 1920s and 1930s, German director and playwright Bertolt Brecht became dissatisfied with conventional Western acting, in which the performers attempted to re-create their characters' emotions and convey them to the audience. Rather than disappear into the role, presenting the character only from the inside, Brecht called on the actor to present the entirety of the character by engaging the role critically, letting the audience see that the actor and the character are not one and the same. Brecht called this technique *Verfremdungseffekt* – a theatrical technique that makes the familiar appear strange and/or the strange appear familiar. The word has also been translated as "alienation" or "estrangement" effect. Many of Brecht's writings were collected and translated by John Willett as *Brecht on Theatre* (New York: Hill & Wang, 1964). One example from that volume, "A dialogue about acting" (1929), is excerpted here. Another leading experimenter of the twentieth-century theater was Polish director Jerzy Grotowski. "The actor's technique" (1967) describes the approach to acting that he developed at the Polish Laboratory Theater, which he founded and directed from 1959 to 1984. Grotowski's intensely physical approach to acting is contrasted with the more internalized "method" acting advocated by American director Lee Strasberg. In "A dream of passion" (1987), Strasberg describes his controversial "emotional-memory" exercise, through which actors draw on their own experience to re-create feelings and sensations on stage. What unites these essays is the intensity with which each director insists on a definition of acting that is something more than mere impersonation or imitation.

Building on this idea performance scholars Frances Harding and Rhonda Blair offer more explicitly theorized ways of thinking about acting. Harding's "Presenting and re-presenting the self: from not-acting to acting in African performance" (1999) applies performance theorist Michael Kirby's model of a continuum between "not-acting" and "acting" to a variety of African performances. Her extended analysis shows that the difference between acting and other types of performing is often a function of context rather than technique or intent. Blair's "Reconsidering Stanislavsky" (2002) explores how recent developments in cognitive neuroscience and neurophysiology can offer new perspectives on the experience of the performer. The so-called Stanislavsky System (or "Method"), the most influential approach to European and American acting in the twentieth century, employs concepts such as "character," "given circumstances," and "feeling" that, notes Blair, are imperfectly understood by most performers. Blair argues that understanding the biological reality that underlies these ideas can enhance the actor's art, but that feminist actors and acting teachers must first overcome their skepticism of biological research, a skepticism that she attributes to an "antibiologism" which Judith Butler (see Chapter 24) and others use (rightly) to challenge essentialist constructions of gender. The search for a biology of acting brings a new dimension to Brecht's call for a scientific theater and Grotowski's idea of the performance space as laboratory, and reminds us of how much performance studies has yet to discover.

27

A DIALOGUE ABOUT ACTING

Bertolt Brecht

(*translated by John Willett*)

The actors always score great successes in your plays. Are you yourself satisfied with them?

No.

Because they act badly?

No. Because they act wrong.

How ought they to act then?

For an audience of the scientific age.

What does that mean?

Demonstrating their knowledge.

Knowledge of what?

Of human relations, of human behaviour, of human capacities.

All right; that's what they need to know. But how are they to demonstrate it?

Consciously, suggestively, descriptively.

How do they do it at present?

By means of hypnosis. They go into a trance and take the audience with them.

Give an example.

Suppose they have to act a leave-taking. They put themselves in a leave-taking mood. They want to induce a leave-taking mood in the audience. If the séance is successful it ends up with nobody seeing anything further, nobody learning any lessons, at best everyone recollecting. In short, everybody feels.

That sounds almost like some erotic process. What ought it to be like, then?

Witty. Ceremonious. Ritual. Spectator and actor ought not to approach one another but to move apart. Each ought to move away from himself. Otherwise the element of terror necessary to all recognition is lacking.

Just now you used the expression 'scientific'. You mean that when one observes an amoeba it does nothing to offer itself to the human observer. He can't get inside its skin by empathy. Yet the scientific observer does try to understand it. Do you think that in the end he succeeds?

I don't know. He tries to bring it into some relationship with the other things that he has seen.

Oughtn't the actor then to try to make the man he is representing understandable?

Not so much the man as what takes place. What I mean is: if I choose to see Richard III I don't want to feel myself to be Richard III, but to glimpse this phenomenon in all its strangeness and incomprehensibility.

Are we to see science in the theatre then?

No. Theatre.

I see: scientific man is to have his theatre like everybody else.

Yes. Only the theatre has already got scientific man for its audience, even if it doesn't do anything to acknowledge the fact. For this audience hangs its brains up in the cloakroom along with its coat.

Can't you tell the actor then how he ought to perform?

No. At present he is entirely dependent on the audience, blindly subject to it.

Haven't you ever tried?

Indeed. Again and again.

Could he do it?

Sometimes, yes; if he was gifted and still naïve, and still found it fun; but then only at rehearsals and only so long as I was present and nobody else, in other words so long as he had in front of him the type of audience I was telling you about. The nearer he got to the first night, the further away he drifted; he became different as one watched, for he probably felt that the other spectators whose arrival was imminent might not like him so much.

Do you think they really wouldn't like him?

I fear so. At any rate it would be a great risk.

Couldn't it happen gradually?

No. If it happened gradually it wouldn't seem to the audience that something new was being gradually developed but that something old was gradually dying out. And the audience would gradually stay away. For if the new element were introduced gradually it would only be half introduced and as a result it would lack force and effectiveness. For this isn't a matter of qualitative improvement but of adaptation to an entirely different purpose; that is to say, the theatre would not now be fulfilling the same purpose better, but would be fulfilling a new purpose, quite possibly very badly at first. What would be the effect of such an attempt to smuggle something in? The actor would simply strike people as 'jarring'. But it wouldn't be his way of acting that would jar them, but he himself. He would grate on them. And yet a jarring element is one of the hallmarks of this new way of acting. Or else the actor would be accused of being too self-conscious; self-consciousness being another hallmark of the same sort.

Have attempts of this kind been made?

Yes, one or two.

Give an example.

When an actress of this new sort was playing the servant in *Oedipus* she announced the death of her mistress by calling out her 'dead, dead' in a wholly unemotional and penetrating voice, her 'Jocasta has died' without any sorrow but so firmly and definitely that the bare fact of her mistress's death carried more weight at that precise moment than could have been generated by any grief of her own. She did not abandon her voice to horror, but perhaps her face, for she used white make-up to show the impact which a death makes on all who are present at it. Her announcement that the suicide had collapsed as if before a beater was made up less of pity for this collapse than of pride in the beater's achievement, so that it became plain to even the most emotionally punch-drunk spectator that here a decision had been carried out which called for his acquiescence. With astonishment she described in a single clear sentence the dying woman's ranting and apparent irrationality, and there was no mistaking the tone of her 'and how she ended, we do not know' with which, as a meagre but inflexible tribute, she refused to give any further information about this death. But as she descended the few steps she took such paces that this slight figure seemed to be covering an immense distance from the scene of the tragedy to the people in the lower stage. And as she held up her arms in conventional lamentation she was begging at the same time for pity for herself who had seen the disaster, and with her loud "now you may weep" she seemed to deny the justice of any previous and less well-founded regrets.

What sort of reception did she have?

Moderate, except for a few connoisseurs. Plunged in self-identification with the protagonist's feelings, virtually the whole audience failed to take part in the moral decisions of which the plot is made up. That immense decision which she had communicated had almost no effect on those who regarded it as an opportunity for new sensations.

('Dialog über Schauspielkunst'. from *Berliner Börsen-Courier*, 17 February 1929)

NOTE

The actress here described was Helene Weigel. Virtually the same account will be found in Brecht's tribute 'Über eine grosse Schauspielerin unserer Nation' printed in the album *Die Schauspielerin Helene Weigel*, Berlin, 1959. The references are to lines 1234ff of *Oedipus Rex*, and if they do not corresond (e.g. the analogy of the 'beater') it is no doubt due to the German adaptation.

The dialogue includes Brecht's first reference to an 'audience of the scientific age', though a note 'Der Mann am Regiepult' in *Das Theater*, Berlin, 1928, no. I had spoken of the producer's duty 'to raise the theatre to the level of science, and present its repertoire to an audience that in *better* surroundings is used to seeing all attempts to involve it in illusions rejected'. It should perhaps be pointed out that *Wissenschaft* in German is a broader term than the English 'science' and that Brecht certainly regarded it as embracing the Marxist view of history as well as the natural sciences.

READER CROSS-REFERENCES

Grotowski – compares his work to Brecht's

Phelan, Kaprow, Strasberg – other experiments in artistic performance

Meyerhold – another early twentieth-century theatre director who experimented with non-realistic acting styles

Gómez-Peña, Lane – performance artists who employ Brechtian techniques

28

THE ACTOR'S TECHNIQUE

Jerzy Grotowski

In 1967 Jerzy Grotowski's Theatre Laboratory performed The Constant Prince *at the Théâtre des Nations in Paris. After a tour of Denmark, Sweden and Norway in 1966, this trip to Paris gave to a greater audience the chance of judging for itself the results achieved by his method. It was during his stay in Paris that Jerzy Grotowski recorded this interview with Denis Bablet, which was then printed in* Les Lettres françaises *(Paris, 16–22 March 1967). Translation: Amanda Pasquier and Judy Barba.*

Jerzy Grotowski, I would first like you to define for me your position with regard to various acting theories as, for example, those of Stanislavsky, Artaud and Brecht, explaining how, through reflection and due naturally to your personal experience, you have come to elaborate your own technique for the actor, defining both its aims and means.

I think it is necessary to distinguish between *methods* and *aesthetics*. Brecht, for example, explained many very interesting things about the possibilities of a way of acting which involved the actor's discursive control over his actions, the *Verfremdungseffekt*. But this was not really a method. It was rather a kind of aesthetic duty demanded of the actor, for Brecht did not actually ask himself: "How can this be done?" Although he has provided certain explanations, these are only general. . . . Certainly Brecht did study the technique of the actor in great detail, but always from the standpoint of the producer observing the actor.

Artaud's case is different. Artaud presents an indisputable stimulus where research relative to the possibilities of the actor is concerned, but what he proposes are in the end only visions, a sort of poem about the actor, and no practical conclusions can be drawn from his explanations. Artaud was well aware – as we know from his essay "Un Athlétisme affectif" in *Le Théatre et son double* – that there is an authentic parallelism between the efforts of a man who works with his body (e.g. picking up a heavy object) and the psychic processes (e.g. receiving a blow, retaliating). He knew that the body possesses a centre that decides the reactions of the athlete, and those of the actor who wants to reproduce psychic efforts through his body. But if one analyses his principles from a practical point of view, one discovers that they lead to stereotypes: a particular type of movement to exteriorize a particular type of emotion. In the end this leads to clichés.

But there was no cliché when Artaud was doing his research and, as an actor, observed his own reactions, seeking an escape from the exact imitation of human reactions and calculated reconstructions. But let us consider his theory. It certainly contains a useful stimulus. However, if one treats it as a technique, one ends in clichés. Artaud represents a fruitful starting point for research and an aesthetic point of view. When he asks the actor to study his breathing, to exploit the different elements of respiration in his acting, he is offering him the chance of widening his possibilities, of acting not only through words but also through that which is inarticulate (inspiration, expiration, etc.). This is a very fertile aesthetic proposition. It is not a technique.

There are, in fact, very few acting *methods*. The most developed is that of Stanislavsky. Stanislavsky propounded the most important questions and he supplied his own answers. Throughout his numerous years of research his method evolved, but his disciples did not. Stanislavsky had disciples for each of his periods, and each disciple stuck to his particular period; hence the discussions of a theological order. Stanislavsky was always experimenting himself and he did not suggest recipes, but the means whereby the actor might discover himself, replying in all concrete situations to the question: "How can this be done?" This is essential. He naturally brought all this about within the setting of the theatre of his country, his time, of a realism which . . .

. . . An interior realism . . .

. . . An existential realism, I think, or rather an existential naturalism. Charles Dullin also devised many good exercises, improvisations, games with masks, or again exercises with such themes as "man and plants", "man and animals". These are very useful for the preparation of the actor. They stimulate not only his imagination, but also the development of his natural reactions. This, however, does not constitute a technique for the formation of the actor.

What then is the originality of your position in relation to these diverse conceptions?

All conscious systems in the field of acting ask the question: "How can this be done?" This is as it should be. A method is the consciousness of this "how". I believe that one must ask oneself this question once in one's life, but as soon one enters into the details it must no longer be asked for, at the very moment of formulating it, one begins to create stereotypes and clichés. One must then ask the question: "What must I *not* do?"

Technical examples are always the clearest. Let us take respiration. If we ask the question: "How should I breathe?", we will work out a precise, perfect type of breathing, perhaps the abdominal type. It is indeed a fact that children, animals, people who are closest to nature breathe principally with the abdomen, the diaphragm. But then we come to the second question: "What sort of abdominal respiration is the best?" And we could try to discover among numerous examples a type of inspiration, a type of expiration, a particular position for the vertebral column. This would be a terrible mistake, for there is no perfect type of respiration valid for everyone, nor for all psychical and physical situations. Breathing is a physiological reaction linked with specific characteristics in each of us and which is dependent on situations, types of effort, physical activities. It is the natural thing for most people, when breathing freely, to use abdominal respiration. The number of types of abdominal respiration, however, are unlimited. And of course there are exceptions. For example, I have met actresses who, because their thoraxes were too long, could not naturally use abdominal breathing in their work. For them it was therefore necessary to find another type of breathing controlled by the vertebral column. If the actor tries artificially to impose on himself the perfect, objective abdominal respiration, he blocks the natural process of respiration, even if his is naturally of the diaphragmatic type.

When I begin to work with an actor, the first question I ask myself is: "Does this actor have any breathing difficulties?" He breathes well; he has enough air to speak, to sing. Why then create a problem by imposing on him a different type of respiration? This would be absurd. On the other hand, perhaps he does have difficulties. Why? Are there physical problems? . . . Psychical problems? If he has psychical problems, what kind of problems are they?

For example, an actor is contracted. Why is he contracted? We are all contracted in one way or another. One cannot be completely relaxed as is taught in many theatre schools, for he who is totally relaxed is nothing more than a wet rag. Living is not being contracted, nor is it being relaxed: it is a process. But if the actor is always too contracted, the cause blocking the natural respiratory process – almost always of a psychical or psychological nature – must be discovered. We must determine which is his natural type of respiration. I observe the actor, while suggesting exercises that compel him into total psycho-physical mobilisation. I watch him while in a moment of conflict, play or flirtation with another actor, in those moments when something changes automatically. Once we know the actor's natural type of respiration, we can more exactly define the factors which act as obstacles to his natural reactions and the aim of the exercises is then to eliminate them. Here lies the essential difference between our technique and the other methods: ours is a negative technique, not a positive one.

We are not after the recipes, the stereotypes which are the prerogative of professionals. We do not attempt to answer questions such as: "How does one show irritation? How should one walk? How should Shakespeare be played?" For these are the sort of questions usually asked. Instead, one must ask the actor: "What are the obstacles blocking you on your way towards the total act which must engage all your psycho-physical resources, from the most instinctive to the most rational?" We must find out what it is that hinders him in the way of respiration, movement and – most important of all – human contact. What resistances are there? How can they be eliminated? I want to take away, steal from the actor all that disturbs him. That which is creative will remain within him. It is a liberation. If nothing remains, it means he is not creative.

One of the greatest dangers threatening the actor is, of course, lack of discipline, chaos. One cannot express oneself through anarchy. I believe there can be no true creative process within the actor if he lacks discipline or spontaneity. Meyerhold based his work on discipline, exterior formation; Stanislavsky on the spontaneity of daily life. These are, in fact, the two complementary aspects of the creative process.

But what do you mean by the actor's "total act"?

It is not only the mobilisation of all the resources of which I have spoken. It is also something far more difficult to define, although very tangible from the point of view of work. It is the act of laying oneself bare, of tearing off the mask of daily life, of exteriorising oneself. Not in order to "show oneself off", for that would be exhibitionism. It is a serious and solemn act of revelation. The actor must be prepared to be absolutely sincere. It is like a step towards the summit of the actor's organism in which consciousness and instinct are united.

In practice, then, the formation of the actor must be adapted to each case.

Yes, I don't believe in recipes.

Therefore there is no such thing as the formation of actors, but the formation of each individual actor. How do you go about this? You observe them? You question them? And then? . . .

There are exercises. We speak very little. During the training each actor is asked to search for his own associations, his personal variants (recalling memories, evoking his needs, all that he has not been able to fulfil).

Do you train collectively?

The starting point of the training is the same for everyone. However, let us take as an example the physical exercises. The elements of the exercises are the same for all, but everyone must perform them in terms of his own personality. An onlooker can easily see the differences according to the individual personalities.

The essential problem is to give the actor the possibility of working "in security". The work of the actor is in danger; it is submitted to continuous supervision and observation. An atmosphere must be created, a working system in which the actor feels that he can do absolutely anything, will be understood and accepted. It is often at the moment when the actor understands this that he reveals himself.

There is therefore total confidence between the different actors, and between them and you.

There is no question of the actor having to do what the producer proposes. He must realize that he can do whatever he likes and that, even if in the end his own suggestions are not accepted, they will never be used against him.

He will be judged and not condemned . . .

He must be accepted as a human being, as he is.

Regarding the actor's integration into the performance, you readily use the term "score" and not "role". This nuance is obviously very important in your work. Could you define exactly what you mean by the actor's "score"?

What is the role? In fact it is almost always a character's text, the typed text that is given to the actor. It is also a particular conception of the character, and here again there is a stereotype. Hamlet is an intellectual without greatness, or else a revolutionary who wants to change everything. The actor has his text; next an encounter is necessary. It must not be said that the role is a pretext for the actor, nor the actor a pretext for the role. It is an instrument for making a cross-section of oneself, analysing oneself and thereby re-establishing contact with others. If he is content with explaining the role, the actor will know that he has to sit down here, cry out there. At the beginning of rehearsals, associations will be evoked normally, but after twenty performances there will be nothing left. The acting will be purely mechanical.

To avoid this the actor, like the musician, needs a score. The musician's score consists of notes. Theatre is an encounter. The actor's score consists of the elements of human contact: "give and take". Take other people, confront them with oneself, one's own experiences and thoughts, and give a reply. In these somewhat intimate human encounters there is always this element of "give and take". The process is repeated, but always *hic et nunc*: that is to say, it is never quite the same.

For each production this score is gradually established between the actor and you?

Yes, in a sort of collaboration.

So the actor is free. How does he manage (and this was one of the great problems underlined by Stanislavsky) to find for each performance the creative state which allows him to execute the score without it becoming too rigid, without a purely mechanical discipline setting in? How can the vital existence of the score and creative liberty of the actor both be preserved?

It is difficult to reply in a few words, but if you will allow me a popularization I shall answer: if during rehearsals the actor has established the score as something natural, organic (the pattern of his reactions, "give and take"), and if, before performing, he is prepared to make this confession, hiding nothing, then each performance will attain its plenitude.

"Give and take" . . . does this include the spectator too?

One must not think of the spectator while acting. Naturally this is a delicate question. First, the actor structures his role; second, the score. At that moment he is seeking a sort of purity (the elimination of the superfluous) as well as the signs necessary to expression. Then he thinks: "Is what I am doing comprehensible?" This question implies the presence of the spectator. I myself am there, guiding the work, and I say to the actor: "I don't understand", "I understand", or "I understand but I don't believe" . . . Psychologists readily ask the question: "What is your religion?" – not your dogmas or philosophy, but your point of orientation. If the actor has the spectator as his point of orientation, then he will, in a sense, be offering himself for sale.

This will be exhibitionism . . .

A sort of prostitution, bad taste. . . . It is inevitable. A great Polish actor from before the war called it "publicotropism". Yet I don't believe the actor should neglect the fact that the spectator is present and say to himself: "There is no one there", for that would be a lie. In short, the actor must not have the audience as a point of orientation, but at the same time he must not neglect the fact of its presence. You know that in each of our productions we create a different relationship between actors and audience. In *Dr Faustus*, the spectators are the guests; in *The Constant Prince*, they are the onlookers. But I think the essential thing is that the actor must not act for the audience, he must act in confrontation with the spectators, in their presence. Better still, he must fulfill an authentic act in place of the spectators, an act of extreme yet disciplined sincerity and authenticity. He must give himself and not hold himself back, open up and not close in on himself, as this would end in narcissism.

Do you believe that the actor needs a long preparation before each performance in order to attain what some people call "a state of grace"?

The actor must have time to cast off all the problems and distractions of daily life. In our theatre we have a period of silence lasting thirty minutes during which the actor prepares his costumes, perhaps goes over certain scenes. This is quite natural. A pilot about to try out a new plane for the first time also seeks solitude for a few minutes before taking off.

Do you think that your acting technique is applicable by other producers apart from yourself, that it can be adapted to ends other than yours?

There again one must distinguish between the aesthetic and the method in my work. Of course in the Theatre Laboratory there are the elements of an aesthetic which is personal to me and which must not be copied by others, for the result would be neither authentic nor natural. But we are an institute for research into the art of the actor. Thanks to this technique, the actor can speak and sing in a very wide register. That is an objective result. The fact that when speaking he has no problems with his breathing is also objective. The fact that he can utilise different types of physical and vocal reactions which are very difficult for many people, that again is objective.

At present there are, then, two aspects in your work: on the one hand the conscious aesthetic of a creator, and on the other the search for a technique in acting. Which comes first?

The most important thing for me today is to rediscover the elements of the actor's art. I was first trained as an actor, then as a producer. In my early productions in Cracow and Poznan I rejected concessions and theatrical conservatism. Gradually I developed and discovered that to fulfil myself was far less fruitful than studying the possibility of helping others to fulfil themselves. This is not a form of altruism. On the contrary, it is an even greater adventure.

In the end the adventures of a producer become easy, but encounters with other human beings are more difficult, more fruitful and more stimulating. If I can attain from the actor – in collaboration with him – a total self-revelation, as with Ryszard Cieslak in *The Constant Prince*, then this is far more fertile for me than just devising a production or, in other words, creating purely in my own name. I have therefore orientated myself, little by little, towards a para-scientific research in the field of the actor's art. This is the result of a personal evolution and not an initial plan.

READER CROSS-REFERENCES

Brecht – to whose work Grotowski compares his own
Barba – close collaborator
Strasberg, Blair – interior work of the actor
De Marinis – compares Grotowski's "score" to the "performance text"
Zimmerman – the actor as a collaborator in the creative process

29

A DREAM OF PASSION

Lee Strasberg

In the emotional-memory exercise, the actor is asked to recreate an experience from the past that affected him strongly. The experience should have happened at least seven years prior to the time that the exercise is attempted. I ask the student to pick the strongest thing that ever happened to him, whether it aroused anger, fear, or excitement. The student tries to recreate the sensations and emotions of the situation in full sensory terms. He must recreate the circumstances which led up to the experience: where he was, who he was with, what he was wearing, what he was doing, and so forth. I tell the actor, "Do not pick a recent experience; not that the recent thing won't work. But the older the experience is, the better it is. If it works, it's going to last for the rest of your life. Whereas, something recent might work now and two years from now it won't. The fact that something has already worked, has existed for a long time and then is recaptured, means it is there for all time."

The actor begins the exercise. He does not tell me the story. He is not to worry about feelings or emotions, only the sensory objects – what he sees, hears, touches, tastes, smells, and what he is experiencing kinetically. The student shouldn't tell me, "I'm in a room." What he must do is describe the sensations as he tries by sense memory to recapture them, just as though he were doing an exercise in concentration.

Some acting teachers misuse this exercise. They want to know the stories. I don't want to know. The less the actor tells me, the better. I only talk to the student if I feel he's having some difficulty or if I want to know where his concentration is.

Here is an example of the procedure in the emotional-memory exercise that was taped at a session I conducted in one of my classes. It begins with the actress saying, "It's cold." We then go on to see if the actress is locating that sensation in different parts of the body – the hairline, etc. The actress then says that she feels a certain kind of cold in certain places.

"Well," I say to her, "take each place separately and try to see if you can remember the kind of cold that existed there. And see if, with the memory, you will be able to recapture some of that cold. And don't worry if it doesn't happen; just make the effort. Don't worry if you cannot swim. You simply keep moving your arms; you won't drown."

As the exercise proceeds, I ask the actress to remember what she was wearing, the material, etc., in an effort to recreate more details. The actress remembers that the material felt cold on her hands.

The exercise then continues as the actress recreates more of the details: the crinkly sound of the ground; later a dusty smell in the air; still later a voice, "shallow, like an echo." As the sound of the voice becomes stronger for the actress, she begins to sob.

"Wait a minute! Wait a minute, wait a minute!" she wails as the emotion breaks through.

In recreating the details of the original emotional memory, the actress recreated the original emotion. (Remember that we did not ask for the story of the original memory – just the details that would help recreate it.) It doesn't matter that the actress has lost words to describe what she's feeling: the playwright will give the actress words on stage. But the actress has tapped into an emotion she can recreate at will.

At this point, I stop the exercise:

"Right. Now, have we already touched the high point of the scene? We've touched it. Okay, that's enough then. That's enough. Look at me. Open your eyes. You want a handkerchief."

I always forget that for these exercises we need Kleenex.

What the actress experienced was the full re-creation of an intense emotional experience. In being able to recreate it and express it, the actress develops the ability to control the expression of her emotions on stage.

In his final period, Stanislavsky made an effort in his research to stimulate the actor's reality and emotion by simple and unforced methods. Unfortunately, Stanislavsky's correct statement that emotion cannot be directly forced has led to the erroneous conclusion that it cannot, therefore, be stimulated. Stanislavsky never gave up the demand that the actor should be capable of living through a part. However, because of the difficulties he encountered, he hoped to stimulate the actor, who was already trained to the emotional response, by means of psychophysical actions.

I have found no difficulty in using the emotional-memory exercise and have developed specific procedures for its use. I demonstrated the way it can be used at the international seminars I gave in Paris, Argentina, and Germany. On every occasion, the observers were startled by the quickness and ease with which it was performed, and at the ease with which the actor could change from one emotion to another. It seemed for the first time to make the actor capable of satisfying those demands for inner precision and definiteness which Gordon Craig was asking for when he demanded that the actor be a "Super ('Über') Marionette." Through the proper use of emotional memory, the actor possesses a skill and flexibility on the stage.

READER CROSS-REFERENCES

Brecht – critical of emotion-based acting
Grotowski, Barba – the demands of the theatrical process on the actor
Gabler, Goffman – the reverse of Strasberg's exercise: drawing on art to perform in life
Blair – neurocognitive basis of the actor's emotional experience

30

PRESENTING AND RE-PRESENTING THE SELF

From not-acting to acting in African performance

Frances Harding

What is universal in performance is the consciousness of performance.
Herbert Blau (1990: 259)

Introduction

This article forms part of a wider study of the performer in African contexts in which I am less concerned with the intention, beliefs, and putative efficacy of any given performance – a focus that receives continual attention from many scholars – than with the techniques, methods, and occasions of behavior that distinguish the two types of performing: *not-acting* and *acting*.

Some studies of African theater and performance (see Drewal 1992) have made use of the performance theories of Richard Schechner, Herbert Blau, and others. The collection of essays edited by Phillip Zarrilli, *Acting (Re)Considered*, has brought together theories of acting which have been developed over several decades. Among the most useful of these for the purposes of this article has been Michael Kirby's methodical exposition of the subtle differences in performing between not-acting and acting ([1972] 1995).

This article attempts to apply to performers in Africa the first section of Kirby's not-acting to acting continuum – the first three stages, which deal with non-acting – and to note how it shades into "acting" with a change of context, even when not initiated by the performers. First are those roles that require minimal skills and are performed by persons whom I shall refer to as "stagehands," recognizing that while in Western theater this designation refers to offstage and largely unseen activity that may not require special skills, this is not always so in an African context. The stagehand is, however, always in a supporting role and cannot sustain a performance independent of a leading character.

While they occupy a conspicuous status for the duration of a performance, stagehands are not themselves perceived primarily as performers but simply as support for the central character. Although they predominantly fulfill a functional role within a performance and thus are "non-matrixed" – to use Kirby's term – in respect to the reasons *why* they are in a staged relationship to a performer, they are, as we shall see, "matrixed." To this extent, they may be described as performers with a bit part or a walk-on part, as this keeps open the possibility of some deliberate intention on their part to present themselves as performers, albeit in a limited way. Even when the "stagehand-performer" deliberately presents her- or himself[l] as a performer, the primary objective and responsibility of the stagehand is to enable the leading actor to perform appropriately, and without worry or concern about the mechanics of costume, location, or timing.

In seeking to ascribe features of reality and pretense as proposed by Kirby to the presentations of performers in Africa, there are, however, two further dimensions that need to be taken into account: The first is the audience–performer relationship in which the interaction between them is a suspension of the *ordinary* rather than a suspension of *reality* and thus constitutes more of a *heightening* of reality in which it is recognized that ordinary people can become extra-ordinary for a period of time. The second feature follows from this and constitutes a preference for multilayered performances whereby any one performer may, within a single performance, be at one point "acting" and at another "presenting the self." Neither the audience nor the performer experiences any difficulty in accommodating a movement between the two. A sustained, uninterrupted representation is not required in order to convince the spectators of the presence of an "other." It is more a case of recognizing that some people have – albeit temporarily (i.e. for the duration of the performance) – the power to move between the presentation of self and the presentation of an "other."

In the case of those whom – in order to emphasize their functional role – I have called stagehands, the notion of an "aside-in-reverse" might help the reader to comprehend the quality of change inherent in playing this role. By this I mean that the percentage of time, within a single performance, that the stagehand-performer is interacting directly with the audience as himself (as in a conventional Western aside) is considerably greater than the time he is playing a role. In these roles, while the stagehand does not "pretend" to be someone else, he is, nevertheless, in several performance forms (the Ibibio puppet theater, the Sapo masks, the Chamba mask) engaged in activities that are "make-believe" and therefore can be said to shade slightly into acting. This exemplifies the crucial point within such performances: the players do not necessarily maintain a single mode of performing throughout a performance, but may move quite frequently between "pretense" and reality. While this might seem Brechtian in its *effect*, in fact it does not serve to remind the spectator that what they are seeing is just a fiction and the character is in reality just an ordinary person, but rather to demonstrate that an ordinary person can become extra-ordinary.

In the second modality I place those performances which have no aspiration to "pretense," focus on presenting an intensification of self, require a high degree of performing skill, and may be either support or lead roles.

The absence of any aspiration to acting and the presence of highly developed skills distinguish this modality from the first, albeit in the case of support roles they are still *part of elaborating* the central act or character. These support performers, recognized as skillful and entertaining in their own right, often use the opportunity to present themselves in such a way as to gain recognition and applause for their skills. However, like the stagehand-performer, they primarily support the central characters and do not upstage central performers. While they may even perform separately – spatially or sequentially – from them, their presence remains dependent on that of the lead performer. This is what distinguishes them from the lead performers. Crucially, they are not acting – i.e. they do not attempt to imply that they are anyone other than themselves, nor that they are in any "time or place different from the spectator" (Kirby [1972] 1995: 43). Lead performers in this modality are those whose acts, displays of skill, or presentations of self are the primary focus of the entertainment. Among them are acrobats, dancers, animal tamers, story-tellers, musicians, snake charmers, strongmen, and praise singers whose performance draws an audience irrespective of any other performers.

Kirby sets out a basic definition of acting: "To act means to feign, to simulate, to repre-sent, to impersonate" ([1972] 1995: 43). He makes a primary distinction between acting that is "active" on the part of the performer, and the manner in which "other qualities that define acting may also be applied to the performer" by onlookers (44). This posits an elementary bifurcation between the active intention of the perpetrator-performer and the active perception of the recipient-spectator. It recognizes a distinction between performers who are deliberately seeking to present the self as "other" and those whose activities are not intended to have any of the connotations of Kirby's definition of acting but who may nevertheless be perceived as acting. This is what Kirby calls "received acting" and precedes two further, more intense, and – crucially – *intentional* degrees of acting which he names as "simple" acting and "complex" acting. These latter categories of performing emphasize the deliberate presentation of an "other" rather than the "self" – in essence, *acting*. I shall consider these stages in detail elsewhere and will here just briefly refer to simple acting. I will conclude this article with an analysis of the presentation of self as other among the Nuba men of Sudan. My example, Nuba personal art, falls at the third point on Kirby's continuum, received acting. In its original context, Nuba personal art formed part of a cluster of seasonal activities but, under contemporary external pressures, has become a double-layered presentation of self in which the performers represent themselves. The practice of self-decoration, which identifies a young man as healthy and physically strong among the Nuba people (see Faris 1972: 19), initially placed them as symbolically matrixed within the society, but was perceived by outsiders in such a way as to constitute received acting, and then, in response, reconstituted and reinforced by the Nuba men themselves to become a form of simple acting.

So that the reader can situate this article into a fuller context, I begin by briefly outlining Kirby's framework and then consider how it can be usefully applied to the experience of African performers.

Kirby's continuum

Kirby has named five stages of the transition from not-acting into acting to describe the range of human behavior that constitutes the presentation of the self "in a special way": "[W]e can follow a continuous increase in the degree of representation from nonmatrixed performing through symbolized matrix, received acting and simple acting to complex acting" ([1972] 1995: 51).

These concepts of performing as representation concentrate on the individual experience for both the perpetrator and the recipient, i.e. performer and spectator. Applying Kirby's framework and methodology to performance in Africa enables an analysis of the attitudes and expectations of the performer in relation to performance to be developed without reference to the degree of belief involved. In the essentially phenomenological experience of performing, belief is not a measure of quality of performance, even if it is of socio-spiritual efficacy:

> Belief may exist in either the spectator or the performer, but it does not affect objective classification according to our acting/not-acting scale. Whether an actor feels what he or she is doing to be "real" or a spectator really "believes" what is seen, does not change the classification of the performance.
>
> (51)

By addressing the phenomenon of performing within a continuum of "not-acting" to "acting," Kirby's framework avoids the sociological overlap between "sacred" and "secular," "old" and "new," "ritual" and "drama," and focuses instead on the craft of performing in its several modes.

Reconciling desire and ability

Not everyone who would like to display the self as *skilled* has equal competence, imagination, or talent, and this necessitates some people occupying "lead" roles while others take up "supporting" roles. Recognition of the relative nature of skill and talent is evident in the widespread use of structured competition in many societies throughout Africa (Horton 1960; Ottenberg 1975). Even within kin-based organizations with responsibility for funerary or other ceremonial rites such as hunters' dances, blacksmiths' dances, or masquerades, there is room for flexibility regarding the extent and nature of individual involvement in performance.

How, then, is the *desire* to display the self and *ambition* to perform reconciled with *ability* within a performance? Happily, in the production of a performance there are many tasks, functions, and roles to be fulfilled, all necessary but not all requiring equal skills or sharing equal responsibility. Those with the talent and the interest may opt to take up a leading role, while those with interest and less ability can opt to take up a supporting role. Peer and community pressure enable the ranking to take place informally at a private, social level and publicly at a competitive level. I have seen a disabled young man dance his rightful share of a funerary dance and still be openly laughed at for daring to get up and dance in public.

The first modality: the stagehand

This ambivalent category of performer fulfills a very necessary role in many performances in African societies – although the skills required may not be of a very demanding nature. These persons are seen on stage, but may not be considered to be either acting or performing. They may not even consider themselves to be "performing," but rather just carrying out a task. They are clearly outside the "informational structure of the narrative" (Kirby [1972] 1995: 44) according to the visual evidence of costuming or masking, yet their presence cannot be ignored and is essential to the performance. This constitutes Kirby's first category of "perceived" performer, which he calls "nonmatrixed" (44). These are those stage persons who "Even if the spectator ignores them as people . . . they are not invisible. They do not act, and yet they are part of the visual presentation" (44). In some instances, they are "supporters"; in others, their task is as "minders" or "attendants," protecting both the performer and the audience (Bravmann 1977: 52). Often, the central performer – for example the masked figure, the stilt walker, or the concealed puppeteer – may have his vision limited by the costume. In such instances, there are guides who lead or conduct performers safely around or out of a performing area. Alternatively, performers may be in an altered state of mind or a trance, and need to be "brought back" or fenced around so that they do not harm themselves. For example, in the *bori* possession cult of the Hausa people of northern Nigeria several women are designated as assistants (Onwuejeogwu 1969: 283).

Every performance requires technical assistance and technical assistants whose task is to make possible the performer's task of entertaining. Such people are "stagehands," a description reflecting their supportive, nonengaged role. They are there to prepare for the performance and to ensure that it runs smoothly. They remove obstacles so that nothing will distract the audience's attention from the performer. They have tasks to fulfill throughout the performance, before, during, and after:

> The preparations for *Isinyago* begin some days before the actual day of performance. The animals are made in the bush preferably in an area where there is plenty of bamboo and grass.
>
> When the makers are satisfied with their work, they prepare a square near the village or homestead where the performance will take place. This square is joined to the actual village square by a clean, stump-free "road" [*sic*]. This is important. Dancing during a dark night and dressed in their masks, the dancers cannot see their way. Their path must be clear to avoid calamities.
>
> (Wembah-Rashid 1971: 40)

Such activities represent the extreme end of the functional aspect of being a stagehand. They also represent the least visible aspect of the stagehand's work. But not all stagehands carry out their work invisible to the audience. Nor do they always play such clearly backstage and offstage roles, but rather usually make a more creative contribution on stage in a number of ways. Describing, for example, a 1914 Ibibio puppet theater constructed from blankets stretched loosely across posts, Percy Amaury Talbot noted the role of such attendants in setting the scene and creating "atmosphere":

> In front stood three men, armed with brushes of palm fibre, with which they continually beat the screen of blankets causing them to quiver, and thus hide any movement made by the real performers as they passed up and down behind. The practical purpose of this little piece of byplay was disguised from the credulous onlookers . . . by the pretext that it was part of the powerful Broom Juju and necessary for the manifestation of the spirits of the play.
>
> (1967 [1923]: 76–7)

What Amaury Talbot refers to as "byplay" is in fact a key task. The support performers are essential to the reinforcement of the implicit narrative of the performance, regardless of how purely functional their role may appear. Their role is a bridge between the nonhuman world of the puppets and the human world of the spectators. If the movements of the puppeteers inside and underneath the stage were not screened, spectators would have to publicly acknowledge the presence of human beings as the active agency mobilizing the puppets. In the Ibibio puppet theater, because their actions are contextualized as having meaning, the "blanket-beaters" become part of the informational structure of the performance and are therefore matrixed.

Nevertheless, however essential they are to the performance, it is never the "custodian" (Fardon 1990: 156), "guide," or "attendant" (Bravmann 1977: 52) that the audience comes to see, for the role of the stagehand is to reinforce the role of the central character.

Although Kirby has pointed out that the Japanese kabuki attendants are not within the "informational structure of the narrative" (45), when we turn to the stagehand in African performance, we find that he is – sometimes implicitly and often ambiguously, as with the Ibibio – incorporated in the structure of the narrative. One key lies in the perception of the performance. Within kabuki performance, there is public recognition that a fiction is being enacted, whereas within masked or puppet performance in the African context, the spectator may be interacting with the puppet performer or the masked figure as bringing a particular kind of reality briefly into being. The spectators' part in the enacted world of the performers is – publicly at least – to acknowledge the puppets or masked figures as spirits, deities, or ancestors.

The hidden manipulators in puppet performances require external assistance, as do many masquerade performers. In these performances, the support performer often interacts with lead masked performers so that they can fulfill their more specialized roles, as for example when the sightlines of the masked figure are partially restricted by costuming. In order to ensure that the masked figure is able to move around safely, that its costume remains secure, and that it does not exceed the behavior appropriate to its characterization, it may need to be guided by another person, a stagehand. Furthermore, as a masquerade performance can last throughout the day, this stagehand/guide must also fan the masked figure to keep it cool, lead it to a place where it can rest and drink, and generally protect it during and between acts. In performance, the stagehand may tie a rope around the middle of the masked figure and then hold on to the end so that both the masked figure and the spectators are protected from each other's excesses. The stagehand – however essential to the success of the performance – is usually uncostumed and relates directly to the masked figure, making no attempt to draw the attention of the audience to himself and often, in fact, ignoring the crowd:

> The masked figure is accompanied by a custodian who leads it into the performing area while striking a small double hand gong. Occasionally he may speak to the creature to coax it into dancing or to warn it against unruly conduct.
> . . . Its dance finished, the mask is led out of the crowd by its custodian.
>
> (Fardon 1990: 156–7)

While fulfilling the task of guiding the masked figure, the stagehand is seen as an ordinary, everyday person, in contrast to the fantastical masked figure. In this way, the self-effacing performance contributes to the mystique of the masquerade character, which purports to behave unpredictably. In order to be perceived as possessing the unpredictable quality associated with supernatural status, the masked figure must be seen to need to be controlled:

> Within the context of Lo Gue . . . it is incumbent on the directors of this masking organisation to control these potentially dangerous elements of its personality . . . [T]o this end a host of talismans will be tucked into the *bamba-da*, the tall peaked white caps worn by the lead griots who play and dance for *Gyinna-Gyinna* and tied to the waist of the attendants of these masked figures. Only the *Gyinna-Gyinna* require human guides, two strong young men who hold onto a sturdy rope tied to the waist of the *djinn*. No other Lo Gue mask requires such attention for no other has the independence of mind or the inherent power to lash out at the living who come to observe this honorific performance.
>
> (Bravmann 1977: 52)

Thus, in spite of the deliberate absence of visual signals (costuming, behavior, etc.) the stagehand is drawn into the "informational structure" of the performance. Why, then, is it useful to call him a "stagehand," suggesting a technical, unseen role, if he is in fact obliquely part of the narrative or characterization? First, and crucially, the possibility of unruly behavior is real; the masked figure in certain circumstances is at liberty to behave in an irrational manner and to cause, perhaps, actual physical harm to people (Drewal 1992: 98). Second, the masked figure's vision is restricted. Thus, I suggest that the *primary* function of the stagehand is practical and the aesthetic or spiritual interpretations follow the *need* for such a figure on stage with the masked figure. However, the aggressive characteristics of the masked figure, the central performer, may be extended to its attendants with "real," immediate effects on the audiences, as among the Chamba: "A braided rope, the tail of the creature, may be worn down the back of the masked figure or else carried by an attendant who uses it as a whip to strike at bystanders" (Fardon 1990: 151; plate 1).

While the functional and spiritual combine on occasion in the role of the stagehand, there is also a further layer of meaningful personal activity involved. In those instances where the stagehand's task as guide, protector, or attendant has been accommodated within the informational structure, the young men who are the supporters of these masks are themselves demonstrating personal attributes, such as strength or skill. They are simultaneously *being* real protectors and *displaying* the self in an advantageous manner. In neither instance are they *acting*, in the sense of adopting a character other than their own – but they are *performing*:

> Sapo daytime masks, which are controlled by associations of young warrior-age men, are said to be "pulled" – that is taken from the forest and brought to town for festive occasions during the dry season. The ability to control these anthropomorphic bush creatures demonstrates *the physical powers and prowess of the young men involved.*
>
> (Lifschitz 1988: 223; italics added)

A link to speech is another option for these non-acting performers:

> The "bush" spirits orate, recite poetry and sing, all in self-disguised voices. They may have a "speaker" or assistant accompanying them who repeats their words in normal speech.
>
> (Lifschitz 1988: 223)

Describing the performances of four masked figures among the Gade people of northern Nigeria, Shuaibu Na'ibi notes that:

> None of these four . . . speak in such a way that people can understand what they are saying, but they put something in their mouths which makes them sound like a bird whistling. Whenever they appear, their followers accompany them, showing them the way and translating what they are saying – for they do not like the people to know that it is only a man inside the . . . costume.
>
> (Na'ibi 1958: 297)

The second modality: support performers and lead performers

So far I have considered those persons whose onstage roles have largely been restricted to *being there* and being either self-effacing or supportive; to restraining violence in the masked figure or even displaying potential violence themselves. There is, however, a second category of support performer. While these roles require more highly developed skills, the primary focus of the performance remains with the lead characters. These performers then move from the first point on Kirby's continuum – nonmatrixed – to the second point, where they occupy a state of "symbolized matrix": their costume, role, or presence is recognized as being within the orbit of deliberately presenting the self in a special way, though still not as *other* than the self.

Support performers

This second modality requires performers to have real skills that present the self advantageously. Recognized as skillful and entertaining in their own right, they use the opportunity to present themselves so as to gain recognition and applause for their skills. Still, like the stagehand-performer, they are primarily there as support for the central characters. They do not upstage central performers and may perform separately and sequentially from the lead characters. Their function remains dependent on the presence of the lead performer and it is this that distinguishes them from the lead performers.

The Tiv people of central Nigeria have an elaborate puppet theater called *kwagh-hir*, meaning "something wonderful." These are usually all-night performances that take place during the dry season. They are mixed-media events with puppetry, masquerades, singers, dancers, and others, including the *shuwa* (narrator) and the *or-usu* (fire-man), whose flaming torch lights up the acting arena and leads the concealed puppeteers in their mobile stages around the perimeter so that each section of the audience can see. The puppet stage, or *dagbera*, is about the size of an average dining table and has enclosed sides concealing the puppeteers underneath. The puppets perform on the top surface but the enclosed sides of the dagbera restrict vision so much that different sounds as well as light are used to guide the puppeteers as they maneuver the mobile stage around to two or three stopping points in the performance arena. The limited sightlines from the dagbera mean that the or-usu must call out to the concealed puppeteers to let them know where to go and brandish his torch in front of the small holes in the front of the dagbera. The shuwa performs between acts, announcing the next one and then standing on the sidelines during the performance.

These or-usu are not self-effacing characters like the masquerade guides we considered earlier. On the contrary, they make much of the opportunity to display their virtuosity. It is the or-usu, or fire-man, who, with his flaming torches, provides a leading light to the hidden puppeteers. Like the masquerade guides, he is technically essential for the expedient fulfillment of the performance; unlike them, he is expected to inject his performance with personal skills that entertain the audience and contribute substantially to the success of the production.

In these puppet performances, there is also a group of singers and sometimes dancers – often older women – who provide a sung accompaniment to the puppet show as well as songs during interludes between each act. Most important, however, is the shuwa, or narrator, who precedes each act with a précis of it. Like the dancers or singers and the or-usu at a kwagh-hir show, the shuwa – who can be either a man or a woman – deliberately presents the self as a skilled performer. Thus in a puppet performance the dancers, singers, the shuwa, and the or-usu are presenting the self as skilled performers, but remain support performers to the puppets and masquerades.

In addition to skilled support performers, there are of course a whole host of skilled, non-acting lead performers. Lead performers are those whose acts and displays of skill are the primary focus of the entertainment. Among them are acrobats, dancers, animal tamers, storytellers, musicians, snake charmers, strongmen, praise singers, puppeteers, and masqueraders. Within Kirby's continuum, these performers have not yet moved from "presenting the self" to presenting an "other." Nevertheless, it is difficult for the performers to maintain a "non-acting" position as they demonstrate their skills.

The lead performer

The non-acting lead performer presents the self in a specific skilled role such as dancer, singer, tightrope walker, wrestler, storyteller, ventriloquist, or musician. Their *intention* is to draw attention to their skills, to themselves, and to entertain the audience. For example, a performer can develop a lead role in a ventriloquist's act:

> In an open space . . . two long stout stakes are driven into the earth, forked or notched at the ends. Between them, from top to top, a long palm-stem is laid, and upon this a row of small fetishes [*sic*] are carefully balanced, one by one. Then tom-toms [*sic*] are beaten, at first slowly and softly but with ever increasing rhythm. When the music grows loud and fast, the little idols [*sic*] begin to dance and talk with the voice of a man. Eggs can also be made to talk in a similar manner.
>
> (Amaury Talbot 1967 [1923]: 75–6)

Alternatively, the performer may demonstrate skills in relation to specific animals, as for example at an agricultural show in Sokoto province, Nigeria, held in the 1950s, where the "hyena-tamers and snake charmers and magicians all come to perform" (*Nigeria Magazine* 1958: 339). Similarly, in Oshogbo, Nigeria, at the festival for Shango, many different forms of entertainment are described, including "tub-thumping" – of a literal sort:

> Pestles and mortar normally used for grinding cassava are properties in this act. Confederates pound heartily whilst Strong Man holds a mortar on his chest.
>   . . . The strong man is also the tumbler and contortionist as well.
>
> (D.W.M. 1953: 302–3)

The magician toys directly with illusion – employing sleight of hand to give an impression of shifting things in an impossible sequence. Again, it is the creation of an illusion that is dependent on actual skill and Bernard Beckerman notes that:

> He (the magician) creates so convincing an illusion of actuality that our eyes accept what our minds hold in abeyance. It is this conflict between eyes and minds that produces the sense of wonder in us.
>
> (1990: 33)

It is only when a performer replaces him- or herself with an illusion that "acting" is said to take place. Richard Schechner has observed that performers are "not-themselves" and "not not-themselves" (1985: 6) and Marvin Carlson restates this, asserting that, within the play frame, a performer "is not herself (because of the operations of illusion), but she is also not not herself (because of the operations of reality). Performer and audience alike operate in a world of double consciousness" (1996: 54).

Illusion, however, is not ostensibly a feature of the performance of the acrobat, whose physical suppleness challenges the restraints of human physiognomy and produces awe and wonder in the spectator:

> At Henshaw town, Calabar, a celebrated play is sometimes given at the time of the full moon. A single slender pole is fixed in the ground. Up this a man climbs till he reaches the top, when he stands on the point and dances *i.e.*, sways to and fro, rippling the muscles of back and waist, and waving his arms. . . . After a while he climbs down head foremost, or springs from the top, turning two somersaults before reaching the ground.
>
> (Amaury Talbot 1967 [1923]: 75)

Similarly, in the streets of Nairobi there are young boy performers who can bend over backwards, stand on their hands, and by bringing their feet through the space between their arms and the ground, hold a matchbox in the toes of one foot and a match in those of the other and light it. They have other tricks such as being able to bend over backward and "walk" their feet more than halfway around their body. Another example is found among the Tiv people of Nigeria, where acrobats can fold up their body into the most extreme contorted positions so that they themselves fit onto a shallow disc the size of a chair seat. Everywhere men – and women, but less so – juggle and bend and spring and in so doing create the illusion of doing the impossible. But it *is* an illusion because it is possible: they do it. To this extent, the acrobat is also drawing attention only to him- or herself – but doing it not only through the display of skill, like the singer or musician, but, like the storyteller, through the creation of an illusion. It is, however, a double illusion that is created by the acrobat. Whereas for the storyteller the element of fiction is primary in the content of the display, for the acrobat the element of fiction is absent, for such performers are the "subject of the performance" (Harrop 1992: 5).

In the all-day *salla* parade that follows the ending of Ramadan in Katsina, northern Nigeria, among the hundreds of performers are scores of young men, *yan tauri* (tough guys), who draw sharp knives and swords across their bare stomachs without cutting themselves. At the same time, a high-pitched squeaking is emitted apparently from a tiny gourd that each performer carries slung on his wrist; he holds it up for the audience to see that he is not squeezing or rubbing it to produce the noise. The claim is that the noise happens automatically when the knife touches the bare flesh. Whatever the truth of the technique, the illusion that there is a direct relationship between flesh, noise, and knife makes impressive entertainment. It is quite different from the snake charmer in the same parade, who lifts the snake and places its head into his mouth. In this case, there is no illusion – the snake really is in his mouth – but the entertainment is no less impressive.

There is another category of performer whose skill is based not on illusion but on a kind of reality that elevates the mind of the listener, and is applauded for that. This particular category is very fully developed in the role of the *omioko* in Idoma inquest inquiries. The

Idoma people live in central Nigeria. In Idoma society, after a death, an inquiry is held to find out who is responsible for the death. This is not undertaken in order to ascribe blame but to find out the social reason for the death.

> The *omioko* were young men with good, vibrant, resonate and powerful voices. They had learned their art through observation and participation and other modes of training. The omioko knew the society and its traditions very well. They were the agents through which the participants spoke both to each other and to the spectators.
>
> (Amali 1985: 23)

The verbal play of the omioko is an example of a key, skilled support role. The omioko is able to move around the inquest arena, not aligning himself spatially or ideologically with any faction, but "moving from one participant to the next in the order in which they spoke" (Amali 1985: 23). In his role, the omioko controls order and focuses the attention of the speakers and the spectators on the performance of the inquest.

The omioko is clearly at the critical midpoint of change on the continuum ranging from support to lead characters. He is an essential character but supposedly only as a transmitter, not creator, of information. He does not move the narrative forward; he does not, theoretically, contribute to the substance of the proceedings. His role is to amplify, elaborate, modify the substantive statements from leading participants in the inquest. Yet there could be no inquest without the omioko, for, as Amali notes: "The omioko's functions added formality and dignity to the occasion" (1985: 23). By his skill and knowledge of the participants and their circumstances and the history of the families involved, he not only orchestrates the proceedings, but may subtly direct them as well.

Another performer who falls into this category, but somewhat differently, is the storyteller, who introduces another element into the experience. Storytellers are recognized and appreciated because of their special skills in the art of *narrating*. The *telling* of the narrative is the personal skill to which the storytellers want to draw the attention of the audience; it takes place in the present tense of the performance. There is, however, also the content of the performance, which may take place in the past or future or in imagined time. Thus, as with song, music, and (to some extent) dance, the content can be appreciated separately from the performer and the performance. In storytelling, there is an emphasis on the non-real elements because this requires in the minds of the listeners the creation of images and characters who do not exist in a phenomenological form for the audience. The storyteller, as John Harrop puts it, is "speaking in his own person" (1992: 5). Yet if – or as – he moves in and out of characterization as the plot progresses, from time to time he can be said to be "acting" in the sense of impersonating an other. Beckerman draws a distinction between what he calls those acts of skill that exist to display skills and those that exist to display skills in order to "achieve an emotional response." Whereas the first category exists for itself and provokes a response of awe and wonder, the latter, or "what I call the illusory or fictive show[,] includes the display of skill but shadows a second realm in the exercise of the perceptible skill. It is such a double-imaged act that is the basis of drama" (1990: 16).

This can be clearly seen in Lele Gbomba's performances:

> Gbomba's theater diminished everything but the *domeigbuamoi*. In the course of his prologue, he stripped himself of his gown, his shoes, his shirt – everything but a pair of blue shorts and a lappa of cloth, and a headtie, which were his only props. Thus, stripped down to his wiry agile frame, a plastic face with enormous eyes, and an incredible modulated voice, Lele Gbomba became his pantheon: a whorish mincing senior wife, brushing off patting hands with outraged stares and limp-wristed swats; a pompous mallam dispensing tedious sententiae to his followers; an English colonial officer stiffly complaining in military cadence: "Oh my God, oh very much, what? Oh light, oh light oh God, my Father!"
>
> (Cosentino 1980: 55)

Many storytellers assist their audiences to imagine the characters about whom they speak by characterizing them in voice and body movement. Thus, while the storyteller is real, those about whom the audience hears may not be real. This involves *illusion* – the creation of perceptions, sensations, expectations, and resolutions about characters who do not actually exist and about events which are not actually taking place. Yet the experiences of the audience are real enough – fear, laughter, sadness. The best of the storytellers, then, like the dancer and the musician and the singer, presents her/himself as the central figure of the performance, and brings into illusory being a whole range of characters who fulfill the narrative. Not all, however, are equally skilled; for example:

> nearly everyone in Mendeland – women and men, chiefs and children – could and did perform these *domeisia* . . . .
>
> Only a few Mende became creative performers of *domeisia*, and fewer still earn the name of *domeigbuamoi*, or "pullers" of the *domei*.
>
> (Cosentino 1980: 54)

Not all storytelling, of course, requires the same degree of dramatization and Spencer (1990) makes a distinction between the Mende *ngawovei* historic narratives in which there is no embellishment or dramatization and the *domei*. Each requires a different performing style and has different aims. The former is delivered in a straight manner, the latter with as much elaboration as the storyteller chooses.

The third modality: "act yourself"

Up until now, I have been considering modalities of performing in which the element of pretense, impersonation, and feigning is minimal or intermittent. Nevertheless, each modality can be discerned from ordinary, everyday activities: the activity is clearly specialized, differentiated, and entertaining. Regardless of either the increasing level of skill required or of their status as support or lead roles, all fall within Kirby's first stage of the continuum: nonmatrixed performing. The performers are people *being themselves*, presenting the self in a special way.

Kirby then defines the next point:

> As we move toward acting from this extreme non-acting position on the continuum, we come to that condition in which the performer does not act and yet his or her costume represents something or someone. We could call this a "symbolized matrix."
>
> (1995 [1972]: 44)

This "symbolized matrix" is often encountered when local people in local dress are seen by visitors for the first time and who may describe the locals as being "in costume" whereas actually the local people are just "dressed." An extreme example of this — and one which gained some international notoreity — was apparent in the presentation of the self practiced by the Nuba people of the southern Sudan, whose display of the socialized self was taken to one form of aesthetic perfection.

Nuba people have developed an aesthetic display of the self in order to celebrate the young healthy body, which is the prerequisite for personal survival and for the survival of the group in the arid conditions of the southeast Nuba mountains (Faris 1972). It is a form of self-presentation that is limited to the nonfarming dry season and to the home villages. Thus it can be said that there is a clear theater of activity and a clear duration of performance within the home culture. The focus of the performance is on the physicality of the young people, essential to the survival of the society.

There are different visual art conventions for men and women. Girls are permitted from an early age to apply a mixture of oil and either yellow or red ocher clay over themselves. The choice of color is regulated by the clan affiliation of the girl. Access to the use of this color is a permanent option in a girl's life, although she is unlikely to use it after her own family is well established. As well as coloring, girls are also subject to a series of one-off bouts of body decoration, which is carried out in three phases. As she develops physically, the girl receives her first set of cicatrizations below her breasts; at the onset of menses, she receives a second set around her navel and across her stomach. Finally, after the birth of her first child and as the child is weaned, she receives the third and final set over her entire back and shoulders. Unlike her socially determined coloring, this decoration is linked directly to the girl's biological development into a physically mature woman. Whereas the cicatrization is linked to the performance of social roles, biologically determined, the application of coloring and oil over the permanent decoration is often done in preparation for the dances that take place in conjunction with, and following, the displays of fighting by the young men.

So to summarize the procedures for the women: first, they have permanent access from an early age to temporary coloring and then a one-off access to a sequence of permanent markings. These two forms of personal display come together at high points of entertainment in a display designed to draw the attention of the young men to the young women and vice versa. For both the young women and the young men, these dances are opportunities to enjoy themselves.

In contrast, the young men do not receive permanent markings but do, through a system of age grades, gradually acquire the permanent right to apply to their bodies temporary clay markings or patterns of specific colors. This is done very frequently throughout the dry season – sometimes more than twice in a day. The color range permitted to the young men keeps pace with their age so access to the full range increases steadily. The applied design itself may be very temporary and sometimes is kept on the body for only a few hours before the young man decides to try out another design. Although the right to use the full range of colors, once acquired, is forever, in practice few men apply the coloring after their most physically perfect years have passed. A specific range of hairstyles for men is similarly linked to age and status and is a longer-lasting, though not permanent, form of decoration and identification. The body and face designs are a personal choice and have no personal ritual significance, but the hairstyles – although they too are personal choice – do have social significance. In performance, natural physical attributes enhanced by artifice, validated by social status, and presented in a display of skill create an aesthetic combining color and kinesis in balanced asymmetry.

These activities of self-decoration constitute what Kirby has called a "symbolized matrix" and, at the point when the decoration and its purpose reach their apogee in the dances, they come into the category of presenting the self "in a special way" (Mude 1983: 2).

The Nuba people experienced in a particularly traumatic way the effects of outside interference. In the 1970s, Leni Riefenstahl, a German photographer famous for her film of the 1936 Olympic Games, recorded on film the personal body art of the young Nuba people. Her photographs were published in two very graphic books, *The Last of the Nuba* and *The People of Kau*, which became very popular outside the Sudan and brought about substantial social changes to the Nuba people. Among these was a steady influx of mainly German tourists who came to see the young men self-decorate and paid them to do it. The Nuba people's awareness of their potential to use their ordinary practice as an entertainment grew and was recorded on the BBC film *South-Eastern Nuba* (1982) as they decorated for tourists and for the camera crew. At one point, on being criticized by his peers for applying a particular color and pattern in the wrong order, a young Nuba man answers, "Oh it will do for the Germans," referring to the BBC television crew as "Germans" – the audience to which they had become most accustomed. This demonstrates a clear understanding of the altered practice of self-decoration and of his own altered role as a painted youth.

Nuba public self-decoration practices have reduced in subtlety of expression as the role of the outsider has had an increasing impact on the society. Nuba people had to accommodate their own perception and practice of body decoration and the accompanying fights and dances to a new group of people, defined only as spectators. These spectators did not have the insider knowledge to see the young people as symbolically matrixed with reference primarily to the rest of Nuba society. This has shifted some Nuba self-decoration practices to a different level of meaning. The body painting is now often carried out as entertainment for outsiders, its meaning for the insiders submerged. The process (self-decorating) and the product (decorated men) have become a performance. Thus the means (body painting) to the end (display of self to peers, ensuring the survival of the group) is seemingly no longer the objective of the practice. Practitioners are no longer carrying out the decoration with a view to identifying themselves within the Nuba group as young, strong, and healthy (Faris 1972) and simultaneously as an aesthetic work, but as people who paint their bodies – albeit with a careless reference to aesthetics. They have moved from doing things with a combined aesthetic, social, and physical focus as part of their experience of growing up and growing older in Nuba society to doing these things in order to fulfill an externally defined role. The original meaning is ignored. It is not lost or changed, nor (possibly) has it become obsolete; it is just deliberately being ignored. People have selected from their daily practices elements that, once isolated, take on new meanings.

The Nuba practices are those in which people are carrying out actions formerly embedded in a social matrix but in which, to the stranger's eye, the performative elements dominate and can be isolated, extrapolated, and re-presented. Implicit in this perception is the notion of strangeness, of dissimilarity to the cultural practices of the observer, and congruence with the observer's expectation of the observed – all converging through the power of the stranger's eye and purse to redefine and recontextualize. Thus, while in the original context the activity may fall under the category of "symbolized matrix," as the performer comes to do it more and more for reasons other than "being" or "becoming," it is transformed into a presentational activity. In deliberately seeking to fulfill a predetermined role and a temporarily redefined identity, the actions come closer to "acting." As Kirby describes it:

> In a symbolized matrix the referential elements are applied to but not acted by the performer . . . As "received" references increase, however, it is difficult to say that the performer is not acting even though he or she is doing nothing that could be defined as acting. . . . When the matrices are strong, persistent and reinforce each other, we see an actor, no matter how ordinary the behavior. This condition, the next step closer to true acting on our continuum, we may refer to as "received acting."
>
> (45)

When the nonmatrixed performers are situated in such a way that observers perceive them as "performing," then, *in spite of* how they may perceive themselves, the performers move closer to what Kirby has called "received acting." Initially framed by Riefenstahl's camera, the men's body decoration practices constituted "received acting." However, taking control of the opportunity, the Nuba men, in their redefined practice of self-decoration, went further. As soon as they opted to self-decorate for outsiders, they moved from *perceived* acting – what Kirby calls "received acting" – to what he calls "simple acting" in which an element of pretense is deliberately employed.

For the cameras and for the outsiders, the Nuba men were "acting" *as the Nuba men defined by Riefenstahl's pictures*; they could also simultaneously interact with each other in asides (even when still within the acting arena) *as the Nuba men they "really" were* – intending to eat and drink, to enjoy themselves, to shop at the market with the money they were earning by "acting" as themselves for the outsiders. Acting became the worktask (Goffman

1959: 72), with the acts themselves, based on the older practices, adjusted to meet the new demands:

> Instead of merely doing his task and giving vent to his feelings, he will express the doing of his task and acceptably convey his feelings. In general then, the representation of an activity will vary in some degree from the activity itself and therefore inevitably misrepresent it. And since the individual will be required to rely on signs in order to construct a representation of his activity, the image he constructs, however faithful to the facts, will be subject to all the disruptions that impressions are subject to.
>
> (Goffman 1959: 72)

Although the "worktasks" (Goffman 1959: 72) have changed, they are worktasks nonetheless. A move from farmer-hunter to actor has been made.

NOTE

1 I have used the male pronoun throughout as almost all performers are male except singers and dancers and a few instrumentalists. The women's Sande Society in Sierra Leone is an exception to the practice of male masking.

REFERENCES

Amali, S.O.O. (1985) *An Ancient Nigerian Drama*, Stuttgart: Franz Steiner Verlag Wiesbaden.

Amaury Talbot, Percy (1967 [1923]) *Life in Southern Nigeria*, London: Frank Carr & Co.

Beckerman, Bernard (1990) *Theatrical Presentation: Performer, Audience, and Act*, London: Routledge.

Blau, Herbert (1990) "Universals of Performance." In *By Means of performance*, edited by Richard Schechner and Willa Appel, 250–72. Cambridge: Cambridge University Press.

Bravmann, Rene A. (1977) "Gyinna-gyinna: making the djinn manifest," *African Arts* 10, 3: 45–50.

Carlson, Marvin (1996) *Performance: A Critical Introduction*, London: Routledge.

Cosentino, Donald J. (1980) "Lele Gbomba and the style of Mende baroque," *African Arts* 13, 3: 54–5.

D.W.M. (1953) "Oshogbo celebrates festival of SHANGO," *Nigeria Magazine* 44: 298–313.

Drewal, Margaret T. (1992) *Yoruba Ritual: Performers, Play, Agency*, Bloomington: Indiana University Press.

Fardon, Richard (1990) *Between God, the Dead and the Wild*, Edinburgh: International African Library.

Faris, James C. (1972) *Nuba Personal Art*, London: Duckworth.

Goffman, Erving (1959) *The Presentation of Self in Everyday Life*, Garden City, NY: Doubleday.

Harrop, John (1992) *Acting*, London: Routledge.

Horton, Robin (1960) "Gods as guests," *Nigeria Magazine*, special issue.

J.O.N. (1958) *Nigeria Magazine* 59: 339–40.

Kirby, Michael (1995 [1972]) "On acting and not-acting." In *Acting (Re)Considered*, edited by Phillip Zarrilli, 43–58. London: Routledge.

Lifschitz, E. (1988) "Hearing is believing: acoustic masks and spirit manifestation," in *West African Masks and Cultural Systems*, edited by Sidney L. Kasfir, 221–9, Tervuren, Belgium: Musée royal de l'Afrique centrale.

Mude, V.I. (1983) "The Tiv ivom dance," *Nigeria Magazine* 54: 2.

Na'ibi, M. Shuaibu (1958) "The Gade people of Abuja Emirate," *Nigeria Magazine* 59: 288–307.

Onwuejeogwu, Michael (1969) "The cult of the bori spirits among the hausa." In *Man in Africa*, edited by Mary Douglas and Phyllis M. Kaberry, 279–97, New York: Tavistock.

Ottenberg, Simon (1975) *Masked Rituals of Afikpo*, Seattle: University of Washington Press.

Schechner, Richard (1985) *Between Theater and Anthropology*, Philadelphia: University of Pennsylvania Press.

Spencer, Julius S. (1990) "Storytelling theatre in Sierra Leone: the example of Lele Gbomba," *New Theatre Quarterly* 6, 24: 349–56.

Wembeh-Rashid, J.A.R. (1971) "Isinyago and Midimu: masked dancers of Tanzania and Mozambique," *African Arts* 4, 2: 38–44.

READER CROSS-REFERENCES

Carlson – self-consciousness as an element of performance

Okpewho – performer training in African oral literature

Goffman – the presentation of self

Schechner, Kirshenblatt-Gimblett – broad applicability of performance studies model

Geertz, C. Bell – on the limits of applying Western theatrical models to non-Western performances

Santino, Ancelet, Fabian – describe other performances to which the formulation acting and not-acting may apply

31

RECONSIDERING STANISLAVSKY
Feeling, Feminism, and the Actor[1]

Rhonda Blair

A few years ago I attended a conference session on feminist theory, theater, and performance. One of the participants, in describing a performance she had seen, told how she was deeply moved by it and then apologized for having had such a response; in short, she seemed to be apologizing for having felt something. In the session as a whole, there was a skeptical stance toward feeling, narrative, and imagination. Though that particular conference session was centered on reception and this essay is centered on the performer, I believe the anecdote is apposite, since a mistrustful attitude toward feeling and the biological body in general has been common in feminist theories of performance since the early 1980s. These anxieties are understandable, given the power of feeling, imagination, and narrative, and the way that these and pseudo-scientific constructions of sex and race in biological bodies have historically been manipulated to oppress women. However, we feminists must move beyond responses based on received information and routinized antiessentialism (which itself is a kind of essentialism). Recent developments in cognitive neuroscience and neurophysiology can provide a fruitful way for reengaging issues of feeling, consciousness, and performance, and concomitantly, for reassessing Stanislavsky's contributions to systematizing the actor's process.

Science is not a final or absolute authority. It is not bias-free, any more than any theoretical construct is (political, literary, or otherwise); for, while hard sciences study perceivable or measurable objects or events, they de facto interpret those objects and events within a specific context. They are subject to scrutiny in terms of the structures of power, domination, and erasure that are embedded in any human activity with a social dimension. However, it is shortsighted and parochial not to consider applications of scientific knowledge and hypotheses that might inform our understanding of theater and performance. Science examines and illuminates things that theater, performance studies, cultural studies, and critical theory do not. Specific to this essay, in the last decades substantial progress has been made in understanding brain function in general. More recently, feminist scientists such as Elizabeth A. Wilson and Anne Fausto-Sterling have significantly advanced our knowledge of or raised fruitful questions about the relationship among cognition, behavior, and sexuality, and how these may be embodied in the brain. These and others lay a groundwork for understanding the species-specific ways in which we operate, as well as the complexity of variations within the species related to broad categories of sex and narrower categories of individual heredity and development.

Wilson describes why feminists must move beyond received skepticism about biological research. In a discussion related specifically to sex difference, but that addresses the more fundamental issue of the relationship between biology and feminist theory (and is therefore a ground for this essay), she states:

> A large part of the difficulty in generating politically engaging feminist critiques of the biological and behavioral sciences must be attributed to feminism's own natural-ized antiessentialism. After all, how can a critical habit nurtured on antibiologism produce anything but the most cursory and negating critique of biology? For example, Ruth Bleier (1984) and Lesley Rogers (1988) – both neurophysiologists – respond to the reductionism of contemporary neurological research on sexual difference by gesturing to the outside of neurology (usually figured as culture or the environment) . . . If the brains of men and women are different, they argue, it is because of postnatal, environmental influence.
>
> (Wilson 1998: 15)

However, Bleier's and Rogers's critique seems to echo not only Judith Butler's endlessly malleable late twentieth-century individual (self as predominantly performative), but also John Locke's late seventeenth-century *tabula rasa*, failing to account for the complex, ongoing interaction between environment *and* biological heredity:

> [The] gesture to a nonneurological culture or environment not only misrepresents the complex relationship between neurology and its outside, but also, by locating malleability, politics, and difference only in the domain of culture or environment, it abandons neurology to the very biologism it claims to be contesting.
>
> (Wilson 1998: 15–16)

For theories of theater and performance to be complete, they must engage developments in science that can illuminate these phenomena, since it is sentient beings with material bodies and brains who are the performers and its percipients. (I make this obvious point because, at the conference at which I presented the earliest version of this paper, a well-established American feminist theorist challenged me to give an example of a law of science; the implication was that such "laws" were primarily culturally conditioned and relative. I used gravity as the example, which I demonstrated by dropping a pencil on the table. My col-league called me to task, since others from a different culture might interpret the event of the falling pencil as the work of spirits, rather than an example of Newtonian physics. Regardless of unseen entities and cultural difference, I trust the pencil to fall every time I drop it, if I'm on the planet and not in an anti-gravity chamber or in outer space.)

The field of cognitive neuroscience has illuminated much about the processes of con-sciousness in the last 20 years. Bringing it to bear on a study of the actor's process is in the tradition of Stanislavsky's own interest in "hard psychology," as evidenced by his study of Pavlov's experiments in reflexology and Ribot's writing on the relationship between sensation and emotion, as well as in his own experimentation and observation in the rehearsal studio. My personal investment in these issues grows out of a desire better to understand the actor's process and possibly why so many of us who are feminist actors or feminists who work with actors keep returning to the fundamentals of the system; to explore the "rightness" of skepticism about feeling and narrative; and also to counter the ways in which Stanislavsky is misread and abused by mainstream theater practitioners. This project was triggered by what began as casual readings in cognitive neuroscience. (For an earlier exploration of some of these questions, see my essay "The method and the computational theory of mind.") I am arguing for the organic nature of some key elements in Stanislavsky's system, calling for feminists to reconsider not only Stanislavsky-based approaches to acting, but also certain ideas of the body, narrative, and consciousness in relationship to the performer's process.

While "realistic" approaches to actor training have often been validly challenged by feminists over the last quarter-century, these critiques typically stop short of a bottom-line materiality since most do not extend beyond cultural, literary, or psychoanalytic studies. One common problem that some feminists have with Stanislavsky is a general discomfort with emotions (or feeling/affect/qualia) because they seem to be overly subjective and conditioned, and therefore suspect (this issue is a variation on the conference presenter's response cited in the first paragraph above). Some criticize Stanislavsky's work for being grounded in a private narrativity, a closed sense of character, and psychological realism. They assert that it reifies a nonexistent "self" at the expense of ignoring socially conditioned aspects of identity; that it is applicable only to specific Western theater forms; that it colludes in mechanisms of representation that serve the ends of decadent late capitalism, reinforcing an ahistorical, non-critical, sentimentalized, or sensationalized view of experience; that it is part of the humanist project of reductively universalizing about experience in order to erase difference; and that, along with realism, it is inherently patriarchal and misogynist. Some say the system consigns us to a naive, anti-intellectual investment in narrative closure, "realistic" mimesis, and continuity that erases difference and ignores social critique.[2] And, in fact, some theater practitioners are guilty of precisely the things cited in feminist critiques, for example, misreading Stanislavsky to justify a decontextualized, hyperpersonalized emotionalism or narcissism. Both camps tend to collapse Stanislavsky with "psychological realism," being acquainted with only a narrow and distorted view of Stanislavsky's theater that ignores the immense range and variety of his work. Perspectives from both camps – "theory" and "practice" – are limited. (I refer the reader to Sharon Carnicke's excellent *Stanislavsky in Focus*, which provides a detailed history of the development of Stanislavsky's work and its dissemination in the US)

In considering an actor's system-based process from the perspective of cognitive neuroscience, specifically how brain structure is materially related to the nature of consciousness, we may gain a more concrete sense of how the actor works. I want to posit that certain fundamental concepts of Stanislavsky-based approaches to acting, though nurtured (and distorted) within Euro-American cultural contexts, are grounded in how the human brain and consciousness are structured. Recent developments in neurophysiology, cognitive neuroscience, and evolutionary biology indicate that Stanislavsky was onto something fundamental about acting. Though he was not the only one devising new approaches to acting that would dominate the twentieth century (see, for example, the discussion of actors such as Elizabeth Robins and Minnie Maddern Fiske in Gay Gibson Cima's *Performing Women*), Stanislavsky was the first to devise and disseminate broadly a systematic approach that connected the actor's behavior, body, emotion, and intelligence. He did this by centering his system in imagination, the given circumstances of the text, and the idea of a character wanting or pursuing something. As we move into the twenty-first century, I want to use new science to reexamine this still-dominant approach to acting in the west and argue that some principles of the system reflect basic characteristics of our biological being.

A Stanislavsky primer

Stanislavsky described the actor's fundamental aim as "the creation of [the] inner life of a human spirit, and its expression in artistic form," which the actor accomplishes by "living the part" (1964: 14). Central to the approach is "reaching the subconscious by conscious means." His goal was to develop a technique to allow "the artistic embodiment of inner emotional experience" (quoted in Toporkov 1979: 9). This process is at its root about expressing a particular human consciousness, or what one might call a "self." Over his lifetime Stanislavsky's thought followed an increasingly concrete trajectory, ultimately focusing on physical means to reach the most compelling embodiment of action and character. The latest phase of Stanislavsky's work currently available in English is the method of physical action. As actor Mikhail Kedrov explains, the method of physical action

> brings great concreteness to the work of the actor. It is based on the indivisible unity of the physical and spiritual life of a person and is built on the correct organization of the actor's life on the stage. The purpose of this method is to penetrate, through logical and correct fulfillment of physical actions, into those complicated, deep feelings and emotional experiences which the actor must call out of himself in order to create the given stage image.
>
> (Quoted in Toporkov 1979: 15–16)

Stanislavsky's thought reached its culmination with the method of active analysis – not, I note, "emotional" or "psychological" analysis. This approach is documented substantially by Maria Knebel, a protegée of Stanislavsky's; unfortunately, her writings have not yet been translated into English, so access to them is limited (Sharon Carnicke is currently engaged in a project to retrieve Knebel's legacy). The goal of both "physical action" and "action analysis" is to create an embodied, conscious, coherently articulated being. In these two late methods, Stanislavsky manipulates principles of action, behavior, imagination, attention, emotion, and memory to help the actor reach what he called the "inner creative state," allowing the actor to engage the work intellectually, physically, and emotionally (and Stanislavsky, free from the constraints of Soviet censorship, would no doubt add spiritually).

Though his view of the relationship between the conscious and the unconscious is problematic (he tends to describe them as discrete entities, rather than as processes that interpenetrate each other neurophysiologically), it is possible to see in his work the idea of a complex consciousness that inhabits the entire body, in which voluntary and involuntary processes and behaviors are not so cleanly separated from each other.

Stanislavsky grounds the actor in material elements of the script and the discovery of a physical score to arrive at a performance: motivated action is supported by given circumstances, which work with imagination (*if*) to arrive at a precise embodiment. Even in his first acting text, *The Actor Prepares*, Stanislavsky declares that emotions are "of largely subconscious origin, and not subject to direct command" (51–52) and focuses rather on kinds of specific information about what has happened or what is happening now in the actor–character's environment or experience, and the action of what she wants to accomplish or avoid. As his thinking developed, Stanislavsky placed increasingly less emphasis on emotion and more on given circumstances and behavior. For example, in the "method of physical actions," the actor is directed to find a physical score that allows her to connect with the action and given circumstances of a script and character, rather than, for example, relying on emotion memory, sense memory, or inner monologue. In short, the actor puts her body where her mind needs to go. This approach emphasizes an actor–character (or a "self") in relationship to an environment (a range of internal and external objects) and is in line with recent views in neuroscience about how body, brain, consciousness, emotion, memory, and behavior are related.

Cognitive neuroscience and Stanislavsky

The writings of neurologist and neuroscientist Antonio Damasio, most particularly *The Feeling of What Happens: Body and Emotion in the Making of Consciousness* (1999), provide an accessible entree into understanding how some principles of acting, especially those based on the later phases of the system, reflect the way our brains function. (Others working in related fields of neuroscience include Patricia Churchland, Gerald Edelman, Francis Crick, Susan Greenfield, and Steven Pinker.) Damasio asserts that the development of a sense of a self is the ground from which consciousness derives. Thus, in order to understand consciousness, we must understand how the sense of a self comes into being. In this regard, Damasio is resonant with Stanislavsky; the work of both is centered on the idea of an aware and sentient self. (Interestingly, the Russian word for consciousness is *samochuvstvo* – literally "self-feeling.") For Damasio the sense of self derives from the organism's sense of its relationship to an object; this mirrors the centrality of the character's relationship to immediate given circumstances in Stanislavsky. Damasio describes this phenomenon as follows:

> The sense of self does not depend on memory or on reasoning and even less on language. The sense of self depends . . . on the brain's ability to portray the living organism in the act of relating to an object. That ability, in turn, is a consequence of the brain's involvement in the process of regulating life [homeostasis].
>
> (Damasio 1999: book jacket)

Damasio's goal is to elucidate "the problem of the self from a biological perspective," through exploring consciousness specifically in relationship to brain structure and function (ibid. 12).[3] He begins with a proposition that, for all organisms, including humans, "Survival depends on finding and incorporating sources of energy and on preventing all sorts of situations which threaten the integrity of living tissues" (23). What distinguishes Damasio from some others who use evolutionary biology and psychology to examine the question of consciousness is that his hypothesis about biologically-driven activity connects behavior, intellect, emotion, and imagination. His view acknowledges complexity and contingency.

Damasio argues that consciousness (which derives from the sense of a self), attention, reason, behavior, emotion, and feeling are physically intertwined in our brains. These terms have correlatives in the vocabulary of the system:

> *self* is resonant with *character*, in the sense of a character aware of herself and her place in the world of the play;
>
> *consciousness* and *reason*, which have to do with the organism's awareness of and response to the environment, are resonant with the character's awareness of and connection to *given circumstances* in the play;
>
> *behavior* is a correlative term for *action* and *intention*, i.e., the organism/character does or attempts certain things out of necessity or desire;
>
> *attention* (a formal term in neuroscience) is what allows the organism to negotiate its environment, sorting through various stimuli and focusing on what might affect it positively or negatively; this is resonant with the actor's *point of focus* or *circle of attention* – that which must hold the individual's concentration to negotiate the performance successfully;
>
> *emotion* and *feeling*, fundamental to consciousness and to acting, are similar in Damasio and Stanislavsky (these will be discussed more specifically later).

Damasio's relational dynamic, centered on the brain's ability to represent "the living organism in the act of relating to an object," echoes Stanislavsky's system: the actor imagines and experiences a fictive self, involved with issues of survival of one kind or another, that ultimately involves, affects, and changes the body. Characters are often engaged with issues of survival and prosperity in one form or another, physically, economically, emotionally, or spiritually. A variation on the "organism-object" dynamic is what the actor plays out in constructing a character: The actor engages the internal (mental) and external objects of the text and its given circumstances, and her own mental objects (derived from memory and personal history); she then accordingly devises a pattern of behavior – a course of action that is related to the character's desire to acquire or avoid something. While this sketch of what the actor does is reductive, it is generally accurate.

The actor connects her body with the physical environment of the studio or stage, and equally importantly, with her imagination. Here Damasio is particularly useful, for he posits a material basis for understanding imagination as an organic, "survival-oriented" function. A key element of his argument is that the evolutionary development of the brain – and thereby consciousness – inextricably links the "world of homeostasis" and the "world of the imagination." The former is the world of inner life regulation, having to do with the maintenance of the organism within the narrow range of parameters within which it can survive; the latter is the world of image-making, in which the organism can imagine possible conditions and outcomes to a given situation, leading it to adjust its behavior to maximize the maintenance of homeostasis. In short, homeostasis – the maintenance of the organism's basic stability – is "a key to the biology of consciousness" (40). Imagination, a result of our brain's evolutionary development, is essential to the fact of our *physicality*, not just our psyches. The links between imagination and the body are grossly evident in our body's responses – blushing, flushing, palpitations, trembling – to embarrassing or frightening situations, imagined or real. Imagination is a basic element of consciousness.

Apropos of theater, in this hypothesis a kind of proto-narrative (i.e., sensing oneself in relationship to an object and sensing that one needs to *do* something about it, whether it be to eat it or run away from it) becomes the beginning of consciousness: the organism is able to imagine a "story" in which it (the "self") encounters an object (external or internal) that causes it to react, thereby causing changes in the organism (168–69). Damasio writes:

> Consciousness begins when brains acquire the power . . . of telling a story without words, the story that there is life ticking away in an organism, and that the states of the living organism, within body bounds, are continuously being altered by encounters with objects or events in its environment, or for that matter, by thoughts and by internal adjustments of the life process. . . . The apparent self emerges as the feeling of a feeling.
>
> (30–31)

That is, the organism becomes aware of and registers the feelings of the neural and chemical events of the body that lead it to define itself – *a* self – only in relationship to objects and events.

Constructing narratives is a core element of the actor's work. Stanislavsky's use of terms such as "throughline of action" and "given circumstances" is all about helping the actor devise an image-based narrative that will carry her successfully through the play. This echoes our daily lives, in which we are constantly engaged in constructing narratives in order to make sense of our experience and to guide our actions. This propensity for making stories, while psychologically and culturally conditioned, is more than just that. The process of proto-narrativizing is embedded in brain structure; the continuity of human consciousness is in fact provided by the flow of nonverbal narratives of a core consciousness. From this perspective, consciousness is "the unified mental pattern [or narrative] that brings together the object and the self." At bottom, consciousness, emotion, and feeling all "depend for their execution on [mental] representations of the organism. Their shared essence is the body" (Damasio: 284). In other words, they are all related to the organism sensing itself, i.e., as being a discrete body/entity either at risk or experiencing pleasure. This makes the "body–mind problem" not a problem at all, for mind – consciousness – is a process of the body.

These ideas influence the way I teach and direct. In an M.F.A. text analysis class, aside from being introduced to straightforward dramaturgical, structural, and historical approaches to analyzing a script, I guide students toward two other principles: imagining a clear progression of where the character is moment by moment physically and "historically" (in the sense of a character's history up to any given moment); and understanding that the efficacy of this "score" is built on their developing a highly personal string of images that can activate their full engagement with the role. In working with actors in rehearsal, I manipulate attention, intention, text-based and personal imagery, and physicality in specific ways to engage the actors with each other, the text, and their environment. These processes differ little, if at all, from Stanislavsky's. What is different is that I operate with the awareness that these processes are reflective of brain structure and function, and that the manipulation of information and physical score allows the actor access to a rich engagement with the material. I have found this approach useful in demystifying the actor's process.

Terms such as "consciousness," "feeling," "emotion," and "self" are often insufficiently defined by theater practitioners and theorists. Damasio's description of various levels of consciousness provides a structure for being more specific. He begins by defining a kind of basic, pre-conscious biological self, the *proto-self* that underlies consciousness. The proto-self

> is a coherent collection of neural patterns which map, moment by moment, the state of the physical structure of the organism in its many dimensions . . . We are not conscious of the proto-self. Language is not part of the structure of the proto-self. The proto-self has no powers of perception and holds no knowledge.

(154)

The proto-self is a first-order, pre-conscious mapping of the organism that allows "relatively simple, stereotyped patterns of response, including metabolic regulation, reflexes, the biological machinery behind what will become pain and pleasure, drives and motivations" (55). Second-order mapping, out of which grows our basic awareness of a self, is in likelihood generated in some combination of the superior colliculi, the cingulate cortex, and the thalamus. These areas effect the enhancement of the object image by activating the sections of the brain responsible for the proto-self and emotions (181). That is, there is no hard and fast separation of cognition, emotions, and basic biological operations of homeostasis. While various functions are centered in different parts of the brain, they are neurophysiologically intertwined.

The most basic level of consciousness, and the one on which our awareness of ourselves depends, is *core consciousness*. This is "the unvarnished sense of our individual organism in the act of knowing" (125):

> You come by this knowledge, this discovery as I prefer to call it, instantly: there is no noticeable process of inference, no out-in-the-daylight logical process that leads you there, and no words at all – there is the image of the thing and, right next to it, is the sensing of its possession by you. . . . The essence of core consciousness is the very thought of you – the very feeling of you – as an

individual being involved in the process of knowing of your own existence and of the existence of others.

(126–27)

This basic level of consciousness is about engendering both the mental patterns we call images of objects (both external and internal) and, in conjunction with this, the "sense of self in the act of knowing" (9). It is "a feeling that accompanies the making of any kind of image" (26), the self's "ceaselessly generated image of the act of knowing first expressed as a feeling of knowing relative to the mental images of the object to be known" (192). "Rationality" and higher intellectual functions – what Damasio calls *extended consciousness* – grow out of this source. These higher functions are centered in the neocortex, the evolutionarily more recent part of the brain. They are built on and cannot exist without the foundation of core consciousness and emotion, which are deeply interdependent and emanate from the subcortex. Representations of emotions derive largely from more primitive, subcortical parts of the brain ("primitive" in the sense of being evolutionarily earlier): the brain stem nuclei, hypothalamus, basal forebrain, and amygdala (79). These are also some of the brain structures responsible for the proto-self, reinforcing the ultimate inseparability of the "layers" of the self.

Damasio posits that emotions are a significant, necessary element in the construction of the narratives of consciousness and that, as such, they are part of the organism's fundamental sense of self. For Damasio, emotions are the states of being that reflect changes in the neural and chemical condition of the organism as it responds to its external and internal environments, i.e., they are substantially preconscious: "Notwithstanding the reality that learning and culture alter the expression of emotions and give emotions new meanings, emotions are biologically determined processes, depending on innately set brain devices, laid down by a long, evolutionary history" (51).

Though what affects us emotionally can vary significantly depending on the environment (including the culture) in which we are raised, there is a cross-cultural sameness in emotional response and expression among humans. This view is borne out, for example, in the studies of Paul Ekman, which document similarities in how emotions manifest themselves in facial expression, regardless of culture; though stimuli may differ, emotional expression in the face is broadly the same, i.e., anger or happiness will be recognizable as anger or happiness. The argument is that, across sex and ethnicity, we are more similar than different in terms of basic human response; emotions, first of all, were and are biological, not "psychological," functions.

Evolutionarily, emotions' two primary functions are to produce "a specific reaction to an inducing situation" and to regulate "the internal state of the organism such that it can be prepared for the specific reaction." Emotions are a high-level component of life regulation "sandwiched between the basic survival kit (e.g., regulation of metabolism; simple reflexes; motivations; biology of pain and pleasure) and the devices of high reason, but still very much a part of the hierarchy of life-regulation devices" (Damasio: 53–54). Emotions and core consciousness require many of the same neural substrates. In fact, absence of emotion in a person is "a reliable correlate of defective core consciousness" (100), as demonstrated in

Damasio's and others' studies of neurological integrity, behavior, and psychology of brain-damaged individuals. (For more on this, see Damasio's *Descartes' Error: Emotion, Reason, and the Human Brain* (1994).) One only has to observe that the conscious state is always accompanied by some coloring of emotion – what Damasio calls "background emotion" and what we might call "mood" or "general state." When we are conscious, there is always something going on with us neurologically and chemically that has an emotional dimension, however low-key or subtle.

Damasio carefully distinguishes between feeling and emotion. Emotions can often exist without consciousness; they are an aspect of the proto-self, which is geared autonomically (in the sense of being self-governing) toward survival. Feelings, on the other hand, begin with a kind of awareness on the part of the organism that it is experiencing an emotion. Interestingly, "it is possible that feelings are posed at the very threshold that separates being from knowing and thus have a privileged connection to consciousness" (Damasio: 43). Feeling is emotion made conscious or, put another way, *consciousness begins with the "feeling of a feeling."* This point is crucial in relationship to the centrality of feeling in Stanislavsky's work and, I daresay, almost any actor's process. The movement from emotion to conscious feeling is an enchained process: the inducer of the emotion (i.e., the internal or external object perceived by the organism) produces an automated emotion in neural sites, which leads to a representation (or image) of emotional changes in the body and brain, which leads to a feeling, which leads to the organism *knowing* the feeling; i.e., becoming aware of the feeling in a second-order processing of the encounter with the object (Damasio: 291). The capacity for feeling takes the organism to the next level in evolutionary development, for

> the process of feeling begins to alert the organism to the problem that emotion has begun to solve. The simple process of feeling begins to give the organism *incentive* to heed the results of emoting. . . . The availability of feeling is also the stepping stone for the next development – *the feeling of knowing that we have feelings*. In turn, knowing is the stepping stone for the process of planning specific and nonstereotypical responses. . . . In other words, "feeling" feelings extends the reach of emotions by facilitating the planning of novel and customized forms of adaptive response.
>
> (284–85)

In short, being aware of feelings allows us to be innovative and creative – conscious, not just automatic – in our responses to the thing causing the emotion. The process of evolution has extended consciousness through the expansion of capacities of longer-term memory, language, and other "higher functions." But the ground of consciousness – the source of second-order representations, the site of imagination leading to conscious action – is found in evolutionarily older neural regions located in the depths of the brain (Damasio: 275).

While using a different vocabulary (e.g., "reaching the subconscious by conscious means"), Stanislavsky began to provide the means for the actor to understand the connections among cognition, imagination, emotion, action, the body, and the sense of a self in a way that resonates with Damasio's description of the inseparability of homeostasis and extended consciousness. There is a

> close linkage between the regulation of life and the processing of images which is implicit in the sense of individual perspective. . . . As for the sense of action, it is contained in the fact that certain images are tightly associated with certain options for motor response. Therein our sense of agency – these images are mine and I can act on the object that caused them.
>
> (Damasio: 183)

Building on core consciousness, extended consciousness allows us to develop an *auto-biographical self* that is composed of a "lived past and anticipated future," emerging from "the gradual buildup of memories of . . . the 'objects' of the organism's biography" (Damasio: 196). Extended consciousness keeps active "the many images whose collection defines the autobiographical self and the images which define the object" (197–98). In short, the auto-biographical self is "a process of coordinated activation and display of personal memories, based on a multisite network" (222). Stanislavsky's textual analysis (to determine given circumstances, which is nothing other than environment and history), psychophysical action, memory, and imagination are variations on Damasio's mechanisms: the actor, in a modified and heightened form that involves both core and extended consciousness, interrelates con-scious elements of history, memory, and given circumstances to unlock imagination and respond "in the moment."

The resonance between Stanislavsky's theatrical principles and Damasio's neuroscientific ones is particularly clear when one focuses on the trajectory of the role of emotion, since consciousness evolved "*within, from*, and *in the vicinity of* the previously available machinery involved in homeostasis, in other words, the machinery of emotion, attention, and regula-tion of body states" (Damasio: 274). Understanding the enchained process linking emotion and conscious feeling can be invaluable to the actor and the acting teacher: the individual processes the object; emotion ensues; the individual becomes aware of the emotion; i.e., feeling and memory arise; attention is enhanced and focused according to the processing of the object and emotion; action is taken. Consciousness has emotion at its root. Theater, which is a quintessence of embodied human consciousness, can benefit by taking this neurobiological knowledge into account.

Conclusion

"Get out of your head" is a phrase used by many acting teachers as a way to admonish actors to be more present to the moment in a scene or a play, to "not think," but to "react" or "respond" – as though a thought were not by definition a powerfully human kind of reaction. Most notable among these teachers is the problematic and brilliant Sanford Meisner, whose book repeats "get out of your head" almost like a mantra. Phrases such as this and the beliefs they reflect are a factor in the anti-intellectualism, narcissism, and mystification that can attach to Stanislavsky-influenced approaches to acting. But they are nonetheless directed at trying to get the actor to engage an imaginary situation as fully and specifically as possible. Rather than "get out of your head," I propose that a more apt and accurate phrase for the actor be, in *certain phases* of her process (along with using every bit of her critical and analytical skills in other phases), "get out of your neocortex." That is, let go of overrationalizing and controlling one's choices (the kinds of processes generated in neocortical regions of the brain) and open up to a scene's immediate given circumstances and one's ability to respond to them spontaneously (the kinds of processes generated substantially in the subcortical regions). And to theorists who continue playing out, knowingly or otherwise, variations on Descartes' error of separating emotion from reason and reason from the body, I would say "get into *all* of your head," not just the neocortex. Let yourself feel at the theater (and in your research), for feelings are part of mind.

Feeling, imagination, and narrative have a primal force in a literal, biological sense, grounded in ancient brain structures at the root of consciousness. This is why theater – performing stories for each other in community – can be so potent and moving. It is a mistake for theorists – feminist and otherwise – to categorize feeling and story as being predominantly social or psychological phenomena, with a negligible or less significant biological component. (Is this possibly because feelings, stories, and bodies can be messy, mysterious, and scary?) I am thankful that we are past the simplistic essentializing about the body and feelings found in some forms of cultural feminism, but it is time to revisit this terrain – because, finally, we *are* bodies with feelings. Referring back to Wilson, feminists have the most to gain by working at the intersections of theory, practice, history, and science. I challenge feminist actors and acting teachers to be more rigorous in their understanding of bodies, consciousness, and feelings as they rehearse and perform. The organism–object model of consciousness allows us to consider an organic basis for the inescapability of the pull to narrativize our experience, as well as the power of engaging a self with the given circumstances of a situation. It lets us understand the body in concrete ways that account for the interpenetration of body, mind, feeling, emotion, and experience. Stanislavsky's experiments led him to devise a framework for an approach to acting that draws directly on how we function as a species, in a way now borne out by cognitive neuroscience and evolutionary biology. If theater is about illuminating the human condition and making us more conscious of what it means to exist – of what it can mean to be human – then our approaches to it must accommodate our history and our experience in every possible way.

NOTES

1 Earlier versions of this research were presented at the Association for Theatre in Higher Education Conference and the American Society for Theatre Research Conference in 2001. It appears here in much-revised form. I would like to thank J. Ellen Gainor and Andrew Sofer for their support.

2 See, for example, Counsell's chapters on Stanislavsky and Strasberg in *Signs of Performance* (1996); various essays in Zarrilli's (1995) *Acting (Re)Considered*, especially Zarrilli's introductory essays and "Part I: Theories and meditations on acting"; Worthen (1992); Diamond (1997); and Aston (1995).

A version of this overview appears in my essay "The method and the computational theory of mind" (2000).

3 This and all other quotations are from Damasio, *The Feeling of What Happens* (1999).

REFERENCES

Aston, Elaine (1995) *An Introduction to Feminism and Theatre*. London: Routledge.

Blair, Rhonda (2000) "The method and the computational theory of mind," in *Method Acting Reconsidered: Theory, Practice, Future*, ed. David Krasner. New York: St. Martin's Press, 201–18.

Carnicke, Sharon Marie (1998) *Stanislavsky in Focus*. London: Taylor & Francis.

Cima, Gay Gibson (1993) *Performing Women: Female Characters, Male Playwrights, and the Modern Stage*. Ithaca: Cornell University Press.

Counsell, Colin (1996) *Signs of Performance: An Introduction to Twentieth-Century Theatre*. London: Routledge.

Damasio, Antonio (1994) *Descartes' Error: Emotion, Reason, and the Human Brain*. New York: Avon Books.

—— (1999) *The Feeling of What Happens: Body and Emotion in the Making of Consciousness*. New York: Harcourt, Brace & Co.

Diamond, Elin (1997) *Unmaking Mimesis: Essays on Feminism and Theater*. London: Routledge.

Ekman, Paul (1992) "Facial expressions of emotions: new findings, new questions," *Psychological Science*, 3: 34–38.

Fausto-Sterling, Anne (2000) *Sexing the Body: Gender Politics and the Construction of Sexuality*. New York: Basic Books.

Stanislavsky, Konstantin (1964) *An Actor Prepares*. New York: Routledge/Theatre Arts Books.

Toporkov, Vasili (1979) *Stanislavsky in Rehearsal: The Final Years*, trans. Christine Edwards. New York: Theatre Arts Books.

Wilson, Elizabeth A. (1998) *Neural Geographies: Feminism and the Microstructure of Cognition*. New York: Routledge.

Worthen, W.B. (1992) "Actors and Objects," in *Modern Drama and the Rhetoric of Theater*. Berkeley: University of California Press, 54–98.

Zarrilli, Phillip B. (ed.) (1995) *Acting (Re)Considered: Theories and Practices*. London: Routledge.

READER CROSS-REFERENCES

Bateson – a cognitive approach to play

Goffman, Gabler – the self as presented in everyday life

Butler – strategically questions the power of biology to determine the self

Strasberg – an emotion-focused, Stanislavsky-based approach to acting

Grotowski – the relationship between the psychological and the physical in acting

Fabian, Conquergood, Turner and Turner – performance as a way of embodying knowledge

Part VII

PERFORMANCE PROCESSES

One of the basic tenets of performance studies is that a performance is not a static finished product. Performances are always in-process, changing, growing, and moving through time. Though a specific performance event may appear to be fixed and bounded, it is actually part of an ongoing sequence that includes the training of the performers, rehearsals and other forms of preparation, the presentation of the performance to a specific audience in a specific time and place, and the aftermath, in which the performance lives on in recordings, critical responses, and the memories of performers and spectators. Performance-studies scholars consider the entire performance process as their object of inquiry.

As Schechner notes, the performance process can be understood as a negotiation among four parties: sourcers, producers, performers, and partakers (Schechner 2006: 250). In "First attempts at a stylized theatre" (1907), Russian director Vsevolod Meyerhold offers his vision of how the work of the author (sourcer), director and designers (producers), and actors (performer) are synthesized into a coherent work of art for presentation to the spectator. Meyerhold, whose boldly kinetic style of acting called "biomechanics" came to symbolize the optimism of the early years of the Soviet Union, describes the particular process by which his Theatre-Studio developed its first production. In African oral literature – a category of performance which includes storytelling, ritual poetry, song, and divination – the individual performer usually enjoys complete control of the performance process, but only after an extended period of training. In "The oral artist: training and preparation" (1992), Isidore Okpewho describes this process, which may be formal or informal and frequently extends over a period of several years.

Semiotician Marco De Marinis, in "The performance text" (1993), takes up the question of when the performance itself can be said to begin and end. By "performance text," De Marinis means "a theoretical model of the observable performance phenomenon, to be assumed as an explanatory principle of the functioning of performance as a phenomenon of signification and communication" (p. 281) – the complete unit suitable for and subject to interpretation. While many performances contain some self-conscious demarcation of a beginning and ending, De Marinis argues that it is ultimately the judgment of the analyst (i.e., the spectator) who determines the boundaries of the performance event. Recognizing the crucial role that the spectator plays in determining the meaning and significance of a performance, Eugenio Barba's "The deep order called turbulence" (2000) explores "The three faces of dramaturgy" which guide a performance toward forging an organic connection with the audience. For Barba, dramaturgy – understood here as the process of composing and preparing a theatrical performance – demands constant attention to both order and turbulence, meticulousness, and chaos. Barba also reminds us that when it is done properly, performance "tires and sometimes hurts" (p. 308).

In "The archaeology of performance," Mary Zimmerman describes how her process of devising theater involves balancing the intellectual demands of a non-theatrical source text with the practical concerns of staging a live performance. Appropriately from the writer-director of *Metamorphoses* (2002), "The archaeology of performance" (2005) explains how the written texts of her plays grow and change in response to the contributions of the actors and designers who serve as her collaborators and to the material conditions under which the performance is prepared.

These five essays illustrate just a few of the many possible approaches to performance processes. Though they differ greatly, all reflect the ways in which a given moment's "performance" bears the hallmarks (and scars) of the process that generated it. Taken collectively, they show us that the *who*, *what*, and *why* of performance cannot be separated from the *how*.

32

FIRST ATTEMPTS AT A
STYLIZED THEATRE

Vsevolod Meyerhold

(translated by Edward Braun)

The first attempts to realize a stylized theatre as conceived by Maeterlinck and Bryusov were made at the Theatre-Studio. In my opinion, this first experimental theatre came very near to achieving ideal stylized drama with its first production, *The Death of Tintagiles*; so I think it is appropriate to describe the work of the directors, actors, and designers on this play, and to consider the lessons learnt during its production.

The theatre is constantly revealing a lack of harmony amongst those engaged in presenting their collective creative work to the public. One never sees an ideal blend of author, director, actor, designer, composer, and property-master. For this reason, Wagner's notion of a synthesis of the arts seems to me impossible.[1] Both the artist and the composer should remain in their own fields: the artist in a special *decorative* theatre where he could exhibit canvases which require a stage rather than an art gallery, artificial rather than natural light, several planes instead of just two dimensions, and so on; the composer should concentrate on symphonies like Beethoven's Ninth, for the dramatic theatre, where music has merely an auxiliary role, has nothing to offer him.

These thoughts came to me after our early experiments (*The Death of Tintagiles*) had been superseded by the second phase (*Pelléas and Mélisande*).[2] But even when we started work on *The Death of Tintagiles* I was plagued already by the question of disharmony between the various creative elements; even if it was impossible to reach agreement with the composer and the artist, each of whom was trying instinctively to delineate his own function, at least I hoped to unify the efforts of the author, the director, and the actor.

It became clear that these three, the basis of the theatre, could work as one, but only if given the approach which we adopted in the rehearsal of *The Death of Tintagiles* at the Theatre-Studio.

In the course of the usual discussions of the play (before which, of course, the director acquainted himself with it by reading everything written on the subject), the director and actors read through Maeterlinck's verses and extracts from those of his dramas containing scenes corresponding in mood to *The Death of Tintagiles* (the play, itself, was left until we understood how to treat it, lest it became transformed into a mere exercise). The verses and extracts were read by each actor in turn. For them, this work corresponded to the sketches of a painter or the exercises of a musician. The artist must perfect his technique before embarking on a picture. Whilst reading, the actor looked for new means of expression. The audience (everybody, not just the director) made comments and assisted the reader to develop these new means. The entire creative act was directed towards finding those inflections which contained the true ring of the author's own voice. When the author was "revealed" through this collective work, when a single verse or extract "rang true," the audience immediately analyzed the means of expression which had conveyed the author's style and tone.

Before enumerating the various new aspects of technique developed through this intuitive method, and while I still retain a clear picture of these combined exercises of director and actors, I should like to mention two distinct methods of establishing contact between the director and his actors: one deprives not only the actor but also the spectator of creative freedom; the other leaves them both free, and forces the spectator to create instead of merely looking on (for a start, by stimulating his imagination).

The two methods may be explained by illustrating the four basic theatrical elements (author, director, actor, and spectator) as follows:

1   A triangle, in which the apex is the director and the two remaining corners, the author and the actor. The spectator comprehends the creation of the latter two through the creation of the director. This is method one, which we shall call the "Theatre-Triangle."

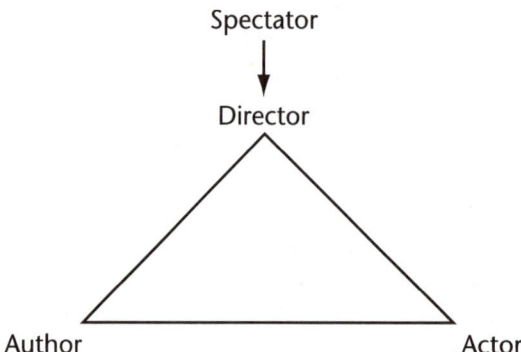

2   A straight, horizontal line with the four theatrical elements (author, director, actor, spectator) marked from left to right represents the other method, which we shall call the "Theatre of the Straight Line." The actor reveals his soul freely to the spectator, having assimilated the creation of the director, who, in his turn, has assimilated the creation of the author.

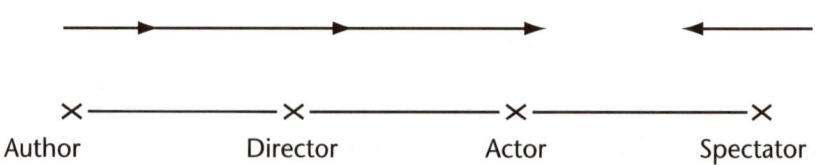

1 In the "Theatre-Triangle" the director explains his *mise-en-scène* in detail, describes the characters as he sees them, prescribes every pause, and then rehearses the play until his personal conception of it is exactly reproduced in performance. This "Theatre-Triangle" may be likened to a symphony orchestra with the director acting as the conductor.

However, the very architecture of the theatre, lacking any provision for a conductor's rostrum, points to the difference between the two.

People will say that there are occasions when a symphony orchestra plays without a conductor. Let us consider Nikisch[3] and the symphony orchestra which has been playing under him for years with scarcely a change in its personnel; take a composition which it has played several times a year over a period of ten years. If Nikisch were absent from the conductor's rostrum on one occasion, would the orchestra play the composition according to his interpretation? Yes, it is possible that the listener would recognize it as Nikisch's interpretation. But would the performance sound exactly as though Nikisch were conducting? Obviously, it would be worse, although we should still be hearing Nikisch's interpretation.

So I contend this: true, a symphony orchestra without a conductor is possible, but nevertheless it is impossible to draw a parallel between it and the theatre, where the actors invariably perform on the stage without a director. A symphony orchestra without a conductor is possible, but no matter how well rehearsed, it could never stir the public, only acquaint the listener with the interpretation of this or that conductor, and could blend into an ensemble only to the extent that an artist can re-create a conception which is not his own.

The actor's art consists in far more than merely acquainting the spectator with the director's conception. The actor will grip the spectator only if he assimilates both the director and the author and then gives of himself from the stage.

By contrast, an orchestral musician is distinguished by his ability to carry out the conductor's directions precisely, by dint of his virtuoso technique and *by depersonalizing himself*.

In common with the symphony orchestra, the "Theatre-Triangle" must employ actors with virtuoso technique, but at all costs lacking in individuality, so that they are able to convey the director's exact concept.

2 In the "Theatre of the Straight Line," the director, having absorbed the author's conception, conveys his own creation (now a blend of the author and the director) to the actor. The actor, having assimilated the author's conception via the director, stands face to face with the spectator (with director and author behind him), and *freely* reveals his soul to him, thus intensifying the fundamental theatrical relationship of performer and spectator.

In order for the straight line not to bend,[4] the director must remain the sole arbiter of the mood and style of the production, but nevertheless the actor's art remains free in the "Theatre of the Straight Line."

The director describes his plan during the discussion of the play. The entire production is coloured by his view of it. He inspires the actors with his devotion to the work, and imbues them with the spirit of the author and with his own interpretation. But after the discussion all the performers remain completely independent. Then the director calls a further general meeting to create harmony from all the separate pieces. How does he set about this? Simply by balancing all the parts which have been freely created by the various individuals involved in the collective enterprise. In establishing the harmony vital to the production, he does not insist on the exact representation of his own conception, which was intended only to ensure unanimity and to prevent the work created collectively from disintegrating. Instead he retires behind the scenes at the earliest possible moment and leaves the stage to the actors. Then, either they are out of accord with the director or the author (if, say, they are not of the new school)[5] and "set fire to the ship," or they reveal their souls through almost improvisatory additions, not to the text but to the mere suggestions of the director. In this way the spectator is made to comprehend the author and the director through the prism of the actor's art. *Above all, drama is the art of the actor.*

If you read any of the works of Maeterlinck, his poetry or his drama, his preface to the last collected edition,[6] his book *Le Trésor des humbles*, where he speaks of the Static Theatre in a tone embodying all the color and atmosphere of his works, you will see that he has no desire to evoke horror on stage; nor does he seek to drive the spectator to such hysteria that he wants to flee in terror. On the contrary, he aims to provoke a fearful yet reasoning acceptance of the inevitability of life, to move the spectator to tears and suffering, and yet to soothe and console him. His first task is "to alleviate our grief by implanting that hope which flags and then springs to life again."[7] When the spectator leaves the theatre, life with all its pain resumes its course, but the pain no longer seems in vain; life flows on with its joys, its sorrows, and its exigencies, but everything acquires meaning because we have seen that it is possible to emerge from the gloom, or at least to endure it without bitterness. Maeterlinck's art is healthy and life-giving. It summons people to a wise acceptance of the might of fate, and his theatre acquires all the significance of a temple. Pastore has good reason for extolling Maeterlinck's mysticism as the last refuge of apostates who refuse to recognize the temporal power of the Church yet cannot bring themselves to discard their free belief in another world. Such a theatre is fit for the presentation of religious subjects. No matter how somber the colors of a work, so long as it is a *mystery*, it contains an indefatigable affirmation of life.

To us it seems that the whole mistake of our predecessors lay in their attempts at frightening the spectator instead of reconciling him with the inevitability of fate. "At the foundation of my dramas" – writes Maeterlinck – "lies the idea of a Christian God together with the ancient concept of Fate." The author hears the words and lamentations of men as a muffled sound, as though they were falling into a deep abyss. He sees men from a vantage-point beyond the clouds as faintly glittering sparks. All he desires is to overhear in their souls a few words of humility, of hope, of compassion, of terror, and to show us the might of the fate which guides our destiny.

Our aim was to ensure that our production of Maeterlinck produced the same effect of reconciliation in the spectator's mind as the author himself intended. A performance of Maeterlinck is a *mystery*; either there is a barely audible harmony of voices, a chorus of soft weeping, of muted sobs and a stirring of hope (as in *The Death of Tintagiles*), or there is an ecstasy which is transformed into a universal religious festival with dancing to the music of organ and trumpets, or a bacchanalia to celebrate a great miracle (as in Act Two of *Sister Beatrice*). The dramas of Maeterlinck are "above all else a manifestation and purification of the spirit." They are "a chorus of souls singing *sotto voce* of suffering, love, beauty, and death." They have a *simplicity* which transports one to the realms of fantasy, a harmony which brings calm, a joy bordering on the ecstatic. It was with this understanding of the spirit of Maeterlinck's theatre that we began work on the rehearsal exercises.

What Muther[8] said of Il Perugino, one of the most fascinating painters of the Quattrocento, seems to me true of Maeterlinck: "The contemplative lyrical character of his subjects, the quiet grandeur and archaic splendour of his pictures could only be achieved by a composition whose harmony is unmarred by the slightest abrupt movement or the merest harsh contrast."

Proceeding from this general evaluation of Maeterlinck's art, our directors and actors intuitively established the following principles during the course of preliminary rehearsals:

I Diction

1   The words must be coldly "coined," free from all tremolo and the familiar break in the voice. There must be a total absence of tension and lugubrious intonation.

2   The sound must always be "reinforced"; the words must fall like drops into a deep well, the fall being clearly audible without any vibration in space. There must be no diffusion of sound, no drawing out of the word-endings (as in the reading of the Decadents' verses).

3   The internal mystical vibration is more powerful than the histrionics of the old theatre, which were invariably uncontrolled and ugly to look at, with flailing of arms, beating of breasts, and slapping of thighs. The internal mystical vibration is conveyed through the eyes, the lips, the sound, and manner of delivery: the exterior calm which covers volcanic emotions, with everything light and unforced.

4   In the expression of the tragic sorrows of the soul the form is dictated by the content. Maeterlinck prescribes one form and no other in order to convey that which is so simple and so long-familiar.[9]

5   The dialogue should never be gabbled; this is permissible only in those *neurasthenic* dramas where much play is made with lines of dots. Epic calm does not exclude tragic emotions, which always possess a certain grandeur.

6   Tragedy with a smile on the lips. I did not grasp fully the need for this until I happened to read the following words of Savonarola:

> Do not assume that Mary cried out at the death of her Son and roamed the streets, tearing her hair and acting like a madwoman. She followed Him with great humility. Certainly she shed tears, but her appearance revealed not so much sheer grief as a combination of *grief and joy*. Even at the foot of the Cross she stood in grief and joy, engrossed in the mystery of God's great mercy.

If an actor of the old school wished to move the audience deeply, he would cry out, weep, groan, and beat his breast with his fists. Let the new actor express the highest point of tragedy just as the grief and joy of Mary were expressed: with an outward repose, almost *coldly*, without shouting or lamentation. He can achieve profundity without recourse to exaggerated tremolo.

II Plasticity

1 Richard Wagner reveals inner dialog through the orchestra; the sung musical phrase lacks the power to express the inner passions of his heroes. Wagner summons the orchestra to his assistance, believing that only the orchestra is capable of conveying what is ineffable, of revealing the mystery to the spectator. Like the singer's phrase in the "Musikdrama," the actor's word in the drama is an insufficiently powerful means of conveying inner dialog. Surely if the *word* were the sole means of conveying the essence of tragedy, everybody would be capable of acting in the theatre. But merely by declaiming words, even by declaiming them well, one does not necessarily *say* anything. We need some new means of expressing the ineffable, of revealing that which is concealed.

Just as Wagner employs the orchestra to convey spiritual emotions, I employ *plastic movement*. But the old theatre, too, regarded plasticity as an essential means of expression; one has only to consider Salvini[10] in *Othello* or *Hamlet*. Plasticity itself is not new, but the form which I have in mind is new. Before, it corresponded closely to the spoken dialog, but I am speaking of a *plasticity which does not correspond to the words*. What do I mean by this?

Two people are discussing the weather, art, apartments. A third – given, of course, that he is reasonably sensitive and observant – can tell exactly by listening to this conversation, which has no bearing on the relationship between the two, whether they are friends, enemies) or lovers. He can tell this from the way they gesticulate, stand, move their eyes. This is because they move in a way unrelated to their words, a way which reveals their relationship.

The director erects a bridge between actor and spectator. He depicts friends, enemies, or lovers in accordance with the author's instructions, yet by means of movement and poses he must present a picture which enables the spectator not only to hear the spoken dialogue but to penetrate through to the *inner* dialogue. If he has steeped himself in the author's theme and grasped the music of this inner dialogue, he will suggest plastic movements to the actor which will help the spectator to perceive the inner dialogue as the actors and he, himself, understand it.

The essence of human relationships is determined by gestures, poses, glances, and silences. Words alone cannot say everything. Hence there must be a *pattern of movement* on the stage to transform the spectator into a vigilant observer, to furnish him with that material which the two people in conversation yielded to the third, the material which helps him grasp the true feelings of the characters. Words catch the ear, plasticity – the eye. Thus the spectator's imagination is exposed to two stimuli: the oral and the visual. The difference between the old theatre and the new is that in the new theatre speech and plasticity are each subordinated to their own separate rhythms and the two do not necessarily coincide. However, it does not follow that plasticity has always to contradict speech; a phrase may be supported by a wholly appropriate movement, but this is no more natural than the coincidence of the logical and the poetic stress in verse.

2 Maeterlinck's images are archaized; the names are like the names on icons; Arkel[11] is like a picture by Ambrogio Borgognoni; Gothic arches; wooden statues, carved and polished like palissander. One senses the need for symmetrical groupings in the manner of Perugino, for thus do they resemble most closely the divine nature of the universe.

"Women, effeminate boys and harmless, weary old men best express the gentle, dream-like thoughts" which Perugino was striving to convey. Is not the same true of Maeterlinck? It is this which prompted an iconic style of portrayal.

The unsightly clutter of the naturalistic stage was replaced in the New Theatre by con-structions rigidly subordinated to rhythmical movement and to the musical harmony of color masses.

An iconic style was employed, too, in the construction of scenery – before scenery was abolished altogether. And since plastic movement acquired primary importance as a means of revealing inner dialog, it was essential that scenery should do nothing to distract attention from this movement. It was necessary to focus the spectator's entire attention on the actors' movements. Therefore, we employed only one backdrop in *The Death of Tintagiles*. When rehearsed against a plain canvas drop, the tragedy produced a powerful impression because the play of gestures was seen in such sharp relief. But when the actors were transferred to a stage with scenery and space in which to move about, the play suffered. Hence we developed the decorative panel. But when we tried it out in a number of plays (*Sister Beatrice, Hedda Gabler, The Eternal Story*[12]) it was a failure.[13] We found that it was no more effective than suspended scenery, against which the effect of plastic movement is dissipated because it is not seen in firm relief. In Giotto, nothing detracts from the fluidity of his lines, because all his work has a decorative rather than a naturalistic basis; equally it must not become merely "decorative" (unless the word be interpreted in the same sense as in the Japanese theatre).

Like symphonic music, the decorative panel serves its own specialized purpose, and if figures are necessary – as in a painting – they must be painted figures, or in the case of the theatre, cardboard marionettes – but not wax, wooden, or flesh-and-blood figures. A two-dimensional decorative panel demands two-dimensional figures.

The human body and the objects surrounding it – tables, chairs, beds, cupboards – are all three-dimensional; therefore the theatre, where the main element is the actor, must find inspiration in the plastic arts, not in painting. The actor must study *the plasticity of the statue*.

These were the conclusions reached at the close of the first cycle of experiments in the New Theatre. A historically vital circle was completed and yielded a fund of experience in stylized production, which gave rise to a new view of the role of decorative art in the theatre.

On learning that the theatre intends to reject the decorative principle, actors of the old school will be delighted, interpreting this as no less than a return to the old theatre. Surely, they will argue, the old theatre was the theatre of three dimensions. So this means – down with the stylized theatre!

My answer is that the placing of the decorative artist firmly in the decorative theatre and the musician in the concert hall signifies not the death of the stylized theatre but its adoption of an even bolder course.

In rejecting the decorative panel the New Theatre has not discarded the technique of stylized production; neither has it rejected the presentation of Maeterlinck in iconic terms. The means of expression must now be architectural, rather than pictorial as they were before. All our plans for stylized productions of *The Death of Tintagiles, Sister Beatrice, Hedda Gabler,* and *The Eternal Story* have been preserved intact, but they have been translated into the terms of the liberated stylized theatre. Meanwhile, the painter has retired to a realm where actors and concrete objects are not admitted, because the aims of the actor and the non-theatrical painter are quite distinct.

(First published in *Teatr, kniga o novom teatre,* reprinted in his *O Teatre* (1913).)

TRANSLATOR'S NOTE

Written late in 1907. According to Volkov, Meyerhold was well acquainted with Wagner's music from an early age. In July 1907 he staged two extracts from *Tristan and Isolde* at Terioki in Finland, just over the border from Petersburg. Later, in October 1909, he produced the full opera at the Marinsky Theatre. [. . .]

NOTES

1 Cf. pp. 82 ff. below.
2 First performed on 10 October 1907 at Komissarzhevskaya's Theatre.
3 Arthur Nikisch (1855–1922), celebrated conductor of the Leipzig Gewandhaus Orchestra.
4 Alexander Blok (*Pereval*, Moscow, 1906, no. 2) fears that the actors "might set fire to the ship of the play," but to my mind, discord and disaster could occur only if the straight line were allowed to become crooked. This danger is eliminated if the director accurately interprets the author, accurately transmits him to the actors, and if they accurately understand him. [Meyerhold's note.]
5 The "Theatre-Triangle" requires non-individualistic actors who none the less are outstanding virtuosi, regardless of their school. In the "Theatre of the Straight Line" individual flair is most important, for without it free creativity is inconceivable. It needs a new school of acting, which must not be a school where new techniques are taught, but rather one which will arise just once to give birth to a free theatre and then die.

"The Theatre of the Straight Line" will grow from a single school as one plant grows from one seed. As each succeeding plant needs a new seed to be sown, so a new theatre must grow every time from a new school.

"The Theatre-Triangle" tolerates schools attached to theatres which provide a regular stream of graduates, who imitate the great actors who founded the theatre, and fill vacancies in the company as they occur. I am convinced that it is these schools which are to blame for the absence of genuine, fresh talent in our theatres. [Meyerhold's note.]
6 Published in Russian in six volumes in Moscow, 1903–9.
7 Hannibale Pastore, "Maurice Maeterlinck," in *Vestnik inostrannoy literatury,* September 1903.
8 Richard Muther, German art historian.
9 In practice, a question arose which I shall not attempt to answer, but content myself by merely stating: should the actor seek to discover the inner content of his part right from the start, give play to his emotions, and then shape it later into some form or other, or vice versa? At the time we adopted the procedure of restraining the emotions until the form was mastered, and that still

seems to me the correct order. People will object that this only leads to the form fettering the emotions. This is not so. Our teachers, the actors of the old naturalistic school, used to say: if you do not want to ruin the part, start by reading it over to yourself, and do not read it aloud until it sounds right in your heart. One should approach a role in a realistic drama by first reading through the text to oneself; in a non-realistic drama one should master first the rhythm of the language and the movement – the same method is right for both. [Meyerhold's note.]

10 Tommaso Salvini: leading Italian Shakespearian actor. He toured in Russia on several occasions from 1880 to 1901.

11 In *Pelléas and Mélisande*.

12 By Przybyszewski.

13 All staged at Komissarzhevskaya's Theatre in 1906.

READER CROSS-REFERENCES

Brecht, Grotowski, Strasberg, Zimmerman – other innovative theatre directors

De Marinis – the relationship between various elements of a theatrical performance

Barba – on the dramaturgical process

33

THE ORAL ARTIST
Training and preparation

Isidore Okpewho

To be an accomplished oral artist, some form of apprenticeship or training is necessary. Essentially two kinds of training are involved in the development of the African oral artist: informal and formal. Informal training entails a kind of loose attachment whereby the future artist happens to live or move in an environment in which a particular kind of oral art is practiced and simply absorbs the skill in it as time goes on. It is possible, of course, for a person to live forever in such an environment and not develop the skill; one's mind or nature has to be predisposed toward art before the skill can successfully take root.

I will illustrate what I mean by informal training with examples from two pieces of research. The first is from a narrator I have been recording since 1980, Charles Simayi from Ubulu-Uno in the southwestern part of Nigeria. When I asked Simayi how he learned the tales he had told me, he replied:

> The events of which I tell, as concerning Ezemu or the border wars – I wasn't eyewitness to these events. It's as it is with you and your father: we were the homegrown ones who served our fathers at home and in the farm. I never went to the city, for they didn't let us go to school in the old days. . . . They said we might get lost if we were taken to school. So, when you sat in the farmhouse with your father and it was raining, they [i.e. father and fellow farmers] would lay aside their whisks and ask you to go and fetch firewood. He and his friends would tell tales of war, and you would listen to them as they told these tales. So that was how I learned those tales about events I was not eyewitness of.

This is one case in which the future artist simply listened to the elders and absorbed the stories he was to tell later on. It is easy to see from Simayi's life why he never needed any kind of formal training to be an accomplished storyteller (acknowledged by his village to be the most outstanding). At the time I met him, he was in his late fifties but had already attained a considerable level of skill in several occupations. He was first and foremost a traditional doctor (medicine man), but in addition he was a farmer, a barber, a builder, a handicrafts maker, and various other forms of artisan. He participated in building the first secondary school in his village, which he helped persuade the local government authorities to locate there. He also built drums, which he hired out to others at very low rates ("simply for publicity, not for money," he told me). He was a member of his village council of elders, one whose advice was highly valued. Although unschooled in Western education, he participated in some of the most delicate missions sent by the ruler of his village to communities far and near. He had therefore shown himself to be a man of many skills, blessed with a sharp natural intelligence. Although he never formally attached himself to anyone to learn the art of storytelling, his "education" in village life more than made up for whatever he may have lost by loose attachment.

From research among the Xhosa of southern Africa, Harold Scheub (1975) reports on similar kinds of preparation. Informal training seems to be the rule among oral artists in this area. "When I specifically asked artists where they had acquired their stylistic tools," Scheub reports, "they said that they were unable to tell. They learned the art, they insisted, by watching others, then making certain elements of performances that they witnessed a part of their own equipment" (17). What Scheub tells us about two kinds of oral performer among the Xhosa is illuminating. The first is a female narrator of folktales (*iintsomi*), who told him:

> I learned from my grandmother. I used to sit and listen to her every night. To my aunt, too. Then I told little *iintsomi*. Very short. About the jackal and the wolf. About the *amaZimu* (man-eating creatures). And then my *iintsomi* got longer and longer. I heard a new *intsomi* and wanted to tell that. I added from this *intsomi* and from that one, and then I was telling longer ones.
>
> (Ibid.)

The second informant is an *imbongi*, or singer of praise poetry (*izibongo*), who spoke along the same lines.

> There's no place to learn *izibongo* except to hear someone saying *izibongo*, and then you learn one word there, and then you hear somebody again at a certain place saying *izibongo*, and you . . . become a *mbongi* because of your interest when hearing the people saying these things. And then you begin to wish to do as they do. . . . Just as in all things, you have to think – I mean to say, when you are interested in anything, then you begin to think, to think, to think, and then . . . the first time you try to start it, then when you start on the next time you will say more. On the next day you will say more. . . . You notice the events that are happening during the time of that chief when he is ruling, or you begin to think about events that happened long ago. And then you just begin to join these things . . .
>
> (22)

From the above statements made by three different oral artists it is reasonably clear what goes on in the informal kind of training. First, the future artist must be a person blessed with a considerable amount of natural genius who possesses an interest in the kind of oral literature that is practiced around him or her. Second, since no formal coaching is involved, these novices must look and listen closely and in this way absorb the ideas, the idioms, and the techniques peculiar to the art. "They must," as Nketia says, "rely on their own eyes, ears, and memory. They must acquire their own technique of learning" (1973: 88). And finally, the process of learning entails that the novices use their imagination to select the relevant materials from the large amount they may have acquired and to increase their store of knowledge as time goes on.

Very much the same things happen in the formal kind of training, except that the process is better organized and the relationship between the trainee and the teacher properly established. In some cases, the type of oral literature involved is a rather special and complex one. The novice may be understudying his or her father or other close relative, and it may be understood that the novice will take over from the senior person at a later stage (e.g. at the death of the latter). In cases where the novice leaves the family house to live with the teacher, it is frequently understood that the novice will perform various kinds of duties (e.g. domestic) not necessarily related to the training. In yet other cases, the novice is trained in a "school" or association established to bring up young persons in a particular form of oral art. Whatever the situation may be, the main difference between the formal and informal kinds of training is that the process is somewhat shorter in the former case. "The lack of systematic formal instruction," as Nketia tells us, "protracts the learning process, which depends too heavily on favourable social conditions" (1973: 89). Formal training is particularly useful for the more complex kinds of oral literature – e.g. some forms of ritual poetry and performances involving the accompaniment of music – on which the future artist could depend as a major source of livelihood. Let us examine briefly some instances of formal training in African oral literature.

Two examples come from the Yoruba of western Nigeria. The first relates to the training in *ijala*, or hunter's poetry, and we may best cite the description of the process by the authority in the subject, Adeboye Babalola. We are first told that for the training to be successful the pupil has to show a deep interest in the chanting of *ijala* poetry, even if he is going to be taught by his own father. This apprenticeship begins, in most cases, in early youth (about the age of six) and lasts about a dozen years. Babalola describes the major stages of his training:

> The first stage of pupilage is a period of merely listening to the ijala chants performed by the teacher in his own house as well as at every social gathering where he entertains people with ijala. The pupil first imitates his teacher when he, the pupil, is on his own and thus he practices ijala-chanting. Subsequently, when he is at a social gathering as the *asomogbe* or *elegbe* (pupil) of his master, he is able to repeat the words of his master's chant almost simultaneously and the sound of the ijala performance then resembles that of choral chanting. The third stage is when the master orders his pupil to give solo performances of ijala chants at social gatherings to which he has taken him. This is obviously a sort of promotion, for the pupil ceases to provide merely an accompaniment to his master's chanting voice.
>
> (1966: 41–2).

After he has gained confidence as a performer, the *ijala* poet ultimately sets up on his own, parting ways with his master either with the latter's consent or without notice (fearing that his master may not voluntarily release him).

Babalola concludes his discussion of the training of the *ijala* poet with a question: How is the poet able to retain so much text in memory and perform steadily without faltering? To this question there is usually a twofold reply. First, practice makes perfect: constant repetition helps the artist to master the text so well that the chances of error are drastically reduced. Second, the chanters admit that they make use of various kinds of medicinal charms (called *isoye*) which aid in the retention of memory. These charms come in the form of magical chants, which are said to instill retention, or of powder taken with food and drink or incised into the poet's bloodstream with a barber's knife. Through these various forms of preparation – i.e. the more practical steps of careful apprenticeship and the less obvious powers of traditional magic – the future *ijala* poet is equipped with the skills he needs for the rather complex demands of a public performance.

The second instance of formal training among the Yoruba relates to *ifa*. This divination poetry is practiced mainly by traditional priests, healers, fortune-tellers, and general counselors on various problems of life. Wande Abimbola, the best authority on this form of oral literature, has carefully sketched the various stages of the training of the *babalawo*, the term generally used for the *ifa* expert (Abimbola 1976: 18–25). To start with, the pupil must in most cases live with the expert and, while training, help in the performance of various domestic chores. Since the art is an extremely complex and demanding one, the training starts at about the age of seven and lasts for about a dozen years. According to Abimbola, the process of becoming a full-fledged *babalawo* is divided into two segments. The first segment entails the actual period of training of the pupil, while the second relates to the ceremonies of initiation of the fully trained *babalawo* into the rites and the secrets of the profession.

The *ifa* divination system may be described briefly. When a client brings a problem to a *babalawo*, the latter listens carefully, then throws either a divining chain (a string of half-nuts) or "sacred palm-nuts" on a divining board. The nuts fall into a combination which signifies one of the 256 *odu* in the divination corpus. Each *odu* is a body of narrative verse, subdivided into a number of chapters known as *ese*. The number of *ese* in each *odu* is limitless, but as a group they embody (from various angles) the answer to the specific problem brought by the client. After the relevant *ese* has been recited, the *babalawo* spells out for the client the sacrifice he or she must perform to obtain a successful solution to the problem.

The first stage of the training of the *babalawo* involves the use of the divining chain. It is followed by training in the use of the sacred palm-nuts – though, since this tool is used less frequently now than the chain, the period of training is considerably shorter. Toward the end of the training period, the pupil learns the various sacrifices (e.g. money, food, clothes) that the client is asked to offer should the *ese* chosen provide the right solution to the problem. But by far the most important part of the training of the *babalawo* is to learn (especially during the first and second stages) the *ese* pertaining to the various *odu*. These narrative verses are committed to memory at a rate commensurate with the capacity of the pupil – one a day, one every other day, and so on. The trainee learns the *ese* independently at his own pace; otherwise, the trainee imitates a master *babalawo* reciting the verses to consulting clients or at appropriate ceremonies. Learning these poems is such a rigorous task that many trainees soon drop out of the program. For trainees in both *ijala* poetry and *ifa* divination, the task of retaining the texts in memory is helped by taking the medicinal *isoye* during meals.

The second and closing stage of the formal training of the *babalawo* is initiation into the profession. This involves a series of ceremonies lasting many days during which sacrifices are offered to the deities of *ifa* and time is spent in entertainment of practicing *babalawo* from far and wide. Secrets of the *ifa* cult are revealed to the initiate, and the entire ceremony is accompanied by dancing and the chanting of various *ese ifa*.

The formal training in the practice and transmission of various forms of the oral tradition shows how seriously this aspect of culture is taken in the traditional society. Such formal training is so strictly organized that we may see the system very much in the same sense as we see schools in modern society. A school of oral literature may be run on a small scale, as in the case of a *babalawo* who has a handful of trainees living in his house and understudying him. But there are schools organized at the larger level of an association or guild of poets with a president at the head of the body. Among the Ruanda of central Africa, for instance, there was until recent times an association of court poets known as the *umutwe w'abasizi*, made up of families officially recognized for the singing of court poetry, i.e. poetry sung for praising kings and recording the history of the royal line. Headed by an *intebe* (president), this association was set up for training young men from those families in the skills of court poetry. In other cases, the state may recognize both the cultural value and the popularity (especially with foreigners) of a category of oral traditions and so set up a "school" where young men can be taught the skills of that art – not only to preserve the culture but also to promote the tourist economy. Such a facility is the school for the training of *griots* (singers) in the island of St. Louis in Senegal.

Modes of training and preparation differ from one society to another and from one type of oral literature to another. But the very fact that some training is involved, whatever its duration, does indicate that oral literature requires a certain level of competence for which the intending artist must be specifically prepared.

REFERENCES

Abimbola, W. (1976) *Ifa: An Exposition of Ifa Literary Corpus*, Ibadan: Oxford University Press.
Babalola, S.A. (1966) *The Content and Form of Yoruba Ijala*, Oxford: Clarendon Press.
Nketia J.H.K. (1973) "The musician in Akan society," in *The Traditional Artisan African Societies*, ed. W.L. d'Azevedo, Bloomington: Indiana University Press.
Scheub, H. (1975) *The Xhosa Ntsomi*, Oxford: Clarendon Press.

READER CROSS-REFERENCES

Grotowski, Strasberg – other forms of performer training
Worthen, Conquergood – on the question of non-literate performance texts
Harding – modes of performing in Africa
Barba – performance composition

34

THE PERFORMANCE TEXT

Marco De Marinis

> The theater is the only place on earth where a gesture, once performed, is never enacted a second time.
>
> Antonin Artaud, *Theater and Its Double*

> We can thus define theater as "what happens between the actor and the audience." All the rest is supplementary – necessary, perhaps, but supplementary.
>
> Jerzy Grotowski, *Toward a Poor Theater*

2.1 Performance as text

I will now definitively shift my attention away from the dramatic text, and turn to the other pole of the transcoding of the theatrical event, i.e. to performance itself, which I have already frequently invoked as /performance text/. To speak of a /performance text/ means to presume that a theatrical performance can be considered a text, even if an extreme example of textuality. This also implies that we conceptualize the semiotics of theater in terms of textual analysis. The textual approach to performance is linked to the increasingly generalized conception of the "text" in semiotic theory over the past few years. The term has now taken on a much broader meaning than allowed by its traditional linguistic and literary application, or even its current usage in textual linguistics. From a semiotic standpoint, the term /text/ designates not only coherent and complete series of linguistic statements, whether oral or written, but also every unit of discourse, whether verbal, nonverbal, or mixed, that results from the coexistence of several codes (and other factors too, as we shall see) and possesses the constitutive prerequisites of completeness and coherence.[1] According to this understanding of textuality, an image, or group of images, is, or can be, a text. A sculpture, a film, a musical passage, or a sequence of sound effects constitutes a text also, or rather, *they can be considered as such* (Metz 1971, 1974: 87). Clearly, therefore, even the units of theatrical production known as performances can be considered as texts, and can thus become the object of textual analysis, provided that they possess the minimal prerequisites for consideration as texts.

To anticipate some of my observations in this chapter, let me say that by /performance text/ is meant a theatrical performance, considered as an *unordered (though complete and coherent) ensemble of textual units (expressions), of various length, which invoke different codes, dissimilar to each other and often unspecific (or at least not always specific), through which communicative strategies are played out, also depending on the context of their production and reception.*[2]

It should be clear that the concepts of /theatrical performance/ and /performance text/ do not completely coincide. /Theatrical performance/ involves theater as a material object, the phenomenal field that is immediately available to perception and to an analytical approach. /Performance text/ refers instead to a *theoretical object* (or an "object of thought," as Prieto defined it in 1975), or to the theatrical event considered according to semiotic-textual pertinence, assumed and "constructed" as a performance text within the paradigms of textual semiotics. We could therefore say that the performance text is a theoretical model of the observable performance phenomenon, to be assumed as an explanatory principle of the functioning of performance as a phenomenon of signification and communication. What is therefore at stake here is the theoretical model of an aspect of the performance-object: its *textual aspect*.[3] The following chapters have the goal of defining and structuring as precisely as possible the textual aspect of the vast category of concrete facts that constitute theatrical performances. As we shall see, however, not all theatrical performances constitute *eo ipso* performance texts. Similarly, not all verbal *discourses* are considered by textual linguistics to constitute *texts*. Having thus attempted an initial narrowing of the range of objects on which the textual-analytical approach can be performed, I will proceed to investigate the properties that are constitutive of performance textuality (its *quidditas*). It is perhaps appropriate to anticipate the main conclusions I will draw: in the long run it is reception (both general and specialized)[4] that determines the coherence and completeness of a theatrical event, and thus qualifies or disqualifies it as a performance text. Hence any performance can be considered a performance text when the interpretive cooperation of the addressee desires (and is able) to "construct" it as such. According to Prieto, "the point of view that gives rise to the pertinence of the way a material object is conceived is never imposed by the object itself" (1975: 131).

2.2 Theatrical performance: A definition

Before continuing, some clarifications must be made concerning the category or class of material objects known as theatrical performances and the criteria according to which the category can be defined.

To begin, I would argue that it is not only *representational theater* that belongs to this class, but also all theatrical phenomena where the so-called *presentational* aspect variously prevails over the representational aspect; where *turning inward* (self-reflexivity or self-referentiality) prevails over turning outward; where production (of meaning, reality, etc.) prevails over reproduction. To eliminate the trait /representation/ from a definition of theatrical performances as a class involves broadening the class sufficiently to include traditional and contemporary phenomena which our current sensibility as audience members or theater specialists tends to include more and more frequently in the domain of "theater": celebrations, ceremonies, rituals (all the "social dramas" described by Duvignaud

[1965]); contemporary avant-garde phenomena such as *"happenings"* and *performance art*; but also traditional genres such as dance and ballet where, as we all know, presentational aspects and self-reflexive abstraction take precedence over representation and the referential function. Even military parades and athletic events belong to this category. Indeed they have been linked to performance since the Renaissance; one has only to remember the case of the eighteenth-century *Opera-torneo*.[5] It is obvious that we are dealing with a field that is far broader and more varied than the category consisting exclusively of *traditional stagings of dramatic texts*, to which some scholars still restrict the class of theatrical performances.[6]

By "representational theater" and "presentational theater" I obviously intend to designate two extremes, two polarities between which, as Valeria Ottolenghi writes:

> It is thus possible to map out the single performance event . . . in relation to the degree that self-displaying elements can be identified within them . . . or signs that refer to something other than themselves.
>
> (1979: 29)

Mentioning in particular the actor's performance, Ottolenghi goes on to state that it is possible to distinguish

> Different modes of self-presentation: from total display of the self (public confession) to the presentation of one's social or professional role (the dancer or the boxer), right up to the complete representation of someone or something other than oneself (a disguise, a character).
>
> (31–2)

This means that while it is very difficult, if not impossible, to find representational performances where there is a complete absence of some presentational and self-reflexive element (given the indispensable fact that a staged event has a real, concrete existence, and that the actor is "truly" there, in the here and now), it seems equally difficult to imagine performances of a presentation type that are completely lacking in representational and symbolic components. [. . .T]he production conventions within which the performances in question are located are extremely important. In representational theater, the *mise-en-scène* functions *on the whole* as a transparent semiotic system of *renvoi*, and as a fictional event, by virtue of the conventional canons that ground it, though it can also obviously contain presentational elements – real actions, concrete objects, and so on – which by themselves, at least to begin with, lack a symbolic aspect. The exact opposite occurs with theatrical events that can be placed mostly or entirely outside the canons of representation. In these cases, the underlying production conventions cause the performance to present itself *generally* as a self-reflexive and nonfictional entity, although it can contain fictional elements that point beyond it. Here I am thinking of events such as "happenings" or performance art, or Grotowski's "para-theatrical acts"; but the same holds true for traditional genres such as ballet, the circus, vaudeville, and the like.[7]

It therefore seems problematical, for different reasons, to use the concept of representation or its opposite to articulate an adequate definition, neither too vague nor too narrow, of the field of theatrical performance. If, on the other hand, we are to transcend the level of purely tautological definitions,[8] as seems necessary, there is no other option than to adopt the communicative-productive perspective, meaning the pragmatic one.

I will begin with Kowzan's definition of the "art of performance":

> [It is] the art form whose product is communicated through time and space, meaning that it requires time and space in order to be communicated. . . . This is what the circumscribed definition of performance implies: *a work of art which must, by necessity, be communicated in time and space.*
>
> (1975: 24, emphasis added)

Obviously, the "autonomous and well-differentiated domain" that this definition circumscribes with respect to the other domains of art is extremely vast. It quite legitimately includes many very disparate forms of performance in addition to theatrical productions in the narrow sense. It is particularly problematic that this definition does not distinguish between theatrical phenomena and other phenomena such as films or television programs, which are certainly performances, but which our "native" competence as theatergoers enables us to recognize intuitively as nontheatrical.

In order to overcome this lack of precision, I will articulate two basic requirements for theatrical communication (in which all the "performance arts" classified by Kowzan are brought together) by developing and honing Kowzan's own hypothesis. These are:

1   *The real physical co-presence of sender and addressee* (the latter is collective, as a rule).[9]
2   *Simultaneity of production and communication.*[10]

Let us say therefore that the class /theatrical performance/ is constituted by all performance phenomena that possess the two properties just articulated.[11] We thus arrive at the following definition: *theatrical performances are performance phenomena communicated to a collective addressee, the audience (physically present at the reception), at the very moment of their production (transmission).* By /production/ is of course meant the production of the theatrical performance *in its entirety and as performance* (meaning, as we will see later, the integration of various partial texts into a single, coherent performance text), and not the production of individual parts of it (individual partial texts, in fact) which can precede, and often do precede, theatrical communication: for example the dramatic text, if one exists, or the staging, the costumes, the music. To insist on the condition of simultaneity between production and communication (between the transmission and reception) means, I believe, to emphasize the discrete and specific aspect of theater – that every theatrical performance (every *single* theatrical occurrence) constitutes an *unrepeatable, unique event*, an ephemeral *production* that is different each time in spite of all attempts at standardization (rehearsals, director's notebooks, *Modellbuch*, repertory theater) and recording (descriptions, graphic transcriptions, audiovisual playbacks). Theater, in short, always involves *event*, as well as code and structure, as we shall see.

2.2.1 Technical reproducibility, repeatability, duplicatability

At this point, it might be useful to articulate some further comments and distinctions in order to avoid possible confusion. In the first place, I would like to emphasize that I understand /unrepeatability/ in the strongest sense; that is, as *non-total duplicatability*. Theatrical performance is therefore unrepeatable, insofar as it is not entirely reproducible (as is the case with film, painting, or novels), but it is nevertheless *usually*[12] possible to replicate it in part. It is no coincidence that in Italian the term /replica/ is used to indicate each single theatrical performance of a play.[13] As for the level of repeatability, this can obviously vary according to each genre, tending to increase in the case of theatrical genres that are highly coded, such as ballet, circus, mime, classical Indian dance, Noh drama, and even Italian director's theater (in the style of the *Teatro Stabile*, for example).[14]

But what are the reasons for this unrepeatability (i.e. "the non-total reproductibility") of theatrical performance? I must return to what I said earlier in Chapter 1 [of the original volume] regarding the total *irreversibility* of the process leading from the dramatic text (or script) to the performance and from there to its eventual graphic transcription. In fact, the non-repeatability of the theatrical performance can be explained in the first place (and not only in the first case, as we shall see) by the lack of a notational system that could unequivocally record the essential characteristics of a given occurrence in order to provide the opportunity of re-delivering it (repeating or reproducing it) as can be done with a musical work, thanks to the existence of sheet music.

At a basic level, therefore, the repeatability of a work seems to depend on whether or not it is suited to transcription into notational language. At least up to now this has not been possible for theatrical performance, since, as we have seen, theater lacks a close equivalent to sheet music. None of the "records" produced before or after a theatrical performance (from the dramatic text to the technical script, from the graphic transcription of a performance to audiovisual recording)[15] fully satisfies the requirements of notationality. These documents cannot therefore be favorably compared to sheet music. As Goodman has pointed out (1968), these "transcriptions" do not succeed in unambiguously determining the class of occurrences that constitutes the exclusive and equivalent examples of a performance text; nor can these transcriptions themselves be determining in an unambiguous way based on a given theatrical occurrence.[16] All this is nevertheless *usually* possible with a musical score. It can therefore be stated that a musical work is in general repeatable, as are literary and architectural works.[17]

But could it also be said that a musical work, a concerto, for example, is *reproducible in its entirety* (or, rather, is capable of precise duplication) in the same way as a film, a photograph, or a literary text? Certainly not.[18] And the reasons for this fact allow us to discover another level of motives that explain and give rise to the unrepeatability of theatrical performance. Indeed, while admitting that the elaboration of a system of complex notation could allow us one day to record and to re-execute a given theatrical occurrence in its totality, determining in an unequivocal way the specific way in which the work must be executed,[19] we would still have to deal with a very different type of reproduction from what is found in cinema, photography, and television (and also from what occurs in painting or sculpture, which can by now be reproduced with the benefit of electronic instruments).[20] While in these cases we can speak of materially identical *copies* (up to a certain point, and in different ways according to the techniques of duplication), in the case of theater, however (and also in the case of musical concerts), we are still faced with renderings that bear an imperfect resemblance to the original, despite the use of a hypothetical system of notation.[21] This depends (and thus we arrive at the second reason for the unrepeatability of theatrical performance) on the "concrete characteristics of theater" (real-life actors etc.): a medium that is not *technically* reproducible, unlike film, television, painting, and literary texts.[22] In sum, it is this very material reproducibility, achievable through different procedures (manual, mechanical, electronic, and so on), which accounts for the possibility of furnishing almost perfect duplicates of works which belong to the autographic arts, i.e. lacking notational systems, and therefore lacking "renderings," as indeed in the case for works of sculpture, painting, cinema, and television. Although the technical reproducibility (or complete duplicatability) of a work is independent of notationality, it nevertheless appears to be closely linked to the work's duration and material persistence, as the examples already given demonstrate. A painting, a sculpture, and even a film or a photograph are examples of texts that last through time and are always materially available. It can thus be stated, in the final analysis, that the non-reproducibility of theatrical performance depends on the ephemeral and transitory quality of its presence.[23]

It is opportune at this point to distinguish between works that are *repeatable*, because they lend themselves to notation, and works that are *technically reproducible* (whether possessing the capacity for notation or not), and to introduce a third level beyond the two already examined:

1   *Partial duplicatability* (e.g. theatrical performance).
2   *Repeatability* (e.g. a musical concert).
3   *Technical reproducibility* (e.g. film).

I must make one final observation on this matter. As already stated, even in the case of technically reproducible (or duplicatable) works, one can never achieve perfect copies, that is, "absolute doubles." And this is on the level of the utterance itself, of the co-text. If we now consider the problem from the point of view of utterance and reception, the concept of total reproducibility is subject to further limitations. It is in fact obvious how even works that are perfectly duplicatable can vary in an unrepeatable manner, because of variations in the practical context, a change in the receiver, or the like. Even if the *text-in-itself* recurs in an identical way, what will always inevitably vary is the *text-in-situation* (thus constituting an unrepeatable event), that is, the "interplay of communication acts" (Schmidt 1973) triggered by the work with the help of a complex set of contextual factors. Consider, for example, the copies of a film projected in different theaters and for different audiences, or readers of various copies of a literary text. Conversely, one could also take, for example, a film seen again by an individual spectator after a lapse of time, or a novel read several times by the same person in different circumstances. More generally,

> it is impossible that two events are identical in every conceivable aspect, given that they must be distinguished if only for their location in time and space. To claim therefore that one is witnessing a repetition it is necessary to presume the irrelevance or accidental quality of the spatiotemporal setting and the possibility that *the same thing* might occur in different places and moments in time.
>
> (Amsteramski 1981: 76)

We must conclude from this that even in the case of works that are technically reproducible (and hence reproduced), *contextual reproducibility* is always impossible. All of this is of course valid *a fortiori* for the theater, where the unrepeatability of the contextual factors (changes of audience, physical space, and the like) is added to and increases the unrepeatability of the contextual element, which has been amply discussed up to this point.[24]

2.2.2 Theater and everyday life

To return to the two principles articulated above and to the pragmatic definition of theatrical performance that can be derived from them, I would like to point out how this definition allows the field of inquiry a broad, even provocative, scope (including, for example, the spectrum of nonrepresentational theatrical phenomena already mentioned, in addition to events not usually considered "theatrical," such as a folk celebration, a game of soccer, or a military parade).[25] Yet the same definition also provides a reliable criterion for making a clear distinction between theatrical performance and other important performance genres which are associated with it according to Kowzan's definition, and which we could describe as "nontheatrical." Cinema and television are the most obvious of these nontheatrical genres, the production of which, like theatrical production, is necessarily implemented through space and time. Because of its technical makeup, cinema never provides simultaneity between textual production and its communication. Although television can provide this simultaneity (through live broadcasting), it does not permit the *real* physical encounter of sender and addressee, also as a result of the specific technical characteristics of the medium. Moreover, in contrast with the unrepeatability of theatrical performance (its merely "partial replicatability"), works created through the medium of film and television are reproducible in full, as we have just seen.

This pragmatic definition also clearly separates theatrical performance from other forms of artistic communication (such as literature, painting, and music), bringing it closer in essence to the interactions of daily life.[26] This similarity is quite meaningful, and in my opinion far from dangerous, if correctly understood. It has already been confirmed in the field of microsociology in Erving Goffman's famous hypothesis of "daily life as performance."

> [Goffman] explicitly draws the analogy between normal interactions experienced by subjects and events that happen on the stage; he speaks of perspectives of theatrical representation, of principles of a dramatic type; "the common social relationship is in itself organized like a staged scene, with an exchange of theatrically exaggerated actions, counteractions and exiting 'lines.' "
>
> (Wolf 1979: 88–9, citing Goffman 1959)

In one of his latest books, Goffman has taken up and developed this aspect from other perspectives:

> Often what the speaker tries to do is to *present dramas to an audience* rather than to convey information to the addressee. It seems that we devote less time to conveying information than to *performing*. This theatricality is not based on the simple display of feelings. . . . The parallel between theatrical performance and conversation is much deeper than that. The point is that ordinarily when an individual says something, he does not state it as a bare assertion of fact. He re-relates it, he re-executes a string of already determined events, for the involvement of his listeners.
>
> (1974: 508; cited in Wolf 1979: 90)

If correctly understood in its metaphorical sense and in its practical usage,[27] Goffman's "dramatic metaphor" proves to be extremely valuable to scholars interested in the type of macro-interaction that constitutes theatrical communication. Goffman does not simply tell us that daily life also involves fiction, lies, pretense, *mise-en-scène*, or that "representation is not confined to the realm of fiction but constitutes an important, essential device in our daily life." He also informs us, above all, that truth and lies, honesty and fiction, pretense and real acts, communication and seduction, and display and concealment constitute the basic materials that theatrical interactions are made of, just like everyday life. If life is also theater (or, more precisely, if it can be read and analyzed through the theatrical metaphor), then theater itself *also* involves *real* life, actions, transformations, and behavior.

> A character staged in a theater is not real in some ways, nor does it have the same kind of real consequences as does the thoroughly contrived character performed by a confidence man; but the *successful* staging of either of these types of false figures involves the use of *real* techniques – *the same techniques by which everyday persons sustain their real social situations*. Those who conduct face-to-face interaction on a theater's stage must meet the key requirement of real situations; they must expressively sustain a definition of the situation.[28]
>
> (Goffman 1959: 254–5, emphasis added)

I fully realize that criticism that can be leveled against my definition of theatrical performance and also against its objective limits. In particular, I could be reproached for limiting myself to a definition of theatrical performance exclusively on the pragmatic-contextual level, and for severely neglecting the co-textual aspects, on the level of both expression and content. But the reasons that militate in favor of my choice are many. (a) A definition of theatrical performance based on content is clearly impossible. As Ertel has recently pointed out (1979: 166), there are no meanings specific to the theater, or which theater is delegated to transmit. But the risk of a content-oriented approach to the theater is, above all, bound to bring the dramatic text to the fore, linking it to the very definition of theater itself. This seems to happen, for example [. . .], when it is claimed that the class of theatrical performances is composed exclusively of productions of dramatic texts.[29] (b) Neglecting the semantic plane for the pragmatic one, the statement for the utterance, the "what" for the "how," my definition intends to restate and confirm a fact that is emerging with increasing clarity from theoretical reflections and experimental practices in contemporary theater. This means that theater is more about *production* than *product*, *process* than *outcome*. It is also obvious by now that *theater* can never be reduced to its *performances*, since there are certain kinds of "performance-less" theater (if we consider theatrical animation, the para-theatrical activities of Grotowski in the 1970s, and the like). When faced with these kinds of theater, traditional critical approaches are completely inadequate and inappropriate since they tend to judge from the outside (and from above) the creative products of a reality (groups, actors) about which nothing is known, and whose working strategies, customs, and cultural traditions are completely ignored (or apparently ignored, given the well-known habit of "critical distance"). (c) The final advantage that can be attributed to my definition is [. . .] that it enlarges the limits of the genre to the greatest extent possible, avoiding the danger of excessive specificity, and thus including (perhaps even merely in a passing way) various phenomena traditionally excluded from consideration but which our *current* sensibility both as audience members and theater scholars would consider as "theatrical," i.e., as linked in some way or from some perspective to the theatrical universe. We can certainly include East Asian rituals of trance or possession, or religious celebrations in the Western tradition, spectator sports, and military displays, but we could also consider the widespread trend toward performance that has been occurring for the past several years in the artistic experiments of the avant-garde. In connection with this trend, the visual arts, music, and literature itself (in the case of "poetry readings") have tended in recent times to come together at least partially under the label of theater – a label that spans different genres – working on the elements of theatricality inherent in the principles defined above, physical display in public, the copresence of sender and addressee, simultaneity of production and communication, and the ephemeral and unrepeatable nature of the work of art understood as event and action.

2.3 Completeness and coherence of the performance text

Since I have now established the meaning of /theatrical performance/ as it is used throughout this [chapter], I will return to the hypotheses of textual analyses that I began to formulate in 2.1. First of all, we must determine under what conditions a theatrical performance (i.e. a theatrical event satisfying the two requirements articulated in 2.2) constitutes a text. In the last section I investigated the properties that constitute *the theatricality* of performance.

I must now examine the properties that constitute its *textuality*, i.e. the properties that transform a theatrical performance – as understood within the paradigms of textual semiotics – into a performance text.

To begin, I must refer back to the previously mentioned generalization of the notion of /text/ in semiotics. My approach to performance is located within a field of textual semiotics of which *Textlinguistik* constitutes only one sector, even if this is currently the most developed sector in the entire field. I would argue that the extension of the categories, theoretical hypotheses, and models of textual linguistics (or discourse analysis) beyond the area in which they were initially elaborated, and above all their application to texts that are mainly, if not entirely, nonverbal, cannot be regarded as easily implemented or to be taken for granted, but must be evaluated one case at a time, unless we intend to proceed in a purely metaphorical way.

Paul Bouissac is undoubtedly one of the scholars who has tried most diligently to utilize the tools and concepts of textual semiotics in the study of nonverbal or mixed communication. Focusing particularly on circus acts in *Circus and Culture* (1976), he attempts to define a "semiotic text" in a sufficiently general way, i.e. in a way that would transcend the particular characteristics of a given expressive medium. Thus, having made the initial claim that "a text can be defined, independently of its physical and symbolic components, by certain formal properties," Bouissac proposes the following definition of /text/:

> any permanent set of ordered elements (sentences, objects, or actions, or any combination of these) whose copresence (or collocation) is considered by an encoder and/or a decoder as being related in some capacity to one another through the mediation of a logico-semantic system.
>
> (126)

This definition is a more abstract reformulation of some "empirical conditions for the identification of a text" expressed by Bouissac on an earlier occasion:

1. Clear-cut boundaries that isolate the message as such, i.e. nonambiguous and formal marks that delimit a finite set of meaningful interwoven elements.
2. A direct or an indirect endurance over time which makes it possible to "read" a message again and again as an "immutable synchrony" or an "achronic present"; the possibility of repetition can be assured because the material of the message is invariable or because it is possible to memorize it exactly.
3. A deep system of relations ensuring the surface coherence of the message; in other words, a structure that accounts for its understandability, i.e. the possibility of building up from its elements a network of relations that includes all the actual terms as well as their relations.

> (90–1)

Leaving aside the second condition (direct or indirect duration in time), which does not appear to be a *preliminary* property of *all* (semiotic) texts but merely a *particular* property of *some*,[30] I will pause to consider the other two conditions, (a) *completeness* of the text, and (b) *coherence* of the "elements" which constitute it. According to claims widely accepted both in linguistic theory and textual semiotics, completeness and coherence represent the principal and constitutive characteristics of textuality. These are the qualities that make a text a text (Conte 1977: 42). Examining completeness and coherence in relation to theatrical performance, in order to see if and how performance possesses these properties, is tantamount to asking if and how a single performance can be enucleated from the continuum of theatrical productions that are part of the "general text" of a given synchrony.[31]

2.3.1 The delimitation of the performance text

Generally, we can consider completeness as a property which is not immanent to units of communication, but which is assigned by the intention (or the attributed intention) of the senders and receivers. This issue concerns the subjective and therefore pragmatic character (context-dependent) of every operation of textual delimitation. Certainly, there are "signs of initial and final demarcation," but these – as Segre notes in connection with verbal texts (1978: 132) – are in reality "evaluated by the observer only with the help of clues of a contextual nature." In effect, to cite Segre again, "the limits of the text are determined by the scholar of the text. . . . It is not therefore possible to define general rules of textual demarcation" (132–3).[32]

To return to the present issue, it seems reasonable to suppose that *an entire* theatrical performance can be considered a complete unit of communication by both poles of the interaction (or at least by the sender). Nevertheless, apart from the possibility of taking into consideration performance texts that are smaller or larger than a single performance (which I will discuss later), it should be pointed out that the actual delimitation of a single theatrical occurrence (and hence of a performance text corresponding to a single, entire performance) is not as easily or intuitively achieved as might appear possible at first glance, as is also true for verbal texts, whether written or oral.[33] In fact, there are numerous examples from ancient times onward of so-called installment texts, or texts that are spread discontinuously in time and/or space beyond the limits that Western culture has, from a certain point in time onward, customarily considered "normal" for *a single* theatrical occurrence. Examples of these serialized performances can be found in the puppet theaters of Sicily and Naples, as well as in the tradition of the Neapolitan *sceneggiate*. Among performances larger than a single performance event, we could include *Renaissance festivals*, at one time the structuring framework for games and theatrical entertainment, which were spread out in a discontinuous way in time and space and yet also constituted a "global" performance, the Great Theater of the World; or the medieval mystery plays and *Sacre Rappresentazioni*, which, as we know, were often performed over a period of days, at different intervals, and sometimes in several places, simultaneously or sequentially.[34] But these references could also include, with better justification, non-Western theatrical traditions, and East Asian traditions in particular. A particularly noteworthy example is the performance format of one day in Noh theater (see Sieffert 1960).

In these cases we are presented with "performances" that fully deserve to be considered unified and complete, if only for the fact that they are so considered by their senders and/or receivers. Yet they do not fulfill the requirements of spatiotemporal demarcation (also linked to the participants' behavior during the communicative act) which Western culture has imposed as "normal," and as the only manner of execution imaginable. I am alluding of course to the traditional *indicators* or *markers* for the *start* of a performance. These are (i) the audience arrives at the performance site, [(ii) the house lights are dimmed], (iii) the curtain is raised and/or the actors emerge, and so on.[35] Traditional indicators or markers for the *end* of the performance are: (i) the actors leave the stage, (ii) [the curtain falls and the house lights are turned on], [(iii) the actors reappear to thank the audience], (iv) the audience leaves the performance site.[36]

To take a contemporary example, let us consider the works of the American director Robert Wilson, which up to this point have all lasted a great deal longer than is customary. *The Life and Times of Joseph Stalin* (1973) went on for twelve hours, *Overture* (1972) for twenty-four hours, and *Mountain and Gardenia Terrace*, which was presented at the Persepoli Festival in 1972 on the slopes of a mountain, lasted seven days and nights. Because of their extreme length (and sometimes also because they cover so much physical space), and because of the unusual slowness and repetitiveness that characterize them, these performances are inevitably experienced in a very discontinuous way. Indeed they demand this kind of reception, and are not damaged by it. The spectators converse with each other, get distracted, eat, even fall asleep. Most important, they come and go constantly, and are absent from the performance for varying periods of time. After observing the audience's behavior during a performance of Wilson's *Stalin* in a New York theater (which lasted from seven o'clock in the evening to seven the following morning), Richard Schechner (1975) mentioned the phenomenon of "selective inattention," pointing out that an unusual pattern of movement was created between the auditorium and the adjacent space (set up as a waiting room for the audience), with audience members passing continuously from one space to the other:

> What happened during *Stalin* was unusual in orthodox American theater, but common in many parts of the world. People chose the parts of Wilson's work that they wanted to listen to carefully and the parts they could miss. Going into the *LePerq space* to rest, exchange opinions, have a drink, or get ready to go back into the auditorium or elsewhere added a dimension to the experience. The social goal of the circuit between the auditorium and the adjoining space was just as important in *Stalin* as the aesthetic viewpoint.
>
> (Schechner 1975: 108)

Clearly, here as in many other similar cases, the traditional criterion based on the audience's entrance and departure proves inadequate, and we must look for other markers defining the beginning and the end.[37] Usually, however, an audience member who leaves early because of boredom, disappointment, or some other reason does not come back to the auditorium. For this individual the performance is finished. Similarly, if an irate audience should abandon the performance space during a hypothetical "avant-garde" performance, this would also mark a conclusion. From that moment onward, theatrical *communication* as such comes to an end, even if the *performance* continues.

To conclude, all that is left is to confirm what I have already said: *it is not possible to articulate general rules for the external demarcation of the performance text* (as is true for all other kinds of texts). The (delimitation) definition of a performance text is obviously founded on specific markers manifest by the text, but, in the long run, when the text is approached for the purpose of analysis, the discretionary powers of the analyst also come into play.[38] Thus the performance text *is a performance unit which the analyst's intention (or the intention of the ordinary audience member) designates as semiotically complete.*

NOTES

[Cross-references, apart from those to "2.1," "2.4," etc., are to other parts of the work from which this reading is extracted. See Acknowledgements.]

1 According to Metz (1970), "manifestation-units," which used to be called *messages*, are almost always *texts*, resulting from the coexistence of various codes or subcodes (Eco 1975: 86), and hence composed of several "interwoven" messages. The multiplicity of codes proper to texts should not be conceived of exclusively on the *horizontal* axis (the text as the sum total of sequentially arranged messages organized by different codes), but above all on the *vertical* axis (the text as a group of messages, each of which is often interpretable on the basis of several codes). The very existence of linear and homogeneous "languages" regulated by a single formal system has by now been definitively questioned (see 2.5).

2 My definition is similar to Ruffini's (1978: 221). In describing the performance text as a group of units I do not intend to designate a static group of paratactical elements, but a unified entity capable of dynamically integrating its own components (hence the emphasis on completeness and coherence), even if not always to the same degree or with the same force. [. . .] I must note, however, that in the case of the performance text, even the constituent "parts" are texts, at a certain level. Hence, while retaining the concept of the unity of the (macro) performance, I can also foresee the possibility of independent analyses of the individual partial texts that constitute it (see 2.7). The expression /performance text/ was introduced by Ruffini (1974, 1976a, and 1976b), but the concept of performance as a complex semiotic text has existed for several years in the field of theater semiotics, under different appellations: see Koch (1969), Bettetini ([. . .] 1977), Pavis (1976, 1980), Gullì Pugliatti (1976), Ertel (1977), Pastorello (1979), Elam (1980), and Ubersfeld (1981). I prefer the term /performance text/ to other possibilities, because it is the only term that avoids the ambiguities or disadvangtages of such expressions as / stage text/ or /theatrical text/. The first of these alternatives emphasizes the dichotomy between dramatic text/*mise-en-scène* which theater semiotics must overcome, selecting performance (or the theatrical transcoding of a dramatic text) as the only focus of inquiry. The other term has been applied too frequently to the written dramatic text, and is no longer genuinely available for other uses.

3 For a discussion of the difference between "theoretical model" and "observable phenomena," see Jansen (1973: 238), who also proposes the notion of "aspect." On the opposition between material object and object of thought, compare Prieto (1975: 131–2) and my own comments in the introduction to [the original] volume. My distinction between theatrical performance and the

performance text is similar, but not identical, to the distinction made in textual linguistics between *discourse* as a concrete occurrence and *text* as a theoretical construct. My approach is quite different from the generative-transformational paradigm in which the distinction between discourse and text is usually couched, and on the basis of which the text becomes a kind of deep structure of discourse, constituting one of its possible manifestations (see, for example, Ballmer 1976: 1; van Dijk 1979: 512; for other definitions of the /text/, see Conte 1977). From now on, when speaking of /textual properties (and components) of performance/, I will always be referring to the properties (and components) of the material object /theatrical performance/ which are pertinent to the performance text as a theoretical object. These properties and components of the performance text can be divided into two categories, located on two distinct levels of the text: (a) physical properties and components, predating the analysis and belonging to the level of concrete discursive manifestation, and (b) theoretical or systemic components, which are not immediately perceptible, and which the analysis must "construct" (codes, textual structures). I must also specify that the term /text/ will be used throughout [the original] volume according to both of its currently accepted uses, i.e. to indicate a theoretical construct as well as a concrete discursive occurrence.

4 See below 3.5 [in original publication] for the distinction between "analysis," "criticism," and "reading."

5 [. . .] For an analysis of the similarities and differences between "ritual theater" and "athletic rituals," see Campeanu (1975: 99). Goffman makes claims similar to Campeanu's (1975: 136), comparing theatrical *performance* to athletic events in terms of *frame analysis*.

6 See, for example, Jansen (1973: 78), Gullì Pugliatti (1976, 1978a, and 1978b), and Serpieri (1977). The adjective /traditional/ is meant to allude to the normative aspirations of "fidelity" to the text, which continually appear in studies of this kind.

7 It is nevertheless very difficult to identify performances in which processes of semanticization and metaphorization are completely absent at the moment of reception. These depend on the conventions of the performance in question as well as on traits of receptive competence. In Chapter 4 [in original publication], I call representational conventions "(quasi-)general conventions," insofar as they are the basis of the vast category of theatrical events known as "representational theater."

8 I am thinking of definitions such as the following: "theater is everything that is designated as theatrical in one way or another." Though more restrictive than these, definitions based on sociological criteria – like Metz's intial definition of cinema as "nothing more than the combination of messages which society calls 'cinematic' " (1974 (1971): 26) – are of the same type [. . .]. Similarly, in the present case, we could say that "theater is the sum total of facts or phenomena which can be designated, thought of, or experienced as 'theatrical' by society as a whole, or by all individuals constituting society." By imposing an initial, if vague, restriction on the range of objects on which analysis can be carried out, a formulation of this type can nevertheless offer a useful point of departure for more descriptive definitions, as I already proposed in De Marinis (1987: 68).

9 In the very frequent case of a multiple sender (take, for example, the standard group of people who create a theatrical production: writer, director, actors, art designer, and other technicians), the copresence of *some* of these individuals is all that is necessary (usually the actors, or puppets with their hidden operators).

10 On theatrical interaction as communication and on its essentially manipulative nature, see below in 6 [in original publication].

11 For the notion of performance as a "show" or "spectacle," see Kowzan. See also Molinari and Ottolenghi for an intial, very general, definition of performance (*spettacolo*) as "everything that is observed by a spectator" (1979: 7). This definition is then narrowed down by the introduction of the concept of *intentionality*: "Some specification regarding the subjectivity of those who prepare a performance should be mentioned. In this case, *a performance is everything that is staged with*

the intention of being observed, but also experienced" (emphasis added). In order to integrate this sender-biased definition with another definition from the receiver's perspective, I would suggest a rough sociological delimitation of the subject, with the claim that /performance/ is "everything within a given synchrony that is designated as performance by society as a whole, or by each individual in that society." See also note 8.

12 Not always, however, as is seen in the case of unique theatrical events, such as "happenings," street acts, or athletic events. Ultimately, a theatrical performance is always unique insofar as it is non-reproducible.

13 The parts that are reproducible in their entirety are obviously the scenery, lights, costumes, and the spoken lines (excluding their supersegmental aspects): components that remain unchanged from each individual performance to the next. Yet they are not completely unchanged if it is true that an alteration in the conditions of enunciation can cause noticeable changes in the "fixed" texts from one show to another. Take, for example, the necessity of adapting scenes to the dimensions of the stage, the placing of the lights, and so on. Eco makes a distinction between individual performances that can be completely duplicated (*doubles*) and performances that are unique in part (1975: 242ff.). For Eco, the existence of "absolute doubles" is problematical and therefore we can speak only of "exact doubles": "there is obviously a precise threshold established by common sense and by our capacities for control: given that a certain number of traits have been preserved, a performance can be considered an *exact double*." The same printed word can often provide a case of exact double; its oral repetitions constitute examples of "partially unique performances." Painting presents a debatable case. Having recognized that in painting and sculpture there are cases of such perfect duplication that the copy cannot be distinguished from the original, Eco negates the possibility of doubles in painting, if "to duplicate is not to represent or imitate (in the sense of 'creating an image of') but to reproduce the same conditions through the same procedures," painting can be replicated only with great difficulty, because the "dense" or "continuous" nature of its sign makes the exact identification of the productive rules of painting very difficult. Essentially adopting Goodman's distinction between *allographic arts* (with the capacity for notation) and *autographic arts* (without notation), Eco tends toward the claim that only works from the allographic category can be completely replicated. As I will clarify later, I prefer to think that the *technical* reproducibility of a work (with the resulting possibility of creating exact doubles) is independent of whether this work can be rendered in notation or not. Conversely, Goodman claims that the allographic arts produce results that are much less similar to each other than those of the autographic arts.

14 In these cases, the difference between two stagings of the same production tends to be less marked, or *almost* nonexistent, though never completely nonexistent. As studies on this topic have confirmed, the possibilities for variation in an actor's or dancer's performance – even if very few and often imperceptible to the nonexpert – are never completely eliminated. If the difference between one performance and another is irrelevant from the theoretical point of view, insofar as it does not affect the principle of the unrepeatability of performance, it can, however, acquire a certain importance on the practical level, in descriptions and analyses of the performance text. In fact, when the differences in question are minimal, the choice of a specific, individual performance may no longer be indispensable for the reconstruction and analysis of the performance (see notes 50 and 82 below [in original publication]). The category of the "textual structure of performance" which I will introduce in the next chapter [of the original publication] will facilitate the distinction between *structural* variations (which bring about a change in the textual structure of performance) and *material* variations (with an invariable textual structure). See in particular note 3 in Chapter 3 [in original publication].

15 On the dramatic text and script, see 1.5 [original publication]. On the description-transcription of the performance text, see 2.4.

16 Obviously, we must be careful not to confuse two separate types of events: different productions

of the same dramatic text on the one hand, and the various individual performances of a specific stage production on the other. On the consequences that the lack of notationality brings to bear on the dramatic text and the technical script, see also Chapter 1, note 32 [original publication].

17 On the "allographic" nature of literature and architecture, see Goodman (1968), who asserts that "a literary script is both in a notation and is itself a work" (210).

18 It is hardly necessary to point out the noticeable differences between various renderings of the same musical score with regard to tempo, timbre, phrasing, and expression. It should be noted, however, that musical notation has a rich and complex history, in which very detailed, rigid scores have given way to "loosely woven" scores allowing greater space for the performer's initiative and for improvization, often dispensing with notational systems in the strict sense. See Lombardi (1980, 1981) for an account of musical writing in the twentieth century as well as the new "notational systems" that it has envisioned.

19 Of all theatrical genres, ballet comes closest to this possibility. As Goodman has observed, Labanotation satisfies the requirements for notation to a large extent. Clearly, however, a transcription need not be exhaustive in order to qualify as a score. For Goodman, "a score need not capture all the subtlety and complexity of performance. . . . The function of a score is to specify the essential properties a performance must have to belong to the work" (212).

20 All of these are autographic arts, that is, having no notational system in the strict sense. Scripts for cinema and television are no exception, and could be compared to the case of the dramatic script, already fully discussed in Chapter 1 [original publication]. As in the case of the dramatic text, the stage directions in the technical film script do not meet the requirements of notationality.

21 Even Goodman continually insists on the fact that if a work belongs to an allographic art capable of notationality, this does not guarantee complete duplicatability.

> The performances of the most specific score are by no means exact duplicates of one another, but vary widely and in many ways. A moderately good copy and the original painting resemble each other more closely than do performances of a Bach suite by Piatigorsky and Casals.
>
> (196)

22 My understanding of /technical reproduction/ is rather different from Benjamin's homonymous concept. Unlike Benjamin, I do not intend it to refer to the possibility of photographic, audio-visual, or sound recording of a work of art, but to the capacity of certain types of work to be duplicated in a more or less precise way and in a greater or lesser quantity of copies.

23 On this issue, see below in 2.4. As the case of opera demonstrates, although ephemerality makes technical reproducibility impossible, it does not prevent repeatability.

24 Regarding the unrepeatability of performance, see Pavis's conception of theater as the result of a collision between *structure* (fiction, conventions, and so forth) and *event* (1980). Amsterdamski's comments on repetition are valuable from the epistemological viewpoint:

> Unlike unrepeatable events, the states of things that are capable of repetition are constructs of our intellect, which elaborates them thanks to its ability to create and to use abstract concepts. . . . The difference between what is repeatable and what is not thus depends essentially on the network of concepts one can use to articulate the real.
>
> (1981: 76–7).

25 The difficulty or impossibility of identifying a receiver (the actant-observer, for Greimas and Cortès [1979]) completely distinct from the sender in phenomena such as folk festivals or ethno-logical rituals could create a problem for the inclusion of these events within my definition of

theatrical performance. In these cases we could speak instead of phenomena of *self-communication* or *self-performance*. But even in circumstances of this kind, we can observe chains of communication and relationships of production and reception, although roles are not as fixed as in traditional performance, and senders can become receivers in the course of the interaction, and vice versa. We must also take into account the presence of the *external spectator* whose gaze establishes a performance relationship even in the case of events that are created for "insiders," and are not originally intended to be communicated to others.

26 My definition reveals the similarity between theater and ordinary human interaction, but these are obviously far from identical categories. My aim is to distinguish the theatrical within performance (see note 11 above). I must emphasize that my definition is a *scientific* one and, as such, concerns what I would call the analyst's *theoretical competence*. As for the ordinary reception of performance, we must postulate a kind of competence containing, in addition to the two basic requirements, other kinds of knowledge (codes and conventions, intertextual frames, co-textual and contextual inferences), without which the spectator would not be in a position to recognize a given theatrical event as such, relating it to the appropriate class, nor to understand and interpret it (see Chapter 7 [original publication]).

27 Both are well clarified by Wolf (91ff.). We must also bear in mind that Goffman's concepts have undergone significant modifications over the years. He is much more likely today to distinguish between theater and daily life than in previous years. See, for example, the close comparison made on the basis of frame analysis between theatrical performance and ordinary, face-to-face interaction in Goffman (1974: 134–44). (For the concept of frame see 4.6.2, below [original publication].)

28 A fairly complex analysis on the similarities and differences between "behavior in real social life" and "theatrical performance" is attempted by Burns (1972), using the history of theater, micro sociology, and ethnomethodology, in order to propose an interdisciplinary inquiry into the "phenomenon of theatricality as it is manifest in theater and in social life" (6). See also 6.6, below [original publication].

29 One of the limits of Ruffini's rigorous and interesting approach lies in the close interdependence he establishes between dramatic text and performance text, defining one through the other, and vice versa.

30 This is a question of the difference between persistent texts and ephemeral texts, or the difference between written texts and oral texts in the field of linguistics (Segre 1978: 133). I also disagree with one of the elements in Bouissac's synthetic definition of /text/ (126), i.e. the *ordered* character of the sum of the elements that constitute a text. I believe that this is a quality of some texts only (verbal texts, and the like), not the constitutive property of all. Given the spatiotemporal multidimensionality (see 2.5) of the performance text, the textual units within it *do not* create an ordered whole.

31 For Kristeva's concept of the "(general) cultural text," see 2.7 and 5.1 [original publication].

32 Eco states a similar position, subordinating delimitation of the text to the pragmatic operation of identifying the topic (1979b: 90). See 2.3.2 for the conditions of coherence in the performance text. Lotman insists on the importance of the opening and closing demarcation of artistic texts (1970: 140).

33 The normal criteria of demarcation (conversational pauses, empty spaces on the page, communicative behavior) do not apply in this case. Two statements uttered at a distance in time and/or in locations very far from each other can constitute a single text. Examples from literature include serialized novels, and "framed" narratives such as *Arabian Nights* and *The Decameron*.

34 Take, for example, the passion plays performed in Europe between the fifteenth and the sixteenth century, involving thousands of spoken lines, hundreds of "actors" and other participants, several days of performance in the town square and possibly in other locations. The passion play performed at Lucerne in 1583 was documented with maps showing the location of each of the

stations in the Weinmarkt during the two days of performance. See Nicoll 1966: figures 58–59 and 62–63, and Konigson 1975: 118–24; 1980: 45–90. Konigson (1975) and Rey-Flaud (1973) provide a systematic discussion of theatrical space during the Middle Ages.

35 I will limit myself to noting the problem of the *exact* beginning of the performance, and hence the exact beginning or the text. According to Guicharnaud (cited in Jansen 1973: 250): "Before the curtain rises, the spectator has the program in his hands. He learns the title, the genre to which the play belongs, the names of the characters, the setting. These details are *already* the work. The performance begins the moment I read in the program '*Tartuffe, or the Impostor*, a comedy in five acts by Moliere.' " This raises a question regarding the relationship between the text proper and the materials that Casetti, Lumbelli, and Wolf in their study of television (1979: 34) call *paratexts:* newspaper presentations and reviews, programs, and oral presentations. For these writers, the function of paratexts is to "predispose the audience . . . to the genre." The function of theatrical paratexts is similar, and will be discussed in Chapters 4 and 7 [original publication]. Nevertheless, I do not share the view that paratexts are part of the performance text. They simply enhance (or confound) its comprehension.

36 These indicators must be understood in chronological sequence. Optional indicators are noted in brackets.

37 I must point out that performances by Robert Wilson, or other contemporary artists, are presented as though already in progress as the audience members begin to enter the auditorium (or other performance site). The stage is fully visible and the actors already present, either immobilized in a kind of *tableau vivant*, or intent on delivering a kind of prologue-overture.

38 Obviously these powers increase in types of theater "with no product," such as street acts and the like. In such circumstances, what can be used as a unit for textual analysis is not the performance, the product (which is often completely absent, or is present only to a minimal degree), but rather the *production*, the entire creative process developed from beginning to end of the "intervention." In other areas of experimentation, the center of attention has shifted from product in the narrow sense to productive process, focusing on the performance "outcome," where *translation* rather than *reduction* occurs. Finally, current theatrical experimentation forces us to rethink the traditional concept of the relationship between theater and performance, according to which the following equation holds true: a theater *is* (only) the performances that it delivers.

REFERENCES

Amsteramski, Sefan (1981) "Ripetizione," *Enciclopedia*, xii, Turin: Einaudi, 76–85.

Ballmer, Thomas T. (1976) "Macrostructures," in Teun A. van Dijk (ed.) *Pragmatics of Language and Literature*, Amsterdam and Oxford: North Holland, 1–22.

Bettetini, Gianfranco (1977) "Appunti per un semiotico del teatro," in Gianfranco Bettetini and Marco De Marinis, *Teatro e comunicazione*, Florence and Rimini: Guaraldi, 9–32.

Bouissac, Paul (1976) *Circus and Culture: A Semiotic Approach*, Bloomington: Indiana University Press.

Burns, Elisabeth (1972) *Theatricality: A Study of Convention in Theatre and in Social Life*, London: Longman.

Campeanu, Pavel (1975) "Un Rôle secondaire: le spectateur," in André Helbo (ed.) *Sémiologie de la représentation*, Brussels: Complexe, 96–111.

Casetti, Francesco, Lumbelli, Lucia, and Wolf, Mauro (1979) *Indagine su alcune regole di genere televisivo*, Milan: Fondazione Rizzoli.

Conte, Maria-Elisabeth (ed.) (1977) *La linguistica testuale*, Milan: Feltrinelli.

De Marinis, Marco (1978) "Lo spettacolo como testo (I)," *Versus* 21, 66–104.

—— (1987) *Il nuovo teatro: 1947–1970*, Milan: Bompiani.

Duvignaud, Jean (1965) *Sociologie du théâtre: Essai sur les ombres collectives*, Paris: Presses Universitaires de France.

Eco, Umberto (1975) *Trattato de semiotica generale*, Milan: Bompiani.

—— (1979a) *Lector in fabula: La cooperazione interpretativa nei testi narrativi*, Milan: Bompiani.

—— (1979b) *The Role of the Reader: Exploration in the Semiotics of Texts*, Bloomington: Indiana University Press.

Elam, Keir (1980) *The Semiotics of Theatre and Drama*, New York; Methuen.

Ertel, Evelyne (1977) "Eléments pour une sémiologie du théâtre," *Travail théâtral* 28–9: 121–50.

—— (1979) "Vers une Analyse sémiologique de la réprésentation théâtrale," *Travail théâtral* 32–3: 164–72.

Goffman, Erving (1959) *The Presentation of Self in Everyday Life*, New York: Doubleday.

—— (1974) *Frame Analysis: An Essay on the Organization of Experience*, New York: Harper and Row.

Goodman, Nelson (1968) *Languages of Art*, New York: Bobbs-Merrill.

Greimas, Algirdas Julien and Courtés, Joseph H. (1979) *Sémiotique: Dictionnaire raisonné de la théorie du langage*, Paris: Hachette.

Gullì Pugliatti, Paola (1976) *I segni latenti: Scrittura come virtualità scenica in "King Lear,"* Florence and Messina: D'Anna.

—— (1978a) "Contributo al processo di segmentazione del testo drammatico in orientamenti deittico-performativi come verifica di ulteriori sopraelevazioni connotative," in *Come comincia il teatro: Dal testo alla scena*, 134–48, Milan: Il Formichiere.

—— (1978b) "Intervento," *Versus* 21: 11–22.

Jansen, Steen (1973) "Qu'est-ce qu'une Situation dramatique?," *Orbis Litterarum* 28: 235–92.

Koch, Walter (1969) "Le Texte normal, le théâtre et le film," *Linguistics* 48: 40–67.

Konigson, Elie (1975) *L'Espace théâtral médiéval*, Paris: Centre National de la Recherche Scientifique (CNRS).

—— (ed.) (1980) *Les Voies de la création théâtrale*, vol. viii, Paris: Centre National de la Recherche Scientifique (CRNS).

Kowzan, Tadeusz (1975) *Littérature et spectacle*, The Hague: Mouton.

Lombardi, Daniele (1980) *Scrittura e suono: La notazione nella musica contemporanea*, Rome: Edipan.

—— (1981) "Spartito preso: a proposito della scrittura musicale contemporanea," in *Spartito preso: La musica da vedere*, Florence: Vallecchi, 9–19.

Lotman, Juri M. (1970) "O modelirujuščem značenii ponatij 'konica' I 'načla' v chudožestvennich tekstach," in *Stat'i Tipologii Kultury* I, Tartu.

Metz, Christian (1970) "Images et pédagogie," *Communications* 15: 162–8.

—— (1971) *Langage et cinéma*, Paris: Larousse; English translation *Language and Cinema*, Approaches to Semiotics 26, The Hague: Mouton, 1974.

Molinari, Cesari and Ottolenghi, Valeria (1979) *Leggere il teatro: Un manuale per l'analisi del fatto teatrale*, Florence: Vallecchi.

Nicoll, Allardyce (1966) *The Development of the Theatre: A Study of Theatrical Art from the Beginnings to the Present* Day, 5th edn., New York: Harcourt, Brace and World.

Ottolenghi, Valeria (1979) "La considerazione genetica," in Molinari and Ottolenghi 1979, 13–53.

Pastorello, Félie (1979) "*L'Opéra de quat'sous* de Bertolt Brecht: mises en scène d'Erich Engel et Gaston Baty," in Denis Bablet (ed.) (1979) *Les Voies de la création théâtrale*, vol. vii, Paris: Centre National de la Recherche Scientifique, 475–543.

Pavis, Patrice 1976) *Problèmes de sémiologie théâtrale*, Montreal: Presses de l'Université du Québec.

—— (1980) *Dictionnaire du théâtre*, Paris: Editions Sociales.

Prieto, Luis (1975) *Pertinence et pratique: Essai de sémiologie*, Paris: Minuit.

Rey-Flaud, Henri (1973) *Le Cercle magique: Essai sur le théâtre en ronde à la fin du Moyen Age*, Paris: Gallimard.

Ruffini, Franco (1974) "Semiotica del teatro: ricognizione degli studi," *Biblioteca teatrale* 9: 34–81.

—— (1976a) "Semiotica del teatro: per una epistemologia degli studi teatrali," *Biblioteca teatrale* 14: 1–27.

—— (1976b) "Analisi contestuale della *Calandria nella rappresentazione urbinate del 1513: I. Il luogo teatrale*," *Biblioteca teatrale* 15–16: 70–139.

—— (1978) *Semiotica del testo: L'esempio teatro*, Tome: Bulzoni.

Schechner, Richard (1975) "Inattenzione selettiva," *Scrittura scenica* 15: 96–113.

Schmidt, Siegfried J. (1973) "Texttheorie/Pragmalinguistik," in Hans Peter Althaus, Helmut Henne, and Herbert Ernst Wiegand (eds.) *Lexikon der germanistischen Linguistik*, Tübingen: Niemeyer, 233–44.

Segre, Cesare (1978) "La natura del testo," *Strumenti critici* 36–7: 131–45.

Serpieri, Alessandro (1977) "Ipotesi terorica di segmentazione del testo teatrale," *Strumenti critici* 32–33: 90–135.

Sieffert, René (1960) "Introduction," in Motokyio Zeami, *La Tradition secrète du Nö*, Paris: UNESCO.

Ubersfeld, Anne (1981) *L'Ecole du spectateur*, Paris: Editions Sociales.

Van Dijk, Teun A. (1979) "New developments and problems in textlinguistics," in Janos S. Petöfi (ed.) (1979) *Text vs. Sentence: Basic Questions of Textlinguistik*, 2 vols, Hamburg: Buske, 509–23.

Wolf, Mauro (1979) *Sociologie della vita quotidiana*, Milan: Espresso Strumenti.

READER CROSS-REFERENCES

Schechner, Kirshenblatt-Gimblett – expanded definition of performance

Worthen, Zimmerman – the relationship between texts, textuality, and performance

Carlson, Parker and Sedgwick – other analyses influenced by semiotics

Bateson – performance and communication

Meyerhold – emphasis on the performance process

Grotowski – whom De Marinis cites as an influence

Barba – occasional collaborator and influence

Goffman, Kaprow – on the blurry boundary between theater and everyday life

Phelan – relationship of video documentation to performance

35

THE DEEP ORDER CALLED TURBULENCE

The three faces of dramaturgy

Eugenio Barba

(translated by Judy Barba)

There exists an invisible revolt, apparently painless yet infusing every hour of work, and this is what nourishes "technique."

Artistic discipline is a way of refusal. Technique in theatre and the attitude that it presupposes is a continual exercise in revolt, above all against oneself, against one's own ideas, one's own resolutions and plans, against the comforting assurance of one's own intelligence, knowledge, and sensibility.

It is the practice of a voluntary and lucid disorientation in the search for new points of orientation.

Apart from nourishing the work, revolt is also nourished by it. I do theatre because I want to preserve my freedom to refuse certain rules and values of the world around me. But the opposite is also true: I am forced or encouraged to refuse them *because* I do theatre.

Storm and meticulousness

The choice to do theatre is often a difficult answer to a difficult situation. It is a way to live a freedom that is only free if the results of our own work succeed in influencing other people and winning them over to our side. It is a way of inventing our own identity, which is revealed to us through work that is both meticulous and stormy.

Some people believe that storm and meticulousness belong in two separate worlds; that technical problems, professionalism, and the craftsman's precision have nothing to do with turbulence and with the impulse towards freedom, destruction, revolt, and refusal.

This is not true.

Extracting the difficult from the difficult

Extracting the difficult from the difficult is the attitude that defines artistic practice. On this depend the incisiveness, the complexity, the dense quality of the result, as well as the moments of difficulty, suffering and illumination, disorientation and reorientation that make up the process.

This attitude illustrates the difference between the organic character of art and the organization of daily tasks which are all the better for having the *easy* extracted from the difficult.

Scylla and Charybdis

Order and disorder are not two opposing options, but two poles that coexist and reinforce one another reciprocally. The quality of the tension created between them is an indication of the fertility of the creative process.

When we attempt to describe this tension, however, the discussion becomes hesitant. The more our explanations stick to what we have experienced in the work, the more they appear fantastic and exotic to the listener. And in trying to transmit experience, there is a risk of misunderstanding.

The easiest way of escaping these problems is through silence. Otherwise we have to navigate between Scylla and Charybdis.

On the one hand there is Scylla, representing the risk of straightening out the route, thus transforming the intricacy of the many paths into one direct line running in the right direction. Everything then becomes clear, even though it does not correspond to our experience. Within the reality of work, creativity is like a stormy sky. It is perceived as disorientation, doubt, frustration, discomfort.

To be master of one's craft signifies above all knowing how to prepare for the storm that will threaten us, and how to resist without resorting to easy or familiar solutions.

"Storm" also means that problems do not present themselves one after another – as when we talk about them – but all or many simultaneously. When the sea and the waves are merely images of the route, every step becomes comprehensible. Everything turns out to be true, yet so abstract that it makes a mockery of experience.

On the other hand, there is Charybdis, with the risk of speaking only of storms and forgetting about the geometry of the compass and the sextant, which make the route possible. It is the risk of becoming anecdote or confession: the process is shown as a random path, confused and shadowy, like magma flowing almost involuntarily into a result without knowing how or why. This too is an aspect of truth, one of its profiles.

To discover the true face behind the reality of the artistic process, you must focus first on one and then the other profile.

The secret complexity of bios

In spite of the disturbing fluctuation between Scylla and Charybdis, with all the misunderstandings that it entails, it is worthwhile to attempt to talk about the way in which a performance grows, takes form, and is transformed. It means questioning oneself about something that has to do with life itself. One has the sensation that they are the same questions as the ones posed by those who investigate the secret complexity of *bios*.

It is this that justifies the interest and the curiosity surrounding the artistic process, with its paradoxes and obstructions. It explains the persistence of certain people to speak of it although well aware that their words will be opaque and the questions will almost always lack answers.

Art and living matter

In artistic terms, the contraposition "organic" and "inorganic" distinguishes work that seems alive, credible, and coherent from that which appears forced, mechanical, arousing in us a reaction of rejection and annoyance. In the natural sciences, however, the contraposition organic–inorganic serves to distinguish the realm of the bios from the mineral realm.

There is an important difference between discussions on nature and on art: in the first case the difference between "organic" and "inorganic" is objective, while in the second it has a purely subjective basis and only acquires an appearance of objectivity when it concerns an opinion shared by many. Or, to express it in terms that might appeal both to skeptics and relativists: discussions on nature have the presumption to be objective, whereas those on art presume that objectivity does not exist.

Another difference is that while the complexity of the natural processes determining *life* often appear as an admirable order, the paths which lead to the *life* of a work of art seem to be dominated by disorder and fortuitousness.

Forging fortuitousness

Many of the solutions that make an impression on the spectator and help to determine the significance of a performance seem to be suggested by fortuitousness. But what we call "fortuitousness" is a complex order in which several forces act simultaneously, a system of relationships that cannot be explored at a single glance.

We could say that in the creative process we must forge our own fortuitousness, just as the Romans used to say that we are the forgers of our own good or bad fortune. But we must not forget the words of Pasteur: "Chance only favors minds which are prepared."

Catastrophe and density

From a technical point of view, how can we disrupt the direction of the work? One way is to concentrate not just on one objective, but to aim in two, three, four different directions simultaneously. Like a sailing boat that wants to go west, while the wind is blowing from the south and the currents are carrying it towards the east. The equilibrium between these tensions is the creative route. The tensions between forces that are divergent, opposed to one another or simply contiguous, can lead to catastrophe. But if we succeed in keeping these forces at bay and discovering the kind of relationship that exists between them – in other words, if we can get them to coexist, interweaving and rearranging them – then we will attain density instead of catastrophe.

Density disorientates the spectators, forcing them to extract the difficult from the difficult and shaking them out of the familiar trains of thought, which constitute a safe home for their ideas.

The technique of disorientation

During rehearsals, the technique of disorientation consists in giving space to a multiplicity of trends, narratives, and directions without bending them, right from the start, beneath the yoke of our choices and intentions. We must follow different tracks, diverging themes, and unconnected associations contemporaneously, and make sure that the stories pursued by the individual actors do not correspond to those of the director and the other actors.

It is an attitude that stimulates and generates a contiguity of material, prospects, and proposals. It is a means of trying out a labyrinthine path between *chaos* and *cosmos*, with sudden swerves, paralyzing stops, and unexpected solutions. It is the growth of a profusion that for a long time appears to obscure the explanatory and narrative clarity in the course of the process.

In this way an apparent confusion is created, a magnetic field with differing forces for each individual actor and for the director, but where each of them can find pretexts, bonds, justifications, interests, obstacles, challenges, and resonances related to the main theme or the nucleus of questions constituting the point of departure.

It implies the creation of a chaotic panorama with many underground rivers along which everyone is free to follow a different route. This freedom already constitutes the seed of a dramaturgy because, if they all navigate according to their own choice, the obligation to follow a common path necessitates the discovery of *relationships* between the various personal motivations. This *search* for coherent relationships is already a *search* for a narrative plot, a coherent dramaturgy.

Three dramaturgies

Working on the dramaturgy does not only involve the text or the story that we want to tell and make visible to the spectators.

There are three different dramaturgies, which should happen simultaneously but can each be worked on separately:

1   An *organic or dynamic dramaturgy*, which is the composition of the rhythms and dynamisms affecting the spectators on a nervous, sensorial and sensual level.

2   A *narrative dramaturgy*, which interweaves events and characters, informing the spectators on the meaning of what they are watching.

3   And, lastly, the one that I call *dramaturgy of changing states*, when the entirety of what we show manages to evoke something totally different, similar to when a song develops another sound line through the harmonics.

In a performance, this *dramaturgy of changing states* distills or captures hidden significances, which are often involuntary on the part of the actors as well as the director, and are different for every spectator. It gives the performance not only a coherence of its own but also a sense of mystery.

The dramaturgy of changing states is the most elusive. There are no technical rules. Furthermore, it is difficult to explain what it involves beyond the perceptible effects: leaps from one dimension to another. For the spectator, actor, and director it is a spring from one state of consciousness to another, with unforeseeable and extremely personal consequences, both sensorial and mental. This leap from one context to another is a perturbation, a change in the quality of energy, which produces a double effect: enlightenment or a sudden vortex that shatters the security of comprehension and is experienced as turbulence.

Turbulence

Turbulence appears to be a violation of order; in fact it is order in motion. It engenders vortexes that upset the current of narrative action. In the absence of these vortexes the continuity, rhythm, and narrative risk lapsing into the obvious, into mere illustration. It is like a succession of notes making a melody, but one which is sung without the wealth of harmonics that bring the voice to life, allowing it to enchant and move.

The dramaturgy of changing states concerns the performance as a physical and sensorial event, as an organism-in-life. It has nothing to do with the written text, with the dramaturgy of the words, in the same way that the vibratory quality of the singing voice has nothing to do with the score.

All this is not possible without the availability of many elements and different seeds, without the will to encourage contiguity and to spread out in several directions simultaneously. This abundance of elements and materials creates confusion, yet its aim is simplicity and coherence.

Coherence

"A writer may well build castles in the air, but they must rest on foundations of granite." This declaration by Ibsen refers to the dramaturgy of words, but emphasizes the dialectic of independence and dependence, anarchy and discipline, on the one hand revolt and on the other the authority of a unifying principle which characterizes every aspect of the three dramaturgies.

The actions of the actors should possess a coherence independent of their context and their "meaning." They should appear credible on a sensorial level and be *present* on a pre-expressive one. The granite foundations are their quality of credibility, their ability to stimulate the attention of the spectator and to be rooted in the body-mind of the actor. They should be based on their own particular independent logic.

There are and have always been actors of prodigious effectiveness who have never fixed the pattern of their actions on stage, who have never thought in terms of a score, who have never consciously worked on a level that they called pre-expressive, avoiding every sign of visible precision that might be controlled from outside.

Why, then, do I insist so strongly on the work of the actor at a pre-expressive level; on the importance of precision in fixing and knowing how to repeat the precise pattern of the actions; on the value of one's independence from the intentions of the director and the writer; on the coherence of one's score and subscore?

I insist not only because I have observed what it is that makes the actor effective, but because the autonomous coherence of the actions (independently of the significance that they assume in the context of the performance) bestows a particular and precious gift on the material which the actor has assembled: it becomes *amphibious*, capable of passing from one context to another without withering away, and able to mutate without losing the roots that keep it alive.

Confusion and con-fusion

During the rehearsal stage, when the actors only follow a personal and coherent thread in their scores, the dramaturgy as a whole may remain confused, even chaotic, for a long time.

Confusion, when it is sought after and practiced as an *end in itself*, is the art of deception. This does not necessarily mean that it is a negative state, one to be avoided. When used as a *means*, confusion constitutes one of the components of an organic creative process. It is the moment in which material, prospects, contiguous stories, and diverse intentions become con-fused, i.e. fuse together, mixing with one another, each becoming the other face of the other.

The intricate lines of the route do not mean that the route aims at intricacy. The profusion and confusion of material and trends are the only way to arrive at the bare and essential action.

Craft and genius

When the work is almost finished, he stops and says that now it can really begin. Those around him express stupor and incomprehension. Meanwhile he disarranges and destroys everything he has done up to that moment. He draws other scenes and figures, which he interweaves or superimposes on the preceding ones, canceling them out. He takes another canvas and on it paints the picture that he has mentally extracted from the difficulties with which he was confronted while working on the previous canvas.

He started out from a dynamic and asymmetric division of a white rectangle, with lines pointing in six directions. Then he peopled it, filled it, applied colors, blotted out forms, reapplied new colors, invented new figures, and transformed others. He painted in haste, then stopped to reflect, began again, glimpsed a solution, and changed his mind. On the canvas, the sun shone on an azure sea. He had made night fall and the entire canvas gradually had become dark. At that precise moment he saw the right path: "Now I can begin. All the mistakes I have made up to now are teaching me the picture I must paint."

In the summer of 1955 Pablo Picasso agreed, contrary to all expectations, to make a film. It was Georges Clouzot, the French director, who had convinced him. The film was to show the painter at work. Contrary to his normal daily schedule, for a whole month Picasso got up early in the morning to go to the film studio in Nice. He agreed to submit to all the technical demands of the filmmaker. He worked in the presence of crowds of "spectators," lighting and sound technicians, electricians, photographers, production staff, director – all the numerous members of a film team.

The film, *Le Mystère Picasso*, is a classic of its genre today. It is presented as a document that allows us to observe what goes on in the head of a genius. He was undoubtedly a genius. But the film reveals above all the craftsman Picasso.

What is the difference?

Humble procedures

In the 1970s, a series of film sequences rejected by Charlie Chaplin was discovered. They were supposed to have been destroyed but had been kept by mistake. With them Kevin Brownlow and David Gill put together a television program that became famous: *Unknown Chaplin*. It showed us Chaplin improvising, searching for a theme for one of his films, starting from nothing, constructing complicated scenes and then discarding them until the right road opened up before him. Meanwhile the camera continued to record hundreds of meters of film which now reveal to us what was going on in the head of that genius. The craftsman yet again.

If we watch *Le Mystère Picasso* or *Unknown Chaplin* in order to deduce something that might be of interest from a professional point of view, we must not allow ourselves to be dazzled by their extraordinary creativity. Their exceptional qualities disclose the humble procedures on which the artist's work is based, whatever the level of the results.

Waste

There is no creative work without waste. The proportion between that which is produced and that which is finally used could be said to correspond to the disproportion of the seeds that are dispersed in nature in order that a single fertilized cell may succeed in engendering a new individual in the animal or plant world.

There is no creative work without waste and there is no waste without the high quality of that which is wasted.

Kipling used to say that you cannot learn to write if you do not learn to discard, and in order to cut a text in a way that is beneficial, the rejected parts must be of an equally high quality to those which remain. In other words, it is no use writing something with the idea that what you write may be thrown away.

Extracting the difficult from the difficult involves creating complexity. This is not an objective in itself but aims at guiding us towards further choices and revealing paths we did not know existed.

This is a paradoxical way of reasoning according to the criteria of economy and accumulation. But it is simple good sense if the criteria are those of the artistic crafts.

In theatre this paradox is mainly present on two different levels of organization: that of the actor and that of the narrative dramaturgy.

Extracting error from confusion

At a certain point in Clouzot's film Picasso appears confused. He is not sure that he will be able to dominate the difficulties that he has created for himself. Slowly, in his eyes, the confusion is transformed into an obvious spider's web of *errors*. At this point he gets his breath back: at last he can begin.

"Truth emerges more often from error than from confusion," said Francis Bacon (not the contemporary painter but the seventeenth-century philosopher). To extract error from confusion, and then *our* own truth from the error, could be a somewhat philosophical way of saying: extract the difficult from the difficult.

Constructing confusion

The capacity to construct confusion is crucial in the theatre's creative process.

From a dramaturgical point of view it implies not being satisfied with what we already know about the performance on which we are working, its story or non-story, the meaning that the writer has given to the text or that we want to express and make visible. It means doing everything to escape the temptation to carry out a previously defined plan, which we usually call "interpretation." When we work on a text, it is important to know how to distance ourselves from it. But the purpose of this detachment, this straying from the path, or pilgrimage, is not to use the text as a pretext. It must be a road which carries us in unimagined directions in order that everything we have discovered while exploring the territories and the themes that have been carrying us away or contradicting our points of departure may build a network of difficulties when we return to face the writer's dramaturgy, confronting us with new questions and unexpected perspectives.

This rule of behavior towards the text or the original theme, towards the meaning that these assumed for us initially, corresponds to a rule guiding the movements of the body: the impulse to move in one direction is preceded by an impulse in the opposite direction, a *sats*. This law of movement of the living organism is amplified by the actor at the pre-expressive level and transformed into one of those stimuli, leaps of energy or micro-vortexes which hold and steer the attention of the spectator sensually and kinesthetically.

Errors as walls and errors as doors

If it is true that it is essential to extract the error from confusion, then we have to ask ourselves what, from a technical point of view, is error.

There are sterile errors that every theatre craftsman has to learn to recognize and correct. These are errors that block the process, like blind walls. On the other hand, there are other types of errors which, as doors, are a threshold, temporary yet fertile.

If we have been able to work at different levels of organization of the performance, then each of these has a life and function of its own. When put together, however, they do not make for harmony but confusion. Every level of organization limits itself to following its own course, and has a certain centrifugal tendency, jealous of its own autonomy. That which possesses its own effective coherency on a particular level of organization – e.g. that of the dynamo-rhythm – loses it on another level, that of the narrative dramaturgy. And vice versa: some actions, a passage or an entire scene, which are essential to the story we are presenting, become an obstacle and counterproductive to the pace of the performance. A performance is built up according to different logics. Something that is right from the point of view of one of these logics becomes "error" when considered from another standpoint.

These "errors" guide us, obliging us to extract a new complexity from those that constituted the previous stages of the work. It is by attempting to respond to these new difficulties, to break down these "doors," that we may experience leaps in perception in ourselves or in the spectator: the dramaturgy of changing states.

At this point a phenomenon occurs which seems strange when we speak of it, but is a sign that the work is on the right course. It is as though the work no longer belongs to us but starts to speak with its own autonomous voice and language, which we have to decipher.

Something similar happens with the work of the individual actors when their physical scores are interwoven with the scores of their fellow actors, with the words of the text, and with the demands of the dramaturgy.

Work tires and sometimes hurts

It is easy to read storm and meticulousness, disorientation and confusion, turbulence and chance which is not fortuitous as formulas for extracting the difficult from the difficult. At the same time it is easy to imagine how, in the reality of the work situation, this process is experienced as doubt, discomfort, and sometimes pain.

During rehearsals, when what seemed already to be a difficult result is treated as a point of departure, some of the actors lose heart. It is always a critical moment for the ensemble. Sometimes the irritation of each against the others prevails and destroys. Yet even this is craftsmanship. Work does not only tire, but sometimes it hurts.

Sadism and masochism are of no use in the artistic process. If they emerge in the web of relationships that make up a group, the result is immediate and bitter destruction.

The drop of water

Why, then, do I work in a way which may bring me distress, cause me unease or wound me or my companions?

In order to create a work that lives and stands alone, that belongs to me, in which I recognize myself, yet which does not need my presence to go on existing in the senses, the memory, and the actions of others.

In order to give the spectators something to remember even after they have forgotten it. Because I long for the bare and essential action: the drop of water that makes the jar run over.

READER CROSS-REFERENCES

Grotowski – close collaborator and influence
Strasberg, Blair – the emotional demands made upon the actor
Sutton-Smith – the rhetoric of chaos
De Marinis – occasional collaborator
Zimmerman – the dramaturgy of devising performance

36

THE ARCHAEOLOGY OF PERFORMANCE

Mary Zimmerman

Most of my time in the theater is spent creating adaptations of nondramatic texts through the process of pre-production and rehearsal. Only once have I ever written a script before beginning rehearsals, and I've never typed a word of a play that didn't already have a scheduled, not too distant opening night. I've never done a workshop of anything or a draft of anything; and I use only the standard four weeks of rehearsal before tech.

I used to think of this process in architectural terms. In my mind my collaborators and I started with a flat line, and through our labor we built something. We tugged that flat line up into an elaborate silhouette of a city. We had "made something out of nothing," and I was very proud of that. But as I have continued to work, my image of our process has undergone a change and it no longer appears to me in architectural, but rather archaeological terms. For me, from the moment a date for first preview has been assigned, I feel that the piece is lying in wait for us, buried underground. I tell my colleagues that we must work carefully in excavating this piece: if we are impatient and nervous and try to dig too fast, we will damage the shape of the piece; but if we are lazy and inattentive to what is emerging, we will arrive on opening night with dust and dirt obscuring its true shape.

The paradox is that the piece is made and shaped by the digging itself: it is both unpredictable and utterly preordained. It is made by who we are, who we are together, the circumstances of production, and the conditions of the world as they exist and change throughout our rehearsal process. We can't know what the piece will become, but it is inescapable.

The process goes like this: I fall in love, or have always been in love, with a particular text, or an episode that I happen to know from a particular text, or the back jacket cover description of a text in the hands of a friend I run into outside of Coliseum Books in New York, or, in one case, the title of a text. Next, I start telling someone at Northwestern, or at the Lookingglass or Goodman Theatre in Chicago, that I want to adapt that text and I trick them into saying they'll produce it. Pretty soon after this, my producers would like some questions answered: How many people in the play? I'm not sure. How long will it be, one act or two? I have no idea. Will it be any good? Can't say.

Yet I'm not completely flinging myself into the void when I start on a play because I'm basing my work on a pre-existing text, or collection of texts, and that is my constant map and guide. When I am devising a performance, the primary factor that determines what goes into the final show is undoubtedly the unconscious and conscious impulses of my own personality in dialogue with the original text: how I read its story, how I can best give that story a body, what I am drawn to, what I feel is beautiful, what formal considerations I value, what I am obsessed with. In other words, my own taste. All of this comes to bear on anyone adapting anything, but in this particular way of devising, in which the script does not precede production, but rather "grows up" simultaneously with it, at least three other factors exert unusual pressure on the final form the script will take: the designs for the play devised by my colleagues and me, the cast of the play, and the events and circumstances of the world during the rehearsal period of the play. The interweaving of these elements creates the "dig."

The design

I begin by gathering my usual designers around me. If the original text is manageable, they read it; but I have a tendency to make plays from source material that could be as many as five thousand pages long. In that case, my designers read around in it as best they can, and listen to me talking as much as I can about what I think is at the heart of the text, what is essential to it, why it is so great, and why we have to do it.

Because of the way the practical calendar of theater production works, my set designer and I must commit to our design before I have written a word of the play, long before I know what settings, events, and characters the set might be called upon to accommodate and represent. Most of the nondramatic texts I am drawn to are written with a flagrant disregard for my designers' convenience. Shakespeare and Chekhov are thinking every moment about someone actually doing their plays on an actual stage and, for the most part, dramatists avoid having characters turn into birds, fly around on carpets, participate in camel trains, split into two monkeys or battle monsters under water and in the sky. However poets, novelists, scientists, and anonymous tellers of ancient myths aren't the least concerned with whether or not what they describe can be realized in the stubbornly material world of the stage, nor with such niceties as unity of time and place. So my set designer has two problems to contend with: the original text was never intended for the stage, and our script of that text does not yet exist.

We try to get around these problems by talking and meeting a great deal. I talk and talk about what I think is moving, beautiful, and funny about the original text; why it is so urgent that we do it; why it is so utterly fantastic. I describe moments that I feel I must see, things that have to happen on stage. The design begins to radiate outward from particular images that seem to be coming forward from the story and presenting themselves. Often I have a strong first idea simultaneous with the idea of doing the text itself. My adaptation of Ovid's *Metamorphoses* was conceived to be performed in water. The idea of doing the myths and the idea of doing them in water were not separate or sequential ideas – they were the same idea. I knew that for *The Notebooks of Leonardo da Vinci* I wanted floor-to-ceiling wooden cabinets which could open up into doors or stairs and also contain all the props for the performance – including very surprising ones such as a field of wheat, a corpse, and several dioramas of anatomical features. Whatever else the set design provides, it must provide an open, even floor because I know there will be a lot of fast traffic. I don't like multiple gradations or levels on floors because my actors will almost certainly be doing things that are physically demanding enough without having to contend with that sort of thing; and in any case, open space is more flexible in terms of what it can "take on" to represent as well. Like everything else in the performance, the set must have a developing arc. It must have, or be, a character, but a character that is pliable and modest, able almost to disappear. Most of all, it must contain things for which I don't as yet have any use, but for which the cast eventually will. It must dare me to find a way to exploit all of its talents and possibilities.

This phase of the process is both deeply pleasurable and extremely critical for me because I know that the set will generate meaning in even greater ways than it would in a conventional process. It will generate text. The design remains relatively unchanged once it is drafted and planned for and the materials for it are purchased – it is the script that remains fluid. The original story is the mother of the set, but the script of that story is in part the child of the design.

In the case of *Metamorphoses* the impact of the set design on the text can't be overstated. As the process got under way, I found myself being drawn to choose particular myths from hundreds of possibilities in great part because they leaned into the set: they could use the water, be amplified by the water, have resonance with it, a dynamic relationship to it. Water is apt for *Metamorphoses* not only because the culture that produced these stories was fundamentally maritime, but also because water is an ancient and cross-cultural symbol of transfiguration. It is an element that transforms almost anything left in it too long, and is itself subject to change: it can easily freeze into a solid or evaporate as steam. Perhaps because it is so transformative and so mutable itself, water easily takes on a wide variety of symbolic resonances. The water in *Metamorphoses* is at times typecast as the sea or as a swimming pool, yet it easily slips into a manifestation of sloppy drunkenness, of grief and tears, of sexual excitement. The fact of the water changed the original stories: an angry father tries to drown his daughter rather than strangle her; a woman sleeps by the edge of the sea instead of in her bed as she awaits the return of her husband; in her grief a girl literally dissolves into tears instead of turning into a bush; a very modern Phaeton floats on a sun-colored raft, describing his troubled relationship to his absent father to a psychotherapist who sits on the deck of his swimming pool.

The water itself became a kind of eloquent text, alternately muted and voluble. At one point in the play, a daughter tricks her father into unwittingly coming to bed with her. Blindfolded, he gropes slowly along the deck as she waits quietly, kneeling in the pool. He reaches one foot out, tentatively suspending it over the still water. When he finally makes the decision to step in, the sudden, violent sound of the breaking surface is the breaking of the world. The subsequent protracted sexual encounter between father and child is all in silence but for the stirring of the water around them, the dripping off of them, the lapping against them. The water is never pretending or acting, it is only behaving. Its natural behavior, utterly indifferent to the unnatural act of father and daughter, creates a tension that is nearly unbearable.

One of the most poignant instances of a set taking the script to an unexpected place occurred in *The Notebooks of Leonardo da Vinci*. The script is entirely made up of Leonardo's writing; there are no made-up characters, dialogue, or plot, and all eight performers play Leonardo. It is a series of vignettes in which the staging and text interact to generate a sort of narrative that accumulates bit by bit. It structures itself around the repetition of the only two childhood memories Leonardo records. One of these is the following:

> Once as a boy, I wandered in the hills above my home; and drawn by my ardent desire, impatient to see the great abundance of strange forms created by that artificer, Nature, I wandered for some time among the shadowed rocks. I came to the mouth of a huge cave before which I stopped for a moment, stupefied by such an unknown thing.

Here Leonardo does a strange thing: he describes precisely and in great detail the position of his body as he looked into the shadowed cave; how his right and left hand were, how his feet and body were positioned. It reminds me of the way I have heard people begin to slow down a story when they are coming close to saying something that is very private or highly charged for them; how they will circle around and stall, adding detailed asides, because what they are approaching is overwhelming. It is also, of course, indicative of how Leonardo is never uninterested in observation, in the appearance of things, even his own physical posture at such a moment. He finally concludes, "After a time there arose in me both fear and desire – fear of the dark and menacing cave; desire to see whether it contained some marvelous thing."

This anecdote was repeated three times in the play in English and almost simultaneously in Italian. Each time it was repeated, both were abbreviated, though with the Italian beginning to dominate, until finally there was no English at all, and only a drastically shortened Italian version. Well, part of the set for *The Notebooks* was a group of 16 small, very deep, removable drawers that all sat within one larger box built into a sidewall. Throughout the course of the play the small drawers were all individually removed and used in various ways. Suddenly, near the very end of our tech, we found ourselves with a large, cave-like opening on the stage – utterly unplanned and unlooked-for. It became very clear that at the end of Leonardo's "life" in the play, he should finally enter that cave: he should cross the threshold on which he had stood so long in memory and step into the "marvelous thing." The actress said the final lines, stepped into the opening, and disappeared.

When a performance is site-specific – that is, made specifically for an environment that already exists – then this "found" rather than conceived design will have the most profound effect on a script, even when that script is an adaptation of a pre-existing text. I devised a performance called *Eleven Rooms of Proust* that took place in three stories of an old, empty factory in Chicago. In this case, the scope and dynamic of the space determined both the design and the development of the text. The factory had enormous rooms that measured 85×150 feet, as well as tiny rooms that were closer to 11×15. At intervals of 40 minutes, groups of 30 spectators were guided through the factory sometimes by live narrators and sometimes by recordings that gave instructions in the form of educational French-language tapes. There were always two audiences in the factory at once. In each of the rooms spectators witnessed scenes and heard text from the seven novels of *Remembrance of Things Past*. The size of the audiences, the intervals between them, and the length of the performance itself were dictated by the layout of the factory: the smallest room of the performance held only 30 people; it took 40 minutes to make sure one audience remained two floors above the next, and the actors needed a certain number of minutes to run back to repeat their roles for an incoming audience.

The experience of devising this piece was as close to ideal as I think I shall ever come. We held every rehearsal for *Eleven Rooms of Proust* in the factory and my set, costume, sound, and lighting designers were present at almost every one of them. The building led the design: rather than come and see how I had staged the action and then figure out how to light it, my lighting designer experimented with different ways to light the architecture, creating hidden recesses and strange shadows, shafts of light coming through distant doors or windows, spotlighting forests of pillars or cluttered ceilings, and then I staged into those compositions.

The size and shape of the rooms created the script: long, dark hallways with lots of doors suggested passages about Odette's hidden life of perpetual rendezvous; stairways implied weariness and struggle. We went into one particular cramped room and discovered a strange, rusted metal box, about five-feet tall and two-feet deep, sitting on four-foot-high legs, with no "front" to it, and immediately felt we were looking at an image of the confined, dark, increasingly narrow existence that Swann feels as he approaches the nadir of his obsession with Odette. We painted the entire small room a sickening red-orange and then (inspired by the years of graffiti carved and scrawled in our booth at a pizza restaurant where we were having a production meeting) we covered every surface of it – the floor, ceilings, and walls, the light switch, molding, door jamb, and conduit – with the word "Odette" written in black marker, sometimes six-feet high, sometimes a half an inch high. We scrawled entire paragraphs, full of punctuation and quotation marks yet containing only one word, over and over: "Odette."

When the audience arrived in this room it was dark. Swann was sitting in the metal box in full tails and top hat, on a little stool, illuminated by a dim fluorescent tube. Under the box, on the floor, lay a winged, naked figure next to a broken arrow. The narrator began to speak: "Even when he could not discover where Odette had gone when she left him, it would have sufficed him, to alleviate the anguish which he then felt. . . ." Swann rose from his stool, unable to stand fully upright, and proceeded to try and arrange himself differently and more comfortably, to no avail. A single bare incandescent lightbulb suspended above the narrator slowly brightened, until the audience could begin to perceive and, one by one, decipher the black writing everywhere surrounding them.

The layout of the factory gave birth to a scene and an event that would not be possible in any other space. The audience, after emerging from the red Odette room, walked across a huge, long, empty space which we took pains to make look unremarkable, dirty, "not important." After peering through an opening into a long dark room for one more scene, the audience was then led onto a loading dock and the aluminum roll-top door was pulled down behind them. There, in the smallest of all the rooms, they watched the narrator describe, for six minutes, the way in which Albertine slept. Albertine was there on the floor at their feet; a real clock ticked on the wall. The narrator whispered so as not to disturb the girl, "I would gaze at Albertine stretched out below me. From time to time a slight, unaccountable tremor ran through her, as the leaves of a tree are shaken for a few moments by a sudden breath of wind." During those six minutes, with the audience safely confined, 14 cast members worked in silence to fill the previously drab "not important" room with over 500 yellow paper flowers that each stood upright on individual wire stems. The audience emerged from the loading dock to be greeted by a landscape: an enormous indoor field of yellow flowers. Elstir, the painter, came forward with his easel, and a narrator began some text about the solitary life of the artist that I later realized was barely heard by most of the spectators, who were in shock.

The penultimate scene of *Eleven Rooms* was a brief bit of text pulled verbatim from Proust but entirely inspired by the architecture of the factory. Were it not for the gifts of the building, this beautiful fragment would never have seen the light of day in performance. The audience sat facing into a room, waiting expectantly for the action to appear in front of them. But, unexpectedly, alongside them, a girl sitting beneath a high window began to speak: "Brief though our lives may be, it is only while we are suffering that we see certain things which at other times are hidden from us. We are, as it were, posted near a high window, badly placed but looking out over an expanse of sea." Here the girl looked up at the window, then rose to open it, saying,

> Only during a storm, when our thoughts are agitated by perpetually changing movements, do they elevate to a level at which we can see, for a time, the whole law-governed immensity which normally, when the calm weather of happiness leaves it smooth, lies beneath our line of vision.

Now the girl addressed the audience, which was at that moment twisted about to look toward the window and her. She said:

> We must forcibly be turned in our comfortable seats in order to see. It may perhaps be true that for a few great geniuses this movement of thought exists all the time, uncontingent upon the agitations of personal grief. Yet can we be sure, when we contemplate the ample and regular development of their joyous creations, that we do not too readily assume from the joyousness of their work that there was also joy in their lives, which perhaps on the contrary, were almost continuously unhappy?

I have been asked a few times to bring *Eleven Rooms of Proust* to different cities, but my would-be producers do not, I think, fully understand the depth to which the script is dependent upon a single abandoned factory in Chicago. Moving it would profoundly change it; disassemble it. It would require a new rehearsal period to make a new or profoundly modified script. It would require stepping again into the unknown.

The cast

When I cast, I am casting an ensemble. With some texts, such as *The Odyssey*, I will be looking for and casting a few particular roles: Odysseus, Penelope, Telemachus, Athena. But for the most part, when I am devising, actors are hired "as cast," meaning that they agree to play whatever comes their way in the as-yet-unwritten script. I hold auditions by finding narrative passages in the original text, or by writing a couple of scenes that may or may not end up in the play but that use a lot of the characters that probably will definitely be in play. Usually the first round looks like the first round of any audition process – although I did once ask the actors to come in prepared to "stage a myth in three minutes." When I call the actors back they come in groups of eight to 12, and I spend 45 with them. I have a series of sort of fun, fast, physical things I do with them, most of which are just excuses for me to spend time with them and ways of making them forget about themselves, but some of which do tell me a lot about how at ease they are in their own bodies. I am really trying to see how they behave in a group: how interested they are or are not in each other. My feeling is, if I enjoy being with them, so will an audience. Who I cast may well end up determining which of the hundreds of potential roles in the original text will end up on stage.

I usually begin rehearsals with the designers' introduction to the set and the ideas for costume design. Then I talk my head off about the original text and why it is so great, etc. Often we will sit around the table and pass a single copy of the text hand to hand, each reading a paragraph or so of some particular passage or episode that I am considering for the play. By the second day I am bringing in bits of text and assigning roles and trying to stage. The way I write is inextricably tied to the way I see the staging, to the gesture of the staging. I know as I am scripting what will be happening in staging or images, and so sometimes words aren't necessary; at other times, lots of words are needed. This is why until very recently I felt that my scripts could not be produced apart from my directing them: the text by itself was to me only one instrument in an orchestra and not necessarily the one always carrying the melody. I knew that moments of intended impact would be empty if the original visual and aural supplement or counterpoint to the text was absent. All of the elements "grew up" together and depended on each other, and I couldn't see separating out one from the others without the entire system of signification just collapsing. For two or three of my texts, I believe that this will always be true; there is no point in trying to publish *Eleven Rooms of Proust* or *The Notebooks of Leonardo da Vinci* because their meaning, the *way in which they produced meaning*, is utterly dependent on all the original theatrical elements working in concert; and if I were to lard the script with the pages and pages of staging notes that tried to sequentially describe what happened simultaneously – well, it would be insufferable to read, and far too boring for anyone to try and reproduce.

I work with a lot of the same actors over and over. They've been through it all many times now, and they act as the calm old quarter horses leading the thoroughbreds – the terrified new actors – to the starting gate. It takes considerable courage for an actor to accept "any part" in an unwritten play in a highly visible venue. Much of what appears in my adaptations, both in terms of text and staging, was created to play to the strength of a particular actor. Sometimes I witness something in the halls on a break, an interaction between the actors that I kidnap and force onstage; sometimes I like to tease my actor friends with the things I make them do in the play. The *Arabian Nights* has two stories in it that were suggested by the performers because they wanted parts in them – and thank God, because they turned out great. When you do *Hamlet*, you run around the country looking for someone to be the perfect Hamlet the script seems to describe; but in this way of working – with texts that are so huge I have lots of options – I can, in part, tailor the script for the actor. I don't think this is particularly radical: I'm sure Shakespeare had some particular actor in mind when he wrote *Hamlet*. I'm sure of it. It works.

Given all of this, my pathetic ego urges me to be clear here: I do write the text. I ask the actors for all sorts of physical improvisation; I come in with the scrap of a staging idea and it is immediately unmasked as impossible or just mediocre by the actors who attempt to embody it, and they invariably improve upon it. But I write the text itself in the hours between rehearsals, trying to be attentive to where the rehearsals and the story are leading me. The most agonizing part of devising for me is the nightly casting session I have to do in my mind. I choose episodes and scenes based on my performers, and almost every night I have to commit to assigning roles for the new, emerging text. I've never had the heart to take back a role once I've given it, so I have to be very careful: often I am not writing the play in order, and so I don't know if I am using an actor too prominently in two scenes that will end up lying side by side. *Metamorphoses* ended up containing a sort of casting mistake in this way: the actor playing Phaeton turns around and plays Eros immediately after. Phaeton's is a very funny scene, and Eros's a very serious one. His first appearance as Eros (admittedly, he is naked) almost always gets a laugh, which, I believe, is because the body of the actor is carrying its comic signification over from the previous scene. There are all kinds of technical flaws like this in my work, in part because there are no first drafts, only the final script, which arrives day by day, bit by bit throughout the rehearsal process and is only completed – I always make this promise – just before going into tech. This method unfortunately results in the text that I have written early on getting hours upon hours of rehearsal – as I desperately try to stall for time – and the very last pieces to be filled feeling rushed and under-rehearsed.

The world

Given all the potential – indeed, certain – pitfalls of working like this, why do it? Why not just write the thing before you start designing and casting and all the rest? I think I've implied part of the answer above: text written in this way has an organic, potentially very powerful relationship to all the other elements of the event – the elements of design and the spirit and personality of the players. Everything is breathing together. But another reason has to do with the text remaining open to the world, part of the world, up to the last possible moment. Theater has a chance to be an art form that can respond very quickly to the events of the world if we let it. It is made up of living human beings who read the paper every day, who are leading lives both inside and outside the "drama" at all times. These people come to rehearsal and they are full of the world. If allowed, they can carry the world inside, into a text in the making that may embrace it.

When the Lookingglass Theatre and I were first devising an adaptation of fairy tales called *The Secret in the Wings*, the first Gulf War was heating up. One of the tales I was considering including, "Three Blind Queens," contained the sentence, "War broke out." In the context of the original text, this line meant nothing, was nothing. It was a plot device to get the three kings out of the picture so that adventures — the story — could happen to the three queens. But when the US forces landed in Kuwait, that line became the most important line possible. The staging and text rearranged themselves so that the first movement of the play was all about the fabulously dull and routine lives of the kings being violently interrupted. The kings spoke in unison a text that was entirely made up:

> The three kings' sons were living their lives, happily, happily living their lives: Getting up in the morning, greeting the day, shaking hands and combing their hair, going about all their princely tasks: visiting their horses and their charioteers, buying up paintings and eating food . . .

This goes on for quite a while in the same vein until the kings arrive at the phrase, "and then one day . . . " and they stop. They repeat the phrase three times, but can't seem to complete it. After a pause, they start over. They go back to the beginning of their speech, cheerfully repeating all their text and their daily tasks, but again stumble and stop on, "And then one day." This happens three times. Finally, the Evil Nursemaid, sitting on a chair fastened high up on the back wall of the theater, utters the end of the sentence — "War broke out" — and dumps a bucket of dirt, garbage, toy soldiers, and stones onto the stage floor from a height of 20 feet. Then she drops the bucket. After the noisy bucket stops rolling around, the entire company stands silent for a minute, as the lights slowly change.

On the nights we performed this in 1993, the entire audience understood what was happening. The theater — like the sweet fantasy of the fairy tale and the routine lives of the kings — had been invaded. The imaginary had been invaded by the real. In complete silence the company, the audience, the crew all shared the same thought. It was just like something else: it was like prayer.

The real reason I devise theater, instead of working from a completed script, is because I believe in the unconscious, and I believe in the will of certain texts to reach the air; and because the intensity of working this way forces me to live under the occupation of the will of these great texts and to submit to them in a way that I find ravishing. When I'm working on *The Odyssey*, or *Arabian Nights*, or the Chinese epic *Journey to the West*, I feel that my real job is to get the hell out of the way of this thing that is coming through me. I confess I have very little memory of actually writing scripts at all. I don't remember ever having done it. The pressure is so great, the time constraint so brutal, that there is no time to calculate, to reason, to justify: you just crack open. There can be no dramaturgy. You can't rely on anything other than what you already are and what the text already is, and what they are in response to each other and all the circumstances of production. There's no time to think up the polite or normal ways to express something theatrically; you have to go with the first idea you get, the one that deeply embarrasses you and that you wouldn't normally bring up, that you would censor were there time for a second thought. I have felt the will of a text asserting itself – I've felt the drive it has towards living, towards life. Musicians talk about this all of the time, that the instrument is playing them. I feel this way in rehearsal: we have all felt the palpable presence of the text entering the room. My job is to be an open door.

READER CROSS-REFERENCES

Worthen – text and authorship
Meyerhold, Barba – other dramaturgical processes
De Marinis – the importance of multiple, nonverbal elements of performance
Kaprow, Grotowski – on artistic experimentation

Part VIII

GLOBAL AND INTERCULTURAL PERFORMANCES

As we have seen, much of what we call culture is in fact performance. A community's performances reflect and embody its values, beliefs, and traditions. Moreover, the concept of performativity suggests that performance can also define and shape those values and beliefs. This explains why understanding performance is critically important in an age when the world's economic, social, cultural, and ideological systems are increasingly interconnected and interdependent. As globalization brings cultures around the world into contact with one another, traditional notions of identity and community have become both more complex and less stable. Performance offers a means to resist the transcultural homogenization of globalization, as well as a means to hasten its arrival.

In "Performing ethnography" (1986), anthropologists Victor Turner and Edie Turner describe their attempts to use performance as a means of teaching their students (and themselves) about other cultures. Rather than simply read accounts of ritual performances, the Turners and their students reenacted rituals in an attempt to gain a more immediate, experiential knowledge of the cultures that produced them. These performances were enacted with the goal of greater intercultural understanding and respect. But for some, the intercultural encounter is inherently inequitable, because one side has the power (economic or military) to dictate the terms of the exchange. In "Of mimicry and man" (1994), Homi K. Bhabha describes the dilemma of those people whose cultures were colonized by the British empire. Though the colonizers encouraged (and often required) their subjects to imitate the customs and culture of Europe, their racist ideology could not allow them to admit the colonized peoples as social equals. Hence, the colonial subject is always configured as a mimicry, an imperfect simulation of the "superior" culture.

The performance artist Guillermo Gómez-Peña further explores the perils of inter-cultural border-crossing in "Culturas-in-extremis", an essay first published as "The new global culture" (2001) and revised for inclusion in *The Performance Studies Reader*. Surveying the grotesque variety of images offered worldwide via film, television, and the internet,

Gómez-Peña describes the challenge of creating oppositional art "against the cultural backdrop of the mainstream bizarre." Another artist whose work expresses opposition to globalization is Bill Talen, aka Reverend Billy. In "Reverend Billy: preaching, protest, and post-industrial flânerie" (2002), Jill Lane describes how the charismatic minister of the "Church of Stop Shopping" uses performance to advocate against the colonization of urban space by the forces of global capitalism.

Drawing, perhaps, on the exuberant resistance of such artists, Dwight Conquergood's "Performance studies: interventions and radical research" (2002) offers a hopeful vision of how performance studies can respond to "a postcolonial world crisscrossed by transnational narratives, diaspora affiliations, and, especially, the movement and multiple migrations of people" (p. 369). Noting that "textualism" – the emphasis on what can be written down – unfairly devalues the knowledge and experience of many subjugate peoples, Conquergood advocates the embrace of performance as a means of knowledge-formation. By emphasizing the connection between artistry, analysis, and activism, performance studies can serve as a force for intercultural equality and understanding.

Finally, Diana Taylor's "Translating performance" (2003) closes this section – and this book – near where we began: with the difficulties of definition. In this excerpt from her influential book *The Archive and the Repertoire: Performing Cultural Memory in the Americas*, Taylor rehearses several arguments that we have seen earlier, but she cites them here with a specific eye toward the global and transnational flow of ideas. Reminding us that how we define our research methodology is crucial to determining the object of our analysis, Taylor celebrates performance studies as a project while pushing us to go further in examining our own assumptions about what we do and where we do it. As her experience as director of the recently formed Hemispheric Institute of Performance and Politics shows, issues of defin-ition are always bound up with issues of translation. Noting, for example, that the word "performance" has no precise analog in Spanish or Portuguese, Taylor challenges us to consider how performance studies can and must transform to meet the demands of a global and intercultural community.

37

PERFORMING ETHNOGRAPHY

Victor Turner with Edie Turner

Anthropological literature is full of accounts of dramatic episodes which vividly manifest the key values of specific cultures. Often these are case-histories of conflicts between lineages or factions, spreading into feuds, vendettas, or head-hunting expeditions. Frequently they describe how criminal behavior is defined and handled. Other accounts describe how illness and misfortune are ascribed to witchcraft or ancestral affliction and reveal tensions and stresses in the social structure. Such descriptions are richly contextualized; they are not flat narratives of successive events for they are charged with meaningfulness. The actors commonly share world-view, a kinship network, economic interests, a local past, and a system of ritual replete with symbolic objects and actions which embody a cosmology. They have lived through hard times and good times together. Culture, social experience, and individual psychology combine in complex ways in any "bit" or "strip" of human social behavior. Anthropologists have always favored the long-term, holistic study of a relatively small society, examining its institutions and their interconnections in great detail, locating the links among kinship, economic, legal, ritual, political, aesthetic, and other sociocultural systems. When they study, say, a particular performance of ritual, they are on the look-out for expressions of shared cultural understandings in behavior, as well as for manifestations of personal uniqueness.

Nevertheless, while it may be possible for a gifted researcher to demonstrate the coherence among the "parts" of a culture, the models he presents remain cognitive. Cognizing the connections, we fail to form a satisfactory impression of how another culture's members "experience" one another. For feeling and will, as well as thought, constitute the structures of culture – cultural experience, regarded both as the experience of individuals and as the collective experience of its members embodied in myths, rituals, symbols, and celebrations. For several years, as teachers of anthropology, we have been experimenting with the performance of ethnography to aid students' understanding of how people in other cultures experience the richness of their social existence, what the moral pressures are upon them, what kinds of pleasures they expect to receive as a reward for following certain patterns of action, and how they express joy, grief, deference, and affection, in accordance with cultural expectations. At the University of Virginia, with anthropology students, and at New York University, with drama students, we've taken descriptions of strips of behavior from "other cultures" and asked students to make "playscripts" from them. Then we set up workshops –

really "playshops" – in which the students try to get kinetic understandings of the "other" sociocultural groups. Often we selected either social dramas – from our own and other ethnographies – or ritual dramas (puberty rites, marriage ceremonies, potlatches, etc.), and asked the students to put them in a "play frame" – to relate what they are doing to the ethnographic knowledge they are increasingly in need of to make the scripts they use "make sense." This motivates them to study the anthropological monographs – and exposes gaps in those monographs in so far as these seem to depart from the logic of the dramatic action and interaction they have themselves purported to describe. The actors' "inside view," engendered in and through performance, becomes a powerful critique of how ritual and ceremonial structures are cognitively represented.

Today, students of social science are familiar with Bateson's concept of "frame," and Goffman's, Handelman's and others' elaborations on it, including Goffman's notions of "framebreaking," "frame slippage," and "fabricated frames." To frame is to discriminate a sector of sociocultural action from the general ongoing process of a community's life. It is often *reflexive*, in that, to "frame," a group must cut out a piece of itself for inspection (and retrospection). To do this it must create – by rules of exclusion and inclusion – a bordered space and a privileged time within which images and symbols of what has been sectioned off can be "relived," scrutinized, assessed, revalued, and, if need be, remodeled and rearranged. There are many cultural modes of framing. Each of them is a direct or indirect way of commenting on the mainstream of social existence. Some use special vocabularies, others use the common speech in uncommon ways. Some portray fictitious situations and characters which nevertheless refer pointedly to personages and problems of everyday experience. Some frames focus on matters of "ultimate concern" and fundamental ethics; these are often "ritual" frames. Others portray aspects of social life by analogy, including games of skill, strength, and chance. Other modes of "play" framing are more elaborate, including theatre and other performative genres. Some social events are contained in multiple frames, hierarchically arranged, frame within frame, with the ultimate "meaning" of the event shaped by the dominant, "encompassing" frame. Frames, in other words, are often themselves "framed." But let's not speak of "meta-frames," except in a play frame! Nevertheless, ribaldry may be the most appropriate "metalanguage" for today's play frames – as Bakhtin argues in his great defense of Rabelais and the "Rabelaisian language" he drew from "the people's second world" – in order to reinstate human good sense in a literature bedeviled by the cognitive chauvinism of intellectual establishments, secular and sacred.

Framing frames perhaps makes for intensified reflexivity. In 1981, one of our Virginia graduate students, Pamela Frese, who has been studying marriage (culturally, structurally, and in terms of social dynamics) in the Charlottesville area – usually in the official role of photographer – elected to cast the entire anthropology department as participants in a simulated or fabricated contemporary Central Virginian wedding. Edith and Victor Turner, for example, were the bride's mother and father, and the bride and groom were identified primarily because they were not in the least a "romantic item." The rest obtained kinship or friendship roles by drawing folded strips of paper from a hat – each slip describing a role: bride's sister, groom's former girlfriend, groom's father's father, bride's drunken uncle, and so on. A Department of Religious Studies graduate student was cast as the minister. Both faculty and students were involved. A "genealogy" of the families was pinned up in the department office several weeks before the event. Almost immediately people began to fantasize about their roles. One of the faculty members declared, as father of the groom, that his "side" of the wedding represented $23 million of "old New England money." This figure, he remembered, was what the heiress whom he nearly became engaged to at Yale was alleged to be worth. Victor Turner was an old proletarian Scots immigrant who made vulgar money by manufacturing a cheap, but usable, plastic garbage can, and who quoted Robbie Burns, often irrelevantly. The Lévi-Straussian principle of "binary opposition" was clearly in evidence.

The "wedding" took place in the large basement of our house at Charlottesville – the "kiva," some called it. Afterwards, there was a "reception" upstairs with a receiving line, real champagne, and festive foods. At subsequent sessions students were asked to describe or, if they wished, to write down their impressions – partly as seen from their own "real" viewpoint. The data is still coming in. Several people took photographs of the different stages of the event. Others taped conversations and registered variations in the decibel level of the group during the reception. All the materials would add up to several full length papers. Pam Frese, the original researcher, will "write up" the whole enterprise. Here, let's consider just the "nesting" of "frames" involved:

1   The encompassing frame is a *pedagogical* one – "everything within this frame is data for anthropological analysis." The formula is "let us learn."

2   Within (1) nests a play frame, with Batesonian "metamessages." (a) The messages or signals exchanged in play are in a certain sense untrue or not meant; and (b) that which is denoted by these signals is non-existent. The formula is: let us make believe.

3   Within (1) and (2) nests a ritual-script – the preparations for the wedding and a Christian form of the wedding service. If this frame had not itself been framed by the override "all this is play," the ritual frame would have had its wider cultural "moral function." Ritual says "let us believe," while play says, "this is make-believe." Without the play frame there would have been a real danger that, in terms at least of Catholic theology, a real marriage would have taken place, for here it is the couple who are the ministers of the sacrament of marriage, not the priest, whose basic role is to confer the blessings of the Church on the couple. Since ritual is "transformative," the couple would have transformed their relationship into that of spouses by the performative utterances of the nuptial liturgy. Truly to "play at" performing a ritual drama is, without suitable precautions being taken, to play with fire. But it was clear that the "serious" ritual frame was being desolemnized and demystified by its own containment in the wider play frame. A reminder of play was the reciting of a poem – an epithalamion by Sappho, in fact – before the service proper began, by a stranger to the group, though a close friend of the "bride." Of course, in a real marriage the couple's intentions are all-important. They must seriously "intend wedlock."

4   Within this frame of fabricated marriage ritual was the frame of the parapolitical structure of the University of Virginia's Department of Anthropology. This frame was

covert but genuine, fabricated like the other frames. At the "wedding reception" it was clear in the behavior of the pretended kin and friends of the groom and bride what the extant pattern was of cleavages and alliances, oppositions and coalitions, between and among faculty and students – a delicate situation we won't dwell on here. However, these artificial rufflings were minor indeed, hardly troubling a genial group of scholars. But under the protection of the play frame and simulated wedding frame, in words, gestures, conversational style, and dress, in reversals of "real-life" roles and manners, one saw everyday departmental politics as a "projective system."

As the evening progressed, frame slippage occurred more and more frequently, and people reverted to their ordinary "selves," though for a few "peak moments" – for example when the champagne cork popped – there was the sort of "ecstasy" that E. d'Aquili and C. Laughlin, in *The Spectrum of Ritual* (1979), write about – the simultaneous "firing" of cerebral and autonomic nervous systems, right brain and left brain, sympathetic and para-sympathetic. It was interesting, too, to observe which persons "stayed in role" longest and who could or could not suspend disbelief in order to play their roles properly. Some, it became clear, thought there was something sacrilegious, some profanation of their own cherished values, in enacting what for them was a religious sacrament. Others, atheists or agnostics, introduced a note of parody or irony into the ritually framed episodes. We were surprised at the wholeheartedness with which some anthropology students played their conventional roles – for example, the "bride," who in real life was having reservations about her own marriage, sewed her own bridal gown. We were also astonished at how well the students understood what phenomenological sociologists would call the "typifications" of American culture, how almost "instinctively" and "automatically" they "knew what to do next" and how to do it, in fact, how "natural" many people find it to act "ritually" given the proper stimuli, motivations, and excuse. It was interesting, too, for us to observe how some participants were almost shocked into recognizing buried aspects of themselves. Others were taken over, "possessed" by what Grathoff and Handelman have called "symbolic types" – priest, bride, bridegroom, and so on, in the domain of ritual liminality; Drunken Uncle, Pitiful Lean and Slippered Pantaloon in the play domain (the "bride's grandfather" – a student played this senile type; in the middle of the service he shouted, "Battlestations! Battlestations!" reliving old wars.)

A few comments on this performance: in practice, the hierarchical nesting of frames was overridden by the subjective responses of the actors, who evidently selected one or another of the frames as dominant. For example, the "bride" caught herself on numerous occasions following the performance talking about her "wedding" as though it was real. Others remained resolutely within the play frame; enacted creative fantasies pivoted on their chosen cultural roles. One woman remained consistently "dotty" throughout the whole ceremony, denouncing the sexual innuendoes of Solomon's *Song of Songs* in loud tones, and remaining generally objectionable during the subsequent reception and "wedding breakfast." Others kept on shifting frames, both during the performance and for some weeks after-wards; some remained "in frame" for several months and continued to call each other by kinship terms derived from the fabricated genealogy. Most participants told us that they understood the cultural structure and psychology of normative American marriage much better for having taken part in an event that combined flow with reflexivity. Some even said that the fabricated marriage was more "real" for them than marriages in the "real world" in which they had been involved.

The fabricated marriage was not our first attempt to "play" ethnography. At the University of Chicago, in seminars we ran in the Committee on Social Thought, our students put on several performances. One was a simulation of the midwinter ceremony of the Mohawk Indians of Canada, directed by David Blanchard, which involved the use of "False Face" masks, "dreaming," trancing, and prophesying. Another "ritual" was a deliberate construct of our students, led by Robert Abernathy, using van Gennep's *Rites of Passage* and Victor Turner's *Ritual Process* and *Forest of Symbols* as "cookbooks" or "how-to" protocols. This "ritual" expressed in terms of symbolic action, symbolic space, and imagery the anxieties and ordeals of Chicago graduate students. It was divided into three stages, each occupying a different space. Each participant brought along a cardboard box in which he/she had to squat, representing his/her constricted, inferior social status. There were episodes, of a sado-masochistic character, representing registration, in which the actors were continually referred between different desks, monitored by sinister rhadamanthine bureaucrats, who constantly found fault with the registrants. Another scene, using multi-media, portrayed a typical student being harangued from a lectern by an "anthropology professor" spouting technical gobbledygook (actually excerpts from published texts), while he was typing his dissertation to the accompaniment of a series of rapid slides of familiar architectural details of the University of Chicago. Finally he "died," and was solemnly buried by a group of his peers clad in black leotards. The scene then shifted from a room in the students' activities hall to a yard in the campus, where the constraining boxes were placed so as to represent a kind of Mayan pyramid which strongly resembled the new Regenstein Library, scene of so many painful graduate attempts at study. The whole group danced around the pyramid, which was set on fire. This "liminal period" was followed by a final rite in another room of the hall, where student papers that had been unfavorably commented upon by faculty were cremated in a grate; the ashes were then mixed with red wine, and two by two the students anointed one another on the brow with the mixture, symbolizing "the death of bad vibes." Finally, all joined together in chanting, "Om, Padne, Om," representing a "communitas of suffering." This production involved music, dancing, and miming, as well as dialogue. Many of the participants claimed that the performance had discharged tensions and brought the group into a deeper level of mutual understanding. It had also been "a lot of fun."

There was one curious further "real-life" development. Victor Turner was contacted by a notorious dean in charge of student discipline, who inquired whether a series of small harmless fires, started in odd corners of the Regenstein Library, could have resulted from the "ritual." He even suggested that some of the participants should be hypnotized by a university psychiatrist to elicit information about "wild-looking" people who participated in the fire dance around the symbolic Regenstein Library. Turner said it was unlikely that one of the actors was to blame for the small fires, since ritual theory suggested that such "rituals of rebellion" (in this case, a "play" rebellion) were cathartic, discharging tensions and allowing the system to function without serious contestation. He then invited the dean to the next seminar, which was an explanation by a Benedictine nun of a new script she had devised for the clothing ceremony of a postulant who would be taking her final vows. This evidently proved too much for the Irish American dean, who no doubt disapproved of Vatican II and all its "liberating" consequences, including taking liberties with the script of traditional ceremonies. Turner never heard from him again.

We have described, in some detail, in a *Kenyon Review* article, "Dramatic Ritual/Ritual Drama: Performative and Reflexive Anthropology" (1980: 80–93), how we experimented with the performance of a social drama described in Victor Turner's books *Schism and Continuity* (1957) and *The Drums of Affliction* (1968), with a mixed group of drama and anthropological students at New York University. This was our contribution to an intensive workshop devoted to exploring the interface between ritual and the theatre, between social and aesthetic drama. In subsequent sessions at NYU, we have experimented, mainly with drama students, in performing Central African and Afro-Brazilian rituals, aided by drummers drawn from the appropriate cultures or related cultures.

These ventures emboldened us to experiment further at the University of Virginia with the rendering of ethnography in a kind of instructional theatre. Our aim was not to develop a professional group of trained actors for the purposes of public entertainment. It was, frankly, an attempt to put students more fully inside the cultures they were reading about in anthropological monographs. Reading written words kowtows to the cognitive dominance of written matter and relies upon the arbitrariness of the connection between the penned or printed sign and its meaning. What we were trying to do was to put experimental flesh on these cognitive bones. We were able, fortunately, to do more than this, for we could draw upon the recent first-hand experience of returning fieldworkers. We therefore cast in the roles of director and *ethnodramaturg* anthropologists fresh from immersion in fieldwork in, for example, New Ireland and the American Northwest Coast. Students were encouraged to read available literature on these areas, and were then given roles in key ritual performances of the cultures recently studied by their returned colleagues.

One of the performances we tried to bring of was the Cannibal (Hamatsa) Dance of the sacred winter ceremonials of the Kwakiutl Indians. Here the director was Dr. Stanley Walens, an authority on the Northwest Coast, whose book *Feasting with Cannibals: An Essay on Kwakiutl Cosmology* (1981) was published shortly after the performance. Walens condensed the long series of rituals composing the Hamatsa ceremony into a short script (see Appendix). My students prepared the ceremonial space, which, again, formed part of the extensive cellarage of my house. Under Walens's guidance they made props, and improvised costumes and body decoration, including face-painting. For speeches, invocations, homilies, myth-telling, ridicule songs, and occasional bursts of competitive dialogue, Walens used Franz Boas's translations of Kwakiutl texts. Walens acted as narrator, chorus, and coordinator throughout.

A similar format was used by Mimi George, the ethnographer who had just returned from her study of Barok ritual in New Ireland. We have no space to discuss these performances in detail, but it might be useful for those who contemplate doing something similar to quote from comments made subsequently by Walens and others. Both, we think, indicate the high reflexive potential of ethnographic performance as a teaching tool,

328

essentially as a means of raising questions about the anthropological research on which they are based, but which the performances transform in the process of dramatic action.

First, then, Walens's commentary:

> The most obvious aspect of putting on the cannibal ritual was perhaps the continual feeling that it was play. The actual ritual must have been far more serious, more cataclysmic in its experiential effect on native observers than it could possibly be on non-natives. The ideas behind the ritual are so cosmic that without the associations that a native makes between those overweening social and cosmic forces, the symbols and actions of the ritual must lose much of their impact.

At the same time, the reactions of the students to the ritual did seem to imply that they picked up on the tenor and timbre of the actual ritual. The sense of aggressiveness, conflict, the controlled display of hostility and destructiveness did come across despite the constant messages from the actors that these were amateurs playing. Of course, there is a dual element of seriousness and play in all drama; one might even wonder about the use of the word "play" to refer to dramatic presentations. Indeed, rituals often seem to focus on the revelation that reality is merely a fiction, a presentation that humans make for one another. Vast secrets are revealed as being mere mechanical tricks; the spirit in the mask turns out to have the same birthmark behind his left knee as does Uncle Ralph. We may marvel at the technical ability of an Uncle Ralph or a Laurence Olivier to make us temporarily suspend belief that we are watching them (indeed that may be the most cogent marvel of drama as a whole) and for a moment to see only a Hamlet, or a cannibal bird, or a Willie Loman. We might ask why that most cosmic of modern plays, *Waiting for Godot*, seems to be one in which the action consists solely of play activity, activity in which all the conventional dramatic moments are negated by statements of their irreality. Contrast how Beckett handles suicide with the way Chekhov or Ibsen does.

In short, the problems encountered in putting on an ethnographic performance are not by nature different from those that an opera or drama director would face. In fact, while preparing the Kwakiutl ritual, I was continually made aware of just how much preparation, training, rehearsal, how many years of stockpiling the paraphernalia, the foods for the feast, the validating gifts, how much patience in achieving the requisite status must have gone into such native ceremonies. Kwakiutl ceremonies are long – the winter ceremonial season lasts as long as four months, consisting of daily ritual activities in hundreds of varieties, all complexly interrelated, and all of which alter the statuses of the participants so that subsequent rituals must take account of the newly acquired or divested statuses of everyone else in the society. We prepared only a minimal amount of food and paraphernalia, and had only the merest mote of performance, yet the amount of preparation time and rehearsal time was tremendous. The amount of camaraderie that arose among us was also astounding; I was not particularly friendly with the people who helped with the preparations before the class, but since then have felt much closer toward them. Perhaps one of the most important aspects of dramatic presentation is the way in which the mutual performance of a fiction unites all its creators.

Another matter is that of performers versus audience. In one sense, we were all the audience for this ritual. The Hamatsa ritual now exists only in a printed form; we tried to approximate this form as much as possible. It was therefore quite unlike the production of a play, where there is a movement toward breathing new life into a form. By nature, living rituals seem to be ever changing. To perform a ritual the same way twice is to kill it, for the ritual grows as we grow, its life recapitulates the course of ours. It becomes the symbol for the society itself. Just as the experimental theatre directors of the sixties and seventies rebelled against the strictures of our society by contravening those strictures in their performance texts, so do Kwakiutl see the cannibal ritual as a symbol of the life and death of their culture, and mourn the demise of their culture in mourning the demise of its ceremonies. Our play presentation then can be seen as a representation of the modern view of primitive ritual as a whole – that it is slightly, if not completely, foolish, that it is primarily a social act, that it is play-acting.

We imagine our own view of the Kwakiutl is the same as their view of themselves. The meaning of the ritual for them is forever unapproachable by us. We experience only the ritual we perform, the one that actually takes place between a group of students, colleagues, and friends in the basement of a house in Charlottesville in December 1981. If we rejoice in our common experience, well and good. We have put on a play, we compare notes, and wait for the reviews. As in any play, we reaffirm, through this particular fiction communally performed, truths communally experienced. We must also question the validity of *that* experience. The situation is not unlike that in which a Plains Indian presents his vision, gained on a solitary quest, to a committee of elders who review it and give it their stamp of approval, or when a ritual of fecundity is given validity through subsequent bestowal of approval by the relevant deific elders. The reviews are important, as important as the production itself, for they define the commonality of the experience.

I wonder if I would have asked these questions about the nature of performance if I hadn't had to put one on. I certainly feel much more aware of the nature of performance *per se* than I did before. It becomes easy to see the messages embedded in rituals that remind the audience that this is a performance – the little skits in the cannibal ritual, or the overblown speeches, the constant revelations by dancers of their human identities. There is an interesting paradox here – in Western drama, the performer's technique should be so good that he conveys through the maximum of artifice the greatest amount of naturalness to his stage character. Both poor mastery of technique and overpresentation of the emotions themselves ("hamming") detract from the illusion of balance between contrivedness and spontaneity that makes for convincing dramatic presentation. Since stage gestures bear no relation to everyday gestures, having by nature to communicate over distances far greater than those normally used in gestural communication, the illusion of naturalness is possible only with carefully controlled artifice. In the cannibal dance too there must be this balance – the cannibal dancer must convey through the balanced use of gesture and action the feeling that he is going to destroy the people in the room. He must make them fear for themselves – is this not the purpose of all drama – by striking a balance between natural human motion and alien motion.

I have often wondered how to convey to my classes an emotion that would be similar in character and degree to that which the audience at a cannibal dance might feel when the cannibal first appears. How do you convey to people that the instrument of their own deaths is present in the room? My classes know me as a cream puff, so I could never begin to pretend to be the type of psychopathic villain that might, in our society's mythology, strike fear into their hearts; I have not prepared them to expect it from me, nor do I possess the acting ability to convey it to them. I think this the most important facet of the cannibal dance — the confrontation each person has with his own death in a living embodiment — and can only feel that it was not conveyed in our play ritual. Douglas Dalton, one of the participating students, giving a somewhat different view, wrote:

> As the ceremony progressed I felt not so much the antagonistic rivalry that was overtly expressed in the ceremony between the bear clan and the killer whale clan, but the fact that we were collectively doing something really important — something essentially correct. There was so much power flowing all over the place in the longhouse [the Charlottesville basement] that night! The spirits were really at work that evening and we had to keep everything in line so all that power wouldn't destroy everything!

The Kwakiutl used to enhance the destructiveness of cannibal dancers, putting on demonstrations of death by using masks, bladders full of blood, and the like. To the audience these must have been very effective; and, of course, there were times when people were really killed.

I keep coming back to this one issue — the nature of artifice and fiction in play performance. I think this is what people in the seminar were most aware of, a universal of drama, not the particular ritual we performed. I also think the questions that lie at the foundation of theatre and theatrical performance lie at the foundation of ritual and ritual performance — questions about the relationship of actors to text, of actors to audience, or fiction to fictive reality, and so on. I have no doubt that the students see some of the dramatic nature of the cannibal ritual — dramatic in both senses of the word: it is effective and it is theatre — and that they can now read ethnography and introject those feelings of theatre into the dry accounts of dances and songs and spirit names which anthropologists have written down. I have breathed life into Kwakiutl ritual just as a director breathes life into a play — but I have done it independently of the intentions of the Kwakiutl authors, just as a play production is independent of the intentions of the play's author.

One has the feeling that rituals are magical, that for some reason as yet unknown to science they can communicate to people, not despite their artificiality, but because of and through their artificiality. Rituals are efficacious and we wonder how. Just as we know that a good stage magician is performing tricks — that is, really not levitating that elephant or sawing that woman in half — we still marvel at the beauty of the illusion and the mastery with which it is presented; so we marvel at the mastery of illusion in ritual while we reaffirm its illusionary nature.

It's obvious from all this that I've been thinking about the question of doubt, in an Augustinian sense, as the basis of ritual. In the chart of frames, each of the inner levels presents more doubt of the outer levels, each contravenes and obviates the outer levels. It is not that religion is so much a statement of belief but that at its most effective it enables us to suspend disbelief in the things that are larger than ourselves, whether they be deities or nature or history or the sacred corpus of anthropological theory. Just as at a ritual we may have had a momentary inkling that there was something greater present than simply a bunch of people playing at ceremony, so in our acting of the cannibal dance we have an inkling of something which transcends the limitations of a particular moment in the history of the anthropology department at the University of Virginia. Compare this finale with Dalton's leap into what he took to be the Kwakiutl view of the Hamatsa ceremony:

> The ritual ended, in fact, with the assurance that the Kwakiutl would continue to keep the world in order in a pledge for next year's ceremony. The bitter rivalry that was expressed in the early parts of the ceremony gave way to a final reconciliation and a true feeling of oneness with the forces of the universe.

Perhaps this is the critical difference between aesthetic theatre and ritual – the actors on stage must always seem to be the characters they portray or they have failed; the ritualist must always seem to be nothing other than what he is, a frail human being playing with those things that kill us for their sport. Stage drama is about the extrapolation of the individual into alien roles and personalities; ritual drama is about the complete delimitation, the total definition of person.

Unlike Walens, Mimi George insisted that the participants in the Barok initiation ritual were not to be instructed in the culture and social structure, but rather assigned ritual roles without preparation. This, in the words of one of the participants, Jean-Jacques Decoster, "provided the feeling of magic that prevailed most of the evening . . . We went through a rite, and didn't just enact a 'savage ritual.' When I went home that evening and my housemates asked me about the stripes painted on my face, my answer was: 'I have just been initiated.'" Mimi George, the director, dramaturg, and fieldworker who prepared the scenario, told us that, despite the alienness of the context, the students were "caught up into the meaning and worth of the ritual." Indeed, she was surprised by the similarity of their performance to its Papuan original. However, she felt that she had not given the actors sufficiently detailed guidance, and was continually beset by the cry, "What do I do now?" What this ritual did bring off was a kind of existential "double-take." At one point the "initiands" beat the Tubuan masked figure. It was then revealed that inside it was merely a human being (in this case Victor Turner). But later, in the garden, in darkness and simulated firelight, the Tubuan glided in unexpectedly to the beat of drums. The demystified "spirit" was dramatically remystified. Decoster notes,

> The moment of greatest intensity was the outdoor ceremony . . . I felt definitely uneasy when we initiands were lined up and facing away from the entity, and it was not Eric (the dancer within the Tubuan) I was turning my back upon, but truly the Tubuan, an unknown and decidedly scary being. In a curious way, the ritual flogging (administered to the initiands by the 'elders') worked as a tension reliever.

Other "initiands" commented on how close they felt to one another as against the uninitiated and already initiated.

We have a thick file of such comments on these and other performances of rituals in other cultures. On the whole they are enthusiastic and encouraging, though not a few echo Waltens's skepticism about whether any culture can be adequately translated into the action-language of another. For our own part, we have not reached any definite conclusions as to the merits of this performative approach to ethnography. Whenever our classes have performed scripts based on our own fieldwork among the Ndembu of Zambia in Central Africa we have undoubtedly learned something about that culture that we failed to understand in the field. For example, when we enacted the girl's puberty ceremony (in which the novice is wrapped completely in a blanket, laid at the foot of the symbolic "milk tree," and is compelled to remain motionless for a long period of time, while a large group of initiated village women dance and sing around her) we were later presented with the following account of her subjective impressions by Linda Camino, the student taking the role of *Kankang'a* (novice, initiand; literally, "guinea fowl").

> Around and around they danced, again and again with punctuated cries and claps. Beneath the blanket I lay still and quiet, firm and "cool," patiently awaiting the next stage, which I knew would be to escort me to my seclusion hut. Then a strange thing happened. Time lengthened, expanded, and my wait seemed interminable, for as the singing and cries of the women grew lustier, as the pulsation of their feet and hands quickened to the driving beat of the insistent drums, I began to fear that they had quite forgotten all about me, guinea fowl. They were having fun; I was not. The drums beckoned me. Their wrenching beats filled my muscles with tension, demanding a response, a response I could not give as guinea fowl. The women's enthusiasm and boisterous cheers challenged me to spring out from the blanket to join them. At this point, a desire to be like those other women, a desire to move my body freely to the sounds of the drums overwhelmed me. I longed to be a woman — alive, vital, responding, moving; not a dull guinea fowl, still before a tree, unseen, stationary, alone.

We were aware of the ambivalence with which pubescent girls had regarded the passage to adult social status, but Camino's comments suggested a hypothesis about how the ritual might have motivated a real Ndembu novice not merely to accept but to strongly desire her new status-role and membership in a community of wives and mothers. Such a hypothesis would have to be tested out, of course, in further field research, but the fact that a simulated ritual could raise it is at least one persuasive argument in favor of performed ethnography. In our experience the most effective kind of performed ethnography is not the simulation of a ritual or a ceremony torn from its cultural context, but a series of "acts" and "scenes" based on detailed observations of processes of conflict.

Rituals, like law cases, should not be abstracted from the frameworks of the ongoing social process in which they were originally embedded. They have their source and *raison d'être* in the ceaseless flow of social life, and in the social dramas within which communities seek to contain that life. By posing the functionally familiar against the culturally exotic in the dynamics of social drama, we can make our students vividly aware both of innate commonalities and of cultural differences in relation to a wide range of human societies. Our recommendation, then, is this: If we attempt to perform ethnography, let us not begin with such apparently "exotic" and "bizarre" cultural phenomena as rituals and myths. Such an emphasis may only encourage prejudice, since it stresses the "otherness of the other." Let us focus first on what all people share, the social drama form, from which emerge all types of cultural performance, which, in their turn, subtly stylize the contours of social interaction in everyday life. In practice, this means setting apart a substantial block of time to familiarize students with the culture and social system of the group whose dramas they will enact. Such instruction should be interwoven with what Richard Schechner might call "the rehearsal process." The resultant instructional form could be a kind of synthesis between an anthropological seminar and a postmodern theatrical workshop. The data should be scripted; costumes, masks, stage settings, and other props should be made carefully, with an eye to cultural authenticity (though heavy-handed realism may not be appropriate). It is highly desirable, whenever possible, to bring in a member of the group studied as a dramaturg or director – or someone in the group who has done fieldwork should be dramaturg or director. We have found that students greatly enjoy these detailed, technical preliminaries. We have also found that nearly all the rituals we have performed involve at least one episode of feasting. If possible, the foods used in the original setting should be provided, cooked in the traditional ways. Foods, food taboos, and ways in which food is shared and exchanged make up a kind of cultural grammar and vocabulary which often give clues, when their symbolism is decoded, to basic attitudes and values of the group and to its social structure.

At least one session should be allocated to a close review of all aspects of the performance seen in retrospect. This should include subjective statements by the actors, the director, the dramaturg, and members of the audience if an audience was thought necessary. Much of the emphasis will be found to be on cultural differences, and the difficulties and delights of playing roles generated by cultures often far different from our own. In these occasions of intercultural reflexivity, we can begin to grasp something of the contribution each and every human culture can make to the general pool of manifested knowledge of our common human condition. It is in dramatics and dynamics most of all that we learn to coexperience the lives of our conspecifics, "our brother man and sister woman," to quote the great bard of Victor Turner's own Scottish culture, Robert Burns.

APPENDIX

Hamatsa (cannibal) ceremony

Meals and covenantal songs
Cries and whistles heard from woods (hamatsas and all helpers)

Ghost dancer appears

Mentions death, excites old hamatsas and spirit retinue

Hamatsas enter from all over – dance four times around fire

new initiate appears – enters excitedly, circles fire four times; he is now very wild, dressed only in hemlock, with no restraining clothes; comes from upper level

People try to encircle hamatsa; he is too wild, enters sacred room, sheds some hemlock branches – burned

Discussion of why hamatsa has escaped

Confession of sins and analysis of ceremonial errors; must be corrected by pledging potlatches, becoming a hamatsa's victim, or becoming an intiate; records are kept of who agrees to be a victim

Adjournment – repurification through smoke

Setting of trap for hamatsa

Hemlock neckring made; all carry hemlock; old man put in center as bait; hamatsa escapes three times – on fourth time all join hands and he is captured; all sing taming songs

Family of hamatsa is on steps of house – acknowledge their pledges

Hamatsa will not enter house – women dance before him enticingly to no avail, entice him with bones and mummified flesh

Screen is set up – hamatsa goes to sacred room

Hamatsa returns

goes counterclockwise four times around fire, each time holding a victim's arm in his mouth and pulling him along; more taming songs, unsuccessful

All hemlock removed, burned

Distribution of property; display of coppers

All spirits appear to dance – faces black; eagle down in their hair and put around the room (carried in dishes like food)

Hamatsa appears

Dances around fire – reappears dressed in cedarbark clothing, a new piece added each time he reappears

House is totally shut up, no chinks or light from outside

Burning of cedar bark

Smoldering bark passed over head of dancer; everyone says "hoip, hoip"; much loud drumming, very rhythmic

Hamatsa dances, squatting and turning

Four more days of ceremony follow, during which time no one enters or leaves the house; no food is served; there is constant singing of power songs

Hamatsa appears wearing cedar bark only

a simulacrum of him is washed and ritually treated, then smoked

Hamatsa still trembles

women sing their most powerful songs simultaneously while men sing songs of wildness

A bloody menstrual napkin from the hamatsa's mother is burned he is made to inhale the smoke; he immediately collapses and has to be carried from the room

Someone has to pledge next year's ceremonials

The ceremonials end.

REFERENCES

d'Aquili, Eugeng, C. Laughlin, and John McManus, eds. (1979) *The Spectrum of Ritual*, New York: Columbia University Press.

Turner, Victor (1957) *Schism and Continuity*, Manchester: Manchester University Press.

—— (1968) *The Drums of Affliction*, Oxford: Clarendon.

—— (1980) "Dramatic ritual/ritual drama: performative and reflexive anthropology," *Kenyon Review* 1, 3: 80–93. Reprinted in *From Ritual the Theatre* by Victor Turner, New York: Performing Arts Journal Publications, 1982.

Walens, Stanley (1981) *Feasting with Cannibals*, Princeton: Princeton University Press.

READER CROSS-REFERENCES

Turner – co-author

Schechner – close collaborator

Worthen – discusses the Turners' practice of ritual reenactment

Goffman, Bateson – significant influences

Fabian, Conquergood – performance as a means toward intercultural understanding

Santino – cites an example of ritual reenactment

38

OF MIMICRY AND MAN

Homi K. Bhabha

> Mimicry reveals something in so far as it is distinct from what might be called an itself that is behind. The effect of mimicry is camouflage. . . . It is not a question of harmonizing with the background, but against a mottled background, of becoming mottled – exactly like the technique of camouflage practiced in human warfare.
>
> Jacques Lacan, "The line and light," *Of the Gaze*[1]

> It is out of season to question at this time of day, the original policy of a conferring on every colony of the British Empire a mimic representation of the British Constitution. But if the creature so endowed has sometimes forgotten its real significance and under the fancied importance of speakers and maces, and all the paraphernalia and ceremonies of the imperial legislature, has dared to defy the mother country, she has to thank herself for the folly of conferring such privileges on a condition of society that has no earthly claim to so exalted a position. A fundamental principle appears to have been forgotten or overlooked in our system of colonial policy – that of colonial dependence. To give to a colony the forms of independence is a mockery; she would not be a colony for a single hour if she could maintain an independent station.
>
> Sir Edward Cust, "Reflections on West African affairs . . . addressed to the Colonial Office", Hatchard, London, 1839

The discourse of post-Enlightenment English colonialism often speaks in a tongue that is forked, not false. If colonialism takes power in the name of history, it repeatedly exercises its authority through the figures of farce. For the epic intention of the civilizing mission, "human and not wholly human" in the famous words of Lord Rosebery, "writ by the finger of the Divine"[2] often produces a text rich in the traditions of *trompe-l'œil*, irony, mimicry, and repetition. In this comic turn from the high ideals of the colonial imagination to its low mimetic literary effects mimicry emerges as one of the most elusive and effective strategies of colonial power and knowledge.

Within that conflictual economy of colonial discourse which Edward Said[3] describes as the tension between the synchronic panoptical vision of domination – the demand for identity, stasis – and the counterpressure of the diachrony of history – change, difference –

mimicry represents an *ironic* compromise. If I may adapt Samuel Weber's formulation of the marginalizing vision of castration,[4] then colonial mimicry is the desire for a reformed, recognizable Other, *as a subject of a difference that is almost the same, but not quite*. Which is to say, that the discourse of mimicry is constructed around an *ambivalence*; in order to be effective, mimicry must continually produce its slippage, its excess, its difference. The authority of that mode of colonial discourse that I have called mimicry is therefore stricken by an indeterminacy: mimicry emerges as the representation of a difference that is itself a process of disavowal. Mimicry is thus the sign of double articulation; a complex strategy of reform, regulation, and discipline, which "appropriates" the Other as it visualizes power. Mimicry is also the sign of the inappropriate, however, a difference or recalcitrance which coheres the dominant strategic function of colonial power, intensifies surveillance, and poses an immanent threat to both "normalized" knowledges and disciplinary powers.

The effect of mimicry on the authority of colonial discourse is profound and disturbing. For in "normalizing" the colonial state or subject, the dream of post-Enlightenment civility alienates its own language of liberty and produces another knowledge of its norms. The ambivalence which thus informs this strategy is discernible, for example, in Locke's Second Treatise, which *splits* to reveal the limitations of liberty in his double use of the word "slave": first, simply descriptively as the locus of a legitimate form of ownership, then as the trope for an intolerable, illegitimate exercise of power. What is articulated in that distance between the two uses is the absolute, imagined difference between the "Colonial" State of Carolina and the Original State of Nature.

It is from this area between mimicry and mockery, where the reforming, civilizing mission is threatened by the displacing gaze of its disciplinary double, that my instances of colonial imitation come. What they all share is a discursive process by which the excess or slippage produced by the *ambivalence* of mimicry (almost the same, *but not quite*) does not merely "rupture" the discourse, but becomes transformed into an uncertainty which fixes the colonial subject as a "partial" presence. By "partial" I mean both "incomplete" and "virtual." It is as if the very emergence of the "colonial" is dependent for its representation upon some strategic limitation or prohibition *within* the authoritative discourse itself. The success of colonial appropriation depends on a proliferation of inappropriate objects that ensure its strategic failure, so that mimicry is at once resemblance and menace.

A classic text of such partiality is Charles Grant's "Observations on the state of society among the Asiatic subjects of Great Britain" (1792)[5] which was only superseded by James Mills's *History of India* as the most influential early nineteenth-century account of Indian manners and morals. Grant's dream of an evangelical system of mission education conducted uncompromisingly in the English language was partly a belief in political reform along Christian lines and partly an awareness that the expansion of company rule in India required a system of subject formation – a reform of manners, as Grant put it – that would provide the colonial with "a sense of personal identity as we know it." Caught between the desire for religious reform and the fear that the Indians might become turbulent for liberty, Grant paradoxically implies that it is the "partial" diffusion of Christianity and the "partial" influence of moral improvements which will construct a particularly appropriate form of colonial subjectivity. What is suggested is a process of reform through which Christian doctrines might collude with divisive caste practices to prevent dangerous political alliances. Inadvertently, Grant produces a knowledge of Christianity as a form of social control which conflicts with the enunciatory assumptions that authorize his discourse. In suggesting, finally, that "partial reform" will produce an empty form of "the *imitation* [my emphasis] of English manners which will induce them [the colonial subjects] to remain under our protection."[6] Grant mocks his moral project and violates the Evidence of Christianity – a central missionary tenet – which forbade any tolerance of heathen faiths.

The absurd extravagance of Macaulay's "Minute" (1835) – deeply influenced by Charles Grant's "Observations" – makes a mockery of Oriental learning until faced with the challenge of conceiving of a "reformed" colonial subject. Then, the great tradition of European humanism seems capable only of ironizing itself. At the intersection of European learning and colonial power, Macaulay can conceive of nothing other than "a class of interpreters between us and the millions whom we govern – a class of persons Indian in blood and colour, but English in tastes, in opinions, in morals and in intellect"[7] – in other words a mimic man raised "through our English School", as a missionary educationist wrote in 1819, "to form a corps of translators and be employed in different departments of Labour."[8] The line of descent of the mimic man can be traced through the works of Kipling, Forster, Orwell, Naipaul, and to his emergence, most recently, in Benedict Anderson's excellent work on nationalism, as the anomalous Bipin Chandra Pal.[9] He is the effect of a flawed colonial mimesis, in which to be Anglicized is *emphatically* not to be English.

The figure of mimicry is locatable within what Anderson describes as "the inner compatibility of empire and nation."[10] It problematizes the signs of racial and cultural priority, so that the "national" is no longer naturalizable. What emerges between mimesis and mimicry is a *writing*, a mode of representation, that marginalizes the monumentality of history, quite simply mocks its power to be a model, that power which supposedly makes it imitable. Mimicry *repeats* rather than *re-presents* and in that diminishing perspective emerges Decoud's displaced European vision of Sulaco in Conrad's *Nostromo* as:

> The endlessness of civil strife where folly seemed even harder to bear than its ignominy . . . the lawlessness of a populace of all colours and races, barbarism, irremediable tyranny. . . . America is ungovernable.[11]

Or Ralph Singh's apostasy in Naipaul's *The Mimic Men*:

> We pretended to be real, to be learning, to be preparing ourselves for life, we mimic men of the New World, one unknown corner of it, with all its reminders of the corruption that came so quickly to the new.[12]

Both Decoud and Singh, and in their different ways Grant and Macaulay, are the parodists of history. Despite their intentions and invocations they inscribe the colonial text erratically, eccentrically across a body politic that refuses to be representative, in a narrative that refuses to be representational. The desire to emerge as "authentic" through mimicry – through a process of writing and repetition – is the final irony of partial representation.

What I have called mimicry is not the familiar exercise of *dependent* colonial relations through narcissistic identification so that, as Fanon has observed,[13] the black man stops being an actional person for only the white man can represent his self-esteem. Mimicry conceals no presence or identity behind its mask: it is not what Césaire describes as "colonization-thingification"[14] behind which there stands the essence of the *présence Africaine*. The *menace* of mimicry is its *double* vision, which in disclosing the ambivalence of colonial discourse also disrupts its authority. And it is a double vision that is a result of what I've described as the partial representation/recognition of the colonial object. Grant's colonial as partial imitator, Macaulay's translator, Naipaul's colonial politician as play-actor, Decoud as the scene setter of the *opera bouffe* of the New World, these are the appropriate objects of a colonialist chain of command, authorized versions of otherness. But they are also, as I have shown, the figures of a doubling, the part-objects of a metonymy of colonial desire which alienates the modality and normality of those dominant discourses in which they emerge as "inappropriate" colonial subjects. A desire that, through the repetition of *partial presence*, which is the basis of mimicry, articulates those disturbances of cultural, racial, and historical difference that menace the narcissistic demand of colonial authority. It is a desire that reverses "in part" the colonial appropriation by now producing a partial vision of the colonizer's presence; a gaze of otherness, that shares the acuity of the genealogical gaze which, as Foucault describes it, liberates marginal elements and shatters the unity of man's being through which he extends his sovereignty.[15]

I want to turn to this process by which the look of surveillance returns as the displacing gaze of the disciplined, where the observer becomes the observed, and "partial" representation rearticulates the whole notion of *identity* and alienates it from essence. But not before observing that even an exemplary history like Eric Stokes's *The English Utilitarians and India* acknowledges the anomalous gaze of otherness but finally disavows it in a contradictory utterance:

> Certainly India played *no* central part in fashioning the distinctive qualities of English civilization. In many ways it acted as a disturbing force, a magnetic power placed at the periphery tending to distort the natural development of Britain's character.[16]
>
> (My emphasis)

What is the nature of the hidden threat of the partial gaze? How does mimicry emerge as the subject of the scopic drive and the object of colonial surveillance? How is desire disciplined, authority displaced?

If we turn to a Freudian figure to address these issues of colonial textuality, that form of difference that is mimicry – *almost the same but not quite* – will become clear. Writing of the partial nature of fantasy, caught, *inappropriately*, between the unconscious and the preconscious, making problematic, like mimicry, the very notion of "origins," Freud has this to say:

> Their mixed and split origin is what decides their fate. We may compare them with individuals of mixed race who taken all round resemble white men but who betray

their coloured descent by some striking feature or other and on that account are excluded from society and enjoy none of the privileges.[17]

Almost the same but not white: the visibility of mimicry is always produced at the site of interdiction. It is a form of colonial discourse that is uttered *inter dicta*: a discourse at the crossroads of what is known and permissible and that which though known must be kept concealed; a discourse uttered between the lines and as such both against the rules and within them. The question of the representation of difference is therefore always also a problem of authority. The "desire" of mimicry, which is Freud's "striking feature" that reveals so little but makes such a big difference, is not merely that impossibility of the Other which repeatedly resists signification. The desire of colonial mimicry – an interdictory desire – may not have an object, but it has strategic objectives which I shall call the *metonymy of presence*.

Those inappropriate signifiers of colonial discourse – the difference between being English and being Anglicized; the identity between stereotypes which, through repetition, also become different; the discriminatory identities constructed across traditional cultural norms and classifications, the Simian Black, the Lying Asiatic – all these are *metonymies* of presence. They are strategies of desire in discourse that make the anomalous representation of the colonized something other than a process of "the return of the repressed," what Fanon unsatisfactorily characterized as collective catharsis.[18] These instances of metonymy are the non-repressive productions of contradictory and multiple belief. They cross the boundaries of the culture of enunciation through a strategic confusion of the metaphoric and metonymic axes of the cultural production of meaning.

In mimicry, the representation of identity and meaning is rearticulated along the axis of metonymy. As Lacan reminds us, mimicry is like camouflage, not a harmonization of repression of difference, but a form of resemblance, that differs from or defends presence by displaying it in part, metonymically. Its threat, I would add, comes from the prodigious and strategic production of conflictual, fantastic, discriminatory "identity effects" in the play of a power that is elusive because it hides no essence, no "itself." And that form of *resemblance* is the most terrifying thing to behold, as Edward Long testifies in his *History of Jamaica* (1774). At the end of a tortured, negrophobic passage that shifts anxiously between piety, prevarication and perversion, the text finally confronts its fear; nothing other than the repetition of its resemblance "in part": "[Negroes] are represented by all authors as the vilest of human kind, to which they have little more pretension of resemblance *than what arises from their exterior forms*" (my emphasis).[19]

From such a colonial encounter between the white presence and its black semblance, there emerges the question of the ambivalence of mimicry as a problematic of colonial subjection. For if Sade's scandalous theatricalization of language repeatedly reminds us that discourse can claim "no priority," then the work of Edward Said will not let us forget that the "ethnocentric and erratic will to power from which texts can spring"[20] is itself a theater of war. Mimicry, as the metonymy of presence is, indeed, such an erratic, eccentric strategy of authority in colonial discourse. Mimicry does not merely destroy narcisstic authority through the repetitious slippage of difference and desire. It is the process of the *fixation* of the colonial as a form of cross-classificatory, discriminatory knowledge within an interdictory discourse, and therefore necessarily raises the question of the *authorization* of colonial representations; a question of authority that goes beyond the subject's lack of priority (castration) to a historical crisis in the conceptuality of colonial man as an *object* of regulatory power, as the subject of racial, cultural, national representation.

"This culture . . . fixed in its colonial status," Fanon suggests, "[is] both present and mummified, it testified against its members. It defines them in fact without appeal."[21] The ambivalence of mimicry – almost but not quite – suggests that the fetishized colonial culture is potentially and strategically an insurgent counter-appeal. What I have called its "identity-effects" are always crucially *split*. Under cover of camouflage, mimicry, like the fetish, is a part-object that radically revalues the normative knowledges of the priority of race, writing, history. For the fetish mimes the forms of authority at the point at which it deauthorizes them. Similarly, mimicry rearticulates presence in terms of its "otherness," that which it disavows. There is a crucial difference between this *colonial* articulation of man and his doubles and that which Foucault describes as "thinking the unthought,"[22] which, for nineteenth-century Europe, is the ending of man's alienation by reconciling him with his essence. The colonial discourse that articulates an *interdictory* otherness is precisely the "other scene" of this nineteenth-century European desire for an authentic historical consciousness.

The "unthought" across which colonial man is articulated is that process of classificatory confusion that I have described as the metonymy of the substitutive chain of ethical and cultural discourse. This results in the *splitting* of colonial discourse so that two attitudes towards external reality persist; one takes reality into consideration while the other disavows it and replaces it with a product of desire that repeats, rearticulates "reality" as mimicry.

So Edward Long can say with authority, quoting variously Hume, Eastwick, and Bishop Warburton in his support, that: "Ludicrous as the opinion may seem I do not think that an orangutang husband would be any dishonour to a Hottentot female."[23]

Such contradictory articulations of reality and desire – seen in racist stereotypes, statements, jokes, myths – are not caught in the doubtful circle of the return of the repressed. They are the effects of a disavowal that denies the differences of the other but produces in its stead forms of authority and multiple belief that alienate the assumptions of "civil" discourse. If, for a while, the ruse of desire is calculable for the uses of discipline, soon the repetition of guilt, justification, pseudo-scientific theories, superstition, spurious authorities, and classifications can be seen as the desperate effort to "normalize" *formally* the disturbance of a discourse of splitting that violates the rational, enlightened claims of its enunciatory modality. The ambivalence of colonial authority repeatedly turns from *mimicry* – a difference that is almost nothing but not quite – to *menace* – a difference that is almost total but not quite. And in that other scene of colonial power, where history turns to farce and presence to "a part," can be seen the twin figures of narcissism and paranoia that repeat furiously, uncontrollably.

In the ambivalent world of the "not quite/not white," on the margins of metropolitan desire, the *founding objects* of the Western world become the erratic, eccentric, accidental *objets trouvés* of the colonial discourse – the part-objects of presence. It is then that the body and the book lose their part-objects of presence. It is then that the body and the book lose their representational authority. Black skin splits under the racist gaze, displaced into signs of bestiality, genitalia, grotesquerie, which reveal the phobic myth of the undifferentiated whole white body. And the holiest of books – the Bible – bearing both the standard of the cross and the standard of empire, finds itself strangely dismembered. In May 1817 a missionary wrote from Bengal:

> Still everyone would gladly receive a Bible. And why? – that he may lay it up as a curiosity for a few pice; or use it for waste paper. Such it is well known has been the common fate of these copies of the Bible. . . . Some have been bartered in the markets, others have been thrown in snuff shops and used as wrapping paper.[24]

NOTES

1 J. Lacan, "The line and the light," in his *The Four Fundamental Concepts of Psychoanalysis*, Alan Sheridan (trans.) (London: The Hogarth Press and the Institute of Psycho-Analysis, 1977), 99.

2 Cited in E. Stokes, *The Political Ideas of English Imperialism* (Oxford: Oxford University Press, 1960), 17–18.

3 E. Said, *Orientalism* (New York: Pantheon Books, 1978), 240.

4 S. Weber, "The sideshow, or: remarks on a canny moment," *Modern Language Notes* 88, 6 (1973), 112.

5 C. Grant, "Observations on the state of society among the Asiatic subjects of Great Britain," *Sessional Papers of the East India Company*, X, 282 (1812–13).

6 Ibid., chapter 4, 104.

7 T.B. Macualay, "Minute on education," in W. Theodore de Bary (ed.) *Sources of Indian Tradition*, vol. II (New York: Columbia University Press, 1958), 49.

8 Mr. Thomason's communication to the Church Missionary Society, 5 September 1819, in *The Missionary Register*, 1821, 54–5.

9 B. Anderson, *Imagined Communities* (London: Verso, 1983), 88.

10 Ibid., chapter 4, 104.

11 J. Conrad, *Nostromo* (London: Penguin, 1979), 161.

12 V.S. Naipaul, *The Mimic Men* (London: Penguin, 1967), 146.

13 F. Fanon, *Black Skin, White Masks* (London: Paladin, 1970), 109.

14 A. Césaire, *Discourse on Colonialism* (New York: Monthly Review Press, 1972), 21.

15 M. Foucault, "Nietzsche, genealogy, history," in his *Language, Counter-Memory, Practice*, D.F. Bouchard and S. Simon (trans.) (Ithaca: Cornell University Press, 1977), 153.

16 E. Stokes, *The English Utilitarians and India* (Oxford: Oxford University Press, 1959), xi.

17 S. Freud, "The unconscious" (1915), *SE*, xiv, 190–1.

18 Fanon, *Black Skin, White Masks*, 103.

19 E. Long, *A History of Jamaica*, 1774, vol. II, 353.

20 E. Said, "The text, the world, the critic," in J.V. Harari (ed.) *Textual Strategies* (Ithaca: Cornell University Press, 1979), 184.

21 F. Fanon, "Racism and culture," in his *Toward the African Revolution*, H. Chevalier (trans.) (London: Pelican, 1967), 44.

22 M. Foucault, *The Order of Things* (New York: Pantheon Books, 1971), part II, chapter 9.

23 Long, *History of Jamaica*, 364.
24 *The Missionary Register*, May 1817, 186.

READER CROSS-REFERENCES

Goffman – belief in social roles

Butler – the performative constitution of identity *vis-à-vis* gender

Harding – describes a colonized people performing for the entertainment of Europeans

Gómez-Peña – globalization and racist discourse

Lane – performance artist Reverend Billy's response to colonization of urban spaces by global capital

Conquergood – performance and colonized or oppressed peoples

Derrida – citation may be understood as an underlying element of mimicry

39

CULTURAS-IN-EXTREMIS

Performing against the cultural backdrop of the mainstream bizarre

Guillermo Gómez-Peña

"You may now experience anything you want, become whomever you wish, or purchase whichever cultural, sexual, spiritual, artistic or political experience you desire. You can impersonate other genders or ethnic identities without having to suffer any physical, social or political repercussions, or be subjected to the rage of the excluded. You don't even need to belong to any 'real' community. And you can do all this from the solitude of your home."

(Note: All words that appear in quotations are temporarily "meaningless.")

Track #1: Uroboro: the spectacle of the mainstream bizarre

The serpent finally bit its own tail. What ten years ago was considered fringe "subculture" is now mere pop. The insatiable mass of the so-called "mainstream" (remember the film *The Blob*?) has finally devoured all "margins", and the more dangerous, "other," thorny, and exotic these margins, the better. In fact, *stricto sensu*, we can say that there are no margins left, at least no recognizable ones. "Alternative" thought, fringe "subcultures," and so-called "radical" behavior, as we knew them, have actually become the mainstream. Nowadays, spectacle replaces content; form gets heightened, more stylized than ever, as "meaning" (remember meaning?) evaporates, or, rather, fades out, boredom sinks in, and everybody searches for the next "extreme" image or experience. Ethical and political implications are fading memories of the past century.

We are now fully installed in what I term the culture of the mainstream bizarre, a perplexing oxymoron, which reminds me of Mexico's ex-ruling party: the Partido Revolucionario Institucional. Nowhere else is this phenomenon more apparent than in mass media and the internet, where so-called "radical" behavior, revolution-as-style, and "extreme" images of racialized violence and sexual hybridity have become daily entertainment, mere marketing strategies of a new corporate chic. From the humiliating spectacle of anti-social behavior performed in US network talk shows to television specials on mass murderers, Aryan supremacists, child killers, religious cults, "extreme" sex and sports, predatory

345

animals and/or natural disasters, and the obsessive repetition of "real crimes" shot by private citizens or by surveillance cameras, we've all become daily voyeurs and participants of a new *cultura-in-extremis*. Its goal is clear: to entice more consumers, extremely jaded consumers, while providing them with the illusion of experiencing vicariously all the sharp edges and strong emotions that their superficial lives lack.

The mainstream bizarre has effectively blurred the borders between pop culture, performance, and "reality"; between audience and performer, between the surface and the underground, between marginal identities and fashionable trends. Where do my collaborators and I stand *vis-à-vis* this new cartography? It's unclear, just like the placement of the new borders.

One thing is clear to us: Artists exploring the tensions between these borders must now be watchful, for we can easily get lost in this funhouse of virtual mirrors, epistemological inversions, and distorted perceptions, a zone where all desires and fears are imaginary, and "content" is just a fading memory. If this happens, performance artists might end up becoming just another "extreme" variety act in the humongous menu of global culture.

What perplexing times for those engaged in critical thinking. Traditionally known for our "transgressive" behavior and our willingness to defy dogmas, cultural borders, and moral conventions, performance artists must now compete in outrageousness with sleazebags Howard Stern, Jerry Springer, and MTV's *Jackass*. Change channel. Independent filmmakers and video artists now must contend with television ads and rock videos whose aesthetic strategies are directly appropriated from independent film and experimental video but with a few small differences: they are twice as technically complex and their budgets are logarithmically bigger. Change channel. Public intellectuals (what does "public" mean in this context?) must now attempt to speak to students or write for readers who may regard Chris Mathews and the performative polemicists of MSNBC as actual public intellectuals. I know. You know. The difference is obvious: "content," but since content *stricto sensu* no longer matters, difference makes no difference. Same with "depth."

In this new convoluted logic, Arafat and the Serial Sniper will be granted equal status and media coverage, as will Mother Teresa and Lady Diana. If Chomsky or Ed Said get invited to present an opposing view to that of Israel on CNN, the real objective of the host will be to disarm them or make them sound like zealots. After all, dissent can also be spectacle. Latino media may be even worse. Submerged in an ocean of celebrity gossip, it invests the banal opinions of "J-Lo," Salma Hayek, or Antonio Banderas about "whatever," including sensitive political issues, with greater weight than those of writers Carlos Fuentes, Richard Rodriguez, or Ana Castillo.

For the moment, performance artists are obsessed with the following questions: If we choose to mimic or parody the strategies of the mainstream bizarre in order to develop new audiences and explore the *Zeitgeist* of our times, what certainty do we have that our high-definition reflection won't devour us from inside out and turn us into the very stylized freaks we are attempting to deconstruct or parody? And if we are interested in performing for non-specialized audiences, what certainty do we have that these audiences won't misinterpret our "radical" actions and our complex performative identities as merely spectacles of radicalism or stylized hybridity? If our new audiences are more interested in direct stimulation than in content, can we effectively camouflage content-as-experience? I have no answers. I only have clues. My dressing room is filled with suspicious mirrors. My computer desktop contains dozens of solipsistic performance scripts. I open one of them:

> *"Dear audience,*
> *I've got 45 scars accounted for*
> *half of them produced by art*
> *& this is not a metaphor.*
> *My artistic obsession has led me to carry out*
> *some flagrantly stupid acts of transgression*
> *including:*
> *Living inside a cage as a Mexican Frankenstein*
> *Crucifying myself as a mariachi to protest immigration policy*
> *Crashing the Met as El Mad Mex*
> *led on a leash by a Spanish dominatrix . . . I mean,*
> *You want me to be more specific than*
> *drinking Mr. Clean to exorcise my colonial demons?*
> *or, handing a dagger to an audience member,*
> *& offering her my plexus?"*

Track #2: The illusion of talking back

Since the new global culture is supposed to be "interactive," we are granted the illusion of talking back. We can call the television or radio station, or e-mail them our opinions. We can post our views in any website we like, join a chat room, or place a classified ad in search of quorum or accomplices. And someone will respond right away. If we are lucky, we may be invited to a talk show to exhibit (or, better said, "perform") our miseries. Students, intellectuals, and civic leaders, along with a bunch of children and housewives randomly chosen by the producer's assistant, may get invited to an electronic town meeting organized by CNN or by the president himself. Our new culture encourages everyone to have an opinion, and express it (not necessarily an informed opinion, just an opinion). Not to act upon it, just to express it, as a kind of placebo or substitute for action. What matters here is the spectacle of participation. No matter how bombastic or "transgressive" our views may be, hey, if they make for good spectacle they will always be welcome – and forgotten immediately.

Citizen participation is encouraged, but not in any significant decision-making process that may effect social change, just in the construction and the staging of spectacle; the great spectacle of the illusion of citizen participation. The cameras are now pointing in all directions. "Normal people" can suddenly become reporters, actors, singers, performance artists, filmmakers, and even porn stars. We don't need to have brains, special talents, or a perfect body. In fact, the more "normal" we look and sound, the better. If we are lucky, we might be cast in a "Reality TV" show, where "everyone is a celebrity." If our camcorders are fortunate enough to catch an act of police brutality or a theft, our tapes might become news. In our new website www.pochanostra.com, the most popular section is called "Aficionado performance artist of the month." There, amateur performance artists get to impersonate their favorite cultural other, stage a performance *tableau vivant* at home, shoot it with a digital camera, and send us the image.

The illusion of interactivity and citizen participation has definitely changed the relationship between live art and its audience. Audiences are increasingly having a harder time just sitting and watching passively a performance, especially younger audiences. They've been trained by television, Supernintendo, video games, and the internet to "interact" and be part of it all, whatever "it" may be. They see themselves as "insiders" and part-time artists. They've got the most recent software to make digital movies and compose electronic music. They burn their own CDs and design their own websites. To them there is nothing esoteric about art. Therefore, when attending a live art event, they wish to be included in the process, talk back to the artist, and if possible become part of the actual performance. These new audience members are always ready to walk on stage at any invitation from the artist and do something, "whatever." If this involves impersonating other cultures or taking off their clothes, the better. It's karaoke time. It's like a live computer game with the added excitement that people, "real people," are watching.

Given this dramatic epistemological shift, artists and art institutions are pressured to redefine our own epistemological relationship with our public. The educational departments of museums are trying to figure out how to design more technologically interactive, performative, and "audience-friendly" exhibits. And experimental artists such as myself are wracking our brains developing new ways to further catch people's attention and implicate new and larger audiences in our performance games. The challenge for performance artists is obvious: If our live "production" is not "exciting," or "interactive," enough, our impatient US audiences have a myriad other options of how to spend their evening.

> "I got to get me a 'real' job, a 9 to 5 job.
> But the question is, doing what?
> How about posing as a model for a computer ad:
> 'El Mexterminator thinks different, y que?'
> Or posing as a wholesome eccentric for a Ben & Jerry's poster?
> I could conduct self-realization seminars for Latino dot-comers:
> 'Come to terms with your inner Chihuahua.'
> Or 'Find your inner Aztec.'
> Or 'The pito within.'
> Or 'How to camouflage your ethnicity to get a better job.'
> (Pause)
> It's tough to find a useful task for a performance artist nowadays."

Track # 3: The Finisecular Freak crosses the Southern border

For years Latin Americans witnessed from the South what we perceived as a First World culture of unacknowledged excesses and gratuitous extremes. But thanks to global media, digital television, the internet, and the black market, today we ourselves are an integral part of this culture, as daily voyeurs and willing participants.

Some examples come to mind:

The popular Mexican comic books known as *mini-novellas* feature the weekly adventures of characters such as a *lucha libre* wrestler with *priapismo* (a permanent erection) who gets kidnapped and sexually attacked by "extraterrestrial nymphos" and "*Pocachondas*," "a horny Indian maiden who loves to torture muscled cowboys." *Cambio de canal*. Spanish-language tabloid television programs such as the recently canceled *Fuera de la Ley* and *Primer Impacto* present a disparate repertoire of extreme body images, framed by "bizarre facts and people." Close-ups of corpses at the scene of the crime or the accident or people with "rare genetic disorders" share the screen with, say, a mob of angry *campesinos* setting a rapist on fire captured by the camcorder of a bewildered tourist, a recent apparition of the Virgin of Guadeloupe, or interviews with witchdoctors and "outrageous artists" such as myself.[1] The old freak show is back in a new high-definition format, and you simply can't take your eyes off the screen. Our lives may suck but the world out there according to Televisa, Telemundo or Univision is still "bizarre, extremely sexy and dangerous."

Cambio de canal. The Mexican talk show with the highest ratings right now, *Hasta en las Mejores Familias*, features, among other topics, guests with "peculiar forms of transexuality," "families engaged in bizarre forms of incest," and "men who love to watch their wives do it with their bosses." Needless to say that most of the guests are working-class *mestizos*, which makes the spectacle even more troubling. With an invited audience that includes people with physical deformities and a "jury" formed by a midget, a deaf-mute, and a drag queen, the guests are encouraged to bite each other's heads off, like in the early Jerry Springer shows. If they get way too violent, a team of flamboyant wrestlers and "gay bodybuilders" (or rather macho bodybuilders performing stereotypical "gay behavior") will bring them back to their senses. It's "radical" according to my own family.

Cambio de canal. But it is definitely Peruvian broadcasting that wins first prize in terms of political incorrectness and humiliation. The most popular comedy program, *Los Cómicos Ambulantes*, features an indigenous troupe of fake transsexuals, overweight women in tangas, and hyper-sexualized midgets, all wearing "Indian" wigs. Their comedic specialty is to make fun of the slang and idiosyncratic behavior of *campesinos* and "dumb *tetonas*" – busty women. During one show I saw, the comedians invited audience members to guess the "weight" of the breasts of a dyed-blonde model, whose "enhanced" body had undergone at least five plastic surgeries. Wearing a microscopic bikini, she looked like a character from a Japanese animé cartoon. For twenty minutes, male audience members stepped in front of the camera to grab her breasts and guessed their combined weight. At the end of the program the model sent a kiss to her "eight-year-old son who is watching the show at home. Jorgito, my love, I see you in an hour. Ciao." There are simply no limits to these shows. Since the genre is so new in Latin America, no legal restrictions have been placed on content, and when the intellectuals or citizen groups complain the ratings simply go up.

At the Mexico City street market of Tepito, as in similar places in São Paolo, Lima, and Bogotá, with enough *conecciones* anyone can find extremely rare pirate videos, from (real or staged) snuff to bestiality with snakes, pigs or rats, to ethnic-specific porn from any culture one can imagine. This "outlaw" global market offers the consumer more variety than the Discovery channels. It appears to defy but in actuality strangely complements the "lawful" one which, as we all know, is also riven with illegalities. In fact, in the global market the borders between legality and illegality are practically non existent.

Track #4: "Extreme sexuality" and other extremely hollow concepts

Twelve years ago performance artists managed to shock the American political class and the mainstream media with their "explicit" sexual language, images, and rituals, and sparked a national conversation about censorship and the role of art. Today, "extreme sexuality" is a hollow concept and a pop cultural genre in HBO, A&E, and Bravo. The kink of Jerry Springer's involuntary performance-artist guests makes Holly Hughes, Tim Miller, *La Congelada de Uva*, or Valie Export look naively chaste. Baroque forms of racialized transexuality, teen prostitution, incest, and family love triangles performed by "normal" working-class Americans are displayed daily on talk shows as part of millennial Americana; while sexual fetishes, hard core S&M, and theatrical sex are regular topics on cable television. It's no big deal.

The margins continue to stretch in the blink of an eye. Howard Stern invites "midget porn stars" and physically challenged women to his television show and asks them to show their breasts on national television. Then (if he finds them "sexy") he offers them a breast enlargement and brings them back to the program after the operation. In another Stern show, titled *I Want to be a Vagina Millionaire*, a guy with a speech impediment and a "midget" have sex with a prostitute as the cameras follow them to the bedroom.

The new "margins" continue to welcome more immigration from the old centers as Anglo males in their thirties, suffused in their never-ending crises of masculinity, attend "circle jerk" seminars sponsored and filmed by HBO. Yuppies in search of intense experiences to shatter their lethargy attend vampire clubs in San Francisco, New York, and London, while financiers and politicians discover the wonders of fetishized S&M. In the porn industry, the kinkiest videos, hotlines, and websites are being marketed to average, middle-class people with boring lives and anesthetized bodies. For the willing consumer of this new sex industry, the unspoken text seems to be: "*I am completely disconnected from my body. I badly need an extreme experience to shake my dormant body up and awaken my senses. Whatever it takes, whatever! . . .*" The great paradox here is that behind the spectacle of "extreme sexuality" lies a profound puritanism, or, as performance theorist Richard Schechner once told me in a letter, "so much staged sexuality amounts to not much actual sensuality."

The sponsors of the mainstream bizarre don't discriminate on the basis of age. Netscape or Yahoo can help lonely suburban teens and kids "navigate" through the user-friendly halls of the great virtual funhouse where online strippers and escorts are already passé. There they can find unimaginable photos to download and video clips to watch: sex with animals, child porn, "juicy cunts under 17," "The Dead Babes" website, and the popular "Couple TV" sites, which feature amateur couples revealing (or rather "performing") "everything" they do at home from making love and taking a shower to defecating. If the young voyeurs get bored with "extreme sexuality," within seconds they can access other daring sites where they can find neo-nazi and KKK paraphernalia, militia manifestos, and right-wing terrorist manuals detailing the formula to construct bombs in the garage. There are truly no limits to our democratic "options." This is the very nature of our new global democracy: Everything is instantly available to us. All we need is a computer, a modem . . . and, of course, lots of spare time to exercise our unlimited "freedoms."

Since performance artists simply can't or don't wish to compete with these readily accessible forms of superficial "transgression," we must then redefine our roles and ask ourselves some tough questions. In this new panorama, what do we mean by "extreme," "radical," or "transgressive"? These words are now empty shells. What is really left to "transgress"? I remember with nostalgia the days when for my Chicano colleagues and I to get naked during a performance piece at a Chicano cultural center would trigger a month-long community controversy. I also remember with a melancholic smile when the Walker Art Center outraged the political establishment for presenting Ron Athey or when Karen Finley was banned in England. Today, things are quite different: Ron gets occasionally invited to direct MTV videos; Karen appears frequently in the television show *Politically Incorrect*; and an HBO film crew follows my Mexterminator project on tour. The image of my collaborator dancer Sara Shelton Mann crucified nude as a transgender mariachi with a strap-on dildo, which would have sparked riots in Mexico just a few years ago, ends up in the final cut. My jaw drops down to my stomach. One of the producers tells me, "Gómez-Peña, I wish you guys had more images like this one."

Is this phenomenon a breakthrough in terms of tolerance for true radical behavior or yet another confirmation that content and difference, in the age of infinite options and multidirectional promises, no longer matter? For the moment, my performance colleagues and I are a bit confused. We are carefully reviewing our image bank, our performance rituals, and, most specially, the language we utilize to frame them.

(I ask someone in the audience)
"Sir, are you in touch with your heart?
Can you see mine, hanging out like a wandering viscera?"
(to someone else)
"Carnal, are you in touch with your genitalia?"
This guy asked me this question at a party the other night:
"What does it mean to be in touch with one's genitalia?"
I answered rhetorically with a question:
"To be sensitive to people's eros

or to engage acritically in sexual harassment?"
(or, in Spanglish, "sexual agárrasment" . . .)
"Is anyone, right this moment, besides me
experiencing incommensurable horniness?"
(Long pause)
"Come on, no one?"
(To another audience member)
"Hey, do you at least know your genetic code?"

Track #5: Altered bodies and wounded bodies

In a culture that glorifies acritically the stylized bizarre, the human body is understandably at the center of it all, for all the wrong reasons. The body is "hot" again, but the spectacle of the altered or wounded body is much hotter. Wherever we turn, we see bodies and body parts reshaped, refurbished, or "enhanced" by implants and prosthetics, steroids and laser surgery, tattoos and piercings; artificial bodies to wear and/or to watch, premiering proudly their liposuctioned asses and "stapled" stomachs, their volcanic breasts and enlarged penises, showing off their reconstructed chins and borrowed noses. These cyborg-ized bodies reconstructed by high technology, in all states of artificial alteration, appear daily in movies, prime-time television, fashion and art shows, ads, and websites. They aren't shocking. These are merely "hip." In this new context, fully tattooed or pierced bodies are no longer a bold counter-cultural statement. We see them on tourist beaches, Ivy League university campuses, spring break specials in the travel channel, and in suburban discos.

The popularization and mainstreaming of these practices have finally permitted anyone, not just eccentrics, bohemians, celebrities, or upper-class dilettantes, to carry out their fantasies, and dramatically alter their bodies. In fact most of us know people or have relatives who have undergone drastic physical transformations within a span of two years or less. And many times we ourselves have fantasized about reshaping or "enhancing" some body part. It's a democratic desire. All races and social classes meet in the new global zone to celebrate the body extreme.

At the same time, the spectacle of bodies wounded or even destroyed by social or political drama went from being a "fringe subculture" (remember *Amok*?) to becoming a cliché. Mutilated, covered with blood, open sores, or prosthetics, "extreme" bodies without identity populate both the corporate mediascape and cyberspace. A vertiginous succession of open bodies, bleeding wounds, dissected abdomens, and missing limbs, whether real or staged, may only cause us to blink our eyes once or twice. Why? I can only speculate: These bodies have been silenced, decontextualized, emptied of drama and emotion, stripped of their humanity and identity. And, as inattentive spectators, we have clearly lost our capability to empathize with them and feel outraged by the violent causes that impacted on them.

The combined spectacle of the altered and the wounded body has generated an interest in the strange intersection of performance (and performative photography), (par-) ethnography, a fringe of cyber-theory, aestheticized porn, forensic medicine, and "role-playing." But the new areas of interest are quite different from last century's fascination with the body extreme. It is clearly no longer the "beautiful" or (fictionalized) "natural" body (with its cultural specificities and ideological implications) or theatricalized nudity as in the films of Fellini, Jodorowsky, or Pasolini. It is definitely not *el cuerpo político* or *el cuerpo cartográfico* as in performance art either. It's the "bizarre" combination of pathology and Eros; of implied violence and high style; of the medical and the criminal realms. It is the morgue, the surgical table, the biogenetic lab, the forensic dossier, as well as the "extreme" sex club, tabloid television, and the porn websites with their myriad subcategories.

The new objects of fascination are a depoliticized "extreme" body, stripped of all implications, and the suffering, erotiziced body of a (willing or accidental) victim. *Loquísimo!* Whether we like it or not, when performance artists "perform," as far as the audience is concerned, our bodies fall in the very same category. Our formidable challenge in this respect is how to rehumanize, repoliticize, and decolonize our own bodies wounded by the media, and intervened by the invisible surgery of pop culture; and to do it in such a way that our audiences are not even aware of it.

> " 'Global' powers are united to form the transnational club of the 'globalized' art network, whose members believe or hope to believe that they are creating a decolonized territory beyond the central art system. Paradoxically, in spite of the newly refurbished diversity of the mainstream, globalization has lead to the re-colonization of the art world and has turned the multicultural landscape into a hip backdrop. The global art world is a colonizer captivated by the strategies of decolonization."
>
> Carolina Ponce de León

Track #6: Collectible primitives in the great international expo

The *modus operandi* of the self-proclaimed "international" art world is not any different from that of corporate multiculturalism or the culture of the mainstream bizarre. In the great art mall of "internationalism," artists, a small number of lucky ones, become ephemeral commodities and trendy neo-primitives. And all we have to contribute to the great multi-culti delicatessen is our ability to generate desire (and a bit of fear) for the global consumer, to perform our stylized (and tamed) "difference" with an obvious understanding of Western "sophistication," and current art trends.

According to the glossy art journals, "internationalism" (*en abstracto*) is the new ism. It portrays the world as a borderless and virginal *mappa mundi digital* where the cultural energy and the art market are constantly shifting from continent to continent, and from country to country, just like the stock market or the programming of the Discovery channel. In this new ball game, more than ever, artists are at the mercy of the global curator, critic, and/or producer. Unlike their postmodern, multicultural, or postcolonial predecessors, the new global impresarios needn't be concerned with ethical or political boundaries. Ethics, ideology, border issues, and postcolonial dilemmas – they all belong to the immediate past, a past too complicated to recall in any serious manner; a past which can merely be sampled as style or excerpted as motif.

The new praxis is to engage in a stylistically "radical" but thoroughly apolitical type of transnational multiculturalism that indulges acritically in mild difference. The new praxis is to witness, document, flatten, "sample," and consume all thorny edges, "alternative" expressions, antisocial behavior, and revolutionary kitsch. One trend or style will follow or overlap with the other as perplexed artists patiently wait to be discovered or rather rediscovered for the hundredth time, this time under a new light, one without implications, continuity, or context. The photo is much sharper; the text much more vague.

The global impresarios scout the virginal *mappa mundi* in search of lite difference and new flavors to stimulate and satisfy their artistic consumers. A combination of political phenomena and the caprices of the impresarios themselves often determine the choice of Otherness. One year it's Cuba, then Mexico, then China, and then the Ivory Coast or South Africa. It's the Buena Vista Social Club syndrome. "Third World" art products are seasonally fashionable so long as they pass the quality-control tests imposed by the new centers. The new Third World or "minority" artist is expected to perform trans- and intercultural sophistication, unpredictable eclecticism, and cool hybridity. The debate is non-existent. In fact, debate is considered passé. Those artists, writers, and curators who decide to problematize this neo-retro-colonial praxis are usually deported back to oblivion or pushed aside to the many other parallel (and semi-invisible) art worlds. After all, no one is truly indispensable in the free market of twenty-first-century art. Besides, the waiting line of young willing Others is immense.

Powerful "international" curators and art critics have effectively depoliticized the border paradigm and the discourse on hybridity, therefore mixing things up is now quite trendy. Daring stylistic juxtapositions of high/low art, Third/First World, shamanic/high-tech, religious/pagan, insider/outsider art have become common curatorial practice, often without any critical backdrop. Borders and identities are now interchangeable, and so are the nationalities and genders of the new *enfants terribles.* It's nomadism for sale, gentrified ethnicity; glossy hybridity and chic radicalism to be experienced first hand.

As artists exhaust our proposals of difference, "rebel" curators venture into the titillating *terra ignota* of "outsider art," the euphemistic term used by the art world to describe the art of prisoners, sex workers, terminally ill patients, "gang members," serial killers, or the mentally impaired, who suddenly become desirable commodities and at times instant celebrities. Unlike in the early nineties, the goal is no longer to "help the outsider." Since compassion is passé and the missionary community arts movement is just a bad memory: the new goal is to voyeuristically observe their crisis and/or borrow their image and artifacts (sometimes permanently) to exhibit them in a museum. The framing, of course, will be done by someone who will never understand the drama of the "outsider."

For the global impresario, embarked on an eternal art safari, there are still lots of extreme emotions and dangerous experiences to explore beyond art, ineffable fringes and sordid realities to discover, document, and bring back to the gallery, the biennial, or the film festival. Delete.

> " 'El Chic-ano Apocalíptico' (As seen in Desperado, Border Wars, and WWF Smackdown)
> Code: Identity morphing microchip embedded in psyche

Features: Undocumented border-crosser. Performs up to ten different identity variations (a feature not included in the "Latino boom" Supernintendo Game): Among others: El Mad Mex, El Narco-shaman, El Techno-bandito, El Mariachi Transvestite, El Binational Boxer, and El S&M Zorro. Body art by authentic Chicano prisoners. Fashion by the Gap.

Programmed characteristics: Theatricalized romanticism, cinematic nostalgia, primeval wisdom, unpredictable sociopathic behavior, and ritualistic sex practices

Products for sale: Action figures, t-shirts, Supernintendo games, "Identity morphing mask," robo-jalapeño phallus, robotic bleeding heart, bottled "Latino Heat." Catalogue available at http://www.pochanostra.com

Prototype financed by Epcot and the Smithsonian Institution."

(Taxonomic information for an "artificial savage" created
in collaboration with anonymous internet users)

Track #7: Performing the Other-as-freak

Performing against the backdrop of the mainstream bizarre has been quite a formidable challenge. My colleagues and I have explored the multi-screen spectacle of the Other-as-freak by decorating and "enhancing" our brown bodies with special effects make-up, hyper-ethnic motifs, hand-made "lowrider" prosthetics and braces, and what we term "useless" or "imaginary" technology (that is, with strictly poetical, ritualistic, or performative purposes). The idea is to heighten features of fear and desire in the Anglo imagination, and "spectacularize" our "extreme identities" so to speak, with the clear understanding that these identities have already been intervened by the surgery of global media.

The composite identities of our "ethno-cyborg"/personae are manufactured with the following formula in mind: one-fourth stereotype, one-fourth audience projection, one-fourth aesthetic artifact, and one-fourth social behavior.

We pose on dioramas as "artificial savages," making ourselves completely available for the audience to "explore" us, smell us, touch us, change our costumes and props, and even replace us for a short period of time. In the last hour of the "show," people get to choose from a menu of possible interactions, which changes from site to site: Among other options, they can whip us, handle us roughly with S&M leashes, "tag" (spray paint) our bodies, and point replicas of handguns and Uzis at us. Some audience members actually invite us to reverse the gaze and inflict violence on them. Curiously, they tend to be the most conservative-looking ones.

Ceding our will to the audience and inviting them to participate in what appears to be "extreme performance games" are integral aspects of the new phase of our work. Some examples come to mind: Once, during a performance at the Caradigian Museum in Wales, a Victorian chanteuse handcuffed to a period dresser played strip poker with male audience members for three hours. She had no problem getting people to participate. In another occasion, during the San Francisco premiere of our "Spanglish lowrider opera" *Califas, 2000,* a nude ranchera singer performed by Colombian ex-prima ballerina gone performance artist Michelle Ceballos, with her face covered by a veil and a strap-on dildo, would get "activated" by audience members through fellatio. Again, people went for it without hesitation. During the international tour of *The Museum of Fetishized Identities*, the performance artist Juan Ybarra politely asked audience members to flagellate him with a flag (of the country where we were performing). Willing audience members immediately formed a line to carry out his instructions. At the opening performance of the Liverpool Biennial, a British-Asian performance artist with her face made up to look like a traditional geisha stood on a platform with a museum sign stating "looking for tender British husband" and asked male audience members to write their phone numbers on her nude body. By the end of the night, her body was completely covered by a phone agenda of excited sexual tourists.

Regardless of the country or the city where we perform, the results of these border performance experiments reveal a new relationship between artist and audience; between the brown body and the white voyeur. Most interactions are characterized by the lack of political or ethical implications. Unlike, say, ten years ago, when audiences were over-sensitive regarding gender and racial politics, our new audiences are more than willing to manipulate our identity, overtly sexualize us, and engage in (symbolic or real) acts of cross-cultural/cross-gender transgression, even violence.

Unless we detect the potential for real physical harm, we let all this happen. Why? Our objective (at least the conscious one) is to unleash the millennial demons, not to pontificate. As performance artists, we wish to understand our new role and place in this culture of extreme spectacle. In the process of detecting the placement of the new borders (specially since September 11) it becomes necessary to open up a *sui generis* ceremonial space for the audience to reflect on their new relationship with cultural, racial, and political Otherness. The unique space of ambiguity and contradiction opened up by performance art becomes ideal for this kind of anthro-poetical inquiry.

NOTE

1 The Latino television tabloid *Primer Impacto* covered my Spanglish performance opera *Califas, 2000*. The cameras concentrated mainly on our nude bodies, "anti-religious message," and "weird aesthetics," which "clearly offended the Latino community." Next day, I *ipso facto* became a one-week outlaw celebrity amongst taqueros, homeboys, and bus chaffers in the Mission District. I also got dozens of e-mails from old friends I hadn't seen in years. It definitely had much more impact that my participation in the Whitney Biennial.

READER CROSS-REFERENCES

Kirshenblatt-Gimblett, Carlson – on performance art
Gabler – the mediatization of culture
Phelan, Faber, Kaprow, Lane – other experimental, oppositional artists
Conquergood, Turner and Turner, Fabian, Taylor – performance as a mode of intellectual inquiry

40

REVEREND BILLY

Preaching, protest, and post-industrial flânerie

Jill Lane

Enter Reverend Billy, a six-foot-tall, imposing, 50-year-old preacher. His booming "Swaggart-expansive" voice greets his flock of urban, East-Village New Yorkers: "Welcome to the Church of Stop Shopping, Children!" In a measured, vibrato baritone, he intones, "In this church we gather to ask the great questions that face us." Pause, slowly extending his emotion-heavy hands: "Is there life after perfect teeth?" Apocalyptic rise: "Will we survive good graphics?" Crescendo: "There is not a person in this room who has not had a loved one chased down and *ki-i-illed* by discounted luxury items!" Huge applause and hollers from the audience. "God help us, *yes*, we will be delivered!" A rising chorus of "Amens." "We will stop shopping yes! We will stop shopping, children!" (Talen 1999a).

Through such abominating semi-ironic preaching, the Reverend has been raging against the noxious effects of consumerism, transnational capital, and the privatization of public space and culture in New York City since 1997. Reverend Billy is the pseudonym of performance artist Bill Talen, whose work as the leader of the "Church of Stop Shopping" represents a fascinating departure for New Left theatre in the era of global capital. Like many political theatre artists in the 1990s and beyond, Talen has faced the challenges posed by the rapidly changing political economy of globalization.

In 1994, the innovative network art-activists of Critical Art Ensemble (CAE) warned in *The Electronic Disturbance* that the current systems of social power may have rendered oppositional art obsolete; the ground against which opposition could be staged has turned "liquid." Arjun Appadurai similarly argues that the competing forces of globalization have created a social scene in which culture and power are produced and disseminated in always-shifting "flows," whose movement rushes through the disjunctures between fluid social landscapes – part material, part imagined – of technology, media, ethnicity, ideology, and finance (1996: 27–47). Numerous other cultural theorists – Zygmunt Bauman (2000), May Joseph (1999), Stuart Hall (1997), Mohammed Bamyeh (2000), among others – follow Appadurai in characterizing our new "global times" as marked by ever more complex, asymmetrical, and asynchronous transnational flows of capital, goods, labor, information, and peoples; these, in turn, have informed the progressive corrosion and decentering of previously stable, if also fictional, categories of national-ethnic boundaries and identities. In this overwhelming scene of social "liquescence" (to borrow CAE's term), how can an artist or activist stage oppositional discourse? How can artists address the devastating effects and casualties of the new global economy, when the representation of power is itself now nomadic, liquid, and on the move? CAE contends that, rather than stage opposition, our only viable option is to create calculated "disturbance" in these networks of power. What role, then, can performance play as a site of such disturbance?

Bill Talen's work as Reverend Billy offers one trenchant set of answers to those questions, revitalizing political street theatre as a sophisticated repertoire – or arsenal – of anti-consumerist theatre techniques. Indeed, Reverend Billy offers us a model of politicized "theater disturbance" that follows, engages, and creatively speaks back to the multiplying sites of privatization that have colonized urban public culture. From his beginnings as a sidewalk preacher protesting the corporate redevelopment of Times Square in New York City, Reverend Billy has taken his theatrical activism to a range of sites, most of which are what he calls "contested spaces": those urban sites that have been recently commodified, or newly condemned, to commercialization. In this vein, he has staged numerous "shopping interventions" in which he and fellow artists perform in commercial spaces themselves – from the Disney Store to Starbucks – in an effort to intervene in (disturb) the seamless corporate architecture and choreography of shopping, or to "re-narrate" them with memories of the lives they displace. Talen also regularly lends the Reverend to a range of staged "political actions" related to the destruction or gentrification of local urban spaces, and of the social memories which they house.

Common to each of these strategies is Talen's commitment to embodied, local actions that can engage the social movement of capital or illuminate the architecture – both public and psychic – of consumerism. Like many left-wing activists, he has committed himself to the local as an answer to capitalist globalization. May Joseph reminds us that "where goods, fashions, cuisine, films, cultural artifacts, and kitsch flow with intensified speed, bodies flow in less efficient ways" (1999: 8). Talen uses this inefficiency, staging the body's awkward resistance and failures to conform to homogenizing choreographies of commodification. For Talen, the body – his own body, and those of his audiences and collaborators – offers a poetics of useful embarrassment: the body inappropriately blocking the smart march of shopping is the first step in answering corporate capitalism and its culture-for-sale.

However, Talen has not indulged in what Bruce Robbins calls "romantic localism," which relies on essentialist notions of place and identity to ground claims for local belonging, community, or action (1998: 3). To the contrary, what is striking about Talen's work is his ability to mobilize community while avoiding such essentialisms. In this sense, the politics and poetics of the Church of Stop Shopping are in keeping with that more hybrid urban experience, alternately dubbed "glocal" by Roland Robertson (1995), "trans-local" by May Joseph (1999), and "cosmopolitical" by Chea and Robbins (1998). Talen uses performance not as a site of prior claims to local identity, but as a site of ongoing, performative self-fashioning that relies on irony to both create community and refuse its fixity in the same gesture.

That ironic self-fashioning is nowhere more apparent than in Talen's signature genre, the comic theatrical service. These performances are structured as "collapsing" comic church services, complete with readings from the saints (or the devils), public confessions, collective exorcisms, the honoring of new saints, donations to the cause, a lively choir, and a rousing sermon. His first series of such services, staged at the Salon Theatre every Sunday in March 2000, was awarded an Obie Award, New York's prestigious recognition of off-Broadway theatre. He followed this with a series at St. Clements Church, *Starbucks out of Hell's Kitchen*, in May 2000, and reprised the genre with his *Spring Revival* at the Salon Theatre (now 45 Bleecker Street) for six Sundays in March and April of 2001. For all the irony that these fake services invoke, each performance is organized around a concrete local issue. For example, one service in 2000 was held to honor the recently bulldozed Esperanza community garden in New York's Lower East Side, another supported efforts to unionize bodega workers, and still others to rally support for a threatened theatre space and a local neighborhood collective. The "saints" who are honored and speak at each service are real activists: Charles Kernaghan, the director of the National Labor Committee; Ricardo Dominguez, Zapatista cyberactivist of Electronic Disturbance Theatre; Alicia Torres, founder of Esperanza Garden. The donations support these causes, and every performance concludes with audience participation in a public action staged outside the theatre.

The Reverend's ability to mobilize "real" communities and to stage meaningful social activism through his exaggerated, comic televangelist satire is one of the most interesting aspects of his work. Talen says that he originally devised his Reverend persona out of a desire to "create a comic spiritual strategy for urban people who normally approach experience . . . through habitual irony" (2000a). As I introduce Reverend Billy's work, I will illustrate several ways that it engages and extends a classic materialist critique and aesthetic for new economic times. In the process, I'll query why this particular persona – the false preacher, the ironic priest in the wrinkled dinner jacket with wild dyed hair – has seemed necessary to this critique. Thus we'll trace the path that has led Reverend Billy, as a theatrical persona, to gradually take on the attributes of a "real" spiritual and social leader for public activism against consumerism and commercial redevelopment in the Lower East Side of New York City – even as everyone is winking when they say "Amen."

[. . .]

Urban memory, or postindustrial flânerie

Talen has committed himself to rescuing realities, memories, and even history itself from the Disneyfication and commodification of experience, past and present. For Talen, like Benjamin before him, the arts of the storyteller are central to this task. Where contemporary urban realities tend to frame, flatten, and commodify experience into consumable information, stories provide alternative structures of memory, alternate modes of keeping – literally, safeguarding – experience for other social uses. The storyteller, writes Benjamin in his famous essay of that title, is one who can, "in the midst of life's fullness . . ., give evidence of the profound perplexity of the living." Stories are, in his view, a form of counsel: "counsel is less an answer to a question than a proposal concerning the continuation of a story which is just unfolding" (1968: 86–7). The Reverend steps into the endangered role of the storyteller; walking through the wreckage of transnational capital he is "constantly asking the question, 'What's the story here?' " (Talen 2000c: 5). Walking the streets of New York, he "finds himself at the center of an ongoing collision of stories" unfolding around him (2000c: 5) and he attempts to voice such perplexity.

This form of storytelling, which appears more often in monologues and theater sermons than in his street preaching, describes the damaged urban landscape, and often attempts to salvage from it the lost memories and lives erased by every next layer of commercial linoleum. These narratives testify to Benjamin's grim projection that, under rampant capitalism and urban rationalization, metropolitan life would be so thoroughly stamped by commodity form as to eliminate all other personal or social imagination; the best the Reverend can do is describe the tightening limits of the imagination in this scene. He asks: "When the corporations own so much square footage, in the sense of psychic space as well as real estate – where does original language begin?" (1998a). In this sense, Talen is a postindustrial *flâneur:* one walking the city, actively trying to see in the new global order of things the diverse realities – lives, memories, bodies – that are rendered everyday more invisible as our forms of social space and public representation are reorganized by commercial culture.

Thus the Reverend describes the experience of trying to make a home – literally – in between giant 150-foot models – Christy Turlington, Michael Jordan, Kate Moss, Brad Pitt. The young, near-naked bodies unfurl down the rubberized billboards that cover the sides of buildings, and even obscure windows of homes and offices. These gorgeous rubberized giants loom tall, towering with air-brushed menace over the blaring traffic and vendors at Houston and Broadway, affirming that we are, indeed, living in the postwar science-fiction films on which so many of us were raised. "Walking down the street is now officially so weird," says Talen, "we have to stop saying the Apocalypse is in the future" (1998d). From down below – or from inside the obscured offices and apartments hidden behind the scrim of advertised knees or cheekbones – the beautiful image giants appear to share in their own erotic product-to-product relations, making us, the beetle consumers driven about by overwhelming desire or fear, almost redundant. "Have they invented a name for this trauma?" asks the Reverend.

As Talen tells these stories, he is interested in their power to re-narrate – momentarily resignify – the spaces that they signal. Talen wants to remember those displaced or erased by the machinations of so-called "progress" and "quality of life." When one of Mayor Rudolph Giuliani's "Quality of Life" sweeps empties a street of social density; when the "New Prosperity" substitutes local idiosyncrasies with "the dotcommed rhetoric of freedom" (2000f); when a place is liquidated of what Talen calls (after Benjamin) "communicable experience" (1968: 84), transforming it from a place where lives were lived and told to an efficient transit to and from labor or shopping, then Talen moves in to re-narrate that space – to act, however momentarily, as its memory.

Talen's materialist critique of the privatization of public life thickens considerably in these narratives. The flâneur, Baudelaire's painter of modern life, walks into the view of

Benjamin's angel of history: walking the city is a textured, bodily practice of rehearsing its social life and memories. The aim of such pedestrian storytelling is not just to invent or retell the good stories of old, but to reveal their ghosted presence in things as they are. As Michel de Certeau writes of pedestrian speech acts, the "long poem of walking" offers a tactic for reinhabiting the panoptic grids imposed by private property and city planning ("urban systematicity," per de Certeau 1988). Talen's stories about walking the city are an archive of counter-memory that index the "rich silences and wordless stories" that saturate urban space, and that are most endangered by the one-dimensional glossy makeovers of franchise facades (2000f: 105–9).

"I miss New York on *this* spot!" cries the Reverend indicating the entryway of a Starbucks shop, in a 2000 sermon entitled *I Love New York* (2000g). From the sidewalk on 9th Avenue to the clean entry of the Starbucks is the portal between New York City and a deterritorialized McWorld, floating in its "Sea of Identical Details." Talen's stories give voice to spatial practices of moving in the new cosmopolitan city. He narrates the physically disorienting experience of stepping through the disjunctures between the city and this newly present McWorld, like sidestepping so many cracks in the sidewalk. He describes the temporal vertigo of oscillating between a material world comprised of the labor and lives of the dead, and the virtual life that is offered us in ultra-brite pixel clarity through dotcom advertisements at every turn. He conjures the lives of those dead, the newly displaced, and the endangered by naming them: old St. Patrick's Cathedral, obscured by billboard advertising; Hakim's Knish and Hotdog Stand, displaced by Times Square redevelopment (2000h); Esperanza Garden, bulldozed in the name of "quality of life" (2000i). "The verbal relics of which the story is composed, being tied to lost stories and opaque acts," writes de Certeau, produce lacunae in the stories. These names – St. Patrick's, Hakim's, Esperanza – are such lacunae, acting as "anti-texts, effects of dissimulation and space, possibilities of moving into other landscapes, like cellars and bushes" (1988: 107). Talen's stories work to insinuate themselves into an increasingly closed public discourse, to make room – habitable space – in the imposed order of things.

Consider a series of short sermons on the cemetery at old St. Patrick's Cathedral, one of which aired on the public radio station WNYC in February 1999 as a "moral advisory," entitled *This Way In*. The Reverend notes that the old cemetery is a kind of "village commons," where even the hurried New Yorker pauses to reflect on the brevity of the small Irish lives that are commemorated there. From St. Patrick's, you have a view of the sky; between the gravestones and clouds, the New Yorker has a solid place from which to imagine eternity. But now, the Reverend testifies, a new imagination has intervened. Rather than see the sky, we see a dotcom ad, four stories high, that instead offers a picture of the sky, with a gigantic door, and a website address. "*This way in . . .*" it reads. It offers, the Reverend says, "an alternative heaven called Intel" whose threat looms over the dead as much as the living. "Children," he cries, "we must have a defense against this blue door." "Our friends, the dead, give us that help. They seem to tell us: 'you are in, you are way in your life now'" (1999c). As de Certeau says, "Haunted places are the only ones where people can live" (1988: 108).

Talen's sermon re-narrates the scene colonized by the advertisement. Like Benjamin in his essay on the storyteller, the Reverend reminds us that advertisements have stripped our capacity to appreciate both the value of human experience and its fundamental unknowability. Talen insists – again, following Benjamin – that the structure of stories and social memory depend on a respect and tolerance for that which is not explained, but lived; "half the art of storytelling," wrote Benjamin, "is to keep a story free from explanation as one reproduces it" (1968: 89). Advertisements, on the other hand, never allow for open imagination, or the unknown: "Nothing human cannot be immediately solved with the purchase of a product," says Talen of the way advertisements distort the structures of storytelling (2000c). Thus the eternity to which those immigrant Irish lives are consigned might yet be brought under commercial control, as suggested by the next dotcom ad to hang over the cemetery some months later: "HTML meets DNA." In a later sermon, the Reverend wondered whether the very remains of those dead were not about to be uploaded to that server blocking our view of the sky (2000f). Another sermon, entitled *Freedom's Got Us Surrounded*, illustrates how Talen engages a materialist understanding of memory and storytelling to serve an anticonsumerist imagination. This sermon, from his 26 March 2000 performance staged at the Salon Theatre in support of unionization of local bodega workers, includes an anecdote about buying coffee at a local deli. As he reaches for the can on the shelf, his arm freezes in mid-gesture, before touching the product. "I'm having a moment of accidental entry into another world," he says, as he narrates a lyrical but lurid vision of the coffee plantation where the beans were grown, replete with underpaid growers and threatening goon squads and the rich children of the overseers flying to resort towns. For some reason he has not been "ushered into that final acquisition, the final reach, touch, grab, and take to the register to pay and bag" (2000a).

This time the fetishized labor of the commodity has been revealed; he is "seeing backward, upstream, into who made this, who worked, who lived, who gave, who was stopped . . ." But why was he offered this special vision? He answers, finally, quietly, as his organist Bill Henry dramatically punctuates the narrative shift with a new chord: "I realized, I was not alone. Next to me is a man. He's been standing there for a long time, but now I see him." The presence of the worker, underpaid and exploited in circumstances comparable to those that produced the sweatshop coffee, has prompted all exploited and fetishized labor to be momentarily revealed. From here, after telling the worker's story, Talen urges the audience out into the streets to join an action in the bodegas.

As his hand freezes on the product, and it reveals its own history and relations of production, that moment of knowledge belongs to a materialist historian. Benjamin, in his much-quoted "Theses on the philosophy of history," writes:

> Thinking involves not only the flow of thoughts, but their arrest as well. Where thinking suddenly stops in a configuration pregnant with tensions, it gives that configuration a shock, . . . a revolutionary chance in the fight for the oppressed past.
>
> (1968: 262–3).

It is precisely this kind of thinking that intervenes in – arrests – the choreography of shopping: "the final reach, touch, grab, take, pay, and bag." Just as the commodity has been stripped of fetishized labor, so too has the choreography of shopping been defamiliarized.

The revolutionary chance in this form of political storytelling lies in the way of thinking, as much as the pregnant content of the thought. As Benjamin so famously reminds us, "To articulate the past historically does not mean to recognize it for what it really was. Rather it means to seize hold of a memory as it flashes up in a moment of danger" (1968: 255). To my thinking, the ultimate value of Talen's storytelling well exceeds its initial activist and propaganda value; its purpose is not just to announce that your coffee harbors unethical relations of labor, or that your local deli sanctions sweatshop hours and wages, although this message is important. The value is pedagogical in a broader sense: it teaches us *how* to recognize these quotidian moments as moments of danger, emergency, and to learn again to hear the fullness and fury of disfigured social lives, caught in the violence of colliding stories, that our everyday behaviors, space, and objects carry.

Negative dialectics: the God that people who don't believe in God believe in

The question that emerges finally is, why a preacher? Benjamin's storyteller wasn't an ironist, after all. Why does Talen's storyteller need a fake collar and waistcoat, the altar-ego; why the tongue-in-cheek amens and halleluiahs?

At first blush, we might imagine that the preacher role is solid satire. Talen offers a send-up of the abominating fundamentalist rhetoric that characterizes the rise of the religious right in the US – from senators like Jesse Helms to televangelists. A corrupt figure like the fallen televangelist Jimmy Swaggart, whom Talen sometimes resembles, is an obvious site from which to deconstruct the ways in which fundamentalist Christianity has been wedded to free-market values, eliding democratic social practice in the name of aggressively conservative "family" values. "Transnationals," says Talen, "are the reigning fundamentalism of our day" (2000b); the persona of Reverend Billy plays ironically against the tight norms of what Linda Kintz, in a related critique, calls "market fundamentalism" (1997). Yet the obvious ground of satire does not fully account for the ways in which Talen's work actually advances certain spiritual notions of community development and social activism.

Bill Talen himself has had a long-term, complex interest in religious practice as a ground for his work in performance, beginning with his youth as a member of a tight-knit Dutch Calivinist community in Wisconsin. While he rejected that upbringing as an adolescent, it no doubt fostered his interest in the power of preaching as a performance form. His later work has often explored the peculiar, energy-creating force of the social oratory that – in a phrase from Laurie Anderson he likes to quote – "hangs between talking and singing." He has been interested too in the power of certain religious stories, especially under the long tutelage of Sidney Lanier, the former Vicar of St. Clements, whom Talen credits with the Reverend Billy concept. Lanier, according to Talen, helped him recognize theatrical preaching as a vehicle for expression beyond satire. In his 2000/2001 artist's residency at the New School in New York City, Talen even taught a semester-long course on preaching in America.

Talen similarly professes enormous admiration for the politicized activism of so many African-American churches, and the preaching of a long line of Baptist preachers, many of whom were models for white televangelists. He has spent ample time at services at the Mariner's Temple Baptist Church, where his own organist and chief collaborator, Bill Henry, both plays organ and practices his faith. The Reverend's relation to these churches is, then, not ironic at all, although he marks his distance from them; "I *will* be the white guy flipping and flopping up there with the African American grandmothers"(2000b). Yet there is a complex irony at work when his often young, disaffected, white audiences in the East Village require this "flopping" white preacher to open a space for their own chorus of "Amens!" and "You tell it brother!" – enthusiastic phrases they too quote from a range of racialized religious sources that they would otherwise be unlikely to indulge. So Talen's keen desire to explore what religion can offer to an atheist, urban Left is still not reconciled with this ironic tone.

We come closer to understanding the Reverend persona and its power, I believe, with the news that Talen finds something spiritual – actually spiritual – in the work of his comedic heroes, Andy Kaufman and Lenny Bruce, performers in whom Talen senses the magnificent proximity of the seriously funny and seriously divine. When asked, point blank, are you a real preacher?, the Reverend does not answer. At best he winks. I am certain that his unwillingness to answer, an unwillingness finally to commit to any form of positive identity, is part of the answer.

Sometimes Talen's unwillingness to fix his role offers strategic opportunity. He can, for example, momentarily "become" the very thing he critiques, and doing so might win him temporary access to the spaces that are otherwise policed and protected for right-wing expression. For example, when Mayor Giuliani tried in the fall of 1999 to withhold public funding from the Brooklyn Museum of Art because the mayor objected to a painting by Chris Ofili, which used elephant dung in the representation of a black Virgin Mary (*The Holy Virgin Mary*, 1996), Reverend Billy was a regular protestor on behalf of the museum. But in this context his religious persona had more power not on the left side of the street, where distinguished activists and artist gave long rallying speeches about freedom of expression. Rather, he literally went to the other side, to test and reveal the limits of free expression.

Stepping behind the police barrier and next to grim women holding signs reading, "Stop funding for Catholic bashing!" the Reverend greeted the group warmly, momentarily becoming an angry Catholic priest. Surrounded by a wall of cross-armed police, he began preaching, in a loud, staccato yell:

> My Children! Let's take the art off the walls and let's have . . . sports! Let's turn the Brooklyn Museum into a . . . Sports Bar! . . . Tear down the art! No more art! I want my Freedom! I want my Sports! And Disney! Thousands of monitors, all with . . . GAMES! It doesn't matter what games, just GAMES! And Elton John! And Chim Chim Cheree! Let's turn the Brooklyn Museum into . . . Times Square!

A place that is only safe for shoppers, Children! Let's go shopping! Praise be! Amen!

(1999d)

Like the Starbucks memo, Billy-as-Catholic-priest can vocalize the underlying ideological assumptions informing Giuliani's campaign, and do so in a space where he might be mistaken for a real right-wing protestor. In this case, however, soon into his sermon, a police officer tried to usher him away from the protestors; she made her own decision as to whether he was a real priest, and whether his message was permissible behind that barricade. Apparently only "real" angry Catholic priests have a right to speech, protected by police-issued permit, in that particular public space.

Talen's actual preaching often sounds like the critique of the culture industry articulated by Adorno and Horkheimer in *Dialectic of Enlightenment* in the 1940s. Like Adorno, Talen reminds us – again and again – that consumer culture cannibalizes public culture and reproduces us all as consumers, duped into imagining we exercise the free choice of individuals. Yet the fact that these critiques are staged through the persona of a comic Christian priest brings Talen closer, I think, to the Adorno who wrote "Negative dialectics" (2000 [1966]), looking for a way to trace that nonconceptuality that is the limit and potential freedom of philosophical thought. "We believe in the God that people who don't believe in God believe in," says Talen of his church; he asks his followers to join in a communal recitation of a long list of such "dis-believes," usually with a great deal of tittering and laughter on their part. Believing in the double negative has a homologous relation to Adorno's insistence that philosophy should strive "by way of the concept, to transcend the concept" (1999d: 65). Talen, along with Lenny Bruce and other relentlessly inappropriate and irreverent comedians before him, does offer a theatrical and political equivalent to negative dialectics in their practice. If dialectics is the "consistent sense of nonidentity," then Talen can't afford a positive identity: the minute he offers a reconciliation, of any kind, of the social contradictions he seeks to reveal, the dialectical potential opened by his work disappears. That negativity – never really being any one thing – becomes a means to an end he cannot name.

In the blur between the real church and real theatre, sustaining this negativity is the Reverend's most genuine, and perhaps most spiritual, act. It is an everyday, renewable sacrifice: he commits himself to an endless negativity in order to make possible new configurations, new revelations, new ways of imagining being in public, being a public, beyond the retail church of shopping.

Conclusion: on magic

Talen joins a range of other performance artists whose potent fictional personas begin to blur and overtake the everyday artist that performs them. Critic José Muñoz notes that because the performance artist Alina Troyano, alias Carmelita Tropicana, appears almost always in character her performance "defies notions of a fixed subjectivity," and, instead, that persona undermines notions of ethnic, racial, or sexual "authenticity and realness in favor of queer self-making practices" (1999: 139). Something similar is at work with Reverend Billy, who is Reverend Billy more often than he is Bill Talen these days, churning in his own performative magic. As long as he doesn't actually become the preacher he now continuously pretends to be, his performances will continue to refract, deconstruct, and open rigid understandings of spirituality and materialist critique, at the same time that they mark, like a social bookmark, a place for a community to momentarily form around him.

Perhaps real fairy godmothers wear wrinkled dinner jackets and have wild dyed hair?

REFERENCES

Adorno, Teodor (2000 [1966]) "Negative dialectics and the possibility of philosophy," in *The Adorno Reader*, edited by Brian O'Connor, 54–78, Oxford: Blackwell.

Adorno, Teodor and Max Horkheimer (1993 [1944]) *Dialectic of Enlightenment*, translated by John Cumming, New York: Continuum.

Appadurai, Arjun (1996) *Modernity at Large: Cultural Dimensions of Globalization*, Minneapolis: University of Minnesota Press.

Bamyeh, Mohammed A. (2000) *The Ends of Globalization*, Minneapolis: University of Minnesota Press.

Barber, Benjamin (1995) *Jihad vs. McWorld*, New York: Times Books.

Bauman, Zygmunt (2000) *Liquid Modernity*, Cambridge: Polity Press.

Bell, Elizabeth (1995) "Somatexts at the Disney Shop: constructing the pentimentos of women's animated bodies," in *From Mouse to Mermaid: The Politics of Film, Gender and Culture*, edited by Elizabeth Bell, Lynda Haas, and Laura Sells, 107–24, Bloomington: Indiana University Press.

Benjamin, Walter (1968) *Illuminations*, edited by Hannah Arendt, translated by Harry Zohn, New York: Schocken Books.

Cheah, Pheng and Bruce Robbins (eds.) (1998) *Cosmopolitics: Thinking and Feeling beyond the Nation*, Minneapolis: University of Minnesota Press.

Critical Art Ensemble (1994) *The Electronic Disturbance*. Autonomedia/semiotext(e), http://www.critical-art.net/ (22 April 2001).

de Certeau, Michel (1988) *The Practice of Everyday Life*, translated by Steven Randall, Berkeley: University of California Press.

Dorfman, Ariel and Armand Mattelart (1975) *How to Read Donald Duck: Imperialist Ideology in the Disney Comic*, translated by David Kunzle, New York: International General.

Giroux, Henry (1999) *The Mouse that Roared: Disney and the End of Innocence*, Lanham, Md.: Rowman & Littlefield.

Hall, Stuart (1997) "The local and the global: globalization and ethnicity," in *Dangerous Liaisons: Gender, Nation, and Postcolonial Perspectives*, edited by Anne McClintock, Aamir Mufti, and Ella Shohat, 173–87, Minneapolis: University of Minnesota Press.

Joseph, May (1999) *Nomadic Identities: The Performance and Citizenship*, Minneapolis: University of Minnesota Press.

Kintz, Linda (1997) *Between Jesus and the Market: The Emotions That Matter in Right Wing America*, Durham, NC: Duke University Press.

Kunzle, David (1991) "Introduction to the English edition," in *How to Read Donald Duck: Imperialist Ideology in the Disney Comic*, by Ariel Dorfman and Armand Mattalart, 11–24, New York: International General.

Muñoz, José Esteban (1999) *Disidentifications: Queers of Color and the Performance of Politics*, Minneapolis: University of Minnesota Press.

National Labor Committee (1996) *Mickey Mouse in Haiti: The Walt Disney Corporation and the Science of Exploitation*, videocassette, New York: National Labor Committee.

—— (1997) "An appeal to Walt Disney," in *No Sweat: Fashion, Free Trade, and the Rights of Garment Workers*, edited by Andrew Ross, 95–112, London: Verso.

The Project on Disney (1995) *Inside the Mouse: Work and Play at Disney World*, Durham, NC: Duke University Press.

Robbins, Bruce (1998) "Actually existing cosmopolitanism," in *Cosmopolitics: Thinking and Feeling Beyond the Nation*, edited by Pheng Cheah and Bruce Robbins, 1–19, Minneapolis: University of Minnesota Press.

Robertson, Roland (1995) "Glocalization: time–space and homogeneity–heterogeneity," in *Global Modernities*, edited by Mike Featherstone, Scott Lash, and Roland Robertson, 25–44, London: Sage Publications.

Starbucks Corporation (2000) " 'Reverend Billy preaches anti-corporate sentiments in NYC Starbucks locations," memorandum, http://www.revbilly.com/starbucksmemo.html (10 October 2001).

Talen, William (1998a) *The Rev's HEAVY Sermon*, http://www.revbilly.com/writings4.html (22 April 2001).

—— (1998b) *The Rev's Sermon from inside the Store*, http://www.revbilly.com/writings3.html (22 April 2001).

—— (1998c) "Disney Invasion #1," uncredited videocapture, http://www.revbilly.com/archives.html.

—— (1998d) "I married a logo: a short essay about Mickey Mouse for Human Drama Lab," unpublished manuscript.

—— (1999a) *The Church of Stop Shopping: A Solo Play in One Act*, unpublished performance text, performed by Bill Talen at the Theatorium and Theatre at St. Clements Church in New York City, May 1999.

—— (1999b) *Invasion Manual for the Anti-Disney Spatathon*, unpublished manuscript, 19 April.

—— (1999c) *This Way In: Short Sermon by Reverend Billy*, unpublished performance text, performed by Bill Talen on WNYC, 7 February.

—— (1999d) Untitled performance, outside the Brooklyn Museum of Art, Brooklyn, NY. Unedited video documentation, by Richard Sandler.

—— (2000a) *Freedom's Got Us Surrounded*, unpublished performance text, performed by Bill Talen, Salon Theatre, New York City, 26 March.

—— (2000b) Personal interview with the author, New York City, 24 July.

—— (2000c) Reverend Billy, unpublished performance text, performed at the Tishman Auditorium, the New School for Social Research, 13 June.

—— (2000d) "Most recent shopping intervention. Halloween October 31st, 2000," http://www.revbilly.com/invasions.html (22 April 2001).

—— (2000e) *Starbucks Invasion Kit*, http://www.revbilly.com/invasionkit.html (22 April 2001).

—— (2000f) *The Basquiat Wall, or Momma I Been Dot-Commed*, unpublished performance text, performed by Bill Talen at the Salon Theatre, New York City, 5 March.

—— (2000g) *I Love New York*, unpublished performance text, by Bill Talen, as part of Starbucks Out of Hell's Kitchen at St. Clements, 18–21 May.

—— (2000h) *There's a Hakim's Knish on Every American Airlines Flight*, unpublished performance text, performed by Bill Talen at the Salon Theatre, New York City, 12 March.

—— (2000i) *Every Story Has a Garden in It*, unpublished performance text, performed by Bill Talen, Salon Theatre, New York City, 19 March.

—— (2001) *Virtually Hip: An Improvisatory Skit for Three People inside $bucks*, http://www.revbilly.com/images/virtual_script.pdf (22 April 2001).

READER CROSS-REFERENCES

Schechner, Geertz – the blurring of the boundary between ritual and theatre

Kirshenblatt-Gimblett, Carlson – on performance art

Gabler – the mediatization of culture

Phelan, Faber, Kaprow, Gómez-Peña – other experimental, oppositional artists

Turner and Turner, Fabian – performance as a mode of intellectual inquiry

Conquergood – performance interventions in response to globalization

Taylor – collaborator with Lane in administration of Hemispheric Institute of Performance and Politics

41

PERFORMANCE STUDIES
Interventions and radical research[1]

Dwight Conquergood

According to Michel de Certeau, "what the map cuts up, the story cuts across" (1984: 129). This pithy phrase evokes a postcolonial world crisscrossed by transnational narratives, diaspora affiliations, and, especially, the movement and multiple migrations of people, sometimes voluntary, but often economically propelled and politically coerced. In order to keep pace with such a world, we now think of "place" as a heavily trafficked intersection, a port of call and exchange, instead of a circumscribed territory. A boundary is more like a membrane than a wall. In current cultural theory, "location" is imagined as an itinerary instead of a fixed point. Our understanding of "local context" expands to encompass the historical, dynamic, often traumatic, movements of people, ideas, images, commodities, and capital. It is no longer easy to sort out the local from the global: transnational circulations of images get reworked on the ground and redeployed for local, tactical struggles. And global flows simultaneously are encumbered and energized by these local makeovers. We now are keenly aware that the "local" is a leaky, contingent construction, and that global forces are taken up, struggled over, and refracted for site-specific purposes. The best of the new cultural theory distinguishes itself from apolitical celebrations of mobility, flow, and easy border crossings by carefully tracking the transitive circuits of power and the political economic pressure points that monitor the migrations of people, channel the circulations of meanings, and stratify access to resources (see Gilroy 1994; Appadurai 1996; Lavie and Swedenburg 1996; Clifford 1997; di Leonardo 1998; Joseph 1999; Ong 1999). We now ask: For whom is the border a friction-free zone of entitled access, a frontier of possibility? Who travels confidently across borders, and who gets questioned, detained, interrogated, and strip-searched at the border (see Taylor 1999)?

But de Certeau's aphorism "what the map cuts up, the story cuts across" also points to transgressive travel between two different domains of knowledge: one official, objective, and abstract – "the map"; the other one practical, embodied, and popular – "the story." This promiscuous traffic between different ways of knowing carries the most radical promise of performance studies research. Performance studies struggles to open the space between analysis and action, and to pull the pin on the binary opposition between theory and practice. This embrace of different ways of knowing is radical because it cuts to the root of how knowledge is organized in the academy.

The dominant way of knowing in the academy is that of empirical observation and critical analysis from a distanced perspective: "knowing that," and "knowing about." This is a view from above the object of inquiry: knowledge that is anchored in paradigm and secured in print. This propositional knowledge is shadowed by another way of knowing that is grounded in active, intimate, hands-on participation and personal connection: "knowing how," and "knowing who." This is a view from ground level, in the thick of things. This is knowledge that is anchored in practice and circulated within a performance community, but is ephemeral. Donna Haraway locates this homely and vulnerable "view from a body" in contrast to the abstract and authoritative "view from above," universal knowledge that pretends to transcend location (1991: 196).

Since the enlightenment project of modernity, the first way of knowing has been pre-eminent. Marching under the banner of science and reason, it has disqualified and repressed other ways of knowing that are rooted in embodied experience, orality, and local contingencies. Between objective knowledge that is consolidated in texts, and local know-how that circulates on the ground within a community of memory and practice, there is no contest. It is the choice between science and "old wives' tales" (note how the disqualified knowledge is gendered as feminine).

Michel Foucault coined the term "subjugated knowledges" to include all the local, regional, vernacular, naïve knowledges at the bottom of the hierarchy – the low Other of science (1980: 81–4). These are the non-serious ways of knowing that dominant culture neglects, excludes, represses, or simply fails to recognize. Subjugated knowledges have been erased because they are illegible; they exist, by and large, as active bodies of meaning, outside of books, eluding the forces of inscription that would make them legible, and thereby legitimate (see de Certeau 1998; Scott 1998).

What gets squeezed out by this epistemic violence is the whole realm of complex, finely nuanced meaning that is embodied, tacit, intoned, gestured, improvised, coexperienced, covert – and all the more deeply meaningful because of its refusal to be spelled out. Dominant epistemologies that link knowing with seeing are not attuned to meanings that are masked, camouflaged, indirect, embedded, or hidden in context. The visual/verbal bias of Western regimes of knowledge blinds researchers to meanings that are expressed forcefully through intonation, silence, body tension, arched eyebrows, blank stares, and other protective arts of disguise and secrecy – what de Certeau called "the elocutionary experience of a fugitive communication" (2000: 133; see Conquergood 2000). Subordinate people do not have the privilege of explicitness, the luxury of transparency, the presumptive norm of clear and direct communication, free and open debate on a level playing field that the privileged classes take for granted.

In his critique of the limitations of literacy, Kenneth Burke argued that print-based scholarship has built-in blind spots and a conditioned deafness:

> The [written] record is usually but a fragment of the expression (as the written word omits all telltale record of gesture and tonality; and not only may our

"literacy" keep us from missing the omissions, it may blunt us to the appreciation of tone and gesture, so that even when we witness the full expression, we note only those aspects of it that can be written down).

(1969 [1950]: 185)

In even stronger terms, Raymond Williams challenged the class-based arrogance of scriptocentrism, pointing to the "error" and "delusion" of "highly educated" people who are "so driven in on their reading" that "they fail to notice that there are other forms of skilled, intelligent, creative activity" such as "theatre" and "active politics." This error "resembles that of the narrow reformer who supposes that farm labourers and village craftsmen were once uneducated, merely because they could not read." He argued that "the contempt" for performance and practical activity, "which is always latent in the highly literate, is a mark of the observer's limits, not those of the activities themselves" (1983 [1958]: 309). Williams critiqued scholars for limiting their sources to written materials; I agree with Burke that scholarship is so skewed toward texts that even when researchers do attend to extralinguistic human action and embodied events they construe them as texts to be read. According to de Certeau, this scriptocentrism is a hallmark of Western imperialism. Posted above the gates of modernity, this sign: " 'Here only what is written is understood.' Such is the internal law of that which has constituted itself as 'Western' [and 'white']" (1984: 161).

Only middle-class academics could blithely assume that all the world is a text because reading and writing are central to their everyday lives and occupational security. For many people throughout the world, however, particularly subaltern groups, texts are often inaccessible, or threatening, charged with the regulatory powers of the state. More often than not, subordinate people experience texts and the bureaucracy of literacy as instruments of control and displacement, e.g. green cards, passports, arrest warrants, deportation orders – what de Certeau calls "intextuation": "Every power, including the power of law, is written first of all on the backs of its subjects" (1984: 140). Among the most oppressed people in the United States today are the "undocumented" immigrants, the so-called "illegal aliens," known in the vernacular as the people *sin papeles*, the people without papers, *indocumentado/as*. They are illegal because they are not legible, they trouble "the writing machine of the law" (de Certeau 1984: 141).

The hegemony of textualism needs to be exposed and undermined. Transcription is not a transparent or politically innocent model for conceptualizing or engaging the world. The root metaphor of the text underpins the supremacy of Western knowledge systems by erasing the vast realm of human knowledge and meaningful action that is unlettered, "a history of the tacit and the habitual" (Jackson 2000: 29). In their multivolume historical ethnography of colonialism/evangelism in South Africa, John and Jean Comaroff pay careful attention to the way Tswana people argued with their white interlocutors "*both* verbally and nonverbally" (1997: 47; see also 1991). They excavate spaces of agency and struggle from everyday performance practices – clothing, gardening, healing, trading, worshiping, architecture, and homemaking – to reveal an impressive repertoire of conscious, creative, critical, contrapuntal responses to the imperialist project that exceeded the verbal. The

Comaroffs intervene in an academically fashionable textual fundamentalism and fetish of the (verbal) archive where "text – a sad proxy for life – becomes all" (1992: 26). "In this day and age," they ask, "do we still have to remind ourselves that many of the players on any historical stage cannot speak at all? Or, under greater or lesser duress, opt not to do so" (1997: 48; see also Scott 1990)?

There are many ethnographic examples of how non-elite people recognize the opacity of the text and critique its dense occlusions and implications in historical processes of political economic privilege and systematic exclusion. In Belize, for example, Garifuna people, an African-descended minority group, use the word *gapencillitin*, which means "people with pencil," to refer to middle- and upper-class members of the professional-managerial class, elites who approach life from an intellectual perspective. They use the word *mapencillitin*, literally "people without pencil," to refer to rural and working-class people, "real folks" who approach life from a practitioner's point of view.[2] What is interesting about the Garifuna example is that class stratification, related to differential knowledges, is articulated in terms of access to literacy. The pencil draws the line between the haves and the have-nots. For Garifuna people, the pencil is not a neutral instrument; it functions metonymically as the operative technology of a complex political economy of knowledge, power, and the exclusions upon which privilege is based.

In his study of the oppositional politics of black musical performance, Paul Gilroy argues that critical scholars need to move beyond this "idea and ideology of the text and of textuality as a mode of communicative practice which provides a model for all other forms of cognitive exchange and social interaction" (1994: 77). Oppressed people everywhere must watch their backs, cover their tracks, suck up their feelings, and veil their meanings. The state of emergency under which many people live demands that we pay attention to messages that are coded and encrypted; to indirect, nonverbal, and extralinguistic modes of communication where subversive meanings and utopian yearnings can be sheltered and shielded from surveillance.

Gilroy's point is illustrated vividly by Frederick Douglass in a remarkable passage from his life narrative in which he discussed the improvisatory performance politics expressed in the singing of enslaved people. It is worth quoting at length:[3]

> But, on allowance day, those who visited the great house farm were peculiarly excited and noisy. While on their way, they would make the dense old woods, for miles around, reverberate with their wild notes. These were not always merry because they were wild. On the contrary, they were mostly of a plaintive cast, and told a tale of grief and sorrow. In the most boisterous outbursts of rapturous sentiment, there was ever a tinge of deep melancholy .... I have sometimes thought that the mere hearing of those songs would do more to impress truly spiritual-minded men and women with the soul-crushing and death-dealing character of slavery, than the reading of whole volumes .... Every tone was a testimony against slavery .... The hearing of those wild notes always ... filled my heart with ineffable sadness .... To those songs I trace my first glimmering conceptions of the dehumanizing character of slavery .... Those songs still follow

me, to deepen my hatred of slavery, and quicken my sympathies for my brethren in bonds.

(1969 [1855]: 97–9)

Enslaved people were forbidden by law in nineteenth-century America to acquire literacy. No wonder, then, that Douglass, a former enslaved person, still acknowledged the deeply felt insights and revelatory power that come through the embodied experience of listening to communal singing, the tones, cadence, vocal nuances, all the sensuous specificities of performance that overflow verbal content: "they were tones loud, long, and deep" (99).

In order to know the deep meaning of slavery, Douglass recommended an experiential, participatory epistemology as superior to the armchair "reading of whole volumes." Douglass advised meeting enslaved people on the ground of their experience by exposing oneself to their expressive performances. In this way, Douglass anticipated and extended Johannes Fabian's call for a turn "from informative to performative ethnography" (1990: 3), an ethnography of the ears and heart that reimagines participant-observation as coperformative witnessing:

> If any one wishes to be impressed with a sense of the soul-killing power of slavery, let him go to Colonel Lloyd's plantation, and, on allowance day, place himself in the deep pine woods, and there let him, in silence, thoughtfully analyze the sounds that shall pass through the chambers of his soul, and if he is not thus impressed, it will only be because "there is no flesh in his obdurate heart."
>
> (Douglass 1969 [1855]: 99)

Instead of reading textual accounts of slavery, Douglass recommended a riskier hermeneutics of experience, relocation, copresence, humility, and vulnerability: *listening to and being touched by* the protest performances of enslaved people. He understood that knowledge is *located*, not transcendent ("let him go" and "place himself in the deep pine woods, and there. . ."); that it must be *engaged*, not abstracted ("let him . . . analyze the sounds that shall pass through the chambers of his soul"); and that it is forged from *solidarity with*, not separation from, the people ("quicken my sympathies for my brethren in bonds"). In this way, Douglass's epistemology prefigured Antonio Gramsci's call for engaged knowledge: "The intellectual's error consists in believing that one can know without understanding and even more without feeling and being impassioned . . . that is, without feeling the elementary passions of the people" (1971: 418). Proximity, not objectivity, becomes an epistemological point of departure and return.

Douglass recommended placing oneself quietly, respectfully, humbly, in the space of others so that one could be surrounded and "impressed" by the expressive meanings of their music. It is subtle but significant that he instructed the outsider to listen "in silence." I interpret this admonition as an acknowledgment and subversion of the soundscapes of power within which the ruling classes typically are listened to while the subordinate classes listen in silence. Anyone who had the liberty to travel freely would be, of course, on the privileged side of domination and silencing that these songs evoked and contested. In effect, Douglass encouraged a participatory understanding of these performances, but one that muffled white privilege. Further, because overseers often commanded enslaved people to sing in the fields as a way of auditing their labor, and plantation rulers even appropriated after-work performances for their own amusement, Douglass was keenly sensitive to *how* one approached and entered subjugated spaces of performance.

The *mise-en-scène* of feeling-understanding-knowing for Douglass is radically different from the interpretive scene set forth by Clifford Geertz in what is now a foundational and frequently cited quotation for the world-as-text model in ethnography and cultural studies: "The culture of a people is an ensemble of texts, themselves ensembles, which the anthro-pologist strains to read over the shoulders of those to whom they properly belong" (1973: 452). Whereas Douglass featured cultural performances that register and radiate dynamic "structures of feeling" and pull us into alternative ways of knowing that exceed cognitive control (Williams 1977), Geertz figures culture as a stiff, awkward reading room. The ethnocentrism of this textualist metaphor is thrown into stark relief when applied to the countercultures of enslaved and other dispossessed people. Forcibly excluded from acquiring literacy, enslaved people nonetheless created a culture of resistance. Instead of an "ensemble of texts," however, a repertoire of performance practices became the backbone of this counterculture where politics was "played, danced, and acted, as well as sung and sung about, because words . . . will never be enough to communicate its unsayable claims to truth" (Gilroy 1994: 37).

In addition to the ethnocentrism of the culture-is-text metaphor, Geertz's theory needs to be critiqued for its particular fieldwork-as-reading model: "Doing ethnography is like trying to read . . . a manuscript" (1973: 10). Instead of listening, absorbing, and standing in solidarity with the protest performances of the people, as Douglass recommended, the ethnographer, in Geertz's scene, stands above and behind the people and, uninvited, peers over their shoulders to read their texts, like an overseer or a spy. There is more than a hint of the improper in this scene: the asymmetrical power relations secure both the anthropolo-gist's privilege to intrude and the people's silent acquiescence (although one can imagine what they would say about the anthropologist's manners and motives when they are outside his reading gaze). The strain and tension of this scene are not mediated by talk or inter-action; both the researcher and the researched face the page as silent readers instead of turning to face one another and, perhaps, open a conversation.

Geertz's now classic depiction of the turn toward texts in ethnography and cultural studies needs to be juxtaposed with Zora Neal Hurston's much earlier and more complex rendering of a researcher reading the texts of subordinate others:

> The theory behind our tactics: "The white man is always trying to know into somebody else's business. All right, I'll set something outside the door of my mind for him to play with and handle. He can read my writing but he sho' can't read my mind. I'll put this play toy in his hand, and he will seize it and go away. Then I'll say my say and sing my song."

> ([1990] 1935: 3)

Hurston foregrounds the terrain of struggle, the field of power relations on which texts are written, exchanged, and read. Whereas Geertz does not problematize the ethnographer's will-to-know or access to the texts of others, Hurston is sensitive to the reluctance of the subordinate classes "to reveal that which the soul lives by" (2) because they understand from experience the ocular politics that links the powers to see, to search, and to seize. Aware of the white man's drive to objectify, control, and grasp as a way of knowing, subordinate people cunningly set a text, a decoy, outside the door to lure him away from "homeplace" where subjugated but empowering truths and survival secrets are sheltered (hooks 1990). In Hurston's brilliant example, vulnerable people actually redeploy the written text as a tactic of evasion and camouflage, performatively turning and tripping the textual fetish against the white person's will-to-know. "So driven in on his reading," as Williams would say, he is blinded by the texts he compulsively seizes: "knowing so little about us, he doesn't know what he is missing" (Hurston 1990 [1935]: 2). Once provided with something that he can "handle," "seize," in a word, apprehend, he will go away and then space can be cleared for performed truths that remain beyond his reach: "then I'll say my say and sing my song." By mimicking the reifying textualism of dominant knowledge regimes, subordinate people can deflect its invasive power. This mimicry of textualism is a complex example of "mimetic excess" in which the susceptibility of dominant images, forms, and technologies of power to subversive doublings holds the potential for undermining the power of that which is mimed (Taussig 1993: 254–5).

Note that, in Hurston's account, subordinate people read and write, as well as perform. With her beautiful example of how a text can perform subversive work, she disrupts any simplistic dichotomy that would align texts with domination and performance with liberation. In Hurston's example, the white man researcher is a fool not because he values literacy, but because he valorized it to the exclusion of other media, other modes of knowing. I want to be very clear about this point: textocentrism – not texts – is the problem.

From her ethnographic fieldwork in the coal camps and "hollers" of West Virginia, Kathleen Stewart documents an especially vivid example of text-performance entanglements: how official signs and local performances play off and with each other in surprising and delightful ways. After a dog bit a neighbor's child, there was much talk and worry throughout the camp about liability and lawsuits:

> Finally Lacy Forest announced that he had heard that "by law" if you had a NO TRESPASSING sign on your porch you couldn't be sued. So everyone went to the store in Beckley to get the official kind of sign. Neighbors brought back multiple copies and put them up for those too old or sick or poor to get out and get their own. Then everyone called everyone else to explain that the sign did not mean them. In the end, every porch and fence (except for those of the isolated shameless who don't care) had a bright NO TRESPASSING, KEEP OFF sign, and people visited together, sitting underneath the NO TRESPASSING signs, looking out.
>
> (1996: 141; see also Conquergood 1997)[4]

Through the power of reframing, social performances reclaim, short-circuit, and resignify the citational force of the signed imperatives. Moreover, Ngũgĩ wa Thiong'o's concept of "orature" complicates any easy separation between speech and writing, performance and print, and reminds us how these channels of communication constantly overlap, penetrate, and mutually produce one another (1998).

The performance studies project makes its most radical intervention, I believe, by embracing both written scholarship and creative work, papers and performances. We challenge the hegemony of the text best by reconfiguring texts and performances in horizontal, metonymic tension, not by replacing one hierarchy with another, the romance of performance for the authority of the text. The "liminal-norm" that Jon McKenzie identifies as the calling card of performance studies (2001: 41) manifests itself most powerfully in the struggle to live betwixt and between theory and theatricality, paradigms and practices, critical reflection and creative accomplishment. Performance studies brings this rare hybridity into the academy, a commingling of analytical and artistic ways of knowing that unsettles the institutional organization of knowledge and disciplines. The constitutive liminality of performance studies lies in its capacity to bridge segregated and differently valued knowledges, drawing together legitimated as well as subjugated modes of inquiry.

There is an emergent genre of performance studies scholarship that epitomizes this text–performance hybridity. A number of performance studies-allied scholars create performances as a supplement to, not substitute for, their written research. These performance pieces stand alongside and in metonymic tension with published research. The creative works are developed for multiple professional reasons: they deepen experiential and participatory engagement with materials for both the researcher and her audience; they provide a dynamic and rhetorically compelling alternative to conference papers; they offer a more accessible and engaging format for sharing research and reaching communities outside academia; they are a strategy for staging interventions. To borrow Amanda Kemp's apt phrase, they use "performance both as a way of knowing and as a way of showing" (1998: 116). To add another layer to the enfolding convolutions of text and performance, several of these performance pieces have now been written up and published in scholarly journals and books (see Conquergood 1988; Becker, McCall, and Morris 1989; McCall and Becker 1990; Paget 1990; Pollock 1990; Jackson 1993, 1998; Allen and Garner 1995; Laughlin 1995; Wellin 1996; Jones 1997; Kemp 1998).

Performance studies is uniquely suited for the challenge of braiding together disparate and stratified ways of knowing. We can think through performance along three crisscrossing lines of activity and analysis. We can think of performance (1) as a work of *imagination*, as an object of study; (2) as a pragmatics of *inquiry* (both as model and method), as an optic and operator of research; (3) as a tactics of *intervention*, an alternative space of struggle. Speaking from my home department at Northwestern, we often refer to the three *A*s of performance studies: artistry, analysis, activism. Or, to change the alliteration, a commitment to the three *C*s of performance studies: creativity, critique, citizenship (civic struggles for social justice). We struggle to forge a unique and unifying mission around the triangulations of these three pivot points:

1 *Accomplishment* – the making of art and remaking of culture; creativity; embodiment; artistic process and form; knowledge that comes from doing, participatory under-standing, practical consciousness, performing as a way of knowing.
2 *Analysis* – the interpretation of art and culture; critical reflection; thinking about, through, and with performance; performance as a lens that illuminates the con-structed creative, contingent, collaborative dimensions of human communication; knowledge that comes from contemplation and comparison; concentrated attention and contextualization as a way of knowing.
3 *Articulation* – activism, outreach, connection to community; applications and inter-ventions; action research; projects that reach outside the academy and are rooted in an ethic of reciprocity and exchange; knowledge that is tested by practice within a community; social commitment, collaboration, and contribution/intervention as a way of knowing: praxis.

Notwithstanding the many calls for embracing theory and practice, universities typically institutionalize a hierarchical division of labor between scholars/researchers and artists/practitioners. For example, the creative artists in the Department of Fine Arts are separated from the "serious" scholars in the Department of Art History. Even when scholars and practitioners are housed within the same department, there often is internal differentiation and tracking, e.g. the literary theorists and critics are marked off from those who teach creative and expository writing. This configuration mirrors an entrenched social hierarchy of value based on the fundamental division between intellectual labor and manual labor. In the academy, the position of the artist/practitioner is comparable to people in the larger society who work with their hands, who make things, and who are valued less than the scholars/theorists, who work with their minds and are comparable to the more privileged professional-managerial class. Indeed, sometimes one of the reasons for forming schools of fine and performing arts is to protect artists/practitioners from tenure and promotion committees dominated by the more institutionally powerful scholar/researchers who do not know how to appraise a record of artistic accomplishment as commensurate with traditional criteria of scholarly research and publication. The segregation of faculty and students who make art and perform from those who think about and study art and performance is based on a false dichotomy that represses the critical-intellectual component of any artistic work, and the imaginative-creative dimension of scholarship that makes a difference. A spurious, counterproductive, and mutually denigrating opposition is put into play that pits so-called "mere technique, studio skills, know-how" against so-called "arid knowledge, abstract theory, sterile scholarship." This unfortunate schism is based on gross reductionism and ignorance of "how the other half lives." Students are cheated and disciplines diminished by this academic apartheid.

A performance studies agenda should collapse this divide and revitalize the connections between artistic accomplishment, analysis, and articulations with communities; between practical knowledge (knowing how), prepositional knowledge (knowing that), and political savvy (knowing who, when, and where). This epistemological connection between creativity, critique, and civic engagement is mutually replenishing, and pedagogically powerful. Very bright, talented students are attracted to programs that combine intellectual rigor with artistic excellence that is critically engaged, where they do not have to banish their artistic spirit in order to become a critical thinker, or repress their intellectual self or political passion to explore their artistic side. Particularly at the PhD level, original scholarship in culture and the arts is enhanced, complemented, and complicated in deeply meaningful ways by the participatory understanding and community involvement of the researcher. This experiential and engaged model of inquiry is coextensive with the participant-observation methods of ethnographic research.

The ongoing challenge of performance studies is to refuse and supersede this deeply entrenched division of labor, apartheid of knowledges, that plays out inside the academy as the difference between thinking and doing, interpreting and making, conceptualizing and creating. The division of labor between theory and practice, abstraction and embodiment, is an arbitrary and rigged choice, and, like all binarisms, it is booby-trapped. It's a Faustian bargain. If we go the one-way street of abstraction, then we cut ourselves off from the nourishing ground of participatory experience. If we go the one-way street of practice, then we drive ourselves into an isolated cul-de-sac, a practitioner's workshop or artist's colony. Our radical move is to turn, and return, insistently, to the crossroads.

NOTES

1 A shorter version of this paper was presented at the "Cultural Intersections" conference at Northwestern University, 9 October 1999. "Cultural Intersections" was the inaugural conference for Northwestern's Doctoral Studies in Culture: Performance, Theatre, Media, a new interdisciplinary PhD program.

2 I thank my Belizean colleague, Dr. Barbara Flores, for sharing this Garifuna material with me. I had the privilege of working with Dr. Flores when she was a graduate student at Northwestern.

3 An earlier version of the Frederick Douglass–Zora Neal Hurston discussion appeared in 1998 (Conquergood 1998).

4 Stewart's experimental ethnography is remarkably performance-sensitive and performance-saturated. Her text is replete with voices, sometimes explicitly quoted, but often evoked through literary techniques of indirect and double-voiced discourse so that the reader is simultaneously aware of the ethnographer's voice and the voices from the field, their interaction and gaps. The students in my critical ethnography seminar adapted and performed passages from the ethnography as a way of testing Stewart's stylistic innovations and textual evocations of performance.

REFERENCES

Allen, Catherine J. and Nathan Garner (1995) "Condor Qatay: anthropology in performance," *American Anthropologist* 97, 1 (March): 69–82.

Appadurai, Arjun (1996) *Modernity At Large: Cultural Dimensions of Globalization*, Minneapolis: University of Minnesota Press.

Becker, Howard S., Michal M. McCall and Lori V. Morris (1989) "Theatres and communities: three scenes," *Social Problems* 36, 2 (April): 93–116.

Burke, Kenneth (1969 [1950]) *A Rhetoric of Motives*, Berkeley: University of California Press.

Certeau, Michel de (1984) *The Practice of Everyday Life*, translated by Steven Rendall. Berkeley: Universityof California Press.

—— (1998) *The Capture of Speech and Other Political Writings*, edited by Luce Giard, translated by Tom Conley, Minneapolis: University of Minnesota Press.

—— (2000) *The Certeau Reader*, edited by Graham Ward, Oxford: Blackwell.

Clifford, James (1997) *Routes: Travel and Translation in the Late Twentieth Century*, Cambridge: Harvard University Press.

Comaroff, Jean and John Comaroff (1991) *Of Revelation and Revolution: Christianity, Colonialism, and Consciousness in South Africa*, vol. 1, Chicago: University of Chicago Press.

—— (1992) *Ethnography and the Historical Imagination*, Boulder, Col.: Westview.

—— (1997) *Of Revelation and Revolution: The Dialectics of Modernity on a South African Frontier*, vol. 2, Chicago: University of Chicago Press.

Conquergood, Dwight (1988) "Health theatre in a Hmong refugee camp: performance, communication, culture," *TDR* 32, 3 (T119): 174–208.

—— (1997) "Street literacy," in *Handbook of Research on Teaching Literacy through the Communicative and Visual Arts*, edited by James Flood, Shirley Brice Heath, and Diane Lapp, 354–75, New York: Macmillan.

—— (1998) "Beyond the text: toward a performative cultural politics," in *The Future of Performance Studies: Visions and Revisions*, edited by Sheron J. Dailey, 25–36, Washington, DC: National Communication Association.

—— (2000) "Rethinking elocution: the trope of the talking book and other figures of speech," *Text and Performance Quarterly* 20, 4 (October): 325–41.

Douglass, Frederick (1969 [1855]) *My Bondage and My Freedom*, introduction by Philip Foner, New York: Dover.

Fabian, Johannes (1990) *Power and Performance: Ethnographic Explorations through Proverbial Wisdom and Theater in Shaba, Zaire*, Madison: University of Wisconsin Press.

Foucault, Michel (1980) *Power/Knowledge*, edited by Colin Gordon, translated by Colin Gordon, Leo Marshall, John Mepham, and Kate Soper, New York: Pantheon.

Geertz, Clifford (1973) *The Interpretation of Cultures*, New York: Basic Books.

Gilroy, Paul (1994) *The Black Atlantic*, Cambridge: Harvard University Press.

Gramsci, Antonio (1971) *Selections from the Prison Notebooks*, edited and translated by Quintin Hoare and Geoffrey Smith, New York: International.

Haraway, Donna (1991) *Simians, Cyborgs, and Women: The Reinvention of Nature*, New York: Routledge.

hooks, bell (1990) "Homeplace: a site of resistance," in *Yearning: Race, Gender, and Cultural Politics*, 41–9, Boston: South End Press.

Hurston, Zora Neal (1990 [1935]) *Mules and Men*, New York: Harper.

Jackson, Shannon (1993) "Ethnography and the audition: performance as ideological critique," *Text and Performance Quarterly* 13, 1 (January): 21–43.

—— (1998) "White noises: on performing white, on writing performance," *TDR* 42, 1 (T157): 49–64.

—— (2000) *Lines of Activity: Performance, Historiography, Hull-House Domesticity*, Ann Arbor: University of Michigan Press.

Jones, Joni L. (1997) "Sista docta: performance as critique of the academy," *TDR* 41, 2 (T154): 51–67.

Joseph, May (1999) *Nomadic Identities: The Performance of Citizenship*, Minneapolis: University of Minnesota Press.

Kemp, Amanda (1998) "This black body in question," in *The Ends of Performance*, edited by Peggy Phelan and Jill Lane, 116–29, New York: New York University Press.

Laughlin, Robert (1995) "From all for all: a Tzotzil-Tzeltal tragicomedy," *American Anthropologist* 97, 3 (September): 528–42.

Lavie, Smadar and Ted Swedenburg, eds (1996) *Displacement, Diaspora, and Geographies of Identity*, Durham: Duke University Press.

Leonardo, Micaela di (1998) *Exotics At Home: Anthropologies, Others, American Modernity*, Chicago: University of Chicago Press.

McCall, Michal M. and Howard S. Becker (1990) "Performance science," *Social Problems* 37, 1 (February): 117–32.

McKenzie, Jon (2001) *Perform or Else: From Discipline to Performance*, London: Routledge.

Ong, Aihwa (1999) *Flexible Citizenship: The Cultural Logics of Transnationality*, Durham: Duke University Press.

Paget, Marianne A. (1990) "Performing the text," *Journal of Contemporary Ethnography* 19, 1 (April): 136–55.

Pollock, Della (1990) "Telling the told: performing like a family," *Oral History Review* 18, 2 (Fall): 1–36.

Scott, James C. (1990) *Domination and the Arts of Resistance*, New Haven: Yale University Press.

—— (1998) *Seeing Like a State*, New Haven: Yale University Press.

Stewart, Kathleen (1996) *A Space on the Side of the Road: Cultural Poetics in an "Other" America*, Princeton, NJ: Princeton University Press.

Taussig, Michael (1993) *Mimesis and Alterity*, New York: Routledge.

Taylor, Diana (1999) "Dancing with Diana: a study in hauntology," *TDR* 43, 1 (T161): 59–78.

Thiong'o, Ngũgĩwa (1998) "Oral power and Europhone glory: orature, literature, and stolen legacies," in *Penpoints, Gunpoints, and Dreams: Towards a Critical Theory of the Arts and the State in Africa*, Oxford: Oxford University Press.

Wellin, Christopher (1996) " 'Life at Lake Home': an ethnographic performance in six voices; an essay on method, in two," *Qualitative Sociology* 19, 4: 497–516.

Williams, Raymond (1977) *Marxism and Literary Study*, Oxford: Oxford University Press.

—— (1983 [1958]) *Culture and Society*, New York: Columbia University Press.

READER CROSS-REFERENCES

Schechner, Worthen, McKenzie, Jackson, Kirshenblatt-Gimblett, J. Bell, Taylor – defining performance studies as an academic discipline

Geertz, Turner, Fabian, C. Bell, Santino – perspectives on using performance to interpret cultures

Turner and Turner – ethnographic performance

Bhabha – performance as it affects colonized or oppressed peoples

Faber, Gómez-Peña, Lane – performance art interventions

42

TRANSLATING PERFORMANCE

Diana Taylor

From June 14 to 23, 2001 the Hemispheric Institute of Performance and Politics convened artists, activists, and scholars from the Americas in Monterrey, Mexico, for its Second Annual Encuentro to share the ways our work uses performance to intervene in the political scenarios we care about.[1] Everyone understood the politics; understanding performance was more difficult. For some artists, *performance* (as it is called in Latin America) referred to performance art. Others played with the term. Jesusa Rodríguez, Mexico's most outrageous and powerful cabaret-performance artist, referred to the 300 participants as *performenzos* (*menzos* means "idiots"). "Performnuts" might be the best translation, and most of her spectators would agree you have to be crazy to do what she does, confronting the Mexican state and the Catholic Church head-on. Tito Vasconcelos, one of the first out gay performers from the early 1980s in Mexico, came onstage as Marta Sahagún, then lover, now wife, of Mexico's president, Vicente Fox. In her white suit and matching pumps, she welcomed the audience to the conference of "perfumance." Smiling, she admitted she didn't understand what it was about and acknowledged that nobody gave a damn about what we did, but she welcomed us to do it anyway. "Per for what?" the confused woman in Diana Raznovich's cartoon asks. The jokes and puns, while good-humored, revealed both an anxiety of definition and the promise of a new arena for further interventions.

Performances function as vital acts of transfer,[2] transmitting social knowledge, memory, and a sense of identity through reiterated or what Richard Schechner has called "twice-behaved" behavior (1985: 36). Performance, on one level, is the object of analysis in performance studies, that is, the many practices and events – dance, theater, ritual, political rallies, funerals – that involve theatrical, rehearsed, or conventional or event-appropriate behaviors. These practices are usually bracketed from those around them to constitute discrete objects of analysis. Sometimes, that framing is part of the nature of the event itself – a particular dance or a rally has a beginning and an end. It does not run continuously or seamlessly into other forms of cultural expression. To say that something is a performance amounts to an ontological affirmation.

On another level, performance also functions as the methodological lens that enables scholars to analyze events as performance.[3] Civic obedience, resistance, citizenship, gender, ethnic identity, and sexual identity, for example, are rehearsed and performed daily in the public sphere. To understand these as performance suggests that performance also

Cartoon by Diana Raznovich. Used courtesy of the artist

functions epistemologically. Embodied practice, along with and bound up with cultural discourses, offers a way of knowing. The is–as distinction underlines the understanding of performance as simultaneously real and constructed, as a practice that brings together what have historically been kept separate as discrete, supposedly free-standing, ontological and epistemological discourses.

The many uses of the word *performance* point to the complex, seemingly contradictory, and at times mutually sustaining layers of referentiality. Victor Turner bases his understanding on the French etymological root *parfournir*, to "furnish forth," "to complete," or "to carry out thoroughly" (1982: 13). For Turner, writing in the 1960s and 1970s, performances revealed culture's deepest, truest, and most individual character. Guided by a belief in their universality and relative transparency, he claimed that populations could grow to understand one another through their performances.[4] For others performance means just the opposite: the constructedness of performance signals its artificiality – it is put on, antithetical to the real and true. While an emphasis on the constructedness of performance may sometimes reveal an antitheatrical prejudice, in more complex readings the constructed is recognized as coterminous with the real. That a dance, a ritual, or a political demonstration requires bracketing or framing that differentiates it from other social practices surrounding it does not imply that the performance is not real or true. On the contrary, the idea that performance distills a truer truth than life itself runs from Aristotle, through Shakespeare and Calderón de la Barca, through Antonin Artaud and Jerzy Grotowski, and into the present. People in business fields seem to use the term *performance* more than anyone else, though usually they mean by it that a person, or more often a thing, acts to potential (see McKenzie 2001). Supervisors evaluate workers' performance on the job; cars, computers, and markets vie to outperform their rivals. Political consultants understand that performance as style rather than as carrying through or accomplishing often determines a political outcome. Science too has begun exploration into reiterated human behavior and expressive culture through memes, which "are stories, songs, habits, skills, inventions, and ways of doing things that we copy from person to person by imitation" (Blackmore 2000: 65) – in short, the reiterative acts that I have been calling performance, though clearly performance does not necessarily involve mimetic behavior.

In performance studies, notions about the role and function of performance also vary widely. Some scholars accept the ephemerality of performance, given that no form of documentation or reproduction can capture the live.[5] Others extend the scope of performance by making it coterminous with memory and history. As such, it participates in the transfer and continuity of knowledge.[6]

Scholars coming from philosophy and rhetoric (such as J.L. Austin, Jacques Derrida, and Judith Butler) have coined terms such as *performative* and *performativity*. A performative, for Austin, refers to cases in which "the issuing of the utterance is the performing of an action" (1975: 6). The reiteration and bracketing I associate above with performance are clear: it is within the conventional framework of a marriage ceremony that the words "I do" carry legal weight. Others have continued to develop Austin's notion of the performative in diverse ways. Derrida, for example, goes further in underlining the importance of the citationality and iterability in the "event of speech," questioning if "a performative statement [could] succeed if its formulation did not repeat a 'coded' or iterable statement" (1982: 326). However, the framing that sustains Butler's use of *performativity* – the process of socialization whereby gender and sexuality identities (for example) are produced through regulating and citational practices – is harder to identify, because normalization has rendered performativity invisible. While in Austin *performative* points to language that acts, in Butler it goes in the opposite direction, subsuming subjectivity and cultural agency into normative discursive practice. In this trajectory, the performative becomes less a quality (or adjective) of performance than of discourse. While it may be too late to reclaim *performative* for the nondiscursive realm of performance, I suggest that we borrow a word from the contemporary Spanish usage of performance – *performático*, or "performatic" in English – to denote it.

One of the problems in using *performance*, and its false cognates *performative* and *performativity*, comes from the extraordinarily broad range of behaviors it covers – from the discrete dance to conventional cultural behavior. However, the word's multilayeredness indicates the deep interconnections of all these systems of intelligibility and the productive frictions among them. As its different uses – scholarly, political, scientific, business-related – rarely engage one another directly, *performance* also has a history of untranslatability. It has been locked ironically into the disciplinary and geographic boxes it defies, denied the universality and transparency that some claim it promises its objects of analysis. These many points of untranslatability are of course what make the term and the practices theoretically enabling and culturally revealing. While performances may not, as Turner has hoped, give us access and insight into another culture, they certainly tell us a great deal about our desire for efficacy and access, not to mention the politics of our interpretations.

In Latin America, where the term finds no satisfactory equivalent in either Spanish or Portuguese, *performance* has commonly referred to performance art. Translated simply but nonetheless ambiguously as "el performance" or "la performance," a linguistic cross-dressing that invites English speakers to think about the sex or gender of *performance*, the word is beginning to be used more broadly to talk about social dramas and embodied practices.[7] People quite commonly refer not to "lo performático" as that which is related to performance in the broadest sense.[8] Despite charges that *performance* is an Anglo word and that there is no way of making it sound comfortable in either Spanish or Portuguese, scholars and practitioners are beginning to appreciate its multivocal and strategic qualities. The word may be foreign and untranslatable, but the debates, decrees, and strategies arising from the many traditions of embodied practice and corporeal knowledge are deeply rooted and embattled in the Americas. The language referring to that corporeal knowledge maintains a firm link to the visual arts (*arte-acción*, *arte efímero* ["art-action," "ephemeral art"]) and theatrical traditions. *Performance* includes but is not reducible to any of these words usually used to replace it: *teatralidad*, *espectáculo*, *acción*, *representación*.

Teatralidad and *espectáculo*, like *theatricality* and *spectacle* in English, capture the constructed, all-encompassing sense of *performance*. The many ways in which social life and human behavior can be viewed as performance come across in them, though with a particular valence. Theatricality, for me, sustains a scenario, a paradigmatic setup that relies on live participants, is structured around a schematic plot, and has a foreseeable (though adaptable) end. As opposed to narratives, scenarios force us to consider the embodied existence of all participants. Theatricality makes that scenario alive and compelling. Unlike a trope, which is a figure of speech, theatricality does not rely on language to transmit a set pattern of behavior or action. Theatrical scenarios are structured in a predictable, formulaic, and hence repeatable fashion. Theatricality, like theater, flaunts its artifice, its constructedness; it strives for efficaciousness, not authenticity. It connotes a conscious, controlled, and thus always political dimension that *performance* need not imply. It differs from spectacle in that theatricality highlights the mechanics of spectacle. A spectacle, I agree with Guy Debord (1983), is not an image but a series of social relations mediated by images. It "ties individuals into an economy of looks and looking" that can appear more invisibly normalizing, that is, less theatrical (Taylor 1997: 119). Both *teatralidad* and *espectáculo*, however, are nouns with no verb and so do not allow for individual cultural agency in the way that *perform* does. Much is lost when we give up the potential for direct and active intervention by adopting these words to replace *performance*.

Words such as *acción* and *representación* do allow for individual action and intervention. *Acción* can be defined as an "act," an avant-garde "happening" (*arte-acción*), a "rally," or political "intervention." The Spanish word brings together both the aesthetic and political dimensions of *perform*. But the economic and social mandates pressuring people to perform in certain normative ways are not included – the way we perform our gender or ethnicity, for example. *Acción* seems more directed and intentional and thus less socially and politically embroiled than *perform*, which evokes both the prohibition against and the potential for transgression. We may be performing multiple socially constructed roles at once, even while engaged in one clearly defined antimilitary *acción*, for example. Representation, even with its verb *represent*, conjures up notions of mimesis, of a break between the real and its representation, that *performance* and *perform* have so productively complicated. While these terms have been proposed instead of the foreign-sounding *performance*, they too derive from Western languages, cultural histories, and ideologies.

Why, then, not use a term from one of the non-European languages, from Nahúatl, Maya, Quechua, Aymara, or any of the hundreds of indigenous languages still spoken in the Americas? *Olin*, meaning "movement" in Nahúatl, might be a candidate. *Olin* is the motor behind everything that happens in life – the repeated movement of the sun, stars, earth, and elements. *Olin* is also a month in the Mexican calendar and therefore enables temporal and historical specificity. *Olin* is also a deity who intervenes in social matters. The term simultaneously captures the broad, all-encompassing nature of performance as reiterative process and carrying through as well as the potential of performance for historical specificity and individual cultural agency. Or maybe adopt *areito*, the term for "song-dance"? *Areitos*, described by the conquerors in the Caribbean of the sixteenth century, were a collective act involving singing, dancing, celebration, and worship that claimed aesthetic as well as sociopolitical and religious legitimacy. This term is attractive, because it blurs all Aristotelian notions of discretely developed genres, publics, and ends. It clearly reflects the idea that cultural manifestations exceed compartmentalization either by genre (song-dance), by participants-actors, or by intended effect (religious, sociopolitical, aesthetic), a compartmentalization that grounds Western cultural thought. It calls into question our taxonomies, even as it points to new interpretive possibilities.

But replacing a word that has a recognizable albeit problematic history – such as *performance* – with another that has developed in a different context and that signals a profoundly different worldview would only be an act of wishful thinking, an attempt to forget our shared history of power relations and cultural domination, a history that would not disappear even if we changed our language. *Performance*, as a theoretical term rather than as an object or a practice, is a newcomer to the field. While it emerged in the United States at a time of disciplinary shifts to engage objects of analysis that previously exceeded academic boundaries (i.e., the aesthetics of everyday life), it is not, like theater, weighed down by centuries of colonial evangelical or normalizing activity. I find its very undefinabilty and complexity reassuring. *Performance* carries the possibility of challenge, even self-challenge, within it. As a term simultaneously denoting a process, a praxis, an episteme, a mode of transmission, an accomplishment, and a means of intervening in the world, it far exceeds the possibilities of these other words offered in its place. The problem of untranslatability, as I see it, is actually a positive one, a necessary stumbling block that reminds us that we – in our various disciplines, languages, or geographic locations throughout the Americas – do not simply or unproblematically understand one another. I propose that we proceed from the premise that we do not understand one another. Let us recognize that every effort toward understanding needs to work against notions of easy access, decipherability, and translatability. This stumbling block stymies not only Spanish and Portuguese speakers faced with a foreign word but also English speakers who thought they knew what *performance* meant.

NOTES

1 The Hemispheric Institute of Performance and Politics is a consortium of institutions, scholars, artists, and activists in the Americas who have explored the intersections of performance and politics (both broadly construed) in the Americas since the sixteenth century. For more information, see hemi.ps.tsoa.nyu.edu.

2 I am indebted to Paul Connerton for this term, which he uses in his excellent book *How Societies Remember* (39).

3 The is–as distinction (an event *is* performance; an event *as* performance) is Schechner's.

4 "We will know one another better by entering one another's performances and learning their grammars and vocabularies" (quoted in Schechner and Appel 1980: 1).

5 Coming from a Lacanian position, Peggy Phelan limits the life of performance to the present: "Performance cannot be saved, recorded, documented, or otherwise participate in the circulation of representations of the representation. [. . .] Performance's being, like the ontology of subjectivity proposed here, becomes itself through disappearance" (1993: 146).

6 "Performance genealogies draw on the idea of expressive movements as mnemonic reserves, including patterned movements made and remembered by bodies, residual movements retatined implicitly in images or words (or in the silences between them), and imaginary movements dreamed in minds not prior to language but constitutive of it" (Roach 1996: 26). See also Connerton's *How Societies Remember* and my forthcoming *The Archive and the Repertoire*.

7 "El performance" usually refers to events coming out of business or politics, while the feminine "la performance" usually denotes events that come from the arts. I am indebted to Marcela Fuentes for this observation.

8 Common usage of *performance* in Latin America now draws from the anthropological and sociological (e.g., the journal *Performance, Cultura e Espetacularidade* from Brazil) as well as from performance art (as in Mexico's Ex-Teresa Arte Actual's *47882 Minutos de Performance*) to highlight the productive entanglement of the various meanings.

REFERENCES

Austin, J.L. (1975) *How to Do Things with Words*, 2nd ed. Cambridge, MA: Harvard University Press.

Blackmore, Susan (2000) "The power of memes," *Scientific American*, October: 64–73.

Connerton, Paul (1989) *How Societies Remember*. Cambridge: Cambridge University Press.

Debord, Guy (1983) *Society of the Spectacle*. Detroit: Black and Red.

Derrida, Jacques (1982) "Signature event context," *Margins of Philosophy*, trans. Alan Bass. Chicago: University of Chicago Press, 307–30.

McKenzie, Jon (2001) *Perform or Else: From Discipline to Performance*. London: Routledge.

Phelan, Peggy (1993) *Unmarked: The Politics of Performance*. London: Routledge.

Roach, Joseph (1996) *Cities of the Dead: Circum-Atlantic Performance*. New York: Columbia University Press.

Schechner, Richard (1985) *Between Theater and Anthropology*. Philadelphia: University of Pennsylvania Press.

Schechner, Richard, and Appel, Will (eds.) (1980) *By Means of Performance*. New York: Routledge.

Taylor, Diana (1997) *Disappearing Acts*. Durham: Duke University Press.

—— (2003) *The Archive and the Repertoire*. Durham: Duke University Press.

Turner, Victor (1982) *From Ritual to Theater*. New York: Performing Arts Journal.

READER CROSS-REFERENCES

Schechner, McKenzie, Jackson, Kirshenblatt-Gimblett, J. Bell – performance studies as a discipline
Carlson, Phelan – definitions of performance
Austin, Derrida, Butler – cited as source, re: performativity
Lane – associate director of the Hemispheric Institute of Performance and Politics
Gómez-Peña – global performance culture

INDEX

Related titles from Routledge

Performance Studies: An Introduction
2nd Edition
Richard Schechner

Praise for the first edition:
'An appropriately broad-ranging, challenging, and provocative introduction, equally important for practicing artists as for students and scholars of the performing arts.' – *Phillip Zarrilli, University of Exeter*

Fully revised and updated in light of recent world events, this important new edition of a key introductory textbook by a prime mover in the field provides a lively and accessible overview of the full range of performance.

Performance Studies includes discussion of the performing arts and popular entertainments, rituals, play and games as well as the performances of every day life. Supporting examples and ideas are drawn from the performing arts, anthropology, post-structuralism, ritual theory, ethology, philosophy and aesthetics.

The text has been fully revised, with input from leading teachers and trialled with students. User-friendly, with a special text design, it also includes:

- new examples, biographies, source material and photographs
- numerous extracts from primary sources giving alternative voices and viewpoints
- biographies of key thinkers
- activities to stimulate fieldwork, classroom exercises and discussion
- key readings for each chapter
- twenty line drawings and 202 photographs drawn from private and public collections around the world.

For undergraduates at all levels and beginning graduate students in performance studies, theatre, performing arts and cultural studies, this is the must-have book in the field.

Hb: 978–0–415–37245–9
Pb: 978–0–415–37246–6

Available at all good bookshops
For ordering and further information please visit:
www.routledge.com

Related titles from Routledge

The Twentieth Century Performance Reader
Edited by Michael Huxley and Noel Witts

The Twentieth-Century Performance Reader provides a pioneering introduction to all types of performance (dance, drama, music, theatre and live art) through the writings of forty-two practitioners, critics and theorists which together reaffirm performance as a discipline in its own terms.

Organised alphabetically, rather than chronologically or according to art form, this reader invited cross-disciplinary comparisons. Each piece is fully supplemented by a contextual summary, detailed cross-references and suggestions for further reading. The editors' introductory essay provides an invaluable analysis of the field, and the definitive bibliography offers an essential reference source.

The reader, which makes it possible to compare major writings on all types of performance in one volume, will be an essential sourcebook for researchers, practitioners and students. It will also be of interest to anyone who enjoys innovative live performance.

Hb: 978–0–415–25286–7
Pb: 978–0–415–25287–4

Available at all good bookshops
For ordering and further information please visit:

www.routledge.com

Related titles from Routledge

Twentieth Century Theatre:
A Sourcebook
Edited by Richard Drain

Twentieth Century Theatre: A Sourcebook is an inspired handbook of ideas and arguments on theatre. Richard Drain gathers together a uniquely wide-ranging selection of original writings on theatre by its most creative practitioners – directors, playwrights, performers and designers, from Jarry to Grotowski and Craig. These key texts span the twentieth century, from the onset of modernism to the present, providing direct access to the thinking behind much of the most stimulating theatre the century has had to offer, as well as guidelines to its present most adventurous developments.

Setting theory beside practice, these writings bring alive a number of vital and continuing concerns, each of which is given full scope in five sections which explore the Modernist, Political, Inner and Global dimensions of twentieth century theatre. *Twentieth Century Theatre: A Sourcebook* provides illuminationg perspectives on past history, and throws fresh light on the sources and development of theatre today. This sourcebook is not only an essential and versatile collection for students at all levels, but also directed numerous devised shows which have toured to theatres, schools, community centres and prisons.

Hb: 978–0–415–09619–5
Pb: 978–0–415–09620–1

Available at all good bookshops
For ordering and further information please visit:
www.routledge.com

Related titles from Routledge

Theatre Histories:
An Introduction
Edited by Philip B. Zarrilli, Bruce McConachie,
Gary Jay Williams and Carol Fisher Sorgenfrei

'This book will significantly change theatre education' – *Janelle Reinelt, University of California, Irvine*

Theatre Histories: An Introduction is a radically new way of looking at both the way history is written and the way we understand performance.
The authors provide beginning students and teachers with a clear, exciting journey through centuries of European, North and South American, African and Asian forms of theatre and performance.

Challenging the standard format of one-volume theatre history texts, they help the reader think critically about this vibrant field through fascinating yet plain-speaking essays and case studies.
Among the topics covered are:

- representation and human expression
- interpretation and critical approaches
- historical method and sources
- communication technologies
- colonization
- oral and literate cultures
- popular, sacred and elite forms of performance.

Keeping performance and culture very much centre stage, *Theatre Histories: An Introduction* is compatible with standard play anthologies, full of insightful pedagogical apparatus, and comes accompanied by web site resources.

ISBN HB: 978–0–415–22727–8
ISBN PB: 978–0415–22728–5

Available at all good bookshops
For ordering and further information please visit:
www.routledge.com